THE
SOCIAL IMPACT
OF
COMPUTERS

THIRD EDITION

THE
SOCIAL IMPACT
OF
COMPUTERS

THIRD EDITION

Richard S. Rosenberg

Professor
Department of Computer Science
University of British Columbia
Vancouver, British Columbia

ELSEVIER
ACADEMIC
PRESS

Amsterdam • Boston • Heidelberg • London
New York • Oxford • Paris • San Diego
San Francisco • Singapore • Sydney • Tokyo

Elsevier Academic Press
525 B Street, Suite 1900, San Diego, California 92101-4495, USA
84 Theobald's Road, London WC1X 8RR, UK

This book is printed on acid-free paper. ∞

Library of Congress Cataloging-in-Publication Data
Application submitted

British Library Cataloguing in Publication Data
A catalogue record for this book is available from the British Library

ISBN: 0-12-597121-4

For all information on all Academic Press publications
visit our Web site at www.academicpress.com

Printed in the United States of America
03 04 05 06 07 08 9 8 7 6 5 4 3 2 1

. . . But not because I am out of sympathy with their feelings about technology. I just think that their flight from and hatred of technology is self-defeating. The Buddah, the Godhead, resides quite as comfortably in the circuits of a digital computer or the gears of a cycle transmission as he does at the top of a mountain or in the petals of a flower.

Robert M. Pirsig, *Zen and the Art of Motorcycle Maintenance*, copyright © 1974 by Robert Pirsig. By permission of William Morrow and Co., Inc.

In memory of my parents, Leibel and Malka, who planted the seed of social concern, helped it grow, but could not see it flower.

CONTENTS

3

CRITICISM AND HISTORY   69

4

THE BUSINESS WORLD   113

5

MEDICINE AND COMPUTERS 173

6

COMPUTERS AND EDUCATION 213

7

GOVERNMENT AND COMPUTERS   249

8

FREE SPEECH ON THE INTERNET   299

9

PRIVACY PROTECTION 339

10

INTELLECTUAL PROPERTY RIGHTS 407

11

COMPUTER CRIME AND SECURITY   439

12

THE ROLE OF GOVERNMENT IN THE NEW MARKET PLACE   465

13

EMPLOYMENT AND UNEMPLOYMENT 519

14

THE INFORMATION SOCIETY 589

15

ETHICS AND PROFESSIONALISM   657

PREFACE TO THE THIRD EDITION

It has been suggested by some of the reviewers of NINETEEN EIGHTY-FOUR that it is the author's view that this, or something like this, is what will happen in the next forty years in the Western world. This is not correct. I think that, allowing for the book being after all a parody, something like NINETEEN-EIGHTY FOUR could happen.

From a press release by George Orwell's publisher Frederic Warburg, from notes dictated by Orwell, author of 1984, in 1949. Copyright, Bernard Crick, George Orwell: A Life (London: Martin Secker & Warburg, 1980, p. 395).

The following paragraph appeared at the beginning of the Preface to the first edition of this book:

> This quotation [above] describes one limit of a future that a rapidly evolving technology makes possible. Will we move towards a society in which government is all-powerful and, by virtue of its mandate to protect the country, assumes extraordinary powers to monitor the daily lives of its citizens, aided by multinational corporations interested in preserving their control and markets? Will technology free the members of advanced industrial (or postindustrial) societies from a scarcity of goods and pave the way for a new age of enlightenment and plenty?

The events of September 11, 2001, referred to extensively in the following pages, have given a new urgency to this concern. The tension in a democracy between individual rights and national security in times of serious terrorist threats, and indeed, terrible actions, has been recently exacerbated. With the rapid growth of the Internet, and associated technology, many of the other concerns described in previous editions demand renewed examination.

If the second edition described the sudden emergence of the Web into a commercial force around the world, in the years that have passed, a number of somewhat surprising events have occurred. The dot.com crash of the early years of the 21st century reminded investors that new technology companies were not immune of the laws of economics and the marketplace. Among the new features of this third edition are the following:

• The structure has been reorganized to reflect the need to devote complete chapters to single, more focused topics. Thus, separate chapters now exist on free speech issues (Chapter 8), intellectual property rights (Chapter 10), and computer crime and security (Chapter 11) rather than a single chapter on the diffuse topic of computers and the law. Thus, the number of chapters has increased from 13 to 15.

• Some of the topics deserving and receiving special attention are the rise of E-commerce and global online business, the role of the Internet in medical treatment, online voting and the rise and shape of E-governance, homeland security and cybersecurity, the legislative struggle to regulate the Internet and the role of filtering software, new threats to personal privacy in the post 9/11 world, the rise and fall of Napster and its technological followers, the increasing importance of intellectual property in the online world, the growing threats of hackers and worms to individual computer security, the concern with cybersecurity, the complex and seemingly endless saga of the U.S. government's antitrust suit against Microsoft, new employment projections from the U.S. Bureau of Labor Statistics, and new case studies for ethical analaysis.

• Many changes have been made to update issues left hanging in the previous edition, such as the results of judicial appeals. Given that most of the references are from online sources, students are encouraged to go online to explore issues at their own pace. In this regard, many interesting and useful online sites are provided in the Appendix. Many more have already been found by new readers.

The social issues are as complex as ever and developments in technology continue to diffuse into the marketplace at an astonishing rate. Wireless access is becoming a fact of life as the cell phone transforms itself into a portable computer with video capability. It is hoped that the third edition of this book will serve as a guide to those interested in making their way through a world increasingly shaped by technological advances.

ACKNOWLEDGMENTS

Many people have helped in the writing of this book, either directly or indirectly: I therefore apologize in advance to anyone I may have omitted. Let me mention, in no particular order, Darrell Evans, Alan Mackworth, Laura Huey, Paul Schuegraf, Susan Prosser, Stephanie Perrin, David Loukadelis, Helen Nissenbaum, Raphael Capurro, Ron Anderson, C. Dianne Martin, Mary Culnan, Marc Rotenberg, Colin Bennett, Cal Deedman, Kelly Gotlieb, David Flaherty, Deborah Wilson, Abbe Mowshowitz, Rob Kling, Robert Ellis Smith, Herbert Lin, Janlori Goldman, Arek Shakarian, Harriet Rosenberg, Richard Lee, David Jones, Jeff Shallit, Leah Findlater, Peter Au, Douglas Johnson, Brian Fuller, Wes Pugh, and Ray Reiter. I also acknowledge the many students at the University of British Columbia, who have asked the right questions.

Of course, I take sole responsibility for the final version of this book. Nothing would have been possible without the constant support and encouragement of my wife, Sheryl, and my children, Aryeh, Rebecca, and Hannah.

— 1 —

COMPUTERS ARE EVERYWHERE

The empires of the future are the empires of the mind.
Winston Churchill (1874 -1965)[1]

INTRODUCTION

You are about to begin the formal study of how computers and associated technologies have affected and will continue to affect societies around the world. In the long history of technological innovation, the computer in some sense is no more notable than such major inventions as the steam engine, the train, electricity and electronics, the telegraph and the telephone, the automobile, the airplane, radio, motion pictures, and television. Yet there is something special about the computer that makes it more than just another machine. Its ability to be programmed to perform an incredible variety of tasks distinguishes it from all others.

The first electronic computers filled large rooms, weighed many tons, and generated vast quantities of heat. Now computers of equal or far greater power sit comfortably on the tops of desks or are carried about in briefcases. Within the last few years, electronics engineers, physicists, and computer specialists have produced powerful microprocessors that can slide easily through a paper clip. Such microprocessors are used in watches, cameras, microwave ovens, portable computers, automobiles, and assembly line robots. Other applications continue to appear at an ever-accelerating rate. Computers are now commonplace in schools, offices, and the home. They generate our checks, our bills, and our receipts. They are used to store and retrieve enormous quantities of information for a wide variety of purposes. They underlie the worldwide network known as the Internet, or perhaps more commonly as the Web. Work and play are equally affected as the following examples show:

- Early in 2002, *Wired News* reported the views of one of the world's most important leaders on the Internet[2]:

> Vatican City—The Internet caters to the best and worst of human nature and needs regulation to stop depravity flooding cyberspace, Pope John Paul said on Tuesday. The 81-year old pontiff, who last year sent his first message over the Internet, praised it as a "wonderful instrument" that should be used to spread the word of God and encourage global peace. However, he warned that while it offered access to immense knowledge, the Internet did not necessarily provide wisdom and could easily be perverted to demean human dignity. "Despite its enormous potential for good, some of the degrading and damaging ways the Internet can be used are already obvious to all," the pope said in a message prepared for World Communications Day."

- A few months later, the Pope went even further in his praise of the Internet[3]:

> Pope John Paul is putting his faith in the Internet. In his weekly address at St. Peter's Square Sunday, the 81-year-old pontiff said: "I've decided, therefore, to propose a big new theme for this year: 'The Internet—a new forum for proclaiming the Gospel'." The leader of the world's Roman Catholics didn't say how much he practices what he preaches—for instance, whether he surfs the World Wide Web. He doesn't have his own e-mail address. But the Vatican does have an active Web site (www.vatican.va), the pope sent his first message over the Internet last year, and there's talk he is searching for a patron saint for Internet users. "Recent progress in communications and information has presented the church with unheard-of possibilities for evangelism," he said.

- Proving that it is never too soon to become familiar with the Internet, this hospital in California has a deal for new babies that is clearly difficult to refuse[4]:

> Babies born at Sequoia Hospital in Redwood City will go home with a birth certificate, a tub of toys and diapers—and a new, unusual perk: a free domain name. In the first program of its kind, Sequoia Hospital is joining Namezero.com, a Los Gatos domain name provider, to offer parents of newborns a chance to register a domain name for their baby where they can build a home page to post pictures and information. "Our folks are real techno-savvy," said Linda Kresge, chief nurse executive of Sequoia. "A lot of folks who have babies here really enjoy connecting with their families. They can get quick information and pictures within seconds." Under the pilot program, which starts today and lasts the rest of the year, new parents will be able to register their babies online with a special password. The first

year will be free as part of the promotion, and continuing the service will cost $29.95 annually.

- The major news event of 2001 was the terrorist attacks in New York and Washington, D.C. on September 11. The repercussions of those events are still with us today and will be so for many years to come. The story was extensively covered in newspapers and television, but how did the Internet deal with this major catastrophe? Consider the following examples of the coverage taken from several sources, first from Cnet, a major Internet news provider[5]:

> People in New York City and around the globe turned to the Internet Tuesday to communicate with their families and to grasp the horrific sequence of terrorist attacks that transformed the World Trade Center and the Pentagon into disaster zones. Unable to connect via wireless and land-line phones, many New Yorkers posted messages on Web sites, signed on to instant chat services and used e-mail to contact loved ones. "There is no phone service in or out of Manhattan, so e-mail is the way to communicate. We are OK," read one e-mail message a worker in New York's Equitable building sent to friends and relatives. "The WTC is just 10 blocks above and we all saw EVERYTHING happen as it unfolded," wrote another New York City worker. "We are all in shock. It is hard to work. We are also trapped in the city we cannot get home." Some concerned New Yorkers even set up personalized Web sites to have friends and family check in with each other and verify each other's well being. Bill Shun built a Web site log asking friends and family from New York City and other affected cities to sign in showing that they were OK.

- The speed with which special purpose sites appeared astonished many, but even so the load almost overwhelmed the capacity, as this report on Newsbytes, a site managed by the *Washington Post,* reveals[6]:

> Web sites are popping up aimed at help people seeking information on friends and family who may have been involved in Tuesday's terrorist attacks in New York. Others are providing information on donating blood and other assistance. Finally, if you were wondering why many Internet sites are apparently overloaded, despite reports that the Internet is surviving the tsunami of Internet surfers logging on in the last 24 hours, here's the reason: "It's not that the Internet as a whole is overloaded, it's just the news and information sites," Ben Butler, a director of the Manchester Network Access Point (MaNAP), a major U.K. peering point, told Newsbytes.

- The British newspaper, *The Guardian,* also reported on the important role played by the Internet in this crisis, as follows[7]:

> The internet is playing a pivotal role in helping friends and relatives determine the whereabouts of people who may have been involved in Tuesday's

tragedy. In addition to support groups and lists of victims supplied by the websites of most major US newspapers, more than 30 independent sites have sprung up. The majority have been set up by internet companies and individuals hoping to bring some cohesion to the search efforts.

One such site, at http://safe.millennium.berkeley.edu, already has over 28,000 people catalogued. Another of the most comprehensive sites is located at www.elbnet.com/wtc, a search engine that collates the information from other databases that have been set up. However, there are fears that because all such sites rely on information volunteered by the public, mistakes or even malicious entries could creep into the databases, causing undue distress.

• Immediately following the disaster, law enforcement officials began taking steps to obtain possible information about the use of the Internet by the terrorists in planning their activities[8]:

Some of the nation's largest Internet service providers were served with federal subpoenas on Tuesday, as investigators combed e-mail accounts for clues as to who might have been behind the terrorist attacks on New York City and the nation's capital. Within hours of terrorist attacks that destroyed the World Trade Center towers in New York City and portions of the Pentagon in Arlington, Va., FBI agents descended upon the nation's largest ISP—AOL Time Warner—with orders to seize information on several user accounts. "Following the tragic events on Tuesday we did cooperate with federal investigators and provided them with information that we hope is relevant and helpful to their ongoing criminal investigation," an AOL spokesman said today. "We're prepared to cooperate with further requests as necessary."

• The search for alien life goes on and the Internet has proven to be a boon for this scientific enterprise[9]:

SETI@Home is a volunteer program that uses the spare computing cycles of ordinary home computers to look for signs of alien life in outer space. Participants download what is essentially a screensaver program, which switches on when computers are idle so it can crunch data. SETI@Home has sifted through billions of radio signals and identified the most likely candidates. Since it started in 1999, SETI@Home has become the biggest distributed computing project in history. Its 4 million participants in 226 countries have crunched an incredible 1.3 million years in computing time—or about 1,000 years of computing time a day. It is also the biggest virtual supercomputer on the planet, averaging 52 teraflops, or 52 trillion floating-point operations a second. The next most-powerful supercomputer is Japan's Earth simulator, which clocks in at 10 teraflops.

• The Federal government responded to the emergency by shutting down most of its Web sites except for one[10]:

For hours after airplanes crashed into the World Trade Center in New York and the Pentagon near Washington, D.C., virtually all official government Web sites remained silent on the unfolding disaster. Only the Federal Emergency Management Agency used its Web site to post information about the government's response. With the Pentagon on fire across the river and the twin skyscrapers collapsing in New York City, FEMA posted an announcement that it was working with Vice President Dick Cheney, National Security Adviser Condoleezza Rice and other top government officials to respond to the apparent terrorist attacks.

• However, several government sites that remained available were not particularly helpful[11]:

But for hours, the White House Web site continued to display a day-old notice that President Bush was concerned about the nation's economy. Finally, about noon, a brief statement by the president was posted. And later in the afternoon, a somewhat longer statement was added. All day, the FBI's Web site featured a story about George "Machine Gun" Kelly, the gangster who in 1933 referred to FBI agents as "G-men." The FBI is the lead law enforcement agency responding to the terrorist attacks. And the Justice Department—whose leader, the attorney general, is the nation's chief law enforcement officer—made no mention of the attacks or its role in responding to them.

• We might consider other, far less important issues when evaluating the contribution of the Internet to modern culture, for example[12]:

More language from Internet culture is to enter the Oxford English Dictionary—but only on its online version because a new printed version is not due for another 10 years. A whole raft of new words are going in from modern culture, but the IT and Net-based ones include: .com, FAQ, HTTP, HTML, homepage, information superhighway, MP3, search engine, spam, smiley face, snail mail [sic], WAP and Y2K. Now hang on here a minute. We did the same story in August last year—new OED words. You're not telling us that HTML wasn't in there before. Well, looking back, no it wasn't. Last time the words included e-commerce, cyber-squatting, dot-com, e-tailer, WAP phones, webcam and—get this—XML.

• As part of the program to enforce airport and airline security, steps have been taken to improve identification procedures. Consider this step, taken by one airline, which may become more common.[13]

Southeast Airlines said it plans to install digital video cameras throughout the cabins of its planes to record the faces and activities of its passengers at all times, as a precaution against terrorism and other safety threats. In addition, the charter airline, based in Largo, Florida, will store the digitized video for up to 10 years. And it may use face recognition software to match faces to names and personal records, the airline said. "One of the strong capabilities of the system is for the corporate office to be able to monitor what is going on at all times," said Scott Bacon, Southeast's vice president of planning. "From a security standpoint, this provides a great advantage to assure that there is a safe environment at all times."

- The Internet's increasing reputation for e-commerce was once again seen in the rapid sale of a famous deck of non-standard "playing cards."[14]

> As he tapped out an e-mail message early one Monday morning in April, Zac Brandenberg had no idea the kind of success he would achieve. At 2:30 a.m. he pushed a button on his keyboard, sending two million copies of the message scampering across the Internet imploring their recipients to "Get the 'Iraqi Most Wanted' Deck of Cards!" . . . Hundreds of millions of e-mail messages about the cards have been sent since, and some 1.5 million decks have been sold by GreatUSAflags.com, a Web site owned by JDR, based in Los Angeles, and its partner, Lionstone International, which is based here. Other companies have sold a total of more than one million decks, making the Iraqi cards one of the fastest-selling fad products in history.

The range of concerns in this limited group of selections is indicative of the degree to which computers have made a major inroad into the national consciousness, especially during the crisis of September 11, 2001. It is difficult to avoid either reading about computers and computer networks such as the Internet, encountering them directly, or having someone tell you about his or her most recent experience with them. Furthermore, we can appreciate their impact without knowing how they work or how to program them, just as we may be able to appreciate the effects of traffic jams or automobile pollution without understanding the principles of the internal combustion engine, or even how to operate a motor vehicle.

A VARIETY OF APPLICATIONS

> It troubles me that we are so easily pressured by purveyors of technology into permitting so-called "progress" to alter our lives without attempting to control it—as if technology were an irrepressible force of nature to which we must meekly submit.—Admiral Hyman G. Rickover

Even the relatively few applications presented here are indicative of how pervasive computers have become. Many of these applications incorporate microprocessors, the basic computing devices that perform decision-making functions when supplied with information from a variety of sensors—voltage, heat, light, and pressure, to say nothing of voice and keyboards. As such, much computer-governed behavior is hidden from view, and thus the true extent of computer penetration into contemporary technology is probably under-appreciated. It is important to recognize that although computers have opened up many new possibilities, for the most part society functioned in much the same way prior to the onset of the "computer age," except for several major exceptions. Checks were processed, taxes collected, students educated, products manufactured, airplanes flown, medicine practiced, people entertained, and wars fought, all without the benefit of computers. Not to deny the many advantages that have accrued from the introduction of computers into all areas of life, some balanced perspective should be maintained. Computers are indeed marvelous inventions that are transforming the workings of society, but their diffusion is accompanied by a variety of real and potential problems. The following applications, chosen from disparate areas, illustrate the flexibility and versatility of computer-mediated equipment. In some instances, computers improve the efficiency of existing processes; in others, they make possible new and innovative ones. New industries have been created—home computers, for example—and others have disappeared—for example, slide rules.

Smart Vehicles

A major effort continues to increase automobile performance and safety in the areas of handling, fuel efficiency, riding comfort, informational aids, and entertainment, as well as wireless Internet connection. Microprocessors have been used for several years to control engine functions in order to improve fuel economy. New systems, control displays, and monitors continue to be introduced. Some questions have arisen about whether or not the average driver really benefits from a growing array of dashboard gadgets. Voice systems have largely disappeared because of driver irritation, as have CRT (cathode-ray tube) displays. Nevertheless, automobile designers foresee an accelerating growth in the incorporation of microprocessors and sensors in automobiles. At present most cars employ microprocessors to perform the following control functions[15]:

- Power train management
- Anti-lock braking
- Onboard diagnostics
- Cruise control
- Automatic climate control
- "Memory" power seats
- Headlights turn on by themselves when needed, windshield wipers sense moisture on the windshield glass, then automatically adapt to existing weather conditions on their own

- Computer-controlled fuzzy-logic that "learns" a motorist's driving habits and preferences, then sets an automatic transmission's shift points to fit a driver's needs based on past driving performance.

Onboard electronics are rapidly becoming a major price component in the manufacturing costs of automobiles. Consider the following[16]:

> Carmakers are spending more on silicon these days, as electronics and software spread throughout motor vehicles, from under-hood control units to driver information systems and rear-seat entertainment modules. It is now estimated that the cost of the electronics in a new car rises by 9-16 percent each year. In the 2001 model year, electronics accounted for 19 percent of a mid-sized vehicle's cost. In the year 2005, it may be 25 percent for mid-sized cars and possibly 50 percent for luxury models.

Computer technology has made possible the inclusion of devices in automobiles to aid driving in a variety of ways—improved safety, quicker diagnoses of current and potential malfunctions, instantaneous location determination, better fuel efficiency, and, of course, continuous Internet connectivity. In somewhat more detail, let us explore these improvements.

The previous quote points to the rapidly growing use of electronics, but their use may be a two-edged sword as discussed in the following[17]:

> You've just started hunting down the road map when you remember that the van comes equipped with a voice-activated telematics system, a two-way wireless communications unit connected to both the Internet and a Global Positioning System (GPS) locator. Punching a button on the dash, you say, "Gas." After a pause, a mechanized voice reads aloud a roster of nearby service stations, including the brand of gas, the distance to each station, even the price per gallon of unleaded regular. Although it's a bit farther away, you choose the third entry on the machine-verbalized "text-to-speech" list because you have that brand's credit card. The electronic voice responds with step-by-step driving directions to your next petroleum oasis.

Note the use of the term "telematics" to refer to the use of onboard communications systems. It is important to remember that the use of cell phones in automobiles has been regulated in some jurisdictions and that connection to the Internet may pose similar safety hazards when used while the vehicle is in motion. But it cannot be denied that access to global positioning systems can reduce fuel consumption by quickly locating efficient routes and therefore reading these routes should probably be done off-road. Telematics is definitely a growth industry. The major provider of such services in the U.S. is OnStar, as the following shows[18]:

> Subscribers to premium telematics services are meanwhile starting to take advantage of more sophisticated features, such as verbal e-mail messages,

digital music, and tailored traffic and weather updates, as well as on-demand news, sports and stock-market reports. And drivers of luxury cars have become accustomed to instrument panels outfitted with color LCD screens that display navigation maps or with other useful driver aids.

"In the five years we've been operating, OnStar has delivered 10 million customer interactions," Huber says. "One out of four General Motors cars has OnStar—that's 5,000 new subscribers every day. And now many other car brands, including Acura, Audi, Honda, Lexus, Saab and Subaru, will offer OnStar services as well." Free for the first 12 months, basic service costs $199 a year, which Huber says is about what it costs annually to keep a cell phone in the car. "To remain competitive, every vehicle in the country will have to be able to deliver at least the basic telematics services," he predicts.

Many concerns have arisen about whether the installation of telematics will improve the competitive advantages of manufacturers. Granted that the range of devices available is impressive and that the services are useful and even necessary for some drivers, the costs continue to escalate, perhaps pushing overall automobile costs beyond market limits. How competitive will telematics make automobile companies, and will they contribute substantially to the bottom line? One answer is provided in the following analysis[19]:

Telematics technologies might deliver an enticing variety of in-car services, which may still revolutionize the experience of driving. But carmakers aren't likely to capture a huge windfall from them. First, the total market won't be as big as predicted in some of the more optimistic forecasts. Second, the vehicle itself won't be critical to every application. Automakers should therefore shift their strategies and focus on dominating a few core telematics applications—not all of them. In the long run, investing primarily in the development of great cars while selectively pursuing telematics will have a much better payoff than pouring funds and management effort into a full offering.

The following is a striking example of the use of telematics in a life and death situation, in which the participants were not able to act consciously because of a terrible accident[20]:

For Patricia Swanson, 37, the service is about safety. On Labor Day weekend in 1999, Swanson, her husband, her two children and her mother were driving along a remote country road in north central Iowa on their way to a parade when a van rammed into their new Chevrolet Venture, propelling it into a ditch where it rolled over two and a half times before coming to a rest upside down.

Her husband, Don, sitting in the driver's seat, was okay. But Swanson's mother was unconscious, hanging upside down from the front passenger seat. Swanson, who was thrown from the van, was also unconscious and her legs were pinned under the van. Her two small children, then 4 and 7 years old, were dangling, held by their seat belts, but they were alert.

There was nothing in sight—just tall fields of soybean and corn. The moment the side-impact air bag deployed, a cell-phone signal was automatically sent to OnStar, at a command center in Detroit, where information about the car owner, and where the automobile had landed, popped up on a screen, prompting a customer-service rep to call for help. A remote voice in the Chevy van informed the family that someone was on the way. Police arrived within about five minutes.

A Sampler of Scientific Applications

The first applications requiring considerable computational speed arose from scientific questions, albeit mediated by military exigencies (namely computations associated with ballistic requirements, as well as the much more important Manhattan project) to produce nuclear weapons. It is not surprising therefore that computers, from supercomputers to personal computers, have become an integral component of scientific investigation whether monitoring laboratory experiments, directing telescopes, counting particles, simulating complex ecological systems, or solving large systems of equations for weather prediction. There is even a project to harness millions of computers around the world to do spare-time computation to determine if we, the Earth, are being bombarded with secret messages from extraterrestrial beings. We briefly describe a few applications in the following standard scientific areas.

Biology

The year 2001 was memorable for many reasons, and none was more important than the completion of the determination of the human genome sequence, which was the result of a competition between the publicly funded Human Genome project and the privately funded Celera Genomics Corporation. On February 16, 2001, the following comments published in *Science* greeted this momentous event[21]:

> For the general public, however, the human genome sequence is of enormous symbolic significance, and its publication . . . this issue and in this week's *Nature* is likely to be greeted with the same awestruck feeling that accompanied the landing of the first human on the moon and the detonation of the first atomic bomb.
>   Why are certain achievements—the first lunar landing, atomic fission, the determination of the human genome sequence—imbued with such emblematic significance? The reason is, I believe, that they change how we think about ourselves. Landing a person on the moon gave us an extraterrestrial perspective on human life; atomic fission gave us the power to create enormous energy reserves and to extinguish all human life on Earth; and now the human genome sequence gives us a view of the internal genetic scaffold around which every human life is molded. This scaffold has been

handed down to us from our ancestors, and through it we are connected to all other life on Earth.

How does the complete human genome sequence affect the way that we think about ourselves? Clearly, the availability of a reference human DNA sequence is a milestone toward understanding how humans have evolved, because it opens the door to large-scale comparative studies. The major impact of such studies will be to reveal just how similar humans are to each other and to other species.

This achievement clearly depended on the use of computers, supercomputers and desktops, running elaborate programs. Of particular interest is the degree to which biological research has been facilitated, and indeed, enabled by mathematical models running on powerful computers. In many research endeavors the role of computers has become central, even leading some researchers to agree with the headline of a *New York Times* article, "All Science Is Computer Science."[22] Consider some of the viewpoints expressed in this piece:

> "Physics is almost entirely computational now," said Thomas B. Kepler, vice president for academic affairs at the Santa Fe Institute, a multidisciplinary research center in New Mexico. "Nobody would dream of doing these big accelerator experiments without a tremendous amount of computer power to analyze the data."
>
> But the biggest change, he said, was in biology. "Ten years ago biologists were very dismissive of the need for computation," Dr. Kepler said. "Now they are aware that you can't really do biology without it."
>
> Researchers have long distinguished between experiments done in vivo (with a living creature) and in vitro (inside a glass test tube or dish.) Now they commonly speak of doing them in silica—as simulations run on the silicon chips of a computer.

One of the emerging fields is bioinformatics, the application of computer algorithms to biological problems. Such areas of computer science as data mining, the extraction of interesting and useful information from masses of data, and visualization, the representation of masses of data in ways to reveal meaningful patterns and relationships, have become valuable research tools in biology and other areas of science.[23]

Physics

For many phenomena, the computer has come to serve as an experimental test bed with computational power being used to simulate the real world. In fact, the needs of scientific computing have been a major motivating force in the development of larger and faster computers, including, of course, supercomputers. However, the simulation of a complex physical phenomenon produces vast quantities of data, which necessitates the development of presentation methodologies such as high resolution graphics. More recently, with increased computing power, resulting from networks of workstations linked to a supercomputer, a new field has emerged—Visualization in Scientific Computing (ViSC) or simply, Scientific Visualization. For example, to study matter under extreme circumstances, such as during a supernova or at the Big Bang, computer models can be important. Almost as important is the means by which the results are presented.

Of course, the principles of quantum physics, long of theoretical interest only, will shortly, by the year 2010 perhaps, have an important role to play in the development of computers based on semiconductors that depend on quantum effects. It will be necessary to understand quantum phenomena that depend on the activities of individual electrons, and so in a neat reciprocal arrangement, supercomputers will be used to study experimentally the phenomena that may well be required in the construction of a future generation of supercomputers.[24]

Quantum computers remain an unrealized research target, but promising steps have been taken. Computer scientists, physicists, and mathematicians have been exploring the nature of computations that could be performed on various models of quantum computers and indeed late in 2001, an interesting result was reported that may or may not be significant. Scientists at the I.B.M. Almaden Research Center, in San Jose, California, announced that they had factored the number 15 into the factors 5 and 3, using a "simple" quantum computer. In somewhat more detail, the description appeared as follows[25]:

> Tiny though they are, the switches that manipulate ones and zeroes in current state-of-the-art computers each consist of billions of atoms. In the quantum computing experiment, the scientists performed the calculation by manipulating single atoms, the submicroscopic equivalent of abacus beads. This confirmed a big advantage: because of the chimerical nature of quantum mechanics, the law that rules the atomic realm, the procedure's multiple steps could be carried out simultaneously.

Building quantum computers would permit the solution of very complex problems far beyond the capacity of today's largest and faster computers, which themselves may be approaching speed limitations. This report goes on to mention such benefits.

> If this kind of quantum parallelism can be extended to a larger scale, an effort far from trivial, numbers hundreds of digits long could be factored with ease. Since many schemes used to protect electronic information are based on the near impossibility of factoring large numbers, building a working quantum computer would be not only a mathematical coup but a cryptographic one as well, potentially putting much of the world's most secret information in jeopardy.

Mathematics

Traditionally, mathematicians, at least pure ones, have required only a pencil and paper (or chalk and a blackboard) to do their work, but more recently, the computer has assumed an important role and thereby changed the way mathematics is done. Consider the following:

• In 1976, Wolfgang Haken and Kenneth Appel used a computer to prove the Four Color Conjecture: that any map can be colored with at most four colors so that no two adjacent regions have the same color. They managed to "reduce" the problem to a large number of cases (1,482), each one of which could be examined by the computer program.[26]

• Late in 1988, a team of researchers lead by Clement Lam of Concordia University in Montreal announced the proof of one example of a conjecture made almost 200 years ago by Carl Friedrich Gauss. The formal statement of this conjecture is that there are no finite projective planes of order 10, which in somewhat simpler terms corresponds to the impossibility of constructing a matrix with 111 rows and columns so that each row has exactly 11 positions filled with ones and any two rows have only one filled position in common. This result required 3,000 hours of computation on a Cray-1, carried out over a 2-year period, during idle time. Note that checking such a result by hand is obviously impossible.[27]

• In many cases, mathematical results are implemented in a computer program to improve the efficiency of existing algorithms or to make possible previously intractable processes. One very famous example is the result achieved by Narendra K. Karmarkar, a mathematician at AT&T Bell Laboratories, in 1984. Without going into any details, we note that in the area of linear programming, which is a mathematical technique used to solve very large problems in scheduling, Karmarkar's result improves speeds by a factor of 50 to 100, so that for a difficult problem for which traditional methods would require weeks to solve, a solution can be obtained in less than an hour, resulting in considerable financial savings. It is interesting that a program incorporating Karmarkar's method was patented by AT&T.[28]

• Current methods in cryptography to ensure the security of transmissions by governments, financial institutions, and others depend on the expectation that very large numbers, used for encoding and decoding keys, are extremely difficult to factor—that is, to determine numbers whose product yields the original number. However, recent results suggest that the optimistic expectation is not warranted. For example, in 1971 a 40-digit number was factored to considerable acclaim. In October, 1988, almost unbelievably, a 100-digit number was factored, and most recently, barely a year and a half later, in an extraordinary achievement by several hundred researchers and about 1,000 computers, a 150-digit number was factored into three irreducible factors. To indicate the magnitude of the computations required, consider that a brute-force method that attempted to factor the number by trying to divide it by every smaller number would take 1,060 years even if each division could be performed in one billionth of a second. A new factoring method was developed, and the problem was subdivided into many smaller pieces to achieve the final answer.[29]

• Some 4 years later, in 1994, a famous, large number, RSA-129, was factored. It had been proposed in 1977 as an example of the security of the RSA encryption scheme, named after its inventors, Dr. Ronald Rivest of MIT, Dr. Adi Shamir of the Weizmann Institute, and Dr. Leonard Adleman of USC. The historical importance of this 129-digit number had stimulated many to attempt its factoring.[30]

High Definition Television (HDTV)

If ever a technology has been promoted as a test of a nation's determination to maintain economic dominance in the face of repeated and growing challenges, it is high definition television (HDTV). However, the term is rife with political, economic, and engineering overtones and for a variety of reasons represents perhaps the most anticipated technology since the personal computer. In brief, HDTV would have about twice the horizontal and vertical resolution of current television, which results in a significant increase in picture quality. This quality is achieved by a doubling of the number of lines transmitted and an increase in the ratio of horizontal to vertical picture size, from 4:3 to 16:9, approximating a film screen.

The route to HDTV has not been smooth, however. About 75% of television stations that should have been broadcasting digitally missed the May 1, 2002 deadline. The reasons for this situation were mainly financial but also technical. By and large, consumers have not been very enthusiastic about HDTV, given the relatively high costs and limited amount of appropriate programming. The "chicken-and-egg" problem is alive and well. It should be noted, however, that in the larger markets, digital broadcasting is available, but it is the smaller markets that face the greatest financial difficulties. In addition to the superior quality of the television image, HDTV has other important technological benefits.[31]

> Policy makers of varying approaches agree that, by using a far smaller sliver of the electronic spectrum, digital significantly frees the airwaves for more productive use by other industries, including wireless communications, whose proponents are clamoring for more licenses. Once digital penetrates 85 percent of the nation's viewing market, the law requires broadcasters to surrender their analog-spectrum licenses back to the government to be reissued to other commercial ventures at auction. As a result, analysts and policy makers agree that the longer the digital transition, the greater the economic overhang. "Spectrum is critical for us to have economic growth," said Blair Levin, a former top official at the Federal Communications

Commission who is a regulatory analyst at Legg Mason. "To the extent it is tied up, it represents a huge drag on the economy."

HDTV was originally conceived as an enhancement of standard broadcast television, whether transmitted directly or over cable or satellite. More recently, the Internet has provided access to film and television content, typically over streaming media systems, that require wide bandwidth to be effective. As increasing numbers of users move from telephone modems at 56.5 kps to cable modems or DSL connections at 10 to more than 20 times the bandwidth, the transmission of full length movies and television shows becomes feasible. However, even new streaming technologies fail to produce picture quality that matches broadcast television.[32]

Solving quality and cost issues in Internet streaming is key to its viability as an entertainment medium capable of competing with other digital delivery platforms, such as cable TV.

Technology innovations in media players address a major piece of the puzzle in delivery of rich data such as video over IP (Internet Protocol), a method for sending data from one computer to another on the Internet. But the potential for delays and data jams on the Internet still exists.

In fact, one of the Web's greatest strengths can be thought of as its weakness when it comes to streaming media. The architecture of the Internet is designed to offer a set of redundant pathways for ferrying "packets" of content—if one byway is jammed, chunks of data can be zapped through another. Though it's a nearly flawless system for sending text, audio and video can suffer hiccups in the stream when they are broken up and rerouted.

Video Games

There is certainly little need to describe video games to anyone, especially young people. During the early 1980s, they suddenly captured a large share of the entertainment market, and later in that decade they made a successful comeback after a difficult period. Teenagers were the prime group to whom advertisers devoted their attention. A number of companies—Atari, Mattel, and Coleco—were prominent in the early days; Nintendo, Sega, and NEC became leading companies in the early nineties. At present the market is largely shared by Nintendo, Sony, and most recently, Microsoft. As their popularity mounted, so did public criticism. Children seemed to be so mesmerized that they would use their food allowance on video games and even steal money to play. Very little sustained criticism has continued to the present day other than a general concern with the mounting costs of both players and game cartridges.

Microsoft's entry into the video-game market has not been auspicious. It introduced the Xbox video-game system in November 2001 but with about 3.5 million in sales worldwide trails badly behind the industry leader Sony, with about 30 million sales, of its PlayStation 2. Nintendo's GameCube falls in between with about 5 million in sales. The competition was so fierce that on May 14, 2002 Sony lowered the price of the PlayStation 2 by one-third to $199; a day later, Microsoft followed suit with a similar price cut. Nintendo's GameCube remained at $199. But there was more to follow. Within the week, Microsoft, following the leads of Nintendo and Sony, announced Xbox Live, a $1 billion online game service.[33]

> Microsoft hopes to create what it describes as the equivalent of an online Disneyland, globally accessible over the Internet, where gamers who subscribe can find partners for dozens of different adventure, racing and sports games . . . While Sony and Nintendo have online plans, networked game playing is peripheral to their video-game strategies. For Microsoft, it has been integral to the Xbox plan from the beginning—the wedge with which Microsoft hopes to gain entry to the nation's and world's living rooms and become an entertainment powerhouse.

The actual games currently available are subject to the kind of criticisms that occurred 20 years ago: too violent, too sexist, too frantic. For example, Sony has a game called State of Emergency, an urban fight against global, capitalistic oppressors. A giant multinational corporation controls the entire country, polluting the environment, taking over the government and the media, and suppressing all dissent. The "only glimmer of resistance is from the Freedom Movement, an underground affiliation of young people who take to the street with their faces masked by bandanas."[34] Making young people the heroes of a video game does not require a stroke of genius.

Social Sciences

Statistical analysis of large data sets; the creation and distribution of linguistic and literary corpi; the modeling of political, historical, economic, and social phenomena; and the collection of historical, archeological, and fine arts image databases are all part of the applications of computers in the social sciences. For example, in the area of historical linguistics, attempts have been made to account for the relationship among modern European and Indian languages by proposing an ancient language from which most evolved. But the nature of this evolutionary process is very difficult to explore because of the sparse data compared with the very large number of possible evolutionary paths: by one estimate, more than 34 million.[35] As an exploratory and hypothesis-testing tool, a computer program has been developed by two linguists and a computer scientist at the University of Pennsylvania. As one of the linguists notes, in defense of this approach[36]:

We've shown what we principally set out to show, that this new computational method for evolutionary tree construction is more powerful and more reliable than any in existence, and that it is especially apt for the testing of hypotheses about the subgroupings of languages. We're hoping this will help lead to new directions of research in historical linguistics.

Other social sciences have benefited as well. The use of networks for communications of all kinds, including the publication of electronic journals, has flourished. For many disciplines, such as anthropology, sociology, psychology, and English, the Internet has provided an experimental testing ground and a source of many interesting social phenomena. Such issues as the formation of virtual communities, the presentation of self, the use of anonymity, gender switching, and the organization of political, social, religious, and other online global groups have stimulated considerable research efforts. Pathological behaviors, such as the so-called Internet addiction, the utterance of threats and sexual harassment, flaming, racism, and more, have found a home on the Internet and become constant topics for research. See Chapters 8, 11, and 14 for more discussion of these topics.

THE INTERNET

Describing the Internet as the Network of Networks is like calling the Space Shuttle, a thing that flies.[37]

In the last few years, the Internet has become a commonplace term in the media. If you are not on the "Net" you must be missing out on something exciting, interesting, and trendy. Providing Internet access is a growth industry. The Internet is yet another interesting example of a technology evolving from rather humble origins to encompass a realm of experience in a manner beyond the expectations of its originators. It is an American creation, and its growth is witness to the vigor and vision of a free and open society, but its future depends on political and economic forces beyond the control of its many millions of users worldwide.

Internet Activities

The range of Internet activities almost beggars description, but a brief overview is necessary to appreciate the worldwide popular success of the Internet. The earliest applications and the basic ones today involve the transfer of files, in one form or another, including text, formatted presentations with sound and video, software, and many other forms. In fact, the success of the Internet is based on the development of protocols, or rules of the road, for transferring files over distributed networks and maintaining the integrity of the files while ensuring their delivery over member systems without planning the route in advance. This means that messages will be rerouted automatically around nonfunctioning subsystems on a regular basis. Messages can be thought of as packets of information with a destination address and a return address. Thus for personal messages, file transfer may be referred to as e-mail, that is, electronic mail. (E-mail users typically refer to traditional mail as snail-mail.) In its simplest form, e-mail has a single sender and a single recipient, similar to ordinary mail. There is also a form of broadcast mail, or one-to-many messaging, typically used by a group of individuals to inform one another but no others. The almost instantaneous transmission times, even worldwide, make e-mail a powerful communication tool.

Remote computing—the ability to access a computer over the Internet on which you have an account—is certainly important but not as much to the general public. However, accessing files remotely and transferring them to a home computer is as important and considerably more widespread. Vast quantities of information, including software, government publications, books in the public domain, pictures, magazine articles, legislation in progress, and much more, are available. Just a few years ago, a variety of search and access tools, such as Archie, Gopher, and WAIS, were available to locate and access files on remote computers. More recently, Web browsers, such as Internet Explorer and Netscape, and search engines, such as Google, Alta Vista, and Yahoo, have proven to be powerful and useful tools for locating, viewing, and downloading files. What has obviously made the Internet a household term is the World Wide Web, or "Web," a linked world network of formatted information, which entered public consciousness in the mid-1990s. Millions of accessible Web sites and pages currently exist, and this number continues to grow, although an increasing number of sites also disappear on a regular basis. The result is an extraordinarily rich information source, with valuable and worthless information indiscriminately mixed. Uninformed users often overlook this distinction.

In somewhat more detail, during 1993, a new application transformed the Internet into a topic of everyday discourse, as well as representing the breakthrough that business seemed to require to take the Internet seriously. The Web was first implemented in 1990 by researchers at CERN (actually the European Laboratory for Particle Physics) to aid fellow physicists to share data and results. In the words of Wayne Roush[38]:

> The idea was that one physics team might create a Web document, or "page," of text using an article or set of data, noting somewhere within the text the existence of, say, a corresponding graphic set up as a separate page in the system. After starting up a program to browse for Web pages, a user could find and read the text and then retrieve the graphic by clicking on the "link" to it (the link, in the form of a word, phrase, or icon, would be highlighted). The user might wish to correspond about the information by electronic mail with the original team, or might develop additional Web documents which could also take the form of color photographs, sound,

and animation that perhaps could be linked to the original text page by the same highlighting process.

The net result is a highly structured document consisting of text and pictures with links to other documents similarly structured. Clicking on a link activates another page at some other site, which contains links. Thus the worldwide collection of Web pages represents a massive collection of information linked in many ways creating a global instance of hypertext.

Probably the most publicized, controversial, and interesting of the early Internet uses is the collection of discussion groups, known as newsgroups or bulletin boards. The term USENET usually is applied to this Internet application and is frequently confused with the Internet itself. The number of newsgroups varies over time, but there are probably between 20,000 and 100,000 devoted to an extraordinarily broad range of topics. A newsgroup can be considered as an electronic forum to which USENET readers can send messages, or postings, on an existing topic, the current thread, or initiate a new topic. The newsgroups form a hierarchy based on their subject areas with the following seven major categories[39]:

CATEGORY	TOPICS
comp	Computer science, hardware, software, hobbyists
misc	Miscellaneous: law, jobs, investments, sales
sci	Sciences, research
soc	Social issues, socializing, cultures
talk	Debates, open-ended topics, endless talk
news	Network information, maintenance, software
rec	Hobbies, recreational information

Alternative hierarchies include alt (sex, privacy, Simpsons, and just about anything else that doesn't fit in elsewhere), gnu (groups related to the Free Software Foundation), and biz (business-related groups). Individual newsgroups are named by a sequence of terms indicating a descent through the hierarchy; so, for example, comp.admin.policy, which falls within the comp major category, is of concern to administrators and deals with policy issues. Some groups are moderated, which means that they have a moderator who must review every posting before distributing it over the network, whereas individual postings are immediately distributed in unmoderated groups. Moderated groups tend to be more focused and less controversial. Unmoderated groups are more chaotic, eclectic, wild, and outrageous, with large numbers of postings and readers.

One way to get a quick feeling for the nature of the USENET is to review some online comments made by experts. Every month, for the benefit of new users, a series of announcements are posted on news.announce.newusers. The following is a selection from such a posting, originally written by Chip

Salzenberg to provide a snapshot of USENET's history, organization, and structure.[40]

> What Usenet is Not
> (1) Usenet is not an organization. No person or group has authority over Usenet as a whole. No one controls who gets a news feed, which articles are propagated where, who can post articles, or anything else. There is no "Usenet Incorporated," nor is there a "Usenet User's Group." You're on your own.
>
> (4) Usenet is not a right. Some people misunderstand their local right of "freedom of speech" to mean that they have a legal right to use others' computers to say what they wish in whatever way they wish, and the owners of said computers have no right to stop them. Those people are wrong. Freedom of speech also means freedom not to speak. If I choose not to use my computer to aid your speech, that is my right. Freedom of the press belongs to those who own one.
>
> (6) Usenet is not an academic network. It is no surprise that many Usenet sites are universities, research labs or other academic institutions. Usenet originated with a link between two universities, and the exchange of ideas and information is what such institutions are all about. But the passage of years has changed Usenet's character. Today, by plain count, most Usenet sites are commercial entities.
>
> (8) Usenet is not the Internet. The Internet is a wide-ranging network, parts of which are subsidized by various governments. It carries many kinds of traffic, of which Usenet is only one. And the Internet is only one of the various networks carrying Usenet traffic.
>
> (10) Usenet is not a United States network. It is true that Usenet originated in the United States, and the fastest growth in Usenet sites has been there. Nowadays, however, Usenet extends worldwide.
>
> What Usenet Is
> Usenet is the set of people who exchange articles tagged with one or more universally-recognized labels, called "newsgroups" (or "groups" for short).
>
> Control
> Every administrator controls his own site. No one has any real control over any site but his own.
>
> If You are Unhappy . . .
> Property rights being what they are, there is no higher authority on Usenet than the people who own the machines on which Usenet traffic is carried. If the owner of the machine you use says, "We will not carry alt.sex on this machine," and you are not happy with that order, you have no Usenet recourse. What can we outsiders do, after all?

There is more. The Internet provides MUDs (Multi-User Dungeons), online role-playing games; IRC (Inter Relay Chat), online written conversation, a precursor of chat rooms available on America Online and Instant Messaging; and phone calls between any two Net users without surcharge, although somewhat lacking in quality and intimacy. The astronomical growth of the Web in terms of numbers of sites and volume of pages has necessarily been accompanied by browsers such as Netscape and earlier, Mosaic, tools to access and explore the wealth of information. In addition, search tools, such as Google, Yahoo, Webcrawler, and Lycos, have been developed to facilitate effective searches for specific information. Finally, the Web has grown so fast largely because of the forum it provides for large and small businesses, organizations of all kinds, government departments of all sizes, and multitudes of individuals to display their wares in a colorful and occasionally interesting manner. One last application is multicasting, which uses the M-bone (multicast backbone) and "enables groups of specially equipped computers to share text, audio and video. A multicast differs from a unicast, in which one computer communicates with one other, and a broadcast, in which one computer communicates with many. In multicasting, many computers can communicate among themselves simultaneously."[41]

The Information Highway: What Is It?

In the early 1990s, the terms Information Highway and Information Superhighway were ubiquitous. The future of the Internet would be the Information Highway, or as it was usually referred to in the U.S., the National Information Infrastructure (NII). Committees were appointed, reports were commissioned, government offices and agencies were created, and detailed plans released. Such efforts were undertaken elsewhere as well, including Canada, Europe, Australia, and Japan. However, it should be noted that as a generally agreed on goal, much of the excitement originally generated by the NII has dissipated, and the term has largely disappeared from the public consciousness. Nevertheless, various components of this highly ambitious project still exist, as do many of the accompanying problems.

Keep in mind a couple of points. The NII, as originally envisioned, is not here yet, although many necessary components are in place. Thus much of the commentary directed toward its promise and potential problems is highly speculative however well-intentioned. Furthermore, the Internet is not the NII, although many of its applications should be available on the NII when it is realized. However, we may be able to anticipate some of the features of the NII by studying the ongoing development of the Internet. The arrival of the Web did seem to suggest that the Internet, from the mid-1990s on, had assumed some of the features hypothesized in various NIH visions. We return briefly to this discussion in Chapter 14.

SOCIETAL ISSUES

For a list of all the ways technology has failed to improve the quality of life, please press three.—Alice Kahn

Technology makes it possible for people to gain control over everything, except over technology.—John Tudor

All technology should be assumed guilty until proven innocent.—David Brower

Issues and Problems

There are many ways to present and discuss social issues arising from the increasing use of computers and computer-based electronic networks such as the Internet. One method is by category, that is, each major application area is studied and the particular problems identified and characterized. Another is to propose a list of areas of social concern, or potential problems, and then to explore each application to determine whether or not it exemplifies one or more of these problems. The results of both approaches could be combined by representing them in a simple diagram that depicts which social issues are of particular concern to which applications or technological innovations. The simple metaphor is to view society as a fabric woven with warp and woof threads. The warp consists of the lengthwise threads of a woven cloth through which woof threads are woven, and the woof consists of the crosswise threads carried back and forth by the shuttle and interwoven with the lengthwise threads of the warp. These definitions are obviously interdependent just as the social issues and applications are. For the purposes of this metaphor, societal, legal, and economic issues are the warp, and computers, technology, and applications are the woof. The dividing lines are not always sharp, however.

Application areas and technological developments include the following.

Robotics and Industrial Automation. The integration of computers and movable electromechanical arms—to perform such tasks as assembling parts, welding, and spray painting—define industrial automation. Robots also may be used for jobs dangerous to humans in hazardous environments such as under the sea, mines, space, and nuclear reactors. Flexible manufacturing systems represent newer ways of organizing production.

Office Automation. The integration of computers, large and small, local and long-distance networks, fax, and printers is transforming the office. Sophisticated word processing, database systems, e-mail, automatic meeting schedulers, management information systems, telecommuting, and portable computing are among the components of what has been called "The Office of the Future."

Telecommunications. The interconnection of computers with communication networks opens up a wide range of possibilities for distributed computing, distributed work, and worldwide information networks for business and government use.

Electronic Financial Transactions. The use of ATMs (Automatic Teller Machines), POSs (Point-of-Sales terminals), and computer communication systems results in electronic financial transactions and may at some point produce the "cashless" society. A dense network linking financial institutions, retailers, wholesalers, and the public is continually changing shopping and banking habits. Commercial transactions on the Internet present special security problems.

Personal Computers. The explosion of computers available for use in the office, school, and home has brought computers from the hands of professionals into the homes of the general public. Marketed as just another consumer item, granted an expensive one, they may have been oversold, but do provide an ever-expanding range of possibilities for the family including games, financial programs, educational programs, and a means to access the Internet and commercial networks.

Microprocessors. The miniaturization of computing power in the form of microprocessors has enabled the computer to be incorporated into an ever-increasing variety of consumer products. Among these are cameras, automobiles, television sets, microwave ovens, fax machines, stereo systems, etc. Improvements in efficiency and repair procedures are changing production practices and servicing strategies. Consumer products can be more energy-efficient and more flexible; that is, more bells and whistles.

E-Mail and Teleconferencing. The use of computer terminals and communication networks permits messages to be sent across the office or across the country and stored in computers or printed and delivered locally as ordinary mail. Combined with fax and teleconferencing, these new communication modes are changing the way companies do business.

AI (Artificial Intelligence). Developments in AI are continually expanding the role computers play in our lives, especially in areas that directly challenge human uniqueness. Once an academic pursuit, AI is achieving varying degrees of economic impact in such areas as expert systems, intelligent robots, and sophisticated diagnostic systems.

Virtual Reality. Recent developments in computer graphics, interfaces, and hardware have opened up the possibilities of real-time interactions in simulated worlds. The proponents claim that shaking off physical limitations will liberate the mind, initiate unpredictable relationships, and usher in an age of unlimited potential, but there are dangers, including threats to self and loss of community.

Internet. The Internet is the current worldwide network linking millions of people and permitting the rapid distribution of text, images, and sounds at low costs. It may be superseded by the Information Highway, that much advertised broadband entertainment network, combining cable, telephone, and broadcasting systems. Such networks are hallmarks of the Information Age.

This list provides a sense of how important computers have become to the functioning of modern society, if any such message is necessary. It now remains to outline an accompanying list of relevant social issues. For some of these, computers are only the current stage in technological development, and so the problems are only existing ones exacerbated. Others are unique to the computer and must be treated as directly associated phenomena. The issues will be characterized by a series of crucial questions highlighting the areas of concern. Among the social issues are the following.

Work. How do all these computer-related developments affect the employment of people? Will the number of available jobs that can sustain both body and mind increase or decrease? How will the skill requirements of jobs change? How well will people accommodate to the increased automation of the workplace? What will happen to the traditional social organization of the office under office automation?

Health. Is long-term health affected by lengthy exposure to VDTs (Video Display Terminals)? Are other computer-related activities problematic? What about the effects of repetitive actions on hand and wrist muscles and nerves? Are there psychological effects associated with "excessive" computer use?

Privacy. Computers permit, indeed encourage, enormous amounts of information to be gathered, stored, processed, linked, and distributed. There is a general concern about how these records are used, about the proliferation of incorrect information, and about access to individual records. Can a claim be made to treat personal information as property, which would require traffickers in personal data to pay for use? Can or should all North American governments regulate the handling of personal information in the private sector as is done in Canada and in many countries in Western Europe?

Centralization of Control. Will computers be used to extend the power of management over employees? Is it inevitable that increased amounts of more accurate information will shift more power to the top of organizations, or will distributed computing lead to distributed responsibility and control? Will governments, even democratic ones, become more powerful and centralized as in Orwell's *1984*, in spite of efforts to minimize their "intrusion into the lives of ordinary citizens?"

Responsibility. Will the widespread use of computers and communication systems fragment society? Will families cluster around their home information systems for entertainment, shopping, education, and even work? In large organizations that are heavily dependent on information technology, will responsibility devolve from people to machines?

The Information Society. How will society change as fewer and fewer people actually produce things and more and more people engage in service activities and information processing? Are we heading to a modern version of "bread and circuses?" Will the home become central to life as information in its broadest interpretation becomes the leading economic commodity? How will access to information be made available?

Human Dignity or Self-Image. How does the computer affect our self-image? Is there a threat to human dignity as machines continue to perform more activities formerly the sole province of people? Is technology an irresistible and autonomous force? Can we maintain human(e) qualities in a computer age?

Ethics and Professionalism. How responsible are computer professionals for their actions? Should they adopt codes of behavior similar to those of doctors and even lawyers? Do computer-mediated situations present new problems for ethical behavior?

National Interests. Does the future economic well-being of a country depend on its achievements in high technology? Should governments play an active role in the marketplace to ensure that technological leadership is maintained? Will success for some countries mean failure for others?

Meritocracy. Will the use of computers accentuate the tensions between the educated and the untrained? Will the work of society be divided between challenging and interesting jobs and routine and boring ones? Will the poor and uneducated view computers as yet another powerful tool for the rich to maintain their status, and will they be right?

Freedom of Expression. In the U.S. the First Amendment guarantees the right of all citizens to say and write what they wish with very few restrictions, but the battle to exercise this right is a never-ending one. The Internet and commercial networks, such as Prodigy and CompuServe, currently form one such battleground. The ease with which all kinds of information can be transmitted on networks immediately raises questions of responsibility and liability. Will content be regulated and how might this work over a global network? (This last question has an answer—yes—The Communications Decency Act of 1996.)

Intellectual Property. In the age of information, the ownership of information assumes major importance. An emerging battleground is the electronic rights for text, images, sounds, hypertext, and multimedia. Will existing information conglomerates reinforce their control or will an emerging grass roots constituency begin to distribute information free of traditional ownership patterns? A recent answer is the "success" of Napster and KaZaA.

Which issues apply to which technological areas? Figure 1.1 is clearly not a precise formulation for many reasons, a primary one being that the definitions are not very precise. It should suggest the general patterns of interaction of social issues and technological innovations. As time goes on, the number of rows and columns, as well as the contents, will vary as new concerns emerge in response to new applications. Thus this formulation is suggestive only and not definitive. It is important to be aware of the possible consequences of technological developments, but this awareness requires a familiarity with the technology, as well as with the economic, political, social, and legal structures of society. Only a beginning is attempted here, but an old Chinese saying is appropriate: "A journey of a thousand miles begins with one step."

Public Opinion

A selection of possible problems associated with computer use in today's society has been presented. The severity of these problems is a matter of debate among computer professionals and social scientists—but how do non-experts, ordinary people, feel about computers? It was not until the late 1950s that the computer emerged as an object of praise and fear. Cartoonists of the period depicted computers or robots as challenging the ability of humans at work and at play. Operators at consoles in front of floor-to-ceiling computers, with flashing lights and whirring tape drives, typed in queries that elicited humorous responses. The cartoons reflected such concerns as possible loss of jobs, threats to human problem-solving skills, personal liberty, and an increasing intrusion into all aspects of human life. Did the cartoonists and editorial writers truly capture the hopes and fears of the general population or did they exacerbate them?

In 1971, *Time* magazine and the American Federation of Information Processing Societies, Inc. (AFIPS) conducted a major survey to determine the

	Work	Health	Privacy	Centralization of Authority	Responsibility	Information Society	Human Dignity	Ethics and Professionalism	National Interests	Meritocracy	Freedom of Expression	Intellectual Property
Robotics	X	X					X		X	X		
Office Automation	X	X	X	X	X	X	X	X		X		
Telecommunication	X		X	X		X		X	X		X	
Electronic Financial Transactions	X		X	X	X			X				
Personal Computers	X	X				X				X	X	X
Microprocessors	X					X				X		X
E-mail	X		X			X			X			
AI	X					X	X		X			
Virtual Reality		X					X	X				
Internet	X		X		X	X			X		X	X

FIGURE 1.1 Social Issues and Computer Technologies.

public's attitude towards computers.[42] Over 1,000 adults from a representative sample of the U.S. population were interviewed on a wide range of topics. The survey results are extensive and lengthy, but the following few observations are revealing:

- Almost half of the working public has had some contact with computers.
- About 90% felt that computers will provide much useful information and many kinds of services.
- 36% felt computers actually create more jobs than they eliminate; 51% believed the opposite.
- 84% wanted the government to regulate the use of computers.
- With respect to privacy, 58% were concerned that computers will be used in the future for surveillance and 38% believed that they were a threat to privacy (but 54% disagreed).

- Only 12% believed that computers could think for themselves, but 23% expected that they might disobey their programmers in the future.
- 54% thought that computers were dehumanizing people, and 33% believed that they were decreasing freedom; 59% disagreed.

On the whole, the general public displayed a reasonable attitude to the ability of computers and the potential threats they posed.

In 1983, Lou Harris and Associates, Inc., conducted a study for Southern New England Telephone entitled *The Road After 1984: The Impact of Technology on Society*.[43] Conducted well into the age of the home computer, this survey should have revealed the opinions of a more sophisticated public. Some highlights follow:

- 67% of the general public believed that personal information was being kept in files somewhere for purposes unknown to them.
- 45% acknowledged that they knew how to use a computer, most at the beginner level.
- 88% believed that the computer would make the quality of life somewhat or a lot better.
- 85% agreed that computers could free up time for individuals to do creative and highly productive work.
- 55% felt that computers could make human robots out of workers by controlling every minute of their day.

In 1994, the Times Mirror Company conducted a broad survey on attitudes towards technology, including computers and online systems, as well as attitudes with respect to the impact of computer-based technologies on social issues. Here are a few findings[44]:

- 31% of all American households have a personal computer, and one in three of these have a modem, permitting communication with an online information system.
- 65% like computers and technology, and 42% think that they give people more control over their lives; 17% say less control.
- 55% worry some or a lot that computers and technology are being used to invade their privacy; 42% say not much or not at all.

There is much more in this survey about uses of computers, working at home, gender differences, children's interests, and detailed profiles of technology users. More information gathered from privacy surveys is reported in Chapter 9, but most surveys have consistently shown over the past few years that the general public is much more concerned about privacy issues than the 55% figure given previously. In fact, about 77% to 80% of respondents have indicated over the past few years that they were very concerned or somewhat concerned about threats to personal privacy.

One area of considerable current interest is the number of regular Internet users and Web browsers (people, not software). Individual Web sites can keep track of the number of visits made but not the number of independent ones, which is an important measure of how popular the site is. In October 1995, A. C. Nielsen, well known for its extensive measurements of television viewing habits, reported that 24 million people in Canada and the U.S. had used the Internet between August and October, and of these, 18 million had accessed Web sites.[45] Survey results reported from MCI Communications and Network Wizards in July 1996 provide the following information: 35 million users worldwide, 186 countries connected, 10 million host computers, 76,000 Web servers, 300% growth in annual traffic, and 2,400% growth in Web servers.[46] Finally, results of a Nielsen poll reported in August 1996 revealed that "the number of North Americans with Internet access jumped from 37 million last August to 55.5 million six months later . . ."[47] Having Internet access is not equivalent to being an Internet user, but this survey does indicate that basic exposure to the Internet, probably the Web, is increasing at a significant rate. The survey also produced some demographic results that revealed a few interesting findings. Among longtime users, 67% are men, 88% own their own computer, 56% have college degrees, and 27% have a household income of at least $80,000.[48] More recent users are less affluent, own fewer computers, have less education, and have a higher representation of women (60% are men).

These and other surveys are intended to answer other questions such as age, frequency of use, type of use, impact on leisure time, and how much money has been spent both to access Web sites and make purchases. Why all the concern about these numbers? The answer is simple: Money. The late 1990s witnessed the so-called dot com boom in which for little apparent reason, thousands of online companies suddenly appeared, flamed brightly on venture capital, and then disappeared, unremembered and definitely unmourned. Since those exciting days, especially for the dot com founders and their mandatory stock options, the Internet and the Web have continued to grow both in size and in uses. How large is it? One regular survey carried out monthly by searchengineshowdown.com characterizes the number of Web pages indexed by the major search engines. Underlying the speed of operation of search engines is the continuous process of indexing web pages and storing these indices in a very large database for quick retrieval. Thus as of the beginning of March 2002, Google indexed 968 million Web pages; AllTheWeb, 580 million; Wisenet, 580 million; Northern Light, 417 million; and AltaVista, 397 million.[49] There are many more statistics available, and their computation usually requires some explanation.

A few more results of Web-use surveys are worth mentioning. Consumers Union, the long-time publisher of *Consumer Reports* magazine, is involved in a project to explore consumer trust on the Internet. In a recent report, the following findings were highlighted[50]:

- Only 29% of users say they trust Web sites that sell products or services; just 33% say they trust Web sites giving advice about such purchases. (Compared to 58% who trust newspapers and television news and 47% who trust the federal government in Washington.)
- 95% say it is important that sites disclose all fees, while 93% attach the same emphasis to statements of the site's policy on using personal information.
- 65% say it is very important that a site display its privacy policy.
- Three in five users (60%) do not know that search engines are often paid to list some sites more prominently than others in their results.

As an introduction to one of the themes of this book, namely computers and the Internet subsequent to the tragedies of September 11, 2001, in New York and Washington, we note one survey from the University of California at Los Angeles' Internet Project. Consider the following highlights[51]:

- 57.1% of e-mail users—more than 100 million Americans—received or sent messages of emotional support, messages of concern for others, or questions about victims of the attacks.
- Of e-mail users, 37.6% received messages of emotional support or concerns about their welfare, and 38.6% sent similar e-mail messages of emotional support.
- 22.9% of Internet users received e-mail messages of support or sympathy from outside the U.S.
- More than half (56.3%) of Americans first learned of the attacks by watching television, compared to 0.8% who learned the news on the Internet (24.9% learned from another person by phone or in person, and 15.5% learned from radio).

The last point is very important and somewhat sobering for Web enthusiasts. When the crunch came on September 11, almost all Americans learned about it not on the Internet (less than 1%) but on television, from friends, and on radio. The Internet may have arrived in the public media and as a means of sharing information after the event, it proved incomparable, but in the early stages, it was nowhere to be seen.

SUMMARY

Computers have become pervasive in contemporary society. They have been used to distribute religious services over networks, provide a site for condolences over the death of rock star Jerry Garcia, and permit people to drink coffee and exchange messages over the Internet at a cafe. There are also problems, such as IBM's failure to provide a working system at the Atlanta Olympics. Designers of some game-playing programs seem to be unable to avoid the use of racism as a feature. The issue of free speech on the Internet has become an ongoing battleground because not unexpectedly this new media has attracted the attention of many interested in material with sexual themes. Major applications also include improved automobile performance, the use of computers to explore the evolution of human language groups, the computer visualization of scientific phenomena, the proof of difficult mathematical theorems, the development of high definition television, and, of course, video games.

In recent years, the Internet and the World Wide Web have become extremely popular as the number of hosts and users has grown very rapidly. From its humble beginnings as a research-oriented computer network funded by the U.S. Department of Defense and later by the National Science Foundation, the Internet has become a global network and a worldwide phenomenon. Advances in telecommunications technology and applications software, as well as U.S. government deregulation legislation has prepared the groundwork for the much advertised Information Highway.

Associated with the benefits of computers are a number of real and potential problems. The many and varied applications of computers, including robotics, office automation, electronic money systems, personal computers, home information systems, and artificial intelligence, have given rise to social problems. Relevant issues include work, health, privacy, responsibility, self-image, and national interests.

From their earliest appearance, computers have aroused feelings of fear, awe, and concern, as revealed in public opinion surveys. Despite increased familiarity, the general public's perception of computers seems still to be conditioned more by media exaggerations than by reality. Recent surveys have shown conflicting estimates in the number of Internet users, but all agree on significant growth rates.

NOTES

1. Collected in online quotation list. Copyright: Kevin Harris 1995.
2. "Pope Loves, Fears the Net." Reuters as reported in *Wired News*, January 22, 2002. Available at http://www.wired.com/news/print/ 0,1294.49910,00
3. Luke Baker. "Pope Gives Internet His Blessing," Reuters, May 12, 2002. Available at http://www.reuters.com/
4. Putsata Reang. "Hospital Offers New Babies Their Own Domain Name," *San Jose Mercury News*, May 23, 2001. Available at http://www.siliconvalley. com/doc/news/svfront/baby052401 [Note this was the original address that is no longer accessible.]
5. Stephanie Olsen. "Net Offers Lifeline Amid Tragedy," Cnet News.com, September 11, 2001. Available at http://news.cnet.com/news/0-1005-200-7132246.html?tag=prntfr
6. Steve Gold. "Help Sites Spring Up In Wake of WTC Assaults – An Update," Newsbytes, September 12, 2001. Available at http://www.newsbytes.com/ news/01/170016.html
7. Owen Gibson. "Web Plays Key Role in Finding Victims," *The Guardian*, September 14, 2001. Available at http://www.guardian. co.uk/Print/0,3858. 4257594,00

8. Staff, Newsbytes. "ISPs Turn Possible Terrorist Communications Over To Feds, Newsbytes, September 13, 2001. Available at http://www.newsbytes.com/news/01/170080

9. Leander Kahner. "Alien Life Search Inches Forward," Wired.com, March 11, 2003. Available at http://www.wired.com/news/technology/0,1282,57992,00.html

10. William Matthews. "Fed Web Sites Silent as New York, Washington Burn," *Federal Computer Week*, September 11, 2001. Available at http://www.fcw.com/fcw/articles/2001/0910/web-sites-09-11-01.asp

11. *Ibid.*

12. Kieren McCarthy. "More Net-speak Enters Oxford English Dictionary," *The Register*, June 6, 2001. Available at http://www.theregister.co.uk/content/6/19724.html

13. Elisa Batista. "Videocams Record Airline Flights," Wired.com, July 18, 2003. Available at http://www.wired.com/news/business/0,1367,59652,00.html

14. Saul Hansell. "E-mail Message Blitz Creates What May Be Fastest Fad Ever," *The New York Times*, June 9, 2003. Available at http://www.nytimes.com/2003/06/09/technology/09CARD.html

15. A study released in October 1994 by Siemens Automotive Corp. and *Ward's Auto World* as reported in Ronald K. Jurgen, "The Electronic Motorist," *IEEE Spectrum*, March 1995, p. 37.

16. Ivan Berger. "Can You Trust Your Car?" *IEEE Spectrum*, March 31, 2002. Available at http://www.spectrum.ieee.org/WEBONLY/publicfeature/april02/ecar.html

17. Steven Ashley. "Driving the Info Highway," *Scientific American*, October 2001. Available at http://www.sciam.com/2001/1001issue/1001ashley.html

18. *Ibid.*

19. "The Road to Telematics," From the *McKinsey Quarterly* to CNET News.com, April 2002. Available at http://news.com.com/2009-1017-877385.html

20. Alec Klein, "Pampered at the Wheel," *The Washington Post*, January 21, 2002, p. AO1.

21. Svante Paabo. "The Human Genome and Our View of Ourselves," *Science*, February 16, 2001, Vol. 291, pp. 1219-1220. Available at http://www-sciencemag.org/cgi/content/full/2915507/1219.html

22. George Johnson. "All Science Is Computer Science," *The New York Times*, Week in Review Section, March 25, 2001.

23. *Ibid.*

24. John Carey and Heidi Dawley. "Science's New Nano Frontier," *Business Week*, July 1, 1996, pp. 101-102.

25. George Johnson, "Efforts to Transform Computers Reach Milestone," *The New York Times*, December 20, 2001, Late Edition – Final, Section A, p. 26.

26. Paul Wallich. "Beyond Understanding," *Scientific American*, March 1989, p. 24.

27. *Ibid.*

28. William G. Wild Jr. and Otis Port. "The Startling Discovery Bell Labs Kept in the Shadows," *Business Week*, September 21, 1987, pp. 69, 72, 76.

29. Gina Kolata. "Giant Leap in Math: 155 Divided to 0," *The New York Times*, June 20, 1990, p. A 8.

30. Gina Kolata. "The assault on 114,381,625,757,888,867,669,235,779,976,146, 612,010,218,296,721,242,362,562,561,842,935,706,935,245,733,897,

830,597,123,563,958,705,058,989,075,147,599,290,026,879,543,541," *The New York Times*, March 22, 1994, pp. B 5, B 6.

31. Stephen Labaton. "Most Commercial Broadcasters Will Miss Deadline for Digital Television," *The New York Times*, April 29, 2002, Late Edition – Final, Section C, p. 6.

32. Stephanie Olsen. "Net Video's Obstacle to a Steady Stream," CNET News.com, May 7, 2002. Available at http://news.com.com/2100-1023-900617.html

33. John Markoff. "Microsoft's $1 Billion Bet on Xbox Network," *The New York Times*, May 20, 2002, Late Edition – Final, Section C, Page 1.

34. Wagner James Au. "Burn Down the Shopping Malls," Salon.com, February 22, 2002. Available http://salon.com/tech/feature/2002/02/22/state_of_emergency.index

35. George Johnson. "A New Family Tree is Constructed for Indo-European," *The New York Times*, January 2, 1996, pp. B 5, B 7.

36. *Ibid.*, p. B 7.

37. John Lester. E-mail signature file, Massachusetts General Hospital. Available in EFF Quotes Collection 9.0 at Web site http://www.eff.org/pub/EFF/quotes.eff

38. Wade Roush. "Spinning a Better Web," *Technology Review*, April 1995. Available at http://www.mit.edu/techreview/www/

39. Brendan P. Kehoe. *Zen and the Art of the Internet: A Beginner's Guide.* (Englewood Cliffs, NJ: Prentice-Hall, 1991).

40. Mark Moraes. "What is Usenet?" Original by Chip Salzenberg. Last change by Mark Moraes on January 16, 1998. Accessed at http://www.faqs.org/faqs/usenet/what-is/part1/

41. Peter H. Lewis. "Peering Out a 'Real Time' Window," *The New York Times*, February 8, 1995, p. C1, C 5.

42. *A National Survey of the Public's Attitudes Towards Computers.* (New York: Time, 1971).

43. Louis Harris and Associates. *The Road After 1984: The Impact of Technology on Society* (for Southern New England Telephone, 1983).

44. *The Role of Technology in American Life.* The Times Mirror Center for the People & the Press, May 1994.

45. Peter H. Lewis. "Technology: Another survey of Internet users is out, and this one has statistical credibility," *The New York Times*, October 30, 1995, p. C 3.

46. Gary H. Anthes. "ISP = Internet Service Problems?" *Computerworld*, July 8, 1996, pp. 53-54.

47. Justin Hibbard. "Net Snares Mainstream," *Computerworld*, August 19, 1996, p. 6. Available at http://computerworld.com/news/1996/story/0,11280,8019,00.html

48. *Ibid.*

49. "Search Engine Statistics," Search Engine Showdown, March 6 2002. Available at http://www.searchengineshowdown.com/stats/sizeest.shtml

50. "A Matter of Trust: What users Want From Web Sites," Consumer Webwatch, January 2002. Available at http://www.consumerwebwatch.org/news/ report1.pdf

51. "Study by UCLA Internet Project Shows E-mail Transformed Personal Communication After Sept. 11 Attack," UCLA News, Press Release, February 7, 2002. Available at http://www.ccp.ucla.edu/pdf/UCLA-Internet-Report-2002.pdf

ADDITIONAL READINGS

A Variety of Applications

Brahm, Robert. "Math & Visualization: New Tools, New Frontiers." *IEEE Spectrum*, November 1995, pp. 19-21.

"Digital Television." Special Issue, *IEEE Spectrum*, April 1995, pp. 34-80.

"Key Technologies for the 21st Century," *Scientific American*, September 1995, 150th Anniversary Issue.

Many Broadcasters Will not Meet May 2002 Digital Television Deadline. General Accounting Office, April 2002. Available at the Web page with URL: http://www.gao.gov/new.items/d02466

Television. Survey. *Economist*, April 13, 2002. Available at the Web site with URL: http://www.economist.com/surveys/index.cfm?category=455022

The Internet and Information Highway

"The Accidental Superhighway: A Survey of the Internet," *The Economist*, July 1, 1995. Available at http://www.economist.com/surveys/internet/index.html

The Challenge of the Information Highway: Final Report of the Information Highway Advisory Council, Industry Canada, 1995. (Ottawa, Ontario: Distribution Services, Industry Canada). Available at <http://info.ic.gc.ca/info-highway/ih.html>.

Jonscher, Charles. *The Evolution of Wired Life: From the Alphabet to the Soul-Catcher Chip – How Information Technologies Change Our World.* (New York: Jon Wiley & Sons, 1999).

National Research Council. *The Internet's Coming of Age.* (Washington, DC: National Academy Press, 2001). Available at http://www.nap. edu/books/0309069920/html

Realizing the Information Future: The Internet and Beyond. Computer Science and Telecommunications Board, National Research Council. (Washington, D.C.: National Academy Press, 1994). Available at http://www.nap.edu/readingroom/books/rtif

"Surveying the Digital Future," The UCLA Internet Report, Year Three, February 2003. Available at http://ccp.ucla.edu/pdf/UCLA-Internet-Report-Year-Three.pdf

Societal Issues

Baase, Sarah, *A Gift of Fire: Social, legal, and ethical issues for computers and the Internet.* Second Edition, (Upper Saddle River, NJ: Prentice Hall, Pearson Education Inc., 2003).

Friedman, Batya (ed.). *Human Values and the Design of Computer Technology.* (New York: Cambridge University Press, 1997).

Johnson, Deborah G. and Nissenbaum, Helen. *Computers, Ethics & Social Values.* (Englewood Cliffs, NJ: Prentice Hall, 1995).

Miller, Steven E. *Civilizing Cyberspace: Policy, Power, and the Information Superhighway.* (New York: ACM Press and Addison-Wesley Publishing Company, 1996).

2

COMPUTERS AND THE HUMAN IMAGINATION

Some men see things as they are and ask why. Others dream things that never were and ask why not.

George Bernard Shaw (1856–1950)[1]

INTRODUCTION

Machines that can move, talk, play games, or mimic human behavior in some other way have held a considerable fascination for people in every era. It is not surprising these days to encounter at the newsstand one or more magazines that report yet another human ability recently achieved by a computer. The mechanisms used to produce such interesting behavior have ranged from steam, clockwork devices, and electromechanical systems to today's mainframes and workstations.

Contemporary depiction of robots is generally favorable—witness the lovable robots of the early *Star Wars* movies and their part in the series' phenomenal success. Only a few years earlier, however, one of the main protagonists in *2001: A Space Odyssey* was a malevolent computer called HAL. Robotic machines, such as those in *Terminator* (I, II, and III) and *Robocop* (I and II), have been perceived both as threats to society in general and humans in particular and as tools or even partners in the process of civilization.

Contemporary artists in many fields have been eager to use computers as partners in the process of creating imaginative works. Music, film, and the visual arts have been the primary beneficiaries (perhaps too strong a term in the opinion of many) of the advances in computer technology. Recently, computers and sophisticated graphics terminals have been used in movie animation to produce extraordinarily complex images. This development will permit directors to combine humans and computer-generated images without recourse to the construction of physical sets or even to produce animated movies entirely by computer. Less interesting results have been achieved in the application of computers to the written or spoken arts. Except perhaps for free verse poetry, where much of the art is in the ear and mind of the beholder, computers and language have not yet meshed successfully.

As a medium for artistic endeavor, the Internet is being employed in a number of interesting ways to extend the scope of creativity instantaneously worldwide. Music can be downloaded, world-famous museums visited, and famous archaeological sites explored, all from one's computer. The possibility of assuming arbitrary identities, including gender switching, may initiate global communities of active participants creating drama without boundaries. Virtual reality, the simulation of artificial worlds that permit people to role-play, is gaining in popularity and will continue to do so as the necessary technology becomes increasingly affordable. On a more mundane level, the explosion of Web pages has stimulated employment for many graphic artists. Terms such as multimedia and electronic art conjure up some of the excitement of the new media. Of course, technology in the employment of mediocre artists will result in mediocre art, but the possibilities of wonderful art available on demand for everyone continue to exist.

There has always been (or so it seems) a curious attraction to artifacts that resemble humans. In our own time, the digital computer has become the test bed for exploring the possibility of artificial intelligence (AI), that branch of computer science concerned with the attempt to develop programs and programmed machines that exhibit intelligent behavior. Indeed, AI has become not only a major branch of computer science but also a growing presence in the marketplace. Where relevant, applications involving AI will be discussed.

THE INTELLIGENT MACHINE IN FACT AND FICTION

Charlie had his way, and I was soon on the show. Charlie was right: Abdullah [a mechanical figure controlled internally by a hidden person] pulled them in because people cannot resist automata. There is something in humanity that is repelled and entranced by a machine that seems to have more than human powers. People love to frighten themselves. Look at the fuss nowadays about computers; however deft they may be they can't do anything a man isn't doing, through them; but you hear people giving themselves delicious shivers about a computer-dominated world. I've often thought of working up an illusion, using a computer, but it would be prohibitively expensive, and I can do anything the public would find amusing better and cheaper with clockwork and bits of string. But if I invented a computer-illusion I would take care to dress the computer up to look like a living creature of some sort—a Moon Man or a Venusian—because the public cannot resist clever dollies. Abdullah was a clever dolly of a simple kind and the Rubes couldn't get enough of him.[2]

Automata and Androids

In his interesting and informative book, *Human Robots in Myth and Science*, John Cohen has traced the human fascination with the possibility of living and thinking artifacts.[3] He describes a variety of instances in antiquity of statues that were supposed to speak and offer advice and prophecies. Hephaestus, also known as Vulcan, god of fire, was accompanied by two female statues of pure gold that assisted him in his activities. In the 15th century B.C., the statue of King Memnon near Thebes supposedly emitted a variety of sounds depending on the time of day. Hero of Alexandria (285–222 B.C.) built mechanical birds that apparently flew and sang.

There are many stories of devices originating in the East that moved and talked. Consider this tale of a robot of the 3rd century B.C. in China.[4]

> King Mu of Chou made a tour of inspection in the west . . . and on his return journey, before reaching China, a certain artificer, Yen Shih by name, was presented to him. The king received him and asked him what he could do. He replied that he would do anything which the king commanded, but that he had a piece of work already finished which he would like to show him. "Bring it with you tomorrow," said the king, "and we will look at it together." So next day Yen Shih appeared again and was admitted into the presence. "Who is that man accompanying you?" asked the king. "That, Sir," replied Yen Shih, "is my own handiwork. He can sing and he can act." The king stared at the figure in astonishment. It walked with rapid strides, moving its head up and down, so that anyone would have taken it for a live human being. The artificer touched its chin, and it began singing, perfectly in tune. He touched its hands, and it began posturing, keeping perfect time. It went through any number of movements that fancy might happen to dictate. The king, looking on with his favourite concubine and other beauties, could hardly persuade himself that it was not real. As the performance was drawing to an end, the robot winked its eye and made advances to the ladies in attendance, whereupon the king became incensed and would have had Yen Shih executed on the spot had not the latter, in mortal fear, instantly taken the robot to pieces to let him see what it really was. And, indeed, it turned out to be only a construction of leather, wood, glue and lacquer, variously coloured white, black, red and blue.

The willingness of people to accept life in objects of stone, metal, or wood seems evidence of some deeply embedded need to believe in the power of either the gods or their specially chosen servants, to create life in any form. The effect is even stronger if the things that move or talk resemble humans. This need has not diminished over the centuries.

The illustrious figures Albertus Magnus (1204–1272) and Roger Bacon (1214–1294) are supposed to have created, respectively, a life-size automaton servant and a speaking head. At the end of the 16th century in Prague, Rabbi Loew reportedly produced a living being—the legendary Golem—out of a clay figure by inserting into its mouth a strip of paper with a magical formula. The creation of life from earth or other inanimate substances is a common theme in both history and literature that reached its apogee, in fiction at least, with Baron Frankenstein's monster some two centuries later.

The golden age of automata perhaps was in Europe in the 18th century. Skilled craftsmen built incredibly lifelike mechanisms that were exhibited to enormous crowds. The more lifelike the appearance, the greater the acclaim. Apparently the most impressive of these automata was a duck built by Jacques de Vaucanson (1709–1782) and exhibited in 1738. A rebuilt version of this automaton was displayed in Milan at La Scala in 1844 amid great excitement. A member of the audience wrote the following:

> It is the most admirable thing imaginable, an almost inexplicable human achievement. Each feather of the wings is mobile . . . . The artist touches a feather on the upper portion of the body, and the bird lifts its head, glances about, shakes its tail feathers, stretches itself, unfolds its wings, ruffles them and lets out a cry, absolutely natural, as if it were about to take flight. The effect is still more astonishing when the bird, leaning over its dish, begins to swallow the grain with incredibly realistic movement. As for its method of digestion, nobody can explain it.[5]

There is no question of such devices exhibiting free will or initiating independent action. However lifelike, the duck was no more than a complex clock mechanism of approximately 4000 parts, and from the moment it began to move, its actions were completely predetermined. We marvel at the incredible ingenuity of the inventor, but at the same time we are aware of the limitations of the invention. Still, the skill of these inventors was mind boggling. Especially impressive are the life-size androids built by Pierre Jacquet-Droz and his two sons near Neufchatel, Switzerland, between 1768 and 1774. One, a "child" android called the Writer, could be mechanically programmed to write any 40 characters of text. Another, the Musician, which had the form of a woman, moved with a marvelous grace replete with subtle gestures that included head motions and a curtsy.

The so-called Chess Player of 1769, built by Baron Wolfgang von Kempelen (1734–1809) was a famous fraud. Costumed as a Turk, the automaton appeared to move the pieces on a chess board and to play quite a good game of chess. It is believed that, unknown to the audience, a person was concealed under the board, though this fact was not actually established during the automaton's lifetime. Edgar Allan Poe, one of those who argued for the hidden person hypothesis, exploited this theme when he wrote the short story called "Maelzel's Chess-Player" in 1838.

The Theme of the Robot

> It is unreasonable . . . to think machines could become *nearly* as intelligent as we are and then stop, or to suppose we will always be able to compete with them in wit or wisdom. Whether or not we could retain some sort of control of the machines, assuming that we would want to, the nature of our activities and aspirations would be changed utterly by the presence on earth of intellectually superior beings.[6]

A robot can be thought of as a mobile computer with sensory, tactile, and motor abilities. Furthermore, it is typically an artifact made in the image of its human creator, who has endowed it with some form of lifelike behavior. It need not, at least in principle, be machine-like. We might argue that Frankenstein's monster was a robot created from a human corpse and given the spark of "life" by the power of lightning.

The relationship between the scientist or inventor and his or her creation has inspired many tales. Two basic plots have emerged. In one, the robot is a subordinate, a servant quick to obey but unable to initiate independent action. The other is concerned with self-motivated behavior, with the robot (or creation) as potential adversary or potential master. Creations of this type have caused trouble through willful disobedience, as exemplified by Frankenstein's monster, and by carrying out a request too zealously and too literally, as shown in the story of the sorcerer's apprentice and in *The Monkey's Paw* by W. W. Jacobs.[7]

Much of the literature in this area relates to the Greek myth of Prometheus, the hero who disobeyed Zeus, stole fire from heaven, and gave it to humankind. This gift permitted people to keep themselves warm, to illuminate the night, and to create tools and other objects, presumably without either the help or permission of the gods. As punishment for this outrageous theft, Prometheus was chained to a mountain top and plagued for eternity by vultures picking at his liver—a torment one might recommend today for the designers of some particularly terrible computer programs. It is often forgotten that the full title of Mary Shelley's *Frankenstein*, published in 1818, is *Frankenstein: or, the Modern Prometheus*. (Remember also that Baron Frankenstein's monster has no name of its own. Thanks to Hollywood, it has become known simply as Frankenstein.)

In her study of robots and androids in science fiction, Patricia Warrick isolates four themes that emerge from Shelley's novel and recur in modern science fiction.[8]

1. The Promethean theme: the acquisition of a hitherto forbidden skill that is now put to the supposed benefit of humankind.
2. The two-edged nature of technology: benefits are frequently offset by unanticipated problems.
3. The precipitous rejection of technology: the monster launches a campaign of terror only after Dr. Frankenstein abandons him.
4. The uneasy relation between master and servant: what is created sometimes turns against the creator and becomes the master.

This last point is perhaps best exemplified in *Erewhon* (1872), by Samuel Butler, which explores the relationship between humans and their machines. The narrator, discussing the reasons given by the society of Erewhon for banishing machines, notes that it is not existing machines that are to be feared, but the fact that they evolve so rapidly and in such unpredictable directions that they must be controlled, limited, and destroyed while they are still in a primitive form. Compare this fear with the sentiment expressed nearly a century later by one of the founders of artificial intelligence in the quotation that began this section. The following quotation from *Erewhon* may serve as a grim commentary on our age[9]:

> True, from a low materialistic point of view it would seem that those thrive best who use machinery wherever its use is possible with profit; but this is the art of the machines: they serve that they may rule .... How many men at this hour are living in a state of bondage to the machines? How many spend their whole lives, from the cradle to the grave, in tending them by night and day? Is it not plain that the machines are gaining ground upon us ...

Other Utopian, or perhaps more precisely dystopian, novels, such as Aldous Huxley's *Brave New World*—written about 50 years later—and George Orwell's *1984*, are more concerned with general issues surrounding the organization of a future society. Nevertheless, the all-powerful computer plays an integral role in these societies, whether it regulates the birth process, as in *Brave New World*, or controls a vast two-way communications network by which Big Brother has access to every person, as in *1984*. The title *1984* has itself become the shorthand term for the perfectly totalitarian society in which all efforts are devoted to maintaining the state against its enemies, both internal and external, real and imagined. "Big Brother is watching you" is the ultimate warning for a society in which there is complete absence of privacy and individual freedom.

In the 20th century, perhaps *the* work of art that most successfully addresses the problem of people and their people-like machines is the play *R.U.R.* (1921) by Karel Capek.[10] In fact the word "robot" made its first appearance in this play, whose title is an abbreviation for "Rossum's Universal Robots." In *R.U.R.* humankind has become so dependent on robots that when the robots revolt, there is no hope. However, the robots do not know how to reproduce themselves, the formula having been lost in the general destruction accompanying their takeover. Thus, the people are ultimately destroyed by their creations, a bitter example of the fourth theme mentioned above.

At variance with the almost universal pessimism expressed so far has been the impact on science fiction of Isaac Asimov's robot stories. Asimov, one of the most prolific writers of our time, wrote a series of short stories dealing with robots and in the process introduced a substantial realignment into the imagined human-robot relationship. In his 1942 story "Runaround," Asimov described "the three fundamental Rules of Robotics—the three rules that are built most deeply into a robot's positronic brain." These govern robot behavior with respect to humans to prevent any harm coming to a human either through an action or lack of action by a robot. The three laws are as follows[11]:

> First Law: A robot may not injure a human being, or, through inaction, allow a human being to come to harm. Second Law: A robot must obey the orders given it by human beings except where such orders would conflict with the First Law. Third Law: A robot must protect its own existence as long as such protection does not conflict with the First or Second Laws.

The working out of implications inherent in these three laws informs the plots of many of the subsequent stories in Asimov's robot series.

The trend of reforming robots has probably reached its peak in the *Star Wars* movies, in which the two robots—R2D2, the chirpy fire hydrant, and C3PO, the prissy, gold-encased English butler—do not appear to have even one malevolent transistor between them. They exist only to serve their masters—humans. In real life another race of robots has appeared in the last few years: those indefatigable workers on the assembly line, the industrial robots. We can conclude with the observation that intelligent artifacts, whether in the form of humans or not, continue to exert a powerful influence on the human imagination. In many ways technology, the product of our minds and hands, is a mixed blessing. Writers have explored this ambivalence for many years, but the issues have sharpened with the appearance of that most marvelous of all inventions, the computer.

COMPUTERS AS A CREATIVE MEDIUM

"The Eureka"

> Such is the name of a machine for composing hexameter Latin verses which is now exhibited at the Egyptian Hall, in Piccadilly. It was designed and constructed at Bridgewater, in Somersetshire; was begun in 1830, and

completed in 1843; and it has lately been brought to the metropolis, to contribute to the "sights of the season . . . ."

The rate of composition is about one verse per minute, or sixty an hour. Each verse remains stationary and visible a sufficient time for a copy of it to be taken; after which the machine gives an audible notice that the Line is about to be decomposed. Each Letter of the verse is then slowly and separately removed into its former alphabetical arrangement; on which the machine stops, until another verse be required. Or, by withdrawing the stop, it may be made to go on continually, producing in one day and night, or twenty-four hours, about 1440 Latin verses; or, in a whole week (Sundays included) about 10,000. During the composition of each line, a cylinder in the interior of the machine performs the National Anthem—
Anonymous, Illustrated London News, 1895

What effects has the computer had, either directly or indirectly, on the arts? "Arts" here means music, drawing and graphics, film, literature, multimedia, and virtual reality. We are concerned with the use of computers in the creative process as a tool or aid or as the very medium for artistic creation, rather than as the subject matter of the work itself. In the best of all possible worlds you would have access to a computer and be able to use it to produce music (with a synthesizer), art (with a graphics system), and perhaps poetry. Second best would be a tape of music, a portfolio of drawings, and a slim volume of computer-generated poetry. Unfortunately, we are in a position only to describe and comment, not to present and demonstrate, but you are encouraged to access the Internet, to search out Web sites that make music, art, film, and literature instantaneously available.

There are a number of issues to keep in mind as we proceed. To what degree is the computer itself creative? This seems to be a question with which the artists themselves have little concern. For those interested in the computer as a tool, there is hardly any reason to attribute special powers of creativity to it. The artist wants to explore ways of creating under his or her initiative. The computer can give the artist a variety of means to extend and augment his or her abilities. Will anything significant emerge from the application of computers to art? The simple answer is "yes, of course." Consider photography and filmmaking as two examples of contemporary arts that have roots in developing and expanding technologies. Consider music played on electronic instruments and manipulated using computer-controlled synthesizers. Consider the possibilities of employing virtual-reality technologies in the making of advanced art. We will explore some of the possibilities in the next few sections.

Music

Music has probably been that art form most amenable to computer experimentation, and the history of computer music is almost as old as that of the first electronic computer. This fact is not very surprising, because even before computers were invented, music could be represented by means of an electronic signal that is readily available for a computer to modify. The original signal itself can be generated by electronic equipment. That is, a complex piece of equipment incorporating signal generators, synthesizers, and microprocessors is like a giant "intelligent" organ that can be used by the contemporary composer.

In the 1950s, electronic music meant tape splicing and other manual rearrangements of sound. It was not until the 1960s that sound synthesizers, high-speed digital-to-analog converters, and sound-generation programs appeared. One of the most famous early works was the "Illiac Suite for String Quartet" by Lejaren Hiller of the University of Illinois. This composition relied on the computer for the generation of random numbers. Music with a strong random component in its performance or composition is called *aleatory* music. For purposes of composition, computers have proven invaluable because the composer is able to set the parameters of permissible variation, and the computer can select the actual path to be followed. Once the program has been designed, the role of the composer is to modify, shape, and select.

However, quite a few discordant sounds have been made as well by critics and the general public. For example, Lars Gunnar Bodin of the Electronic Music Studio of Stockholm has written, albeit more than 20 years ago, "in spite of great efforts in time and money, relatively little of artistic significance has been produced in computer music."[12] The composition of music using electronic aids has been subject to criticism similar to that once directed at the mechanical reproduction of music. The German writer E. T. A. Hoffman (about whose life and stories Jacques Offenbach composed the opera *Tales of Hoffmann*) wrote the following in 1816[12]:

> To set to work to make music by means of valves, springs, levers, cylinders, or whatever other apparatus you choose to employ, is a senseless attempt to make the means to an end accomplish what can result only when those means are animated and, in their minutest movements, controlled by the mind, the soul, and the heart. The gravest reproach you can make to a musician is that he plays without expression; because, by so doing, he is marring the whole essence of the matter. For it is impossible that any impulse whatever from the inner man shall not, even for a moment, animate his rendering; whereas, in the case of a machine, no such impulse can ever do so. The attempts of mechanicians to imitate, with more or less approximation to accuracy, the human organs in the production of musical sounds, or to substitute mechanical appliances for those organs, I consider tantamount to a declaration of war against the spiritual element in music; but the greater the forces they array against it, the more victorious it is. For this very reason, the more perfect that this sort of machinery is, the more I disapprove of it; and I infinitely prefer the commonest barrel-organ, in

which the mechanism attempts nothing but to be mechanical, to Vaucanson's flute player, or the harmonica girl.

An important aspect of the creation of computer-related art is the availability of the necessary hardware, typically a specially equipped workstation, and the appropriate software. For music, the Musical Instrument Digital Interface (M.I.D.I.) sound synthesis system has been the relatively low-cost system of choice for many musicians. A typical M.I.D.I. system consists of a method for generating signals at given frequencies, a process to shape and modify these signals, and finally a sound chip to create the synthesized music that can be converted to analog form and played back through a speaker.[14] Apparently, using M.I.D.I. is not straightforward and has been difficult for many musicians to learn.

However exciting the creation of music using computers may be, the important news for the past few years has been the downloading and online trading of music files. This topic will be discussed more extensively in Chapter 10, in the context of intellectual property rights, but at this point some of the technical issues will be explored. The most common format for storing music in a computer is as an MP3 file. MP3 is an abbreviation for the Moving Pictures Experts Group, Audio Layer 3, an organization that sets international standards for digital formats for audio and video. But what are MP3's?[15]

> MP3s are digital audio files that have been shrunken down while still maintaining their original sound quality. Before there were MP3s, digital audio files took hours to download. But on a 56K modem, most MP3s can download in just a few minutes. MP3s are widely recognized as the most popular format for storing and listening to music on the World Wide Web.

MP3's are traded, downloaded, saved, and transferred to (burned onto) CD's. There is an enormous black market industry in trading music via Web sites, ferocious counterattacks from music industry associations, an emerging growth of point-to-point rather than central service facilities, and pressure on governments to enforce existing laws, pass more stringent laws, and to mount massive education campaigns. That music would become a focal point for Web activity is not surprising, in retrospect, but the passions aroused by millions of aficionados, who believed it to be their natural right to download music, wherever it was located, for free, was unexpected. More later.

Visual Arts

Turning to drawing, graphics, and video art, we find, up to fairly recently, considerable inventiveness but a certain sameness of technique. Facile use of a new and powerful tool may be the problem. As in music, we may have to look to the future for the emergence of real art and not just the obvious exploitation of an available technology. One of the early and important artists to use computers was A. Michael Noll. In an article written in 1967, he makes the point that even though the computer must be programmed to perform each action, its speed, decision-making ability, and large memory give it great power even to the point of appearing to produce the unexpected.[16] The computer permits the artist to explore many possibilities and, in some sense, demonstrates a measure of creativity.

In the interest of exploring this notion, Noll programmed a computer to generate a picture composed of pseudo-random elements resembling paintings done by Piet Mondrian, a well-known 20th-century artist. The computer-generated picture was displayed, along with a Mondrian painting, for the benefit of 100 subjects, who were asked which they preferred and which was in fact the Mondrian. 59% preferred the computer picture and only 28% could identify the Mondrian picture. An interesting fact is that people found the Mondrian too precise and machine-like in its placement of the picture elements, whereas the randomness in the placement of the corresponding picture elements in the computer picture was found pleasing.[17]

Another early computer artist is Charles Csuri at Ohio State University. He began in 1964 to use a mainframe computer and has continued to the present day, but he is not interested in using paint programs. He "wants the full power of a sophisticated computer at his fingertips, which lets him sculpt images in three dimensions, view them from any angle, set them in motion, and alter them in ways that often blur the distinction between special effects and art."[18] Csuri's view on the role of the computer in the creation of art is interesting and valuable, given his experiences over many years. He insists that, "Just because the computer can do perspective and beautiful shadows and shininess, or make things look like glass, you still need to have an esthetic sensibility, you need a sense of culture and history. That has not changed."[19]

The relationship between art and technology has always been uneasy. It has taken many years for photography to be recognized as art, and the suspicion remains that the photographer achieves most by selection rather than by creation, since the camera seems to do most of the work. Thus, it is not surprising that acceptance of such a marvelous piece of equipment as a computer should be resisted by both the public at large and the artist. But change is inevitable, given the nature of our times. Too frequently the computer is used as an overpriced electronic paintbrush. Most of the results could hardly be termed "fine art": repetitive patterns, distorted images of human forms, and randomly placed patches of randomly generated lines. However, many artists have used the computer in a creative and exciting way.

One of these is Harold Cohen, who almost 30 years ago designed a program called Aaron in order to study the way people both produce and understand drawings. Not surprisingly, Cohen has discovered that much of the enjoyment and appreciation of a work of art is brought by the viewer.

Many times he has been asked if what is being displayed is indeed art. What may be surprising is that Aaron itself has "advanced from drawing squiggly lines to painting portraits that look handmade and are hung in major art museums."[20] Surprisingly, in spite of all the accolades for Aaron, Professor Cohen is somewhat ambivalent about how to characterize his program's performance:

> "Most everybody else does consider it to be creative," Cohen said. "I personally do not, because I have rather stringent views on what creativity would demand. But it's considered creative enough that the president of the American Association for Artificial Intelligence cited it in his inaugural address last year as one of the only creative programs in existence."
>
> "All the time in the back of mind is the question of machine autonomy," Cohen said. "The problem I would face if I ever figured out how to do it, in giving Aaron as it were its own head, is I might hate what it does."
>
> "If the program did a drawing in August that it couldn't have done when I stopped programming it in January [2001]," he said, "then I'll consider it creative."[21]

Another artist, Hubert Hohn,[22] in reaction to the idea of the computer as a sophisticated tool, has decided to, "try to define a computer aesthetic based on the unique properties of the machine . . . . I want to see what happens when a computer is allowed to be itself—not forced to function as a paintbrush or a camera or a lump of charcoal."[23] Letting the computer be itself in this case involved writing a simple program to print out the current state of memory as a structured array of 0s and 1s and attaching titles such as "SELF PORTRAIT," or "THE MACHINE EXAMINES THE STATE OF ITS MEMORY IN THE ACT OF EXAMINING THE STATE OF ITS MEMORY", or, "THE MACHINE SEEKS THE ORIGIN OF ITS CONSCIOUSNESS." In some sense the titles have assumed an importance far beyond the work itself.

In the last few years, the hardware and software have improved so dramatically that the computer has become a major factor in the production of graphic art. Even the Internet has become an integral component of many works of art. One example employs the FBI's surveillance program, called Carnivore (See Chapter 9 for more about this program), to make a point about the insidiousness of monitoring the Internet communication of all the customers of a chosen Internet service provider. A group of artists has developed a program that represents the traffic on a network in the form of continuously changing colors, shapes, and sounds.[24] This project opened for display at Princeton University during January, 2002.

Themes in this new art are a mixture of exploring general fears of technology in today's society, provoking such fears, exploitation of the technology itself as a window and even a door into alternative domains of experience, and playing with images, sounds, and textures in unpredictable ways.

Some of the earliest applications appeared in advertising, and this trend has continued in the relatively new area of Web pages. Thousands of Web sites are in active competition to attract first-time viewers and to maintain their interest. One method is to design flashy graphics, but unless the content is equally compelling, first-time viewers may well not return. In any case, a lucrative application area has appeared for graphic artists to practice their craft and many talented designers have been attracted.[25]

Of course, the events of September 11, 2001 cast a pall over most artistic endeavours. They have also raised some serious questions about the nature of art, in general, in a time of political and social crises. The National Coalition Against Censorship (NCAC), together with Art Now, launched a Web site to present artistic responses to the tragedy. A variety of purposes are served by the existence of this site that go beyond the display of works of art[26]:

> In building this national archive, project coordinators wanted to include not just artworks that commemorate, but also those that raise questions about meaning and civic consciousness. They wanted to expand public focus beyond New York City to increase visibility for local artists who are responding to the tragedy.
>
> "We wanted to go beyond the idea of art as healing and look at works that deal with foreign policy and media images," said Rebecca Metzger, who is coordinating the Art Now website.
>
> NCAC launched the Art Now discussion forum to replicate live debates and to create a virtual place where artists might connect and collaborate with each other.

To further emphasize the important role that the Internet has assumed in the world of art, we briefly describe some examples of recent exhibitions:

- 0101010: Art in Technological Times. [March 2001, San Francisco] This week the San Francisco Museum of Modern Art will open one of the most ambitious exhibitions in its history, a show filled with animated "paintings," virtual reality art, cyborg sculptures and other technological creations. . . . In an unusual move, none of the five online art projects will be viewable in the museum. People will have to see them at their own computers, as the works are meant to be seen, Ross said, who acknowledged that some in the art community wouldn't mind if Web-based art wasn't part of the show at all.[27]
- Casting a Net: A Survey of Internet Art. [December 2001, McLean, Virginia] If you're with-it enough to have a broadband Internet connection, Flash 4 and 5, Shockwave, QuickTime and RealPlayer on your home computer, you need not show up at the gallery at all. You can see the show whenever you want, at www.mcleanart.org. But if the Internet's great hope is that it allows each of us to be independent media producers, do we even need

galleries to show it? Plenty of media artists could give a hoot about taking part in a survey like "Casting a Net." But for time-strapped artgoers too busy to surf on their own, a gallery or museum can provide a handy cache of pre-screened work.[28]

- 20th Ars Electronica Festival. [September 2001, Linz, Austria] So much new innovation is unfolding in the realm of digital art. Because of this, the debate about the art is, in a way, less important than the structures and institutions that enable digital artists to work and surprise us with their new directions. . . . Ars will focus more on workshop-like sessions that feature young artists and other up-and-comers.[29]

As with so much of the material in this book, much more could be said. Fast becoming an important factor in picture-making is three-dimensional imagery. Increased computing power has enabled software to be created to present 3-D pictures in such areas as medicine, advertising, games, engineering, the military, and science.[30] One possibly dangerous implication of this technology is that the ability to manipulate digital images can destroy all confidence in the fidelity of photographic evidence. Obviously, altering photographs or creating photographs that depict events that did not occur can have devastating impact for historical research, news reporting, and of course in the courts. At the very least, a healthy skepticism must now be maintained[31]:

> Photographs appeared to be reliably manufactured commodities, readily distinguishable from other types of depictions. They were generally regarded as causally generated, truthful reports about things in the real world, unlike more traditionally handicrafted images, which seemed notoriously ambiguous and uncertain human constructions. The emergence of digital imaging has irrevocably subverted these certainties, forcing us all to adopt a far more wary and vigilant interpretive stance. The information superhighway will bring us a growing flood of visual information in digital format, but we will have to take great care to sift facts from the fictions and the falsehoods.

The reference to the information superhighway is well-taken, but from another point of view the ability to visit the world's museums remotely via the Internet provides heretofore unavailable opportunities.

Finally, something must be said about the incredible growth in digital photography. The price of cameras is right and their flexibility unmatched. The quality of the photographs is steadily improving; furthermore, the ability to view the pictures on computers and to alter their appearance with readily available software opens up possibilities for the amateur photographer previously only available to professionals, with the concerns mentioned above of course. And such photographs can be easily sent over the Internet to friends and relations.

Film

Some would say that movies are *the* exciting domain of contemporary arts. They are another fairly recent art form. In their early years, movies were seen mainly as popular entertainment, and profits were the main motive for their production. Almost inadvertently, artists were attracted to this new medium and succeeded over time in producing important and serious artistic endeavors. However, there has always been an uneasy peace between the goals of profit and art. Many of the experimental efforts in film have emerged from a stream outside the commercial film industry.

One of the earliest and most important filmmakers to use the computer as an integral part of the creative process is John Whitney. Fully aware of the potential of computers as early as the 1940s, Whitney observed that

> the best computer art did not compare well with lacework from Belgium made a century ago. But the computer possessed a unique capability of making very complex pattern flow. One could plan exacting and explicit patterns of action and distinctive motions as intricate as lace, but in a way no Belgian lacemaker would ever have imagined.[32]

Whitney created a number of films, with music, generated by computer. They are characterized by the complex development of geometric themes in a rhythmic pattern accompanied by an original musical score. He had no illusions about the role of computers in the creation of art and very bluntly stated his beliefs that computers would never create "meaningful" art. The crucial issue in creativity is judgment, not calculation.

It is altogether fitting that the real breakthrough in the application of computers to the making of films was made by Walt Disney Studios in *TRON* (1982). Long the world leader in animated feature films, Disney Studios recognized that the state of the art in computer animation was sufficiently well developed for computers to make a major contribution to filmmaking. The traditional Disney animation system required that many people work over long periods of time to produce thousands upon thousands of drawings. Developments in graphics, however, both in hardware and software, have permitted generation by computer of representational three-dimensional scenes. In all previous movies based on fantasy or science fiction, very complex models—usually quite small—were designed and built. Actors were positioned and cleverly photographed against these models to give the illusion of vast reaches of space, giant castles, enormous space ships, and other constructs of the projected future or distant past. Of course many other techniques have been employed in the composition, photography, and editing of films, and computers have played an important role in these phases as well. As for *TRON*, although in its time it was a technological success, its artistic failure limited its influence.

In July 1984, *The Last Starfighter* was released. It included about 25 minutes of computer-generated film, compared to about 5 minutes in *TRON*. The computer scenes were generated by Digital Productions, using a Cray X-MP. This machine replaced the earlier Cray-1 (used in the making of TRON) and was needed in such prodigious computations as those for the hero's spaceship *Gunstar*, which required 750,000 polygons and achieved an extraordinarily realistic effect. [Interestingly enough, it is a more difficult challenge to represent soft objects such as flowers and people than spaceships and robots.]

A Lucasfilm division called Pixar (founded by George Lucas, the creator of the enormously popular and successful *Star Wars* series), set up to carry out research and development in advanced computer graphics, was purchased in 1986 by Steven Jobs and is now an independent company. It has made a number of important contributions to such movies as *Star Trek II: The Wrath of Khan* and *Return of the Jedi*, as well as producing award-winning animated shorts such as *The Adventures of Andre* and *Wally B.*, and culminating with the five-minute *Tin Toy,* the first computer-generated film to win an Academy Award. Although the computational efforts to create even short films are prodigious, the fundamental creative act still resides in the human animators, who must design the original figures, environment, and of course, story line. The appearance of the very successful film *Who Framed Roger Rabbit?*, a full-length movie integrating hand-drawn animated characters with humans, serves as a reminder of how much is yet to be achieved by computer animation systems. The long period of time involved in producing traditional animated movies, however, to say nothing of the associated high costs, certainly provides impetus for further research.

The past few years have seen this challenge being met. The production of such successful films as *Casper, Terminator 2, Jurassic Park, The Mask, Forest Gump, Toy Story*, and *Jumanji*, has finally indicated that completely automated animation is possible and that an entire film of high quality is well within reach; in fact *Toy Story* may very well be that film. One technique that has been employed successfully is called *morphing*, the continuous deformation of one image into another. It was an integral part of the treatment of the android in *Terminator 2*, that repeatedly reconstructed itself from the results of episodes of drastic dismemberment, and permitted Jim Carrey's face to undergo the most startling transformations in *The Mask*, but that old question remains[33]:

> *The Mask* is not so much a movie, more a feature-length demo reel for the wonders of digital conjuring on screen. . . . You end up enthused by the product but wondering, before you take out your cheque book, whether you should not wait a little longer while they improve the story-packaging.

Toy Story is 77 minutes long and every frame was computer generated[34]:

> Each one of its 1,560 shots was created on Silicon Graphics and Sun work-stations by artists working from some 400 computer-generated mathematical models and backgrounds. The shots were then edited using Avid editing systems and painstakingly rendered by powerful Pixar-developed RenderMan software. (That software consumed 300 Mbytes per frame, provided by 117 Sun SPARC 20s. Four years in the making, the 77-minute film required 800,000 machine-hours just to produce a final cut.)

Interestingly enough, this enormous expenditure in computer resources was produced by Disney, the world leader in traditional animation methods. And even more surprising, the film was an artistic success with many critics rating it as one of the best of 1995. The success is a result of a good story with funny dialogue and excellent characters, well-served by the exciting and extremely effective animation. In a surprisingly wonderful continuation of great animated films, the 2001 Academy Award for animated feature films (a new category) went to *Shrek*, a lovable ogre. The future looks more than promising for the application of technology to the making of movies.

The past few years have inevitably featured more advances in the application of technology to filmmaking. In the film *Gladiator* (2000), the Roman Coliseum was peopled with the images of a small number of actual individuals reproduced many times over. *The Matrix*, a 1999 movie, contained scenes of incredibly choreographed fights, possible only by the use of computer systems. These techniques reached a more advanced level almost two years later in the acclaimed movie *Crouching Tiger, Hidden Dragon* (2000), with its wonderful rooftop sword fights.

In addition to the direct technological impact on filmmaking, it is necessary to comment, however briefly, on a few other issues. One of these is the portrayal of hackers by Hollywood, apparently a growth industry. Consider the films *WarGames* (1985), *Real Genius* (1985), *Sneakers* (1992), *Goldeneye* (1995), *Hackers* (1995), *The Net* (1995), *The Matrix* (1999), and *Antitrust* (2001).[35] In these movies, the portrayal of hackers varies from malevolent evil doers, to innocent high school boys, to Internet-savvy women, to idealists combating large fictional software corporations. And indeed, some of them have done very badly at the box office. For example, a quick summation of the plots suggests reasons for the failure of *Hackers* and *The Net*. *Hackers*: "Stringy-haired youths compete to obtain secret virus information;" *The Net*: "Assassin seeks to obtain secret virus information on floppy disk. In the process, he wipes out the main character's credit card history, driver's license and passport information."[36] Flashy computer graphics do not make up for a weak plot.

In preparation for the next section, we turn to a much anticipated movie in mid-2001, Steven Spielberg's *A.I.*, about a boy who is actually artificial, that is, an apparent living instantiation of an artifact driven by A.I. software. The film is based on a short story written by the British science fiction writer, Brian Aldiss, titled, "Supertoys Last All Summer Long," in 1969. The story was purchased in 1982 by the director Stanley Kubrick, who died in 1999, without having produced a screenplay. However, he had shared his vision with Spielberg, who eventually brought it to the screen with decidedly mixed results. It represents one of the very few financial and critical failures in Spielberg's overwhelmingly successful career.[37] The boy, David, is made in a factory and brought to live with a couple, who very much want a child, even an artificial one. David wants to know who he is if not a real boy, and his journey of discovery forms the substance of the movie. Unfortunately, the short story does not scale up to a full-length film, and very little light is shed on the nature of A.I.

With all the advances in animation, the next challenge is to animate realistic humans, and recent evidence shows progress in that direction. Such achievements raise serious issues such as[38]:

> When computer graphics imaging (C.G.I. is the industry shorthand) becomes detailed enough, and when voice synthesis software becomes smooth enough, filmmakers will be faced with their own version of the great cloning debate. Is it right to make dead actors work again, to make living actors do things they didn't do in front of a camera, or to create actors out of whole pixels, who might take on an existence of their own?

In July 2001, the movie *Final Fantasy* opened with probably the most lifelike computer-generated characters, so-called "synthespians." This process will continue and one day a film will appear in which everything is computer generated. Will it matter?

Finally, there is an area in which the application of current computer technology to films has aroused some controversy, namely the colorization of black-and-white movies. For a generation raised with color television and primarily color movies, black-and-white images do not seem to be attractive, or at least this is what Turner Entertainment, the current owner of such classic movies as *The Maltese Falcon, Casablanca, Miracle on 34th Street*, and *It's a Wonderful Life*, maintains.[39] Consider the following summary of two positions, keeping in mind that the owner of a work of art, or any property for that matter, has complete control over his or her possession[40]:

> The Directors Guild of America has protested colorization on the grounds that its members' works of art are being tampered with. [They] defended black-and-white films as an art form, meriting the preservation granted to historical films or national landmarks. The colorists' position is that they are simply offering the public an option; those who prefer the black-and-white can simply turn down the color control on their television set.

CONTEMPORARY VIEWS OF THE MACHINE

All life is an experiment. The more experiments you make the better.—
Ralph Waldo Emerson (1803–1882)[41]

We are living in an age of science and technology. The newsstand has exploded with computer and technology magazines such as *MacWorld, PC World, Wired, Internet World, Virtual Reality*, and others, whose covers advertise stories on biotechnology, artificial life, new theories of the universe, and, inevitably, computers. In addition to the purely technological articles on how microprocessors will revolutionize our lives, stories on intelligent machines appear with regularity. We are told how computers will do the work of doctors, lawyers, and other professionals, and that robots will soon be making regular appearances in our homes and in our places of work and play.

The public at large is infatuated with the robot. The immensely popular R2D2 and C3PO of the by-now classic *Star Wars* series, are totally dedicated to the well-being of their human masters. They are the complete antithesis, of, say, Frankenstein's monster and are, in fact, a realization of the kind of robot proposed by Isaac Asimov. We are now in the era of the robot as friend and servant. Some voices have been raised in warning about the possibility of massive unemployment resulting from the introduction of robots into the assembly line. The counterargument is that robots will be engaged in boring and dangerous activities and thus free people to realize their full potential in other areas of life. In any case, robots are on the way. We are even being encouraged to attribute robotic qualities to household devices that incorporate microprocessors, sensors, and actuators—manufacturers inform us in their advertisements that our televisions, microwave ovens, cameras, and other pieces of everyday equipment have an "electronic brain" that can think (for us) and therefore act for us.

Intelligent machines may be a mixed blessing, as you will recall from that powerful motion picture, *2001: A Space Odyssey*. A computer called HAL (each letter in the name only one letter removed from IBM) begins acting unpredictably as it tries to ensure the success of the space mission, believing that it is in jeopardy because of the actions of the human crew. It causes the death of four men before it is dismantled by the one remaining human. As its circuits are progressively disconnected it appeals piteously to be allowed to continue functioning. It even promises to be good in the future. All this is to no avail, as it has in fact violated Asimov's First Law and must be punished.

This impressive film leaves us with the assured feeling that we humans will retain ultimate control because we can "pull the plug." The popular media generally present a favorable viewpoint toward robots or intelligent machines: These machines will secure more leisure time for everyone and liberate people from dangerous work; they will mine the seas, explore space, and bring prosperity to all. However, some nonscientific observers think that if machines become intelligent enough they will develop a sense (a strategy) of self-preservation that will cause them to defend their existence. From Hollywood, the frequent creator and arbiter of mass taste, has come a series of beings illustrating such diverse themes as the destruction of humans (*Terminator*, played by Arnold Schwarzenegger) and their protector (*Terminator 2*, with the protecting android again played by Arnold confronting a more advanced killing model). More recently, *Screamers* shows what happens when robots designed for special tasks of directed destruction somehow mutate and destroy humans indiscriminately, yet another instance of the slave turning on the master. These movies and many others are all products of the human imagination as typically revealed in science fiction, and while the vision of the future they present is possible, at root it is clearly more fiction than science. However, there is a scientific discipline concerned with the development of intelligent machines, namely, artificial intelligence or AI.

ARTIFICIAL INTELLIGENCE: A BRIEF INTRODUCTION

All great ideas are dangerous.—Oscar Wilde (1854–1900)[42]

Machines and Living Things Compared

In a paper written in 1955, Anatol Rapoport points out the strong relationship between the level of technology and contemporaneous mechanical models of living things.[43] He first defines a technological "phylum," in comparison with a biological phylum, as characterized by a principle of operation. He then goes on to distinguish four technological phyla that came into being successively. The first phylum is the tool that serves primarily to transmit muscular forces; the second is clockworks that operate under the principle of stored mechanical energy, released subsequently and perhaps gradually; the third is heat engines that operate on supplied fuels; the fourth is machines that operate on the principle of storing and transmitting information.

Because tools do not operate independently, they have rarely been compared to living things, although weapons are often personified in mythology, for example, King Arthur's Excalibur and Siegfried's Nothung. The second phylum, however, has suggested living things, especially in such complex realizations as mechanical dolls and animals. (In fact, for Descartes, animals were equivalent to highly complicated automata that lacked only souls to differentiate them from humans.) The main difficulty with clockworks is that their source of energy is too unlike the source of energy of living things to allow for a strong comparison. The analogy to living things becomes much stronger when we turn to heat engines powered by such fuels as coal and oil. "It became apparent that machines could be constructed which did not need to be 'pushed' but only 'fed' in order to do work." [43a]

In the early 20th century, the development of the telephone switchboard served as a technological model for the central nervous system. This model, together with the physiological research on the reflex arc, suggested—mainly to the early behaviorists—that "behavior was . . . a grand collection of units called reflexes," to use Rapoport's words.

It was with the arrival of the fourth phylum, however, best represented by the general purpose digital computer, that the possibilities of "thinking machines" became most likely, at least in the opinion of the most devoted practitioners of AI. Here is a machine of such structural and behavioral complexity that comparisons to the human brain invite serious analysis. Computers are applied to an incredibly wide variety of tasks, including many that were formerly the sole province of humans. This gradual encroachment on a private domain has undoubtedly indicated to many people that it is only a matter of time until no exclusively human activities or skills remain. As has often been pointed out, whereas the first industrial revolution replaced man's muscle, the second is replacing his hand and brain.

Few disciplines can have their historical beginnings as precisely determined as AI can. In the summer of 1956, a number of researchers met at Dartmouth College to discuss issues of mutual concern focused on the central question of how to program machines (digital computers) to exhibit intelligent behavior. Among the attendees were Marvin Minsky, John McCarthy (who is said to have suggested the term artificial intelligence), Allen Newell, and Herbert Simon (subsequently a Nobel laureate in economics). They gave impetus to, and shaped the direction of, research for years to come. The story of their motivations, how they attempted to realize them, and the major developments—a tale of almost epic dimensions—is recounted by Pamela McCorduck in her book *Machines Who Think*.[44] A shorter version is presented here.

There are a number of reasons to introduce AI at this point. First, it represents the current best attempt, together with cognitive science, to understand the nature of intelligent behavior. Second, the computational models it has developed have had an impact on a variety of disciplines such as linguistics, psychology, education, and philosophy. Third, and probably most important, is its current visibility in the public eye as a developer of systems for providing "senses" for industrial robots, natural language interfaces for databases, expert systems for chemistry, medicine, financial planning, and so forth. Aside from the typical, sensational claims made for AI in the public media, there are some solid achievements and, more importantly, some hope for significant accomplishments in the future.

A Short History of Artificial Intelligence

A number of events coincided after the Second World War to give rise to the new discipline called AI. Most important, of course, was development of the digital computer, significantly accelerated by the needs of war research. An important paper written in 1943 by Warren McCulloch and Walter Pitts, called "A Logical Calculus of the Ideas Immanent in Nervous Activity,"[45] stimulated a number of people to explore the possibilities of achieving intelligent behavior from a machine. In 1948 Norbert Wiener's *Cybernetics* appeared. This book was subtitled *Control and Communication in the Animal and the Machine* and arose from Wiener's wartime research in designing mechanisms to control antiaircraft guns.[46] Researchers interested in intelligent behavior were stimulated to apply the principles of feedback, whereby a system's desired goals are compared to its current situation in order to drive the system closer to where it should be.

Much of the early research could be characterized by its reference to such terms as *adaptive, learning*, or *self-organizing*. That is, what seemed to be required was the application of powerful and general learning principles to a system with very little built-in knowledge. There were hopes of simulating certain aspects of the neuronal structure of the brain, based both on the McCulloch and Pitts work and that of the psychologist Donald Hebb. However, by the early 1960s the directions for the next 20 years were firmly in place. Basically, work on learning systems was abandoned, especially in North America, and the effort turned toward determining how knowledge could be represented in a computer and furthermore how it could be used to solve problems, play games, "see" the world, communicate in natural language, and even infer new knowledge.

Right from the outset of this new direction, two streams developed that were sometimes complementary and sometimes antagonistic. One arose from parallel developments in psychology that signaled a movement away from the then dominant theoretical position of behaviorism toward the newly emerging field of information processing or cognitive psychology. Here the metaphor of information processing by computer was applied to the human system and the heretofore restricted domain of the human mind. Practitioners designed models, constructed programs, and carried out experiments in an attempt to answer questions about how humans think, solve problems, use language, and see the world.

The second stream was concerned with the building of computer programs to exhibit various aspects of human behavior. When a computer is programmed to solve problems, it is not obviously necessary that the methods used have anything, or much, in common with how people do it. Researchers in AI may be influenced in designing their programs by a variety of sources, of which perceived human methods is one and introspection, hardware architecture, available software, and computational limitations are others. It may turn out that the programs developed are suggestive of mechanisms underlying human performance, but this result is not the primary aim of the researchers.

In the early 1960s, programs were developed to play games such as checkers and chess, communicate in English, prove theorems in logic and geometry, and recognize simple patterns. Their level of performance was not very high in general, but there were indications that a new enterprise had been launched that promised to make a major contribution to the study of intelligent behavior. In these early years, AI was sometimes viewed as a somewhat less-than-respectable branch of computer science. Since then, however, the founding fathers, as they are sometimes called—John McCarthy, Marvin Minsky, Allen Newell, and Herbert Simon—have all been awarded Turing Awards. The Turing Award is given annually to outstanding figures in computer science by the Association for Computing Machinery (ACM), the major association of academic computer scientists in the United States.

In the mid-1960s, much of the research effort was devoted to robotics or integrated artificial intelligence. We can mention here that a number of hand-eye systems were built consisting of a computer-controlled mechanical arm and television camera, as well as one mobile robot called Shaky. Out of this period came a renewed interest in the major components of intelligent behavior, namely vision or image understanding, natural language understanding, problem solving, game-playing, and so forth. It became quite clear that the major issues underlying much of the research in AI could be characterized—but not solved, of course—by two words: representation and control. That is, it will be necessary to represent vast amounts of knowledge in the computer even to carry out rather simple tasks. Of course, knowledge is not enough; how and when to use it—control—is of paramount importance.

In pursuit of these goals, new programming languages have been developed. LISP, designed by John McCarthy, was among the earliest and clearly the most important. More recently, the language Prolog (*Programmation en Logique*), primarily developed by Alain Colmerauer and his group in France and building on seminal work by Robert Kowalski in London, has also achieved worldwide support. Some of the principles incorporated in these languages have been adopted by other language designers. A history of ideas for AI would show that many formerly esoteric notions arising from AI research have become commonplace in other fields. This has become a major important and useful side effect of the research.

During the 1970s, the earlier research areas continued to develop, with new branches emerging. Among the latter are expert systems, knowledge engineering, advanced question-answering interfaces to databases, and a variety of new applications. The work in expert systems involved the design and building of large programs to incorporate specialized knowledge and inference mechanisms to advise and assist users of the system. Thousands of such systems have been developed, primarily for business applications, such as diagnosis, maintenance, fault determination, financial prediction, design, and process monitoring. There are also applications in medicine, geology, physics, and many other scientific disciplines. Typically, teams of researchers, both computer scientists and domain experts, work together to extract and reformulate the specialized knowledge. Programs are written, tested, and modified until they achieve a satisfactory level of performance. For example, one of the most successful systems, R1/XCON, was developed by Digital Equipment Corporation (subsequently absorbed by Compaq, itself taken over by Hewlett-Packard) to configure complex computer systems.

Recent Artificial Intelligence

During the 1980s, AI evolved in several interesting directions. Expert systems (ES) have continued their diffusion into the business sector as the most visible evidence of the AI enterprise. Companies large and small set up groups to design and implement ES in the hopes of improving performance and maintaining corporate knowledge beyond the work life of individual employees. Most companies have used special high-level programming languages called shells for the implementation of ES, and many seemed to be satisfied with the results.[47] Other approaches and applications include fuzzy logic, favored by some Japanese manufacturers as a way to improve washing machine performance; data mining or data discovery, "extracting previously unknown information from existing data, often with the help of another AI program, using statistical and visualization techniques to discover and present knowledge in a form that is easily comprehensible to humans;"[48] genetic algorithms that use evolutionary strategies to solve problems; and intelligent agents, programs that cooperate to solve a variety of real-world problems such as intelligently exploring the Web to discover resources that satisfy the needs of individual users.

With respect to more technical aspects, a greater emphasis has been placed on putting AI on a firmer theoretical foundation through the increasing use of logic as both a representational language and a computational one. A range of human activities, such as common sense reasoning, reasoning in the face of uncertainty, diagnosis of faulty systems, and learning under a variety of conditions has been formalized and modeled using a variety of different logics and statistical theories. The favored language for implementing AI programs, LISP, has been superseded in many parts of the world by Prolog, a language with a built-in problem solver, based on formal theorem-proving in logic. Prolog is the most popular example of a programming approach called logic programming, an attempt to take traditional logic, a passive descriptive language, and add a control structure to transform it into a problem-solving language. Current research is focused on developing distributed, or parallel, implementations as well as incorporating a system of constraints to increase problem solving efficiency.

The 1980s and 1990s also witnessed a return, albeit in a modified form, to the neural networks of the 1950s and 1960s. In their current incarnation, such terms as connectionism and parallel distributed processing have also been applied to research in this area. Once again the goal is to design individual neurons, geometries, learning rules, and training procedures to construct large networks to learn interesting and complex behaviors. The primary emphasis is on learning, and the motivation derives in part from the availability of cheap microprocessors, which permit the construction of relatively large, fast networks. In addition, the behavior of such networks has attracted the attention of researchers from such disciplines as physics, mathematics, and psychology, in addition to AI. Some interesting results have been reported but connectionism remains controversial, as some of these results have not been adequately explained. Furthermore, many in the AI community are familiar with the devastating criticism launched against the previous generation of neural networks, known as perceptrons, by the distinguished AI researchers Marvin Minsky and Seymour Papert.[49]

In a somewhat lighter vein, but probably more accessible to the public, have been reports of the remarkable progress in chess-playing programs. Particularly noteworthy is a program called Deep Thought, which, in late 1988, achieved the distinction of being the first program to defeat a grandmaster, Bent Larsen of Denmark. Subsequently it was defeated by the then world champion Gary Kasparov and former world champion Anatoly Karpov. Nevertheless, its overall level of performance is now world caliber and improving. Deep Thought was developed at Carnegie-Mellon University by five graduate students and employs a special-purpose chip that permits it to examine about 750,000 moves per second. Thus, success has been achieved not through the incorporation of explicit, deep chess knowledge, but rather because of increases in brute-force speed made possible by advances in computing technology. By 1996, Deep Thought, now supported by IBM and referred to as Deep Blue, could look at more than 100 million moves per second and engaged Gary Kasparov in a series of heavily publicized matches. In a stunning victory, reported and debated worldwide, Deep Blue won the first match decisively on February 10. After some reflection about what had happened, Kasparov recovered quickly, won the next game, drew two, and won the final two decisively, taking the match four points to two.

This match aroused considerable attention and focused world attention, for a brief time, on the issue of machine versus human intelligence. Within days after the match had concluded, *Time*'s cover story asked the hoary question, "Can Machines Think?"[50] Kasparov, in discussing his opening-game loss, reports that when Deep Blue made its pawn sacrifice, he was stunned; "What could it mean? I had played a lot of computers but had never experienced anything like this. I could feel—I could *smell*—a new kind of intelligence across the table."[51] This sense of awe did not last once he realized that this "surprising" move was just the product of Deep Blue's remarkable computational speed. It was necessary to "confuse" the program by presenting it with situations without any "concrete goals to calculate towards." If it can't find a way to win material, attack the king, or fulfill one of its other programmed priorities, "the computer drifts planlessly and gets into trouble." Thus, the answer to *Time*'s question, at least for now, is no.

The following year, in early May, the rematch took place. An improved Deep Blue lost the opening game, won the second game, drew the next three, and then won the match, 3.5 to 2.5 points, when Kasparov resigned after only nineteen moves in the decisive sixth game. "Machine Beats Man" was the headline. Another victory for computers. Man had been bested at chess and fallen in a game long hailed as a supreme test of human intelligence. Vishwanathan Anand, one of the world's great players, described Kasparov's dilemma before the match[52]:

> He had two options: to play like Kasparov or to play like "Mr. Anti Deep Blue." The former runs the risk of playing to the strengths of the machines, the latter that the human ends up as disoriented as the machine. Humans, too, play weaker in unfamiliar situations and though they may find their way around better, machines can compensate for that with brute force.

Well, he had played like the latter and he lost.

On October 19, 2002, the world champion Vladimir Kramnick played to a 4–4 tie with the program Deep Fritz. Kramnick had become world champion by defeating Kasparov two years previously. After having won the first game, Kramnick blundered badly in the second and lost. It is interesting that whereas Deep Blue examined about 200 million moves per second, Deep Fritz was limited to about 3 million moves per second. "However, programmers said Fritz was designed to look more intelligently at the moves ahead, rather than using Deep Blue's brute-force method."[53]

One last match must be briefly described, between Kasparov and Deep Junior, an Israeli chess program, during February 2003[54]:

> Garry Kasparov's US $1 million, six-game match in New York City last month against Deep Junior, the Israeli chess program, added yet another case to an evolving pattern: all such competitions in the past two years have been draws. Last year, Vladimir Kramnik, second on the international chess rating list, just below Kasparov, split a match with the German program Deep Fritz; then, just before the New York match, Evgeny Bareev, ranked eighth, did the same with the British program HiarcsX.

What does this pattern say about the 50-year quest for excellence in computer chess? That software is improving, that human players have still not learned to tune their play against it, and that either computers can think or chess does not involve thinking. From the purely subjective point of view—the only point of view by which intelligence can be judged, say many—the machines seem not merely sentient, but even to have a personality. The only way to tell man from machine is by man's penchant for blunders.

Now and the Future

There are critics of the AI enterprise, and their arguments range from questioning the morality of doing research that can be used by government in surveillance activities to concern about the possibly false philosophical principles that underlie AI. The former position is held by Joseph Weizenbaum, once of the Massachusetts Institute of Technology. Much of the early research in AI, well into the 1970s in the U.S., was in fact funded by the Advanced Research Projects Agency (ARPA) of the Air Force, and through the 1980s by its successor, DARPA (Defense ARPA). Additional funding came from the Strategic Defense Initiative (SDI, popularly known as "Star Wars") as well as more traditional sources such as the National Science Foundation (NSF) and the National Aeronautics and Space Administration (NASA). This heavily defense-oriented association led some critics to suggest that the major beneficiary of the research would be the defense establishment. For example, an important research area in the early 1970s was speech recognition. In this process a computer, programmed to receive the electrical signal resulting from the transformation of the acoustic speech wave, produced first a representation in words and second a representation of the underlying meaning. It was Weizenbaum's claim that one of the goals of this research was to enable U.S. security agencies to monitor conversations automatically and determine whether or not they posed a risk to government.

His argument was also broader, in that he criticized the entire AI enterprise for attempting to produce what he called an "alien intelligence." That is, while programs that could engage in a broad range of behavior might be possible, they would not be desirable because they would be fundamentally at odds with the human experience and spirit. Not surprisingly, this opinion was immediately and vigorously challenged by leading researchers in the field. However, recent developments in the aftermath of September 11 have renewed this and similar criticisms, as increased funding by the Defense Department has been directed toward projects whose goal is to detect potential terrorist activities at the cost of threatening individual privacy.

Criticism on the basis of philosophical principles was launched by Hubert Dreyfus, a philosopher at the University of California at Berkeley. He argued that the goals of AI were impossible in principle and that researchers were either misguided or were misleading the community at large. He and his brother Stuart, a distinguished applied mathematician, have criticized the extravagant claims made for expert systems, countering them with the contention that human expertise is too deep, too intuitive, too broad, and too open-ended to be captured by a computer program. The Dreyfuses (mainly Hubert) argue that because the dominant stream of Western philosophy, analytic philosophy, is bankrupt, any applied research based on it, such as AI, will not succeed. These criticisms are considerably weakened when applied to neural networks, about which the Dreyfuses have reserved judgment.

Another philosopher, John Searle, has long criticized AI researchers for what he calls their commitment to "strong AI," the belief that computers can be programmed to exhibit intelligent behavior equivalent to that of humans, or in Searle's words,[55]

> Many people still think that the brain is a digital computer and that the conscious mind is a computer program, though mercifully this view is much less widespread than it was a decade ago. On this view, the mind is to the brain as the software is to the hardware. There are different versions of the computational theory of mind. The strongest is the one I have just stated: the Mind is just a computer program. There is nothing else there. This view I call Strong Artificial Intelligence (Strong AI, for short) to distinguish it from the view that the computer is a useful tool in doing simple simulations of the mind, as it is useful in doing simulations of just about anything we can describe precisely, such as weather patterns or the flow of money in the economy. This more cautious view I call Weak AI.

The charges have largely been ignored within the AI community and occasionally angrily denounced as being ill-informed. Other philosophers, however, such as Daniel Dennett[56] and John Haugeland[57] have found useful ideas in AI.

When all is said and done, AI has become an important factor both in computer science and in society at large. Clearly the development of intelligent or even pseudo-intelligent machines will have a significant impact on our future. The role of AI in the various areas investigated in this book will be assessed, for it has become much more than an academic discipline. Furthermore, note that it will not be necessary for sophisticated systems to be developed before their impact is felt. The premature use of pseudo-intelligent machines may introduce the unfortunate possibility of people being forced to adapt to machines that are not really very smart at all.

SUMMARY

The human fascination with artifacts that mimic human behavior is longstanding and has inspired tales and legends from many cultures. Particularly noteworthy are the automata built by the Jacquet-Droz family of Switzerland between 1768 and 1774. The theme of robots and their ambiguous relation to their human creators has been expressed in such works as *Frankenstein, R.U.R.*, and *2001: A Space Odyssey*. In the 20th century Isaac Asimov, in his robot stories, and George Lucas, in his *Star Wars* series of movies, have presented robots whose sole purpose has been to serve their human masters.

Many artists, musicians, and filmmakers consider the computer to be a new and powerful tool for the creation of art. Supercomputers are being used to generate extraordinarily realistic film images, doing away with the need for special models and special photographic effects.

In the mid-1950s, a new scientific discipline made its appearance. Its goal was to develop computer programs to exhibit intelligent behavior. Its name is artificial intelligence and its contributions to technology will be significant. AI techniques are currently being used in vision systems for robots, natural language interfaces for databases, and expert systems for many applications. An early match pitting world chess champion Gary Kasparov against IBM's computer program Deep Blue ended with a decisive win by Kasparov, after he had lost the first game. Other matches followed with results less favorable toward humans. Once again, debate raged among the general population as well as philosophers and computer scientists about whether or not computers can or could think.

NOTES

1. Collected in online quotation list. Copyright: Kevin Harris 1995.
2. From *World of Wonders* by Robertson Davies. © 1975. Reprinted by permission of Macmillan of Canada.
3. John Cohen. *Human Robots in Myth and Science* (London: Allen & Unwin, 1977).
4. Joseph Needham. "Science and Civilization in China." *History of Scientific Thought, Vol. 2.* (Cambridge, United Kingdom: Cambridge University Press, 1956), p. 53.
5. John Kobler. "The Strange World of M. Charliat," *Saturday Evening Post*, March 25, 1955, p. 70.
6. Marvin Minsky. *Information.* (San Francisco. Scientific American, 1966), p. 210.
7. W. W. Jacobs. *The Monkey's Paw.* (New Rochelle, NY: Spoken Arts *Records* SA1090, 1970).
8. Patricia S. Warrick. *The Cybernetic Imagination in Science Fiction.* (Cambridge, MA: MIT Press, 1980).
9. Samuel Butler. *Erewhon.* (New York: New American Library, 1960), p. 180.
10. Karel Capek. *R.U.R.* (London: Oxford Universe Press, 1923).

11. Isaac Asimov. "Runaround," in *I, Robot*. (London: Granada, 1968), pp. 33–51.
12. Lars Gunnar Boden, as cited in Leopold Froehlich, "Give Tchaikovsky the News," *Datamation*, October 1981, p. 136.
13. E. T. A. Hoffman. "Automata," in E. F. Bleiler (Ed.), *The Best Tales of Hoffman*. (New York: Dover, 1967).
14. Lawrence B. Johnson. "PC Makers Are Focusing on Fine-Tuning the Sound," *The New York Times*, December 11, 1995, p. C3.
15. "About MP3," MP3.com Help. Available from the Web page with URL: http://help.mp3.com/help/category/aboutmp3s.html
16. A. Michael Noll. "The Digital Computer as a Creative Medium," *IEEE Spectrum*, October 1967. Reprinted in Zenon W. Pylyshyn (Ed.), *Perspectives on the Computer Revolution*. (Englewood Cliffs, NJ: Prentice–Hall, 1970), pp. 349–358.
17. *Ibid.*, pp. 354–355.
18. Paul Trachtman. "Charles Csuri is an 'Old Master' in a New Medium," *Smithsonian*, February 1996, pp. 56–60.
19. *Ibid.*, p. 57.
20. Steven R. Holtzman. "Painting by Number," *Technology Review*, May/June 1995, p. 60.
21. Mark K. Anderson. "'Aaron': Art for the Machine," *Wired News*, May 12, 2001. Available at http://www.wired.com/news/culture/0,1284,43685,00.html
22. Hubert Hohn, "The Art of a New Machine or Confessions of a Computer Artist," *Technology Review*, November–December 1988, pp. 64–73.
23. *Ibid.*, p. 67.
24. Noah Shachtman. "Turning Snooping Into Art," *Wired News*, January 5, 2002. Available at http://www.wired.com/news/print/0,1294,49439,00.html
25. Glen Rifkin. "Increasingly, Top Designers Are Drawn to the Web," *The New York Times*, November 27, 1995, p. C7.
26. Kendra Mayfield. "Art Now: Beyond the Healing," *Wired News*, January 18, 2002. Available at http://www.wired.com/news/print/0,1294,49617,00.html
27. Jason Spinqarn-Koff. "010101: Art for Our Times," *Wired News*, February 28, 2001. Available at http://www.wired.com/news/culture/0,1284,41972,00.html
28. Jessica Dawson. "Internet Art: More Click Than Point," *The Washington Post*, December 20, 2001, p. C05.
29. Steve Kettmann. "Ars Electronica Ousts the Critics," *Wired News*, September 1, 2001. Available at http://www.wired.com/news/culture/0,1284,46462,00.html
30. Peter Coy with Robert D. Hof. "3-D Computing," *Business Week*, September 4, 1995, pp. 70–73, 76–77.
31. William J. Mitchell. "When Is Seeing Believing?" *Scientific American*, February 1994, p. 73.
32. John Whitney. *Digital Harmony*. (New York: McGraw-Hill/Byte Books, 1980), p. 30.
33. Nigel Andrews in *The Financial Times*, as quoted in Glenn Zorpette. "An Eye-Popping Summer," *IEEE Spectrum*, October 1994, p. 19.
34. Burr Snyder. "The Toy Story," *Wired*, December 1995, p. 147.

35. Andrew Brandt. "How Hollywood Portrays Hackers," CNN.Com (From PCWorld.Com), May 4, 2001. Available at http://www.cnn.com/2001/TECH/internet/04/05/hacking.hollywood.idg/index.html

36. Ty Ahmad-Taylor. "Using Some of That Crazy Internet-Type Stuff in Films," *The New York Times*, October 9, 1995, p. C5.

37. Brian Aldiss. "AI and a Life: Like Human, Like Machine," *New Scientist*, August 11, 2001. Available at http://www.newscientist.com/ (An account is required.)

38. Dave Kehr. "When a Cyberstar Is Born," *The New York Times*, November 18, 2001.

39. Mark A. Fischetti. "The Silver Screen Blossoms into Color," *IEEE Spectrum*, August 1987, pp. 50–55.

40. *Ibid.*, p. 50.

41. Collected in online quotation list. Copyright: Kevin Harris 1995.

42. *Ibid.*

43. Anatol Rapoport. "Technological Models of the Nervous System." Reprinted in K. M. Sayre and F. J. Crosson (Eds.), *The Modeling of Mind.* (New York: Simon & Schuster, 1968), pp. 25–38.

43a. *Ibid.*

44. Pamela McCorduck. *Machines Who Think.* (San Francisco: Freeman, 1979).

45. Warren McCulloch and Walter Pitts. "A Logical Calculus of the Ideas Immanent in Nervous Activity," *Bulletin of Mathematical Biophysics, 5, 1943*, pp. 115–133.

46. Norbert Wiener. *Cybernetics: Control and Communication in the Animal and the Machine, Second Edition.* (New York: Wiley, 1961).

47. Edward Feigenbaum, Pamela McCorduck, and H. Penny Nii. *The Rise of the Expert Company.* (New York: Times Books, 1988).

48. Otis Port. "Computers That Think Are Almost Here," *Business Week*, July 17, 1995, p. 69.

49. Marvin Minsky and Seymour Papert. *Perceptrons: An Introduction to Computational Geometry*, (First Edition, 1969) *Second Edition.* (Cambridge, MA: MIT Press, 1988).

50. Robert Wright. "Can Machines Think?" *Time*, April 1, 1996, pp. 50–53, 56–60.

51. *Ibid.*, p. 57.

52. "Deep Blue Wins." Kasparov vs. Deep Blue, The Rematch, May 11, 1997. Available at the Web site with URL: http://www.research.ibm.com/deepblue/home/html/b.html

53. Alan Boyle, "'Man vs. Machine' match ends in tie," MSNBC News & Associated Press, October 19, 2002. Available at http://www.msnbc.com/news.820304.asp?cp1=1

54. Philip Ross, "The Meaning of Computers and Chess," *IEEE Spectrum*, March 1, 2003. Available at http://www.spectrum.ieee.org/WEBONLY/wonews/mar03/chesscom.htm

55. John R. Searle. "The Mystery of Consciousness," *The New York Review of Books*, November 2, 1995, p. 60.

56. Daniel Dennett. *Brainstorms.* (Montgomery, VT: Bradford Books, 1978).

57. John Haugeland. *Artificial Intelligence: The Very Idea.* (Cambridge, MA: MIT Press [A Bradford Book], 1985).

ADDITIONAL READINGS

Computers as a Creative Medium

Atkins, Robert. "The Art World & I Go On Line," *Art in America*, December 1995, pp. 58–65, 109.

Braham, Robert. "The Digital Blackout," *IEEE Spectrum*, July 1995, pp. 51–63.

"Circuits: Digital Photography Special," *The New York Times*, May 23, 2002.

Fisher, Marshall John. "Pixels at an Exhibition," *The Atlantic Monthly*, December 2001. Available at http://www.theatlantic.com/issues/2001/12/fisher.html

Hapgood, Fred. "The Media Lab at 10," *Wired*, November 1995, pp. 142–145, 196, 198.

Heim, Michael. *The Metaphysics of Virtual Reality*. (New York: Oxford University Press, 1993).

Pickover, Clifford. *Computers and the Imagination: Visual Adventures Beyond the Edge*. (New York: St. Martin's Press, 1991).

Riding, Alan. "Video Artists Meet Today's Software," *The New York Times*, December 26, 1995, pp. B1–B2.

Taylor, Dave. "Creating Web Pages," *Computerworld*, October 16, 1995, pp. 104–105, 109, 112.

Vacca, John R. "The Outer Limits, Virtual Reality on the Internet," *Internet World*, March 1995, pp. 42–44, 46–47.

Artificial Intelligence: A Brief Introduction

Dennett, Daniel C. *Consciousness Explained*. (Boston: Little, Brown and Company, 1991).

Dreyfus, H. L. *What Computers Can't Do, Second Edition*. (New York: Harper & Row, 1979).

Feigenbaum, E. A. and McCorduck, P. *The Fifth Generation*. (Reading, MA: Addison-Wesley, 1983).

Goldsmith, Jeffrey. "The Last Human Chessmaster," *Wired*, February 1995, pp. 120–123, 167–170.

Hebb, D. *The Organization of Behavior*. (New York: Wiley, 1949).

Kurzweil, Ray. *The Age of Spiritual Machines: When Computers Exceed Human Intelligence*. (New York: Viking, 1999).

Penrose, Roger. *Shadows of the Mind: A Search for the Missing Science of Consciousness*. (New York: Oxford University Press, 1995).

Rosenberg, Richard S. "Artificial Intelligence in the Real World: A Critical Perspective." *Proceedings of the Ninth Canadian Conference on Artificial Intelligence*, AI '92, May 11–15, University of British Columbia, Vancouver, BC, pp. 22–29.

Searle, J. *Minds, Brains and Science*. (Cambridge, MA: Harvard University Press, 1984).

Sterling, Leon and Shapiro, Ehud. *The Art of Prolog*. (Cambridge, MA: The MIT Press, 1986).

"The Grandmaster's Nemesis." *The Economist*, December 23, 1989, pp. 95–96.

von Neumann, J. *The Computer and the Brain*. (New Haven, CT: Yale University Press, 1958).

Weizenbaum, J. *Computer Power and Human Reason*. (San Francisco: Freeman, 1976).

Winograd, T. and Flores, F. *Understanding Computers and Cognition: A New Foundation for Design*. (Norwood, NJ: Ablex, 1986).

3

CRITICISM AND HISTORY

The clock not the steam engine is the key-machine of the modern industrial age. For every phase of its development the clock is both the outstanding fact and the typical symbol of the machine: even today no other machine is so ubiquitous . . . .

The clock, moreover, served as a model for many other kinds of mechanical works, and the analysis of motion that accompanied the perfection of the clock, with the various types of gearing and transmission that were elaborated, contributed to the success of quite different kinds of machines . . . .

The clock, moreover, is a piece of power-machinery whose "product" is seconds and minutes: by its essential nature it dissociated time from human events and helped create the belief in an independent world of mathematically measurable sequences: the special world of sciences.

—Excerpt from *Technics and Civilization* by Lewis Mumford, copyright © 1934 by Harcourt Brace Jovanovich and renewed 1961 by Lewis Mumford, reprinted by permission of Harcourt Brace & Company.

INTRODUCTION

Computers did not suddenly appear. Technological innovation does not arise from thin air. There are strata of previous technological achievements and economic and human resources. We frequently assume that our times are unique and that only our particular genius could have brought forth such wonders. Many craftsmen, inventors, and scientists laid the necessary groundwork for the modern computer. Its history extends from the invention of the abacus to the designing of the Jacquard loom and beyond. The brief history presented in this chapter is not a substitute for a more complete one but should serve to indicate the excitement of the quest for powerful computers, especially since the Second World War.

There is a time when the operation of the machine becomes so odious, makes you so sick at heart that you can't take part; you can't even passively take part, and you've got to put your bodies upon the gears and upon the wheels, upon the levers, upon all the apparatus and you've got to indicate to the people who run it, to the people who own it, that unless you're free, the machine will be prevented from working at all. —Mario Savio, Berkeley, December 2, 1964

For many, this quotation was the rallying cry of the protest movement of the 1960s and early 1970s in the United States. It seemed to express the feelings of young Americans that the state was a powerful, oppressive machine grinding up its young to further its single-minded aims. Interestingly, the late 1990s and early 2000s witnessed a revival of a movement against perceived global capitalism that echoed the efforts of the 1960s, accompanied by a similar rhetoric urging the necessity of hurling one's body into the very core of the enemy. The relevant topic in this chapter is not politics, but rather this perception of technology in control and people as victims. It is necessary and important to confront the criticisms raised, if not to answer them completely.

COMMENTS ON TECHNOLOGICAL CHANGE

Technological progress is like an axe in the hands of a pathological criminal.—Albert Einstein (1879–1955)[1]

The following two points of view—two caricatures, perhaps—define the conflicting poles of the debate:

Computers are just tools. We as their inventors and users decide what we shall do with them. They are more complex and have greater potential than other tools but you should never forget that ultimately that is what they are. All statements to the contrary are alarmist.

A computer is not just another tool. Computers can carry out activities that previously only people could do. Furthermore, by virtue of their enormous speed and capacity they can give unpredictable results when applied in new areas. They already endanger privacy, employment, even freedom. Although previous tools posed some of these difficulties, the computer represents not just more of the same but an obvious quantum jump.

You may not yet have formed an opinion on this issue. In fact it may be premature to expect it. Even if you agree with the first viewpoint, you might in daily life be expected to defend that view again and again as the computerization of society proceeds and new issues crop up. Computers are here and now. Can we still shape our own destiny?

Computers are in a real sense a natural continuation of technological development, and there exists a large body of commentary on the effects and dangers of technology itself. Important scholars have provided a number of incisive insights and warnings.

Machine analogies can be readily perceived in human situations. For Lewis Mumford, the slave population involved in building the pyramids can be seen as a mega-machine, the individual humans analogous to cogs and gears, each performing a limited repeatable task. Siegfried Giedion views the assembly line in a similar manner. In one of his most damning criticisms of modern technology he shows how bread has evolved from nourishing food to a convenient, well-packaged, food product. The claim that technology is neutral and merely a tool that can be used for good or ill is subjected to a major critique by Jacques Ellul. Norbert Wiener points out that just by virtue of its size and speed the computer can go beyond being a tool and in some sense create a new reality. These critics have been concerned with technology in general, with computers only the most recent development.

In an important article published in 1969, John McDermott describes technology as "the opiate of the educated public, or at least its favorite authors."[2] He gives a representative list of the fruits of the cornucopia as seen by a number of the so-called prophets of technology, as follows[3]:

> An end to poverty and the inauguration of permanent prosperity (Leon Keyserling), universal equality of opportunity (Zbigniew Brzezinski), a radical increase in individual freedom (Edward Shils), the replacement of work by leisure for most of mankind (Robert Theobald), fresh water for desert dwellers (Lyndon Johnson), permanent but harmless social revolution [and] the final come-uppance of Mao-Tse-Tung and all his ilk (Walt Rostow), and, lest we forget, the end of ideology (Daniel Bell).

This brief characterization of points of view should be fleshed out. In all the uproar over the wonders of technology, there should be a place for a few wise voices with a message of caution and concern. This book explores the impact of recent computer developments. Beyond the initial, obvious benefits, future problems may indeed lurk. It is worth listening to the group of critics, historians, and commentators that includes Mumford, Giedion, Ellul, and Wiener—the old, but honorable, guard as well as Weizenbaum, Postman, and Birkerts, the newer critics. In addition, a call to arms from a rather unexpected source, Bill Joy, a co-founder and former Chief Scientist of Sun Microsystems, will conclude this section.

Lewis Mumford

A major social critic and the grand old man of the environmental movement, Mumford is also a distinguished historian of technology. In a long series of books beginning in 1922, he was especially concerned with establishing the continuity of craftsmanship and technology down through the ages. Furthermore, he attempted to catalog and analyze the variety of forces technology brings to bear against the maintenance of humanity in everyday life. Power, centralization, autocracy, mechanization, and control are a few of the key words that only begin to suggest the many issues that exercised him for so many years. It is difficult to do justice to a lifetime of scholarship in so brief a space.

Here we are concerned with Mumford's analysis of the impact of computers and automation. He is disturbed not so much by the physical replacement of workers as by the elimination of the human mind and spirit from the process of production. The spirit suffers because of the elevation of computer decision making and the parallel subordination of individual initiative. The system or organization becomes all-knowing and all-powerful. The individual—whether as scientist, engineer, manager, or consumer—must abide by the established rules even if there is a loss of a human way of life.

For Mumford, the computer itself and its role in automation is just one more step along a road of constrained human choice. He has traced the enslavement of people from the building of the pyramids, under an organizational scheme that he likens to a machine, to the development and refinement of the modern assembly line. It is not inevitable that technology be used to enslave society (even assuming that we feel enslaved), because decisions as to its use must frequently be made consciously. If we have the knowledge and the will, we can structure society so that spontaneity and choice are encouraged and even rewarded. But if computers are left to make what are fundamentally human decisions, the consequences may be indeed serious, because computers may be programmed to return only those results desired by the leaders and managers.

In contrast to these perceived limitations in computers, strenuously challenged of course by most computer enthusiasts, Mumford offers a paean to the human brain[4]:

> Unfortunately, computer knowledge, because it must be processed and programmed, cannot remain constantly in touch, like the human brain, with the unceasing flow of reality; for only a small part of experience can be arrested for extraction and expression in abstract symbols. Changes that cannot be quantitatively measured or objectively observed, such changes as take place constantly all the way from the atom to the living organism, are outside the scope of the computer. For all its fantastic rapidity of operation, its components remain incapable of making qualitative responses to constant organic changes.

Siegfried Giedion

The major work of the architectural and social critic Siegfried Giedion, *Mechanization Takes Command*,[5] appeared in 1948, before computers had achieved a significant presence. He is concerned with the process by which traditional human activities have gradually been assumed by machines to the obvious detriment of the final product. He is interested in "the elimination of the complicated handicraft."[6] An important example is the making of bread, long a central enterprise of human existence. From the beginnings of agriculture and the cultivation of wheat, the preparation of bread has been a necessary and honorable activity. The connection of humans with the organic is well exemplified through bread, its manufacturing (i.e., making by hand), distribution, and consumption. Riots have been provoked by scarcity of bread or slight increases in its price. The images conjured up by the simple phrase "the breaking of bread" are suggestive of basic human relations: sharing, participating, a sense of community, a willingness to understand, and a desire to reaffirm historical continuity.

The problem is, the quality of mass-produced bread today is highly suspect. For the most part in North America, it looks and tastes like cardboard. Few remember, or even care, what a treat real bread can be. The story begins with the mechanization of kneading, clearly a strenuous activity requiring pulling and pushing and the use of feet as well as hands. In the late 18th century, the French pharmacologist Antoine Augustin Pametier described kneading as a process in which flour, yeast, water, and air are sufficiently well mixed to produce a new substance. It is clear that kneading is physically difficult and an obvious candidate for mechanization. Mechanical rotary kneaders were developed as far back as the Romans, and experiments continued through the Renaissance into the industrial era. Surprisingly, however, complete mechanization did not take place until after 1925, with the introduction of the high-speed mixer in the United States. Whereas early machines simulated the action of human hands, the high-speed mixer has an agitator that "usually consists of two arms attached to simple steel bars, which perform sixty to eighty revolutions a minute."[7] In explaining why they have not been widely adopted in Europe, Giedion notes that the more delicate European wheats cannot accommodate the tremendous speed and shocks produced by these mixers. Beyond the efficiency of using the mixers in the United States, there was a stronger motivation: "The main reason seems to have been that the energetic mixing made possible the manufacture of a bread even whiter than before."[8]

The final stage in the process is baking. Again, over time a satisfactory form of oven evolved. It resembled an egg, a shape that proved economical and advantageous for uniform heat distribution. However, there were limitations involved in the method of heating, the means for sweeping out embers, and the problems of dealing with large quantities of bread. And so the shape, size, and method of heating evolved: steel plates replaced brick and gas heaters replaced coal. Still, mechanization was not complete because what was needed was an assembly line process to measure and allocate the ingredients, to mix them into dough, and to cut, weigh, mold, and position the individual portions on a conveyor belt ready for the oven. As early as 1840, the French had achieved the mass production of bread.

Other aspects of the mechanization process should be mentioned. Two basic ferments were used to make the dough rise, yeast and leaven. These underwent a number of chemical transformations to speed up the fermentation process, increasing the weight of the bread. For example, carbonic acid increased the speed of fermentation and human labor was thereby reduced. Additional chemicals were added to make bread look whiter. These additives were used as long ago as the mid-18th century. Even the milling process to produce the flour was altered to produce a whiter, cleaner product. At the beginning of the 19th century, artificial bleaching was introduced to decrease the aging process and improve the whiteness. More recently, vitamins have been added to replace the nourishment lost through the actions of the previous processes.

As a result of all these innovations, in North America the bread factory has largely replaced the bakery. The small, egg-shaped oven has become the 100-foot tunnel oven. The complete process has been mechanized, from the mixing, in several stages, to the dividing, the rounding into balls, the molding, the placing into pans, and the high-speed fermentation to, finally, the baking of the bread in the oven on an endless conveyor belt. The cooling process is accelerated by artificial means, and the bread is sliced, packaged, and distributed.[9] One question remains: What has happened to the quality of the bread?

The technological process has certainly produced a bread of uniform quality, which, it is argued, the public demands, as the following quotation shows[10]:

> The bread of full mechanization has the resiliency of rubber sponge. When squeezed it returns to its former shape. The loaf becomes constantly whiter, more elastic, and frothier . . . Since mechanization, it has often been pointed out, white bread has become much richer in fats, milk, and sugar. But these are added largely to stimulate sales by heightening the loaf's eye-appeal. The shortenings used in bread, a leading authority states, are "primarily for the purpose of imparting desirable tender eating or chewing qualities to the finished product." They produce the "soft velvet crumb," a cakelike structure, so that the bread is half-masticated, as it were, before reaching the mouth.

The story of bread teaches that in the face of increased mechanization there is a strong tendency for the natural to suffer. But is it inevitable? Visitors to San Francisco rave about its sourdough bread, which is mass-produced. French bread is world famous for its taste, texture, and smell and is usually sold by small, family-owned bakeries. Thus, technology is inextricably woven into the social fabric of a culture. If it is important to maintain the quality of bread, independent of issues of mass production and distribution, it will be maintained. Therefore, to understand how technology affects the quality of life it is necessary, at the very least, to understand how public opinion is formed and shaped and how it manifests itself in the accommodation of the new. However, there is one critic of technology who argues that we don't have a real choice.

Jacques Ellul

A French sociologist, Jacques Ellul became one of the world's foremost critics of technology. His major work, published in France in 1954, appeared in the United States in 1964 under the title *The Technological Society*.[11] He presents a very grim picture, indeed. He views technology as an irresistible, mysterious force, far more menacing than either Mumford or Giedion have supposed. It has an ability to change every aspect of life that it encounters. First, it is necessary to understand what Ellul means by *technique*. It is similar to Giedion's *mechanization* but much stronger[12]:

> The term *technique*, as I use it, does not mean machines, technology, or this or that procedure for attaining an end. In our technological society, *technique is the totality of methods rationally arrived at and having absolute efficiency* (for a given stage of development) *in every field of human activity*. Its characteristics are new; the technique of the present has no common measure with that of the past. (Emphasis added.)

The sense of the term should become clearer as we continue.

Ellul argues that although techniques derive from crafts and methods prior to the 18th century, there has been a quantitative change, and technique has taken on a life of its own with its own internal logic. Initiated by the labors of past generations, it has somehow become a separate force with potentially terrible consequences. He presents four explanations of why technique was under control until the 18th century.

1. Only certain constrained areas were amenable to technique.
2. Other areas of life such as leisure, social intercourse, sleep, prayer, and play were more predominant.
3. Technique was local and spread slowly.
4. The geographical and historical isolation of societies permitted, indeed required, the flourishing of many different types of techniques.

The situation is different now—we face the new and terrible power of technique and its unremitting campaign against human individuality. Progress still depends on the individual, but only within the terms defined by technique. Thus, efficiency is of prime concern, and aesthetics and ethics are sacrificed. Progress is a concept inherent in the system and is largely unrelated to the desires or wishes of the people.

It almost seems as if technique is some kind of living, breathing monster out of control—our control at least—with its own aims and its own means of achieving them. What are some of the features of this monster?[13]

> [Technique] has been extended to all spheres and encompasses every activity, including human activities. It has led to a multiplication of means without limit. It has perfected indefinitely the instruments available to man, and put at his disposal an almost limitless variety of intermediaries and auxiliaries. Technique has been extended geographically so that it covers the whole earth. It is evolving with a rapidity disconcerting not only to the man in the street but to the technician himself. It poses problems which recur endlessly and ever more acutely in human social groups. Moreover, technique has become objective and is transmitted like a physical thing; it leads thereby to a certain unity of civilization, regardless of the environment or the country in which it operates.

Here, in brief, are some of the characteristics of technique as it operates currently.

Rationality. Aspects of management such as standardization, division of labor, and quality control.

Artificiality. Technique creates an artificial world, denying and eliminating the natural world.

Automatism of Technical Choice. The human has no role to play. Technique acts and people observe.

Self-augmentation. Technique changes and evolves with no help or direct intervention by people.

Monism. Technique forms a single whole and its various components are self-reinforcing.

The Necessary Linking Together of *Techniques.* An historical necessity operating in which the technique at one stage must follow the one at a previous stage.

Technical Universalist. Geographic—technique has been spread by commerce, war, and the export of technicians. Qualitative—technique has taken over the whole of civilization.

The Autonomy of Technique. A good example is the functioning of an industrial plant as a closed system that is independent of the goals and needs of the society in which it exists.

Since it is not really made clear how technique has evolved, it is certainly not clear what, if anything, can be done. In contradistinction to Ellul's unrelieved pessimism, evidence can be offered of how much life has improved over the years. The obvious decreases in hunger and sickness, the lengthening of the life span, and the increase in literacy are proof of the fruits of technology. Ellul's critics would grant that all is not roses but on balance the good brought by technology far outweighs the ills.

Norbert Wiener

Called the father of cybernetics, Norbert Wiener was an important mathematician who had a deep concern about the possible social impact of his work. Cybernetics and automation are intimately related, as engineering is related to mathematics and physics. In fact, the subtitle of Wiener's very influential book, *Cybernetics*, is *Control and Communications in the Animal and Machine*.[14] The central notion in cybernetics is feedback. In this process, an action is maintained by continuously reducing the monitored difference between the current state and the desired state. This principle underlies much of industrial automation, hence Wiener's anguish over the fruits of his labor. He views automatic equipment as equivalent to slave labor, which means that humans in competition with the mechanical slaves must accept economic conditions equivalent to theirs. That is, employers will not pay their human workers more than the costs associated with robots performing equivalent work. He prophesied a period of serious unemployment when the new technology becomes pervasive.

Wiener was much less pessimistic about the future in the second edition of this book, which appeared some 13 years after the first. He felt that many of his concerns were starting to be accepted by the business world. The relation between technological change and unemployment is perhaps the central issue in assessing the impact of technology. There appears to be a general consensus that, initially, technological innovation may result in the loss of jobs but eventually more jobs are created than lost. (We return to this question in Chapter 13.) Wiener was troubled also by the ability of computers to produce unintended and unanticipated results. The problem results from a combination of factors, including the speed of the computer, the inadvisability of interfering with it during its computation, the narrowness of the program's scope, and the limitations of the data. Note that none of these elements has anything to do with whether a computer can exhibit intelligent behavior. The fundamental point is that computers operate so much faster than do humans that there is a basic mismatch in their interaction. We had better be very sure that the computer is doing what we have desired and intended.

Wiener offers a strategy much easier stated than carried out[15]:

> Render unto man the things which are man's and unto the computer the things which are the computer's This would seem the intelligent policy to adopt when we employ men and computers together in common undertakings. It is a policy as far removed from that of the gadget worshipper as it is from the man who sees only blasphemy and degradation of man in the use of any mechanical adjuvants whatever to thoughts.

Wiener feels that computers can ultimately be controlled for the benefit of society. But this sentiment seems to be expressed more as a caution—against the possibility of a terrible future if computers are not used wisely—than as a realistic expectation.

Joseph Weizenbaum

More than 25 years ago, Professor Weizenbaum published a book, *Computer Power and Human Reason*,[16] that served as a warning about the possible dangers of computers replacing humans in decision-making situations. He introduced the term *alien intelligence* to argue that no matter how intelligent computers may appear to be by virtue of advances in artificial intelligence, they should never be involved in human affairs:

> The concept of an intelligence alien to certain domains of thought and action is crucial for understanding what are perhaps the most important limits on artificial intelligence. But that concept applies to the way humans relate to one another as well as to machines and their relation to man. For human socialization, though it is grounded in the biological constitution common to all humans, is strongly determined by culture. All human cultures differ radically among themselves.[17] Every human intelligence is thus alien to a great many domains of thought and action. There are vast areas of authentically human concern in every culture in which no member of another culture can possibly make responsible decisions. It is not that the outsider is unable to decide at all—he can always flip coins, for example— it is rather that the *basis* on which he would have to decide must be appropriate to the context in which the decision is to be made.[18]

Although this argument has been viewed as an assault on the more arrogant segment of the AI community, the book itself presents an extended argument for the virtues of human reason and judgment over the power of computers and calculation. Weizenbaum heaps abuse upon computer hackers and the mentality that would view humans as replaceable by smart machines or perhaps as nothing more than smart machines. As such he continues in the tradition of those who value humans and human society above all and who are alarmed by the degree to which society seems ready to accept technology and all its supposed benefits with little question.

Neil Postman

Mr. Postman has long been concerned with the relationship among culture, literacy, and technology with a general viewpoint that things are getting progressively worse. As he states in the introduction to his book, *Technopoly*[19]:

> In fact, most people believe technology is a staunch friend. There are two reasons for this, First, technology *is* a friend. It makes life easier, cleaner, and longer. Can anyone ask more of a friend? Second, because of its lengthy, intimate, and inevitable relationship with culture, technology does not invite a close examination of its own consequences. . . . Stated in the most dramatic terms, the accusation can be made that the uncontrolled growth of technology destroys the vital sources of our humanity. It creates a culture without moral foundation. It undermines certain mental processes and social relations that make human life worth living. Technology, in sum, is both friend and enemy.

Except for the last sentence quoted, Mr. Postman is in the tradition of Ellul in believing that technology at its worst is destructive of human values and, in spite of its obvious benefits, in many cases extracts an enormous price in return. Ellul has argued that there are no good and bad sides to technology, or rather *technique* in his terms, because technology does not really respond to human needs and desires, especially in its more advanced forms. However, Postman is willing to grant that there are benefits, but what exactly does his term Technopoly (the T is Postman's usage) encompass? He classifies cultures into three types, namely, tool-using, technocracies, and Technopolies, examples of which can be found in today's world. Technocracies are based on belief in modernity, the scientific method, rationalism, the power of knowledge, and secularism, in the sense that what people are able to accomplish and believe in is in no way limited by what God's design may be. Although his argument is lengthy, Postman claims that the U.S. was certainly a technocracy by the end of the 18th century.

Currently, the U.S. is the only country in the world to have become a Technopoly, albeit a young one. Postman suggests a couple of dates to mark this transformation: the rise of Henry Ford's empire being one and the Scopes "monkey trial" another. The first period is really the beginning of automation, the transformation of the workplace and the fundamental shift in the U.S. economy. The second is more of a mind jump and a continuation of the process of science and technology triumphing over religion and mystical beliefs. As for a definition, Postman offers the following: "the submission of all forms of cultural life to the sovereignty of technique and technology."[20] At another point he writes, "Technopoly, in other words, is totalitarian technocracy. . . . And it does so [eliminating alternatives to itself by making them invisible] by redefining what we mean by religion, by art, by family, by politics, by history, by truth, by privacy, by intelligence, so that our definitions fit its new requirements."[21] This is a bleak picture, consistent with Ellul's worst case.

Sven Birkerts

One last critic will be presented, Sven Birkerts, a writer, a critic, and a teacher. Though his concerns do not appear to be of the same magnitude as the others, they are very real and very worrisome, especially for literate people who worry about a generation or more that has been informed by electronic media and has little feeling for the printed word. Unfortunately, and with some irony, Birkerts's argument will be appreciated only by those who need no convincing, whereas those who might benefit from books seem lost to them and the cultural and historical matrix in which they are immersed. Thus, in the introduction to his 1994 book, *The Gutenberg Elegies*, he notes: "As the printed book, and the ways of the book—of writing and reading—are modified, as electronic communications assert dominance, the 'feel' of the literary engagement is altered. Reading and writing come to *mean* differently; they acquire new significations."[22] As noted, the argument as developed can make sense only to those already sharing many of Birkerts's very strong convictions. Here in a nutshell is his central concern[23]:

> For, in fact, our entire collective subjective history—the soul of our societal body—is encoded in print. Is encoded, and has for countless generations been passed along by way of the word, mainly through books. I'm not talking about facts and information here, but about the somewhat more elusive soft data, the expressions that tell us who we are and who we have been, that are the record of individuals living in different epochs—that are, in effect, the cumulative speculations of the species. If a person turns from print—finding it too slow, too hard, irrelevant to the excitements of the present—then what happens to that person's sense of culture and continuity?

It is curious that the Internet community defines itself by its impatience with traditional media, its conviction that the Internet represents a new frontier, a break with the past, a venture without traditional constraints. Books are the past, digital flows of information are the present, and as for the future, more and faster is all that matters. Subtleties, nuances, layers of meaning and inferences, the richness of language are casualties of the technological imperative for speed, efficiency, sensation, and endless gadgets and toys.

Bill Joy

Mr. Joy, former Chief Scientist and Corporate Executive Officer of Sun Microsystems, is also a leading designer of Solaris software and Java technology, and co-chair of the Presidential Commission on the future of IT. He would seem to be the archetypical technology guru and advocate, and yet . . . In an article published in *Wired* in April, 2000, Mr. Joy wrote openly of his concerns, and indeed fears, about the future impact of technology. His article was subtitled, "Our most powerful 21st-century technologies—robotics, genetic engineering, and nanotech—are threatening to make humans an endangered species."[24] The following selections indicate the scope of his concerns and the degree to which a sophisticated mind such as his can be awakened by advances in technology to which he himself has made major contributions.

But now, with the prospect of human-level computing power in about 30 years, a new idea suggests itself: that I may be working to create tools which will enable the construction of the technology that may replace our species. How do I feel about this? Very uncomfortable. Having struggled my entire career to build reliable software systems, it seems to me more than likely that this future will not work out as well as some people may imagine. My personal experience suggests we tend to overestimate our design abilities.

But if we are downloaded into our technology, what are the chances that we will thereafter be ourselves or even human? It seems to me far more likely that a robotic existence would not be like a human one in any sense that we understand, that the robots would in no sense be our children, that on this path our humanity may well be lost.

It is most of all the power of destructive self-replication in genetics, nanotechnology, and robotics (GNR) that should give us pause. Self-replication is the modus operandi of genetic engineering, which uses the machinery of the cell to replicate its designs, and the prime danger underlying gray goo in nanotechnology. Stories of run-amok robots like the Borg, replicating or mutating to escape from the ethical constraints imposed on them by their creators, are well established in our science fiction books and movies. It is even possible that self-replication may be more fundamental than we thought, and hence harder—or even impossible—to control.

Because of his stature in the field, Joy's piece aroused considerable attention. The response of Raymond Kurzweil, the renowned inventor, is noteworthy for its total dismissal of Joy's fears, as the following illustrates[25]:

Kurzweil was, unintentionally, the person who scared Sun Microsystems co-founder Bill Joy so thoroughly that Joy felt the urge to warn the world about possible advances in a controversial *Wired* magazine article.

"I guess (our conversation) alarmed Bill and started him on a course he's still on," Kurzweil said, calling Joy's advice to relinquish future technologies "unfeasible, undesirable, and basically totalitarian."

These views of the social critics range from apprehension to horror. The easy response to them is, "yes there have always been problems, yes there will be more problems, but we are in control of our own destiny." The debate will continue and will probably increase in intensity as the presence of computers both singly and in networks is more strongly felt. In all likelihood, the discussion will turn on whether or not the computer in its most prevalent form—the microprocessor—represents a quantitative change in technology. The final word in this section, reminding us that concern about technology is not a recent phenomenon, goes to the 19th-century social philosopher John Stuart Mill, who suggests the following image[26]:

Suppose that it were possible to get houses built, corn grown, battles fought, causes tried, and even churches erected and prayers said by machinery—by automatons in human form—it would be a considerable loss to exchange for these automatons even the men and women who at present inhabit the more civilized parts of the world, and who assuredly are but starved specimens of what nature can and will produce. Human nature is not a machine to be built after a model, and set to do exactly the work prescribed for it, but a tree, which requires to grow and develop itself on all sides, according to the tendency of the inward forces which make it a living thing.

The Ring of Optimism

The fact is, that civilization requires slaves. The Greeks were quite right there. Unless there are slaves to do the ugly, horrible, uninteresting work, culture and contemplation become almost impossible. Human slavery is wrong, insecure, and demoralizing. On mechanical slavery, on the slavery of the machine, the future of the world depends.[27]

As most of this book is a study in success of the computer in its incredibly wide variety of forms and applications, we hardly need to pause to praise it. Nevertheless, these few words of cheer should be welcome as a clear statement of technology as the servant of the people who invent it, develop it, and employ it to serve the needs of everyone. About 100 years later, this view was reinforced by Herbert Simon, winner of the Nobel prize in economics in 1978 and one of the fathers of artificial intelligence. Simon views technological change from the unique combined vantage point of economist, computer scientist, and cognitive psychologist. In a ringing challenge, Simon presents probably one of the most optimistic and encouraging statements of the technological vision[28]:

It is to realize, perhaps for the first time in human history, that we are a part of the world; that we are a part of this vast machinery; that man is not outside nature, that man is not above nature, but that man is a part of nature.

If we can make peace with ourselves on those terms, it will have at least one desirable byproduct: As we design new technology, as we make use of our knowledge about the world and the knowledge that we are gaining about ourselves, about our thinking processes, through research in AI and cognitive simulation, we will realize that we have to apply our technology in a way that keeps man's peace with the universe in which he lives, instead of conceiving our technology as a weapon with which man can wage war on the rest of nature.

One can almost hear the trumpets. But of course, Simon is not a solitary voice. George Gilder, Nicholas Negroponte, Alvin and Heidi Toffler, James Naisbitt, Kevin Kelly, John Perry Barlow, Andrew Grove, Howard Rheingold, and many others are projecting, to varying degrees, future visions of the technology harvest. Common to many is the centrality of networks, the economic power of information, and the new frontier of virtual communities with new political structures. Witness the following print media cover stories from the mid-1990s:

Newsweek
- February 27, 1995. Technomania: The Future Isn't What You Think: Cyberdemocracy, Intelligent Agents, Online Sex, Tracking a Hacker, Virtual Surgery, Interactive Movies and Music
- December 25, 1995/January 1, 1996. The Year of the Internet

Time
- Spring 1995. Special Issue: Welcome to Cyberspace: Strange Sounds and Sights, Intimate Strangers, Haves vs. Have-Nots, Confessions of a Cyberholic, Virtual Washington, It's a Wired, Wired World
- July 3, 1995. Cyberporn. Exclusive: A new study shows how pervasive and wild it really is. Can we protect our kids—and free speech?

Scientific American
- Special Issue 1995. The Computer in the 21st Century: Products and Services for Computer Networks, Networking, Government in Cyberspace, Computers, Networks, and the Corporation, Civil Liberties in Cyberspace

Business Week
- Special 1994 Bonus Issue. The Information Revolution: How Digital Technology is Changing the Way We Work and Live, The Information Economy, The Enabling Economy, The New Face of Business, The Information Society.

A common theme runs through all these stories: big changes are on the way and while there may be some minor problems, the future is unbounded, replete with an ever-increasing stream of technological goodies. It did not take very long for the bubble to burst; witness these cover stories:

Fortune
- October 9, 2000. The Future of the Internet: Everything is about to change again. Your Connected Car is Ready to Roll, The FCC Tries to Keep up, Hot Wired to the Web, Cybersecurity.
- October 30, 2000. [Just two weeks later] Lessons from the Dot-Com Crash: It all seemed so grand! We were changing the world! We were rich . . . Now What?? Dot-Coms: What Have We Learned? Fallen Idols.

Business Week
- March 26, 2001. Rethinking the Internet. Patience, please—the Net obviously won't change everything. It's power to transform will play out unevenly, and in stages.

- August 13, 2001. Lessons from the Telecom Mess: Here's how to get the $700 billion industry on track. Deregulation simply isn't working. The rollout of broadband net connections is going to be slow, costly and incomplete.

One final and important version of the optimistic vision has been articulated by the Progress and Freedom (PF) Foundation, which suddenly became known in 1995 because of its connection to then Speaker of the House of Representatives, Newt Gingrich. Its mission statement includes the following:

> Progress is the belief that Mankind has advanced in the past, is presently advancing, and will continue to advance through the foreseeable future.
>
> No idea is more American, no idea has played a more central role in the development of Western, and more recently, American Civilization. No idea is more important to our collective future, and no idea has suffered more from the cultural nihilism of the past 30 years than the idea of progress. . . .
>
> . . .That explains the mission of The Progress & Freedom Foundation: To restore, to renew and to recreate America's sense of its future, a future woven inextricably with the ideas of progress and freedom. It has been said that "The best way to predict the future is to create it." Creating ideas that will define America's future is what the Foundation has set about to do since its inception in April 1993.[29]

The PF Foundation is probably best known for a document it released in 1994, titled, "A Magna Carta for the Knowledge Age."[30] Its four coauthors—Ms. Esther Dyson, Mr. George Gilder, Dr. George Keyworth, and Dr. Alvin Toffler—are widely known. Dr. Keyworth, a former Science Advisor to President Ronald Reagan, is chairman of the PF Foundation; Ms. Dyson is a prominent computer consultant and a former president of the Electronic Frontier Foundation, and Mr. Gilder and Dr. Toffler are very well-known writers, lecturers, and futurologists. The term Magna Carta was very cleverly chosen to indicate that the document contains a list of new rights appropriate for our new and exciting time. One thing to keep in mind, however, is that the original Magna Carta was an agreement, in 1215, between the barons and King John of England over respective rights and powers and indeed only by default was relevant to the lives of most of the common people. This is not to deny the obvious importance of the Magna Carta in the history of achieving civil liberties. This modern Magna Carta envisions a revolutionary change as the Knowledge Age arrives, as the following excerpt from the Preamble demonstrates:

> But the Third Wave, and the *Knowledge Age* it has opened, will not deliver on its potential unless it adds social and political dominance to its accelerating technological and economic strength. This means repealing Second Wave [based on oil, steel, and auto-production] laws and retiring Second

Wave attitudes. It also gives to leaders of the advanced democracies a special responsibility—to facilitate, hasten, and explain the transition.

As humankind explores this new "electronic frontier" of knowledge, it must confront again the most profound questions of how to organize itself for the common good. The meaning of freedom, structures of self-government, definition of property, nature of competition, conditions for cooperation, sense of community and nature of progress will each be redefined for the Knowledge Age—just as they were redefined for a new age of industry some 250 years ago.

Of concern to the authors are such issues as the ownership of property (different), the marketplace (even more open), freedom (more and different), community (different and more diverse), and the role of government (much less regulation and more competition, increasingly distributed and decentralized). Such sentiments are emphasized in the final words of the authors:

> Yet there are key themes on which this constituency-to-come can agree. To start with, liberation—from Second Wave rules, regulations, taxes and laws laid in place to serve the smokestack barons and bureaucrats of the past. Next, of course, must come the creation—creation of a new civilization, founded in the eternal truths of the American Idea.

More trumpets.

A BRIEF HISTORY OF COMPUTERS

Computers in the future may weigh no more than 1.5 tons.—*Popular Mechanics*, 1949

The next few pages will sparkle with such catchy names as ENIAC, EDVAC, UNIVAC, EDSAC, MARK 1, and others. They are the names of the earliest real computers, developed about 60 years ago. How they came to be is a fascinating, long, and involved story. There is a problem inherent in an abbreviated history—it may appear to be a series of inventions that were historically inevitable. The social forces, the burgeoning requirements of applied mathematics, and the demands made during times of war and peace—including the computation of ballistic tables, navigational aids, and census statistics—are discussed in the Additional Readings.

Before the Twentieth Century

Computing probably began with counting, and counting began with fingers and sticks and stones. The abacus, one of the oldest calculating devices, was known to the Egyptians as early as 460 BC and is still used today in many parts of the world. There are two classes of computing machines—*analog* and *digital*. An abacus is a digital device in which the positions of individual beads on wires represent numbers. In analog machines, the instantaneous value of a continuously varying physical quantity such as a length, voltage, or angular position represents a number. Before it was rendered obsolete by the pocket calculator, the slide rule was probably the most commonly used analog computing device. Its operation makes use of the fact that the product of two numbers is equivalent to the sum of their logarithms. By using a length on a stick to represent the logarithm of a number, multiplication is carried out by positioning two sticks appropriately. A traditional watch with face and hands is analog (no matter what process is used for positioning the hands), whereas one with only numbers, that change in discrete jumps, is digital. In this history the analog computer is a minor player.

Brian Randell, editor of *The Origins of Digital Computers*, divides their history into two streams: mechanical digital calculation and sequence control mechanisms.[31] These are the two major concerns of computation—how to actually perform a calculation and how to control sequences of calculations. Counting, the former, was of primary concern historically.

For centuries, wheels with teeth or cogs in a linked train have been used to deal with addition that involves carries. The complete story includes the development of number systems, leading to the use of the decimal system in Europe. John Napier (1550–1617), best known as the inventor of logarithms, probably was the first person to use the decimal point in arithmetic operations. Until quite recently, the credit for inventing the first calculator was given to the famous French philosopher Blaise Pascal (1623–1662). It is supposed that his impetus was to aid his father in performing calculations. In any case, at age 19 he designed his first machine and by 1645 he had achieved a patent on it. The currently recognized first inventor, however, is Wilhelm Schickard of Tübingen (1592–1635), who apparently sent a set of drawings of a calculating machine to Kepler, the famous astronomer, in 1623. Who was first is not particularly important, since the idea and the necessary technology were in the air. The historical record is probably incomplete. The real importance of a new invention is heavily dependent on the social environment in which it occurs.

Some 30 years after Pascal's invention, Gottfried Leibniz (1646–1716), a great mathematician and universal thinker, designed the Leibniz wheel, a crucial component of mechanical calculators. His machine, which was not constructed until 1694, permitted multiplication and division as well as addition and subtraction and was much more efficient than previous devices. As useful calculating devices were developed, the impetus grew to refine and improve them in order to carry out even more complicated computations. Leibniz himself raised the banner for the relief of drudgery through technology[32]:

Also the astronomers surely will not have to continue to exercise the patience which is required for computation. It is this that deters them from computing or correcting tables, from the construction of Ephemerides, from working on hypotheses, and from discussions of observations with each other. *For it is unworthy of excellent men to lose hours like slaves in the labor or calculation which could safely be relegated to anyone else if machines were used.* (Emphasis added.)

Charles Babbage: The Difference Engine and the Analytical Engine

Over the next century a number of refinements took place in the basic calculator, but it was not until the mid-19th century that a generally successful calculator became available. Charles Babbage (1792–1871), a most remarkable man—mathematician, inventor, and initiator of scientific management—flourished in this period. He clearly deserves the title father of the computer, although his story is one of generally unfulfilled ambition. In 1821, he became interested in building a "Difference Engine" to automate the calculation of algebraic functions by using successive differences. A story describes the moment of its inception. Apparently, Babbage was checking some calculations with John Herschel (the son of Sir William Herschel, the discoverer of Uranus) when Babbage remarked, "I wish to God these calculations had been executed by steam." Herschel simply replied, "It is quite possible." (Steam was the major power source of Babbage's time.)

In 1835, before his Difference Engine was completed, Babbage conceived of a much more powerful, general purpose computer that he called the Analytical Engine.[33] In the end, neither machine was completed, for a variety of reasons—lack of sufficient financial resources, technical requirements beyond the skill available, and a design that underwent too-frequent changes. There is little doubt, however, that Babbage at this early date envisioned a machine of such scope that its power, if not its design, would not be realized for more than a hundred years. His design included a memory store, an arithmetic unit, punched card input and output, and a mechanism that provided enough power of control to do iteration and branching. Following his death, others tried to build similar machines with little success. When successful machines were finally built, some of their designers were aware of his work; others were not. In the final analysis, Babbage appears to have been a cranky genius with ideas impossible to realize—for both economical and technical reasons—in his time.

It is worth elaborating briefly on one of the reasons usually offered for Babbage's failure to realize his vision, namely, the inadequacy of the technology of his time to produce the mechanical components to the necessary tolerance. In 1991, on the 200th anniversary of Babbage's birth, the Science

Museum of London put on display the first full-sized working model of his Difference Engine No. 2. The initial motivation was based on the following proposal from Professor Allan Bromley of Sydney Australia[34]:

> My studies of the design of Difference Engine No. 2 convince me that it would have worked. The logical or mathematical design is simple and elegant. The mechanical design had been refined by Babbage's many years of design experience and incorporates many neat devices to ensure that the mechanism could not, by accident, become deranged and the calculation fall into error. The calculating, printing and control mechanisms all exhibit a similar elegance of design. *All parts should function correctly, separately and in unison, if made to the accuracy known to have been attained for the parts of the earlier Difference Engine.* (Emphasis added)

No history of this period would be complete without mention of Augusta Ada, Countess of Lovelace (1816–1852), the only child of the poet Lord Byron, and a person of some mathematical ability. In 1840, when Babbage presented a series of lectures in Italy on his machine, they were attended by a young engineer, L. F. Menabrea. Ada translated his notes on the lectures and added comments of her own. Her work is the major account of the Analytic Engine. She may also have been the first programmer—she included a program to compute Bernoulli numbers, an important task for many physical problems. Her description of the engine is quite lyrical, not surprising for the daughter of a poet.[35]

> We may say most aptly that the Analytical Engine weaves *algebraic patterns* just as the Jacquard loom weaves flowers and leaves. Here, it seems to us, resides more originality than the Difference Engine can be fairly entitled to claim.

It appears that even the idea of a computer provoked in her mind the possibility that people might readily believe in the creative powers of such machines. She was at pains to disabuse the public of such a thought.[36]

> It is desirable to guard against the possibility of exaggerated ideas that might arise as to the powers of the Analytical Engine. In considering any new subject, there is frequently a tendency, first, to *overrate* what we find to be already interesting or remarkable; and, secondly, by a sort of natural reaction, to *undervalue* the state of the case, when we do discover that our notions have surpassed those that were really tenable.
>
> The Analytical Engine has no pretensions whatever to *originate* anything. It can do whatever we *know how to order it* to perform. It can *follow* analysis; but it has no power of *anticipating* any analytical relations or truths. Its province is to assist us in making *available* what we are already acquainted with.

What did Babbage achieve in the end? He did not build his Analytical Engine, but he did anticipate much of what would follow even if his work for the most part had little direct influence on the achievements of the 20th century. He failed to realize his vision, probably because of his restless mind, political difficulties, and the lack of an obvious need for the projected computing power. He continually designed more advanced machines while the struggle was still on to realize his earlier designs. Still, his intellectual achievement was monumental.

Control of Computation

Ada's reference to the Jacquard loom relates to the second theme in our history of computers—sequence control mechanisms. The problem was twofold: (a) how to represent numbers and develop a mechanism for performing arithmetical operations on them, and (b) how to carry out sequences of calculations without human intervention, which could only restrict operational speeds. The automata discussed in Chapter 2 were generally controlled by a rotating pegged cylinder or a disc with holes, much like contemporary music boxes. The problem of how to actually control a process by a mechanism essentially external to that process first arose in the weaving industry.

It was probably a man called Basile Bouchon who in 1725 used a perforated tape to control the weaving of ornamental patterns in silk. This idea was refined over the years by a number of inventors, including Jacques Vaucanson, the creator of the remarkable mechanical duck. The most important contribution was made by Joseph Marie Jacquard (1752–1834). Building on the work of Vaucanson, Bouchon, and others, he designed a system of control that used a connected sequence of punched cards. The holes in the card determined whether or not vertical hooks controlling the warp threads were used in the pattern being woven. By the end of the 19th century, looms with 400 or 600 hooks were quite common. As early as 1812, there were approximately 11,000 Jacquard looms in France.

In 1836, Babbage adopted the Jacquard card mechanism not only for entering numbers into the machine but most importantly for controlling the sequence of operations necessary to carry out the calculations. It was easier to punch up a set of cards, he reasoned, than to make changes directly within the central core of the computer. Once the cards were made they could be used again whenever the particular computation was desired. Clearly this was much easier than physically altering the computer itself. Babbage anticipated the notion of a fixed machine performing computations under the direction of a program. It is interesting that a technological advance in one area turned out to be influential in quite another one. The story resumes in the United States, where for the most part the electronic computer was first invented and subsequently refined.

Near the end of the 19th century in the United States, the demands made on the Census Office became quite burdensome. The 1870 census was the first to make use of mechanical equipment of a rather simple kind. The key figures were John Shaw Billings, who was in charge of the 1880 census, and Herman Hollerith (1860–1929), who worked for the Census Office from 1879 to 1883 and later supplied the tabulating equipment for the 1890 census. There is some controversy over who should be given credit for the tabulating machine concept. It seems that Billings suggested the idea of using punched cards to represent information but Hollerith actually built the machine. Billings apparently mentioned that he was inspired by the Jacquard loom principle. In any case, the machines, patented by Hollerith in 1889, won a competition and were used in the 1890 census to punch and process approximately 56 million cards. Hollerith's machines, in an improved version, also were used in the 1900 census. However, relations between his company and the Census Bureau (the name was changed in 1903) deteriorated so much that for the 1910 census the Bureau used its own machines, which were developed by James Powers.

After Hollerith left the Census Office, he formed a company in 1896 called the Tabulating Machine Company. In 1911 it merged with two other companies to form the Computer-Tabulating-Recording Company. Thomas J. Watson, Sr., formerly with National Cash Register, became president in 1914. Ten years later he changed the company's name to International Business Machines (IBM). In the same year in which Hollerith's company carried out the mergers, James Powers formed his own company, Powers Tabulating Machine Company, on the basis of patents received while he was employed by the Census Bureau. This company eventually merged with Remington Rand in 1927. Thus, the rivalry of Powers and Hollerith at the turn of the century gave rise to two companies that were rivals in the development of the electronic computer.

Birth of the Modern Computer

Babbage's machine did not die with him—his son attempted to raise money to complete it. (All that remained were a number of incomplete sections.) Others were influenced. Percy Ludgate, an Irish accountant, attempted to build his own Analytical Engine in 1903. He died in 1922 leaving only a 1909 sketch describing his design. The Spaniard Leonardo Tores Y Quevedo (1852–1936) wrote an interesting paper in 1914 outlining a program-controlled device in the spirit of Babbage's Analytical Engine. He was also well known for his endgame chess-playing automata. As we move into the 1930s, the story starts to become rather complicated. Historians are still uncovering and evaluating claims for machines and devices. Furthermore, secret work done during World War II, especially work on the Colossus project undertaken in England, is only now being gradually declassified. It was a very exciting and interesting time—social and political conditions were ripe for the building of the first computer.

Before the first digital computer was developed there were a variety of analog computers in operation designed to solve specific problems. The most important of these, called the differential analyzer, was built at the Massachusetts Institute of Technology (MIT) by Vannevar Bush in 1931. Its purpose was to solve differential equations arising from several areas of mathematics. More important, perhaps, was its influence on computational endeavors elsewhere. For example, a version of the differential analyzer was built at the Moore School of Electrical Engineering at the University of Pennsylvania between 1933 and 1935. This effort provided the crucial experience from which the first electronic computer emerged some ten years later. As a side effect, MIT's commitment to analog computers, at the expense of digital ones, probably began at that time.

Electromechanical Computers

It is generally agreed that the first electronic computer was built at the Moore School under the direction of John Mauchly (1907–1980) and John Presper Eckert, Jr. (1919–1995). Called ENIAC (Electronic Numerical Integrator and Computer), it was built between 1943 and 1946. There were others, however, who claimed to be the first. The common factor of such claims was that the device was not electronic but electromechanical; that is, it relied on a mixture of electrical and mechanical components. Unfortunately, the first of those had very little impact on the development of computers in general. In fact, it was not until after World War II that the important work of Konrad Zuse (1910–1995) became known. He began in Germany to design electromechanical calculating aids in 1934; by 1938 he had produced the Z1, a somewhat unreliable mechanical computer. With the help of Helmut Schreyer he succeeded in building the Z3, "a floating point binary machine with a 64 word store. This computer, since it was operational in 1941, is believed to have been the world's first general purpose program-controlled computer."[37] Zuse continued his work during the war, but resources were not made available to extend his design. He made another important contribution with the design (in 1945) of a programming language called Plankalkul. This work also was not as influential as it should have been because it was unknown at the time. In the United States, important work on digital computers was initiated at the Bell Telephone Laboratories in New Jersey under the direction of George Stibitz. It is not surprising that Bell would be interested in computers, nor that they would be based on the relay circuit technology already in place in the telephone system. Stibitz and his associates began their research in 1937 and produced the first model, called the Complex Number Computer, in 1940. This so-called Model I was followed by a number of computers over the years: Model II, the Relay

Interpolator, Model III, a relay calculator, the Ballistic Computer, and finally, Model V in 1946. This last model was a general-purpose computer under program control. Even though it was slow, it did permit programs to be changed easily and was quite reliable as well.

Another important early development in computer technology was the work of Howard Aiken (1900–1973). In 1937, while an instructor at Harvard, he convinced IBM to begin the design of a computer. Together with three IBM employees—C. D. Lake, F. E. Hamilton, and B. M. Durfee—Aiken built the Harvard Mark 1, or Automatic Sequence-Controlled Calculator, in 1944. Basically a mechanical computer, it was more than 50 feet long, perhaps the largest ever built. More important than the machine itself, probably, was the fact that it was an entry point for IBM into the world of computers. After this machine, Aiken went on to build a series of machines at Harvard based on mechanical components. When questioned many years later about his reluctance to use electronic components, he replied that he knew that electronics were the way to go but that they were unreliable at first and he preferred the dependability of mechanical systems. At IBM the development of machines continued with the Pluggable Sequence Relay Calculator, installed in 1949, and the SSEC (Selective Sequence Electronic Calculator), completed in 1948 under the direction of Wallace Eckert. The series of computers that followed launched IBM into world leadership.

ENIAC: The First Electronic Computer

The work of Aiken and Stibitz was well known to the designers of the ENIAC, as was that of John W. Atanasoff, who had built a special-purpose computer to solve systems of simultaneous linear equations. In fact, Mauchly visited Atanasoff at Iowa State University in 1941 to see his computer and invited him to come to the Moore School. There has been much controversy about how much ENIAC owed to Atanasoff. Mauchly in later years called Atanasoff's computer a "little gizmo." A court ruling in 1973, resulting from litigation between Honeywell and Sperry Rand over the ENIAC patent, was not clear-cut. The ruling, issued in October of 1973, stated, "Eckert and Mauchly did not themselves first invent the automatic electronic digital computer but instead derived the subject matter from one Dr. John Vincent Atanasoff."[38] Nevertheless, the judge acknowledged Eckert and Mauchly as the inventors of ENIAC, and Atanasoff's work did not change the ENIAC patent claims.

Two of the participants have written books about the development of this first electronic computer.[39] Herman Lukoff, an engineer, and Herman Goldstine, a mathematician, together with Arthur Burks and John von Neumann, were involved in the development of the ENIAC and successor machines. The Moore School had gotten involved with computers—albeit analog ones—in 1933, with the construction of a differential analyzer.

John Mauchly, a physicist interested in the possibilities of electronic means of computation, joined the Moore School in the fall of 1941. Eckert, an electrical engineer employed as an instructor at the Moore School, was supportive of Mauchly's interests. In August 1942 Mauchly wrote a memo, "The Use of High Speed Vacuum Tube Devices for Calculating," which has been called by Randell, editor of *The Origin of Digital Computers* "surely one of the most important documents in the history of computers."[40] The Moore School had by this time become involved with the Ballistics Research Laboratory of the U.S. Army Ordnance Department. Captain Herman Goldstine, acting as liaison officer, helped convince the U.S. government to sign a contract with the Moore School in 1943 to develop an electronic calculating machine for computing ballistic tables. The machine was completed in the fall of 1945 and dedicated on February 14, 1946.[41] It was a monster. Incorporating over 18,000 vacuum tubes, 70,000 resistors, and 10,000 capacitors, 100 feet long, 10 feet high, and 3 feet deep, it consumed 140 kilowatts in operation.

Thus, 1996 was the 50th anniversary of the public unveiling of ENIAC. This event has been celebrated in a number of ways and certainly was an appropriate time to consider the impact of this remarkable machine. On a sad note, the last three major computer pioneers, whose work began in the 1930s, namely John Atanasoff, John Presper Eckert, and Konrad Zuse, all died in 1995.

The Stored Program Concept

The next major step was to control the computer's actions by means of a program stored in its memory. If this could be done, programs could be manipulated just like data. Even more important, the computer could become involved in the preparation of programs themselves through the development of assemblers, compilers, and operating systems. (The latter are themselves programs, such as Windows, that reside in the computer and permit the running of user-written programs.) As in many other areas of computer invention, the question of who was responsible for the stored program concept is somewhat unclear. Currently, there is general agreement that John von Neumann is the person to whom most of the credit belongs. Some facts are clear: The idea did emerge in the ENIAC group and it was expressed in print in a draft report dated June 30, 1945, written by von Neumann, on the proposed EDVAC. Von Neumann (1903–1957) was one of the supreme geniuses of the 20th century. He made major contributions to such diverse areas as the foundations of mathematics, quantum mechanics, game theory, hydrodynamics, and the foundations of computer organization and software. Contemporary computers have been described as von Neumann machines. However, there is some question about the origin of the ideas in the 1945 report.

Apparently, the stored program concept emerged in group discussions during the ENIAC project. Von Neumann first became involved with work at the Moore School when taken there by Goldstine in August of 1944. It is his opinion that von Neumann did make the major contribution, but it is unfortunate that the draft report did not acknowledge the work of others, and thus became known as the von Neumann report. Goldstine claims that von Neumann did not expect it to be widely circulated before he produced a revised version. Others have not been so agreeable.

Mauchly himself tried to set the history straight. In late 1979 he stated that as early as April of 1944 he and Eckert had planned to include both programs and data in the same memory. Furthermore, they discussed these plans with von Neumann in September of that year when he first came to the Moore School.

> We started with our basic ideas: there would be only *one* storage device (with addressable locations) for the *entire* EDVAC, and this would hold both data and instructions. All necessary arithmetic operations would be performed in just *one* arithmetic unit. All control functions would be centralized.[42]

Von Neumann quickly understood the nature of these ideas and reformulated them in his own terms, using such biological references as organs and neurons. Mauchly insists that von Neumann was merely rephrasing ideas developed by himself and Eckert. In any case, the von Neumann report does contain the first known program for a stored program digital computer; it happens to be a sorting program.

The Moore School went on to complete the EDVAC and deliver it to the Ballistics Research Laboratory near the end of 1951. Mauchly and Eckert left to form their own company, the Electronic Control Company, in late 1946. (The name was changed to Eckert-Mauchly Computer Corporation in 1947.) Problems with patent disputes and the constraints of the university environment had led to this separation. They conceived UNIVAC (a Universal Automatic Computer) but its development required continued research supported by contracts. In 1949, they completed a computer called BINAC—the first operational stored-program electronic computer that used magnetic tapes rather than punch cards—for the Northrup Aircraft Company. In 1950, Eckert and Mauchly sold their company to Remington Rand because of financial problems. The following year the UNIVAC I was completed and used for the computation of the 1950 U.S. census. In 1955, Remington Rand merged with the Sperry Corporation and continued to manufacture the UNIVAC series. (The UNIVAC name was discontinued in 1983.)

Developments in England

In 1946, von Neumann and Goldstine went to the Institute of Advanced Studies at Princeton University and began to work on a new computer, the

IAS. The early 1950s saw the beginnings of the computer explosion, as computers were developed at a number of research institutions in the United States and elsewhere.

The MARK 1, developed at Manchester University, in England, under F. C. Williams and T. Kilburn, was probably the first stored program computer to be operational. It was a rather primitive machine and is important mainly for the concept it embodied and for the fact that its development was fairly independent of the Moore School effort.

Another significant project in England was the computer built at Cambridge University under the direction of Maurice Wilkes, called EDSAC (Electronic Delay Storage Automatic Calculator). This machine was based on the EDVAC principles—Wilkes had attended an important series of lectures at the Moore School in 1946. The EDSAC has been called the first practical stored program computer to be completed. It executed its first program in May 1949.[43] Finally, the classified work done at Bletchley Park during World War II has recently been disclosed. A computer called COLOSSUS was developed there under the leadership of Professor Newman and Mr. Flowers, with a major contribution by Alan Turing (1912–1954).[44] Turing was later involved with the ACE computers built at the National Physical Laboratories at Teddington.

No history of computing would be complete without mention of Alan Turing. His name has been associated primarily with a theoretical construct called the Turing machine, which he created to explore general issues of computation. More recently his contributions to the design of actual computers, especially his work on a highly-secret coding machine called Enigma, have been made public. From a theoretical and a practical perspective, Turing is certainly one of the fathers of the modern computer. A film called *Enigma*, loosely based on these events, appeared in 2002.

The Rise of IBM

The age of the computer had arrived and growth was explosive. IBM quickly established its dominance and its name became synonymous with the computer. How this happened has been debated, but no one disputes the fact that IBM, with all its ups and downs, has remained the major company in the field and has been so for many years, both in the United States and worldwide. More recently, IBM has been less dominant in the wider information-processing industry because of the importance of personal computers, their associated software, and the phenomenal growth of the Internet. Of all the factors contributing to IBM's success, the most important was probably its organizational structure, which was highlighted by a large, well-motivated, and dedicated sales staff. The company stressed a well-trained and responsive sales and service division. Its availability and concern did much to carry its customers through the early uncertainties of the commercial computer age. In the 1960s, the industry was described as IBM and the Seven Dwarfs. The dwarfs in 1967 were Sperry Rand (later Sperry Corporation), Control Data Corporation, Honeywell, RCA (Radio Corporation of America), NCR (National Cash Register), General Electric, and Burroughs. In 1971, General Electric sold its computer hardware operation to Honeywell but maintained its computer services division and has recently shown strength in specialized computer equipment. RCA sold its computer operations to Sperry in 1971. Consolidation continued into the 1980s and 1990s; in 1986, Sperry merged its computer operations with Burroughs to form UNISYS, Honeywell sold its computer business to Groupe Bull (France), with a share to Japan's NEC, and on May 6, 1991, AT&T acquired NCR for $7.4 billion. Change continued throughout the 1990s.

In the mid-1990s, the number two company in the world was Fujitsu, far behind IBM in data processing revenues. Among the 10 leading companies in data processing revenue in 1995, six were American—IBM (1), Hewlett-Packard (3), Digital (6), AT&T (7), Compaq (8), and EDS (9); and four were Japanese—Fujitsu (2), NEC (4), Hitachi (5), and Toshiba (10). Just four years previously, Groupe-Bull (France), Siemens (Germany), and Olivetti (Italy) were in the top 10, while Compaq, EDS, and Toshiba were not. A number of U.S. companies, among the most prominent names in the early computer industry, were in serious decline. For example, Control Data, once second only to IBM, dropped to number 92 worldwide with revenues of $524 million. Other companies that lost significant market share were Wang, Data General, Unisys, and Texas Instruments (all United States), Siemens (Germany), Olivetti (Italy), and Groupe-Bull (France).

By the early 2000s, the leading companies were a mixture of the old and new and included companies involved in hardware, software, services, and computer-related telecommunications. The top 10 companies (included in the above categorizations,) in terms of revenues, as of mid-2002, were IBM ($83.4 billion), Hewlett-Packard ($75.25 B, including the recently absorbed Compaq, which had previously absorbed Digital Equipment), Verizon Communications ($67.3 B), Hitachi ($60.1 B), AT&T ($51 B), Deutsche Telekom ($51 B), SBC Communications ($45.2 B), NEC ($44.4 B), Fujitsu ($44.2 B), Dell Computer ($31.2 B), and Microsoft ($27.7 B).[45] To emphasize the importance of software and in particular Microsoft's significance, we note that while IBM's revenue's fell 7.5% between mid-2001 and mid-2002 and its profits of $7.16 billion were 8.6% of revenues, Microsoft's revenues rose 12.9% and its profits of $6.4 billion were an incredible 23% of revenues.

Computers have traditionally been categorized by size and power, with supercomputers at the top, then mainframes, followed by minicomputers, workstations, and personal computers (PCs) at the bottom. There are no precise dividing lines, and as the power of personal computers continues to increase, the other categories tend to recede or even disappear, so that very powerful PCs have come to dominate all levels of computers. In spite of all these changes, IBM remains a dominating force in the industry and, in spite of various setbacks, is likely to hold its position into the foreseeable future. It has continued to be a presence in services, servers, proprietary software, and of course, the diminishing market for mainframes, as well as supercomputers. Much of its success over the past decade is the responsibility of its recently retired chairman, Lou Gerstner, who joined IBM in 1993. One important measure of IBM's ability to recreate itself, in spite of possibly crippling setbacks is its shift from primarily a mainframe company (so-called "Big Iron"), to a much more diversified one. Questions have been raised about the effect of such a powerful force on other companies in the industry and, more importantly, on the development of the field itself. Indeed, many of IBM's practices over the years have become *de facto* standards. Of course, a similar observation has been made about Microsoft, whose influence on Information Technology (IT) has been far greater than IBM's over the past few years.

The Rise to Dominance of Microsoft

In this section, a familiar retelling of the Microsoft tale will be presented. Later in this book (Chapter 12), the seemingly endless antitrust suit against Microsoft by the U.S. Justice Department and several U.S. states will be recounted, but for now consider the origins of a true American success story. Bill Gates was born in Seattle in 1955 and was introduced to computers in 1968, when he entered prep school. Gates's early years have been described as follows[46]:

> In 1973, Gates entered Harvard University as a freshman, where he lived down the hall from Steve Ballmer, now Microsoft's chief executive officer. While at Harvard, Gates developed a version of the programming language BASIC for the first microcomputer—the MITS Altair.

> In his junior year, Gates left Harvard to devote his energies to Microsoft, a company he had begun in 1975 with his childhood friend Paul Allen. Guided by a belief that the computer would be a valuable tool on every office desktop and in every home, they began developing software for personal computers. Gates's foresight and his vision for personal computing have been central to the success of Microsoft and the software industry.

Actually, a few interesting details have been omitted from the official story. Gates and Allen had promised MITS the software before they had written it.[47] When the first IBM PC was produced in 1981, Microsoft licensed MS-DOS (Microsoft Disk Operating System) to IBM, in one of the great business deals of all time, made possible because of IBM's dismissal of the importance of software as rather insignificant compared to the importance of hardware.

Given the success of IBM and the quick development of clones, Microsoft soon became a major player in the industry. It went public in 1986, making Bill Gates a millionaire, and in the following year, Windows appeared for the first time.[48] By the time Windows95 appeared, Microsoft was a major force and its application software—Word, Excel, PowerPoint—were *de facto* industry standards. It was also in 1995 that Microsoft acknowledged the importance and long-lasting presence of the Internet. Thus, development of Internet Explorer, the now-dominant Web browser, began, but the story will be continued later in the book.

THE EMERGENCE OF THE CHIP

If the aircraft industry had evolved as spectacularly as the computer industry over the past 25 years, a Boeing 767 would cost $500 today, and it would circle the globe in 20 minutes on five gallons of fuel.[49]

If the automobile business had developed like the computer business, a Rolls-Royce would now cost $2.75 and run 3 million miles on a gallon of gas.[50]

The History

The modern computer developed from a mechanical calculator into an immense electronic machine with thousands of vacuum tubes that occupied a large room. The power requirements were enormous and the issue of reliability was of paramount concern. When ENIAC was completed in 1946, it was generally believed that only a very few computers would be necessary to serve the computational needs of the nation. Developments were already underway, however, to change the basic structure of computers. As early as 1945, Bell Laboratories began research to develop electronic devices useful for telecommunications. Leading this research team were William Shockley, John Bardeen, and Walter H. Brattain. They were awarded the Nobel prize for physics for their invention, in 1947, of the point contact transistor. This device was not an instant success, because it operated over a limited range of frequencies, could amplify only to a limited degree, had limited stability, and was expensive to manufacture. It would have been difficult to predict at this point the shape of things to come.

As an electronic component, the disadvantages of the vacuum tube are that it generates a great deal of heat in operation, requires considerable power, and occupies a relatively large space. The advantages of the semiconductor are striking: low power requirements, minimal heat generation, and above all, microscopic size. The semiconductor, as its name suggests, has conductive properties that lie between those of a conductive material such as copper and an insulating material such as plastic or rubber. The first transistor was made of germanium, as was the second, called the junction transistor. Both were developed by Bell in 1951. Eventually silicon came into wide use, first for transistors and later for integrated circuits, or chips.

Over the next few years developments were rapid, and prices fell correspondingly. The basic motivation for miniaturization, however, did not derive from the requirements of computer engineers. It sprang from the basic need of the U.S. space and missile programs for compact, durable, and light components. Developments were further accelerated by a combination of advances in scientific knowledge and the growth of scientific entrepreneurship.

Transistors were first used in hearing aids in the early 1950s. It was not until 1955 that the first all-transistor radios appeared. Much more importantly, in that same year IBM introduced a computer in which over 1000 large tubes had been replaced by more than 2000 tiny transistors. In addition to the virtues of the transistor already noted, there is one additional important point that had great implications for the future.[51]

> The great advantage of the transistor, an advantage scarcely appreciated at the time, was that it enabled one to do away with the separate materials—carbon, ceramics, tungsten and so on—traditionally used in fabricating components. At the same time the transistor raised the ceiling that sheer complexity of interconnections was beginning to place on system design. . . . The transistor was the first electronic component in which materials with different electrical characteristics were not interconnected but were physically joined in one structure.

The next natural step was to include more than one transistor in the same physical structure. Once this idea was articulated, developments took place very rapidly. The integrated circuit includes—on a single chip of silicon—transistors, diodes, resistors, and capacitors, all connected in a functional circuit.

Once it was introduced, the integrated circuit business grew rapidly worldwide, with nearly $1 billion in sales in 1970 and $3.6 billion in 1976. These figures are dramatic in more ways than one since there has been a corresponding reduction in prices over these years and an increased number of active elements per circuit. For example, the cost per bit (binary digit) of random-access memory has declined an average of 35% per year since 1970.[52] Furthermore, from a single bit per circuit in 1959, the growth curve has been from 1K in 1970, to 4K in the mid-1970s, to 16K in the late 1970s, to 32K shortly after, followed by 64K in the early 1980s, to the 256K-bit memory in 1983, to the 1 megabit DRAM in the late 1980s, the 4 megabit DRAM in the early 1990s (selling for about $12[53]), and the 16 megabit DRAM in the mid-1990s. (The letter K is an abbreviation for 1024 but is typically used to mean 1000; a megabit is one million bits; DRAM means Dynamic Random Access Memory.) The benefits of integrated circuits are as follows:

- They are cheaper.
- Labor and materials are saved by not having to make large numbers of connections.
- The integrated connections are more secure; hence, less maintenance is required.
- Power and space requirements are drastically reduced, resulting also in savings on cooling fans and transformers.
- Quality control is improved.

In 1964 Gordon Moore, one of Robert Noyce's colleagues at Fairchild, suggested that the complexity of integrated circuits would continue to double every year. Moore's law is apparently still in effect and augurs well for improvements over the next few years.

The Microprocessor

So far we have discussed the development of circuits that have either been preprogrammed to carry out well-defined functions or are available for memory purposes. One of the most significant technological innovations of our time took place in 1971 at Intel, a semiconductor company founded two years earlier by Robert Noyce and others in Santa Clara, California. M. E. Hoff, Jr., a young engineer, invented an integrated circuit that is essentially equivalent to the central processing unit of a computer. Consider the following description[54]:

> Hoff's CPU [Central Processing Unit] on a chip became known as a microprocessor. To the microprocessor, he attached two memory chips, one to move data in and out of the CPU and one to provide the program to drive the CPU. Hoff now had in hand a rudimentary general-purpose computer that not only could run a complex calculator but could also control an elevator or a set of traffic lights, and perform any other tasks, depending on its program.

Intel brought out its first microprocessor chip, the 4004, in 1971. A larger model, the 8008, followed in 1972. Near the end of 1973 came the second generation 8080 chip, more than 20 times faster than the 4004. This last chip formed the basis for the personal computer bonanza that followed. Other companies—such as Rockwell International, National Semiconductor, Texas Instruments, and Motorola—soon entered the microprocessor derby.

In early 1989, Intel introduced its new microprocessor, the i486, successor to the 386 (technically the 80386) and two to four times faster. At that time, Intel sold a less advanced version of the 386, the 386SX, to computer manufacturers for $89 while the new i486 sold for $950. 386SX-based computers could be bought for $1500, a remarkable price given their power, and yet another indication of the rapid pace of development. One more startling indication is that although the 386 contained 375,000 transistors, the i486 had over one million. Less than one year later, TRW and Motorola (which makes the 6800 series of chips for the Apple Macintosh and Sun computers, among others) announced a "superchip" with about four million transistors[55]:

> Two hundred million operations per second mean the [chip] is the computational equivalent of some supercomputers that fill an entire room, require elaborate refrigeration systems and weigh several tons . . . . Commercial successors of the superchip could find use in a wide variety of applications where high speed, small size and great computing power and reliability are needed. Among these are computer-aided design, medical diagnosis, plant process control and complex imaging.

New chips continue to appear at a regular rate, including Intel's Pentium chip, the microprocessor of choice for most of the world's personal computers, and the Power PC chip developed by Motorola for Apple's Power Macintoshes. Motorola's Power PC 620, available in 1996, has nearly seven million transistors and is about the size of a fingertip.[56] Powerful computers are required to help design, build, and verify the increasingly complex chips under development. Such incredible increases in power and decreases in size seem to occur with such regularity in the computer industry that we tend to forget how remarkable these achievements are and how great an impact they continue to have on our lives. For example, Intel has a Pentium 4 processor that runs at speeds up to 2.53 GHz (literally 2.53 billion cycles per second). Furthermore, this processor powers home computers, an incredible technological achievement.

The Semiconductor Business

> Technological innovation and scientific discovery generated much of the Nation's economic growth over the past 50 years, creating millions of jobs, and improving the quality of life. For example, about two-thirds of the 80% gain in economic productivity since 1995 can be attributed to information technology.—The Budget of the United States Government for Fiscal Year 2003

The semiconductor business is perhaps the crowning jewel of the American industrial system. Its important early growth period was fostered by the

U.S. Department of Defense, which subsidized developmental costs. As it coincided with the emergence of scientific entrepreneurship, the U.S. lead was ensured. The semiconductor industry has an economic impact far beyond its own domain, because of the multiplier effect. That is, a piece of equipment depending on semiconductors is likely to cost many times more than the integrated circuit itself.

That almost mythical community, Silicon Valley (named for the basic material of semiconductors) is a region running from Palo Alto south to San Jose along San Francisco Bay. Home of a number of chip manufacturers, personal-computer companies, and peripheral-device companies, it has achieved worldwide fame as a source of innovation and expertise in the incredible explosion of microelectronics technology. Its achievements have been so overwhelming that other regions of the United States and the world have sought to plant seeds for their own Silicon Valleys.

The tradition of scientific entrepreneurship in the Valley is not new. As far back as 1939, David Packard and William Hewlett formed an electronics company, Hewlett-Packard, which in 2001 had total revenues of over $43.1 billion. The initial impetus of the phenomenal postwar growth of Silicon Valley came from William Shockley, one of the inventors of the transistor. He left Bell Laboratories and moved to Mountain View, California, to set up Shockley Semiconductor Laboratory in 1955, which attracted a number of young, ambitious engineers and physicists. One of these was Robert Noyce, who (with seven others) left Shockley two years later to form Fairchild Camera and Instrument. The Silicon Valley syndrome of old companies spawning new ones was well under way. Indeed, after a few years, the next generation of offspring was born: National Semiconductor in 1967, Intel—founded by Noyce—in 1968, and Advanced Micro Devices in 1969. These are among the "Fairchildren" of Fairchild alumni. Not only has the semiconductor flourished in Silicon Valley; a whole range of computer-related companies have found the atmosphere congenial.

Even on its own terms, the semiconductor market, including memory chips and microprocessors, has grown enormously, but erratically; for example, worldwide sales in 1995 increased about 42% over 1994 to $144 billion but then fell the following year to about $132 billion.[57] The next serious crash in sales occurred between 2000 ($204.4 billion) and 2001 ($139 billion), coinciding with the worldwide "dot.com" crash. The U.S. has of course been the major world player, with a share of worldwide sales of approximately 50%, compared with Japan at about 30%.[58] One final point is the remarkable fact that, "In 2001, the semiconductor industry will manufacture about 60 million transistors for every man, woman, and child on Earth, and by 2010, this number should be 1 billion transistors."[59]

The Personal Computer

Almost exactly 30 years after the first electronic computer made its appearance, the first personal computer (PC) was marketed. Since then, sales have been phenomenal. In the United States, sales for 1981 (excluding software and peripherals) reached $1.4 billion; they were up to $2.6 billion in 1983, and approximately $6 billion in 1985. Worldwide sales were $6.1 billion in 1982 and soared to $37.4 billion in 1989. By 1994, the top 10 PC manufacturers in the U.S. had combined sales of almost $40 billion. (See Chapter 14 for more recent statistics.) All this has been made possible by the microprocessor, but the idea of making a computer at a price low enough to sell to an individual, coupled with the belief that the computer would have sufficient appeal for that individual, is a product of American scientific and business genius.

The major early success story of the personal computer, discounting IBM's achievements, Compaq's success in riding on IBM's coattails, and more recently, Dell's achievements in becoming number one in sales, is Apple. Founded in Silicon Valley by Steven Wosniak and Steven Jobs, then in their early twenties according to the by-now familiar Valley legend, Wosniak built the first machine in his parents' garage. Interestingly, Jobs left Apple (or was pushed out) in 1985, and in 1987 announced a new computer from his company, NeXT, Inc. (He has of course since returned to Apple.) The first Apple machine was marketed in 1976, and by 1983 its sales had exceeded $1 billion, climbing above $11 billion by 1995 and propelling it to 11th place in the worldwide computer market. (Compaq, growing faster, had climbed to number six and was number two in 2001 before being taken over by Hewlett-Packard.) Recently, however, Apple has experienced financial problems and has carved out its own niche market, with one of the few non-Windows operating systems.

We are living in a time when computers are numbered in the millions. It was recently announced that, "Approximately 1 billion PCs have been shipped worldwide since the mid-70s, according to a study released . . . by consulting firm Gartner."[60] And there is more:

> Seventy-five percent of these machines have gone into professional, or work-related, environments, while the other 25 percent have been for personal, or home, use. Approximately 81.5 percent of PCs shipped have been desktops. The next billion, though, should ship much more quickly. Declining prices, the growth of the Internet, and the rapid adoption of computers in the developing world will likely double the number of PCs shipped by 2007 or 2008.

Of the 1 billion that have been shipped, about half are still in use and of course most of them are in the U.S., to which almost 40% have been shipped. As we can see from the figures above, PCs are no longer the private preserve of the government, large businesses, and research institutions.

Extraordinary power is becoming available to a wide segment of society. (Recall the new Pentium 4 processors.) How that power will be distributed and used, and to what ends, is a question yet to be answered. However, one application of that distributed power that is rapidly achieving the status of the familiar and the commonplace is the Internet.

New Computer Technologies

Computers are getting faster, smaller, even cheaper, but there are limits to the current silicon-based technology. In anticipation of such limits and to develop even faster and smaller machines, scientists and engineers are involved in many pursuits, but among the most interesting are biological and quantum computing. It should be kept in mind that both of these technologies will not be practical for many years to come, if ever. One example of a biological, or DNA, computer was reported near the end of 2001, as follows[61]:

> Following Mother Nature's lead, Israeli scientists have built a DNA computer so tiny that a trillion of them could fit in a test tube and perform a billion operations per second with 99.8 percent accuracy. Instead of using figures and formulas to solve a problem, the microscopic computer's input, output and software are made up of DNA molecules—which store and process encoded information in living organisms. Scientists see such DNA computers as future competitors to their more conventional cousins because miniaturization is reaching its limits and DNA has the potential to be much faster than conventional computers.

There is some hope that such a microscopic computer could be inserted directly into the body to perform therapeutic functions.

Quantum computing brings together researchers in physics, mathematics, and computer science to exploit the uncertainty of quantum phenomena to create very fast computations. Some researchers view quantum computing as an inevitable outcome of current directions in miniaturization. For example, consider the following[62]:

> Mr. Nolte, a physics professor at-Indiana's Purdue University, points out that if Moore's law is projected to 2020, transistors in microprocessors would need to be so miniaturized that they would operate on only a single electron. Given the improbability of that scenario, Mr. Nolte believes, silicon's momentum must slow, and photonic computing take up the slack. Ultimately, Mind at Light Speed proposes, three generations of architectures of light will create an "intelligent optical fabric that will drape the world."

On December 20, 2001, a significant event was announced at the IBM Almaden Research Center in San Jose, California[63]:

In an important milestone toward making powerful computers that exploit the mind-bending possibilities of calculating with individual atoms, scientists at the I.B.M. Almaden Research Center, in San Jose, Calif., are announcing today that they have performed the most complex such calculation yet: factoring the number 15. The answer itself was no surprise: 3 and 5, the numbers that divide into 15, leaving no remainder. But the exercise that led to that simple result—the first factoring of a number with an exotic device called a quantum computer—holds the promise of one day solving problems now considered impossible, and cracking seemingly impenetrable codes.

Research in quantum computing is a rapidly growing research area, but the possibility of actually building a quantum computer is still quite remote.

THE INTERNET

Is it a fact, or have I dreamt it—that, by means of electricity, the world of matter has become a great nerve, vibrating thousands of miles in a breathless point of time?—Nathaniel Hawthorne, *The House of the Seven Gables*

The Internet is a vast computer network, linking computer networks around the world, so therefore a network of networks. As described in Chapter 1, it originated from ARPANET, an experimental network financed by ARPA (Advanced Research Products Agency of the Department of Defense) in the late 1960s. Its purpose was to link geographically distributed researchers with shared interests via a relatively high-speed network to facilitate collaborative efforts. Its design was motivated by the necessity to function even during wartime conditions and it is therefore very resistant to interruptions, however serious. Its growth over the first few years was slow, as more and more researchers came online. In fact by 1977, there were only about 100 hosts on ARPANET. Although ARPANET itself was discontinued in 1990, other networks such as CSNET, founded by the National Science Foundation in 1980, and BITNET a year later, took up the burden for a much wider audience than Defense Department researchers. Notable events include the introduction of the UNIX operating system in 1969 (Ken Thompson and Dennis Ritchie at AT&T Bell Labs), the first e-mail program that same year (Larry Roberts), and the beginning of work on TCP/IP (Transmission Control Protocol/Internet Protocol) (Vinton Cerf and Robert Kahn) in 1974. Another definition of the Internet, therefore, is the network of all networks that communicates by means of TCP/IP.[64]

The growth of the Internet began to take off in the late 1980s as the number of hosts seemed to increase exponentially. The Internet Software Consortium estimated that there were over 16.1 million hosts worldwide on the

Internet as of January 1997. By January 2000, that number had grown to over 72 million, and as of January 1, 2003, the number had grown by almost 100 million to 171.6 million.[65] Compare this number to the figure for July 1989, namely 130,000. What is more difficult to determine is the number of people who have access to the Internet and its multitude of offerings. Various companies attempt to survey the number of Internet users on a regular basis, for advertising purposes. One of these has estimated that 605.6 million people were on the Internet worldwide as of September 2002. Of these, 182.67 million were in the U.S. and Canada, 190.91 million in Europe, and 187.24 in Asia/the Pacific.[66] These results are described as an "educated guess."

In addition, commercial networks such as America Online, Microsoft, and CompuServe have millions of customers and can also access the Internet. It is the apparent success of the Internet that gave rise to a vision—the Information Highway, a somewhat dated name currently—of a broadband network linking homes, schools, government, and business with a two-way communication system, able to download movies in real time.

SUMMARY

There is a rather simple dichotomy between the view that technology is neutral, just a tool, and the view that it can create serious problems independent of the intentions of the developers. Critics of the unrestricted use of technology include Lewis Mumford, who is very concerned about the dehumanizing aspects of automation; Siegfried Giedion, who argues that technology in the pursuit of efficiency may be achieved at the loss of quality and traditional human skills; and Jacques Ellul, who presents an enormously pessimistic view of technology (or *technique*) as an all-powerful force independent of human control. More recently, Joseph Weizenbaum, Neil Postman, and Sven Birkerts, among others, have focused on computers and related technologies and expressed their concerns about negative impacts. Surprisingly, Bill Joy of Sun Microsystems has also raised concerns about the future impact of technology.

Charles Babbage, an irascible genius of 19th-century England, essentially invented the concept of the modern computer. He was unable to build it because of political and financial problems as well as his continual design changes, which inhibited actually focusing on a given model.

The modern electronic computer generally is acknowledged to have been invented at the Moore School of Electrical Engineering, University of Pennsylvania, by John Mauchly and John Presper Eckert in 1945. Called ENIAC, it was funded by the Department of Defense and motivated by the computational needs of wartime research and development. Other contributions were made in the United States, England, and Germany, and their history is only now becoming clear. IBM (a name synonymous with the computer) has had major growth and a huge impact on the industry and, despite its ups and downs, still leads in sales in most categories, not including personal computers, associated software, and Internet-related technologies.

The major triumph of technology in the third quarter of the 20th century may well be the integrated circuit, usually called the chip. Another phenomenon of our times is the personal computer, which provides enormous computing power at relatively low cost and small size. But the 1990s have also been witness to the growth and incredible popularity of the Internet, as it has moved out of the research environment into mainstream consciousness and use. The future impact of these technological innovations is impossible to predict, but the opportunities they present will have a significant impact on society, for both good and ill. A good source for information about the Internet, not surprisingly, is the Internet Society.[67] Given the Internet's importance, many of the issues to be discussed in this book will be motivated by concerns arising from its use.

NOTES

1. Collected in online quotation list. Copyright: Kevin Harris 1995.
2. John McDermott. "Technology: The Opiate of the Intellectuals," *New York Review of Books*, July 31, 1969, p. 25.
3. *Ibid.*
4. Lewis Mumford. *The Myth of the Machine: The Pentagon of Power.* (New York: Harcourt Brace Jovanovich, Inc., 1970), p. 273.
5. Siegfried Giedion. *Mechanization Takes Command.* (New York: Oxford University Press, 1948).
6. *Ibid.*, p. 5.
7. *Ibid.*, p. 172.
8. *Ibid.*
9. For a detailed description, see Samuel A. Matz, "Modern Baking Technology," *Scientific American*, November 1984, pp. 122–6, 131–4.
10. *Op. cit.*, Giedion. *Mechanization Takes Command*, p. 198.
11. Jacques Ellul. *The Technological Society*, 1964; reprint ed. (New York: Vintage, a division of Random House, 1967).
12. *Ibid.*, p. xxv.
13. *Ibid.*, p. 78.
14. Norbert Wiener. *Cybernetics: Control and Communications in the Animal and Machine, Second Edition.* (New York: MIT Press and Wiley, 1961).
15. Norbert Wiener. *God and Golem.* (Cambridge, MA: MIT Press, 1966), p. 73.
16. Joseph Weizenbaum. *Computer Power and Human Reason.* (San Francisco: W. H. Freeman and Company, 1976).
17. *Ibid.*, p. 224.
18. *Ibid.*, p. 226.

19. Neil Postman. *Technopoly: The Surrender of Culture to Technology.* (New York: Vintage Books, A Division of Random House, 1993), p. xii.

20. *Ibid.*, p. 52.

21. *Ibid.*, p. 48.

22. Sven Birkerts. *The Gutenberg Elegies: The Fate of Reading in an Electronic Age.* (Boston: Faber and Faber, Inc., 1994), p. 6.

23. *Ibid.*, p. 20.

24. Bill Joy, "Why the Future Doesn't Need Us," *Wired*, April 2000. Available at http://www.wired.com/wired/archive/8.04/joy.html

25. Declan McCullagh, "Kurzweil: Rooting for the Machine," *Wired News*, November 3, 2000. Available at http://www.wired.com/news/technology/ 0,1282,39967,00.html

26. John Stuart Mill. *On Liberty.* (Boston: Ticknor and Fields, 1863), p. 114.

27. Oscar Wilde. *The Soul of Man Under Socialism and Other Essays.* (New York: Harper Collins, 1970), p. 245.

28. Herbert A. Simon, "Prometheus or Pandora: The Influence of Automation on Society," *Computer*, November 1981, p. 91.

29. The Progress and Freedom Foundation, "Mission Statement." Available at http://www.pff.org/pff/miss.html on February 20, 1996.

30. The Progress and Freedom Foundation, "Cyberspace and the American Dream: A Magna Carta for the Knowledge Age." Release 1.2, August 22, 1994. Available at http://www.pff.org/pff/position.html on February 21, 1996.

31. Brian Randell, ed., *The Origins of Digital Computers, Selected Papers.* (New York: Springer-Verlag, 3rd edition, 1982), pp. 1–7.

32. Gottfried Liebniz, as quoted in Herman H. Goldstine, *The Computer From Pascal to von Neumann.* (Princeton: Princeton University Press, 1972), p. 8.

33. A letter from Babbage to Adolphe Quetelet, dated April 27, 1835, is apparently the earliest known reference to the Analytical Engine. For a fascinating study of the torturous process of historical attribution as well as the pitfalls of publication, see J.A.N. Lee, "On Babbage and Kings" and "How Sausage Was Made: And Now for the Rest of the Story," *IEEE Annals of the History of Computing*, 17(4), Winter 1995, pp. 7–23.

34. Doron Swade, *The Difference Engine: Charles Babbage and the Quest to Build the First Computer.* (New York: Viking, 2001), p. 223.

35. Countess Lovelace's translation of "Sketch of the Analytical Engine invented by Charles Babbage, Esq. By L. F. Menabrea, of Turin" [1842] appeared in *Taylor's Scientific Memoirs*, Vol. III, together with her editorial notes. It is reprinted in B. V. Bowden, ed., *Faster Than Thought: A Symposium on Digital Computing Machines.* (London, England: The Pittman Press, 1971) (original edition, 1953), p. 368.

36. *Ibid.*, p. 398.

37. Randell, *Ibid.*, p. 160.

38. As quoted in Nancy Stern, *From Eniac to Univac.* (Bedford, MA: Digital, 1981), p. 4. The original source is E. R. Larson, Findings of Fact, Conclusions of Law and Order for Judgment (sic), File No. 4-67 Civ. 138, Honeywell Inc., vs. Sperry-Rand Corp. and Illinois Scientific Developments Inc., U.S. District Court, District of Minnesota, Fourth Division, Oct. 19, 1973.

39. Herman Lukoff, *From Dits to Bits: A Personal History of the Electronic Computer*. (Portland, OR: Robotics, 1979). Herman Goldstine, *The Computer From Pascal to von Neumann*, (Princeton, NJ: Princeton University Press, 1972).

40. Randell, *Ibid.*, p. 297.

41. See the Spring 1996 issue of *IEEE Annals of the History of Computing* 18(1) for several papers "Documenting ENIAC's 50th Anniversary."

42. John Mauchly, contribution to "Reader's Forum," *Datamation*, October 1979, p. 217.

43. Randell, *Ibid.*, pp. 379–380.

44. John A. N. Lee and Golde Holtzman. "50 Years After Breaking the Codes: Interviews with Two of the Bletchley Park Scientists," *IEEE Annals of the History of Computers*, 17(1), 1995, pp. 32–43.

45. "IT 100/200 Scoreboard," *Business Week*, June 24, 2002. Available at *http://bwnt.businessweek.com/it100/* Figures for Fujitsu and NEC are obtained from their financial report available at http://pr.fujitsu.com/en/ir/annual/pdf/p20.pdf and http://www.nec.co.jp/ir/en/library/annual/2001/five-y.pdf respectively.

46. William H. Gates, Chairman and Chief Software Architect, Microsoft Corporation, 2002. Available at http://www.microsoft.com/billgates/bio.asp

47. "History of Microsoft," September 7, 2001. Available at http://www.piesoftwareinc.co.uk/textonly/microsoft.html

48. "Microsoft History," 1995. Available at http://www.maccare.com.ar/pc_ing.htm#Microsoft%20History

49. Hoo-min D. Toong and Amar Gupta. "Personal Computers," *Scientific American*, December 1982, p. 87.

50. "The Computer Moves In," *Time*, January 3, 1983, p. 10. Copyright 1983 Time Warner Inc. Reprinted by permission.

51. F. G. Heath. "Large Scale Integration in Electronics," *Scientific American*, February 1970, p. 22.

52. Robert N. Noyce. "Microelectronics," *Scientific American*, September 1977, p. 67. This influential paper presents important reasons for the success of the integrated circuit.

53. Jaikumar Vijayan and Stewart Deck. "Glut of Memory Chips Pushes Prices Down," *Computerworld*, February 19, 1996, p. 32.

54. Gene Bylinsky. "Here Comes the Second Computer Revolution," *Fortune*, November 1975. Reprinted in Tom Forester, ed., *The Microelectronics Revolution*. (Cambridge, MA: The MIT Press, 1981), p. 6.

55. "Computer Superchip 'Impressive'," *The Vancouver Sun*, January 4, 1990, p. B4.

56. Hutcheson and Hutcheson, p. 62.

57. "Stats: World Market Sales and Shares," Semiconductor Industry Association. Available at http://www.semichips.org/downloads/ACF84.pdf

58. *Ibid.*

59. "Industry Facts & Figures," Semiconductor Industry Association. Available at http://www.semichips.org/pre_facts.cfm

60. Michael Kanellos. "PCs: More Than 1 Billion Served," Cnet News, June 30, 2002. Available at http://news.com.com/2100-1040-940713.html

61. "Researchers Build Tiny Computers from DNA," Reuters, Cnet.com, November 21, 2001. Available at http://news.cnet.com/news/0-1003-200-7946153.html?tag-prntfr

62. Mark Williams. "Photonic Computing Takes a Quantum Leap," A book review of David Nolte, *Mind at Light Speed: a New Kind of Intelligence* (New York: The Free Press), 2001. Available at http://www.redherring.com/insider/2002/0410/2275.html

63. George Johnson. "Efforts to Transform Computers Reach Milestone," *The New York Times*, December 20, 2001, Section A, p. 26.

64. Stan Kulikowski. "Timeline for a Network History." As posted on comp.society.cu-digest, June 10, 1993. Message-ID: <1993June24.233217.3449@chinacat.unicom.com

65. "Internet Domain Survey," Internet Software Consortium, 2003. Available at http://www.isc.org/ds

66. "How Many Online," NUA Internet Surveys, September 2002. Available at http://www.nua.com/surveys/how_many_online/index.html

67. The Internet Society is a nongovernmental international organization for global cooperation and coordination for the Internet and its internetworking technologies and applications. The Society's individual and organizational members are bound by a common stake in maintaining the viability and global scaling of the Internet. They comprise the companies, government agencies, and foundations that have created the Internet and its technologies as well as innovative new entrepreneurial organizations contributing to maintain that dynamic. Visit their home pages to see how Internet innovators are creatively using the network. The Society is governed by its Board of Trustees elected by its membership around the world. Available at http://www.isoc.org

ADDITIONAL READINGS

Comments on Technological Change

Bell, Daniel. *The Coming of the Post-Industrial Society*. (New York: Basic Books, 1983).

Benedikt, Michael. *Cyberspace: First Steps*. (Cambridge, MA: The MIT Press, 1991).

Frankel Boris. *The Postindustrial Utopians*. (Cambridge, United Kingdom: Polity Press, 1987).

Kelly, Kevin. *Out of Control: The Rise of Neo-biological Civilization*. (Reading, MA: Addison-Wesley, 1995).

Kuhns, William. *The Post-Industrial Prophets*. (New York: Harper & Row, 1971).

Masuda, Yoneii. *The Information Society as Post Industrial Society*. (Bethesda, MD: World Future Society, 1981).

Mander, Jerry. *In the Absence of the Sacred: The Failure of Technology & the Survival of the Indian Nations*. (San Francisco: Sierra Club Books paperback edition, 1992).

Negroponte, Nicholas. *Being Digital*. (New York: Alfred A. Knopf, 1995).

Nora, Simon and Minc, Alain. *The Computerization of Society*. (Cambridge, MA: The MIT Press, 1981).

Reinecke, Ian. *Electronic Illusions: A Skeptic's View of Our High-Tech Future*. (New York: Penguin, 1984).

Shallis, Michael. *The Silicon Idol: The Micro Revolution and Its Social Implications*. (New York: Oxford University Press, 1984).

Stoll, Clifford, *Silicon Snake Oil*. (New York: Doubleday, 1995).

Winner, Langdon. *Autonomous Technology: Technics-out-of-Control as a Theme in Political Thought*. Cambridge, MA: MIT Press, 1977.

Winner, Langdon. *The Whale and the Reactor: A Search for Limits in an Age of High Technology*. (Chicago: University of Chicago Press, 1986).

A Brief History of Computers

Aspray, William. *John von Neumann and the Origins of Modern Computing*. (Cambridge, MA: MIT Press, 1990).

Augarten, Stan. *Bit by Bit: An Illustrated History of Computers*. (New York: Ticknor & Fields, 1984).

Blohm, Hans, Beer, Stafford, and Suzuki, David. *Pebbles to Computers: The Thread*. (Toronto, Canada: Oxford University Press, 1986).

Burks, Alice R. and Burks, Arthur W. *The First Electronic Computer: The Atanasoff Story*. (Ann Arbor: The University of Michigan Press, 1988).

Flamm, Kenneth. *Creating the Computer: Government, Industry, and High Technology*. (Washington, DC: The Brookings Institution, 1988).

Garr, Doug. *IBM Redux: Lou Gerstner & the Business Turnaround of the Decade*. (New York: HarperBusiness, 1999).

Gates, Bill. *The Road Ahead*. (New York: Penguin Books, 1996).

Hinsley, F. H. and Stripp, Alan (Eds.). *Codebreakers: The Inside Story of Bletchley Park*. (New York: Oxford University Press, 1993).

Hyman, Anthony. *Charles Babbage, Pioneer of the Computer*. (Princeton, NJ: Princeton University Press, 1982).

Lavington, Simon. *Early British Computers*. (Bedford, MA: Digital Press, 1980).

Lee, J. A. N. *Computer Pioneers*. (Los Alamitos, CA: IEEE CS Press, 1995).

Lundstrom, David. E. *A Few Good Men From Univac*. (Cambridge, MA: MIT Press, 1987).

Metropolis, N., Howlett J., and Rota, Gian-Carlo. *The History of Computing in the Twentieth Century*. (New York: Academic Press, 1976).

Mollenhoff, Clark R. *Atanasoff: Forgotten Father of the Computer*. (Ames: Iowa State University Press, 1988).

Polson, Ken. "Chronology of Events in the History of Microcomputers," 1996. Availble at http://www.islandnet.com/~kpolsson/comphist.htm on September 26, 1996.

Rojas, Paul and Hashagen, Ulf. *The First Computers: History and Architecture*, (Cambridge, MA: MIT Press, 2002).

Wallich, Paul. "The Ghosts of Computers Past," *IEEE Spectrum*, November 2002. Available at http://www.spectrum.ieee.org/WEBONLY/publicfeature/nov02/gost.html

Williams, Michael R. *A History of Computing.* (Englewood Cliffs, NJ: Prentice-Hall, 1985).

The Emergence of the Chip

Braun, Ernest and MacDonald, Stuart. *Revolution in Miniature: The History and Impact of Semiconductor Electronics.* (Cambridge, United Kingdom: Cambridge University Press, 1978).

Hanson, Dirk. *The New Alchemists: Silicon Valley Fever and the Micro-Electronics Revolution.* (New York: Avon, 1983).

Hayes, Dennis. *Behind the Silicon Curtain: The Seductions of Work in a Lonely Era.* (Boston: South End Press, 1989).

Rogers, Everett M. and Larsen, Judith K. *Silicon Valley Fever: Growth of High-Technology Culture.* (New York: Basic Books, 1984).

Siegel, Lenny and Markoff, John. *The High Cost of High Tech: The Dark Side of the Chip.* (New York: Harper & Row. 1985).

The Internet

Anthes, Gary H. "The History of the Future," *Computerworld.*, October 3, 1994, pp. 101, 104–105.

Berners-Lee, Tim. *Weaving the Web: The Original Design and Ultimate Destiny of the World Wide Web.* (New York: HarperSanFrancisco, 1999).

"Internet & Beyond," Special Report, *Byte*, July 1995, pp. 69–92.

Kehoe, Brendan P. *Zen and the Art of the Internet: A Beginner's Guide.* (Englewood Cliffs, NJ: Prentice-Hall, 1991).

Kroll, Ed. *The Whole Internet: User's Guide and Catalog.* (Sebastopol, CA: O'Reilly 1992).

Mitchell, William J. *City of Bits: Space, Place and the Infobahn.* (New York: HarperCollins, 1995).

4

THE BUSINESS WORLD

American business has a voracious appetite for more and better information.

Mark Klein, "Information Politics," *Datamation* (Cahners Publishing Co.), August 1,1985.

INTRODUCTION

A major part of the June 5, 1971, issue of *Business Week* was devoted to a serious overview of computers in business.[1] The underlying sentiment was that computers are wonderful tools but they must satisfy traditional business principles; they must be used wisely, and they tend to generate their own special problems. Technology is changing rapidly, prices are falling, machines are getting faster and smaller, and software to deal with many of the pressing problems of business will soon be available. Minicomputers (minis) were the big news, much cheaper than mainframes but with more computing power for the dollar. And computers were being used everywhere:

- *Process Control and Manufacturing.* Steel plants, automobile factories, the aerospace industry
- *Education.* Business schools, high schools, elementary schools
- *Financial Institutions.* Banks, credit card systems, the stock market
- *Government.* Social security administration, research, defense department (3200 computers and the electronic battlefield), economic modeling

A list for today would be similar but much longer, as would be the list of concerns and aims. Our purpose in this chapter is first to trace the evolution of data processing systems, as they were once called—their problems, their uses, and their future. The term data processing (DP) has evolved into the more ambitious concepts of information processing (IP), or information technology (IT), or even information and communications technology (ICT). And of course, industry managers need management information systems or knowledge-based systems. These will provide instant information, decision-making advice, forecasts, statistics, graphs, and tables. With a computer on the office desk or a laptop aboard the airplane, the manager can access all these forms of business information directly, or so the story goes. Computers and associated technologies have thus changed the way companies are managed, with such descriptions, for example, as the virtual corporation and the re-engineering of the company having received considerable attention several years ago.

Among the potential future benefits of computers, none has been as acclaimed as the automated office. There has been a call for the office to be transformed by computers and communication networks to decrease paperwork and increase productivity. The personal computer, which has slipped into every nook and cranny of the company, will continue to play an important role. Networking, both within companies and globally, is becoming a major factor in the business world. Also of increasing importance is the Internet and especially the World Wide Web as a necessary advertising and sales tool, offering many potential benefits. The impact of computerization on the organizational structure of companies is of course an issue, as are the fears of some office workers about the potential industrialization of the office and the accompanying loss of jobs.

It is impossible to cover all the material that could comfortably fall under the general category of computers and business, but beyond a brief review of the early applications, there are some issues that demand coverage. One major issue is the use of the Internet by traditional businesses to further their aims. As with many new technologies, it is not always obvious what the best ways are to employ Internet technology in order to improve business operations and ultimately sales and profits. In what follows, various applications will be described and possible future ones explored. For some businesses, the Internet is the *raison d'etre* of the enterprise, rather than a useful tool. Of course, the boom of the late 1990s was followed by the sobering dot.com crash of 2000 and beyond. Thus the role of the Internet as just a new marketing tool as well as a new source of products and services will be examined. Other areas of interest include a review of the Year 2000, or so-called Y2K, phenomenon with its predictions of dire consequences to the industrialized countries as the date advanced from 1999 to 2000, some discussion of the developing theory and reality of E-commerce, and some examples of successful online companies.

The Year 2000 (That Never Was)

But all is not efficiency, productivity, and organization: What about the advertised chaos that was predicted to herald the year 2000? Because computers began to be used heavily in the 1960s, a shortcut was introduced with respect to the computation of ages, years, and dates in innumerable databases. Simply put, if Mary was born in 1953 and it is currently 1997, her age can be computed by subtracting 1953 from 1997 (within one year). It requires less computer memory, a vital concern in the 1960s, 1970s, and 1980s, and less computation to carry out the subtraction as 53 from 97, if only two digits are stored for the year of birth and the current year. In many thousands of databases, both public and private, this latter strategy was followed for 40 years with the result that a simple and effective process, if not amended, was anticipated to result in chaos in the year 2000 and beyond if remedial steps were not taken. [The age in the previous example will not be 47. It could be −53, it could be zero if negative results have been excluded,] or it could cause a system crash if negative results permeate the database. To deal with this apparently simple problem would require a very expensive fix. The Gartner Group, Inc, made the following predictions:[2]

• Worldwide costs to address the Year 2000 change: $300 billion to $600 billion. This cost includes inventory and finding and fixing date fields as well as testing. It does not include changing forms to accommodate the extra date field.
• Fix-it costs per line of code: $1. This cost does not include documentation, training, and final implementation testing.

The Gartner forecast was disputed at the time, of course, especially the prediction that correcting the problem would provide an enormous boost for mainframe sales, but there did exist a general agreement that it was a serious problem that had to be addressed and one whose solution would not be cheap.[3] Just to reinforce the concern, here are some reasons that investors could have suffered from Year 2000 problems because all transactions are heavily dependent on the accurate recording and use of dates[4]:

• Clearing and settlement of transactions could break down.
• Stocks held electronically and checking accounts could be wiped out.
• Customers might be denied access to their accounts.
• Deposits or trades might not be credited to an account, and customers' funds would not be available.
• Interest might not be properly credited to accounts.

As it turned out, the first days of 2000 arrived and very little happened. That is to say, the following front page story in the *New York Times* was typical[5]:

Despite a few sputters and glitches, the world's computers appear to have survived the year 2000 rollover without major problems—and with humanity's faith in technology intact, at least for another day.

Yet the day arrived without the kind of catastrophic problems once feared, of widespread power failures or planes crashing.

Thus after a worldwide expenditure of about $300 billion to anticipate and correct the problem, by various estimates, very little happened. One hypothesis is that if it were not for this massive effort, real catastrophes would have occurred; another is that the dangers were actually considerably less than advertised and that many consultants, software companies, and others profited from scare tactics. Even other concerns about the "confusion" over whether or not 2000 was a leap year turned out to be overstated. All in all, the following overview by the well-known financial consultant Edward Yourdon seems to capture the right balance[6]:

- Potential Y2K problems have been fixed.
- Potential Y2K problems were exaggerated.
- Many potentially faulty systems were turned off for New Year's or run manually.
- I have no regerets or apologies for the preparations I made or the precautions I took—no more so than I regret the money I spent last year on automobile insurance, health insurance, and fire insurance, none of which turned out to be necessary.

THE EARLY YEARS: DATA PROCESSING SYSTEMS

It is a capital mistake to theorize before one has data.—Arthur Conan Doyle

The computer is almost synonymous with business. After use in military applications, the first computer sales were to business. Since then (almost 50 years ago) business, in all its multifarious interests, has become the major user of computers. Some of the uses are obvious: payroll, accounts receivable, sales records, inventory control—management of all the basic records and computations needed to operate a business. As computer technology evolved and was in fact actively spurred on by the rising expectations of the business community, the range of uses expanded rapidly to meet both perceived and anticipated needs.

The Evolution of Data Processing

Cyrus Gibson and Richard Nolan described the goals of managers in introducing computer facilities and the resulting organizational problems that have arisen.[7] They were interested in methods and techniques for improving these facilities in response to the changing requirements of a company. In 1974, they argued that there are four stages of electronic data processing (EDP) growth and that it follows the classic S-curve from an initial to a mature phase. The first stage, accounting applications, reflects the replacement of manual methods by the computer with the primary goal of cost savings. Succeeding stages are characterized by a flowering of new possibilities that exploit the power and speed of computers. Stage 2 shows a "proliferation of applications in all functional areas" such as cash flow, budgeting, inventory, and sales. Stage 3 is consolidation, as the applications of Stage 2 are accommodated and control is emphasized. In Stage 4 more sophisticated software appears, focused on the database with a variety of online activities, as well as financial and simulation models.

It is instructive to remember, again, that not too many years ago when the population was not much smaller than it is today, bills were received, payments were acknowledged, payrolls were computed and disbursed, and society functioned more or less as it does currently, without computers. The arrival of the computer, however, meant that management had the potential systems capacity to engage in an enormous variety of new activities. This power would translate into quicker, more, and possibly better service for the customer; more (not always better) controls; better forecasts; and new ways of evaluating information. A new version of Parkinson's Law, that work expands to fill the time available, has arisen: Applications expand to fill the computer power available. (A corollary might be that ambition expands even faster.) For example, simulation and financial models represent complex applications made possible only by computers.

Simulation models are used to study complex systems for which exact mathematical analysis is too difficult. Companies trying to gauge market trends or determine crucial factors in the production process may decide to develop computer programs that simulate the situations of interest. Such programs are designed to simulate relevant features of the real world and study their interaction, because the world is too complex and cannot usually be modified to serve desired purposes. Care must be taken that important and relevant variables are recognized and properly interrelated. The underlying model must be carefully constructed and subsequently evaluated to ensure that the results produced are meaningful and significant.

Simulation is a powerful tool for science, government, and industry, but it must be used carefully. In the early 1970s, a considerable controversy arose in the wake of the publication of *The Limits to Growth,* a report that warned of a coming breakdown of the industrial world due to shortages in fuels and raw materials.[8] The report, based on a simulation model, was criticized for ignoring certain information, badly estimating the importance of some of the parameters, and ignoring crucial relations among selected variables. Currently a similar debate rages over the greenhouse effect and the concern that unless we curtail the production of carbon dioxide, a byproduct of industry and automobiles, we will have to confront the effects of higher temperatures around the world. If company policy is to be based on the results of simulations, management must be convinced of their accuracy—a non-trivial requirement. Even so, the use of simulations has become another important weapon in management's operational and planning arsenal.

Financial planning models depend on sophisticated mathematical models that have been designed to predict medium- and long-term events. Such models have become quite useful and important and would not be possible without computers. Their construction requires mathematical, financial, and programming skills. As computer systems have become more powerful these models have taken on a new significance. They can be responsive to changing world conditions and permit managers to make quick decisions. It is interesting to consider the current situation in which the major financial institutions all depend on sophisticated financial models to carry out their activities. To the best computer programs go the spoils.

One of the major advances of the 1970s was the development of online systems. An online system permitted almost instantaneous access to, and response from, the computer in contrast to the previous batch systems that required overnight runs to process daily activities. For example, a banking system permits online access with which the teller can update an account directly from a terminal or personal computer. With online systems, management can have rapid access to personnel information, customer information, and sales information. It should be noted that an online system typically permits access to several hundred, if not thousands of users. Such a facility requires a large mainframe computer, or more recently, a distributed system with many small and powerful computers linked in a client-server configuration. These days, of course, home banking is being encouraged for clients, to take advantage of the Internet from the comfort of their homes. The growth in home banking certainly suits bank customers and has many advantages for banks and merchants as well.

Gibson and Nolan pointed out a number of the problems associated with the growth of EDP systems in general. One of the earliest was the location of the data processing division within the company organization and the implications of this decision. A data processing center could be a branch of the financial division, a service center accommodating a number of departments, or an autonomous division with its own vice president. Each of these had its own advantages and disadvantages for the company, for middle management, and for the employees. Not uncommonly, the first computer appeared in the finance department, since there were immediate applications in accounting. Soon other departments such as sales, marketing, production, and research saw in the computer an important and necessary instrument. In some cases the large investment in computing resources was jealously guarded by the financial department, and part-time release of resources to other departments may not have been sufficient. Pressure arose for either a central independent computer facility or center to which all divisions or departments would have equal access, or a computing facility directly responsible to other users. In the former case, the center would be just another company division responsible to the president and in competition for resources in its own right. In the latter, the center would be a service department expected to provide whatever might be required and dependent on its clients for its budget. Clearly, different organizational roles imply differing degrees of responsibility. Computer professionals may be either technicians or part of the executive hierarchy. The arrival of powerful personal computers certainly changed the structure of this situation forever.

Five Generations of Computers

One of the best overviews of the early evolution of computer systems has been provided by Frederic G. Withington, a vice president at Arthur D. Little Inc., and a long-time student of data processing systems.[9] He outlines five generations of computers, the first being 1953–1958 and the last 1982–ongoing. (The first three generations run from 1953 to 1974, the year the article was written. The last two represent predictions whose accuracy can be better determined as time goes on.) The names of Withington's generations are instructive.

The first three periods, gee whiz, paper pushers, and communicators, represent the initiation and consolidation phase—new hardware, new software, traditional applications, changing organizational structure, and consolidation of the new technology. Withington predicted that the fourth generation, information custodians, would be characterized by very large file stores (databases), general-purpose data manipulators, and centralized control with logistic decisions moving to headquarters and tactical decisions moving out. The forecast was actually quite accurate, with a couple of exceptions. The software did not evolve as rapidly as expected, although time-sharing systems did predominate. In the area of hardware, Withington did not, and could not be expected to, anticipate the personal computer explosion.

The last generation, action aids (beginning about 1982), he supposed would make use of new hardware such as magnetic bubble, laser-holographic technology, and distributed systems. Laser-holographic technology has yet to make its presence felt in the computer industry. Most computer companies have given up on magnetic bubble memories, but distributed systems have become the predominant architecture, albeit several years after the predicted date. Less centralized computing was anticipated, but the overwhelming integration of computing and communications could hardly have been expected. Furthermore, developments in office automation promise to revolutionize the basic operation of business. Other important contributions will include management information and decision analysis systems; aids to managers and executives at every level of the company; and direct marketing applications, advertising, and consumer measurements over the Internet.

IT Industry Evolution

One last view of the evolution of IT (Information Technology) presents "four waves of change." These persist from their years of initiation into the indefinite future as new waves wash over them and add to their effects. This view is more complex than the previous one, which seems to suggest a more-or-less linear sequence of successively more advanced technologies, with their associated organizational impacts. Table 4.1 presents a summary of the discussion in "IS Priorities: As the Information Highway Begins."[10]

We seem to be in the age of the Information Society or at least the beginning of what many would characterize as the Internet Age, a definite precursor to the fully blown vision encompassed in the term, Information Society.

Guidelines for Growth

The transition from computer management to data resource management is an important step. Clearly, the situation changes as the range of applications grows, access diversifies via remote terminals and independent workstations, and more and more activities depend on the ready availability of information. In a natural way, the computer is thus transformed into a multifunctional information resource that is no longer the preserve of a designated division but is far-reaching and integrated into all the operations of the organization. Information in a variety of forms is now accessible, on

TABLE 4.1

EVOLUTION OF INDUSTRY INFORMATION TECHNOLOGY

Technology	Focus	Years of Duration	Number of Users
Mainframes and Minicomputers	Large institutions	From 1964–1981 (until about 2010)	10,000,000 worldwide
PCs, LANs open systems	Individuals at work at school, at home	From 1981–1993 (until past 2030)	Over 80,000,000
Information highways	Pervasive IT connectivity	From 1993–2010 to?	Over 100,000,000
Information society	Converged, all-digital multi-media context	From 2010–? to to?	Over 150,000,000

modern systems, by all levels of management as well as other employees, whether or not they are technically sophisticated, or have financial, managerial, marketing, or sales expertise.

In 1979, Richard Nolan extended the stages of data processing growth from four to six.[11] He considered the growth in knowledge and technology, organizational control, and the shift from computer management to data resource management to be a necessary broadening of computer applications. It is obvious that the growth of knowledge exerts an important influence on the direction and nature of further developments. In terms of organizational control, management must determine a balance between tight and so-called slack control. In fact, this balance will vary depending on the stage of growth. For example, to facilitate growth the control should be low and the slack should be high, but as the system matures, both should be high. Nolan bases his results on a study during the 1970s of many companies that passed through all the stages except the last one.

And what of the predictions for the 1990s and beyond? The 1980s witnessed enormous technological and organizational changes as companies struggled to accommodate an endless flow of new hardware and software. Arguments have raged about centralization versus decentralization (when most of the computing power was localized in mainframes) fulfilling user needs or management's directives, control, massive investment in technology with little obvious payoff, aging and fragile software investment, and an unpredictable and rapidly changing world economy. Given the basic and continuing importance of information to management, it is worth paying attention to the words of Peter Drucker, one of the world's foremost experts on management theory and practice. In a 1988 paper, Drucker notes that for the most part computers are still being used to facilitate traditional computational efforts; that is, to "crunch conventional numbers," but that as a company, especially a large one, moves from "data to information, its decision processes, management structure, and even the way its work gets done begin to be transformed."[12] Consider Drucker's definitions[13]:

> Information is data endowed with relevance and purpose. Converting data into information thus requires knowledge. And knowledge, by definition, is specialized. . . . The information-based organization requires far more specialists overall than the command-and-control companies we are accustomed to.

Drucker argues that, to stay competitive, companies "will have to convert themselves into organizations of knowledge specialists."

If this all sounds a bit too theoretical so far, perhaps we should turn to an industry practitioner:[14]

> As the companies reorganize for the '90s they are also exploding some myths. Chief among these is the notion that decentralization, the theme of

the 1980s, will be the favored organizational approach to the emerging global marketplace. The pundits couldn't be more wrong, the executives reveal. Centralized control will increase, new centralized functions and entrepreneurial teams will arise.

As the 1990s approached, there seemed to be a considerable difference of opinion about the directions that business organizational structures would move in response to developments in information systems. Interestingly enough, when 50 U.S. information systems executives were asked to rate 18 issues in order of importance they chose the following (in descending order of importance)[15]:

• Rapport and credibility with senior management
• Knowledge of the business
• Strategic systems opportunities
• Long-range vision and plan
• Skills mix and motivation of IS personnel.

The final words in this section will go to Richard Walton, distinguished and informed scholar of information system design and implementation. In a book written about 15 years ago but still relevant, Walton makes the claim, consistent with the previous comments, that the effective implementation of advanced information technology (IT) in organizations "is a function of integrating the technical aspects of IT systems *and* [emphasis added] the social aspects of the organization."[16] To elaborate, we include a few additional comments, recognizing that they barely do justice to this important book, which proposes a detailed framework for the implementation of advanced IT.[17]

He notes that certain principles have been recognized early on in the implementation of IT:

• Project champions
• Top management support
• Good relationships between developers and user departments
• User involvement
• Adequate organizational resources
• Communication
• Supportive organizational climate.

But more recently, these principles have been extended in the following ways:

• Top management should do more than merely support projects it approves. IT should develop and promulgate a broad version of IT, a vision capable of inspiring and guiding specific IT projects.

• Users are increasingly viewed as legitimately influencing design as well as installation activities.

• Advanced IT has "dual potentialities." For example, IT "can either routinize work or it can widen the discretion of users; it can strengthen hierarchical control or facilitate self-management and learning by users."

Information Technology and Productivity

In recognition of significant difficulties associated with the automation of the office, *Fortune* devoted the cover of its May 16, 1986, issue to the provocative claim, "The Puny Payoff from Office Computers."[18]

> Have the millions of computers purchased by U.S. businesses brought any overall improvement in productivity? Surprisingly, the best information available says no. . . .[O]n a national scale, business's investment of hundreds of billions of dollars in computers has failed to bring about a discernible improvement in productivity.

A number of reasons have been proposed to support this claim. These include the argument that computerization involves a long learning curve, that it may require a reorganization of the work process to realize significant gain, and simply that computers have been oversold so that they are misapplied in many applications. From another point of view, only the massive adoption of computers has prevented businesses from hiring many more people to maintain the same productivity levels.

Almost five years later the problem had not gone away, as a survey by the consultants Index Group reports, "the problem looming largest in the minds of corporate computer jockeys is convincing their colleagues to change their business practices to take advantage of office automation."[19] The startling statistic is that between the years 1980 and 1989, while the share of office equipment as a percentage of capital equipment rose from 3% to 18%, the productivity of office workers remained essentially unchanged. Over the same period the productivity of blue collar workers has increased substantially. We will have more to say about the difficult subject of productivity measurement later, but one final observation from the Index Group is particularly relevant: "Only about one-third of [computer] projects alter business practices. Most of the rest merely turn paper shufflers into computer-printout shufflers."[20]

More recently, productivity has reportedly increased but adequate tools and measures have not been available, so the by-now familiar misconception that productivity has not increased is unjustified. Professor Bakos of the University of California at Irvine presents the following reasons for the unacknowledged productivity gains:[21]

• It is ludicrous to blame computers for inadequate productivity in that period [the 1980s]. Computer investments in the 1970s and 1980s pale in comparison to the trillions of dollars of machinery, buildings and other assets that had accumulated over several decades.

• Any earlier move [prior to the 1990s] between computers and productivity would have been dwarfed by the impact of movements in oil prices and interest rates, changes in the tax code or fluctuations in the economy.

• Much of the productivity shortfall of the 1980s was a mirage anyway. Our tools for measuring productivity—designed for counting bushels of wheat and Model Ts off Ford's assembly line—are blunt when called upon to measure the tremendous improvements in service, quality, convenience, variety and timeliness.

• [A] recent comprehensive study of productivity of 380 large firms that together generate yearly sales in excess of $1.8 billion . . . found that computers . . . were significantly *more* [original emphasis] productive than any other type of investment these companies made.

If we can agree that computers have boosted productivity, the question that must be asked is why. There are no definitive answers but there are some possible ones. The real payoffs come about because the effective use of computers requires a substantial reorganization of the work process. In another study that attempts to determine the reasons for the wide fluctuations in computer-buying behavior by large companies, the authors suggest the following:[22]

> The biggest reason for business's computer-buying behavior was that companies had to reorganize their business practices to take advantage of the new technology and had to tailor new software for their workers. They faced significant adjustment costs, and the process was painfully slow.

Two interesting answers to the productivity question seem to follow from this conclusion:[23]

• The road to technical progress will need to be cleared by managers solving the intractable problems of corporations just as they have since the age of the Medicis.

• Why [have] the so-called social returns from the spread of computer technology—increased wealth or leisure from greater productivity . . . been so slow to materialize? At first companies simply applied computer speed to old-fashioned work designs—paving the cowpaths, as it were. Really turbocharging productivity required basic redesign of work. And that took time.

A detailed examination of these issues was published in 1994 and invoked a mathematical model, resulting in the following conclusion:[24]

The reason that neither supernormal returns nor unmeasured output, under generous but plausible assumptions, lead to large effects on productivity is that the share of computers in the capital stock is simply too small. The authors conclude that there is no computer productivity paradox; computing equipment should not have been expected to have made a large contribution to growth in the past two decades.

Without going into much detail at this point, it is necessary to clearly state that there is a positive link between IT and productivity, in spite of many articles in the popular press, over many years, to the contrary. In fact it would be surprising if vast amounts were spent on IT in the 1980s and 1990s with little impact on the bottom line. In Chapter 13, we will present a more thorough examination of issues related to technology, productivity, and jobs, but for now consider the following[25]:

> In recent years, the relationship between information technology (IT) and productivity has become a source of debate. In the 1980s and early 1990s, empirical research on IT productivity generally did not identify significant productivity improvements. More recently, as new data are identified and more sophisticated methodologies are applied, several researchers have found evidence that IT is associated not only with improvements in productivity, but also in intermediate measures, consumer surplus, and economic growth.

INFORMATION TECHNOLOGY AND NEW BUSINESS MODELS

> Knowledge is of two kinds. We know a subject ourselves, or we know where we can find information on it.—Samuel Johnson
> Knowledge itself is power.—Francis Bacon (1561–1626)

It is not my intention to provide a comprehensive overview of information technology (IT) or information systems (IS) in business, even if that were possible given space constraints. Rather it will be possible only to indicate the current state of certain aspects of IT, such as groupware, workflow, and knowledge management, and to highlight possible trends. My purpose therefore is to present a number of current issues and approaches to integrating IT in the workplace and even more to bring the story up to date.

General Background

In mid-1994, the cover of *Fortune* magazine read, "Managing in a WIRED WORLD."[26] This announcement seemed to herald the arrival of computer networks as a major organizational theme in the management world. This special report, also subtitled as *Fortune's* guide to Information Technology, surveyed such issues as managing, dealing with information overload, a survey of stationary and portable PCs, the role of telecom, or the office communication network, an overview of new products, ideas, and, of course, investments. A sampler of opinions followed to capture the swirl of issues surrounding the management problems of the mid-1990s[27]:

- Bill Raduchel, chief information officer of Sun Microsystems: "E-mail is a major cultural event—it changes the way you run the organization."
- Susan Falzon, a principal at CSC Research & Advisory Services in Cambridge, Massachusetts: "When work is carried out through networks, an organization's structure changes whether you want it or not. I can't find a single case where it doesn't happen. . . . In a network, supervision changes. There's less supervision of the content of the work, more supervision of a person's overall performance and career."
- Robert Walker, chief information officer at Hewlett-Packard: "With the ability to share information broadly and fully without filtering it through a hierarchy, we can manage the way we always wanted to. . . . Every month H-P's 97,000 employees exchange 20 million E-mail messages."
- Warns Helene Runtagh, CEO of General Electric Information Services, "The worst of all worlds is clinging to hierarchical behavior while bringing in network-based communications. You're in for a decade of chaos, frustration and poor financial results."

You might think that by examining a company's expenditures in IT and its overall performance it would be possible to determine what the best strategy might be with respect to the optimal deployment of computing resources. This is just what Paul Strassmann, a chief information officer at several major corporations and a writer for *Computerworld*, did, using data derived from a study of *Computerworld's* Premier 100 companies over a period of two years. These companies are renowned for their effective use of IT. Some of Mr. Strassmann's conclusions are given here[28]:

- They don't show any trend towards massive outsourcing.
- Excellent corporations deploy information technology in several ways. Many rely on mainframe computing, using older machines. Some spend a great deal on server hardware and PCs. Some devote up to half their budgets to systems development and systems engineering, and others coast along on program maintenance.
- Excellence is gained through the accumulation of company-specific know-how, for which company-based information management is indispensable.

In a following report, Mr. Strassmann makes the claim that expenditures in IT are not the determining factor in a corporation's success: "After twenty years of research I have found that computers do indeed add a great deal of value to well-managed companies. But, computers are not an unqualified blessing. Identical machines, with identical software, will make things worse if the enterprise is mismanaged."[29] He goes on to state that,[30]

> The proof of these assertions is that computer expenditures and corporate profits show no correlation whatsoever. I can state also that it is unlikely that any such relationship can be ever demonstrated. Computers are only a catalyst. Business values are created by well organized, well motivated and knowledgeable people who understand what to do with all of the information that shows up on the computer screens. It would be too much to hope that such a phenomenon would be a universal characteristic of all businesses.

These last remarks were based on a 1994 study of 500 corporations in the U.S., Canada, and Europe. A scatter plot of Return on Equity versus Information Technology spending per employee for a statistically unbiased sample shows no correlation, as mentioned.

In Chapter 2, Isaac Asimov's three rules for robotics were given as an example of how technology could be constrained to serve people but not harm them, by building into the "positronic brains" of robots a fundamental limitation on their exercise of power. Well, a project manager at a large company proposed a similar set of laws to govern the relationship between users and their information systems (IS)[31]:

- *Law No. 1*: IS can't harm the business, or through inaction let the business come to harm.
- *Law No. 2*: IS must obey the orders given it by a user, except where such orders conflict with the first law.
- *Law No. 3*: IS must always protect its own existence, except where this would conflict with the first and second laws.

The first law encourages a proactive stance for IS, the second a reexamination of underlying assumptions prior to the initiation of new applications, and the third, among other things, would discourage outsourcing (a position consistent with Strassmann's findings).

To continue with this emphasis on the value of promoting a human-centered approach to the management of IT, we turn to the important work of Thomas Davenport, a partner and director of research at Ernst & Young's Center for Information Technology and Strategy in Boston. Mr. Davenport has written at length about the importance of people in the managing of IT and the benefits to be gained when their abilities, skills, and concerns are effectively addressed and employed. With the focus on gathering, storing, manipulating, and disseminating information using computers and computer networks, a simple idea is occasionally lost, namely that much of what is valuable and important does not reside in machines but rather is part of the working intellectual capital of organizations and resides in the people themselves. In Davenport's own words, here are a few of the ten "Information Facts of Life"[32]:

1. Most of the information in organizations—and most of the information people really care about—isn't on computers.
2. Managers prefer to get information from people rather than computers; people add value to raw information by interpreting it and adding context.
4. All information doesn't have to be common; an element of flexibility and disorder is desirable.
6. If information is power and money, people won't share it easily.
8. To make the most of electronic communications, employees must first learn to communicate face-to-face.
10. There's no such thing as information overload; if information is really useful, our appetite for it is insatiable.

Knowledge Management

This section is the first in this chapter to discuss a number of labels that have been applied to the employment of IT in the corporation, in conjunction with a specific management strategy that is claimed to improve efficiency, productivity, competitiveness, and whatever else seems important at the time. Thus knowledge management, the virtual corporation, the re-engineered corporation, and other similar terms have been fashionable, with more and varied approaches ready to make their appearance. They are based on a variety of beliefs in the importance of knowledge to the successful corporation, the need to access and employ that knowledge, and the role of IT in that undertaking.

From a regular column by Joseph Maglitta in *Computerworld*, we learn that knowledge management is "the emerging discipline of systematically and actively managing and leveraging the vast stores of knowledge and information that exist in a typical company. 'Knowledge' refers to systems, processes, and know-how."[33] The answer to the question, "How does it affect IS [Information Systems]?" provides a boost to the development of technology, namely, "Depending on the organization and culture, technology groups lead knowledge management efforts or play an integral role as enabler. Some backers say knowledge management offers a promising, natural next stage of evolution for many IS groups."[34] The recognition of the value of company information is not a new idea, but its identification, extraction, and employment in a number of areas including sales and marketing by means of advanced IT *is* new.

More than six months later, Maglitta attempted to characterize the importance of knowledge management as follows[35]:

> Although approaches vary, knowledge management in general tries to organize and make available important know-how, wherever it's needed. This includes processes, procedures, patents, reference works, formulas, "best practices," forecasts and fixes. Technologically, intranets, groupware, data warehouses, networks, bulletin boards and videoconferencing are key tools for storing and distributing this intelligence.

Recent descriptions of knowledge engineering have incorporated newer technologies into their characterizations. For example, consider the following[36]:

> Over the past few years, just as groupware applications shifted from proprietary client/server models to a platform-agnostic Web model, knowledge management's embrace of Web technologies has extended its usefulness and cut costs. Web-based knowledge management systems require no (or minimal) change to users' desktops and can be simpler to install and administer. More recently, knowledge management systems started using XML to identify relevant data elements and extract knowledge from them both in and out of the organization. XML offers document schemas and tags, allowing readers to collect meta-information about each piece of information. For example, a data object marked "" in a help desk application is more likely to have useful answers than one marked ".

Workflow and Groupware

Two recent developments in IT facilitate the tracking and monitoring of work, Workflow, and the efforts of individuals to cooperate on projects, Groupware. Both of these seem to have unlimited potential for enhancing the work process in an important way, if employed in a spirit of commitment to basic human values. But first we examine the state and promise of these technologies.[37]

> WORKFLOW software automates and tracks the flow of documents and work processes through a company. The focus is on how work normally moves through an organization—the process—instead of on the specific information. There is a consensus today that you can break workflow products down into four groupings:
>
> • *Production workflow*: deals with transaction-oriented, high-value, repetitive processes such as insurance claims or accounts receivable. . .

- *Collaborative workflow*: deals with high-value, non-repetitive, generally nontransactional-oriented processes such as new product development, sales-force automation or technical document assembly. . .
- *Administrative workflow*: deals with low-value processes generally connected to routine office work such as travel expense reporting, budgeting and purchase approvals. . .
- *Ad hoc workflows*: deals with low-value processes, generally connected to routine office work such as FYI routing, review and approval. Lots of ad hoc products are e-mail-based.

The trend is to include, or rather embed, workflow software in a broad range of applications programs so that it can be used directly in the programming environment. As more software is implemented in an object-oriented framework, workflow components will be integrated as a system of rules. Another perspective on workflow is based on the following definition by Thomas Koulopoulos, author of *The Workplace Imperative*,[38] who describes it

> As a toolset for the proactive analysis, compression, and automation of information-based tasks and activities. Think of the office environment as an information factory, or more specifically, a process factory. . . . The connection of . . . office tasks creates a value chain that spans internal and external task boundaries. In this architecture, workflow attempts to streamline the component of the factory by eliminating unnecessary tasks, saving time, effort, and costs associated with the performance of those tasks and automating the remaining tasks that are necessary to the process.

So far the emphasis has been on the technological aspects of workflow but as previously mentioned, nothing will work unless "human factors" are taken into account. Thus the following considerations are crucial to the success of the workflow process[39]:

- *Involving the Users.* [You] mustn't underestimate the importance of soliciting input from the actual users of the system. . . . An added benefit of involving users while designing the workflow is that you build in user support and ownership of the application from the start.
- *Setting Expectations.* It is important that you set realistic expectations for your users. . . . If expectations have been set acknowledging that there will be problems initially but that over the course of a few weeks it will get easier, and if the potential benefits are clearly explained, people are more likely to get over the hurdles quickly.
- *Training.* . . . these are group solutions which rely heavily on everyone knowing exactly how the application works and what is expected of them.
- *Importance of Piloting.* Try to select a representative group as your pilot so that you can determine the issues most likely to affect the organization at large.

- *Building Buy-in at all Levels.* In order for strategic workflow applications to succeed, you need buy-in at the top. . . buy-in at the executive level. . . . [b]uy-in at the management level is equally important. . . . You absolutely must have buy-in at the user-level.
- *Rewarding Usage.* Users must perceive an added value to using the new application.

Say the word groupware to information systems professionals and the response is likely to be Lotus Notes, software that permits individuals at different locations to share online ideas and writing projects. So for some, groupware is related to collaborative computing, or "information technology used to help people work together more efficiently," or "computer-based systems that support groups of people engaged in a common task and that provides an interface to a shared environment."[40] There appear to be two major current approaches that depend on such existing and independently effective technologies as e-mail, bulletin boards, discussion forums, electronic meeting and scheduling programs, shared databases, and multiauthoring document tools. The two approaches are characterized as follows[41]:

- *GroupSuite Model.* [It] parallels the desktop suite model in which several products are tightly integrated and provide a [somewhat] common user interface into a suite of applications. These products typically provide the basic functionality most companies are looking for today in Groupware including group calendar and scheduling, electronic forms, information sharing, email and workflow automation. . . . GroupSuites strive to provide group productivity by providing ubiquitous access to information, tools for document sharing and tools that organize information in a meaningful way. [Best example is Novell's GroupWise]
- *Information/Communication (InfoComm) Model.* In this new model the user is presented with relevant information regardless of its origin, where it is located, or the application. Users are capable of storing, accessing, managing, and analyzing information from a wide variety of sources without having to think about where it is physically stored and what applications are needed to manipulate it. . . . It may be stored on a server in another department or even on a worldwide web server at some other company. In this new environment the user is only concerned with the information. The best example of this model today is Lotus Notes.

The potential power of such collaborations is enormous, and the growth in popularity of the Web provides an additional possibility for organizations that wish to foster distributed collaborative computing.

Virtual Corporation

As this discussion proceeds, keep in mind that our aim here is not an in-depth exploration of the modern business organization, but rather an

introduction to the role of computer and telecommunications technology in
that organization. As such, the emphasis is on identifying the uses to which
computers have been put, how successful these have been, their impact on
the social environment, and reasonable projections of future developments.
The tools, applications, and approaches discussed so far provide ways to
perform work better, to improve the monitoring process, and to take
advantage of valuable company knowledge, presumably with the goal of
transforming the corporation in some fundamental manner. The corporate
transformational models that have been proposed over the past few years
rely heavily on these tools. The so-called virtual corporation, the result of a
strategy for converting an inertia-bound company into a flexible, adaptive,
efficient, and productive one, adopts the word "virtual" in part from
its use in computer technology as a software-implemented, real-world
phenomenon. *The Virtual Corporation* is the title of a book by William
Davidow and Michael Malone[42] that both introduced the term and defined its
potential. As we might expect, it is not particularly easy to define this rather
abstract and elusive concept. First, however, it is necessary to define the
simpler notion of a virtual product, namely, "The ideal virtual product or
service is one that is produced instantaneously and customized in response to
customer demand."[43] In somewhat greater detail, the following is offered[44]:

> A virtual product (the term will be use to mean both physical products and
> services) mostly exists even before it is produced. Its concepts, design, and
> manufacture are stored in the minds of cooperating teams, in computers,
> and in flexible production lines. While the *perfect* virtual product can never
> exist, there is little doubt that many will come close. . . formerly well-
> defined structures [are] beginning to lose their edges, seemingly permanent
> things starting to continuously change, and products and services adapting
> to match our desires. . . the ability to make them will determine the suc-
> cessful corporations of the next century.

Based on this idea of a virtual product, the virtual corporation can be
thought of as a highly adaptive, highly flexible organization, which can
respond rapidly to changing market conditions, changing technology,
changing demand, and changing regulations in order to design, develop,
test, and market the perceived right product or service at the right time. It is
as if in the context of automobile production, new designs would result in
the instantaneous creation of appropriate assembly lines with the
simultaneous disappearance of no-longer-needed ones. Design, development,
and production teams would appear as needed and diffuse into the
corporation at large when their mission has been accomplished. Davidow
and Malone offer the following formulation[45]:

> It will appear almost edgeless, with permeable and continuously changing
> interfaces between company, supplier, and customers. From inside the firm

the view will be no less amorphous, with traditional offices, departments, and operating divisions constantly reforming according to need. Job responsibilities will regularly shift as will lines of authority—even the very definition of employee will change, as some customers and suppliers begin to spend more time in the company than will some of the firm's own workers. . . . will require taking a sophisticated information network that gathers data on markets and customer needs, combining it with the newest design methods and computer-integrated production processes, and then operating this system with an integrated network that includes not only highly skilled employees of the company but also suppliers, distributors, retailers, and even consumers.

Business Week recognized the arrival of the "Virtual Corporation" as a "new model that uses technology to link people, assets, and ideas in a temporary organization. After the business is done, it disbands."[46] In this overview, the virtual corporation is characterized as "a temporary network of companies that come together quickly to exploit fast-changing opportunities." In more detail, five important features are highlighted:

• *Technology.* Informational structures will help far-flung companies and entrepreneurs link up and work together from start to finish. The partnership will be based on electronic contracts to keep the lawyers away and speed the linkups.

• *Excellence.* Because each partner brings its "core competence" to the effort, it may be possible to create a "best-of-everything" organization. Every function and process could be world-class—something no single company could achieve.

• *Opportunism.* Partnerships will be less permanent, less formal, and more opportunistic. Companies will band together to meet a specific market opportunity and, more often than not, fall apart once the need evaporates.

• *Trust.* These relationships make companies far more reliant on each other and require far more trust than ever before. They'll share a sense of "co-destiny," meaning that the fate of each partner is dependent on the other.

• *No Borders.* This new corporate model redefines the traditional boundaries of the company. More cooperation among competitors, suppliers, and customers makes it harder to determine where one company ends and another begins.

In 1996, the book *Going Virtual*[47] touted the virtues of the virtual organization, providing a detailed how-to manual for executives who still want to achieve a lean, flexible organization. The possibly enduring mantra to be derived from this guide to the eager-to-change is, "Transitioning to a virtual organization is like redesigning an airplane while it's flying. Don't become so focused on your destination that you fail to keep the airplane up in the air."[48]

One last example should be instructive with respect to the current possibilities for creating virtual organizations with many thousands of employees. The story is about the largest manufacturing contract ever awarded ($200 billion) for stealth fighter airplanes, to Lockheed Martin Aeronautics, by the U.S. Defense Department in late 2001.[49] A few details of this contract follow:

> More than 80 suppliers will be working at 187 locations to design and build components of the Joint Strike Fighter. . . . All told, people sitting at more than 40,000 computers will be collaborating with each other to get the first plane in the air in just four years.

What is supposed to make this all possible is the most recent incarnation of the virtual corporation, namely,[50]

> Management experts have long talked about the so-called virtual corporation: a company that focuses on what it does best and farms out the rest to specialists who can do better. Now a new generation of Net-collaboration technologies is making it easier for companies to work hand-in-hand with their partners to bring new products to the market in record time—and on penny-pinching budgets. These jazzy new technologies could take the Web a step closer to delivering on its potential.

Reengineering

Almost in tandem with the advice to produce the "Virtual Corporation" was the more popular challenge to "reengineer the corporation," by using a variety of methods to transform a moribund organization into a dynamic, responsive one. Again, technology—computers and telecommunications systems—will play a necessary and vital role. The gurus of this call to arms are Michael Hammer and James Champy,[51] chairmen of influential management consulting firms, whose book *Reengineering the Corporation* came out in 1993 as a manifesto for change; indeed the word manifesto appeared in the subtitle of their book. They leave no doubt about the kind or magnitude of the change they say is absolutely required:

> Business reengineering means putting aside much of the received wisdom of two hundred years of industrial management. It means forgetting how work was done in the age of mass market and deciding how it can best be done now. In business reengineering, old job titles and old organizational arrangements—departments, divisions, groups, and so on—cease to matter. They are artifacts of another age. What matters in reengineering is how we

want to organize work today, given the demands of today's markets and the power of today's technologies.[52] . . .

Reengineering, we are convinced, can't be carried out in small and cautious steps. It is an all-or-nothing proposition that produces dramatically impressive results. Most companies have no choice but to muster the courage to do it. For many, reengineering is the only hope for breaking away from the ineffective, antiquated ways of conducting business that will otherwise inevitably destroy them.[53]

The idea caught on. *Fortune's* cover story on August 23, 1993, trumpeted: "Reengineering the Company: It's Hot, It's Happening, It's Now, How it Works—and Doesn't." Some four months later, *Business Week's* cover announced, "The Horizontal Corporation: Hierarchy is dying. In the new corporate model, you manage across—not up and down. Here's how."[54] Inside the magazine, a plethora of organizational models was described, with such entertaining names as Starburst, a graph with multi-colored nodes; Shamrock, a three-leafed shamrock; Pizza, a graph in a pizza shape with a center and radial arcs connecting sub-centers; and Inverted Pyramid, labeled from top to bottom with operate, enable, and create. Clearly, a major attempt was in progress to recreate organizational models for the Information Age. Hammer and Champy describe how work will change in the reengineered company as follows[55]:

- Work units change—from functional departments to process teams.
- Jobs change—from simple tasks to multi-dimensional work.
- People's roles change—from controlled to empowered.
- Job preparation changes from training to education.
- Focus of performance measures and compensation shifts—from activity to results.
- Advancement criteria change—from performance to ability.
- Values change—from protective to productive.
- Managers change—from supervisors to coaches.
- Organizational structures change—from hierarchical to flat.
- Executives change—from scorekeepers to leaders.

And finally, a few remarks about the role of IT in reengineering from the perspective of the early 1990s (and these are not surprising)[56]:

- A company that cannot change the way it thinks about information technology cannot reengineer. A company that equates technology without automation cannot reengineer. A company that looks for problems first and then seeks technology solutions for them cannot reengineer.
- Reengineering, unlike automation, is about innovation. It is about exploiting the latest capabilities of technology to achieve entirely new goals.

- . . . the real power of technology is not that it can make the old processes work better, but that it enables organization to break old rules and create new ways of working—that is, to reengineer.
- The sheer capacity of increasingly affordable computing power creates new application possibilities for companies. [original emphasis]

More recently, a new term has achieved currency, Business Process Reengineering or Innovation (BPR or BPI). Actually, it "has been practiced as a formal discipline since the early 1920s. Then it was known as 'Methods and Procedures Analysis,' always searching for new ways of restructuring work flows or improving business organization."[57] This term seems to have superseded Hammer and Champy's original idea of reengineering and has been defined as follows[58]:

> Business Process Innovation (BPI), also called Reengineering, is an approach to dramatically improve operating effectiveness through redesigning critical business processes and supporting business systems, as opposed to incremental improvement. It is a radical redesign of key business processes that involves examination of the fundamental process itself. It looks at the details of the process, such as why the work is done, who does it, where is it done and when. By focusing on examining the process of producing the output, it is an examination of the process's ability to add value.

Given the enormous amount of publicity associated with BPR, it is appropriate and even necessary to conclude this section with the cautionary voice of Paul Strassmann, who has been around long enough to be wary of the latest fad, no matter how enthusiastically it has been hailed as a cure for many illnesses, real and imagined[59]:

> Reengineering is certainly not a breakthrough in management thinking, but a convenient bandwagon on which management and consultants could readily hop in search of a quick remedy to unfavorable financial health of U.S. industrial corporations that had been festering for a long time. A wholesome by-product of this rush is the long overdue reinstatement of the primacy of business process analysis that was neglected during three decades of over-emphasis on computer systems and prior to that two decades of socio-psychological experimentation. It has also freed funds for innovative computer-aided business analysis tools which make business process improvement and systems analysis much easier to do.

What's on the Horizon? The Real-Time Economy

In years to come, experts predict, many companies will use information technology to become a "real-time enterprise"—an organisation that is able to react instantaneously to changes in its business. And as firms wire themselves up and connect to their business partners, they make the entire economy more and more real-time, slowly but surely creating not so much a "new" but a "now" economy.[60]

The idea of a real-time economy is growing in importance as the technology makes possible the rapid accumulation and analysis of data and the equally rapid transformation into marketing and manufacturing policy and service strategies. Examples will be given in the remainder of this chapter but for now consider the following[61]:

> To advocates of the concept, the real-time enterprise is a giant spread-sheet of sorts, in which new information, such as an order, is automatically processed and percolates through a firm's computer systems and those of its suppliers. Thus a simple inquiry such as, "When is my order being shipped?" can be answered immediately, and not six phone calls and three days later, explains Vinod Khosla, a partner with Kleiner Perkins Caufield & Byers and one of the most notable advocates of the real-time concept. Many consumers have already encountered real-time business without realising it, for instance when they order a Dell computer. The firm's website allows customers to check the status of their order at any time.

As with all major business transformations, there will be false starts, misdirections, bad assumptions, system failures, both internal and external resistance, and just plain mistakes, but the momentum is building and future directions seem clear.

E-COMMERCE AND E-MANAGEMENT

In the ordinary business of life, industry can do anything which genius can do, and very many things which it cannot.—Henry Ward Beecher

In this section, a wide range of somewhat disparate topics will be covered. Two major themes will be pervasive, namely, e-commerce, the all-encompassing term for doing business over the Internet, and e-management, the use of computer and networked-based technologies to improve all aspects of management. Of course, in discussing the nature of e-commerce, it will be necessary to explore the successes as well as the failures, the so-called dot.com crash. While no stock market advice will be offered, some thoughts about the crash and the anticipated recovery will be presented. Of course, the tragic events of September 11, 2001, have also had an impact on the economy as well as many other aspects of life. All in all, complexity abounds.

E-Commerce

> The Internet is so big, so powerful and pointless that for some people it is
> a complete substitute for life.—Andrew Brown

The use of the Internet to sell products and services efficiently and more
economically seemed to be an idea whose time had come. The following
quotation is taken from a special report on the future of e-business[62]:

> The economy is stuck in the doldrums, thanks largely to the broken prom-
> ises of technology. Dazzled by seemingly limitless returns, bankers had
> funded hundreds of companies, all going after the same dubious markets.
> Heedless, individual investors clamored to get into the stock market, driv-
> ing share prices to unheard-of levels. Soon, the overheated market crashed,
> turning the new heroes of business into goats and scoundrels. Now, disillu-
> sionment reigns, and nobody knows what's going to happen next.

Although it seems to refer to stock market events in the early years of the
21st century, this quotation actually applies to England in 1850, with the
technology of interest being railroads, not computers. The point is that all
technologies have a difficult birth, a tumultuous infancy, and a trying
adolescence. A review of the early era of retail operations and the role of
computers offer further examples of this.

By its very nature, selling requires identifying those who will buy as well
as those who might buy. Manufacturers make products but retailers must
sell them, taking advantage of their closeness to the consumer and their
knowledge of what sells. The largest retailers in the world have discovered
that very large, carefully arranged stores can not only sell but earn
enormous profits as well. Witness the stunning success of Wal-Mart, the
world's largest retailer, and indeed the largest company in terms of
revenues, with sales of almost $220 billion in 2001. As noted in "A Survey
of Retailing,"[63] computers have finally begun to pay off after more than
a decade and a half of capital investment. Some of the benefits are
obvious, namely, inventory control, accurate sales statistics, general store
management, and itemized profit margins. But there are many additional
benefits as the growth of massive retail giants around the world has
coincided with the growing importance of IT to this branch of the
business world.

Many of the more sophisticated applications depend on the fact that with
computers, "a well-managed retailer should no longer be lumbered with
stock that may not sell, or run out of items customers want to buy."
"Computers have at last enabled clever retailers to exploit the closeness to
the customer and control of the shelves that have always been their strongest
points," and "Computers have allowed retail managers to exercise closer
control over much more extended store chains."[64] The success of Wal-Mart,

whose first store opened in 1962, is based to a great degree on the informed use of computers. From its inception in Arkansas, Wal-Mart used computers to construct a distribution system to gain the attention of major producers who had no reason to pay attention to a relatively small company. Computers played a major role in the following way[65]:

> By the early 1980s Wal-Mart had not only set up computer links between each store and the distribution warehouses; through a system called EDI (electronic data interchange) [more later], it also hooked up with the computer of the firm's main suppliers. The distribution centers themselves were equipped with miles of laser-guided conveyor belts that could read the bar codes on incoming cases and direct them to the right truck for their outward journey. The final step was to buy a satellite to transmit the firm's enormous data load. . . .
>
> The first benefit was just-in-time replenishment across hundreds of stores. This has since been refined further, using computer modeling programmes to allow the firm to anticipate sales patterns. The second benefit was cost.

Many companies are modernizing their sales systems, after having addressed the automation of "manufacturing, inventory control, purchasing, and accounting."[66] Key issues in assembling a modern sales system are the following[67]:

• *Opportunity management systems* help sales reps manage sales opportunities, track those in the sales pipeline, and make forecasts.
• *Sales configuration systems* help companies put together accurate orders by configuring products, pricing, and financing in conjunction with each other.
• *Marketing encyclopedia systems* maintain repositories of all marketing information, including product literature and pricing. Sales reps can even call up videos of reference accounts to pitch products to potential customers.
• *Team sales solutions* require telemarketing and field sales integration tools, while low-end sales configuration software supports rapid order entry.
• *Sales management systems* provide traditional account management so companies can keep track of data in a variety of ways.

The consumer information accumulated by large companies in enormous databases has become an invaluable resource for targeting customers, predicting trends, setting trends, and tailoring buying and distribution in a more precise fashion. Given this background, we can return to issues arising from more recent events.

With all the attention paid to e-commerce, it is worth noting that it is still a rather minor player in the overall economy. Recent reports from the

U.S. Census Bureau reveal that in retail trade, the sector in which e-commerce has been given most attention, it has had very little impact so far. The numbers for 2000 show "e-commerce sales. . . that account for 0.9 percent ($29 billion) of total sales."[68] However, in manufacturing, the same source indicates that, "Manufacturing leads all industry sectors with e-commerce shipments that account for 18.4 percent (777 billion) of the total value of manufacturing shipments."[69] It should also be noted that in spite of the pervasiveness of the Internet and its overwhelming acceptance by the general public, almost all e-commerce is behind the scenes, in business-to-business (B-to-B) activities. The same source indicates that indeed 94% of e-commerce is B-to-B. Here are the highlights as the Census Bureau sees them for 2002[70]:

- E-commerce is pervasive among the industry groups in each sector.
- B-to-B e-commerce dominates.
- E-commerce grew in all sectors.
- The dollar value of e-commerce in each sector is concentrated in a handful of industry groups.
- Electronic Data Interchange (EDI) plays a critical role in supporting B-to-B e-commerce.

In addition to government statistics, many surveys are conducted by consulting companies to help other companies plan their e-commerce strategies. For example, eMarketer consolidates the results of surveys and reports on most aspects of e-commerce as well as other technological issues. It estimates that "online retail sales will generate $50.3 billion in revenue in 2002."[71] It seems that most of the analysis available treats e-commerce as not just the wave of the future for retail trade but also as an unmitigated benefit for the economy at large. One dissident voice is Edward Leamer, an economist at the University of California, Los Angeles, who was recently quoted as follows[72]:

> "The fundamental question is: Where did the profits go?" Leamer said in a recent telephone interview. "My number one hypothesis is it has to do with New Economy tools, both the Internet and communication devices." His theory is pretty straightforward: The Internet shrivels profits by turning earnings that formerly went to businesses into savings that go directly into customers' pockets. In other words, while consumers may benefit greatly from the abundance of discounts on the Internet, it leaves the firms offering them barely able to cover operating costs. . . . The UCLA economist pushes his theory a step further. When a firm's profits disappear, then suppliers all the way down the chain—even if they don't use the Internet—must scale back their prices—leading to lower profits all around. "If firms don't make profits, they don't invest," Leamer said. "If you don't get the investment, you don't get the growth in the economy."

At this point in the chapter, a few government and private sector sources will be examined to flesh out the picture as a necessary background to the next section dealing with the dot.com disaster.

Economic Impact of IT

Hal Varian, a professor at the University of California, Berkeley, is internationally renowned for his research on the role of IT in modern economies. His work is important both for corporate and public policies. For example, in his paper, "Economics of Information Technology," he ranges widely to determine how industries that are technologically intensive differ from more traditional ones. Using Microsoft as an example, he argues that there will be far less competition and far more concentration in the software industry. Another important factor in Microsoft's dominance is the existence of a proprietary standard that makes it difficult for competitors to compete. However, the recent Microsoft antitrust settlement may change this situation. Note that in the hardware sector there is considerable competition, as no one company dominates. It might be recalled that in the days when IBM dominated the computer industry, considerable debate raged about whether or not its establishment of *de facto* standards was beneficial or harmful. Varian concludes his paper with the following point[73]:

> Better information for incumbents, lock-in, and demand- and supply-side economies of scale suggest that industry structure in high-technology indus-tries will tend to be rather concentrated. On the other hand, information technology can also reduce minimum efficient scale thereby relaxing barri-ers to entry. People value diversity in some areas, such as entertainment, and IT makes it easier to provide such diversity.

International Electronic Commerce

So far, the overview has been focused on the U.S.—not very surprising given both the importance of the U.S. in IT and the overall focus of this book, but casting a wider net in this instance should prove beneficial. Clearly, the Internet, in principle, does not respect national borders, and in fact many of the issues discussed in this book will deal with the conflict between a global phenomenon and national laws in such areas as free speech, privacy rights, intellectual property rights, and others. For the present, we wish to identify some of the issues, from a U.S. point of view, which arise in a world in which international electronic commerce plays an ever important role. A U.S. government agency, the General Accounting Office, has provided a necessary discussion of these issues and has raised the following relevant questions in a 2002 report[74]:

> (1) What is international electronic commerce? (2) What data on inter-national electronic commerce (IE. . .++C) does the U.S. government collect?

(3) What is being done to remove obstacles and facilitate consumer and business use of international electronic commerce? (4) What are some of the efforts being made to adapt the legal framework for international electronic commerce transactions? and (5) How do international trade agreements and negotiations address barriers to international electronic commerce?

Very briefly, the report includes the following answers[75]:

1. The term "international electronic commerce" has no commonly accepted definition. Different institutions use the term "electronic commerce" to describe different things.
2. The U.S. government does not produce an official statistic for the value of international electronic commerce. Current government statistics for electronic commerce are drawn only from selected industries: namely, manufacturing, merchant wholesale trade, selected industries, and retail trade.
3. Policymakers are working on how to facilitate consumer use of international electronic commerce. They recognize that the adoption of international electronic commerce will depend in part on consumers' confidence that they will be treated fairly in online transactions and that their personal information will be protected.
4. Ongoing trade negotiations are addressing barriers that reduce the efficiency of conducting business and consumer transactions in Internet services, information technology products, express shipments, and other components of international electronic commerce.

Global Online Retailing

In the previous section, issues related to international e-commerce were briefly presented from the U.S. government point of view. The private sector obviously has its own concerns. One major source of relevant information is a report produced by the large consulting company, Ernst & Young, based on a survey conducted in October and November of 2000 on consumers and retail companies in 12 countries, including the U.S., Canada, Germany, France, South Africa, and Brazil.[76] As might be expected, the bottom line takes prominence with concern for growth and market share also critical issues. Among the major findings are the following:

• More people are buying online. Of the consumers participating in our study, almost two-thirds worldwide have purchased items online in the past 12 months.

- Consumers are making more online purchases, and shoppers worldwide are increasing their spending.
- Books, CDs, and computer equipment are still the top-selling products online, but consumers are beginning to move into new categories. "High-touch" products like apparel are beginning to make an impact and therefore represent a significant selling opportunity.
- While Amazon.com is still the consumers' favorite site worldwide, several traditional brick-and-mortar retail brands are now in the top 10.
- More than half of all shoppers say they visit the store less often because they shop online. As online retailing becomes more widely accepted, the demographic profile of the online shopper is beginning to look more like that of a "typical" on-land consumer.
- The majority of customers also expect to find lower prices online, yet they often do not.
- As in previous years, shipping costs are the biggest concern of online buyers; it ranks as the number-one factor discouraging online buying and the number-one reason for abandoning a shopping cart.

Dot.com Successes and Failures

For most people, the Internet is a vast collection of sites with addresses that have the appearance www.xxx.com, where the xxx stands for amazon, ebay, yahoo, microsoft, dell, or thousands of other familiar names. The years 1994 and 1995 witnessed the first growth of the World Wide Web (hence the prefix, www), or just the Web. The challenges for traditional retailers were how to use the Web to augment existing practices, to replace certain parts of the operation, or to create entirely new forms of selling to attract the large and growing online market. As the number of retail outlets on the Web began to grow, the reputation of the Web as a "get-rich-quick" place also began to grow at an even more frantic pace. Dot.com millionaires were created overnight; companies with no ostensible business plans or expectations of profits were greeted as high flyers; valued employees of dot.com "success" stories were rewarded with stock options promising great wealth; and of course stock markets trumpeted the unlimited value of these new and exciting companies.

The late 1990s witnessed a somewhat frenzied stock market boom, fueled in a major way by the apparently unlimited prospects of Internet-based companies whose names glittered with the magic dot.com suffix. Some observers were troubled by the obvious but seemingly easily ignored fact that most of the dot.com companies were losing money at a furious rate. In response, *nouveaux riches* executives repeatedly called for patience and argued that in the new Web world of business, traditional economics did not apply. In a piece in the *Washington Post* in July 2002, the well-known columnist Richard Cohen recalled a meeting of the World Economic Conference in Davos, Switzerland, in 1999[77]:

> The dot-comers were there in force, cocks of the walk all, especially the venture capitalists who were making a fortune backing the new technology. Someone asked a question: Who repealed the laws of economics that hold that, sooner or later, you have to make a profit? A venture capitalist booed the questioner. "You don't get it," he hissed. Others took up the chant. "You don't get it." I was stunned. I was humbled. Inwardly, I confessed they were right. I didn't get it. Why? Because at the heart of the new age— of dot-com this and dot-com that—is the computer. It does something in a way we do not understand and cannot see. When you hit a typewriter key, you see what happens. But the computer is different. It remembers what you did. It moves money. It enabled Enron to sell power, which you could not see in the first place, and then water and then everything. The economy was functioning in the ether and people were getting rich without producing anything at all, including profit.

The booming stock market encouraged the widely-held belief that there was no downside to buying dot.com stocks. Then early in the year 2000, economic reality began to set in, as money from venture capitalists began to dry up in the face of little income, no profits, and rapidly mounting losses, and the bankruptcies began to mount. From January 2000 through April 2002, at least 835 Internet shutdowns and bankruptcies occurred, of which 303 (36%) were in business, 423 (51%) in consumer areas, and 109 (13%) in general areas.[78] The cover of *Fortune*, October 30, 2000, seemed to say it all. It pictured a man reading a newspaper, *The Daily Net*, his dog beside him, and in the background a pile of rubble made up of computer parts. Among the parts, partially obscured, is the sign, HUBRIS.COM. The man is saying: "It all seemed so grand! We were changing the world! We were rich . . . Now what??" The dog is thinking: "Quit whining and get a *real* job!" The newspaper's cover reads: "12 ways the dot-coms changed business." Inside the magazine is another full-page illustration of the same man and dog in the middle of the detritus of a party, long over, with the banner, "Dot-Coms Forever." The man is saying: "Someone please tell me what happened here . . ." The dog is thinking: "I am one hurt puppy."

The lessons seemed to be that the dot.coms were oversold but they were surely the wave of the future, that they were not immune from the requirement to show profits sooner rather than later, and that just having a presence on the Web, however attractive, was not enough. The simplest way to describe this chastised view is a return to established business practices; i.e., in spite of the advanced technology underlying the new enterprise, it must have a solid business foundation. Witness the advice that the consulting firm, Ernst & Young, has for dot.com survival:[79]

- Appoint non-executive directors who are experienced business people
- Actively seek the opinions of shareholders, suppliers and customers
- Incorporate their opinions into the business strategy
- Control cash-flow rigorously
- Identify, measure and act on the key drivers of success ensuring the whole business understands them
- Trust in teamwork and build a balanced team
- Create a customer-centric business
- Deliver on your customer promises

How did the American public view the dot.com crash? Fortunately, the Pew Internet & American Life Project conducted a poll during February, 2001, in which the major findings are given as follows[80]:

- 67% of Americans say a major cause of the dotcom downturn was because investors' desire to turn quick profits led to too many business risks.
- 56% say that Internet companies lacked clear plans for attaining profitability.
- 39% blame the youth and inexperience of some of the Internet firms' executives.

It should be mentioned that each of these possibilities was presented to subjects as a possible reason for the dot.com problems.

One might well ask what, if any, are the dot.com success stories? On December 27, 1999, Jeff Bezos was named *Time* magazine's Person of the Year. Bezos is the founder and chief executive of Amazon.com, probably the best known Web retailer. Amazon has attracted large numbers of visitors, has sales in the hundreds of millions of dollars, and has rarely made a profit in any quarter; yet its continued existence and growth seem to be a fact. In 2001, Amazon reported a loss of $567 million on total sales of $3.12 billion, up 13% over 2000. Another important indicator of future success is that Amazon "served 25 million customer accounts in 2001, compared to 20 million in 2000 and 14 million in 1999."[81]

Somewhat smaller, but much more successful, is eBay, the online auction site. eBay is the prime example of a business concept that made full use of the Internet and that could not have existed otherwise. eBay has been profitable from the outset. In 2001, its profit was about $90 million on net revenues of $748 million generated by 42 million users. eBay has become a fixture on the Web and a way of life for many around the world. Its success seems to be based on experienced and well-qualified managers exploiting a great idea in a thoroughly professional manner.

E-Management

What is a management information system (MIS)? There are many varied conceptions and definitions depending on who is doing the defining and for what purpose. Back in 1974, one of the foremost figures in the development of MIS, Gordon B. Davis, supplied a definition of what MIS should be[82]:

> An integrated man/machine system for providing information to support the operations, management and decision-making functions in an organization. The system utilizes computer hardware and software, manual procedures, management and decision models, and a database.

In 1985, some 11 years after this definition, Davis and coauthor Margrethe Olson provided the following definition of MIS[83]:

> An integrated, user-machine system for providing information to support operations, management, analysis and decision-making functions in an organization. The system utilizes computer hardware and software; manual procedures; models for analysis, planning, control and decision making; and a database.

It is fairly clear that, at least in the view of Davis and Olson, not much had changed in 11 years—a somewhat surprising situation given such enormous technological developments as PCs, networking, workstations, spreadsheets, word processing, laser printers, fiber optics, Fax machines, cellular phones, and more. In any case, MIS is not easily characterized. An MIS must incorporate expertise from a variety of areas such as organizational theory, economics, accounting, statistics, and mathematical modeling, to say nothing of computer hardware and software. It sounds incredibly ambitious, and it is. In the view of many, the open-ended expectation engendered by such descriptions is one of the major reasons why any working MIS is felt somehow to be short of the mark, no matter what it actually accomplishes.

What are the components of such systems and what functions do they (or are they supposed to) perform? One way of viewing an MIS is as a pyramid structure. At the bottom is the routine transaction processing that occupies a good deal of the computer power of the system (recall that such activities as payroll and accounting were the first application of computers, beginning in the mid-1950s). The next level is concerned with supporting day-to-day activities at the operational level, whereas the third level represents a jump to tactical planning and decision making. At the top level, the MIS concept is fully expressed, with a wide array of resources for strategic planning and management decision making.

The pyramid—transactions, inquiries, planning, and decision making—sits on top of the data. Where do the data reside? The problems of representation, structure, organization, and integrity of data have occupied much attention in both the research and business communities. Gradually, the notion of a database management system (DBMS) has evolved, and this concept is fundamental to MIS. The DBMS must be responsible for manipulating data, on demand, by the variety of application subsystems supported by MIS. DBMS theory is currently a very active research and development area, with relational databases the most commonly used. The decision-assisting models at the top level of the pyramid have evolved into a major component of MIS, usually referred to as decision support systems (DSS).

As we might expect, a number of criticisms have also surfaced. Many of these revolve around the issue of centralization versus decentralization of the information resources, of the computer facilities, and of the analysis and modeling systems. In a sense, certain of these problems have become academic in an age of distributed computing brought in by advances in computer technology and communications. But the organizational issues remain—of access, and of smaller specialized databases versus larger uniform ones. In a paper examining the changes in MIS over the 15-year period from 1980 to 1995, the authors admit that[84]

> The areas of progress are significant and substantial. Yet the surprising lack of progress over the past 15 years is disturbing. MIS has an increasingly polyglot set of reference disciplines. The cumulative tradition in the field is still elusive, however, it is emerging in some research areas. More MIS research is carried out and published, but only read by MIS researchers themselves, bringing in to question relevance to practitioners. When added to the fact that important new issues have arisen, the future of the MIS research community appears to remain problematic.

Recent proposals have suggested that the time may be fast approaching when most executives sitting at their own desks will be able to call up any data they desire, in any form they wish, from personal computers that are part of a large, complex computer network. However, until that time arrives, a number of issues still need to be considered. In a book published in 2002,[85] Thomas A. Stewart proposes a number of reasons that knowledge management has not been successful. These arguments would seem to apply as well to MIS. Consider the following advice that Stewart offers to organizations considering undertaking a knowledge management effort[86]:

1. What is the work group? The first task of knowledge management is to select what one might call a unit of analysis or a unit of management. Then place primary responsibility for the content of knowledge management there. This is not necessarily a functional unit. Cross-functional project teams, for example, clearly need a "knowledge space" that is shared.
2. What does the group need to know? It's important to distinguish between information and knowledge. Information tends to be transient;

knowledge, abiding. Every work group needs information management and information resources, which range from magazine subscriptions to databases. You can find out what people need by asking them, and then arrange the fastest, cheapest, most effective way to get it to them.

3. Are you a standardizer or a customizer? For a company that reuses knowledge, reinventing the wheel is a no-no, so it's good knowledge management to build a virtual storehouse containing the specs for every wheel ever invented. But an encyclopedia of corporate know-how is doomed to become an expensive failure for a shop where invention is the necessity. . . . One of the great dangers of knowledge management technology is that it can lead you to invest in systems for reusing knowledge when innovation is central to your company's value proposition. If nothing else, that's a waste.

Providing direct access to executives to useful information has yet to be realized.

Decision Support Systems and Executive Support Systems

One direction that developments in MIS have taken is toward decision support systems (DSS). An early definition of DSS follows[87]:

Decision Support Systems . . . represent a point of view on the role of the computer in the management decision making process. Decision support implies the use of the computer to:

1. Assist managers in their decision processes in semistructured tasks.
2. Support rather than replace, managerial judgment.
3. Improve the effectiveness of decision making rather than its efficiency.

Rockart and De Long wrote a book in 1989 titled *Executive Support Systems*[88] and since then the designation ESS has become more commonly used. Whatever the name, the idea of executives having hands-on access to information via PCs or terminals is not yet generally acceptable, but gradually more and more upper management executives are demanding to see the data prior to massaging by their support staffs. There are good reasons for this growth, as Rockart and De Long note[89]:

1. Use of information technology to support executives makes good managerial sense. Despite the complex, unstructured, and unpredictable nature of their work, there are many logical applications of IT which can effectively support executive tasks.
2. The technology, both hardware and software, is rapidly improving. Applications for managers that were technically impractical and too costly only a few years ago have now become significantly easier to implement.
3. More and more top managers have become computer literate . . . many middle managers who have come to rely heavily on computers in their jobs are now being promoted to the executive ranks.

Of course there are a number of arguments against the adoption of ESS, including the following: as currently structured, ESS do not fit today's management styles or needs; further, they cannot provide the type of information needed most by executives—verbal, anecdotal, nonformal, and therefore difficult, if not impossible, to capture in a program; there are potentially negative properties associated with the new technology—manipulating numbers via spreadsheets and simulations may mislead as to what is actually being accomplished, and communication facilities are useless unless a desire to communicate exists; consequently, many attempts to implement working ESS have failed.[90]

Expert Systems

Probably the greatest commercial impact of artificial intelligence (AI) was in the area of expert systems (ES). In the 1980s and 90s, ES became the most visible and highly publicized product of the entire AI enterprise. Indeed, they can be characterized as an almost independent discipline. They have been applied in a wide and growing number of domains including medicine, education, finance, industry, and the military. In their simplest form, they consist of a body of knowledge, typically quite narrow but necessarily deep, and a reasoning apparatus, or engine, that is able to use this knowledge to perform a range of activities including answering questions, predicting events, offering warnings, or identifying meaningful patterns.

Beyond this rather limited overview, work in ES can be divided into two broad categories: implementation of specific expert systems employing so-called shells, and research in diverse areas associated with basic problems in AI such as knowledge representation, reasoning in general and reasoning with respect to uncertainty, and knowledge acquisition among domain-specific experts, programmers, and others operating within the constraints of a commercially available ES shell. The emphasis on knowledge acquisition dominates because of the need to translate informal expertise into the requirements of the shell's knowledge representation formalism. The inference strategy and problems of uncertain information are predetermined within a given shell and therefore must be accepted by the user.

The availability of shells of varying degrees of complexity has resulted in an explosion of ES. Many companies, from the very small to the very large, have built ES to capture some part of their corporate expertise. Systems abound, as described by Feigenbaum, McCorduck and Nii,[91] in such major companies as IBM, Digital Equipment, Toyota, American Express, Sears, Frito-Lay, and Texas Instruments, and are increasing at a rapid rate. Probably the most well-known and the most successful early systems were XCON (eXpert CONfigurator) and XSEL (eXpert SELector), developed at Digital Equipment (since then acquired by Compaq, itself recently acquired by Hewlett-Packard) to configure computer systems automatically and to assist interactively in the selection of saleable parts, respectively. The applications are seemingly endless but the following are representative: medical diagnosis, computer configuration, mineral prospecting, oil well analysis, stock market decision making, financial analysis and planning, insurance analysis, electromechanical faultfinding and repair, and military analysis and decision making.

With the appearance of the Internet, a variety of AI applications have emerged that deal with Web-specific applications such as natural language interfaces to search engines, Web crawlers that search more intelligently for specified objects characterized in arbitrary ways, and systems that can discover more meaningful patterns in vast amounts of recovered data. Pattern recognition and natural language understanding are traditional major areas of research in AI, but what is different now is that statistical methods enabled by enormous computational power have produced better results in working systems.[92]

Expert systems are also referred to as knowledge-based systems (KBS), with the subtle implication that other business software is somehow devoid of, or seriously impoverished with respect to, basic business knowledge. Of course, all software must incorporate "knowledge" in a variety of forms to perform adequately. The claim for ES is that it is an approach that explicitly separates knowledge from how it is used so that incremental growth can take place in a coherent fashion. In addition, the acquisition of knowledge as an ongoing joint enterprise of specialists and programmers is a unique contribution. Of particular significance to executives is the growth of sophisticated ES in financial planning. Such systems represent yet another important component in the gradually growing tool kit of computing resources for executives.

THE OFFICE OF THE FUTURE

> A paperless office has about as much chance as a paperless bathroom.—
> Anonymous

Office Automation

What is sometimes called the "electronic office" will be brought about by "office automation" or by the use of "office information systems." It will eliminate paper, promote electronic communication, isolate workers and break down social interaction, reproduce industrial automation in the office, increase the monitoring and surveillance of workers, decrease wasted time in preparing documents, and generally improve productivity. Such are the claims made by both proponents and critics.

What is included under the general term "office automation"? The definition we use, taken from Mowshowitz some years ago, is given here[93]:

> Office automation is the use of information technology in an office environment to create, process, store, retrieve, use, and communicate information in the performance of managerial, professional, technical, administrative, and clerical tasks.

Although not part of the definition, the most common reason for introducing office automation is to *improve* performance, but there are other reasons, such as to facilitate a new service that would be impossible without the technology, or to reinforce management's control. In any case, this definition does capture a general overview of office automation. More specifically, some of the office functions made possible by computers and associated technology follow, but first let's look at a spectrum of traditional office activities:

- Answering the telephone and handling messages
- Typing written and dictated material
- Filing and retrieving material
- Copying letters and reports
- Opening and handling mail
- Scheduling meetings and travel plans
- Billing and accounting
- Processing internal memoranda
- Miscellaneous—organizing parties, selecting gifts, buying take-out lunches

In addition, higher-level functions include the following:

- Conducting research
- Monitoring market changes
- Drafting original documents
- Utilizing resource people
- Dealing with middle and upper management

What are the current and proposed functions of the electronic, or automated, office? They are many and diverse, but a number have been mentioned by most observers. Consider the following categories:

Word Processing. This application involves the use of computer-aided facilities to enter, manipulate, and edit text, employing word-processing software on computers with access to local and wide area networks, as well as the Internet.

Electronic Mail or E-mail. This is a system for transmitting messages in text, sound, pictures, and films, typically over the Internet. It is clearly one of the major applications of the Internet and the application most attractive to the average user.

Database Management Information Retrieval. The ability to store and retrieve large amounts of information under a variety of conditions has made computers irreplaceable in the office and has created a new industry— the marketing of information.

Spreadsheets. No single application, with the exception of word processing, has had as great an impact on companies. Employees from all levels of the organization are able to model cash flow, expenses, accounts receivable, and other economic factors in order to explore a variety of what-if scenarios. Thousands of variables can be included. The demands of spreadsheet users for ever more powerful personal computers became a driving force in the PC industry.

Desktop Publishing. The ability to produce sophisticated in-house brochures, newsletters, advertising material, and reports has saved businesses considerable amounts of money, driven the development of low-cost laser printers, challenged traditional composition and printing methods, and facilitated grassroots publishing.

Computer-Aided Design/Computer-Aided Manufacturing (CAD/CAM). Economical tools have been developed to permit engineers and draftsmen to design and manufacture new products using desktop computers. These are programs that facilitate the drawing and manipulation of precise and detailed diagrams, in 3D and color on high-resolution monitors.

Expert Systems and Decision Support. As discussed previously, these systems are assuming increasing importance for management, and the ability to run them on PCs and workstations will accelerate this process.

Graphics. The development of special programs, high-speed processors, and high-resolution color monitors and laser printers has resulted in the widespread use of graphics in design, documents, and video.

Teleconferencing. The use of telecommunication systems permits simultaneous communication over long distances via audio, computers, video, or combinations of these for distributed meetings.

Activity Management. This category includes systems such as electronic tickler (reminder) files and automated task-project management to track, screen, or expedite schedules, tasks, and information.

Instant Messaging. The online, real-time, synchronous communication system known as instant messaging has become increasingly popular in offices (but probably not as popular as with young teenage girls and boys) and provides yet another communication tool with advantages and disadvantages.

The Wireless or Portable Office. There is no reason for the office to be fixed in a building. The briefcase can contain a portable computer, printer, and fax system connected wirelessly through a cell phone, permitting the same kind of connectivity available in the office.

Other possibilities include the following:

- Electronic blackboards for broadcasting messages
- Electronic calendars for scheduling
- Computerized training to provide employees with up-to-date information and introduce new skills via CD-ROM, VCRs, and interactive systems
- The home office as a means of increasing the flexibility of work arrangements

and, of course

- The design, implementation, and use of Web sites on the Internet for advertising, marketing, and sales

If all this sounds rather overwhelming, it should, because one of the major components of the so-called information revolution is the electronic office. Much of the work force is currently engaged in white-collar jobs, and what happens in the office matters a great deal. Most white-collar workers use computers, and the market for information technology is enormous and growing. Recently, IBM and Steelcase, the office furniture company, introduced Bluespace, their joint vision of the office of the future, which includes the following highlights[94]:

- *BlueScreen:* This touch screen, which sits adjacent to the computer monitor, puts users in control of their physical and virtual environments. Interactive icons allow users to adjust—with the touch of a finger—temperature, airflow or lighting to suit their preference. Users can direct heat to cold feet, adjust humidity levels, increase volume of white noise, or modify lighting based on preference or the focus of their work. Interactive icons help employees share projects, better communicate with their team members, and access real time news feeds.
- *Monitor Rail:* This patent-pending moving rail consists of a work surface that travels the length of the work space and a dual monitor arm that almost rotates to a complete circle, allowing the users to be positioned anywhere in the area.
- *Everywhere Display:* A display projects information onto any surface, be it a wall, desktop, or floor, transforming everyday objects into interactive displays, and untethering employees from their desktop computers. Wireless computer-processed sensing technologies enable touch sensitivity, allowing fingers to act as cursors, even on walls or desktops. A guest badge in the office vicinity automatically helps cloak confidential information by prompting the Everywhere Display to project a generic image.

- *Threshold:* Designed in response to a need for increased privacy control, this patent-pending moveable work surface, ceiling and wall act as a "technology totem" that provides on-demand visual and territorial privacy to the user. Color-coded lighting at the top of the threshold in blue, red and green alerts colleagues when an employee is away, busy or accepting visitors. An integrated front panel display on the threshold can visually communicate what each employee wants to share with colleagues, such as current projects and scheduling.

On the Road to Better Communications

In the early days, computers were locked away in antiseptic rooms guarded by a cadre of initiates who were the sole custodians of programming, data preparation, and result reporting. As the number of people who had direct access to the computer increased, greater demands were made on the managers of computer facilities to provide easier access and better, more readable output. The development of first time-sharing systems, and later the Internet and Web, gave most employees better access to fellow employees and managers within the organization, and of course to the outside world as well. Accompanying greater connectivity have been improvements in software and hardware quality as well as rapid innovations in capabilities.

Graphics and Imaging

Since the business of management is to make decisions based on all the available information, it is important to reduce the effort of gathering, processing, and displaying that information. Recently, technology and software developments have combined to make graphics facilities widely available to both information processing professionals and executives. For most managers, graphics presentation is a needed relief from pages of texts and tables. As someone has remarked, a computer image is worth a thousand printouts. The benefits claimed for computer graphics are straightforward: saving of time in the production, interpretation, and communication of data, and assistance in management decision making provided by visual information that is much easier to assimilate. Interactive graphics systems also encourage managers to explore the available information more extensively. Graphs, charts, and bar diagrams are readily available.

We should distinguish between graphics—the creation and manipulation of computer-generated images—and imaging—the representation of paper documents as special computer files. An important early instance of imaging began in 1988 when American Express included with its billing statements "laser-printed, reduced facsimiles of the original receipts, including signatures. The reproduced forms were not photocopies, but rather digitized electronic images printed in the billing statements."[95] Scanners are used to convert documents directly into computer files that can then be manipulated—printed, included in other documents, retrieved, and mailed electronically. The uses of computer graphics are very widespread, including CAD/CAM applications, architectural design, multimedia, desktop publishing, geographical maps, and scientific visualization.

Many of these applications serve the important purpose of condensing and distilling large amounts of data in order to improve the decision-making process. Therefore, graphics are rapidly becoming an important component of the automated office as well as an important management tool and thus a means to improve productivity. Decreasing costs and improved power are also significant factors in the widespread use of graphics equipment.

E-Mail

At its simplest, e-mail is the sending of a message from one computer to another or to many other computers, over a network, perhaps over a long distance. But what makes e-mail so successful is its ease of use, its low cost, its asynchronous nature that permits delayed response, and its universal acceptance. There are problems in its use, however, and these will be described. The editor-in-chief of *Datamation*, Kevin Strehlo, hails e-mail as a transforming technology. He also calls it "the glue that binds most virtual organizations," claims "that having had an unchanging e-mail shingle for quite some time has kept me from losing touch with key professional acquaintances," and admits that, "even my personal life is being dominated by e-mail today."[96]

In some cases, e-mail may be *too* successful, to the degree that measures must be taken for self-preservation. It is easy to be overwhelmed by a large stream of e-mail—the term information overload seems appropriate. How can anyone deal with a large volume of messages on a regular basis without having it detract from other aspects of work and play? The U.S. technology researcher, Gartner Inc., carried out a survey of 330 corporate e-mail users early in 2001. Some of the interesting results follow[97]:

- During workdays, 53 percent of users check their e-mail six or more times a day, according to Gartner, while a whopping 34 percent check e-mail constantly throughout the day.
- U.S. users receive an average of 22 e-mail messages a day. However, only 27 percent of these require immediate attention and 37 percent are what the research group calls occupational spam, meaning gratuitous e-mail from co-workers like messages reading simply "OK!"
- All this e-mail checking eats up time, Gartner reported, with the average user spending 49 minutes a day just managing their mail.
- 42 percent of U.S. users check their business e-mail while on vacation, while 23 percent check e-mail over weekends.

For the average home user, spam has become the major curse of the Internet. It is a major nuisance to be flooded with messages promoting sex, viagra, quick money-making schemes, and much, much more. As we might expect, there are technological solutions, namely filtering and sorting, but these have their drawbacks. Some systems will place messages in predefined folders organized by subject matter and source. What is lacking so far is the ability to sort on the basis of importance to the recipient where the notion of importance is both context-sensitive and time-sensitive, but work on this is in progress. In addition, during 2003, Congress held hearings and began work on legislation to limit the vast and growing spam problem.

In a final cautionary note from Paul Strassmann, although somewhat dated, he states that "I have found no correlation whatsoever between the extent of e-mail availability and the information productivity of firms, as measured by the ratio of economic value-added/estimated total cost of information," and further cautions firms to "view e-mail as part of a much larger package of how people share information, rather than as an isolated application."[98]

PDAs (Personal Digital Assistants)

The evolution of computers from mainframes to minicomputers to workstations to personal computers to laptops seems to have culminated in a class of very small, palm-sized computers called personal digital assistants (PDAs), or pen-based devices. In 1993, Apple introduced its first version in this class called the Newton, with a well-advertised handwriting recognition program. There were some problems with the technology—most significantly that it did not work very well, in fact it was nearly useless—but Apple and other companies such as AT&T, Hewlett-Packard, Fujitsu, Motorola, Casio, and Sony have persisted. One surprising success story, at least in terms of sales, is Palm Computing's Pilot. Apple introduced its MessagePad 120 in 1995 with improvements in handwriting ability, much more computing power, better desktop synchronization, and more application software. They have found favor in applications requiring mobility, appointment scheduling, note-taking, and where portability is a premium. Although there continues to be resistance because of unfulfilled promises and limited performance, PDAs are clearly a part of the computing picture and their use will increase as technology improves, especially in the area of wireless connectivity.

Instant Messaging

As mentioned above, instant messaging (IM) has gradually moved into the workplace as yet another form of useful communication. Gartner Inc. characterizes it as follows[99]:

> Whether it's for B2B, customer relationship management or a group of friends who want to chat live, instant messaging (IM) is gaining recognition as a useful application. IM, which enables two or more online users to communicate immediately and in real time, is made possible by a special piece of client software that reaches out to a central server and registers the user as being online. This user registration and mapping to his or her screen name is the "identity vessel." The user is then invited, or able to invite others, to join a conversation.

IM can be used for informing clients in a personal way about new products and services as well as by employees involved in online meetings—far less expensive than current videoconferencing. Gartner defines the "bottom line" in this way[100]:

> Gartner believes IM will be a critical technology for identity portability. IM screen names will become far more important than they are to today's IM users. By 2003, we believe vendors that require rich and easy authentication must prepare for IM screen names to bear the token of identity. By 2004, Gartner expects that 60 percent of real-time Internet-enabled communication between users via any means, including voice, text or call-and-response, will be driven through IM technology.

There are some privacy issues related to the use of IM. While messages transmitted over IM systems are not typically cached, or saved, in the manner in which e-mail messages are, they could be, and with the increasing number of IM users at work, they probably will be. As of early 2002, "about 16.9 million people 'ping' others at work."[101] Privacy issues will be discussed in more detail in Chapter 9.

The Intranet

The cover of *Business Week*, February 26, 1996, advertised a special report on "The Intranet" (not another feature piece on the Internet). Also on the cover: "The Internet revolution has come home—to internal corporate networks. Cheap flexible 'intranets' are spreading everywhere—and becoming a new management tool."[102] If 1995 has been hailed as the year of the Internet, then for many companies, 1996 was the year of the intranet, an Internet-like structure or internal Web, providing all the features of the World Wide Web but accessible only within the company. Claims are rampant that intranets are a much more efficient means to distribute company information of all kinds rather than traditional systems. Consider the following features of intranets and their benefits[103]:

Application Feature Set

- rapid prototyping (can be measured in hours or days)
- scalable (start small, build as needs, requirements allow)
- easy navigation (internal home page provides links to information)
- accessible via most computing platforms
- can integrate distributed computing strategy (localized web servers residing closer to the content author)
- can be tied in to "legacy" information sources (databases, existing word processing documents, groupware databases)
- extensible to a variety of media types (audio, video, interactive applications)

Benefits to These Features

- inexpensive to start, requires little investment either in dollars or infrastructure
- significantly more timely and less expensive than traditional information (paper) delivery
- distributed computing strategy uses computing resources more effectively
- users familiar with link metaphor from surfing experiences
- open platform architecture means large (and increasing) number of add-on applications available

These benefits have not been lost on information technology managers, but there are associated problems. For example, "multiple browser support" will be a fact of life, "hardware upgrades" will still be required, "application development" is still necessary, "re-engineering" to take advantage of the intranet is mandatory, "management" will still have to be concerned with new security problems, the new technology will demand "integration with legacy systems," and there will be no way to avoid the usual "screwups and restarts."[104]

Videoconferencing and Teleconferencing

Traditional videoconferencing involved rented or leased television studios and closed-circuit television to link geographically distributed individuals. It was a very expensive way to exchange information and not a very productive one either. The latest technology of choice is called desktop videoconferencing, a technology that currently depends heavily on LANs (Local Area Networks). As Peter Cassidy notes, "Given the complexity of the application, which carries voice, video, and a mix of data, there is no single solution for rolling out desktop videoconferencing. In fact, moving too quickly now could preempt the benefits that will accrue once standards for LAN-mediated videoconferencing technologies are finally in place."[105] The technical quality is not equivalent to broadcast television, because desktop systems operate at 15 frames per second, not 30 per second, but the convenience of being able to interact with colleagues from the comfort of your own workstation outweighs the somewhat jerky images on the screen. Also, bandwidth requirements may severely compromise the other functions delivered by the LAN. Many developments are underway to address some of the current problems, including the use of ISDN lines, international standards to improve interoperability, and reduced hardware and software costs.

One event has quite unexpectedly stimulated considerable interest in videoconferencing. Following the terrorist attacks on the World Trade Center by hijacked airplanes, air travel declined substantially, and one byproduct was a renewed interest in videoconferencing. Hal Varian wrote in late 2001, describing the past difficulties involved in the establishment of a viable videoconferencing market, that the crucial factor is the concept of network externalities, defined by the economist Jeff Rohlfs as, "a good or service exhibits network externalities when its value to a potential purchaser depends on how many other people have purchased it."[106] That is, unless a threshold is achieved, a particular good or service will not become viable. Mr. Varian goes on to make the following comments:

> Videoconferencing never achieved critical mass because it has always been more attractive to hop on a plane. Real-time face-to-face meetings are costly, but that's the way business has been done for centuries, and it is hard to change ingrained patterns of behavior. Those companies that have experimented with videoconferencing have had mixed success. Low-cost videoconferencing is flaky enough that you can't really count on its working, and the high-quality technology is still pretty expensive.

This is a technology that is worth following, given the enormous repercussions if it becomes well established.

EDI (Electronic Data Interchange) and B2B

As more companies have computerized their internal operations, it has become inevitable that intercompany communications would move from paper (mail) and telephone to the computer. This process is encouraged by the globalization of industry and the growth of worldwide communications networks. It seems to make good business sense that companies that depend upon one another should be able to facilitate this interaction by computer networks, that is, electronic data interchange (EDI) or what is currently referred to as business-to-business (B2B) exchange. As in many other areas, EDI growth is fueled by the need to obtain a competitive advantage and to respond to customer needs. Many companies and government agencies now require that all suppliers and customers use EDI. A formal definition of EDI was provided by Phyllis Sokol, a pioneer in EDI standards[107]:

> Electronic data interchange (EDI) is the INTER-COMPANY COMPUTER-TO-COMPUTER communication of STANDARD BUSINESS TRANSACTIONS in a STANDARD FORMAT that permits the receiver to perform the intended transaction.

Instead of generating a transaction on paper and then mailing it to a receiver, who then enters the data into a computer and runs an application program, the sender generates the transaction by computer, transmits it via a computer network, and the receiver simply has to run the application program on this transmitted data. By the previous definition, the data must be transmitted both in a standard form and for standard business transactions. Thus electronic mail would not be considered part of EDI because it is unstructured. Traditional modes of EDI are currently being challenged by the use of Web-based formatting languages such as XML and SHTML. The potential for large-scale use of B2B is still great: "It is expected to explode: B2B e-commerce could reach $5.7 trillion by the end of 2004, and fully half of that will flow through exchanges [specialized transaction domains]."[108]

Data Mining and Knowledge Discovery

Imagine a chain of supermarkets that builds up a database of purchases with complete details about date, time of day, store address, geographic location, items purchased, associated prices, coupons used, sales items, cashier identification, payment method, if credit card then kind, and if point-of-sale card then issuer. In very little time, an enormous database, or data warehouse, emerges. Of course, no imagining is necessary as almost every major retailer has such a warehouse. It is an article of faith that such massive collections of data must be useful beyond such obvious purposes as keeping track of the relative popularity of house brands versus national brands or the frequency of use of different credit or debit cards. The process of extracting useful information out of this mass of data "ore" is called data mining, an obvious analogy. Here is more precise definition[109]:

> Data mining, *the extraction of hidden predictive information from large databases,* is a powerful new technology with great potential to help companies focus on the most important information in their data warehouses. Data mining tools predict future trends and behaviors, allowing businesses to make proactive, knowledge-driven decisions. The automated, *prospective analyses* offered by data mining move beyond the analyses of past events provided by retrospective tools typical of decision support systems. Datamining tools can answer business questions that traditionally were too time consuming to resolve. They scour databases for hidden patterns, finding predictive information that experts may miss because it lies outside their expectations.

Many companies are involved in providing products to perform data mining. Given the data warehouse, data mining requires large computer systems, typically with multiprocessor or parallel hardware, and appropriate algorithms, derived from research efforts in Artificial Intelligence, related to learning, and from ongoing work on large databases. In the context of retail marketing just mentioned, data mining could reveal hidden patterns that would not otherwise be apparent, and this possibility is what drives research and investment. The rewards may be great. Consider the following[110]:

Automated prediction of trends and behaviors. Data mining automates the process of finding predictive information in large databases. Questions that traditionally required extensive hands-on analysis can now be answered directly from the data—quickly. A typical example of a predictive problem is targeted marketing. Data mining uses data on past promotional mailings to identify the targets most likely to maximize return on investment in future mailings. Other predictive problems include forecasting bankruptcy and other forms of default, and identifying segments of a population likely to respond similarly to given events.

Data mining continues to be a very active area of research in AI and databases. Retail activities on the Internet provide a very economical means for collecting large amounts of data on Internet shoppers. Issues of privacy related to Internet commerce and browsing will be discussed in depth in Chapter 9. One final comment on the importance of data mining for business[111]:

> In essence, data mining represents an umbrella or catch-all for a wide variety of techniques that aim at examining large quantities of data in search of easy-to-overlook relationships or hints that prove to have business or scientific value. . . . It appears that interest in data mining is not waning and that at a minimum, its use in the current application areas such as direct marketing campaigns, fraud detection, and development of models to aid in financial predictions will only intensify.

SOCIAL ISSUES

> The increasing usage of the Internet further complicates the social contract between employee and employer.[112]

Significant changes are occurring in the organizational structure of companies as a result of information technology. It is also affecting the nature of office work. The actual role of the technology is not always easy to identify, however. The crucial factors in evaluating the office environment are the attitude of management, its goals, its methods, and its expectations for the new equipment. Ostensibly, the primary reason for introducing, and continuing the introduction of, computers and communications systems is to increase productivity. More machines should mean fewer people doing the same work and therefore an increase in individual productivity. As sales expand, additional people or even more equipment may be necessary. The very presence of the computer creates the real possibility of providing a wide range of new services to the public and new tools to management. Thus productivity may not increase as rapidly as expected and staff reductions may not necessarily take place. Nevertheless, management may succeed in implementing, by means of the technology, a number of its tactical as well as strategic goals.

From one point of view, management's long-term goal is to control every aspect of the production process, whether in the factory or the office. Of course, this position derives from an analysis of factory work, in which things are the end result of the process. In the office, it is not so easy to measure either productivity or control, but several issues have arisen that indicate to some that control is the foremost concern. Among these are electronic monitoring, health, and deskilling. These issues will be extensively discussed in Chapter 13, but an introduction will be made next with respect to the previously discussed reengineering process. The Internet offers access to information directly related to work objectives, but it also permits access to social, political, and entertainment material that management may feel is not an appropriate activity from nine to five.

Reengineering and People

One of the original founders of the reengineering movement was Thomas Davenport, now a distinguished professor at the University of Texas. In a remarkable article published in late 1995, he offers his unique insight on the incredible success of reengineering from the late 1980s to the mid 1990s, when its popularity substantially decreased. Admitting that it was clearly oversold as a basic answer to all the ills of U.S. corporations, he claims that one of the major problems was that it was frequently implemented in complete disregard for its impact on employees, their feelings, and even their very jobs. "Reengineering didn't start out as a code word for mindless bloodshed. It wasn't supposed to be the last gasp of Industrial Age management."[113] Professor Davenport's most relevant and provocative remarks follow[114]:

> When I wrote about "business process redesign" in 1990, I explicitly said that using it for cost reduction alone was not a sensible goal. And consultants Michael Hammer and James Champy, the two names most closely associated with reengineering, have insisted all along that layoffs shouldn't be the point. But the fact is, once out of the bottle, the reengineering genie quickly turned ugly.

> So ugly that today, to most business people in the United States, reengineering has become a word that stands for restructuring, layoffs, and too-often failed change programs. . . .

> Reengineering treated the people inside companies as if they were just so many bits and bytes, interchangeable parts to be reengineered. But no one wants to "be reengineered." No one wants to hear dictums like, "Carry the wounded but shoot the stragglers"—language that makes workers feel like prisoners of war, not their company's most important assets. . . .

The 1994 CSC Index "State of Reengineering Report" had the answer: 50% of the companies that participated in the study reported that the most difficult part of reengineering is dealing with fear and anxiety in their organizations; 73% of the companies said that they were using reengineering to eliminate, on average, 21% of the jobs; and, of 99 completed reengineering initiatives, 67% were judged as producing mediocre, marginal, or failed results.

In 1996, the term downsizing, a byproduct of reengineering, gained common currency, as several large, very profitable, high-technology companies announced sizable workforce reductions. More recently, with downturns in the high-tech sector, especially the telecom industry, downsizing has become a basic fact of life.

Appropriate Use of the Internet

Should there be guidelines within corporations as to who should have access to the Internet and what if any restrictions should be imposed on what employees can access during working hours? Given that the workplace, the computers, and the communication costs are borne by management, it seems on the surface that management should, and indeed has, the responsibility to set guidelines, but what is not so clear is how management should determine if the guidelines are being followed. In an informal poll of 153 visitors to *Computerworld's* Web site during February of 1996, 25% agreed that "it should be the IS department's responsibility to monitor on-line use," while 75% disagreed. In addition 53% of respondents acknowledged that their "company [had] a policy for end users who go on the Internet," while only 23% of these enforced it.[115] The following is a checklist of concerns that should be taken into account by management before it implements a monitoring strategy, according to Computerworld's reporter, Alice LaPlante[116]:

- *Create a policy that's in line with your corporate culture.* Employees who are used to autonomy will resent restrictions and monitoring more than those who are accustomed to stringent control of corporate resources.
- *Remember that full benefits of the Internet have yet to be realized.* A staffer who appears to be wasting time surfing Web sites could be looking for innovative ways to improve job performance, serve customers more effectively, or generate new revenue.
- *If you intend to monitor employee usage of the 'net, the Electronic Communications Privacy Act requires that you publicize that policy.* It's possible that simply notifying your employees of your policy may be sufficient to protect you legally, but it's always better to get consent, says Barry Weiss, a partner at Gordon & Glickson, a law firm in Chicago.
- *Beware of being too dictatorial.* IS erred in that direction during the PC revolution; the result was virtual anarchy among users. An attempt to rein in users too tightly could instigate a similar revolt.

Software exists to determine the Web sites visited by employees as well as what is downloaded from those sites. Presumably, employees that use company time to download pornography will be discouraged if informed that management has installed such monitoring software and is prepared to use it. There are of course other activities that might not please management such as exploring entertainment sites or participating in nontechnical newsgroups or listservs. However, a flexible and non-punitive management policy may encourage a culture in which playtime does not detract from work and may even result in quality work because of improved employee morale.

A recent study of Internet abuses identified the following 11 categories: "general e-mail abuses, including spamming, chain letters, harassments, etc.; unauthorized usage and access; copyright infringement/plagiarism, newsgroup postings on non-work-related topics; transmission of confidential data; visiting sexually explicit sites; hacking of Web sites; uploading or downloading large non-work-related files; general browsing for non-work-related purposes; attempting to avoid detection at work by using external ISPs; and conducting personal business using work resources."[117] Most organizations have implemented acceptable use policies (AUP) with varying degrees of success.

Epilogue

Business has changed since September 11, 2001. Possible terrorist threats have raised the profile of security specialists. The stock market has been very volatile and high-tech stocks especially so. However, about one year prior to this event, *Fortune* magazine produced a special issue titled, "The Future of the Internet."[118] The introduction contained the following words: "More recently we've marked time by the emergence of new technologies—the Industrial Revolution, the Information Age. But this time the metaphor is neither a pure technology nor a physical object, though it embraces both. It is an idea. Welcome to the Age of the Network. . . . Driven by advances in speed, capacity, and mobility—as well as by the functional mutations sure to arise when a communications system is both ubiquitous and always on—the real upheavals of the Network age are ahead of us."[119] Now, more than three years after this declaration, the future is even cloudier, and with the collapse of the telecom market, uncertainty is everywhere. Nevertheless, the Internet and the Web continue to excite and to promise a future of great possibilities.

SUMMARY

The history of computers is very much intertwined with their role in business. From their earliest use in payroll and accounting to more recent applications in knowledge-based decision making, computers have become an integral component of the business community. Some of the business applications include financial planning, processing orders, billing, simulations, and real-time computing.

Information processing has taken several organizational forms, in response to both technological developments and management structures. There have been many attempts to provide models to characterize the growth of data processing, with varying degrees of success. With the arrival of PCs and workstations, a certain measure of chaos has occasionally entered the picture.

Management information systems (MIS) have been advertised and anticipated for several years. They are supposed to support a variety of management and decision-making functions and they have succeeded in part, although not perhaps as the integrated systems envisioned by the data processing pioneers. More recently, MIS has evolved into decision support systems, executive information or support systems, and expert systems, the last being an application of work in artificial intelligence.

Opening up more ways of serving computing needs is the growth in distributed computing. From large mainframes to networks of minicomputers linked to mainframes, to PCs linked to minis linked to mainframes, to PCs linked to workstations in host-server systems, the opportunities are boundless, but with many associated difficulties. Of paramount consideration is the communications hardware and software necessary to make such systems work.

As noted, PCs and workstations have appeared on the scene in large numbers, bringing computing power to everyone's desk (and home), but usually with little planning and overall control, at least until recently.

The so-called office of the future features electronic mail, word processing, database management, spreadsheets, desktop publishing, CAD/CAM, scheduling, instant messaging, and occasionally teleconferencing. The impact on employment and work structure has yet to be understood. A number of other technological advances are entering the world of business. Among these are graphics (for generating images and presenting data in novel and informative ways) and electronic data interchange to facilitate communication among companies. Progress has also been made in natural language interfaces to databases as well as voice communication and speech synthesis.

The Internet and the World Wide Web have begun to demonstrate their commercial possibilities. The Internet itself has served as a model for the distribution of computer resources within companies, the so-called intranet. In a surprisingly short time, the Web has assumed increasing importance as a new medium for commercial enterprises such as Amazon and eBay.

NOTES

1. "Business Takes a Second Look at Computers," *Business Week,* June 5, 1971, p. 59.
2. Peter de Jager. "If You Start Now... You Just Might Make It," *Computerworld,* November 20, 1995, p. 97.
3. Craig Stedman. "Controversy Roils Over Year 2000 Conversion Toll," *Computerworld,* December 18, 1995, pp. 1, 111.
4. Leah Nathans Spiro. "Panic in the Year Zero Zero," *Business Week,* August 12, 1996, pp. 72–73.
5. Steve Lohr. "1/1/00:Technology and 2000—Momentous Relief; Computers Prevail in First Hours of '00," *The New York Time,* January 1, 2000, Late Edition—Final
6. Edward Yourdon. "Assessment of the Y2K Situation," Ed Yourdon's Web Site, January 1, 2000. Available at http://www.yourdon.com/index2.html
7. Cyrus F. Gibson and Richard L. Nolan. "Managing the Four Stages of EDP Growth," *Harvard Business Review,* January-February 1974, pp. 76–88.
8. D. H. Meadows, D. L. Meadows, J. Randers, and W. W. Behrens III. *The Limits to Growth.* (New York: Universe, 1972).
9. Frederic G. Withington. "Five Generations of Computers," *Harvard Business Review,* July-August 1974, pp. 99–102.
10. IS Priorities as the Information Highway Begins, a Special Advertising Supplement in *Computerworld,* May 22, 1995. Table 4.1 is based on Figure 1 and the associated discussion.
11. Richard L. Nolan. "Managing the Crisis in Data Processing," *Harvard Business Review,* March-April 1979, pp. 115–126.
12. Peter F. Drucker. "The Coming of the New Organization," *Harvard Business Review,* January-February 1988, p. 46.
13. *Ibid.,* pp. 46–47.
14. Ralph Carlyle. "The Tomorrow Organization," *Datamation* (Cahners Publishing Co.), February 1, 1990, pp. 22, 23.
15. Clinton Wilder. "Foreign and U.S. Execs See Eye-to-Eye on Top IS Issues," *Computerworld,* May 22, 1989, p. 63.
16. Richard E. Walton. *Up and Running: Integrating Information Technology and the Organization.* (Boston: Harvard Business School Press, 1989).
17. *Ibid,* pp. 1–2.
18. William Bowen. "The Puny Payoff From Office Computers," *Fortune,* May 26, 1986, pp. 20–24.
19. "Managing Computers, a Lot to Learn," *The Economist,* March 3, 1990, pp. 64–65.
20. *Ibid.,* p. 65.
21. J. Yannis Bakos. "Are Computers Boosting Productivity? Yes!" *Computerworld,* March 27, 1995, pp. 128, 130.
22. Timothy F. Bresnahan and Shane Greenstein. "The Competitive Crash in Large-Scale Commercial Computing," National Bureau of Economic Research Working Paper No. 4901 as reported in Rob Norton, "What Slowed the PC Revolution," *Fortune,* March 6, 1995, p. 38.

23. Rob Norton. *Ibid.*

24. Stephen D. Oliner and Daniel E. Sichel. "Computers and Output Growth Revisited: How Big Is the Puzzle. *Brookings Papers on Economic Activity*, 1994, 2. An Editor's summary is available at http://www.brook.edu/dybdocroot/es/commentary/journals/bpea_macro/1994_2.htm

25. Erik Brynjolfsson and Shinkyu Yang. "Information Technology and Productivity: A Review of the Literature." In Marvin V. Zelkowitz (Ed.) *Advances in Computers, VOL. 43* (San Diego, CA: Academic Press, 1996), pp. 179–214.

26. "Managing a WIRED WORLD," Cover Story, *Fortune*, July 11, 1994.

27. As quoted in Thomas A. Stewart, "Managing in a Wired Company," *Fortune*, July 11, 1994, pp. 44, 46, 47, 48.

28. Paul Strassmann. "The Myth of Best Practices," *Computerworld*, December 18, 1995, p. 88.

29. Paul Strassmann. "Computers Don't Make Money, People Do," *Computerworld*, February 19, 1996. Available at http://www.strassmann.com/pubs/people-do.html on March 31, 1996.

30. *Ibid.*

31. Michael Gentle. "Sci-Fi Lessons for IS and Users," *Computerworld*, December 11, 1995, p. 37.

32. Thomas H. Davenport. "Saving IT's Soul: Human-Centered Information Management," *Harvard Business Review*, (72:2), March-April 1994, p. 123.

33. Joseph Maglitta. "Smarten Up," *Computerworld*," June 5, 1995, p. 85.

34. *Ibid.*

35. Joseph Maglitta, "Know-How, Inc.," *Computerworld*, January 15, 1996, p. 73.

36. Pete Loshin. "Knowledge Management," Computerworld.com, October 22, 2001. Available at http://www.computerworld.com/printthis/2001/0,4814,64911,00.html

37. Amy Malloy, Laura Hunt, and Lory Dix. "So What's All This About Workflow?" *Computerworld*, October 30, 1995, pp. 93, 97.

38. Theodore M. Koulopoulis. *The Workplace Imperative.* (New York: Van Nostrand Reinhold, 1995). As quoted in Ronni T. Marshak, "The Business Imperative for Workflow & Business Process Reengineering," an advertising supplement in *Fortune*, February 19, 1996.

39. *Ibid.*, Marshak.

40. Nina Burns. "Groupware: A CNI Overview," Creative Networks, Inc., 1995. Available at http://www.cnilive.com/cni008.htm

41. *Ibid.*

42. William H. Davidow and Michael S. Malone. *The Virtual Corporation: Structuring and Revitalizing the Corporation for the 21st Century.* (New York: HarperCollinsPublishers, 1992).

43. *Ibid.*, p. 4.

44. *Ibid.*

45. *Ibid.*, pp. 5, 6.

46. "The Virtual Corporation," cover story, *Business Week*, February 8, 1993, pp. 98–103.

47. Ray Grenier and George Metes. *Going Virtual: Moving Your Organization into the 21st Century*. (Upper Saddle River, NJ: Prentice-Hall Professional Technical Reference, 1996).

48. William E. Eager. "Virtual Realities," *Computerworld*, April 1, 1996, p. 90.

49. Faith Keenan and Spencer E. Ante. "The New Teamwork," *Business Week e.biz*, February 18, 2002, PP. EB 12–EB16.

50. *Ibid.*

51. Michael Hammer and James Champy. *Reengineering the Corporation: A Manifesto for Business Revolution*. (New York: HarperBusiness, a Division of HarperCollinsPublishers, 1993).

52. *Ibid.*, p. 2.

53. *Ibid.*, p. 5.

54. "The Horizontal Corporation," *Business Week*, December 20, 1993, pp. 76–81.

55. *Ibid.*, Hammer and Champy, pp. 65 ff.

56. *Ibid.*, pp. 83 ff.

57. Paul A. Strassmann, "The Roots of Business Reengineering," *American Programmer*, June 1995. Available at http://www.strassmann.com/pubs/reeng/roots.html

58. "Business Process Innovation: What Is It? Available at http://www.abs.uci.edu/depts/facil/renovate/bpi_what.html

59. *Ibid.*, Strassmann, June 1995.

60. "The Real-Time Economy," Survey, *The Economist*, January 31, 2002. Available at http://www.economist.com (Click the Surveys link and click the Business link.)

61. *Ibid.*

62. Robert T. Hoff with Steven Hamm. "How E-Biz Rose, Fell, and Will Rise Anew," *Business Week*, May 13, 2002.

63. "A Survey of Retailing: Change at the Check-Out," *The Economist*, March 4, 1995, p. 5.

64. *Ibid.*, p. 4.

65. *Ibid.*, p. 6.

66. Emily Kay. "Selling Enters the Information Age," *Datamation*, May 1, 1995, p. 38.

67. *Ibid.*, p. 40.

68. "E-commerce 2000." *E-Stats*, U.S. Department of Commerce, March 18, 2002. Available at http://www.census.gov/eos/www/papers/estatstext.pdf

69. *Ibid.*

70. *Ibid.*

71. eMarketer.com, June 3, 2002. Available at thttp://www.emarketer.com/estat-news/estats/ecommerce_b2c/20020603_doc

72. Michael Kahn, Reuters. "Is the Internet Short-circuiting the U.S. Economy?" DigitalMass.com, April 11, 2002. Available at http://digitalmass.boston.com/news/2002/04/11/internet_economy.html

73. Hal Varian. "Economics of Information Technology," December 16, 2001. Available at http://www.sims.berkeley.edu/~hal/Papers/mattioli.pdf

74. "International Electronic Commerce: Definitions and Policy Implications," U.S. General Accounting Office, March 2002, Report GAO-02-404. Available at http://www.gao.gov/new.items/d02404.pdf

75. *Ibid.*
76. "Global Online Retailing," An Ernst & Young Special Report, 2001. Available at http://www.ey.com/global/vault.nsf/US/2001_Retail_Study/ $file/GOR.pdf
77. Richard Cohen. "A Computerized Smoke Machine," *The Washington Post,* July 23, 2002, p. A17.
78. "Dot Com Shutdowns Rate Continues to Slow Amid Signs the Market's "Cyberphobia" Is Beginning to Slow," Webmergers.com, 2002. Available at http://www.webmergers.com/editorial/article.php?id=58
79. "How to face the Future as a Dotcom," Ernst & Young, October 23, 2000. Available at http://www.ey.com/global/gcr.nsf/UK/News_Room_-_How_to_ face_the_future_as_a_dotcom
80. "Risky Business: Americans see greed, cluelessness behind dot-com's comeuppance," Pew Internet & American Life Project, March 16, 2001. Available at http://63.210.24.35/reports/pdfs/PIP_Dotcom_Woes_Report.pdf
81. Amazon.com Annual Report," 2001. Available at http://media.corporate-ir.net/media_files/nsd/amzn/reports/ 2001AnnualReport.htm
82. Gordon B. Davis. *Management Information Systems: Conceptual Foundations, Structure, and Development,* (New York: McGraw-Hill, 1974), p. 5.
83. Gordon B. Davis and Margrethe H. Olson. *Management Information Systems: Conceptual Foundations, Structure, and Development, Second Edition.* (New York: McGraw-Hill, 1985).
84. Paul E. Cule and James A. Senn. "The Evolution From ICIS 1980 to AIS 1995: Have the Issues Been Addressed?" Proceedings of 1995 Americas Conference on Information Systems, August 25–27, 1995, Pittsburgh. Available at http://hsb.baylor.edu/ramsower/acis/papers/cule.htm
85. Thomas A. Stewart. *The Wealth of Knowledge: Intellectual Capital and the 21st Century Organization.* (New York: Currency Doubleday, 2002).
86. Thomas A. Stewart. "The Case Against Knowledge Management," Business2.0.com, February 2002. Available at http://www.business2.com/articles/mag/print/0,1643,36747,FF.html
87. P.G. Keen and M.S. Scott Morton. *Decision Support Systems: An Organizational Perspective.* (Reading, MA: Addison-Wesley, 1978), p. 13.
88. John F. Rockart and David W. De Long. *Executive Support Systems: The Emergence of Top Management.* (Homewood, IL: Dow Jones-Irwin, 1989).
89. *Ibid.*, pp. 6–7.
90. *Ibid.*, pp. 7–9.
91. Edward Feigenbaum, Pamela McCorduck, and H. Penny Nii. *The Rise of the Expert Company.* (New York: Times Books, 1988).
92. Jennifer Kahn. "It's Alive," *Wired,* March 2002. Available at http://www.wired.com/wired/archive/10.03/everywhere_pr.html
93. Abbe Mowshowitz. "Social Dimensions of Office Automation," in Marshall C. Yovits (Ed.), *Advances in Computers, Vol. 25.* (New York: Academic Press, 1986), p. 336.
94. "IBM and Steelcase Announce Global Initiative to Design Office of the Future," Steelcase.com, January 14, 2002. Available at http://www.steelcase.com. Search with the term, "Office of the Future."

95. "Imaging: Changing the Way the World Works," Special Advertising Section, *Business Week*, April 2, 1990, p. 105.

96. Kevin Strehlo. "E-Mail Can Change Your Life," *Datamation*, April 15, 1995, p. 9.

97. "Gartner: No Rest for the Work E-mail Addict," Itworld.com, July 2, 2001. Available at http://www.itworld.com/Tech/2987/IDG010702gartner/

98. Paul A. Strassmann. "E-mail is Only One Path to Success," *Computerworld*, January 9, 1995, p. 35.

99. "Beyond Chat: IM Comes of Age," Gartner, Inc. 2001. Available at http://enterprise.cnet.com/enterprise/0-9534-717-5210496.html?tag=st.ne.1005bynd-cht.cn

100. *Ibid.*

101. Shannon Henry. "The Instant-Mess Age," *The Washington Post*, July 21, 2002, p. H01.

102. Amy Cortese. "Here Comes the Intranet," *Business Week*, February 26, 1996, Cover, pp.76–79, 82–84.

103. Lee Levitt. "Intranets: Internet Technologies Deployed Behind the Firewall for Corporate Productivity," Intranet Society, INET'96 Annual Meeting. Available at http://www.process.com/intranets/wp2.htm

104. John Gantz. "Intranets: A Thicket of Hidden Costs," *Computerworld*, May 6, 1996, p. 37.

105. Peter Cassidy. "Special Report: Videoconferencing, The Next Best Thing to Being There," *LAN Times*, December 1995. Available at http://www.wcmh.com/lantimes/95dec/512a079a.html

106. Hal R. Varian. "Videoconferencing May Get Much-Needed Critical Mass," *The New York Times*, October 4, 2001, Section C, p. 2.

107. Phyllis K. Sokol. *EDI: The Competitive Edge.* (New York: Intertext Publications/Multiscience Press, McGraw-Hill, 1989).

108. Spencer E. Ante and Arlene Weintraub. "Why B2B Is a Scary Place to Be," *Business Week*, September 11, 2000, pp. 34–37.

109. Kurt Thearling. "An Introduction to Data Mining: Discovering Hidden Value in Your Data Warehouse," Pilot Software (Dun & Bradstreet). Available at http://santafe.edu/~kurt/dmwhite.pdf

110. *Op cit.*, Thearling, p. 2.

111. Karim K. Hirji. "Exploring Data Mining Implementation," *Communications of the ACM*, Vol. 44, No. 7, July 2001, pp. 87–93.

112. Murugan Anandarajan. "Internet Abuse in the Workplace," *Communications of the ACM*, Vol. 45, No. 1, January 2002, p. 54.

113. Thomas H. Davenport. "The Fad That Forgot People," *Fast Company*, Number 1, November 1995. Available at http://www.fastcompany.com/fastco/Issues/first/Reengin.htm

114. *Ibid.*

115. Alice LaPlante. "'Net Cops," *Computerworld*, March 11, 1996, pp. 81–83.

116. *Ibid.*, p. 83.

117. Keng Siau, Fiona Fui-Hoon Nah, and Limei Teng. "Acceptable Internet Use Policy," *Communications of the ACM*, Vol. 45, No. 1, January 2002, pp. 75–79.

118. "The Future of the Internet," Fall 2000 Special Issue, *Fortune*, October 9, 2000.

119. *Ibid.*, p. 90.

ADDITIONAL READINGS

Introduction

Nocera, Joseph. "The Story of '00," *Fortune*, August 19, 1996, pp. 50–52, 54, 58, 60, 62. "Year 2000 Computing Challenge," United States General Accounting Office, September 2000. Available at http://www.gao.gov/new.items/ai00290.pdf

The Early Years: Data Processing Systems

Allen, Brandt. "Make Information Services Pay Its Way," *Harvard Business Review*, January–February 1987, pp. 57–63.
Drucker, Peter. *The New Realities*. (New York: Harper & Row, 1989).
Vincent, David R. *The Information-Based Corporation* (Homewood, IL: Dow Jones-Irwin, 1990).
Verity, John W. "Rethinking the Computer," *Business Week*, November 26, 1990, pp. 116–119, 122, 124.

Information Technology and New Business Models

"A Business Researcher's Interests: Business Process Reengineering/Innovation," a Web site maintained by Yogesh Malhotra, sponsored by the Association for Information Systems, Available at http://www.pitt.edu/~malhotra/interest.html
Champy, James. *X-Engineering the Corporation: Reinventing Your Business in the Digital Age* (New York: Warner Books, 2002).
"Engineering's Digital Era," Special Report, *Business Week*, July 16, 2002. Available at http://www.businessweek.com/technology/tc_special/engineer.htm
Hammer, Michael. *The Agenda: What Every Business Must Do to Dominate the Decade* (New York: Crown Business, 2002).
Hammer, Michael with Steven A. Stanton. *The Reengineering Revolution: A Handbook*. New York: HarperCollins, 1995.
Strassmann, Paul. "Spending Without Results," *Computerworld*, April 15, 1996, p. 88.
"Survey: The IT Industry," *The Economist*, May 8, 2003. Available at http://www.economist.com/surveys/showsurvey.cfm?issue=20030510&CFID=122 31330&CFTOKEN=5d3a6-c5ed9f71-ddf1-426a-a608-74116c6dae34
"Trends Shaping the Digital Economy," Trends Report 2001, The Software & Information Industry Association, 2001. Available at http://www.trendsreport.net/trends2001.pdf
Wiig, Karl M. "What Future Knowledge Management Users May Expect," *J. Knowl. Management* (3:2), 1999, pp. 155–165. Available at http://www.emeraldinsight.com/pdfs/jkm1.pdf

E-Commerce and E-Management

Brandel, Mary. "Videoconferencing Slowly Goes Desktop." *Computerworld*, February 20, 1995, p. 81.

"E-commerce 2001 Highlights," United States Department of Commerce, E-Stats, March 19, 2003. Available at http://www.cwnsus.gov/eos/www/papers/2001/2001estatstext.pdf

"End-User Training and Learning," several papers in *Communications of the ACM*, 38 (7), July 1995, pp. 24–79.

"An Overview of Data Mining at Dunn & Bradstreet," DIG White Paper 95/01, Data Intelligence Group, Pilot Software, Cambridge, MA, September 1995. Available at http://santafe.edu/~kurt/wp9501.pdf

"OECD Guidelines for Protecting Consumers From Fraudulent and Deceptive Commercial Practices Across Borders," OECD, June 11, 2003. Available at http://www.oecd.org/pdf/M00041000/M00041900.pdf

Port, Otis. "Computers That Think Are Almost Here," *Business Week*, July 17, 1995, pp. 68–71, 73.

"Possible Anticompetitive Barriers to E-Commerce: Wine," Federal Trade Commission, July 2003. Available at http://www.ftc.gov/os/2003/07/winereport2.pdf

Spector, Robert. *Amazon.com: Get Big Fast.* (New York: HarperCollins, 1997).

Sproull, Lee and Kiesler, Sara. *Connections: New Ways of Working in the Networked Organization.* (Cambridge, MA: The MIT Press, 1991).

Thearling, Kurt. "From Data Mining to Database Marketing," DIG White Paper 95/02, Data Intelligence Group, Pilot Software, Cambridge, MA, October 1995. Available at http://santafe.edu/~kurt/wp9502.pdf

"The Accidental Superhighway: A Survey of the Internet," *The Economist*, July 1, 1995. Available at http://www.economist.com/surveys/internet/index.html

"Electronic Commerce and the Internet," special section. *Communications of the ACM* 39 (6), June 1996, pp. 22–58.

"A Survey of the Software Industry," *The Economist*, May 25, 1996. Available at http://www.economist.com/surveys/software/index.html

The Office of the Future

Flynn, Nancy. *The ePolicy Handbook: Designing and Implementing Effective E-Mail, Internet, and Software Policies.* (New York: Amacom, 2001).

Ricadela, Aaron. "Microsoft Shows off the Office of the Future," *InformationWeek*, September 26, 2002. Available at http://www.informationweek.com/story/IWK20020926S0001

Tsakindou, Evdoxia. "How to Talk With Your Computer," *Siemens Webzine*, March 12, 2001. Available at http://w4.siemens.de/FuI/en/archiv/zeitschrift/heft1_99/artikel04/

Social Issues

"Corporate Information Technology Policies and Procedures Survey," Gordon & Glickson PC, Chicago, IL, May 1996. Available at http://www.ggtech.com/pdf/96041.pdf

Dern, Daniel P. "Just One More Click . . ." *Computerworld*, July 8, 1996, pp. 93, 96.

Scheier, Robert L. "Let Go!" *Computerworld*, June 3, 1996, p. 82.

MEDICINE AND COMPUTERS

The potential for new computing and telecommunications technologies to reduce the cost of delivering health care, while facilitating broad structural changes in the health care industry, may presage a rapid expansion in the application of information technologies to the health care system.[1]

INTRODUCTION

Medicine is, at its root, skilled people helping people. Doctors skilled at diagnosis and treatment are expected, in our society, to recognize the health problems of their patients, recommend the best ways to treat them, monitor this treatment, and adjust it if necessary until full health returns or a stable condition is achieved. In the course of this process it may be necessary to prescribe changes in diet, administer drugs, use equipment to monitor various body functions, or perform surgery—in short, to apply any necessary technology to meet the perceived needs of the patient. This model for health care in the United States stresses treatment rather than preventive methods and is eager to employ expensive and sophisticated technology. Examples of the latter are open-heart surgery, dialysis machines, reproductive technologies, and body-scanning devices.

The computer has been used in this system in a variety of ways. It has found a natural home in the health delivery system and has supported a kind of medical practice that emphasizes and depends upon high technology. These computers and computer networks have responded to the deeply felt concerns of hundreds of thousands of health care professionals working within the current system. On the other hand, some are concerned that loss of humanity and increase in alienation might result from the growing dependence on machines and the more and more frequent replacement of human contact with computer interfaces.

The most natural and earliest use of computers in medicine was in record keeping, billing, and payroll, as has been true in other areas of society. In medicine, however, record keeping serves a function beyond its immediate mundane use. The ability to access medical records in an information system can serve a research as well as a required therapeutic function. And with the growth of the Internet it is now possible to access records from anywhere in the world. Beyond this very important function, the Internet also permits, indeed encourages, the establishment of kindred groups of patients and health professionals, to exchange information, offer advice, and support those in need. Medicine itself can be practiced remotely and over the past few years, considerable attention has been paid to the emerging discipline called telemedicine.

Other important application areas for computers are cross-sectional image analysis systems, medical education, and library access and research. Visually impaired, hearing impaired, and physically disabled people have been major beneficiaries of technological developments. The computer and (even better) the microprocessor have opened up a number of possibilities otherwise beyond their reach. There are now automatic devices for communication and for answering the telephone or the door. Other devices can monitor the ill and alert doctors or nurses if help is needed. Besides these uses, computer programming itself is an occupation that is well-suited for home-bound people. Video games are being used in therapy for patients suffering from brain disorders as a result of strokes, tumors, and degenerative diseases. The games help improve hand-eye coordination, patient alertness, attention, concentration, memory, and perceptual motor skills. There are plans to tailor software more specifically to rehabilitation purposes in the video game context. All in all, medicine and technology sounds like a marriage made in heaven.

The arrival of the Internet, and more specifically the Web, has added a new dimension to the doctor-patient relationship as well as to the patient's own ability to educate herself or himself. As a ubiquitous source of information, the Web abounds with reputable sites sponsored by medical associations, educational institutions, hospitals, medical journals, and individual physicians. In addition, there are less official and somewhat more suspect sites managed by patient groups, survivor organizations, and anyone who claims some degree of medical knowledge. Impenetrable medical journals and textbooks have given way to information presented on the web in a language available to non-specialists, with surprising results. Many patients, having consulted the Web, attempt to engage their doctors in e-mail conversations based on their newly acquired expertise. Such activities place a significant burden on doctors to respond in a timely and effective manner. It is also likely that a self-educated patient will not obtain a complete picture and thus physicians will be expected to fill in the blanks—again a drain on limited time. To summarize, this often difficult relationship will have to accommodate new strains, perhaps for the better, however, as patients use the Web to improve their understanding of their own medical circumstances.

MEDICAL INFORMATION SYSTEMS

> However, there is still no system that comprehensively facilitates the flow of all types of health information and symmetrically addresses the needs of clinicians, administrators, policy makers, patients, and consumers.[2]

On the surface, information systems appear to include just computer databases that store information, programs to process user queries, and more programs to present the results in a variety of forms. However, special demands on medicine have resulted in the development of information systems with additional appropriate properties. It may literally be a matter of life and death that medical records be accurate, complete, and current. This requirement is the most basic, but there are a number of subsidiary ones beyond patient care, namely administration, accounting, monitoring and evaluation of service, research, and resource allocation.

A Very Large Medical Information System

Figure 5.1 is a schematic diagram of an implemented information system developed by the U.S. Department of Defense (DOD) for its worldwide medical service. DOD announced the Composite Health Care System (CHCS) in 1988, to be installed at 754 locations worldwide, ranging from large military hospitals to small clinics.[3] The system was intended to automate patient administration, patient scheduling, nursing, order entry, clinical dietetics, laboratory, radiology, and pharmacy services. Each facility would have communications, maintenance, and operations support. Furthermore, it would be able to interact with other DOD systems, such as the National Disaster Medical System and VA System, food service, medical logistics, and tactical automation system.

The U.S. General Accounting Office (GAO) has reviewed CHCS for several years in terms of cost-benefit analysis, success in reaching stated goals, and recent technological developments in medical care systems. It describes CHCS briefly in the following manner[4]:

> CHCS is a comprehensive medical information system that Defense has developed to provide automated support to its military medical treatment facilities. As shown in Figure 5.1, the system is multi-faceted and complex, composed of nine integrated modules and shared capabilities, such as order-entry, results retrieval, and electronic mail. The modules are used to create and update the integrated patient database, which can be accessed by all authorized users.

This system actually has been implemented in 526 medical treatment facilities worldwide and represents a considerable investment of about $2 billion. It is probably one of the most advanced medical information systems

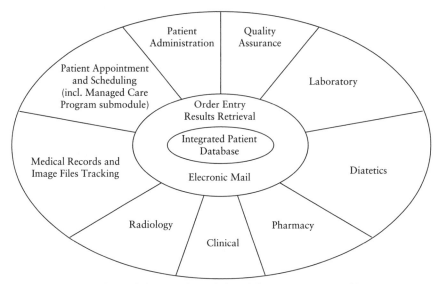

FIGURE 5.1 Shared Capabilities and Modules of the Composite Health Care System. (From "Medical ADP Systems: Defense Achieves Worldwide Deployment of Composite Health Care System," United States General Accounting Office, GAO/AIMD-96-39, April 1996. Accessed from the Web page with URL: http://www.gao.gov/monthly. list/ai96039.pdf on May 21, 1996.)

in existence, and while GAO is concerned with its costs and certain functions, it is the capabilities of CHCS that are of the most interest. A very brief overview of the various modules follows[5]:

> **Capabilities shared by most CHCS modules** include *order-entry*, which allows the entry of patient orders by healthcare providers and ancillary support personnel; *results retrieval*, which allows direct access to test results performed under any module; and *electronic mail*, which allows users to communicate with each other.
>
> The **Dietetics** module manages the order and delivery of patient dietary instructions.
>
> The **Clinical** module manages orders for patient care and the retrieval of test results. It contains checks against the patient's medical record for risks and contraindications, and issues a warning if necessary.
>
> The **Laboratory** module manages data associated with clinical and anatomical pathology, and blood/chemical tests. This includes ordering tests, processing specimens, documenting test results, and supporting quality controls.
>
> The **Patient Administration** module manages the registration of patients and their medical records.
>
> The **Patient Appointment and Scheduling** module manages appointment schedules for clinics and healthcare providers. Its Managed Care Program submodule supports enrollment, provider network management, and healthcare finder activities.

The **Pharmacy** module manages the ordering and filling of prescriptions. It checks for drug interactions and allergies, and includes an automated inventory control capability.

The **Radiology** module manages the ordering and scheduling of diagnostic, radiologic, nuclear medicine, and radiation therapy testing, as well as the reporting of test results.

The **Medical Records and Image Files Tracking** module manages and tracks patient medical records and images.

The **Quality Assurance** module supports the identification and documentation of recurring problems related to patient care, and tracks their solutions and resolutions. It also provides management of provider case lists and training to support the credentialing process.

Recent Developments in the Military System

A medical information system ultimately depends on the structure and content of the patient record for all the purposes it is intended to serve. Beyond the system discussed above, in 1998, the U.S. government—actually the Department of Veterans Affairs (VA), the Department of Defense (DOD), and the Indian Health Service (IHS)—initiated the Government Computer-Based Patient Record (GCPR), "which would allow health care professionals to 'share clinical information via a comprehensive lifelong medical record'."[6] The intention was to create this comprehensive medical record for millions of American soldiers and veterans that could be accessed by the Composite Health Care System described above, as well as by the other agencies. In somewhat more detail,[7]

> GCPR is intended to allow physicians and other authorized users at the agencies' health facilities to access data from any of the agencies' other health facilities by serving as an interface among their health information systems. . . . As envisioned, the interface would compile requested patient information in a temporary or virtual record while appearing on the computer screen in the format of the user's system. GCPR would divide health data into 24 categories, or "partitions," including pharmacy, laboratory results, adverse reactions, vital signs, patient demographics, and doctors' notes.

Not surprisingly, progress was slow and the costs were increasing. Another General Accounting Office report, about a year later, noted that the recommendations from the previous report had not been acted upon and that goals should be scaled back.

Computer-Based Patient Record

In 1991, the National Academy Press produced a study of the computer-based patient record (CPR) which argued for its importance and necessity. A second edition was published in 1997.[8] It is clear that advances in technology have improved the possibility of achieving the CPR, an ever elusive goal. Of course, the most significant and potentially far-reaching advance is the Internet, but more on this topic later in this chapter. As of 1997, the authors of one of the papers describes the state of the art in this way[9]:

> However, comprehensive information system products that seamlessly integrate data and coordinate processes across the entire continuum of health care services do not exist. Most health care information system vendors, whether their products were formerly based in the inpatient or the outpatient side, are working to extend their products to cover the needs of integrated delivery systems.

The patient record is fundamental to the multi-use medical information system and it has proven to be an elusive target. One of the difficulties is that technologies change, ambitions grow, costs increase, and management allegiances alter. A study by the U.S. Institute of Medicine formulated five conditions that would be helpful in achieving the development and diffusion of a successful CPR[10]:

1. The uses of and legitimate demands for patient data are growing. Part of this growth can be attributed to increased concern about the content and value of clinical therapies and a recent intense focus on health services research.
2. More powerful, affordable technologies to support computer-based patient records are now available.
3. Increasingly, computers are being accepted as a tool for enhancing efficiency in virtually all facets of everyday life.
4. Demographic factors such as an aging population (which results in a growth in chronic diseases) and the continued mobility of Americans create greater pressures for patient records that can manage large amounts of information and are easily transferable among health care providers.
5. Pressures for reform in health care are growing, and automation of patient records is crucial to achievement of such reform.

The report made strong recommendations on improving the CPR, including a commitment to the CPR as the standard for medical care.

The (Almost) Digital Hospital

The Georges Pompidou European Hospital, in Paris, opened in 2000. "At the heart of this ambitious model is the electronic patient record, or EPR."[11] This particular author argues that it has been difficult to implement the EPR in large part due to human factors:

> Finding a comfortable interface between people and machines (That is, making it easy for doctors and nurses to enter and use data) is a continuing

challenge. In addition, financial and productivity incentives for adopting EPRs are not always clear, and training staff to use them is time consuming, expensive, and often must be customized for the peculiarities of each hospital.

Protecting the Medical Record

Of course a pervasive problem in the use of the EPR, or CPR, is the privacy and security of the record. Medical information is among the most sensitive of all personal information and deserves the highest level of protection. More details will be provided in Chapter 9, but for the present we turn to a book published by the National Academy Press, which reports the results of a study on just these issues.[12] The concern with privacy has been seen as an important factor impeding the dissemination of systems based on the use of the EPR. This study made several recommendations in the context of a thorough exploration of relevant issues. The first of these advocated adoption of a set of technical practices and procedures developed in the study. Among these are the following, for immediate implementation[13]:

- *Individual authentication of users.* To establish individual accountability, every individual in an organization should have a unique identifier (or log-on ID) for use in logging onto the organization's information systems.
- *Access controls.* Procedures should be in place for ensuring that users can access and retrieve only that information that they have a legitimate need to know.
- *Audit trails.* Organizations should maintain in retrievable and usable form audit trails that log all accesses to clinical information. The logs should include the date and time of access, the information or record accessed, and the user ID under which access occurred.
- *Protection of remote access points.* Organizations with centralized Internet connections should install a firewall that provides strong, centralized security and allows outside access to only those systems critical to outside users.
- *System assessment.* Organizations should formally assess the security and vulnerabilities of their information systems on an ongoing basis.

Of course, this advice is appropriate for any computer system and particularly one which processes such sensitive information.

Key Information Technologies for Health Care

In 1995, the research arm of the U.S. Congress, the Office of Technology Assessment (OTA), issued a particularly relevant report with the title, *Bringing Health Care Online*.[14] Coincidentally, the OTA closed on September 29, 1995, after 23 years of operation during which it produced many important and relevant studies of technological impact. A list of diverse technologies that are quite relevant for health care is provided in

Table 5.1. These technologies are divided into groups, starting with the collection of data by a number of new techniques involving different modalities and onsite data entry. Once collected, issues of storage medium, data compression (for medical images), and structured archiving arise. The stored data is useful in so far as it can be readily accessed independent of distance and size; thus, issues of telecommunication networks and protocols are of prime importance. Finally, use must be made of the data, which requires programs to synthesize, analyze, and infer relevant information. Such disciplines as artificial intelligence, data mining, database theory, and decision support systems are also involved.

The obvious advantages of computer-based patient records over paper records include that "the health care delivery process could be fully documented, health information could be unfettered," and "care-giving, research, and data administration could be knit together."[15] These observations are well known, but it is clear that they represent some of the major benefits of information technology in the medical system and need to be emphasized. Once stored digitally, information is accessible from many points and available for many purposes.

As we have seen, many reasons have been given for the importance and usefulness of medical information systems, but perhaps one additional reason might be offered: Medicare. In 1968, Medicare was introduced to help the elderly pay their medical bills. Medicare payments have become a crucial factor in hospital finances and the entire health care system, accounting for about 40% of hospital billings in 1987. Tight restrictions on Medicare payments, however, because of the federal government's decision to limit hospital payments to a fixed amount to treat each illness, as well as pressure by major corporations to limit the costs of large insurance carriers, have forced the health care system to tighten its operations. Thus, hospitals are encouraged to treat illnesses as quickly and cheaply as possible to recover a greater proportion of their costs. This situation has motivated the development and implementation of medical information systems to help reduce costs and at the same time improve the quality of care.

Medical Databases

The National Library of Medicine (NLM) is the "principal resource for the collection, organization, and retrieval of scientific literature in the health and biomedical fields."[16] The library has long been concerned with the application of computers to information retrieval and in 1964 introduced MEDLARS (Medical Literature Analysis and Retrieval System), its computerized retrieval and technical processing system. This system maintains data files, provides online retrieval services, and produces computer-photocomposed publications. It includes "over 40 online databases containing about 18 million records." One of these

TABLE 5.1

KEY INFORMATION TECHNOLOGIES FOR HEALTH CARE

Human-computer interaction	handheld computers
	handwriting recognition
	personal digital assistants
	speech recognition
	automated data collection
	structured data entry
Storage, processing, and compression	computer-based patient records
	magnetic stripe cards
	smart cards
	picture archiving and communications systems
	medical imaging
	political storage
	image compression
	digital signal processors
	object-oriented software design
Connectivity	clinical information systems
	cabled, optical, and wireless networks
	Internet and electronic mail
	World Wide Web
	Integrated Services Digital Network (ISDN)
	frame relay
	Asynchronous Transfer Mode (ATM)
	client-server computing
	messaging and coding standards
	proponetary and consensus standards
	Medical Information Bus
Security	passwords
	fault tolerant computers
	redundant disk (RAID) systems
	authenticators
	encryption
	firewalls
Data distillation	decision support systems
	pattern recognition
	artificial neural networks
	knowledge based systems
	relational databases
	knowledge discovery
	natural-language processing
	encoders and groupers

Source: U.S. Congress, Office of Technology Assessment, Bringing Health Care Online: The Role of Information Technologies, OTA-ITC-624 (Washington, DC: U.S. Government Printing Office, September 1995), Table 2-1, p. 44. Also available at URL: http://www.wws.princeton.edu/~ota/

databases, MEDLINE (MEDLARS online), first came into service in 1971 to provide online capability. The MEDLINE database is actually Index Medicus® online, "the monthly subject/author guide to articles in 3,000 journals."[17] Currently, the term MEDLINE is used to describe the database, not the online service, and in fact is the largest and most extensively used of all the Library's databases. It currently has "over 11 million references to journal articles in life sciences with a concentration on biomedicine."[18] Other databases contain information on ethical topics, cancer, chemical substances, epilepsy, health planning and administration, history of medicine, and toxicology. The online network consists of over 14,000 institutions and individuals in the United States.

In the mid-1980s, the NLM introduced PC-based software, Grateful Med, that permits the search of almost the entire MEDLARS database via a user-friendly interface. On April 16, 1996, a new version, Internet Grateful Med, was introduced, which permits health professionals around the world to access MEDLINE via the Internet and the World Wide Web.[19] Internet Grateful Med was retired in September 2001 and replaced by a new system, PubMed. As the rate of growth in medical knowledge continues to increase at a rapid rate, access to a comprehensive database such as MEDLINE becomes an indispensable aid to providing medical care. As the then National Library of Medicine director Donald A. B. Lindberg, M.D., noted, "Even a disciplined physician who reads two medical journals a night for an entire year before going to bed would find that he had fallen behind on his reading by over 550 years. Medline will be an indispensable tool for medical professionals to stay current with the latest in medical information."[20]

MEDICAL APPLICATIONS

Improving the health care of Americans through the discovery and implementation of new medical technologies has been an explicit goal of the federal government for over a century. Since the 1970s, however, the government has also underwritten a less visible effort—the attempt to identify which health care interventions, among those in current use, work best.[21]

The computer has found a welcome home in medical diagnosis, treatment, and as an aid to the disabled or physically disadvantaged. Powerful tools have become available for exploring parts of the body previously accessible only through surgery. For patients in intensive care or on life-support systems, the availability of microprocessors has relieved nurses of the responsibility of constant surveillance. In such applications, the computer is indispensable because of both its computational power and its decision-making ability.

Body Imaging

Until fairly recently there were two basic methods for identifying and investigating problems within the human body: X-rays—with or without the use of ingested or inserted dyes or radioactive tracers—and surgery. Both methods have obvious drawbacks. Surgery is a traumatic invasion of the body and should be reserved for situations that demand the actual removal of diseased or damaged organs or tissues or the correction of problems. Its use as an exploratory tool should be minimized. Over the past 30 years a number of methods for producing images of various parts of the body have been developed, employing both invasive and noninvasive means. Probably the best known is the computerized axial tomography or computer-assisted tomography (CAT) scanner.

CAT Scanners

The term *tomography* refers to "any of several techniques for making X-ray pictures of a predetermined plane section of a solid object, by blurring out the images of other planes."[22] In an ordinary X-ray picture, the X-ray source produces a diverging beam that passes through the body and falls on a photographic plate. Although it has proven to be an invaluable tool, conventional X-ray does have limitations in that there is little sense of depth, and soft tissues show up somewhat blurred. The CAT scanner uses X-rays to produce sharp, cross-sectional images of the human body. The patient lies horizontally on a table and is placed in the center of the apparatus, which consists of an X-ray source and collimator (a device to focus the beam) on one side, a detector and data acquisition system on the other. The body is kept stationary in the scanner while the apparatus rotates around a given section, generating X-rays that are registered by the detectors as they pass through the body. There is attenuation of the beams as they pass through body structures of varying densities. The actual cross-sectional image is produced by using a computer to carry out a complex summation of the various measurements made. Although a number of algorithms for producing cross-sectional images have been known for years, it is only when using a computer that the computation becomes feasible.

More recent advances in technology have increased the rate at which pictures can be taken: "The original scanners in 1978 took 2 minutes per slice and had very rough images. The new scanners today can do a series of 30 images in a few seconds and have much sharper images."[23] Another advance in the technology has been the spiral or helical CAT scanner. The entire chest can be scanned in the time it takes for one breath.[24] The CAT scanner has been hailed as a major, almost revolutionary advance in medical diagnosis. In terms of safety, the X-ray exposure necessary to produce a cross-sectional image is no greater than that for a conventional

X-ray. Most major hospitals have acquired CAT scanners even though the price is around $1 million. In fact it has become something of a controversial item, adding to the criticism of the unseemly haste with which hospitals have competed to purchase the latest and most expensive equipment. However, there is no denying that it has proven to be an important diagnostic tool.

Nuclear Magnetic Resonance (NMR) or Magnetic Resonance Imaging (MRI)

NMR (also known as Magnetic Resonance Imaging, MRI) produces images similar to those obtained by CAT scanners but also permits the actual observation of certain internal processes such as the movement of blood, the reaction of cancerous tumors to a particular therapy, the presence of multiple sclerosis, the action of heart and blood vessels, and various problems in tendons, ligaments, and cartilage.[25] All these observations can be accomplished without X-rays, the injection of hazardous dyes, or the use of radioactive isotopes. Nuclear magnetic resonance has been used for many years by chemists to analyze uniform solids and liquids. In its medical application, the patient is placed inside a large cylindrical magnet. In the plane of radiation, the magnetic field can vary between 1500 and 15,000 gauss (more than 15,000 times the magnetic field of the earth). Under the influence of the large magnetic field, the atomic nuclei of hydrogen, phosphorous, and other elements act as tiny bar magnets and align themselves in the direction of the field. When the radio frequency (RF) is removed, the tiny magnets return to their original positions and in the process emit characteristic RF signals. An antenna in the cylinder detects the radio waves and transmits them to a computer to be analyzed and presented as an image. Further information can then be obtained, because the computer can also determine the rate at which the nuclei return to their original positions. It is even possible to obtain a sequence of images of the human heart with the valves opening and closing.

There are some disadvantages, however. Among these are cost—an NMR system sells for about $1.5 million, about 50% more than a CAT scanner. The system must be isolated from extraneous electromagnetic signals and magnetic substances. The system may be hazardous to people with artificial joints and pacemakers. The long-term effect of high magnetic fields on the body is unknown. Pregnant women are currently being excluded from examination by NMR, pending further research on the risk. It is being introduced more slowly than the CAT scanner, but the future holds much promise for its use.

Positron-Emission Tomography (PET) Scanners

As is often the case, new technology follows rapidly on the heels of the old, say CAT scanners. The use of a PET scanner requires the subject to ingest, or be injected with, a radioactive isotope, typically of oxygen, carbon, and nitrogen. The system detects the radioactive decay by means of special scintillation counters. These isotopes are called positron emitters, because as they decay they release positively charged particles that are annihilated after collision with electrons. Gamma rays result whose direction of travel can be detected very precisely, thereby revealing a great deal about the relevant body tissue. The patient is placed inside a ring structure containing a number of gamma ray detectors. The directions are identified and the computer comes into play to construct a cross-sectional image of the distribution of the positron emitter. The PET scanner has an advantage over the CAT scanner in that it is able to reveal the functioning of organs and tissues, not just their outline.

The PET scanner can be used to (a) monitor blood flow in certain areas of the heart (cardiology), (b) assess the intake of sugar in cancerous tumors of the brain (neurology), determine the size and growth of cancerous tumors (oncology), and (c) study chemical reactions that may suggest schizophrenia or Alzheimer's disease. There are many fewer PET scanners than CAT scanners in use, and many of the results obtained so far are still experimental.

There are some problems associated with the widespread use of PET scanners. Short-lived isotopes are necessary to prevent the patient from receiving too large a dose of radiation while the scan is in progress. Isotopes with such short half-lives (between 2 and 110 minutes) must be produced on-site by a cyclotron. The need to have a cyclotron on hand increases the costs enormously, on the order of $2 million for a PET installation. Furthermore, at the present stage of development the interpretation of the data is a very complex process. It still requires the efforts of specially trained chemists, mathematicians, physicists, computer scientists, and doctors. Both PET and CAT scanners are subject to the criticism that they expose the body to excessive radiation from either gamma rays or X-rays.

The benefits of PET scanners have become more evident over the years. For example, consider the following[26]:

> P.E.T. has demonstrated that it is a clinically proven, cost effective, and safe method for imaging colon cancer, lung cancer, lymphoma, brain cancer, heart disease and neurological disorders such as Alzheimer's Disease. P.E.T. is also a useful tool in determining whether exploratory surgery, radiation therapy, organ transplantation or other procedures may be necessary.

A Future Scenario

In a special issue of the *Communications of the ACM (Association for Computing Machinery)*, the following scenario is presented as one possibility for the future role of computational bioimaging[27]:

> Upon arrival at the hospital, patients will press their fingers onto sensors that identify them through DNA analysis, then move down a short corridor

in which they are scanned by a number of imaging devices, before arriving in a waiting room (there will probably still be waiting rooms in our medical future). Together with their physicians, they will view fully registered, multimodal, high resolution, interactive, 3D visualizations of their anatomical selves (structure) as well as their functional selves (electrical, mechanical, and chemical). Immediately highlighted will be possible abnormalities in structure and function. Physicians will then be able to manipulate and further analyze various suspect regions and simulate possible treatments, from drug and gene therapies to minimally invasive surgical reconstructions.

Storage of Images

As a variety of techniques have emerged for producing images of the body, an interesting problem has arisen. Large numbers of images must be stored, cataloged, and made readily available for future reference. For example, "A 300-bed hospital generates about 1 gigabyte (8×10^9 bits) of picture information every day and is legally bound to hold it for three to seven years—30 years in the case of silicosis or black lung disease, illnesses that may have relevance to future lawsuits."[28] Diagnostic imagers could have been designed to produce digital output, which would have facilitated the storage of the images and their transmission over networks, but for commercial reasons this was not done; in addition, when scanners were first introduced, high resolution monitors were not generally available and film processing techniques and handling were. More recently, a number of hospital and medical research centers in the U.S., Japan, and Europe have begun to implement and routinely use picture-archiving and communication systems (PACS). In more detail, a definition follows[29]:

> PACS accepts pictures or images, with associated text, in digital form and then distributes them over a network. The components of a PACS include control computers and a communication network, interfaces to imaging devices, storage media, display stations, and printers.

Some of the problems impeding the rapid growth of PACS are the quality of the resolution of digital images compared to film, the inability to view multiple digital images rapidly, and the high cost of equipment compared to film systems of requisite quality. To deal with these issues, radiologists will have to accept digital images even though they are concerned about the possibility of extraneous details being introduced during computation. Another looming problem is the vast number of images that must be stored.

The real payoff of PACS is the ability to transmit quality images over varying distances: local-area networks (LANS) linking scanners, data storage devices, and display stations in one department; wide-area networks for linking LANs within hospitals and medical centers; and teleradiology networks for national and worldwide distribution. PACS had their heyday in the 1980s and as with many other computer technologies, the Internet has had a major impact. The idea is that the scanners themselves produce images in a form compatible with Internet transmission.[30]

Electronic Monitoring

For the patient in the intensive care unit of a hospital, the immediate world is full of electronic hums and beeps, flashing lights, and video monitors. Many activities performed by nurses in the past are now being carried out by a combination of sophisticated electronics, microprocessors, and software. Many body functions can be monitored automatically and compared to desired (or dangerous) levels by specialized equipment that emits signals to warn nurses and other staff if an emergency arises. This system relieves nurses of the stressful and tedious work of sitting at the bedside of critically ill patients who are often unconscious. The patient can be assured of constant monitoring and the nurse can apply himself or herself to patients who are more aware of nursing efforts.

The electronic Intensive Care Unit, or eICU, is beginning to make an appearance. Sentara Healthcare, a chain of hospitals in southeastern Virginia, has developed an eICU with the ability to manage ICU patients remotely, including the direct observation of the patient, all monitoring devices, laboratory results, as well as the ability to order new tests, changes in treatment, and to issue warnings about possible signs to observe. In somewhat more detail, the system provides the following capabilities[31]:

> Sentara's eICU receives information on occupants of four ICUs at three Sentara institutions—a total of about 50 patients. Virtually all the bedside data—from vital signs and current prescriptions to the settings of ventilators and intravenous pumps—come to the eICU in real time. Also available in electronic form is the history of the patient's illness and treatment, lab results and chart notes made by the doctors and nurses doing the hands-on care. Video and audio links give the eICU staff the ability to look at the patient and talk with caregivers. "This is something that's added on top of the care. We amplify the effect of the bedside team; we don't replace it," said Gene H. Burke, the Sentara critical-care physician in charge of integrating VISICU's system into the hospital operations.

Is the practice of medicine becoming increasingly dehumanized? How far have we moved away from the image of the doctor or nurse hovering near the patient, deep in thought, full of compassion? Perhaps this image is overly romantic and has little to do with the actual quality of care. It is difficult to assume a critical stance when sophisticated monitoring systems that are responsive to the slightest changes in the well-being of patients are in use and there is less dependence on overworked and tired medical staffs.

Robot Surgery

It might have been expected that as the technology of micromanipulators and visions systems improved sufficiently, robot-like devices would be developed to aid surgeons in performing delicate operations. And indeed, such is the case. Even more, the possibilities of performing such surgery remotely, over large distances, has also become a reality. One example is an operation performed in August of 2000 by Dr. Donald Galen at the Reproductive Surgery Center in San Francisco.[32] The system he used "allows doctors to perform surgery by controlling miniature hands inserted into the body through 1-centimeter incisions. Surgeons control the robotic appendages with joysticks and tiny cameras attached to the probes that translate the operation into a 3-D computer image." Dr. Galen seems to be quite optimistic about this system and is quoted as saying, "The 3-D graphics display gave me an amazing view of the operative field, and the hand controls provided precise control over the instruments. In fact, I was able to suture with more precision than with conventional surgery."

About one year later, surgeons in New York operated a remote-controlled robot in an operation on a woman in Strasbourg, France. Her gall bladder was removed. The surgeons in New York sat[32a]

> in a cockpit-like console equipped with joysticks to manipulate the robot via transoceanic fiber optic cables. The robot had three "arms"—two holding instruments and another containing a laparoscope, or a tiny camera embedded in flexible tube. The surgeons moved the camera with simple voice commands (up, down, left, right) and watched the procedure on a video monitor.

In a statement that is typical of those issued whenever a machine performs a function heretofore in the exclusive province of humans, the founder and chief technology officer of Computer Motion, the company that manufactured the robotic surgical system, Yulun Wang, cautioned, "It's important to recognize that these robots don't replace doctors, they're tools for the doctors."[32b]

Computers in Medical Education

Aside from the use of computer-aided instruction in medical schools (the importance of which should not be overlooked), a significant and interesting application has been medical robots. These devices are shaped like humans, covered with synthetic skin, and are chock full of electronics that simulate a variety of human functions. Controlled by computers, they are used to provide students with an opportunity to perform diagnostic tests before they are experienced enough to interact usefully with human subjects. As advances are made in robotics, these robots will become more sophisticated and more challenging for students. Improved computer graphics and multimedia have resulted in medical simulations that also provide excellent teaching aids.

Medical Expert Systems

At the heart of medical practice is the diagnosis, that somewhat mysterious process by which a doctor assimilates medical evidence—in the form of family history, symptoms, the results of tests, and direct verbal reports—and determines a course of treatment along with further tests to ascertain whether the patient is in fact suffering from a particular ailment. Although there have been significant advances in medicine, the determination of the nature, cause, and treatment of disease and disability is still often more art than science. The process depends heavily on the experience, knowledge, and skill of the attending physicians and sometimes on just plain luck. The educational process depends on teaching diagnostic skills by example, occasionally in stressful situations, with the hope that the novice will learn from the experienced.

In the past few years there has been a considerable effort to apply artificial intelligence techniques to the area of medical decision making. There are several components to this research program: the acquisition of medical knowledge, the problem-solving system or inference engine that captures the decision-making strategy of the best doctors, a means of adding new knowledge and modifying old, and finally, a facility for natural communication. The earliest medical expert system, MYCIN, was designed at Stanford University in the early 1970s to recommend the appropriate antibiotics to treat bacterial infections. (MYCIN is a typical suffix for the names of antibiotics, for example, streptomycin and aureomycin).[33] More recently, expert systems have been developed for more general-purpose use such as in the offices of general practitioners. Such a system is the "Explain software package developed by G. Octo Barnett of Harvard Medical School's Laboratory for Computer Science; it includes 2200 diseases and 5000 symptoms in its knowledge base."[34]

COMPUTERS AND THE DISABLED

For some individuals with disabilities, assistive technology devices and assistive technology services are necessary to enable the individuals—

(A) to have greater control over their lives;
(B) to participate in, and contribute more fully to, activities in their home, school, and work environments, and in their communities;

(C) to interact to a greater extent with individuals who do not have disabilities; and

(D) to otherwise benefit from opportunities that are taken for granted by individuals who do not have disabilities.[35]

The processing power of computers and indeed of microprocessors has found a ready application in devices and systems to aid the paralyzed, the sensory impaired, and the severely disabled. And not a moment too soon, given the surprisingly large number of disabled people in the U.S. and elsewhere. Some interesting and challenging results of a survey of 32,000 households in November, 1997, which excluded people in institutions, are as follows[36]:

- In 1997, 52.6 million people (19.7 percent of the population) had some level of disability and 33.0 million (12.3 percent of the population) had a severe disability.
- About 10.1 million individuals (3.8 percent of the population) needed personal assistance with one or more ADLs [Activities of Daily Living. For example, getting in or out of bed or a chair, bathing, and dressing] or IADLs [Instrumental ADLs. For example, going outside, keeping track of money and bills, preparing meals, and doing light housekeeping].
- Among the population 15 years old and over, 2.2 million used a wheelchair. Another 6.4 million used some other ambulatory aid such as a cane, crutches, or a walker.
- About 7.7 million individuals 15 years old and over had difficulty seeing the words and letters in ordinary newspaper print; of them, 1.8 million were unable to see.
- The poverty rate among the population 25 to 64 years old with no disability was 8.3 percent; it was 27.9 percent for those with a severe disability.
- Out of a total population of 267.7 million non-institutional individuals, 52.6 million (or 19.7 percent) had some type of disability.
- Among those with a disability, 33.0 million (or 12.3 percent of the total population) had a severe disability and 10.1 million (or 3.8 percent of the total population) needed personal assistance with one or more ADLs or IADLs.

The impact of computer technology is likely to be so significant that the visually impaired will be helped to (albeit dimly), the hearing impaired to communicate, the physically disabled to move (albeit slowly and with difficulty), and the paralyzed to interact with the world, for both work and play. Technologies that can be used "to increase or improve functional capabilities of individuals with disabilities"[37] are called assistive technologies. Some obvious examples are motor-driven wheelchairs, hearing aids, computer keyboards with oversized keys, voice-activated electromechanical systems, and remote-controlled devices.

The Visually Impaired

A 2002 report from the National Eye Institute of the National Institutes of Health announced that blindness stemming from age-related eye disease is a growing phenomenon: "Over one million Americans aged 40 and over are currently blind and an additional 2.4 million are visually impaired. These numbers are expected to double over the next 30 years as the Baby Boomer generation ages."[38] The leading causes of blindness in the U.S. include diabetic retinopathy, age-related macular degeneration, cataracts, and glaucoma.

Most advances in the treatment of blindness are still experimental. For the visually impaired, help comes in two forms: technology to improve access to information, and a means for providing a crude form of vision. In the former case, an important development was the Kurzweil Reading Machine and other reading machines. A book or printed page is placed on its glass top. A scanning mechanism converts the print images to electrical signals that are processed by a computer program whose output device is a voice synthesizer. Such programs incorporate a large number of English phonological rules (how text might be directly converted to appropriate sound) and exceptions (under what conditions the general rules fail). The voice or voices are sometimes difficult to understand, but users report that in a very short time they become quite comfortable with one or more variations. In addition, controls allow the user to vary the pitch, spell out the letters in words that have not been understood, repeat previous words, and increase the number of words scanned per minute.

For years, vision researchers have been experimenting with artificial eyes, retinal implants, and even cortical implants. In particular, work is proceeding along the following three fronts[39]:

- Enhanced vision, which refers to aids that process the image for maximum visibility and then present the information to still viable parts of an individual's seeing retina.
- Prosthetic vision, which presents processed visual information to the inner retina or visual pathways through electrical stimulation of the surviving neurons.
- Artificial vision, which processes and interprets visual information and presents the result to the individual through another sensory modality.

Digital Hearing Aids

About 28 million Americans have some form of hearing disability or loss; they may suffer from one or more of the following[40]:

- Difficulty hearing conversations, especially when there is background noise.
- Hissing, roaring, or ringing in the ears (tinnitus).
- Difficulty hearing the television or radio at a normal volume.
- Fatigue and irritation caused by the effort to hear.
- Dizziness or problems with balance.

Apparently, about 1.5 million hearing aids are sold annually in the U.S. but many are unused because of their general ineffectiveness in many situations. Recently, digital hearing aids have been introduced with the expectation that they will provide improved performance. Digital circuitry will be able to vary the amplification profile of the hearing aid to take into account more precise information about the range of individual hearing loss and the sound characteristics of typically encountered environments. The NIH document referred to above characterizes digital devices as follows:

> **Digital/Programmable:** The audiologist programs the hearing aid with a computer and can adjust the sound quality and response time on an individual basis. Digital hearing aids use a microphone, receiver, battery, and computer chip. Digital circuitry provides the most flexibility for the audiologist to make adjustments for the hearing aid. Digital circuitry can be used in all types of hearing aids and is typically the most expensive.

Current research on such devices is concerned with such areas as "the application of new signal processing strategies and ways to improve sound transmission and reduce noise interference, as well as psychophysical studies of the impact of abnormal hearing function on speech recognition."[40a]

Other Assistive Technologies

Most people will remember having seen the world's most famous physicist, Stephen Hawking, using a device to produce speech, because he is unable to do so on his own, given his affliction with ALS (amyotropic lateral sclerosis; also known as Lou Gehrig's disease). ALS is a progressive motor neuron disorder that profoundly affects the muscular system and has forced Hawking into a wheelchair at an early age as well as reduced his speech to unintelligibility and finally silence because of an emergency tracheotomy. He was using a speech synthesizer, a device that takes text as input and produces speech, albeit clearly non-human, as output. There are a number of such systems commercially available, probably the most common being software that enables users to communicate in rudimentary speech with their computers. One of the best known systems is Words-Plus, used by thousands of people worldwide. Most companies currently in this market are quite small, mainly because of the nature of the market they serve: "The severely disabled are a highly segmented group, making them a difficult target for a firm interested in mass markets. A company that makes products for the partially blind is not likely to also manufacture devices for the deaf or those in wheelchairs."[41]

Artificial limbs have had limited purposes, usually cosmetic or to provide limited mobility or grasping. But with the arrival of microprocessors, large-capacity memories, accurate and durable sensors, and strong, light, and flexible materials, the artificial limb has been transformed into a device that more closely approximates the natural limb. One of the most advanced artificial limbs, the C-Leg, manufactured by the German company, Otto Bok, uses "microprocessors, strain gauges, angle detectors, hydraulics and electronic valves to recreate the stability and step of a normal leg."[42] A more detailed description follows:

> The C-Leg is, in effect, a wearable computer, although Otto Bock and other prosthetic-device makers avoid the phrase. Beneath its carbon fiber composite shell are two microprocessors that receive data from a string of sensors at a rate of 50 times a second. The processors' sophisticated software coordinates a mechanical and hydraulic system that allows the leg to switch seamlessly from a rigid position that supports the user's weight to a relaxed position that allows the user to walk in a way that closely imitates a natural gait.

Alzheimer's disease (AD) is a terribly debilitating affliction that is not part of normal aging. Unfortunately it can only be definitively diagnosed by examining the brain of a potential victim in a post mortem procedure, but the accuracy of diagnoses made on living individuals has been improving. The following statistics are AD for the year 2000[43]:

> AD is the most common cause of dementia among people age 65 and older. It presents a major health problem for the United States because of its enormous impact on individuals, families, the health care system, and society as a whole. Scientists estimate that up to 4 million people currently suffer with the disease, and the prevalence (the number of people with the disease at any one time) doubles every 5 years beyond age 65. It is also estimated that approximately 360,000 new cases (incidence) will occur each year and that this number will increase as the population ages.

A very ambitious research program, in the area of assisted cognition, is underway with the goal of providing assistance to Alzheimer's patients without the need for human intervention. As a field of study, assisted cognition depends on such research areas and technologies as artificial intelligence, Global Positioning Systems, sensor networks, and infrared ID badges. The goal of the research is to develop systems of sufficient ability to aid AD patients in the early stages of the disease in order to postpone the time at which they must be moved from their homes to a care facility. One of the leading researchers, Henry Kautz, at University of Washington, notes that the realization of this goal is still 20 to 30 years away.[44]

The Disabled at Work

In 1990 a comprehensive law was passed in the U.S., the Americans with Disabilities Act (ADA), requiring employers, public institutions, and private companies to provide facilities sufficient to enable people with disabilities to enjoy all the benefits that the rest of society currently enjoys and usually takes for granted. Although the ramifications of this law are likely to be far-reaching and unpredictable, it is clear that the computer, or at least the microprocessor and associated input/output devices, will play an important role. It will be important that all forms of equipment produced for the general public be designed so that the physically disabled will also benefit from its use. This requirement has added urgency given that more than 55 million Americans have disabilities as of 2002. Specially designed computers with oversized keyboards and large monitors, and special communication networks will allow the severely disabled to work and be educated at home. Speech synthesizers have been improved and their price lowered so that screen displays can be spoken for the benefit of people with visual impairments, software is available to translate from English to Braille for printing, light pens and joy sticks can replace or augment keyboards (although adequate software is still in short supply), and speech recognition technology is an active research area for people with and without disabilities.

Other applications of microprocessors to aid the disabled include their use in wheelchairs to improve control, and electronic mail or specialized telephone equipment to permit the deaf to communicate. Part of the motivation for a revitalized concern for the disabled was the passage by Congress of the Workforce Investment Act of 1998, containing Section 508, Electronic and Information Technology. Among the provisions of this section are the following[45]:

> (A) DEVELOPMENT, PROCUREMENT, MAINTENANCE, OR USE OF ELECTRONIC AND INFORMATION TECHNOLOGY—When developing, procuring, maintaining, or using electronic and information technology, each Federal department or agency, including the United States Postal Service, shall ensure, unless an undue burden would be imposed on the department or agency, that the electronic and information technology allows, regardless of the type of medium of the technology—
> (i) individuals with disabilities who are Federal employees to have access to and use of information and data that is comparable to the access to and use of the information and data by Federal employees who are not individuals with disabilities; and
> (ii) individuals with disabilities who are members of the public seeking information or services from a Federal department or agency to have access to and use of information and data that is comparable to the access to and use of the information and data by such members of the public who are not individuals with disabilities.

Section 508 took effect on June 21, 2001.

In the several years since the passage of the ADA, the possibility of large-scale resistance from employers has not occurred, even though the Act was necessarily accompanied by [bureaucratic apparatus] to ensure compliance. In April 2001, the Supreme Court agreed to hear two cases that related to provisions of the ADA. One case involved a disability claim based on a worker at a Toyota plant who suffered from carpal tunnel syndrome, a major affliction among workers, including computer users, whose primary work activities involve frequently repetitive motions. The decision, which may affect millions of workers, came down on January 8, 2002[46]:

> In a unanimous ruling narrowing the reach of the law that requires reasonable accommodations for disabled workers, the justices said a U.S. appeals court used the wrong standard by looking at whether an impairment prevented an employee from doing a specific, job-related manual task. In the opinion cheered by business groups, Justice Sandra Day O'Connor said the proper test involved whether the impairments prevented or restricted someone from performing tasks "that are of central importance to most people's daily lives."

The decision basically says that Congress intended the Act to apply only for serious disabilities that are long term and not for those that limit the ability to perform ordinary tasks in only a minor way: "Merely having an impairment does not make one disabled for purposes of the ADA," the court declared. "Claimants also need to demonstrate that the impairment limits a major life activity."[47] Thus the courts will not uphold minor limitations on access for the disabled.

Access to Libraries

Libraries have long taken a leading rule in providing access to a wide range of information resources for the disabled. Access to the Internet has become yet one more service that libraries are expected to provide and this responsibility translates into appropriate computers and interfaces. As mentioned, it is now quite common to encounter magnified letters on computer screens, oversized keyboards, and raised platforms to accommodate wheelchairs. Other technological aids, or assistive technologies, are voice interfaces and Braille displays. Also of concern is the form of the user interface, because depending on the nature of the disability, users may or may not be comfortable with graphics or text or sound. On January 16, 2001, the American Library Association Council (ALA) approved the policy, Library Services for People with Disabilities, to ensure that U.S. libraries provided the necessary service to disabled users, whether mandated by law or within the ALA's control. The policy covers such areas as library facilities, accessibility of the collection, availability of assistive technologies, and the availabilty of publications in alternative formats.[48]

A Very Personal Computer

The first cardiac pacemaker was implanted in a human in 1958, in Sweden, and the second a year later in the United States. These early devices emitted pulses in a fixed, regular pattern to overcome the condition known as heart block, in which the body's method for stimulating the heart operates intermittently. Unfortunately, this fixed-rate system of stimulation could occasionally cause the heart to beat too rapidly (tachycardia), resulting in death. Advances in design resulted in pacemakers that operated only on demand, when the body's natural stimulation failed. Eventually, pacemaker technology benefited from developments in microelectronics, and programmable microprocessors are currently being implanted. Physicians can vary such features as sensor-amplifier sensitivity, energy output per pulse, pulse width, pulse frequency, and delay between chamber pulses. In addition, system diagnostics are available over telephone lines to permit doctors to check the behavior of the pacemaker. Another innovation is a pacemaker that adjusts its rate in response to the patient's physical activity. One model determines this activity by measuring body motion and another is triggered by changes in blood temperature.[49]

Another serious heart disorder that is benefiting from new technology is called fibrillation, in which the heart suddenly goes into a chaotic state that restricts or stops circulation and can lead to death within a few minutes. Since action must be taken quickly, implantable defibrillators could save many lives by automatically detecting the onset of an attack. One current drawback is that they must be implanted during open-chest surgery, a traumatic and expensive operation. Under testing is a procedure for implanting the electrodes into the heart transvenously, similarly to the way pacemaker leads are implanted.[50] In July 1995, an atrial defibrillator was tested for the first time, as part of a national clinical trial. The device was being tested for "functionality, programmability, and data collection."[51] The next important technology under investigation is a single device to combine a pacemaker, a device to control arrhythmia, or irregular beat, and a defibrillator. A recent survey of pacemaker developments predicts improvement in the analysis of arrhythmia, "based on greater circuit sophistication and the ability to link information from the atrial and ventricular leads into an independent determination of rate from an artificial sensor."[52]

The next decade holds much promise as the computational power of microprocessors increases. For example it is expected that soon five channels of information will be available to pacemakers, or to use a more general term, implantable cardiac devices; these sources of information are "atrium, ventricle, two artificial sensors and an antitachycardia sensing channel specifically for the detection of tachycardia." [Early this century, pacemakers will have five channels to deliver shocks to stimulate the heart in various regions and for various purposes.]

MEDICINE AND THE INTERNET

> The use of telecommunications to deliver health services has the potential to reduce costs, improve quality, and improve access to care in rural and other underserved areas of the country.[53]

The Internet has begun to have an impact on the practice of medicine and more is promised as one of the major payoffs of the Information Age. The transmission of records, including medical images, is a fact of life and has permitted doctors to share knowledge and experiences over long distances. The term telemedicine has come into use to describe the host of medical services available over the Internet. Not surprisingly, the growth of telemedicine has been accompanied by a number of problems, both social and legal, including privacy and accuracy of medical records, the licensing of physicians, the efficacy of long-distance treatment, and the allocation of costs. The Internet has also fostered the creation of self-help and advice groups to facilitate the sharing of medical information among patients and relatives of patients. Of course doctors and other health practitioners have found the Internet to be an invaluable resource as well. Although the topic of telemedicine is the main focus of this chapter, other issues will be presented first to lay the groundwork.

Doctors and E-mail

One of the first byproducts of the growth of e-mail and a large population of users was the querying of physicians by their patients. As a followup of an appointment, asking a question, reporting a symptom, describing information discovered in an Internet search, or for a host of other reasons, sending an e-mail message to a doctor seems like a good idea. It certainly avoids being put on hold by the receptionist, but is it of any benefit to the doctor? If sufficient number of patients start to e-mail their doctor on a regular basis, his or her time may be compromised. For example, Dr. Adam Schneider, an internist, is not averse to using a computer as a regular part of his practice; in fact, "he is the one who configures all the computers for his practice."[54] But with all his expertise, he discourages use of e-mail and prefers that patients telephone him: "There are too many variables with e-mail as opposed to a patient picking up the phone," he said. "It's not, in my mind, as effective as the telephone."

Far more patients than doctors wish to use e-mail for communication. Doctors seem to be reluctant for a number of reasons including the following:[55]

> The doctors' concerns are many. Some are worried about the risks to doctor-patient confidentiality, while others are concerned that an electronic paper trail might increase their exposure to malpractice liability.

Other concerns go to the heart of medical practice in an era of managed care, when doctors find time for patients increasingly scarce and reimbursement rates diminishing. Give patients your e-mail address, some doctors say, and you are inviting trouble: they will overtax your already burdened day, and one sympathetic response could cascade into a flow of demands and questions.

In 1997, the American Medical Information Association (AMIA) produced a document, "Guidelines for the Clinical Use of Electronic Mail with Patients."[56] Below is a summary of the communication guidelines.

Summary of Communication Guidelines

- Establish turnaround time for messages. Do not use e-mail for urgent matters.
- Inform patients about privacy issues. Patients should know:
Who besides addressee processes messages
   During addressee's usual business hours.
   During addressee's vacation or illness.
That message is to be included as part of the medical record.
- Establish types of transactions (prescription refill, appointment scheduling, etc.) and sensitivity of subject matter (HIV, mental health, etc.) permitted over e-mail.
- Instruct patients to put category of transaction in subject line of message for filtering: "prescription," "appointment," "medical advice," "billing question."
- Request that patients put their name and patient identification number in the body of the message.
- Configure automatic reply to acknowledge receipt of messages.
- Print all messages, with replies and confirmation of receipt, and place in patient's paper chart.
- Send a new message to inform patient of completion of request.
- Request that patients use autoreply feature to acknowledge reading provider's message.
- Maintain a mailing list of patients, but do not send group mailings where recipients are visible to each other. Use blind copy feature in software.
- Avoid anger, sarcasm, harsh criticism, and libelous references to third parties in messages.

The non-medical parts of these guidelines could certainly be used in other contexts in which privacy, courtesy, and accuracy are important.

Doctors' Use of the Internet

The American Medical Association carried out a survey of 977 physicians, between August and December 2001, to determine the role of the Internet in their practices. The results indicate that the Internet has become an important factor in the practice of medicine. Among the most interesting findings in the survey are the following[57]:

- More than three-quarters (78 percent) of physicians surf the Web.
- Two-thirds of online physicians access the Web daily—an increase of 24 percent since 1997.
- The average number of hours a physician uses the Web per week jumped from 4.3 in 1997 to 7.1 in 2001.
- Approximately 3 of 10 physicians using the Internet currently have a Web site.
- The percentage of physicians aged 60 or older using the Internet increased from 43 percent in 2000 to 65 percent in 2001.

A majority of doctors have turned to the Internet precisely because so many of their patients are Internet users. This trend will continue. And it will expand. As reported on February 22, 2001, "three companies that operate most of the nation's managed care drug plans agreed yesterday to establish a joint system to make it easier for doctors to send prescriptions to pharmacies electronically or over the Internet."[58] The benefits of this system should be a substantial reduction in illegible or misinterpreted prescriptions and therefore an increase in the well-being of patients. Pharmacists will waste considerably less time in verifying illegible prescriptions.

Health Information on the Internet

As in may other areas of life, the Internet is a source of incredible amounts of information related to health issues. Some of the information is useful and helpful, while other information is inaccurate, misleading, and even dangerous. For the layman, the problem is to distinguish the quality of the contents of arbitrary Web sites. This concern resonates with most health care providers and professionals. In an article in the British Medical Journal, the authors report on a number of errors found in information at medical Web sites: "Somebody who doesn't know enough about a topic might think they have everything they need when there might be certain crucial things missing. It is very, very variable."[59] The authors go on to say that, "Our study shows that features of Web site credibility have only slight or at best moderate correlation with accuracy of information in five common health topics."

The survey company, Harris Interactive, regularly reports on people who go online to search for health information. It refers to them as "Cyberchondriacs." The highlights of a poll conducted in March 2002 are given as follows[60]:

- 80% of all adults who are online (i.e., 53% of all adults) sometimes use the Internet to look for health care information. However, only 18% say they do this "often", while most do so "sometimes" (35%), or "hardly ever" (27%).
- This 80% of all those online amounts to 110 million cyberchondriacs nationwide. This compares with 54 million in 1998, 69 million in 1999 and 97 million last year.

- On average those who ever look for health care information online do so three times every month.
- A slender majority (53%) of those who look for health care information does so using a portal or search engine which allows them to search for the health information they want across many different websites. About a quarter (26%) go directly to a site that focuses only on health-related topics and one in eight (12%) goes first to a general site that focuses on many topics that may have a section on health issues.

In mid-2003, the Pew Internet & American Life Project reported on Internet medical resources and their use patterns. Result of this survey reinforce the belief that increasing numbers of Americans are obtaining health information from the Internet. Consider the following highlights[61]:

- Fully 80% of adult Internet users, or about 93 million Americans, have searched for at least one of 16 major health topics online. [For example, specific disease or medical problem, certain medical treatment or procedure, diet, nutrition or procedure]. This makes the act of looking for health or medical information one of the most popular activities online, after email (93%) and researching a product or service before buying it (83%).

Among other things, Internet users:

- Search for health information at any time of the day or night.
- Research a diagnosis or prescription.
- Prepare for surgery or find out how best to recover from one.
- Get tips from other caregivers and e-patients about dealing with a particular symptom.
- Give and receive emotional support.
- Keep family and friends informed of a loved one's condition.
- Find humor and even joy in a bad situation.
- Women are more likely than men to seek health care and health information, so it is no surprise that they lead the way with Internet health. Some 85% of online women have searched for at least one of these 16 health topics, compared to 75% of men. Wired women are also considerably more likely than wired men to have sought information on multiple health topics.
- Although very large numbers of Internet users conduct health searches, most do so infrequently. Eight out of ten of those who have conducted health searches say they do so every few months or less frequently than that. Indeed, on a typical day, just 6% of Internet users look for health or medical information online (by contrast, 49% use email, 19% research a product or service, and 5% buy a product online). More than half of those who recently conducted searches did so on behalf of someone else—a spouse, child, friend, or other loved one—not for themselves.
- In addition to information searches, Internet users are increasingly going to disease- or situation-specific support sites and using email to discuss health issues with family, friends, and (to a lesser degree) doctors.

So far the discussion has focused on the availability, to the general public, of medical information on the Internet with little about the possibilities of actual online treatment and therapy. Next we turn to this area, usually referred to as telemedicine.

Telemedicine

From a report, "Bringing Health Care Online: The Role of Information Technologies," by the now-defunct Office of Technology Assessment, "Telemedicine can be broadly defined as the use of information technology to deliver medical services and information from one location to another."[62] It is clear that the quality of medical care is not uniformly distributed across most countries or even within countries because of lack of expertise, lack of economic resources, and lack of political will. There is now a general belief that the use of information technology, especially communications technology as manifested on the Internet, provides the means to deliver high-quality medical care to those regions previously ill-served. Thus telemedicine has the promise to reduce costs of medical delivery, to increase general access, and to improve the quality of care. But some issues must be resolved if the benefits of the widespread diffusion of telemedicine are to be realized. Therefore, consider the following issues[63]:

Reimbursement for Services
A critical issue for telemedicine is whether and how it will be reimbursed by Medicare/Medicaid and other third-party payers. In rural areas, up to 40 percent of physicians' patient base consists of Medicare/Medicaid patients. As one congressman testified at a 1994 hearing on rural health care:
Telemedicine is particularly important to rural health delivery systems. . . . However, without the assurance of payment for telemedicine services, the full potential of telemedical technology will never be realized. . . . This administrative roadblock prevents the development and expansion of these systems in rural America.

Lack of Research/Experience
Another barrier to telemedicine is the lack of research demonstrating its safety and efficacy, clinical utility, and cost-effectiveness. This is a problem for potential users, payers, and policy-makers. No one knows for certain which medical conditions are best suited to the use of telemedicine. . . . Early experiments in telemedicine were terminated before they produced answers concerning its cost, impact on access, and effects on quality of care. Those projects did not end because they failed to achieve their objectives. Instead, the reasons included:

1) lack of familiarity and limited experience with the systems,
2) lack of institutional commitments to sustain them when outside funding ran out,
3) lack of incentives for physicians to use the systems,
4) limitations of the technology, and
5) poor system planning and design.

Telecommunications Infrastructure
The technology exists to provide a wide variety of telemedicine services over regular telephone lines. In many rural areas, however, the telecommunications infrastructure does not provide a medical facility with sufficient bandwidth to carry the necessary signals for interactive video teleconsultations. . . . Delivering health care to the home is increasingly important for people who need convalescent or chronic care. A public network that can provide two-way video, high speed data transfer, and graphics is required before a wide range of health services can be delivered directly to the home.

Legal/Regulatory
Remote diagnosis and treatment across state lines could bring differing laws and regulations into conflict. Telemedicine raises a number of legal issues related to privacy/confidentiality, licensing and credentialing, and liability that could represent significant barriers to its broader diffusion.

• *Privacy and Confidentiality*
Privacy in health care information has been protected in two ways: 1) in the historical ethical obligations of the health care provider to maintain the confidentiality of medical information, and 2) in a legal right to privacy, both generally and specifically, in health information.
Confidentiality involves control over who has access to information.

• *Physician Licensing*
Physicians must be licensed by the states in which they practice. Telecommunication facilitates consultations without respect to state borders and could conceivably require consultants to be licensed in a number of states. This would be impractical and is likely to constrain the broader diffusion of telemedicine programs. In July 1994, the State of Kansas passed legislation requiring that out-of-state physicians who provide consultations using telemedicine be licensed in Kansas. The licensing problem for telemedicine could be addressed by the implementation of national licensing standards or the classification of physicians practicing telemedicine as consulting physicians, thereby circumventing state rules. For a start, such a national license could be provided to physicians who provide consultations to *underserved* populations.

• *Liability*
The liability implications of telemedicine are unclear. At least two aspects of telemedicine could pose liability problems. One is the fact that, in a remote consultation, the specialist does not perform a hands-on examination, which could be regarded as delivering less than adequate care. The second aspect is that the use of compressed video, in which repetitious information is eliminated as the data are converted from analog to digital and back, may raise the issue of diagnosing with less than complete information. On the other hand, telemedicine may, in fact, decrease the threat of malpractice suits by providing better record keeping and databases, and the fact that taping the consultations will automatically provide proof of the encounter. Tapes could also help to prove the innocence of providers who are falsely accused.

This degree of detail is necessary to illustrate that what appears to be an obviously worthwhile and effective technological solution to a pressing need may be accompanied by a host of problems, some relatively easy to solve and some very difficult. Interestingly, most of the problems are not technical in nature. Most studies of telemedicine have recognized these problems and have called for cooperation among state and federal agencies, and professional organizations. Thus a report issued by the Western Governors' Association recognized six barriers to the successful implementation of telemedicine[64]: Infrastructure Planning and Development, Telecommunications Regulation, Reimbursement for Telemedicine Services, Licensure and Credentialing, Medical Malpractice Liability, and Confidentiality. To provide a flavor of the kind of steps necessary to make telemedicine a commonly available medium for health care delivery, consider the following recommended actions to deal with the licensure barrier.

It is recommended that a broadly-based task force be established to draw up a "Uniform State Code for Telemedicine Licensure and Credentialing (similar in principle to the Uniform Commercial Code)."[65] This task force would have to be concerned with a variety of licensing issues such as licensing of doctors to practice telemedicine, licensing of the networks themselves with respect to their adequacy, and reciprocity issues for interstate licensing. Those advocating a more rapid adoption of telemedicine argue that these barriers must be overcome so that people living in rural areas, especially, will be able to benefit from improved medical care. Furthermore, health care professionals will be in much closer and effective contact with their colleagues, thus alleviating concern with isolation and lack of familiarity with current medical theory and practice.

How have these ideas and goals evolved? The National Research Council reported on a study carried out in 1999 titled, *Networking Health: Prescriptions for the Internet*.[66] The study was very far-ranging and suggested the following possibilities for the Internet, some of which already exist:

- Enable consumers to access their health records, enter data or information on symptoms, and receive computer-generated suggestions for improving health and reducing risk;
- Allow emergency room physicians to identify an unconscious patient and download the patient's medical record from a hospital across town;
- Deliver care instructions to a traveling businessperson who begins to feel chest pains while in a hotel room;
- Enable homebound patients to consult with care providers over real-time video connections from home, using medical devices capable of transmitting information over the Internet;
- Support teams of specialists from across the country who wish to plan particularly challenging surgical procedures by manipulating shared three-dimensional images and simulating different operative approaches;
- Allow a health plan to provide instantaneous approval for a referral to a specialist and to schedule an appointment electronically;

- Enable public health officials to detect potential contamination of the public water supply by analyzing data on nonprescription sales of antidiarrheal remedies in local pharmacies;
- Help medical students and practitioners access, from the examining room, clinical information regarding symptoms they have never before encountered; and
- Permit biomedical researchers at a local university to create three-dimensional images of a biological structure using an electron microscope a thousand miles away.

In response to the development of a new form of medical practice, doctors have been concerned about how their responsibilities may have changed and what may now be expected of them. In 1999, the World Medical Association (WMA) adopted a statement with respect to medical practice in the new environment.[67] One crucial element is to ensure that doctors do not permit the technology to affect the basic ethics of medical practice and so the following clause appears:

> Telemedicine must not adversely affect the individual physician-patient relationship. When used properly, telemedicine has the potential to enhance this relationship through increased opportunities to communicate and improved access by both parties. As in all fields of medicine, the physician-patient relationship must be based on mutual respect, the independence of judgement [sic] of the physician, autonomy of the patient and professional confidentiality. It is essential that the physician and the patient be able to reliably identify each other when telemedicine is employed.

There is much more that is valuable and necessary in this document and the WMA recommended that all national bodies adopt it.

SOCIAL ISSUES

> In the evolving information infrastructure, there may be a unique role for the federal government to play to assure that CHI [Consumer Health Information] "systems" are not used as tools to breach issues of patient confidentiality and privacy. The public should be able to access CHI in completely anonymous (e.g., at home or privately in libraries) or confidential (clinical practice settings) ways.[68]

Perhaps the most serious charge against the use of computers in medical care, or in the health delivery system, is that they tend to dehumanize the patient-physician relationship. This argument suggests that doctors will shunt patients toward computers to increase their income by treating more patients. For the foreseeable future, computers will not be treating people directly; they will be an adjunct to doctors, complementing their knowledge.

But what about large information systems, in which the patient is just a record to be scanned, modified, and, of course, billed? It is certainly possible for patients to be treated in a dehumanizing way in a large medical center. The question is whether or not the use of computers aggravates this situation. Critics of computers in medical care argue that by their very nature the machines, and the organizational structure in which they are embedded, tend to centralize control, diminish individual responsibility, and inevitably will decrease the human quality in the relationship. On the other hand, information systems that assume much of the routine clerical work in hospitals and offices should free conscientious physicians to spend more time with their patients.

Hardly anyone could disagree with the important applications made feasible by computers in body imagery, education, and devices for the disabled. Surely the ability to diagnose internal problems by relatively noninvasive means is an incalculable benefit. But even here, the haste with which hospitals rush to acquire million-dollar machines makes many uncomfortable. The motivation seems to be a concern with status and prestige rather than the therapeutic benefits. CAT scanners seem to typify a large-machine mentality at the heart of the U.S. medical system. It is easier to purchase a large machine than to provide preventive medical care for the less fortunate members of the community. In the case of microprocessor-based equipment for the disabled, there should be no argument against the significant and beneficial changes made in the lives of such people. However, there seems to be an imbalance in that relatively large amounts of money have been made available for treatment and equipment for relatively few individuals. On the other side it is argued that costs are high in the initial experimental phases, but in the long run many will benefit.

Let us explore these issues a bit further, given their importance and impact on the health care of the American public. Two obvious questions are how much has technology improved the overall level of health care and how much does medical technology contribute to the rising costs of health care. These are both very complex questions and no ready answers are available.

Genetic Testing

One area of medical technology that has not been mentioned yet is genetic testing. The information derived from performing a wide range of genetic tests has considerable impact that affects individuals and society in many ways. For example consider the following issues associated with genetic testing reported in a mid-1990s study[69]:

- They have the ability to predict risks of future disease. Seldom however, does the predictability approach certainty.
- Often no independent test is available to confirm the prediction of a genetic test; only the appearance of the disease itself confirms the prediction.

- The results may confront prospective parents with options regarding reproduction, including, artificial insemination, prenatal diagnosis, termination of
pregnancy, in utero treatment, or cesarean section instead of vaginal delivery.
- The results provide genetic information relevant to the future health of
relatives.
- For many genetic disorders, no interventions are yet available to cure,
prevent or ameliorate future disease. For some others, the interventions
that are being tried have not yet been demonstrated to be safe and effective.
- People identified as at risk of disease may experience psychological distress, discrimination and stigmatization.
- Because the frequencies of disease related alleles differ between ethnic
groups, the appropriateness of many tests, and the interpretation of the
results, is influenced by the ethnicity of the person being tested.
- Most health care providers have received little training in genetics.
- The number of medical geneticists and genetic counselors to whom
patients can be referred is likely to remain too small to cope with the potential volume of testing.

As more and more genetic information is accumulated, the potential for
beneficial uses as well as misuses mounts. This rather simplistic observation
has not been lost on the scientific community, especially since the
remarkable achievement announced on February 12, 2001. A draft sequence
of the human genome had been achieved by both the U.S. government-
sponsored Human Genome Project and the private company, Celera
Genomics. Ethical issues related to the use of genetic information and the
role of technology in genetics are coming to public attention and will remain
there for years to come.

SUMMARY

The practice of medicine is slowly being affected by the use of computers in
record keeping, diagnosis, treatment, the Internet, and research.

Beyond the direct application of storing patient records, medical
information can serve a variety of needs, including medical research.
Computer databases, which can be searched more easily than manual ones,
can uncover trends and access individual records at a distance. Systems vary
in range of functions, ease of use, and ability to accommodate new data-
processing responsibilities. In medical diagnosis, computers play a vital role
in the new area of body imaging, which includes such systems as CAT
scanners, PET scanners, and NMR systems. Other important computer
applications are the automated electronic monitoring of patients and the use
of medical robots for teaching purposes.

The linking of computers to communication systems and to physical
manipulators has provided new opportunities for disabled people to escape

the boundaries of their beds and homes. The Kurzweil Reading Machine helps visually impaired people to access material not available in Braille automatically and quickly. Other aids for people with disabilities are still in the experimental stage. New microprocessor-driven pacemakers are being used to deal with various cardiac problems. In addition, they facilitate long-distance patient monitoring and treatment.

The Internet has begun to be used for experiments in telemedicine—the delivery of health care over long distances. A variety of issues must be dealt with, however, before telemedicine can become more commonplace, such as legal responsibility and cost-sharing.

Some commentators have expressed concern that an increasing use of technology in the medical delivery system will lead to dehumanization of the doctor-patient relationship. Large expenditures for medical technology have also been criticized as an allocation of resources away from the important needs of preventive care.

NOTES

1. U.S. Congress, Office of Technology Assessment. *Bringing Health Care Online: The Role of Information Technologies,* OTA-ITC-624. (Washington, DC: U.S. Government Printing Office, September 1995), p. 14. Available at http://www.wws.princeton.edu/~ota/
2. *Ibid.*, p. 30.
3. "DOD's New Health Care System," *SIGBIO Newsletter,* 10(3) September 1988, p. 81.
4. From "Medical ADP Systems: Defense Achieves Worldwide Deployment of Composite Health Care System," United States General Accounting Office, GAO/AIMD-96-39, April 1996, p. 2. Available at http://www.gao.gov/monthly.list/ai96039.pdf
5. *Ibid.*, pp. 18–19.
6. U.S. General Accounting Office. "Computer-based Patient Records: Better Planning and Oversight by VA, DOD, and IHS Would Enhance Health Data Sharing," Report to Congressional Committees, April 2001. Available at http://www.gao.gov/new.items/d01459.pdf
7. *Ibid.*
8. Richard S. Dick., Elaine B. Steen., and Don E. Detmer (Eds.) *The Computer-Based Patient Record: An Essential Technology for Health Care, Revised Edition.* (Washington, DC: National Academy Press, 1997). Summary available at http://www.nap.edu/catalog/5306.html
9. Paul C. Tang and W. Ed Hammond. "A Progress Report on Computer-Based Patient Records in the United States." In Richard S. Dick et al. (Eds.). *The Computer-Based Patient Record: An Essential Technology for Health Care, Revised Edition,* 1997. Also available at http://bob.nap.edu/html/computer/commentary.html#us

10. "Summary." In Richard S. Dick et al. (Eds.). *The Computer-Based Patient Record: An Essential Technology for Health Care, Revised Edition*, 1997. Also available at: http://bob.nap.edu/html/computer/commentary.html#summary

11. Giselle Weiss. "Welcome to the (Almost) Digital Hospital," *IEEE Spectrum*, March 2002, pp. 44–49.

12. National Research Council. *For the Record: Protecting Electronic Health Information*. (Washington, DC: National Academy Press, 1997). Available at http://bob.nap.edu/html/for/contents.html

13. *Ibid.*

14. *Op cit.*, *Bringing Health Care Online: The Role of Information Technologies*.

15. *Ibid.*, p. 41.

16. U.S. Congress, Office of Technology Assessment. *MEDLARS and Health Information Policy*, OTA-TM-H-11 (Washington, DC: U.S. Government Printing Office, September 1982).

17. The National Public Library. Available at http://www.nlm.nih.gov/publications/factsheets/nlm.html

18. "Medline Is No Longer Available Through Internet Grateful Med (IGM)," United States National Library of Medicine. January 31, 2002. Available at http://www.nlm.nih.gov/databases/freemedl.html

19. "Internet Grateful Med' Goes on the World Wide Web," Available at http://www.nlm.nih.gov/new_noteworthy/press_releases/igmpr.html

20. *Ibid.*

21. U.S. Congress, Office of Technology Assessment. *Identifying Health Technologies That Work: Searching for Evidence,* OTA-H-608 (Washington: U.S. Government Printing Office, September 1994). Available at http://www.ota.nap.edu/pdf/data/1994/9414.pdf

22. Richard Gordon, Gabor T. Herman, and Steven A. Johnson. "Image Reconstruction From Projections," *Scientific American,* October 1975, pp. 56–61, 64–68.

23. "Computerized Axial Tomography," MedExpert.net, November 3, 1998. Available at http://www.medexpert.net/medinfo/catscan.htm

24. "Tomography (CT Scan)," Radiology Channel, January 3, 2002. Available at http://www.radiologychannel.net/computerizedtomography/

25. "What You Should Know About Magnetic Resonance Imaging," The Magnetic Resonance Imaging Center, The University of Iowa Hospitals and Clinics. August 28, 1995. Available at http://vh.radiology.uiowa.edu/Patients/PatientDept/RadiologyBrochures/MR/MRI.WhatYouShouldKnow.html

26. "What is PET?" University of Iowa PET Imaging Center, August 14, 2002. Available at thttp://pet.radiology.uiowa.edu/

27. Christopher R. Johnson. "Computational Bioimaging for Medical Diagnosis and Treatment," *Communications of the ACM*, Vol. 44, No. 3, March 2001, pp. 74–76.

28. William J. Dallas. "A Digital Prescription for X-Ray Overload," *IEEE Spectrum*, April 1990, pp. 33–36.

29. *Ibid.*, p. 33.

30. Robert B. Lufkin and Anne Scheck. "Fasten Your Seatbelt: MRI in for a Wild Ride, *Diagnostic Imaging*, 1996. Available at http://www.dimag.com/feature.htm

31. David Brown. "Intensive Care, From a Distance," *The Washington Post*, June 2, 2002, p. A01.

32. "A Cut Above Traditional Surgery," *Wired News Report*, August 15, 2000. Available at http://www.wired.com/news/technology/0,1282,38250,00.html

32a. Julia Sheeres. "Surgeons Here, Patients There." *Wired News Report*, September 19, 2001. Available at http://www.wired.com/news/medtech/0,1286,46946, 00.html

32b. *Ibid.*

33. Bruce G. Buchanan and Edward H. Shortliffe (Eds.). *Rule-Based Expert Systems: The MYCIN Experiments of the Stanford Heuristic Programming Project.* (Reading, MA: Addison-Wesley, 1984).

34. John A. Adam. "Medical Electronics," *IEEE Spectrum*, January 1996, pp. 92–95.

35. "Technology-Related Assistance for Individuals with Disabilities Act of 1988 as Amended in 1994," Public Laws 110-407 and 103-218, Section 2. Findings and Purposes. Available at http://www.gsa.gov/coca/tech_act.htm

36. Jack McNeil. "Americans With Disabilities," Current Population Reports, 1997 (Issued February 2001). Available at http://www.census.gov/prod/2001pubs/ p70-73.pdf

37. Alber M. Cook and Susan M. Hussey. *Assistive Technologies: Principles and Practice.* (St. Louis, MO: Mosby-Year Book, Inc., no date). Available at http://www.asel.udel.edu/at-online/publications/chapter.html

38. "More Americans Facing Blindness Than Ever Before," National Eye Institute, National Institutes of Health, March 22, 2002. Available at http://www.nih.gov/ news/pr/mar2002/nei-20.htm

39. Gislin Dagnelie and Robert W. Massof. "Toward an Artificial Eye," *IEEE Spectrum*, May 1996, pp. 20–29.

40. "Hearing Aids," National Institutes of Health, NIH Pub No. 99-4340, February 2001. Available at http://www.nidcd.nih.gov/HealthyHearing/tools/pdf/ HearingAids.pdf

40a. *Ibid.*, p. 192.

41. David Colker, "Giving Disabled a Voice," *The Los Angeles Times*, April 8, 2002. Available at http://www.latimes.com/technology/la-000025027apr08.story? coll=la%2Dheadlines%2Dtechnology

42. Ian Austen. "A Leg With a Mind of Its Own," *The New York Times*, January 3, 2002, Late Edition—Final, Section G, p. 1.

43. *Progress Report on Alzheimer's Disease, 2000*, National Institute on Aging, National Institutes of Health, 2001. Available at http://www.alzheimers.org /pubs/prog00.htm

44. Mark Baard. "AI to Assist Alzheimer's Patients," Wired.com, June 24, 2002. Available at http://www.wired.com/news/print/0,1294,53028,00.html

45. "Workforce Investment Act Laws and Regulations," U.S. Department of Labor Employment & Training Administration, (No date). Available at http://www.doleta.gov/usworkforce/asp/act.asp

46. "Court Restricts Employees Disability Claims," Reuters, Cnet.com, January 8, 2002. Available at http://news.cnet.com/news/0-1005-200-8407357.html?tag=prntfr

47. Edward Walsh. "High Court Narrows Disabilities Act's Scope," *The Washington Post*, January 9, 2002, p. A01.

48. "Library Services for People With Disabilities Policy," American Library Association, September 28, 2001. Available at http://www.ala.org/access_policy. html

49. Elizabeth Corcoran. "Medical Electronics," *IEEE Spectrum*, January 1987, pp. 66–68.

50. Karen Fitzgerald. "Medical Electronics," *IEEE Spectrum*, January 1989, pp. 67–69.

51. "Atrial Defibrillator Tested for the First Time in Milwaukee," Doctor's Guide to the Internet, July 28, 1995. Available at http://www.pslgroup.com/dg950731.htm

52. Seymour Furman. "A Brief History of Cardiac Stimulation and Electrophysiology—The Past Fifty Years and the Next Century," from Keynote Address at NASPE (the North American Society of Pacing and Electrophysiology), 1995. Available at http://webaxis.com/heartweb/history3.htm

53. *Op cit.*, *Bringing Health Care Online*, p. 161.

54. Katie Hafner. " 'Dear Doctor' Meets 'Return to Sender'," *The New York Times*, January 6, 2002, Late Edition—Final, Section G, p. 1.

55. *Ibid.*

56. "Guidelines for the Clinical Use of Electronic Mail With Patients," American Medical Informatics Association, 1997. Available at http://www.amia.org/ pubs/other/email_guidelines.html (Reprinted from the *Journal of the American Medical Informatics Association*, Vol. 5, Num. 1, Jan/Feb 1998.)

57. Robyn Greenspan. "Physicians Net Usage UP," CyberAtlas, July 22, 2002. Available at http://cyberatlas.internet.com/markets/healthcare/0,,10101_ 1430741,00.html

58. Milt Freudenheim. "A Plan to Send Prescriptions Electronically," *The New York Times*, February 23, 2001, Late Edition—Final, Section C, p. 2.

59. "Experts Raise Alarm Over Health Info on Internet," Reuters, SiliconValley.com, March 8, 2002. Available at http://www.siliconvalley.com/docs/news/reuters_ wire/17011101.htm

60. "Cyberchondriacs Update," The Harris Poll #21, Harris Interactive, May 1, 2002. Available at URL://http://www.harrisinteractive.com/harris_poll/index. asp?PID=299

61. "Internet Health Resources," Pew Internet & American Life Project, July 16, 2003. Available at http://www.pewinternet.org/reports/pdfs/PIP_ Health_Report_July_2003.pdf

62. *Op cit., Bringing Health Care Online*, p. 159.

63. *Ibid.*, pp. 177–184.

64. "The Western Governors' Association Telemedicine Action Report," 1995. Accessed at http://www.arentfox.com/telemed.western.html

65. *Ibid.*

66. National Research Council. *Networking Health: Prescriptions for the Internet.* (Washington, DC: National Academy Press, 2000). Available at http://books.nap.edu/html/networking_health/

67. "Statement on Accountability, Responsibilities and Ethical Guidelines in the Practice of Telemedicine," World Medical Association, October 1999. Available at http://www.wma.net/e/policy/17-36_e.html

68. Kevin Patrick and Shannah Koss. "Consumer Health Information White Paper," Health Information and Application Working Group, Committee on

Applications and Technology, Information Infrastructure Task Force, May 15, 1995. Available at http://nii.nist.gov/chi.html

69. "Interim Principles Task Force on Genetic Testing," NIH-DOE Working Group on Ethical, Legal, and Social Implications of Human Genome Research, March 1996. Available on the Web site http://infonet.welch.jhu.edu/policy/genetics/

ADDITIONAL READINGS

Medical Information Systems

Bennahum, David, "Docs for Docs," *Wired*, March 1995, pp. 100, 102, 104.

Grossman, Jerome H. "Plugged-In Medicine." *Technology Review*, January 1994, pp. 22–29.

Kennedy, Maggie. "Integration Fever." *Computerworld*, April 3, 1995, pp. 81, 84–85.

Kolata, Gina. "New Frontier in Research: Mining Patient Record," *The New York Times*, August 9, 1994, p. A10.

Medical Applications

Blanck, Peter David. "Celebrating Communications Technology for Everyone," *Federal Communications Law Journal*, Vol. 47, Num. 2, December 1994. Also available at http://www.law.indiana.edu/fclj/v47/no2/blanck.html

"The Cutting Edge of Virtual Reality," *The Economist*, March 24, 2001. Available at the Economist Web site, http://www.economist.com. Note that access must be paid for.

Ditlea, Steve. "RoboSurgeons: *Technology Review*, November/December 2000. Available at http://www.technologyreview.com/articles/ditlea1100.asp

"Magnetic Resonance Imaging FAQs," FONAR, Melville, NY, March 5, 1996. Available at http://www.fonar.com/faq.html

Computers and the Disabled

Kotler, Steven. "Vision Quest, Half Century of Artificial Research Has Succeeded. And Now this Blind Man Can See," *Wired*, September 2002. Available at http://www.wired.com/wired/archive/10.09/vision_pr.html

Norman, Richard A., Maynard, Edwin M., Guillory, K. Shane, and W. Warren, David J. "Cortical Implants for the Blind," *IEEE Spectrum*, May 1996, pp. 54–59.

Stipp, David. "New Hope for the Heart," *Fortune*, June 24, 1996, pp. 108–112.

"When the Americans With Disabilities Act Goes Online: Application of the ADA to the Internet and the Worldwide Web," National Council on Disability, July 10, 2003. Available at http://www.ncd.gov/newsroom/publications/adainternet.html

Wyatt, John and Rizzo, Joseph. "Ocular Implants for the Blind," *IEEE Spectrum*, May 1996, pp. 47–53.

Medicine and the Internet

"Innovation, Demand, and Investment in Telehealth," United States Department of Commerce, Technology Administration, June 19, 2002. Available at http://www.ta.doc.gov/reports/TechPolicy/Telehealth-020619.htm

Moore, Samuel. "Extending Healthcare's Reach," *IEEE Spectrum*, January 2002, pp. 66–71.

Patrick, Kevin and Koss, Shannah. "Consumer Health Information 'White Paper'," Information Infrastructure Task Force, Working Draft, May 1995. Available at http://nii.nist.gov/chi.html

Scanlon, Bill. "The Internet Preps for a Medical Miracle," Interactive Week, March 19, 2001. Available at http://www.zdnet.com/zdnn/stories/news/0,4586,2696791,00.html

Telemedicine Information Exchange. Available at http://tie.telemed.org/

"Transforming Health Care Through Technology," President's Information Technology Advisory Committee, February 2001. Available at http://www.itrd.gov/pubs/pitac/pitac-hc-9Feb01.pdf

"Vital Decisions: How Internet Users Decide What Information to Trust When They or Their Loved Ones Are Sick," Pew Internet & American Life Project, May 22, 2002. Available at http://www.pewinternet.org/reports/pdfs/PIP_Vital_ Decisions_May2002.pdf

"Wired for Health and Well-Being: The Emergence of Interactive Health Communication," Science Panel on Interactive Communication and Health, Department of Health and Human Services, April 1999. Available at http://www.health.gov/scipich/pubs/report/wired-pb.pdf

Social Issues

"A Survey of the Future of Medicine," *The Economist*, March 19, 1994, pp. 1–18.

"Avoiding the Crisis: Protecting the Confidentiality of Patient Data in a Healthcare Information Network Environment," Gordon & Glickson PC, 1995. Available at http://www.ggtech.com/pdf/96032.pdf

Lewontin, Richard. *It Ain't Necessarily So: The Dream of the Human Genome and other Illusions*. (New York: New York Review of Books, 2000).

Magnusson, Paul. "Give Medicare a Shot of Managed Care," *Business Week*, June 24, 1996, p. 122.

National Research Council. *For the Record: Protecting Electronic Health Information*. (Washington, DC: National Academy Press, 1997). Available at http://www.nap.edu/catalog/5595.html

Symonds, William C. "Whither a Health-Care Solution? Oh, Canada," *Business Week*, March 21, 1994, pp. 82–83, 85.

6

COMPUTERS AND EDUCATION

[A]lthough new interactive technologies cannot alone solve the problems of American education, they have already contributed to important improvements in learning. These tools can play an even greater role in advancing the substance and process of education, both by helping children acquire basic skills and by endowing them with more sophisticated skills so that they can acquire and apply knowledge over their lifetimes.

U.S. Congress Office of Technology Assessment, *Power On! New Tools for Teaching and Learning,* 1988.

INTRODUCTION

In 1866, the blackboard was hailed as a revolutionary device certain to have a significant impact on the educational process. Since then, "revolutionary" changes have appeared more frequently: radio in the 1920s, film in the 1930s and 1940s, language laboratories and television in the 1950s, beginning in the 1960s, the computer, and in the mid-1990s, the Internet and the World Wide Web. Claims for the last two have been mounting ever since. Computers and the Internet will allow students to learn at their own pace. They will not be judgmental, impatient, or unsympathetic. Appearance, social class, and race are irrelevant.[1] The teacher will be free to devote quality time to those with real need while others acquire information, review material, take tests, or even play games. The computer will keep track of the student's progress, produce grades and averages, suggest additional material, and alert the teacher to any potential or actual problem. More and more material will be made available on an ever-increasing number of subjects on the Web. The computer itself and the Web will excite students, igniting their native curiosity and natural desire to learn. New programming languages and systems will appear, opening up innovative and challenging environments. In short, it is claimed, teaching and learning will never be the same.

In spite of the near saturation of computers in the classroom and the near universal connectivity of schools to the Internet, the controversy persists with respect to the ultimate value of computers and education. There seems to be little doubt that the Web is a source of information without parallel, but access should never be equated with anything beyond just that, the ability to download possibly relevant content. The rough equivalence is borrowing a book from the library and confusing this first modest step with actually having read the book. Having is not reading and reading is not knowing. With these cautionary remarks in mind, we will examine the growth in computers in the classroom, the kinds of programs being used in the service of certain explicit and frequently unstated goals, and the diverse response to the rapid growth of technology in the schools. Of equal if not greater importance is the training and motivation of teachers. In this domain, statistics are plentiful and in what follows, some highlights and interesting results will be presented.

The growth in the number of computers in use in U.S. schools during the 1980s was significant. From 1981 to 1987, the percentage of schools with at least one computer grew as follows: Elementary schools, from 10% to 95%, Junior high schools, from 25% to 97%, Senior high schools, from 43% to 98%.[2] The total number of computers in public schools rose from 250,000 in 1983 to 2.4 million in 1989 to 3.5 million in 1992.[3] Student computer use in school and at home was reported by the Bureau of the Census in early 1995 for data gathered in 1993. For purposes of comparison, data from 1984 and 1989 are also included. Among the highlights are the following[4]:

- In 1993, more than two-thirds of all students in grades 1–12 used a computer either at home or at school, with a majority, 66 percent, using a computer at school.
- The percentage of students in grades 1–12 using a computer at school more than doubled between 1984 and 1993, increasing from 31 to 66 percent. Twenty-seven percent of students used a computer at home in 1993, up from 13 percent in 1984.
- Whites were more likely than blacks or Hispanics to use a computer either at home or at school, both in grades 1–6 and in grades 7–12. In 1993, approximately 40 percent of blacks and Hispanics in grades 1–6 did not use computers at all compared to 20 percent of their white counterparts.
- Between 1984 and 1993, the proportions of students in grades 7–12 who used a computer either at home or at school increased at similar levels across family income. On one hand, the gain for low income students can be explained primarily by their increased use of computers at school, which rose 32 percentage points; on the other, the gain for high income students can be explained by their increased use of computers at school,

which rose 30 percentage points, and at home, which rose 29 percentage points.

We now turn to the results of more recent surveys. The source of much information about education in the U.S. is the National Center for Education Statistics (NCES). It issues regular comprehensive reports on many aspects of education, including computer related issues. NCES commissioned a major survey in the spring of 1999 to determine how teachers use computers and the Internet. The first finding is that "99 percent of full-time regular public school teachers reported they had access to computers or the Internet somewhere in their schools."[5] They use these resources for the purposes listed in Table 6.1 with percentages of teachers shown.

In more recent years, the number of computers in classrooms and Internet connections in schools as well as classrooms has increased dramatically. Two measures should serve to illustrate this dramatic growth. From 1998 to 2001, the average number of students per instructional computer fell from 6.3 to 4.2 and the average number of students per internet-connected computer fell from 19.7 to 6.8.[6] From 1994 to 2000, the number of schools with Internet access rose from about 35% to about 98%; for instructional rooms, the increase was from about 3% to 77%. Some selective statistics follow[7]:

> The total computer usage rate of students at school increased from 59 percent in 1993 to 69 percent in 1997. The rate for grades 1 to 8 increased from 69 percent in 1993 to 79 percent in 1997. The school computer usage rate in 1997 was 70 percent for students in high school and 65 percent for undergraduate students in college. At that time, sizable percentages of students used computers at home, though fewer actually used them for schoolwork. About 43 percent of elementary school children used computers at home and about 24 percent used them for schoolwork. Students at the high school and undergraduate levels were more likely than elementary school children to use home computers for schoolwork.

It is clear that the number of computers has been increasing dramatically over the years and that more and more students have been using them both at school and at home. It remains to explore how much time students spend at the computer, that is, how integrated computer use is in the curriculum at large, how effective computers are in the education process (a very difficult question to answer), and how newer technologies such as connection to the Internet are being used.

A comprehensive survey released in August 2002 by the Pew Internet & American Life Project provides detailed information on the topics at hand.[8] Consider the highlights of this report, the results of extensive interviews with "14 gender-balanced, racially diverse focus groups of 136 students

TABLE 6.1

TEACHERS USING COMPUTERS AND THE INTERNET FOR A VARIETY OF PURPOSES WITH VARYING SKILL LEVELS

School and teacher Characteristics	Create instructional materials	Administrative record-keeping	Communicate with colleagues	Gather information for planning lessons	Multimedia classroom presentations	Access research and best practices for teaching	Communicate with parents or students	Access model lesson plans
1. All public school teachers with access to computers or the Internet at school	39	34	23	16	8	7	7	6
Teachers' feeling of Preparedness:								
2. All Public School Teachers	78	51	50	59	36	37	25	34

1. Percent of Teachers Indicating They Use Computers or the Internet "A Lot" at School to Accomplish Various Objectives: 1999

2. Percent of all Teachers Who Reported Using Computers and the Internet for Various Activities at School, by How Well Prepared They Felt to Use Computers or the Internet for Instruction: 1999

*Sources:*1. U.S. Department of Education, National Center for Education Statistics. April 2000. "Teacher Use of Computers and the Internet in Public Schools." Washington, DC: NCES 2000-090. Available at http://nces.ed.gov/pubs2000/2000090.pdf

2. U.S. Department of Education, National Center for education Statistics. June 2001. *The Condition of Education 2001*, Washington, DC: NCES 2001-072. Taken from Table 39-1, p.160. Available at. http://nces.ed.gov/pubs2001/2001072.pdf

drawn from 36 different schools." It should be kept in mind that what is being presented are the students' views, not those of their teachers.[9]

- Internet-savvy students rely on the Internet to help them do their schoolwork—and for good reason.
- Internet-savvy students describe dozens of different education-related uses of the Internet.
- The way students think about the Internet in relation to their schooling is closely tied to the daily tasks and activities that make up their young lives. In that regard, students employ five different metaphors to explain how they use the Internet for school:
  - The Internet as virtual textbook and reference library.
  - The Internet as virtual tutor and study shortcut.
  - The Internet as virtual study group.
  - The Internet as virtual guidance counselor.
  - The Internet as virtual locker, backpack, and notebook.
- Many schools and teachers have not yet recognized—much less responded to—the new ways students communicate and access information over the Internet. . . . Students perceive this disconnect to be the result of several factors:
  - School administrators—and not teachers—set the tone for Internet use at school.
  - Even inside the most well connected schools, there is wide variation in teacher policies about Internet use by students in and for class.
  - While students relate examples of both engaging and poor instructional uses of the Internet assigned by their teachers, students say that the not-so-engaging uses are the more typical of their assignments.
- Students say they face several roadblocks when it comes to using the Internet at schools. In many cases, these roadblocks discourage them from using the Internet as much, or as creatively, as they would like. They note that:
  - The single greatest barrier to Internet use at school is the quality of access to the Internet.
  - While many students recognize the need to shelter teenagers from inappropriate material and adult-oriented commercial ads, they complain that blocking and filtering software often raise barriers to students' legitimate educational use of the Internet.
  - Since not every student has access to the Internet outside of school, the vast majority of students report that their teachers do not make homework assignments that require the use of the Internet.
- [S]tudents' concerns can inform several policy debates about technology and education.
  - Students want better coordination of their out-of-school educational use of the Internet with classroom activities. They argue that this could be the key to leveraging the power of the Internet for learning.
  - Students urge schools to increase significantly the *quality* of access to the Internet in schools.

- Students believe that professional development and technical assistance for teachers are crucial for effective integration of the Internet into curricula.
- Students maintain that schools should place priority on developing programs to teach keyboarding, computer, and Internet literacy skills.
- Students urge that there should be continued effort to ensure that high-quality online information to complete school assignments be freely available, easily accessible, and age-appropriate—without undue limitation on students' freedoms.
- Students insist that policy makers take the "digital divide" seriously and that they begin to understand the more subtle inequities among teenagers that manifest themselves in differences in the quality of student Internet access and use.

All these remarks are very encouraging and quite sophisticated as well, given the ages and experiences of the students. On the down side is the history of technological innovations in education and the extravagant claims made for each wave, followed by reassessments and reevaluations of the early enthusiastic reception. Consider Table 6.2, produced by Joseph Becker for the now-defunct Office of Technology Assessment. He attempts to characterize the waves of enthusiasm for the early introduction of computers into the schools. Given that the characterization ends in 1994, the reader is encouraged to supply his or her favorite slogans for the past few years. Professor Becker amended this table a few years later.[10]

Before engaging in an exploration of the influence of the Internet and the Web on education, it is worth reviewing past and present attempts to use computers in significant ways as part of the education process. Computer-assisted instruction is a well-known term, but what does it include and how well has it worked? A well-publicized, much acclaimed computer learning environment is provided by the language LOGO. It arose out of research carried out by artificial intelligence researchers. The LOGO environment is supposed to liberate the young from the constraints of traditional educational methods. Although less popular currently, lessons of cooperation and the development of problem-solving skills are a LOGO legacy worth considering briefly.

From the elementary school to the university, computers are playing an ever-increasing role both as part of traditional education and as a new focus for investigation. The popularity of the Internet seems to present unlimited possibilities for extending and improving education, if only schools can connect—a non-trivial problem given the costs of more sophisticated equipment and more sophisticated expertise. Nevertheless, yet another technology is being hailed as the solution to what ails education and, indeed, as a necessary next step to prepare students for the information-rich society that awaits them in this century. Along the way, vocal critics have appeared who challenge the very use of computers in the classroom, especially among

TABLE 6.2

TIMELINE OF CHANGES IN THE PREVAILING WISDOM OF "EXPERTS" ABOUT HOW
TEACHERS SHOULD USE COMPUTERS IN SCHOOLS

	1982
Teachers are told to:	*Teach students to program in BASIC.*
Rationale:	"It's the language that comes with your computer."
	1984
Teachers are told to:	*Teach students to program in LOGO.*
Rationale:	"Teach students to think, not just program."
	1986
Teachers are told to:	*Teach with integrated drill-and-practice systems.*
Rationale:	"Individualize instruction and increase test scores."
	1988
Teachers are told to:	*Teach word processing.*
Rationale:	"Use computers as tools, like adults do."
	1990
Teachers are told to:	*Teach with curriculum-specific tools (e.g., history databases, science simulators, data probes).*
Rationale:	"Integrate the computers with the existing curriculum."
	1992
Teachers are told to:	*Teach multimedia hypertext programming.*
Rationale:	"Change the curriculum—students learn best by creating products for an audience."
	1994
Teachers are told to:	*Teach with Internet telecommunications.*
Rationale:	"Let students be part of the real world."

Source: From H. J. Becker, "Analysis and Trends of School Use of New Information Technologies," Office of Technology Assessment contractor report, March 1994.[11]

younger children. These critics will be heard from later in this chapter, as will those who dispute their claims.

TECHNOLOGY IN THE SCHOOLS

> Available data suggest that in secondary schools, computers are used relatively infrequently for teaching and learning in traditional academic subjects, far less than in classes focused on teaching students *about* computers.[12]

Any discussion of computers in education in the 1980s and 1990s is inevitably sprinkled with an alphabet soup of names: CBE, CAI, CAL, and

CML. CBE is a very general term standing for computer-based education and includes all the others as subcategories. The basic division is along instructional and non-instructional lines. The major component of non-instructional uses is data processing, including record keeping, inventory control, and attendance and employment records. Some of the non-instructional applications are described as follows:

Computer-Assisted Testing (CAT). The computer is used solely as a testing medium. It is possible to take advantage of the computer's abilities to provide imaginative tests or merely to use it as a substitute for manual testing.

Computer-Assisted Guidance (CAG). The computer is used as an information-retrieval system to provide career guidance for graduating students. It does not add to students' skills or knowledge but may encourage them to take certain courses to help with their future career plans.

Computer-Managed Instruction (CMI). The teacher uses the computer to plan a course of study, tailored for the student, that consists of computer sessions, readings, and testings. The computer will keep track of the student's performance and provide regular reports, highlighting problems and accomplishments. (In Great Britain, this application is called computer-managed learning, CML.) In somewhat more detail, CMI is based upon a set of well-defined learning objectives, often tied in with a particular set of textbooks. The computer is used to test mastery of these objectives and provide learning prescriptions for each child, based upon individual placement within the objectives. After each prescription is followed, the child is retested and a new set of learning prescriptions is generated, based upon the test results.

These applications are useful and important, but the most interesting and potentially far-reaching work is being done in the areas of CAI and CAL (computer-assisted learning). Before launching into a detailed examination of some of the important work in this area, it may be helpful to first present a brief overview. In an historical survey of computer applications in education, Kurland and Kurland define the following phases in the development of early educational computing:[13]

CAI Delivery Systems. As computers moved from the office to the classroom, the earliest of the major CAI systems was begun in 1959. The underlying intellectual foundation was behavioral learning theory, and these systems had the flavor of programmed learning, that is, a bit of new material, a few questions, a review, and then more of the same. The technology was based on large, time-sharing systems with centralized software development.

The Micro Invasion and the Decentralization of Computers. The major systems such as PLATO had little market penetration when microcomputers made their appearance in the early 1980s. At first the style of software followed the previous systems, but then diversification rapidly took place and new styles emerged.

LOGO and the Emergence of the Computer as a Tool to Think With. The computer and appropriate software to facilitate new ways of thinking was the next development, led by Seymour Papert of the Massachusetts Institute of Technology (MIT). LOGO was first implemented on mainframes and later, in the early 1980s, on microcomputers.

The Computer Literacy Movement—Schools Attempt to Regain Control. The movement was toward awareness of computers (history, components, applications, and some social issues) and computer programming (LOGO, Basic, and Pascal). There was a growing concern, however, with the superficiality of the approach.

The Computer as Tool—Word Processing and Personal Productivity. The emphasis on programming was decreasing and more attention was directed, in the mid-1980s, toward application programs to assist productivity in writing, business, and general education through word processing, databases, and spreadsheets.

Incorporation of Computers Into the Mainstream Curriculum. Microcomputer software was being introduced at an enormous rate and two views were in competition: to strengthen the existing curriculum or to change it in response to the new technology, including video and CD-ROMs as well as very powerful microcomputers and networks.

Now we can return to a more leisurely examination of the dimensions and scope of CAI, still a component of computer applications in education, although the sheer presence of the Web has seemingly overshadowed more formal and structured approaches.

Computer-Assisted Instruction (CAI)

Simply put, CAI is the use of the computer directly in the instructional process as either a replacement for or complement to books and teachers. CAI has been a factor in education for a long time—since the 1960s at least—as a much-heralded but never quite perfected educational system. Because of the premature introduction of CAI software, many educators have become quite cautious about the claims for such systems. However, with the pervasiveness of microcomputers and access to the Internet, the demand to install CAI systems, or at the very least to elevate computers to a more prominent role in schools, has become quite insistent.

There are several varieties of CAI. In the basic mode of drill and practice, the computer asks a question, receives the answer, and provides an appropriate response. If the student's answer is correct, positive feedback is provided, usually in the form of an affirming comment to the student. If the answer is incorrect but belongs in a class of expected answers, a variety of responses may be selected. Finally, if the answer is incorrect and the system cannot deal with it, it must repeat the original question, and supply the answer, or go on to a new but similar question. In the second case, the question may be repeated with an encouraging remark, or a new question is posed based on the student's perceived difficulty. Because the computer can be programmed to keep track of each student's individual performance over a long period of time, at any given session it can work on those areas that need special attention and also boost the student's ego by reinforcing performance in areas of past success. Clearly, drill and practice is helpful when simple facts are to be learned in a structured context. Most available CAI software is of the drill-and-practice mode, but with considerable variation and ingenuity.

Tutorial systems for CAI are much more complex, since in this context new information is being delivered. At each stage the program can supply some general piece of information—a fact, an example, or a question to test the student's comprehension. As the major purpose of tutorial programs is to teach, they must have some way of determining what the student probably knows, what his or her difficulties are, and how the material can best be presented. In such programs, the knowledge is typically represented in a tree structure, and the presentation involves following the branches exhaustively. By precisely defining a local context, this tree organization helps identify the problems that the student may be having.

There are other issues involved with this approach to CAI. For instance, more than one answer to a question may be acceptable, and the program must be prepared to deal appropriately with different responses. Furthermore, it must be able to produce sequences of questions that explore some area in detail, and such sequences may depend on the nature of the intervening questions. Clearly, the preparation, design, and realization of tutorial programs is a complex task, and it is not surprising that the overall quality of such programs could be better than it is. As the material to be presented becomes more difficult, the problem of presenting it also becomes more of a challenge. Tutorial programs are increasingly useful, as they allow more flexible input by the student. This input may include the ability to ask limited questions. Once again the influence of artificial intelligence is becoming more important, as programs are being designed that communicate more readily with users. In addition to facility in natural language, the more advanced programs will need abilities in model building, problem solving, knowledge representation, and inferencing.

Simulations are useful for studying processes that are so complex that it is difficult to determine the specific impact of individual variables. For example, suppose we are interested in studying traffic flow at a busy intersection. A computer program can be written to capture the important features of the intersection—the traffic light sequence, and estimates of traffic density in each direction—defined by the average expected occurrence of a vehicle in a given small time interval. How is the backup of traffic related to the arrival rates and the traffic light patterns? To facilitate this investigation, a simulation program will accept values for the input numbers and then display the resulting behavior as it unfolds over time, preferably using graphics. In more advanced applications, students will be able to construct the simulation domain themselves out of a building-block set of components, to study not only the system behavior but how well it has been modeled. As the simulation unfolds, the system may ask the student about decisions involved in selecting values and about expectations that the student has about its behavior. Simulations are designed for more than the acquisition of factual knowledge. They encourage students to discover for themselves how something works. They have been used extensively in the physical and biological sciences as a substitute for or supplement to actual laboratory experiments, as well as in the social sciences to model such processes as presidential elections.

As video games established an incredible appeal and excitement outside the educational establishment, it was inevitable that the schools would begin using them to teach children. Games minimize any fears children may have about sitting in front of a terminal (if any such fears exist). They can be tailored to young children and to teenagers, who are enormously fascinated by them. They are challenging, almost hypnotic, and—if properly handled— can be an open door to most other forms of CAI. Some games can be combined with a question-and-answer feature to reinforce certain concepts. Others can be presented as a kind of puzzle for which the student must figure out the steps to a solution. How significant an impact games will have on education is still an open question.

Computer-Assisted Learning (CAL)

Some teachers use technology to support more student-centered approaches to instruction, so that students can conduct their own scientific inquiries and engage in collaborative activities while the teacher assumes the role of facilitator or coach. Teachers who fall into the latter group are among the most enthusiastic technology users, because technology is particularly suited to support this kind of instruction.[14]

CAL promotes a vision of the computer as a learning resource and as a stimulus for the imagination of the child, a powerful friend able to follow commands and respond to requests. A major early figure in CAL was Seymour Papert, Leg Professor of mathematics and of education at the Massachusetts Institute of Technology. He has made major contributions in cognitive psychology and artificial intelligence. Earlier in his career, he worked with Jean Piaget, the eminent child psychologist. From these experiences emerged some important ideas on how children might learn by using a computer—an ideal instrument, given its power to stimulate and to be whatever the child desires. The programming language Papert designed, LOGO, permits even young children to do very inventive things. In its heyday, in the 1970s and 1980s, it was hailed as a revolution in learning, and teaching as well, that would substantially transform the classroom environment.

One very important aspect of the use of LOGO in schools is its impact on the social environment. The traditional classroom has one teacher and many learners, and the flow of knowledge is directed from the teacher to the students. In an environment rich in self-discovery, new and interesting possibilities arise. For example, students can help one another to learn by sharing individual knowledge, by asking interesting questions, and by working together in common pursuits. Papert speaks to this issue in *Mindstorms*.[15]

> By building LOGO in such a way that structured thinking becomes power- ful thinking, we convey a cognitive style one aspect of which is to facilitate talking about the process of thinking. LOGO's emphasis on debugging goes in the same direction. Students' bugs become topics of conversation; as a result they develop an articulate and focused language to use in asking for help when it is needed. And when the need for help can be articulated clearly, the helper does not necessarily have to be a specially trained pro- fessional in order to give it. in this way the LOGO culture enriches and facilitates the interaction between all participants and offers opportunities for more articulate, effective, and honest teaching relationships.

The notion of a "LOGO culture" is quite interesting, for it suggests a shared language, common interests, and common goals. This LOGO culture may more properly be spoken of as a subculture of the rapidly growing computer culture, in which children can share ideas and enthusiasms.

Evaluation of Education Technologies

In late 1995, the RAND Corporation's Critical Technologies Institute (CTI) completed a study of educational technology for the U.S. Department of Education. A report, presented by James Kulik of the University of Michigan, attempted to evaluate the then-current state of computer-based instruction by a careful survey of a number of independent studies. Although the studies surveyed employ differing definitions of computer-based instruction and evaluate the success of programs in differing ways, it still seems possible to draw some conclusions about the effectiveness of educational technology. As Professor Kulik states, "At least a dozen meta- analyses have been carried out to answer questions about the effectiveness of computer-based instruction. . . each of the analyses yielded the conclusion that programs of computer-based instruction have a positive record in the evaluation literature."[16] In somewhat more detail, he states the following[17]:

- Students usually learn more in classes in which they receive computer-based instruction. The analyses produce slightly different estimates of the magnitude of the computer effect, but all the estimates were positive.
- Students learn their lessons in less time with computer-based instruction. The average reduction in instructional time was 34% in 17 studies of college instruction, and 24% in 15 studies of adult education.
- Students also like their classes more when they receive computer help in them.
- Breaking studies of computer-based instruction into conventional categories clarifies the evaluation results. One kind of computer application that usually produces positive results in elementary and high school classes is computer tutoring. Students usually learn more in classes that include computer tutoring. On the other hand, precollege results are unimpressive for several other computer applications: managing, simulations, enrichment, and programming.

Another RAND study suggested more reasons that it is difficult to make definitive statements about the contributions that educational technology can make to the overall learning process. Thus the following comment is quite revealing[18]:

The review that we made of evidence of the effectiveness of educational technology reaffirmed our initial impressions. By traditional evaluation standards, the most satisfying evaluation data are those generated in laboratory or controlled clinical settings using well-specified and implemented treatments and readily measured outcomes. When technology is removed from such settings and becomes more nearly a tool to be used by students and teachers than a treatment in itself, or when the outcomes sought become richer and less precisely measurable, assessment becomes much more difficult and the results less satisfying from a technical point of view.

This study does provide evidence that schools with sufficient technological resources can create interesting, challenging, and effective environments. Exactly how educationally effective is difficult to determine, as is the cost-effectiveness of the technology. Thus, it is not surprising that definitive statements about educational technology are scarce, and detailed recommendations for action are limited in number and scope. Nevertheless, a few of the findings of this study are interesting, seemingly obvious, trivial, and provocative, even suggesting directions for future research[19]:

1. Educational technology has significant potential for improving students' learning.
2. Extensive use of technology in schools has the potential to promote significant school restructuring and expand the time and motivation for student learning.

4. Data from a study by the IEA [International Education Association] in 1992 suggested the availability of technology in schools serving poor, minority, and special needs populations did not appear to lag substantially behind the averages of schools taken as a whole. However, to the extent that technology enables learning outside the school, large disparities in the access of students of different class and ethnicity to technology is a matter of concern.

6. The costs of ubiquitous use of technology are modest in the context of overall budgets for public elementary education but moving to such use requires significant and potentially painful restructuring of budgets.

7. When technology is deeply infused in a school's operations, teachers tend to assume new roles and require new skills. There is a strong consensus among the experts we consulted that neither the initial preparation of teachers nor the current strategies for continued professional development have been effective in developing these skills.

A major survey of more than 4,000 teachers from U.S. schools, including elementary, middle, and high schools, was carried out in 1998 and reported in 2001. Obviously, it is difficult to characterize such a large study in the limited space available but the following points are of considerable interest[19a]:

Frequent use of computers by middle and high school teachers and their students in math, science, social studies, and English is . . . still very much a rare phenomenon. Outside of word processing, very few teachers have their students make frequent use of computers during class. Students in lower-ability classes are often given computer games and drills related to the subject area of their class, but it is primarily those rare classes of other students and other teachers who use more sophisticated computer software as resources and tools for doing productive and constructive academic work. The teachers' philosophy of education certainly plays a role in determining whether she will use computers and how they will be used, but there are even stronger factors at work in determining whether teachers will make use of computers during class time for constructivist learning approaches. Specifically, those stronger factors are the teacher's own technical expertise and professional experience in using computer applications, the number of computers in their own classroom, and their personal involvement in their profession, both within their school building and beyond. Each of those factors, explored only in a small way in this paper, appear to be stronger determinants of constructivist uses of computers during class than the teacher's philosophy itself.

Will computers continue to play a "niche" role in the academic education of secondary students? . . . with continued development of the capability of computer hardware, the Internet infrastructure, and applications software; with increasing numbers of classrooms having sufficient computer access to this technology; with the increasing experience and expertise of teachers in using computers; and with the facilitating influence of the teachers most professionally active among their peers, the niche may be growing.

A more recent, extensive review of CAL was conducted for the New Zealand Department of Education; the overall results are not favorable.[20]

> Overall, the effectiveness of computer-assisted learning has not been conclusively demonstrated. To date, it has been shown to be less effective, on average, than other forms of intervention in education. In considering the results of evaluative research in computer-assisted learning, one has to avoid confounding the medium with the method. Generally, computer-assisted learning software is under pinned by an older, neo-behaviourist theory of learning, one that has been displaced in the classroom by more social constructivist views of learning. Particularly in New Zealand primary classrooms, the approach of the software may differ considerably from widely accepted classroom pedagogy.

In somewhat more detail, the criticism is directed at issues of cost effectiveness, the lack of results that compare cost efffectiveness among programs, the lack of success in improving reading, although applications in basic mathematics skills were favorable, and little evidence of the acquired knowledge being generalizable to other areas of instruction. It must be noted that in this vast domain of technology and education, it is difficult to determine results of lasting value. Long-term studies are rare and, given the enormous number of variables, experimental results are difficult to generalize. The number of interested parties is large and they often have conflicting motives. Given all these concerns, it is important to be cautious, and skeptical as well, about claims and predictions. What is fashionable may not be beneficial and may not endure.

COMPUTERS IN HIGHER EDUCATION

> A teacher affects eternity; he can never tell where his influence stops.—
> Henry Adams (1838–1918)
> Teachers open the door, but you must enter by yourself.—Chinese Proverb

Computers first made their presence felt in education at universities, both as research tools and as objects of study. Not long after the first electronic computer, ENIAC, was built at the Moore School of the University of Pennsylvania, students were being instructed in the intricacies of computer design and programming. Electrical engineering departments turned their attention to transistors, semiconductors, integrated circuits, and communications. New departments of computer science were founded, to instruct students in the care and feeding of computers—that is, programming—and to carry out research in such areas as operating systems, the theory of computation, numerical analysis, and artificial intelligence. Many important innovations have come from the universities—time-sharing systems, programming languages (such as LISP, Pascal, and Basic), graphics devices (SKETCHPAD), numerical packages, and a variety of intelligent systems. The universities have filled an important function in training large numbers of computer professionals and in introducing several generations of other students to computers long before computer use became fashionable in the wider society. This role was recognized quite early by computer companies. Among these, IBM was the most prominent in recognizing the fact that early exposure to a given computer system would be a major influence in subsequent choices made by the students when they established themselves in the outside world. This realization produced a strategy that worked exceedingly well and contributed to IBM's early dominance in the computer industry.

More recently, computer companies including IBM, Apple, Hewlett-Packard (H-P), Silicon Graphics, Dell, and Sun have again begun to respond to opportunities at the universities. These range from special purchase plans for students and faculty, and outright gifts of hardware, software, and maintenance, to joint development projects including software and operating systems for existing machines, and the design and development of new machines and networks. A number of universities require their students, upon beginning their studies, to purchase computers under very favorable financial arrangements. These include Carnegie-Mellon University, MIT, Dartmouth, Drexel University in Philadelphia, Clarkson College in Potsdam, New York, and Rensselaer Polytechnic Institute in Troy, New York. In addition, most students are entering university with their own computers and Internet connections. Another growing trend is the availability of campus wireless access and the increasing number of students, and faculty, with portable computers being used during lectures and at other times.

The intention is clearly that every student be able to use a computer and the Internet in a variety of interesting ways beyond programming: to check for assignments in a course, to prepare and submit answers to assignments (via a file accessible only to the instructor), to browse the catalog file of the library and reserve books, to take tests and exams, and to exchange messages, via electronic mail, with fellow students and professors. All this can be done from a computer in the student's own room, on or off campus, from one of the many work stations distributed around campus, or from a laptop if a wireless or plug-in connection is available. Hard copies can be produced from fast printers near the work stations or from the student's own printer. Such systems require extensive and sophisticated computer networks permitting thousands of users to simultaneously use computers and access the Internet. Of course, special-purpose systems, such as WebCT, have been developed to facilitate course preparation, including the online availability of material as well as many of the functions mentioned above.

With all the investment in technology at universities and colleges, the obvious question arises: Is there an improvement in the educational process? Clearly, differences exist between providing specialized knowledge in computer science and providing the necessary technology to improve the education of all students, independent of field of study. Other related issues are costs of information technology, of the training of teachers, of maintenance and upgrading, and of communications systems. Some of these IT issues in universities deal with management more than teaching and learning. Thus, the Campus Computing Project reports that, "Over one-fifth (21.2 percent) of the campuses [responding] report that they have a 'single/initial sign-on campus portal' up and functioning as of fall 2002. Another fifth (20.4 percent) report that the campus portal is 'under development' or being installed in the current year. Just under a third (29.5 percent) of the participating campuses indicate that portal issues are now 'under review/discussion' at their institutions."[21]

In another important survey of U.S. college campuses, some of the major concerns are given as follows[22]:

Two overall findings for all respondents are especially notable:

1. IT Funding Challenges has become the number-one IT-related issue in terms of its strategic importance to the institution, its potential to become even more significant, and its capture of IT leaders' time and attention. This is not surprising given the state of the U.S. economy, the draconian cuts in college and university budgets (especially in the public sector), and and the growing need for resources to support an established IT infrastructure while continuing to make new investments to keep up with technological change.

2. Security and Identity Management is not only on the top-ten list of IT-related issues that are of strategic importance, growing in significance, and demanding the campus IT leader's time, but is now among the top-ten in human and fiscal resource consumption.

The challenges for university administrators are clear but for students many other issues dominate. The Pew Internet & American Life Project has carried out a survey to discover the technology concerns of college students. Among the findings are the following[23]:

College students are early adopters and heavy users of the Internet
- One-fifth (20%) of today's college students began using computers between the ages of 5 and 8. By the time they were 16 to 18 years old all of today's current college students had begun using computers—and the Internet was commonplace in the world in which they lived.

- Eighty-six percent of college students have gone online, compared with 59% of the general population.
- The great majority (85%) of college students own their own computer, and two-thirds (66%) use at least two email addresses.

College students say the Internet has enhanced their education

- Internet use is a staple of college students' educational experience. They use the Internet to communicate with professors and classmates, to do research, and to access library materials. For most college students the Internet is a functional tool, one that has greatly changed the way they interact with others and with information as they go about their studies.
- Nearly four-fifths of college students (79%) agree that Internet use has had a positive impact on their college academic experience.
- Almost half (46%) of college students agree that email enables them to express ideas to a professor that they would not have expressed in class, but, some interactions are still primarily face-to-face: Only 19% of students said they communicate more with their professors via email than they do face-to-face.
- Nearly three-quarters (73%) of college students say they use the Internet more than the library, while only 9% said they use the library more than the Internet for information searching.
- About half of all college students (48%) are required to use the Internet to contact other students in at least some of their classes.
- Two-thirds (68%) of college students reported subscribing to one or more academic-oriented mailing lists that relate to their studies. They use these lists to carry on email discussions about topics covered in their classes.
- More than half (58%) of college students have used email to discuss or find out a grade from an instructor.
- Nearly two-thirds (65%) of college students who email professors say they report absences via email.

College social life has been changed by the Internet

- The college experience is not only about learning in the classroom, it is also about encountering new social situations and gaining new social skills. College students use the Internet nearly as much for social communication as they do for their education. But just as they use the Internet to supplement the formal parts of their education, they go online to enhance their social lives.
- 42% of college students say they use the Internet primarily to communicate socially.

It is clear that technology in general and the Internet in particular are basic parts of college life for virtually all students and faculty. Special expertise is neither required nor expected. The burden on IT administrators to provide adequate portal environments is clear as the smooth functioning of college life is at stake. An obvious question arises: If so much of college life is conducted over the Internet, is physical presence necessary? More on this topic later in the chapter.

One last addition to university life should be mentioned, namely, the use of the Internet for such an unethical purpose as plagiarism. Simply put, plagiarism is the use of someone else's words or work as your own without proper attribution. It can be a single sentence or two in an essay, or the entire essay. Plagiarism problems have become an issue as well in programming courses, where copying and modifying existing programs is relatively straightforward. How prevalent plagiarism is at the university level is debatable but it is generally recognized as a serious problem, exacerbated by the ease with which material can be downloaded from the Internet for free or by visiting sites that can produce complete essays for a price. In response to the new Internet reality, software has been developed that can track down plagiarized material by searching the Internet. Another response is to include anti-plagiarism material in course curricula in a more serious and coherent manner.

The Virtual University

Given that universities are at the forefront of technological innovations, it is to be expected that new forms of delivering instruction at the post-secondary level are emerging. More and more universities are turning to the Web as a way to provide instruction to supplement the typical lecture system. In fact, entire courses have been placed on the Web, permitting students access to lecture material at any time and from any place. Students have been encouraged to treat the course Web site as a living document by adding their own links to material discovered in the process of doing assignments or carrying out research projects. Thus, every student can potentially benefit from every other student's efforts. In such a situation, education can become a genuinely cooperative enterprise involving teachers and students alike. There is more. Courses mounted on the Web are also available around the world, so that one might expect to see international competition among universities. In fact, many universities now accept admission applications over the Web. There is a danger of uniformity as the globally renowned universities make their presence felt everywhere. How will local colleges and universities compete? They will have to provide a variety of services— hands-on experiences, local special conditions, direct personal attention— not available to distant institutions. Educational institutions will have to be flexible, imaginative, and perhaps lucky, to survive in a networked world.

Before the Internet, and of course the Web, were in common use, many universities and colleges offered an educational opportunity for students unable to attend in person; the common term used was distance education, and it primarily depended on the mail system with in-person visits for tests and exams at designated sites. As mentioned above, the virtual, or online, university presents unique opportunities for remote, even global educational opportunities. One important issue that has been studied is how effective student communications are in this mode of education. One estimate is that, "by the year 2007 almost 50% of all learners in post-secondary education will be enrolled in some type of distance learning; it is safe to state that distance learning and especially Internet-based distance learning has 'arrived.'"[24] This limited experiment reported some interesting results, which should be kept in mind as the virtual university grows. For example, consider this interesting issue: "Many publishers are rushing to provide on-line content related to texts. Faculty often think that making their notes or lecture slides available will help students. But our data suggest that the on-line content was not used extensively and our measure of use of on-line content was not a good predictor of student's performance. Before more effort goes into making on-line content available, we need to know more about the use and effectiveness of such material."[25]

Electronic Publishing

It is the job of professors not only to transmit knowledge by teaching but to add to knowledge by publishing their research findings in journals and monographs. Traditionally, these hard-copy media have been a relatively slow way to disseminate knowledge, and they have become increasingly expensive, especially journals, as rising subscription costs have been countered with falling numbers of subscribers, thereby establishing a deadly spiral. For many scholars, the Internet offers a way out of this dilemma by providing rapid turnaround in the refereeing process, and reduced printing and mailing costs because paper has been removed from the process. In fact it is possible to only download or print individual articles of interest rather than entire journals, also a cost-saving measure. It may be possible for universities to become publishers of scholarly information as well as course material. These activities are happening now and will only increase as the advantages of electronic publishing become more obvious and a variety of technical and legal problems are resolved.

A scholarly paper, published in 2002, on legal issues related to online universities, focused on copyright questions.[26]

> The first major obstacle impeding the growth of purely Online universities is the legal battle over intellectual property. Putting a university course Online poses many unique copyright issues, especially when it comes to whether a university or a professor owns the copyright to the entire course. In fact, the law is so unsettled in the course-ownership area, that the U.S. Copyright Office did not even attempt to address the issue in a report to Congress about distance education copyright law. The problem centers on whether teaching falls under a university professor's "scope of employment" for purposes of copyright law. Copyright law's "work-for-hire" doctrine gives employers ownership of the works that their employees create when it is: a) "a work prepared by an employee *within the scope of his or her employment*" or b) "a work specially ordered or commissioned . . . if the parties expressly agree in a written instrument signed by them that the

work shall be considered a work made for hire." [Copyright Act of 1976, 17 U.S.C. § 101 (1976 & Supp. 2000)] This portion of the note will suggest that for-profit, solely-instructional institutions of higher education can claim copyright ownership of Internet courses via the work-for-hire doctrine, but that nonprofit, research-based universities and colleges cannot. Furthermore, this note will conclude that in order to maintain the integrity of academic freedom that is inherent in the employment relationship between a professor and a research-based university, courts must insist on maintaining a distinction between the two types of institutions.

University Research

Universities that have forged research and development contracts with computer vendors often argue that the relationship is beneficial for both parties because it keeps universities at the cutting edge of technologies, to say nothing of acquiring computers at bargain prices, and permits computer and software companies to experiment with new ideas in a relatively sophisticated market. However, the growing relationship between universities and big business raises serious questions about autonomy, ethics, and responsibility. Can a university researcher simultaneously be responsible to his or her university, discipline, students, and corporate sponsor? What about the free and open circulation of research results when industry has proprietary interests? Going one step further, a number of university researchers have themselves formed companies, to develop commercial applications of their own research efforts and to consult with industry in their areas of expertise. This development is not new and there are arguments in favor of cooperation between academia and business, but there are also potential dangers. Researchers must be careful not to exploit their students' work for financial gain or use results achieved with the help of government funds for private profit. Computer science is quite a lucrative field and there is considerable temptation for university researchers with these backgrounds to jump into the marketplace.

Another important player in the university computing research environment is the U.S. government, in two major forms, the National Science Foundation (NSF) and the Department of Defense's (DOD) Defense Advanced Research Projects Agency (DARPA). NSF funds basic research in the sciences but its level of funding is considerably below that provided by DOD. For example, most of the federal funding for computer science at the prestigious universities, the University of California at Berkeley, Carnegie-Mellon, MIT, and Stanford, comes from DOD. Furthermore, the military tends to support applied research related to various mission-oriented projects. Thus, to a significant degree the goals of the defense establishment shape the nature of research undertaken at the major universities of the country and hence the academic curriculum. Of course, the events of

September 11 have exacerbated this situation as research in a variety of anti-terrorsim technologies, including facial recognition, detection of weapons, data mining, and others, have been funded with the additional, obvious incentive that one's country is under threat.

Computer Literacy and the Internet

> I find television very educational. The minute somebody turns it on, I go to the library and read a good book.—Groucho Marx (1890–1977)

The idea that people should be knowledgeable about computers in today's society hardly seems controversial. However, the details of various proposals to implement this idea have aroused some disagreement. The term commonly used to characterize a heightened awareness about computers and their role in society is computer literacy. Comparisons with the notion of general language literacy are unavoidable and frequently misleading.

Various definitions of the term have been proposed, some of which draw parallels to literacy as it refers to language skills and a minimal level of competence in some domain. Ronald Anderson and Daniel Klasson of the Minnesota Education Computing Consortium (MECC) define computer literacy as "whatever understanding, skills, and attributes one needs to function effectively within a given social role that directly or indirectly involves computers."[27] The given social role is meant to encompass general well-being as well as specific achievements.

In the schools, at all levels, the debate continues over the definition, importance, and relevance of computer literacy. Critics are wary of pandering to the newest, flashiest technology. In a delightful parody several years ago, Bill Lacy, the then president of Cooper Union, described the repercussions of the introduction of the pencil (later in colors and with eraser) into medieval Europe. Its introduction in schools met with the following responses: "Just because they have a pencil doesn't mean they have a lot of education going on," and "I don't know why my kid needs a pencil to learn French. We *are* French." Evaluating the claims made for computer literacy in the midst of the widespread publicity surrounding computers is not an easy task. Schools are under pressure by parents to provide their children with the best chance for a prosperous life, and that certainly includes computers.

Many universities and colleges are requiring as a condition of graduation that students take at least one course in what is sometimes called computer appreciation. Typically, this course includes an introduction to computer programming; a survey of computer applications, such as a word processor, a spreadsheet, and a database program; a familiarization with a few associated social issues; and of course an introduction to the Internet and the World Wide Web. It is felt that every person, to be a functioning and responsible citizen, must be aware of the role of computers in contemporary society. The debate about the usefulness of computers in the curriculum turns on such issues as the intellectual content of computer literacy courses, the benefits of computer programming for the average student, the supposed transferability of computer skills, improved job prospects, and the usefulness of the Internet in schools and later in work. Definitive answers are not yet available, but a number of voices have been raised against the uncritical acceptance of the concept of computer literacy for everyone. Other issues arise at the primary and secondary school level, in relation to computer programming, computer-assisted instruction, and computer games.

Many commentators have argued that for most people, learning to program is neither necessary nor beneficial. The long term-trend is toward sophisticated, user-friendly software as in word-processing and financial-planning programs. Programming is not a skill easy to acquire or practice. It is unlikely that very many people, besides professionals and eager hobbyists, will program on their own. Thus, for every student to learn how to program skillfully should not be the major aim of the computer literacy movement.

The primary emphasis in computer literacy should be in the historical, economic, legal, and philosophical areas. Computers must be seen in their historical context—as part of an ongoing technological process. The economic and legal implications of their use are a rich source of material for exploring many important social issues. It would be a mistake to focus on the computer itself, because treating even such a marvelous machine in isolation can only result in superficial understanding. This is a real danger, if computer literacy courses are taught by programmers with little experience in other areas. The pressure to offer such courses may result in ill-conceived projects. Public pressure is a reality, however, and many schools have responded with such courses, and even programs, in computer literacy. The popularity of the Internet has added further fuel to the debate. It is seen by some as a wonderful educational and research tool that increases student access to information beyond that provided by teachers and local libraries. Others see it as a colossal waste of time, a vast melange of flash and glitter, requiring considerable experience and sophistication to be useful. Its potential is unlimited, however, and with careful instruction and discipline it is an invaluable resource and a major addition to the intellectual climate both inside and outside of educational institutions.

Education is usually considered in the context of educational institutions— elementary schools, high schools, vocational schools, colleges, and universities— but considerable learning goes on in the workplace as well as in company-sponsored classrooms. Many people have a vision of lifelong learning as a combination of institutionalized instruction and the individual pursuit of knowledge. Traditionally, libraries have played a very important role in enabling motivated individuals to pursue their interests in a self-directed manner. Now with the emergence of the Internet, and the explosive growth of information, it is not unrealistic to consider that self-education is accessible beyond the confines of formal institutions.

ISSUES AND PROBLEMS

> I know of no safe depository of the ultimate powers of society but the people themselves; and if we think them not enlightened enough to exercise their control with wholesome discretion, the remedy is not to take it from them, but to inform their discretion by education.—Thomas Jefferson, letter to William Charles Jarvis, 1820

One of the fundamental criticisms leveled against computer-assisted instruction (CAI) is that an infatuation with hardware has minimized the concern about the educational merits of the courses. Critic after critic has bemoaned the poor quality of the material. As the market has grown, the rush to produce software has resulted in a lowering of quality. Perhaps there also exist some serious problems with educational theory itself, and it is unreasonable to expect CAI to produce wondrous results. Another problem frequently ignored is the difficulty of obtaining qualified teachers who know how to use available hardware and software to their best advantage.

Other important issues include the impact of computers and computer use on the social organization of the classroom, as a byproduct of such aids to computer learning as LOGO, the tendency of the new technology to exclude girls and women or to minimize their contributions, and the role of technology in aiding the disabled.

Impact of CAI

Because of the many dimensions of the instructional process, it is difficult to determine the effectiveness as well as the drawbacks of educational technology. This observation was made earlier but it is useful to be reminded that powerful technologies do not operate independently of the environment in which they are immersed. In analyzing data obtained from a "study of social and organizational factors affecting technology and school reform," Barbara Means reports that two of the nine schools reviewed, with seemingly similar motivations, resources, and skills, diverged strikingly in the results achieved. She was thus led to make the following recommendations for the successful implementation of educational technology[28]:

- Jointly developed school goals and technology's place in fulfilling them
- Adequate technology access provided in regular classes

- Technical support readily available and non-judgmental
- Professional growth opportunities, recognition, and rewards provided for exemplary technology use by regular teachers
  - Technology use as a choice, not by fiat
  - Mechanisms for teacher choice in what technology to use and how to use it
  - Opportunities provided for teachers to work together
  - Supported time for teachers to learn to use technology and to design technology-supported learning activities.

Technology will not be effective unless the people issues are taken into account in a meaningful way. One of the long-time leaders in the field, Professor Emeritus Alfred Bork, offered a number of comments about how to improve interactive learning on the Internet. He describes the problems in terms of a number of flaws that currently exist and that must be overcome in order to reap the benefits of the technology. Among these flaws are the following[29]:

- Flaw 1 – The courses only work for small numbers. A major problem we face in learning today is increasing numbers of students.
- Flaw 2 – Lack of adequate interactions with students. Students need individualized help for effective learning, adapted to their individual needs.
- Flaw 4 – Insufficient storage of student information. Skilled human tutors start a session with a student with considerable previous experience, and they make use of this information to guide the tutorial situation. Current Internet systems store very limited student information.
- Flaw 5 – Many students do not learn with existing materials. We need learning systems in which ALL students succeed, learning to the mastery level.
- Flaw 6 – Learning is too expensive. Present online material, with twenty student groups each with an instructor, is too expensive for today. Further, it does not scale easily to much larger numbers.
- Flaw 7 – Insufficient consideration of lifelong learning. Most of the online material developed has been based on existing university courses, as we have noted.
- Final comments. There are fatal flaws in current Internet learning materials, as expressed here. This does not represent an Internet or World Wide Web problem, but a problem in the types of material designed for the Internet now. We need a new learning paradigm.

LOGO and the Classroom

The claims for the virtues of LOGO have been loud, insistent, and consistent since the late 1970s when it was first introduced. For example, two strong supporters, Maddux and Johnson, made the following claims for teaching children to program in LOGO[30]:

- Logo can provide a success [sic] experience for children who are accustomed to failure.
- Interesting things can be done with Logo by children who have received only a brief orientation to the language.
- The self-correcting nature of programming eliminates the need for adult correction for students who are sensitive to such correction.
- Logo may help promote social interaction and peer acceptance among children who are deficient in these important characteristics.

But perhaps the most controversial claim is that LOGO will improve general problem-solving abilities, that there will be a transference from programming skills to conceptual skills in other disciplines, and that LOGO will unlock the natural curiosity and desire to learn inherent in all children, independent of their social and economic backgrounds—a sweeping claim, to say the least. Is there any evidence in support of this?

An important early study of LOGO was carried out in two classrooms in an independent school in Manhattan by researchers from Bank Street College's Center for Children and Technology, between September 1981 and February 1984. One classroom included eight- and nine-year-olds, and the other, eleven- and twelve-year-olds, all of mixed socioeconomic backgrounds and achievement levels. Space does not permit a discussion of the experiments and methodology of this lengthy and careful study, so we will limit our presentation to a report of the most salient results.[31]

1. Teachers had a great deal of difficulty deciding on their approach to the use of LOGO in the classroom, between a structured environment and an environment to promote self-discovery.
2. Over the course of two years, students varied greatly in their interests and accomplishments. Teachers had difficulty in reaching those students who did not naturally take to the language.
3. Many students found the underlying logical structure of LOGO formidable and were unable to overcome their difficulties to the point that they could write even simple programs.
4. Teachers had difficulty rationalizing the role of LOGO into the ongoing classroom work. "Is Logo a legitimate part of the curriculum? And, if so, does it fit in as programming or math, or does it belong elsewhere? What can students be expected to learn from their efforts involving Logo: specific programming or math concepts, general problem-solving skills, or both?"

In the Introduction to the second edition of *Mindstorms*, Seymour Papert briefly and unapologetically responds to his critics, first by claiming that problems that may have arisen in applying ideas discussed in the 1980 edition are probably related to the mode of presentation rather than to the ideas themselves. Furthermore, to those academic critics whose response to Papert's apparent claims that "'working with computers' would *cause* change in how children think," was to engage in experiments to prove him wrong, he responds with the following[32]:

> I make no such claim anywhere in the book, but I may have made a mistake in waiting until chapter 8 before saying emphatically that I was not making it. What I was saying, and still say, is something slightly more subtle: I see Logo as a *means* that *can, in principle*, be used by educators to *support the development* of new ways of thinking and learning. However, Logo does not in itself produce good learning any more than paint produces good art.

Gender Issues

Prior to the arrival of the computer, girls were not expected to do well in science and mathematics, and these expectations were often self-fulfilling, as the educational system did not encourage their participation in these areas. Some of the computer concerns related to gender are equal access, gender bias in expectations, and stereotypical computer programs and games. Experiments conducted at the University of British Columbia in 1993 attempted to explore the following widely held views about boys with respect to computer games[33]:

Commonly held views about boys	Research results
(a) electronic games and boys' behavior while playing them contain elements of aggression, violence, competition, fast-action, and speed;	(a) while violent games are popular, many boys prefer games that challenge them mentally;
(b) electronic games encourage anti-social, "loner" behavior; and	(b) there appears to be little connection between anti-social behavior and electronic game playing; and
(c) boys who play electronic games are susceptible to becoming so devoted to playing games that they neglect other areas of their lives, such as school, physical activity, and family.	(c) many boys who play electronic games have interests also in music, programming, reading, and school.

So boys are actually more open and have a wider range of interests than is usually recognized. One can only hope that the game-playing software companies would recognize this observation and act accordingly.

The Technological Fix

Computers are a valuable and undoubtedly useful tool. They have an important role to play in the educational system, as they do in the rest of society. But they are only one part of the educational process. As Joseph

Weizenbaum has said, "Children may not be motivated in school because they're hungry or they've been abused at home or for any number of reasons. Simply introducing computers avoids the question of why children may not be motivated in school. It converts a social problem into a technological problem and then tries to solve it by technical means."[34]

In a study on the future impact of technology on education, the question is asked: "Is there a 'down side' to technology?" The following responses are provided as possible areas of concern[35]:

- Downsizing of the teaching force as staffing patterns are altered. (Many workshop participants felt that major changes in staffing. . . would be challenged by teachers and administrators who faced possible job loss.)
- Greater inequalities in knowledge and skills among different groups of students due to differential access to technological resources. Will adding more technology to the most technologically advanced schools exacerbate discrepancies between the technology "haves" and "have-nots," creating inequalities in access to information between students who attend the "have not" schools and students who attend the "have" schools?
- Concerns about whether learning through technology is always the best way for students to learn. Will an over-emphasis on technology mean that students who would benefit from direct, traditional instruction get lost in the shuffle of changing approaches to teaching and learning?
- Potential harmful influences from opening the sheltered class to the outside world. Telecommunications networks could give students easier access to questionable or dangerous elements, such as pornography on the Internet.

Another major voice raised in concern about the high expectations being placed on technology to solve many of the ills of the current education system is Larry Cuban, Professor Emeritus at Stanford University. In an interview conducted in mid-2000, when asked to elaborate on his frequent characterization as a critic of "techno-enthusiasts," Cuban responded,[36]

When I refer to "techno-enthusiasts" or "technophiles" I'm talking about folks who believe that schools can be saved by information technology. These enthusiasts usually say kids learn faster, better and more with the machines and that the technology is an instrument for reform. They do not question at all the pervasive story used to justify educational technology—that, unless we have technology in our schools, kids won't be able to get jobs in an increasingly computerized world. I believe this is a misguided way to think about schooling. We worry about teaching keyboarding today but it won't be needed when voice activation becomes common in a few years. The dogma will only be replaced when people realize how quickly it is all changing. Kids don't need years of computer exposure to succeed. People with no computer background generally catch on in a few weeks—a few months tops.

His closing response to a suggestion that perhaps technology should be temporarily forgotten for now, is the following[37]:

> Not necessarily but we need to ask the right questions. What are the goals of schooling? Do we care most about literacy? Social development? Other goals? The school community needs to reach a consensus, then ask, "Now, how might the technology help us reach these goals?" Finally, once you know where you want to go and how technology might help, you need to look at the structure of the school and how time is used and see what might need to change in order to meet the goals. The questions really break down into:
>
> 1. What are we after?
> 2. How can technology help?
> 3. What do we have to change to make use of it?
>
> Teachers themselves vary in their beliefs. They don't necessarily agree with one another about whole language vs. phonics, arithmetic vs. "new math." We need to leave them some choice. Technology can help drive change. Sometimes it's a catalyst. But it is not driving most school reform efforts. And I can imagine a fine school that uses no computer technology at all. We need to be honest and open to debate about value conflicts—not determined that wiring schools and sending teachers to workshops is the only right answer.

Henry Jay Becker has responded to Cuban's concerns, employing results of his major research project, "Teaching, Learning and Computer Survey (TLC)," conducted in 1998, including more than 4,400 teachers in over 1,100 schools, covering grades 4 to 12. This project was discussed earlier in the chapter. The following are some of Becker's evaluations of Cuban's positions[38]:

> On the issue of whether computers are generally a central vehicle of instructional activities in classrooms, the data suggests that Cuban remains correct at this time. . . . Thus, in a certain sense Cuban is correct—computers have *not* transformed the teaching practices of a majority of teachers, particularly teachers of secondary academic subjects. However, under the right conditions—where teachers are personally comfortable and at least moderately skilled in using computers themselves, where the school's daily class schedule permits allocating time for students to use computers as part of class assignments, where enough equipment is available and convenient to permit computer activities to flow seamlessly alongside other learning tasks, and where teachers' personal philosophies support a student-centered, constructivist pedagogy that incorporates collaborative projects defined partly by student interest—computers are clearly becoming a valuable and well-functioning instructional tool. [*original emphasis*]

Finally, in early 2003, a report was released which evaluated the massive investment in computers and the Internet in the British school system. It had been commissioned by the Department for Education and was carried out between 1999 and 2002, involving 60 schools. Clearly, one of its strengths is that it lasted for a three-year period and is therefore more than just a snapshot. The results were described by one major newspaper as follows[39]:

> Equipping schools with a million computers and connecting them all to the internet has had little if any impact on standards, according to a study commissioned by the Department for Education. Despite what the report called "unprecedented levels of Government investment"—including more than £1 billion over the past five years—it could find "no consistent relationship" between computer use and pupil achievement in any subject at any age. Its most optimistic conclusion was that computers could help to raise the national test scores of primary school children by a meagre three marks in English if they used the equipment regularly—usually for word processing—either at school or at home. In science, on the other hand, 11-year-olds were likely to perform worse if computers were used in the classroom.

Of course, as stated in the report, there were many caveats included to position the results in a less pessimistic form, but the outcomes are relatively clear and consistent with many other studies. Many factors are necessarily involved in determining the effectiveness of technology in the classroom, as we have noted above. Expectations are high, given the costs, and the critics tend to be marginalized because they are not team players. It is an exciting time, but excitement is no substitute for solid results, ongoing evaluations, adequate training, and well-understood and explained pedagogies.

Final Comments

The limitations of technology in providing the answer to educational problems are revealed in a simple insight underlying what has come to be called the Comer process, after Dr. James Comer, a Yale University psychiatrist: "A child's home life affects his performance in school, and. . . if schools pay attention to all the influences on a child, most problems can be solved before they get out of control. The Comer process. . . encourages a flexible, almost custom-tailored approach to each child."[40] These observations seem so obvious and so unglamorous compared to high technology that it is not surprising that it has taken so long for adequate attention to be paid to them. One interesting point with respect to the arguments made for technological solutions is that there are other claims to massive expenditures to maintain the educational infrastructure. Will there be enough money to satisfy all the basic needs of the educational system?

If all else fails, however, the Internet offers many opportunities to achieve so-called academic credentials The following was received in the mail by the author during 2003:

GET YOUR UNIVERSITY DIPLOMA

Do you want a prosperous future, increased earning power, more money and the respect of all?
Call this number: **X - XXX - XXX - XXXX** (24 hours)

- There are no required tests, classes, books, or interviews!
- Get a Bachelors, Masters, MBA, and Doctorate (PhD) diploma!
- Receive the benefits and admiration that comes with a diploma!
- No one is turned down!

Confidentiality assured!

It is hoped that the computer, properly used, can be a liberating force, fostering what Ivan Illich, a well-known critic of technological fixes, calls conviviality.[41] Illich does not mention computers explicitly, but they clearly have the potential to be tools for conviviality par excellence through the growing use of electronic mail, multimedia, teleconferencing, and other information and communication resources, such as the Internet and the World Wide Web.

SUMMARY

Computers are rapidly becoming a pervasive feature of the educational scene. Will they transform education or are they just one more educational novelty, as were radio, film, and television?

Almost all the schools in America have computers and Internet connections. They are used to teach programming and such subjects as arithmetic, geography, history, and so forth. Computer-based education can be divided into a number of categories. The major areas are computer-assisted instruction (CAI) and computer-aided learning (CAL).

CAI includes such activities as drill and practice, tutorial (in which new material is presented), simulation (a means to explore the behavior of complex systems), and games. CAL uses the computer itself as the center of the learning experience, not as a tool to acquire knowledge in other areas. It is argued by CAL's foremost proponent Seymour Papert, one of the creators of the programming language LOGO, that an understanding of some of the important principles associated with programming can improve a child's performance in other areas of the curriculum. However, some reported experiments have not supported this claim.

At universities, computers are being used in almost every area of instruction. Some universities are requiring that incoming students purchase or lease their own microcomputers. They are used for word processing, assignments, library searches, and communicating with fellow students and professors. Comprehensive communication systems to support the growing number of computers have been initiated at most universities. The growing relationship between universities and the Department of Defense is of some concern, given the amount of military funding received by computer science researchers. Also of concern is the degree to which industry is cooperating in joint research efforts with faculty members and the impact of such efforts, as well as the military influence, on the academic program.

Computer literacy is a controversial area with many opinions about whether or not it constitutes a legitimate discipline. Other areas of computer applications in education have not yet proven their value. They seem to improve the rate of acquisition of knowledge in certain fact-driven areas, but even here they seem to be no more cost effective than other methods of instruction or remediation. The Internet, as in many other areas, is becoming an increasingly important factor in education. Access to a vast extended library is just one of the many ways that students and their teachers can use computers to participate in a shared learning experience.

Finally, there is a basic concern on the part of some that computers will be viewed as a technological fix to educational problems that are rooted in socioeconomic difficulties.

NOTES

1. Recall the famous *New Yorker* cartoon of a few years ago, with a dog at a terminal speaking to another dog: "On the Internet, nobody knows I'm a dog."
2. *Power On! New Tools for Teaching and Learning*, OTA-SET-380. U.S. Congress, Office of Technology Assessment (Washington, DC: U.S. Government Printing Office, September 1988), p. 36.
3. *Teachers and Technology: Making the Connection*, OTA-EHR-616. U.S. Congress, Office of Technology Assessment (Washington, DC: U.S. Government Printing Office, April 1995), p. 92. Also available at http://www.ota,nap.edu/pdf/data/1995/9541.PDF
4. "The Condition of Education, 1995," U.S. Department of Commerce, Bureau of the Census, October Current Population Surveys, January 30, 1995. Available at http://www.ed.gov/NCES/pubs/CoE95/05txt.html
5. U.S. Department of Education, National Center for Education Statistics. April 2000. "Teacher Use of Computers and the Internet in Public Schools."

Washington, DC: NCES 2000-090. Available at http://nces.ed.gov/pubs2000/2000090.pdf

6. "Access Improving," *Education Week, May 9, 2002*. Available at http://www.edweek.org/sreports/tc02/chart.cfm?slug=35tracking-c1.h21

7. U. S. Department of Education, National Center for Education Statistics, *Digest of Education Statistics, 2001*, 2002. Available at http://nces.ed.gov/pubs2002/digest2001/ The statistics are taken from Chapter 7, Libraries and Educational Technology, available at http://nces.ed.gov/pubs2002/2002130g.pdf

8. Pew Internet & American Life Project. "The Digital Disconnect: The Widening Gap Between Internet-Savvy Students and Their Schools," August 14, 2002. Available at http://www.pewinternet.org/reports/pdfs/PIP_Schools_Internet_Report.pdf

9. *Ibid.*

10. Henry Jay Becker. "How Are Teachers Using Computers in Instruction," Meetings of the American Educational Research Association, April 2001. Available at http://www.crito.uci.edu/tlc/FINDINGS/special3/How_Are_Teachers_Using.pdf The following "Expert" wisdom was added in 2001:
(1996) The Web: Finally research is fun
(1998) Learning by producing: Publish student work on Web
(2000) Technology is not important; it's just a tool for reform.

11. *Ibid.*, p. 104.

12. *Ibid.*, p. 103.

13. D. Midian Kurland and Laura C. Kurland. "Computer Applications in Education: A Historical Overview," in Joseph F. Traub, Barbara J. Grosz, Butler W. Lampson, and Nils J. Nilsson, *Annual Review of Computer Science, Vol. 2* (Palo Alto, CA: Annual Reviews Inc., 1987), pp. 317–358.

14. *Op cit., Teachers and Technology*, pp. 1–2

15. Seymour Papert. *Mindstorms: Children, Computers, and Powerful Ideas.* Second Edition, New York: Basic Books, A Division of HarperCollinsPublishers, 1993, p. 180. (First Edition, 1980)

16. Arthur Melmed (Ed.). "The Costs and Effectiveness of Educational Technology: Proceedings of a Workshop," Critical Technologies Institute, RAND Corporation, DRU-1205-CTI, November 1995. Available at http://www.ed.gov/Technology/Plan/RAND/Costs/cover.html

17. *Ibid.*, Section: Effectiveness.

18. Thomas K. Glennan and Arthur Melmed. "Fostering the Use of Educational Technology: Elements of a National Strategy," RAND Corporation, MR-682-OSTP, 1996. Available at http://www.rand.org/publications/MR/MR682/contents.html

19. *Ibid.*, Chapter Five, Summary and Conclusions.

19a. *Op cit.*, Henry Jay Becker, "How Are Teachers Using Computers in Instruction?"

20. "A Review of the Literature on Computer-Assisted Learning, Particularly Integrated Learning Systems, and Outcomes With Respect to Literacy and Numeracy," New Zealand Ministry of Education, June 19, 2003. Available at http://www.minedu.govt.nz/index.cfm?layout=document&documentid=5499&CFID=118793&CFTOKEN=66927972

21. "Campus Portals Make Progress; Technology Budgets Suffer Significant Cuts," The Campus Computing Project, October 2002. Available at http://www. campuscomputing.net/pdf/2002-CCP.pdf

22. "Fourth Annual EDUCAUSE Survey Identifies Current IT Issues," EDUCAUSE, Number 2, 2003. Available at http://www.educause.edu/ir/library/pdf/ EQM0322.pdf

23. "The Internet Goes to College: How Students Are Living in the Future With Today's Technology," Pew Internet & American Life Project, September 15, 2002. Available at http://www.pewinternet.org/reports/pdfs/PIP_College_ Report.pdf

24. Scott B. Wegner, Kenneth C. Holloway, and Sandra K. Wegner. "The Effects of a Computer-Based Instructional Management System on Student Communications in a Distance Learning Environment," *Educational Testing & Society*, 2(4) 199, pp. 146–153. Available at http://ifets.ieee.org/periodical/ vol_4_99/wegner.pdf

25. *Ibid.*

26. Elizabeth D. Kaiser. "The Legal Implications of Online Universities," 8 RICH. J.L. & TECH. 19 (Spring 2002). Available at http://www.law.richmond.edu/ jolt/v8i3/article19.html

27. Ronald E. Anderson and Daniel L. Klasson. "A Conceptual Framework for Developing Computer Literacy Instruction," (St. Paul: Minnesota Educational Computing Consortium, November 5, 1980), p. 7.

28. *Ibid.*, "The Costs and Effectiveness of Educational Technology: Proceedings of a Workshop," November 1995, Implementation Issues and Strategies Section.

29. Alfred Bork. "What Is Needed for Effective Learning on the Internet? *Ed. Tech. & Soc.* 4(3) 2001. pp. 139–144. Available at http://www.ics.uci.edu/~bork/ effectivelearning.pdf

30. Cleborne D. Maddux and D. LaMont Johnson. *Logo: Methods and Curriculum for Teachers* (Binghamton, New York: The Haworth Press, 1988), p. 13.

31. Jan Hawkins. "The Interpretation of Logo in Practice," in Roy D. Pea and Karen Sheingold (Eds.), *Mirrors of Kinds: Patterns of Experience in Educational Computing* (Norwood, NJ: Ablex., 1987), pp. 3–34.

32. *Ibid.*, *Mindstorms*, p. xiv.

33. Joan Lawry, Rena Upitis, Maria Klawe, Ann Anderson, Kori Inkpen, Mutindi Ndunda, David Hsu, Steve Leroux, and Kamran Sedighian. "Exploring Common Conceptions About Boys and Electronic Games," Technical Report 94–1, March 1994, Department of Computer Science, University of British Columbia, Vancouver, Canada, V6T 1Z4.

34. Joseph Weizenbaum as quoted in Alison B. Bass. "Computers in the Classroom," *Technology Review*, April 1987, p. 61.

35. *Education and Technology: Future Visions*, U.S. Congress, Office of Technology Assessment, OTA-BP-EHR-169, (Washington, DC: U.S. Government Printing Office, September 1995). Available at http://www.ota.nap.edu/pdf/data/1995/ 9522.PDF

36. "Interview with Larry Cuban," Conducted by Judy Salpeter, Editor, *Technology & Learning*, June 15, 2000. Available at http://www.techlearning.com/ db_area/archives/TL/062000/archives/cuban.html

37. *Ibid.*

38. Henry Jay Becker. "Findings from the Teaching, Learning, and Computing Survey: Is Larry Cuban Right?" Revision of a paper written for the January, 2000, School Technology Leadership Conference of the Council of State School Officers, Washington, DC, July 2000. Available at http://www.crito.uci.edu/ tlc/findings/ccsso.pdf

39. John Clare. "Internet in Schools Fails to Improve Results," *The Daily Telegraph*, January 10, 2003. Available at http://www.millennium-debate.org/ tel10jan034.htm

40. Michel Marriott. "A New Road to Learning: Teaching the Whole Child," *The New York Times*, June 13, 1990, pp. A1, B8.

41. Ivan Illich. *Tools for Conviviality* (New York: Harper & Row/Perennial Library, 1973).

ADDITIONAL READINGS

Introduction

"Reinventing Schools: The Technology is Now," Washington, DC: National Academy of Sciences, 1995. Available at http://www.nap.edu/nap/online/tech-gap/welcome.html

"Computers in Education: A Brief History," The Technological Horizons in Education Journal, 2002. Available at http://www.thejournal.com/ magazine/vault/ articleprintversion.cfm?aid=1681

Computers in the Schools

"21st Century Teachers," President Clinton's Educational Technology Initiative, May 1996. Available at http://www.ustc.org/21stcentury/index.html.

"Learning for the 21st Century, A Report and Mile Guide for 21st Century Skills," Partnership for 21st Century Skills, 2003. Available at http://www.21stcenturyskills.org/downloads/P21_Report.pdf

Marshall. James M. "Learning with Technology: Evidence That Technology Can, and Does, Support Learning," Cable in the Classroom, May 2002. Available at http://www.ciconline.org/uploads/CIC_REPORT.pdf

"Visions 2020: Transforming Education and Training Through Advanced Technologies," U.S. Department of Commerce, Technology Administration, September 9, 2002. Available at http://www.ta.doc.goc/reports/TechPolicy/ 2020Visions.pdf

Computers in Higher Education

"Building a Nation of Learners: The Need for Changes in Teaching and Learning to Meet Global Challenges," Business-Higher Education Forum, 2003. Available at http://www.acenet.edu/bookstore/pdf/2003_build_nation.pdf

Byrne, John A. "Virtual B-Schools," *Business Week*, October 23, 1995, pp. 64–65, 68.

Clark, Tom. "Virtual Schools: Trends and Issues," Distance Learning Resource Network, October 2001. Available at http://www.wested.org/online_pubs/virtualschools.pdf

"ECAR Study: Trends in Wireless Communications in Higher Education," Educause Center for Applied Research, August 2002. Available at http://www.educause.edu/ir/library/pdf/EDU0218.pdf

"The Future of Networking Technologies for Learning," Office of Educational Technology, U.S. Department of Education, May 24, 1995, Available at http://www.ed.gov/Technology/Futures/

Learning to Work: Making the Transition From School to Work, U.S. Congress, Office of Technological Assessment, OTA-EHR-637, (Washington, DC: U.S. Government Printing Office, September 1995). Available at http://www.ota.nap.edu/pdf/data/1995/9548.PDF

"The Learning Connection," Benton Foundation, Winter 1995. Available at http://cdinet.com/cgi-bin/lite/Benton/Goingon/learning.html

Riel, Margaret and Becker, Hank. "Beliefs, Practices, and Computer Use of Teacher Leaders." (No date). Available at http://www.crito.uci.edu/tlc/findings/aero/aero_leaders.pdf

Rothman, David. "TeleRead: A Virtual Central Database Without Big Brother." In Robin P. Peek and Gregory B. Newby (Eds.) *The Electronic Frontier*, Cambridge, MA: The MIT Press, 1996. Available at http://www.clark.net/pub/rothman/teleread.html

Issues and Problems

Cuban, Larry. *Oversold and Unused: Computers in the Classroom* (Cambridge, MA: Harvard University Press, 2001). Available at http://hup.harvard.edu/pdf/CUBOVE.pdf

Miller, Leslie, Chaika, Melissa, and Groppe, Laura. "Girls' Preferences in Software Design: Insights from a Focus Group," *Interpersonal Computing and Technology: An Electronic Journal for the 21st Century*, 1996. Available at http://www.helsinki.fi/science/optek/1966/n2/miller.txt

Gokhale, Anuradha A. "Collaborative Learning Enhances Critical Thinking," *Journal of Technology Education*, (7:1), Fall 1995. Available at http://scholar.lib.vt.edu/ejournals/JTE/jte-v7n1/gokhale.jte-v7n1.html

"Purchases of Degrees From Diploma Mills," U.S. General Accounting Office," November 21, 2002. Available at http://www.gao.gov/new.items/d03269r.pdf

— 7 —

GOVERNMENT AND COMPUTERS

All government, indeed every human benefit and enjoyment, every virtue, and every prudent act, is founded on compromise and barter. We balance inconveniences; we give and take—we remit some rights that we may enjoy others. . . . Man acts from motives relative to his interests; and not on metaphysical speculations.

Edmund Burke, Speech on Conciliation with America, March 22, 1775

INTRODUCTION

Governments exist to serve their citizens, and presumably computers are playing a role in this endeavor. How, and for what purposes, do governments use computers? Their primary activity is record keeping—the gathering, entering, maintenance, processing, and updating of files on individuals, families, organizations, and companies. The government might actually be thought of as *the* great record keeper, whose insatiable appetite for information arises from the belief that the continual accumulation of information inevitably leads to the provision of better services. The U.S. government is the single largest user of computers in the world. Many of the applications are well known—taxation, social security, census, law enforcement, national security and defense, energy, health, education and welfare, agriculture, and so forth.

Clearly, the government is more than simply a user of computers. By virtue of being such a major purchaser of computer technology, the government tends to set standards and shape the form of future developments. The needs of the Census Bureau played an important role in the early development of the computer. In carrying out its responsibility for the nation's security, the Department of Defense (DOD) has spurred research and development in integrated circuits, programming languages, operating systems, security methods, and fault-tolerant designs. The National Aeronautics and Space Administration (NASA) is concerned with such issues as miniaturization, low power consumption, high reliability, and resistance to the effects of vibration and weightlessness.

These technical innovations are important and have done much to make the United States the leading technological country in the world, but more recently there has been an attempt to paint the federal government as too big, too intrusive, too remote and unresponsive, and a danger to individual rights. In this context, technological sophistication may be seen as a threat, assisting an all-powerful government bent on discovering more about its citizens by means of modern technology and thereby controlling their behavior. This extreme viewpoint is usually seen as characterizing the far right segment of the U.S. political spectrum, but it also is consistent with views expressed by many long-time Internet users, who are very concerned about government attempts to prevent non-regulated encryption schemes from being publicly used. In addition, the government has attempted to regulate content published on the Internet as prescribed in the Telecommunications Act of 1996 (see Chapter 8 for a detailed discussion). Curiously, this area of government intervention *is* supported by many religious fundamentalist and conservative organizations.

The election of a republican majority in both houses of Congress in 1994 seemed to signal a general public consensus to "downsize" government. Of particular interest, former speaker of the House, Newt Gingrich, believed that the new interactive technologies would permit a smaller government to determine more directly the wishes of the electorate and to perform its information processing more efficiently and effectively. The terms Cyber-democracy or E-democracy have been proposed as a way of characterizing a new form of democracy facilitated by national information networks such as the once-favored National Information Infrastructure, or Information Highway. *Time* magazine was not overly taken with this vision of the future, noting that,[1]

> One problem with all this enthusiasm about electronically wiring the citizenry to the Washington policymaking machine is that in a sense it's already happened. Politicians are quite in touch with opinion polls and have learned not to ignore all the radio talk-show hosts, with their ability to marshal rage over topics from Hilary to the House post office. . . . "Electronic Town Halls" have always faced one major rhetorical handicap: the long shadow of America's Founding Fathers. The Fathers explicitly took lawmaking powers out of the people's hands, opting for a representative democracy and not a direct democracy.

It has yet to be determined whether real economies of scale can be achieved by advanced technologies, but even earlier, the Clinton administration had limiting the launched its National Performance Review with the goal being to control the growth of government. Technology—primarily information-processing systems, the Internet, and the World Wide Web—is expected to play the major role in limiting the growth of the government. It is not yet clear whether these efforts are more than window dressing or represent a realistic attempt to make government more responsive.

Another area of growing importance is the increasing involvement of computers in the political process. This new development in the use of computer technology makes it possible to produce detailed mailing lists of voters who will likely respond as desired to specific issues. The use of computer models to predict voter behavior is also increasing in popularity, and of course every candidate of substance has a Web site, replete with speeches, position papers, voting profiles, and endorsements. Opinions are solicited from interested browsers, thereby providing issues of most concern to a group of potential supporters. What has been surprising is that even as recently as the 2002 federal elections, the use of political Web sites has not been as widespread as expected.

The public has understandably been concerned about the well-publicized voting problems, which reached their peak during the presidential election of 2000 and the unfortunate occurrences in Florida. One potential answer for many of these problems seems to be the Internet, that is, the use of remote access to vote, perhaps from the convenience of one's home or else from a more traditional polling station with computers. Studies on Internet voting, as well as trials, have been launched around the world, with mixed results. The promise exists, but security and verification problems in addition to other issues remain. Several studies have been conducted to determine under what conditions Internet voting would be feasible and offer a compelling alternative to present methods.

Computer applications related to the nation's defense include the computerized battlefield, and the use of computers in war games, security needs, and cryptographic development. Traditionally, the nation's defense has involved engagements overseas to deter aggression, punish transgressors, and save innocent victims. The events of September 11, 2001, have significantly increased responsibilities so that Homeland Defense has assumed a substantial share of defense resources. Additional issues related to securing the U.S. at home will be discussed in further chapters.

Many other areas of activity that involve computer applications and the role of government will be dealt with later in this book. Because government is intricately involved in so many phases of society, it is inevitable that government-related issues turn up in many areas. In relation to computers and the law, such issues as the legal protection of software (Chapter 10), the use of computers by law enforcement agencies, and computer crime (Chapter 11), are paramount. In this regard, the events of September 11, 2001 are of paramount importance.

The federal government is also being called upon to take an active role in promoting and aiding the development of manufacturing strategies for American industry (Chapter 12). In the communications industry, the Telecommunications Act of 1996 will have significant repercussions with respect to the computer networks spanning the country. Finally, one of the major concerns of the public is the question of privacy of computer records (Chapter 9). This extremely important issue includes the debate over the competing interests of the marketplace versus the government in the protection of individual privacy. Consider the following role envisioned for government in a book published by the National Research Council in 1996[2]:

> Regardless of political sentiments about its role in general, government at all levels will inevitably be a major player. Government agencies at state and federal levels participate in almost every information-related role pursued by the private sector publisher, user, network manager, innovator. Governments have additional responsibilities by virtue of their constitutional obligations as arbiter, regulator, convener, and even leader in the interest of equity and an efficient, productive society. The federal government has unique responsibilities with respect to the transnational issues arising in the global information infrastructure (GII) and advancing the national technology base through support for research and development.

INFORMATION PROCESSING: COMPLEXITY AND BUREAUCRACIES

> The Paperwork Reduction Act of 1995 requires the Office of Management and Budget's Office of Information and Regulatory Affairs (OIRA) to set a goal of at least a 10-percent reduction in government wide paperwork burden for fiscal year 1996 and goals for each agency that reduce burden to the "maximum practicable" extent. It also requires agencies to follow certain procedures in developing information collections, including a 60-day notice and comment period.[3]

Information Technology in the Federal Government

As mentioned above, the U.S. federal government by virtue of its sheer size determines many of the trends in information technology. Among the budget documents produced by the government is one called Analytical Perspectives. The one for the fiscal year 2003 is over 700 pages long and contains some very interesting information about the increasingly important role played by information technology (IT) in the governance of the country. For example, it is estimated that IT expenditures, or as the document puts it, "the government's investment in IT," for 2003 will be about $50 billion.[4] This number compares with a figure of $23.5 billion in 1994, some 10 years earlier. The growth seems to be accelerating as forecasts for fiscal year 2007 provide an estimate of $63.3 billion.[5] Furthermore, most of the expenditures (nearly 70%) will be spent by five departments: Defense, Treasury, National Aeronautics and Space Administration, Transportation, and Justice. The U.S. government is clearly the largest buyer of IT in the world.

The budget is a valuable source of information about the government's intentions in making its operation more efficient. Hence, consider the following selection[6]:

> Under the Administration's IT management reforms, federal agencies will no longer pursue the costly strategy of automating paper intensive procedures that have long outlived their worth. Instead, the 2003 Budget focuses on using information technology to:
> - Simplify and integrate processes across redundant or duplicative programs, so as to make it easy for citizens to get service,
> - Directly improve the management of programs, so as to achieve better program outcomes,
> - Ensure sound security of government information systems,
> - Eliminate redundant or non-productive IT investments, and
> - Bring successful e-business practices to government administrative operations, such as effective procurement and human capital management strategies.

A serious question exists about whether or not there is a real payoff in terms of efficiency, productivity, and improved service from increased expenditures in IT. The Office of the Management of the Budget, within the White House, has "implemented IT decision-making practices that review IT investments across agencies to resolve six issues that have previously limited productivity improvements[7]:

1. Automation of existing outdated processes, instead of fixing underlying management problems or simplifying agency procedures to take advantage of new e-business and Egovernment capabilities.
2. Duplicative IT investments. Multiple departments and agencies buy the same IT items, resulting in redundant investments and operations that make it difficult and time consuming for citizens to interact with the federal government.
3. Few IT investments have significantly improved mission performance. Although agencies have made progress in implementing capital planning and investment control, agency budget decisions and management practices rarely linked IT investments to program performance improvement.
4. Few agencies have plans demonstrating and documenting the linkage between IT capabilities and the business needs of the agency. Lack of such "enterprise architecture" plans can lead to IT investments that

cannot work together, which further retards information flows across agencies and across the government.

5. Many major IT projects do not meet cost, schedule, and performance goals. Under the Federal Acquisition Streamlining Act (FASA), agencies must report and track progress against cost, schedule, and performance goals for IT and other capital projects, which is implemented through Administration budget guidance.

6. Major gaps exist in agency and governmentwide computer-related security. Under the Government Information Security Reform Act, agencies submitted reports to OMB based on annual assessments by CIOs and Inspectors General. The assessments show gaps both within and across agencies, which suggest that federal agency missions may be put at risk by a broad range of security problems.

The last point will be of prime importance for the foreseeable future. The events of September 11, 2001, have made security the first issue of concern in both government and the private sector.

Automated Bureaucracy

Even before computer systems became prevalent, governments were regularly subject to the criticism that they were too bureaucratic. The most straightforward interpretation of this charge is that bureaucracies frequently are so concerned with rules and procedures that they forget that their purpose is to deal with people and their problems. Thus, it is feared that computer systems will serve bureaucratic interests, not the public's, by further shielding government workers from direct responsibility. Furthermore, how do such systems affect the quality of decisions? Are citizens still assured of due process when computers are part of the decision-making process? Can the high-level policy makers in Congress and the executive branch be sure that the bureaucracy is held accountable?

It may be useful to provide more detail on the activities of the Office of Management of the Budget (OMB), given authority over federal information functions under the Paperwork Reduction Act of 1980. Within OMB, the Office of Information and Regulatory Affairs (OIRA) was established with specific authority over "general information policy, reduction of paperwork burden, federal statistical activity, records management activities, the privacy and security of records, agency sharing and dissemination of records, and the acquisition and use of automatic data processing and telecommunications and other information technology for managing information resources."[8] With respect to information policies for the federal government, the 1980 Act specified the following[9]:

1. The development, implementation, and oversight of uniform information resources management policies and guidelines

2. The initiation and review of proposals for legislation, regulations, and agency procedures to improve information management

3. The coordination, through budget review and other means, of agency information practices
4. The promotion of greater information sharing among agencies through the federal information locator system (FILS), the review of budget proposals, and other means
5. The evaluation of agency information practices
6. The oversight of planning and research regarding the federal collection, processing, storage, transmission, and use of information.

These information policies are meant to accomplish the main purpose of the Paperwork Reduction Act—to reduce the amount of paper the government handles. Just transforming paper into computer memory is not the answer. More computers do not necessarily mean less information is handled; in fact, quite the opposite may be the case. Thus, OMB is obliged by the Act to determine, "whether the collection of information by an agency is necessary for the proper performance of the functions of the agency, including whether the information will have practical utility for the agency." Beyond its responsibility for paperwork clearance, OMB must[9a]

- Prepare an inventory of all information collection activities
- Assign agencies as the primary collectors for other agencies
- Determine the goals for the reduction of information collection
- Monitor compliance with the recommendations of the Commission on Federal Paperwork
- Design and operate FILS [Federal Information Locator System], and
- Report to Congress on an annual basis.

A major thrust of the Act is to reduce the paperwork burden on the general public by minimizing the government's requirements for information. In 1986, the Act was amended by the Paperwork Reduction Reauthorization Act, which called for additional reductions in the collection burden[10]:

1. [OMB was] directed to establish goals for agencies to reduce Federal paperwork burdens by five percent for each of the next four consecutive years beginning with FY 1987,
2. [the Act] clarified the treatment of paperwork requirements contained in regulations as being similar to other information collections, and
3. expanded the opportunities for meaningful public comments on agency information collection.

Continuing in this vein and not deterred by the lack of success, Congress passed the Paperwork Reduction Act of 1995 (PRA) that[11]

establishes a broad mandate for agencies to perform their information resources management activities in an efficient, effective, and economical manner. To assist agencies in an integrated approach to information resources management, the Act requires that the Director of OMB develop and implement uniform and consistent information resources management policies; oversee the development and promote the use of information management principles, standards, and guidelines; evaluate agency information resources management practices in order to determine their adequacy and efficiency; and determine compliance of such practices with the policies, principles, standards, and guidelines promulgated by the Director.

In mid-1996, the GAO released a report casting serious doubts on the paper reduction enterprise; in fact, it was noted that the burden placed on the general public had "increased significantly since 1980, both government wide and in particular agencies."[12] One agency alone, the Internal Revenue Service, "accounted for about 80% of the total paperwork burden of nearly 7 billion hours."

Another GAO report released in 2002 reveals that in spite of a massive investment in information technology (IT) over the years, major problems still exist in satisfying the amended and recodified PRA of 1995. Consider the following concerns[13]:

In brief, the data indicate that federal paperwork increased by almost 290 million burden hours during fiscal year 2001—the largest 1-year increase since the PRA was amended and recodified in 1995. As was the case in previous years, this record increase is largely attributable to IRS, which increased its paperwork estimate by about 250 million burden hours during the year. Most of the increases that IRS described involved changes that had been made at the initiation of the agency—not because of new statutes.

Federal agencies providing information to OMB identified more than 400 violations of the PRA that occurred during fiscal year 2001. Those same agencies identified only slightly fewer violations than last year, indicating that the overall decline in the number of violations during the past 2 years has stopped. Some of these PRA violations have been going on for years, and they collectively represent substantial opportunity costs. As we have said for the past several years, we believe that OMB can do more to ensure that agencies do not use information collections without proper clearance.

Over the years, that government agency most criticized for its inefficiencies and increases in paperwork, as mentioned above, is the Internal Revenue Service (IRS). It should also be noted that by virtue of its basic activities, the IRS should be a major beneficiary of IT.

Problems and Hopes at the Internal Revenue Service (IRS)

The activities of the IRS affect every taxpayer in the country, a rather large number given that some 120 million individual returns were filed annually in the 1990s, with 129 million in 2002. Reports of problems at the IRS appear with some regularity—witness 1985 when problems with the computer system threatened to bring operations to a halt. As discussed above, the IRS was identified by the GAO as having a high-risk IT problem, and the press has not overlooked such major difficulties. Thus, *Business Week* warned, "Perhaps most troubling, the agency's vaunted Tax Systems Modernization (TSM) program—designed to replace its outdated system with a state-of-the-art network employing digital imaging—is in disarray."[14] Here are more details about the TSM problem from the GAO[15]:

> How can IRS design, acquire, and maintain computerized systems that streamline operations and are secure? By the end of fiscal year 1995, IRS will have spent over $2.5 billion on its $8 billion TSM initiative to streamline selected tax processing functions. Yet, the overall design of TSM remains incomplete, and IRS is continuing to automate existing functions with limited demonstration of how or if the pieces of the system will fit together to improve tax processing. Given such concerns and budget constraints, the Congress reduced IRS' fiscal year 1995 budget request by $339 million. In making decisions on IRS' fiscal year 1996 budget, the Congress will need to know whether the management of TSM has improved.

In fact, Congress cut the IRS budget by an additional $160 million for 1996. It is somewhat ironic that the IRS, which should be a prime beneficiary of electronic networks as a means of automating its enormous workload as well as providing a convenient and efficient service to its captive clientele, should be having so much difficulty implementing an appropriate system to do just that. In July of 1996, the IRS informed "1.2 million companies that they must begin paying business taxes electronically by year's end."[16] Many of these companies did not know about these electronic filing requirements, nor did they have proper software. The IRS continues its unfortunate record of alienating the public, into the network age.

Recent evaluations of the IRS have been somewhat more encouraging: "Overall, since the mid-1990s IRS has seen increased workload, decreased staffing, and significant changes in the allocation of resources between taxpayer assistance programs and its compliance and collection programs."[17] In somewhat more detail, consider the following[18]:

- Between 1995 and the end of 2001 IRS's workload, measured by returns filed, increased by about 10 percent while aggregate staffing declined by about 14 percent.
- Over the same time, there was a significant internal reallocation of resources with a disproportionate decline in compliance and collection program staffing to accommodate more emphasis on taxpayer service, such as telephone assistance, and to information systems operation and investment.
- Electronic filing of returns increased but not enough to reduce paper returns sufficiently to free significant processing resources for use elsewhere.

- The reallocation of resources shows signs of beginning to produce more accurate service for taxpayers, but the compliance and collection programs have seen large and pervasive declines in performance indicators such as audit rates, collection cases closed, enforcement actions such as liens and levies, and raw productivity (measured by cases closed per unit of staff time without adjusting for possible quality changes).

The results of the 2002 tax filing season are quite revealing in terms of the progress made and the increasing role of the Internet in this activity. The highlights of five key areas, given as follows, supports the view that after many difficult years, the IRS has accommodated to the diffusion of a technology that permits people the convenience of filing from home.[19]

- Processing—Available evidence indicates that IRS was able to smoothly process about 131 million individual income tax returns and about 99 million refunds in 2002. This assessment is based on IRS's performance in 2002 compared with its performance in 2001 and its goals for 2002 as well as other evidence, such as testimony from the tax practitioner community.
- Electronic Filing—The number of individual income tax returns filed electronically grew from about 40.2 million in 2001 to about 46.9 million in 2002, an increase of about 16.5 percent, and the percentage of individual tax returns filed electronically reached 35.9 percent. This 16.5-percent increase over the number of returns received electronically in 2001 was more than IRS's goal of 15 percent and continued the upward trend in the number of returns filed electronically since 1995.
- Telephone Service—IRS's performance measures showed that IRS provided more accessible and accurate telephone service in the 2002 filing season than in 2001 and met most of its telephone service performance goals. IRS achieved these results despite an increase in calls due to the rate reduction credit.
- Walk-in Assistance—Despite data limitations, there was enough evidence to suggest that the accuracy of tax law assistance provided by IRS's walk-in sites improved in 2002 compared with 2001, although the level of accuracy (about 50 percent) was still low.
- Internet Web Site—Our assessment and external assessments indicated that IRS's redesigned Web site, which became operational in January 2002, was easier to access and more user friendly, although there are certain aspects of the site that need attention.

It does appear that over the years, the IRS has finally responded to ongoing criticism and is engaged in a program of improvement that has yielded measurable results. Its history represents a significant case study of the complexities of IT, hailed as an obvious solution to a host of apparent problems. Air traffic control systems have also appeared to be an obvious beneficiary of IT, as air traffic has grown substantially over the years.

Trouble With Air Traffic Control Systems

As another example of the problems involved in implementing sophisticated information systems, especially those operating in safety-critical environments in real-time, no better example could be chosen than air traffic control systems, previously identified as high-risk by the GAO. In 1988, the cost of the Federal Aviation Administration's (FAA) Advanced Automation System (AAS) was estimated at $2.6 billion, an estimate that more than doubled to $5.9 billion by 1993, reaching $6.9 billion the following year.[20] By mid-1995, no new systems had yet been installed, with 1998 given as a target for the delivery of the first system: "The aviation agency is under renewed pressure to update its creaky 30-year-old backup systems. This is because the FAA has been going through a formal air traffic control system modernization effort since 1981 but still doesn't expect final delivery of the first of 20 systems until 1998."[21] The FAA, recognizing the serious problems it faced because of increasing failures in old mainframes, announced in late July 1995 that it would "begin installing new mainframes at air route traffic control centers in October 1997, more than a year earlier than it planned."[22] These systems, however, would still be running old software because "[t]he FCC said it could no longer wait until new software is written as part of its planned $4.8 billion overhaul of the nation's air traffic control system."[23] Thus, the hardware part of the IT equation is being addressed, but the state of software remains a serious problem.

Just to gain an appreciation of the size of the task that the FAA confronts, consider that its air traffic control system handles 220 million flights annually. Of these, "246,000 are delayed because of weather, 4,000 are delayed because of equipment failures," and in further support of its improvements, the FAA claims that ["air traffic control systems are 99.43% reliable."][24] In addition to safety issues, the FAA must now deal with very serious security issues arising from the increased threat of terrorism. Homeland security as an integral component in the defense of the nation will be discussed later in this chapter.

E-GOVERNANCE AND THE FUTURE

> Specifically, federal agencies have implemented an array of e-government applications, including using the Internet to collect and disseminate information and forms, buy and pay for goods and services, submit bids and proposals, and apply for licenses, grants, and benefits.[25]

Such terms as E-Government, E-Democracy, and E-Governance have become as ubiquitous as E-Business. That is, government is expected to employ whatever technologies are available in order to increase efficiencies of operation, be more responsive to the needs of citizens, and engage in new supportive activities now made feasible. The expectation is strong that because the Internet has affected so many areas of life, it must affect government and in a powerful manner. Of course, the term government applies to different levels—municipal, state, and federal—and to different functions—executive, legislative, and judicial—to say nothing of national and global governments. In this section, the notion of E-government will be discussed and possible benefits explored. Important Internet applications in politics and voting will be reserved for a later section.

The Shape of E-Government

As we shall see, the idea of E-government is a work in progress. The notion is of a government readily accessible to its citizens by means of the Internet. Thus government services and information are provided and individual payments and information are received and acted upon, all by electronic means. All of this seems both natural and necessary and is being implemented by many countries around the world. But what is more difficult to integrate into current activities is the attractive idea of determining the will of the citizenry on a regular basis. Democratic governments, once elected, are assumed to have a mandate to carry out their policies until the next election. However, the Internet offers the real possibility of sampling the electorate's position on any issue, at any time. Such a possibility harkens back to the beginnings of direct democracy in the Athenian *agora*, or marketplace. The real question then arises: What could or should be done with such potentially available information?

Proponents of the Internet playing a major rule in governance have spoken of the "Electronic Agora" as a way of giving voice to the people beyond the infrequent and diffuse electoral process. This concern is part of the more general idea of empowering citizens[26]:

> Technological innovation in government has long been an oxymoron. Bureaucrats hate change—and the very concept of streamlining. But what happens when the immovable object meets an irresistible force called the Internet? The cheap computing, fast connectivity, and easy-to-use interfaces that characterize the Web are just too powerful to ignore as tools for making government more efficient.
>
> Among other things, they allow citizens to take over tasks—such as deciding what types of benefits or grants they should apply for—that once were the domain of clerks. Give government agencies the ability to easily share data and communicate, moreover, and they'll enjoy the same productivity gains that the Net has produced for businesses.
>
> Over the past couple of years, the push for e-government has taken on a new sense of urgency. A ballooning federal budget deficit and the looming

retirement from the taxpaying ranks of the massive baby-boom generation mean that over the next 20 years, governments at all levels will probably have to accomplish far more with relatively stagnant revenues and resources (except for the military, of course).

It is not surprising that there is some difference of opinion about what constitutes an E-government initiative. One recent report by an organization called the Performance Institute proposed the following definition to characterize one kind of initiative: "Citizen-centered e-government initiatives strategically employ information technology to provide government products or services to intended users resulting in enhanced value."[27] The report goes on, at length, to provide examples of E-government initiatives as well as characterizing the methods used and their effectiveness as follows[28]:

2. Agencies generally fail to use mission-aligned IT performance measures to justify, manage and evaluate the success of e-government
3. Agencies need to become more creative and willing to "blow up" old program structures with technology. . . .
5. E-Government is increasingly focusing on the citizen again, but not all e-government initiatives are "Citizen-Centered"
6. CIO's are assuming an appropriate role of "enabler" of agency business processes and are more integrated with the rest of the agency's leadership
7. More program managers are playing leadership roles in e-government, but more needs to be done to engage all program managers in e-government leadership roles. . . .
10. Establishing clear priorities is paying off in generating attention to and sufficient funding for key e-government initiatives.

The Council for Excellence in Government is a private Washington organization, which released a report with the provocative title, "E-Government: The Next American Revolution."[29] This report describes the finding of two large surveys conducted in late 2000 and early 2001 on the topic of the importance and inevitability of E-government. The American population seems to support the concept of E-government very strongly, but of course no well-defined description exists. It just appears to be obvious that the growing adoption of Internet technology must be a good thing. The report includes a set of guiding principles for "What should e-government be?" and these certainly seem reasonable[30]:

1. Easy to use, connecting people with federal, state, regional, local, tribal, and international governments according to their preferences and needs
2. Available to everyone, at home, at work, in schools, in libraries and other convenient community locations
3. Private and secure, with the appropriate standards for privacy, security, and authentication—generating trust—required for e-government to grow and serve the public

4. Innovative and results-oriented, emphasizing speed and harnessing the latest advances in technology
5. Collaborative, with solutions developed collectively and openly among public, private, nonprofit, and research partners, on the basis of their experience and expertise
6. Cost-effective, through strategic investments that produce significant long-term efficiencies and savings
7. Transformational, harnessing technology through personal and organizational leadership to change the way government works, rather than merely automate existing practices.

So far the emphasis in this section has been on what is expected of governments and how they can fulfill their responsibilities with respect to the needs and expectations of their citizens. But what do individuals, organizations, and companies of technologically advanced countries such as the U.S. want and need? The results of an extensive survey, carried out by the Pew Internet & American Life Project, were reported in April of 2002. Almost 2,400 americans, of whom 1,450 use the Internet, were surveyed and in addition, an in-depth survey was conducted of 815 people who use government Web sites. The summary of findings begins as follows: "Web presence is not optional for governments in the United States. Citizens are online and learning to demand answers at Internet speed. Government budget-writers require that the cost-savings potential of the Internet be mastered. At the same time, laws and executive orders mandate the provision of at least some services online."[31] Among the highlights are the following[32]:

- Fully 68 million American adults have used government agency Web sites—a sharp increase from the 40 million who had used government sites in March 2000 when we first polled on the subject.
- They exploit their new access to government in wide-ranging ways, finding information to further their civic, professional, and personal lives.
- Some also use government Web sites to apply for benefits, engage public officials, and complete transactions such as filing taxes.
- 42 million Americans have used government Web sites to research public policy issues. 23 million Americans have used the Internet to send comments to public officials about policy choices.
- 14 million have used government Web sites to gather information to help them decide how to cast their votes.
- 13 million have participated in online lobbying campaigns.
- Most government Web site visitors are happy with what they find on the sites; 80% of them say they find what they are seeking on the Web sites.
- Half of government Web site users (49%) say the Internet has improved the way they interact with the federal government.
- 16% of those who use government Web sites had filed taxes online.
- The most frequently cited service that government users would like to have is to be able to access their Social Security account information.

There seems to be little doubt that the increasing use of the Web by governments in the U.S. has made government information and services readily available to individuals, and they have certainly taken advantage as the Pew Internet survey has shown. But serious questions remain about other important uses that are being overlooked. In particular, "there is concern among academics, activists, and even some elected officials that government Web sites might focus too much on providing services, and not enough on facilitating Americans' civic involvement. This service orientation, they argue, treats citizens as consumers rather than owners of government, and thus inhibits public engagement with the nation's political life."[33]

The discussion so far has focused on institutional Web sites, but of course elected officials maintain individual sites in order to present their accomplishments and goals and to receive questions, criticisms, and even praise from their constituents. A report produced by the Congressional Management Foundation described most of the 605 congressional personal sites as fair to poor.[34] Such sites are deficient in providing useful objective information; instead they contain press releases, photographs of the politician at events, and promotional material. What is lacking is "basic legislative information such as position statements, rationales for key votes, status of pending legislation, and educational material about Congress."[35]

In mid-December 2002, President Bush signed the Electronic Government Act of 2002,[36] which mandates a set of policies to implement a wide range of electronic government services. Note that the title of the Act reads as follows:

A bill to enhance the management and promotion of electronic Government services and processes by establishing an Office of Electronic Government within the Office of Management and Budget, and by establishing a broad framework of measures that require using Internet-based information technology to enhance citizen access to Government information and services, and for other purposes.

The Act creates the Office of Electronic Government, with the Administrator appointed by the President. This Administrator assists the Director of the OMB by implementing specified requirements of the Act. For example, his functions include the following[37]:

- Advising the OMB Director on the resources required to effectively operate information systems
- Recommending to the Director changes in government-wide strategies and priorities for electronic government
- Promoting innovative uses of information technology (IT), especially initiatives involving multi-agency collaboration
- Helping to establish policies which set the framework for IT standards and guidelines for interconnectivity and interoperability, categorizing gov-

ernment electronic information to enhance search capabilities, and computer system efficiency and security

• Sponsoring dialogue with leaders on electronic government in the executive branch agencies, and legislative and judicial branches; in state, local, and tribal governments; and with representatives from the private, non-profit, and academic sectors to encourage collaboration and share best practices

• Oversee the development of an integrated, standardized, Internet-based system (a portal) for providing government information and services to the public from a single point, organized by function, as provided for in Section 204 of the Act.

It will be interesting to see how well the Act fulfills its intentions as it takes effect and becomes part of existing bureaucracies.

State and Local Governments

It is obvious that citizens interact with their state and local governments more frequently than they do with the federal government. Unfortunately, up to fairly recently, Web sites constructed at the local level have been less heavily used than those at the federal level. The Pew Internet survey referred to above made the following points[38]:

• Federal and state Web sites are more popular than local Web sites: 80% of government Web site users have visited federal sites, 76% have visited state sites, and 41% have visited local government Web sites.

• Generally, seekers find the information they want more easily on federal (68%) and state (69%) Web sites than they do on local government sites (46%). Federal and state sites get higher evaluations from these Internet users.

A subsequent Pew Internet report dealt specifically with the use of the Internet at the civic level and the claims made by local officials for associated benefits. The survey was carried out during July 2002 and among the more interesting findings, including the importance of e-mail for every level of interaction, are the following[39]:

• 88% of local elected officials in this broad national sample use email and the Internet in the course of their official duties.

• 90% of online local officials use email in their official duties at least weekly and 61% use it daily for such purposes.

• 79% of all municipal officials in this survey say they have received email from citizens or local groups about civic issues. Some 25% receive email from constituents every day.

• 61% of online local officials use email to communicate with citizens at least weekly. 21% do so every day.

- 75% of online local officials use the Web for research and other purposes in the course of their official duties at least weekly and 34% use it daily for such purposes.
- 73% of online officials note that email with constituents helps them better understand public opinion.
- 56% of online officials say their use of email has improved their relations with community groups.
- 54% of online officials say that their use of email has brought them into contact with citizens from whom they had not heard before.
- 32% have been persuaded by email campaigns at least in part about the merits of a group's argument on a policy question.
- 21% agree that email lobbying campaigns have opened their eyes to "unity and strength of opinion" among constituents about which they have been previously unaware.
- 61% of online officials agree that email can *facilitate* public debate. However, 38% say that email alone cannot carry the weight of the full debate on complex issues.

Municipal Web sites typically carry such features as "city staff directories, meeting agendas with minutes, information on receiving municipal services, calendars for meetings/events, access to zoning/city planning, budget/tax information,"[40] and much more. Another study of so-called "urban e-government" reported on "a detailed analysis of 1567 city government web sites in the 70 largest metropolitan areas" and found that sites were increasingly available and the range of associated services had grown substantially.[41]

1. 49 percent of websites offer services that are fully executable online, up from 25 percent last year
2. the most frequent services are requesting services, requesting information, paying traffic tickets, and filing complaints
3. 93 percent of websites provide access to publications (up from 64 percent in 2001) and 77 percent have links to databases (up from 38 percent last year)
4. 38 percent show privacy policies (up from 14 percent in 2001), while 25 percent have security policies (up from 8 percent last year)
5. 82 percent of government websites have some form of disability access, which is up from 11 percent last year
6. 2 percent of sites have commercial advertising, about the same as last year
7. 11 percent of websites charge user fees for the ability to execute particular online services, while 2 percent have premium sections requiring payment for entry
8. 8 percent of city government websites have restricted areas requiring user names and passwords to access
9. 17 percent of city government websites have foreign language translation features (up from 7 percent last year)

One further, somewhat disturbing point from this study should be noted: "However, at the same time, there is growing reliance on user fees and premium service areas that limits access. Some cities also are creating 'restricted areas' requiring user names and registration for accessibility. These features need to be assessed very carefully in order to determine how they will affect the ability of ordinary people to access electronic government."

Accessing Governments Elsewhere

It is not surprising that in other countries, citizens also access, or wish to access, their governments using the Internet. Space does not permit a detailed comparison but a few interesting findings will be reported. The global management and technology services company, Accenture, reported in 2002 on the results of its third survey of a group of countries, comparing their performance in the domain of E-government. 169 national government services across nine major service sectors were compared for 23 countries: "Human Services, Justice & Public Safety, Revenue, Defense, Education, Transport & Motor Vehicles, Regulation & Democracy, Procurement and Postal."[42] The countries were ranked using a measure called Overall Maturity—a combination of two other measures, Service Maturity and Customer Relationship Management (CRM). Here are the definitions given of these two measures.[43]

> • Service Maturity measures the level to which a government has developed an online presence. It takes into account the number of services for which national governments are responsible that are available online (Service Maturity Breadth), and the level of completeness with which each service is offered (Service Maturity Depth).
> • CRM is a measure of the sophistication of service delivery, thereby helping citizens get the best value from their online interaction with government. There are five measures of CRM: Insight, Interaction, Organization Performance, Customer Offerings, and Networks.

The winner for the third time was Canada, followed closely by Singapore, and then the U.S. Canada's progress is consistent and it "continues to advance toward its stated goal of providing Canadians with electronic access to all federal programs and services by 2004." It is impossible to summarize the detailed information in this long report but the following passage does raise some interesting points.[44]

> At the highest level, the findings show that the governments surveyed are becoming increasingly sophisticated, both in their articulation of what eGovernment is, and in how best to implement eGovernment initiatives to maximize benefits to citizens, businesses and government alike. Blanket statements exhorting all agencies to "get online" without a blueprint for

what this means and how this can improve both service delivery and administrative effectiveness are disappearing. In their place are detailed action plans that encompass all the requirements of a successful eGovernment program and address stakeholder needs. In the early stages of eGovernment, the gap between rhetoric and reality was a yawning chasm as political leadership articulated an ambitious vision with little consideration of the pragmatic considerations and complexity involved in bringing that vision to life. In these early stages the unintended effect was more rather than less complexity in dealing with government.

We, as citizens, are just starting to feel comfortable with making contact with our governments over the Internet. Whether or not the future holds real changes in the way democratic governments operate remains to be seen. However, although technology opens up many possibilities, in the final analysis, the choices are ours. One last example of a democracy planning to employ information technology in a creative fashion is the United Kingdom, where the House of Commons Information Committee delivered a report with a recommendation that[45]

the following set of principles for information and communication technologies [ICT] be adopted for the House:

A. The House is committed to the use of ICT to increase its accessibility and to enable the public, exercising its right to use whatever medium is convenient, to communicate with Members and with Committees of the House.

B. The House is committed to using ICT to enhance the professionalism of Members [and] their staff in all aspects of parliamentary life.

C. The House is committed to the use of ICT to increase public participation in its work, enabling it to draw on the widest possible pool of experience, including particularly those who have traditionally been excluded from the political and parliamentary process.

D. The House recognizes the value of openness and will use ICT to enable, as far as possible, the public to have access to its proceedings and papers.

E. The House will develop and share good practice in the use of ICT by other parliamentary and governmental bodies both within the United Kingdom and elsewhere, and will work in collaboration with outside bodies.

These principles are worthy of being emulated.

THE POLITICAL PROCESS

As the happiness of the people is the sole end of government, so the consent of the people is the only foundation of it.—John Adams

Politics is the art of looking for trouble, finding it, misdiagnosing it, and then misapplying the wrong remedies.—Groucho Marx

In their simplest applications, computers have been used to register voters prior to elections and to tabulate the results on election night. As a consequence of the nationwide census taken every ten years, election boundaries must be redrawn to reflect the new population distribution. Computers play an important role in this process of reapportionment and have aroused considerable controversy for their alleged technological contribution to gerrymandering. They are also employed to compute the output of public opinion polls, predict the outcome of elections, and maintain detailed lists of political supporters. More recently, candidates and political parties have placed their opinions and positions on the Web to make them readily available to current supporters and to attract new ones. Fears have been voiced that the political party with sufficient money to afford the best computer and telecommunication resources and designers will have a major advantage in the electoral process. But then again, what has really changed? The skillful use of financial resources has always been a major determining factor in the outcome of political contests.

Beyond the use of computers and the Internet for the purposes listed above, there are on the horizon possibilities that could radically transform the entire electoral process as well as the functioning of government itself. As mentioned above, in a wired world, citizens could be regularly polled for their opinions, with the use of adequate security procedures. They could in fact cast votes on a number of issues, an extension of the referendum process usually in place for congressional elections in some states or for call-back votes in others. This form of instantaneous democracy is a powerful tool, whose operation must be carefully studied before it is implemented. That is, great care must be taken not to have technology drive potentially radical changes in both the electoral process and the governing process, without considerable study and discussion.

This section will focus on two main issues: the use of the Internet by political parties, citizen groups, incumbents, and challengers in the basic process of getting elected, and the ostensibly straightforward process of voting and counting votes. Discussion of the latter topic is clearly motivated by the events associated with the counting of votes in Florida during the 2000 presidential election. The apparent difficulties encountered by many voters, with the subsequent voiding of many ballots, resulted in a controversial outcome. A host of studies was undertaken to determine if computers and the Internet could substantially improve the voting experience and the accuracy of the outcome to reflect the intentions of the voters, while maintaining a secure system. The results of most studies is caution on relying too much on imperfect technologies.

Getting Elected

It requires a great deal of money to get elected to political office, and indeed the role of fund-raiser has achieved a high profile in election campaigns.

Traditionally, supporters have been identified and then canvassed for contributions before and during the campaign. But increasingly sophisticated fundraising methods have been developed that take advantage of computer power. Mailing lists of supporters are carefully organized in terms of ethnic background, income, education, age, sex, and opinion on a number of issues. Also stored in the computer are texts of fundraising letters, each focusing on a particular issue. Such systems are maintained by the political parties and by corporate political-action committees (PACs), legislated by Congress to collect money for political candidates. Whenever a political issue surfaces, the appropriate letter form is selected and "personally" addressed by the computer to those supporters with an appropriate profile.

These techniques have also been used to mobilize support for political causes, in which case letters and telegrams are solicited rather than money. A system for this purpose requires a moderately-sized computer, considerable storage, a high-speed printer, folding-sealing-stamping equipment, and people to do data entry. Of course, currently many voters and supporters, if not most, can be reached over the Internet, with substantial savings in paper and postage. The ability to target voters along ethnic, regional, religious, or any other lines results in more efficient fundraising and more effective pressure tactics. But the public should be aware of what lies behind current solicitation practices.

One analysis of the 2002 political campaign, while cautious about claiming too much, identified a number of interesting and innovative applications[46]:

- Websites—In 2002, 70% of major candidates for major races (Congressional and above) had websites as opposed to less than 60% in 2000.
- Online fundraising on campaign sites went from under 25% in 2000 to over 55% this year and preliminary estimates are that the amounts of money raised about doubled.
- Online tools—Traditional online tools such as campaign newsletters and action alerts are now a standard feature of most major campaigns and they have become visually very appealing. These are the first meaningful steps toward truly widespread online organizing which has enormous potential.
- E-mail—Although most are still using in-house lists, campaigns have figured out the cost benefit (almost free) of using email and they are frequently mailing every name they can find, occasionally with the 'mass personalization' that will become commonplace.
- Rapid Response—In the past it was only presidential campaigns that were know for their near instantaneous response to their opponents' charges and the media's questions. With the ability to access email from virtually anywhere, rapid response is now standard in most major campaigns.

A Washington-based communications company, the Bivings Group, surveyed the readiness of Republican and Democratic incumbents in Congress for the

2002 election, with respect to their use of the Internet. It is somewhat surprising to discover that the Internet has not become as ubiquitous or as useful as one might have expected. For example, consider the following findings[47]:

- Less than 30 percent of the campaign committees for incumbent U.S. Senators and Representatives have a functional website specifically for the 2002 election.
- The campaign committees for incumbent U.S. Senators are more than twice as likely to have a 2002 campaign websites than U.S Representatives.
- 42 percent of the campaign committees for incumbent U.S. Senators and Representatives that are up for re-election in 2002 have no Web presence.
- The campaign committees for Republican incumbents are 52 percent more likely to have current 2002 websites than Democratic campaign committees.
- While 76 percent of all live campaign websites included in this study provided sufficient contact information, only 60 percent provide information regarding how to volunteer to assist the campaign.
- Only 42 percent of all live campaign websites included in this study would accept secure online donations.

Somehow, in spite of the obvious virtues of the Web, on the whole, politicians have been quite cautious in how they have chosen to use it. The following is a particularly trenchant observation[48]:

> But when the tech bubble burst, the political Web bubble went with it, and the same business model that failed e-commerce, search engines, and other sites—draw eyeballs now, worry about revenue later—also failed. People did use the Internet to learn about politics. . . . But most people wanted simple news, not a site "delivering democracy to your desktop," as voter.com promised. Online polls bombed as accurate gauges, cranks dominated Internet chat rooms, and ultimately users tilted toward trusted sites such as NYTimes.com and CNN.com.

How Does the Voter Want to Vote?

Nowadays, people are asked their opinion about everything: their favorite soap opera, sitcom, and politician. There are public polls such as Gallup, Harris, and Roper, and many private ones are conducted for elected officials as well as candidates. The computer is now used to store survey results and to perform sophisticated statistical analyses and projections. Over the years, models have been constructed that can predict with reasonable accuracy, on the basis of a careful sampling of voter preferences, the outcome of elections on the local, state, or federal level. A danger of such models is that both elected officials and candidates for political office will begin to tailor their opinions in the directions determined by the models. A basic problem for elected officials will be heightened—to vote their conscience or to represent the political views of their constituency, when these are in conflict.

There were not many experiments in electronic polling of people at their homes prior to the widespread popularity of the Internet. In Columbus, Ohio, in the early 1980s, about 30,000 homes, under an experimental system called QUBE, now terminated, were wired to a central computer by a two-way communication system. QUBE was used to sample public opinion in a quick and painless fashion. A question put to the subscribers appeared on their television set. Viewers would press either the yes or no button on their handsets as the vote was being taken. Each home on the network was briefly scanned, the votes accumulated, and the results would appear on the screen in a few seconds. Could (or should) such a polling method be used within the current political system? Consider the comments at the time of political scientist, Jean Bethke Elshtain, in criticizing this voting model as an[49]

> interactive shell game [that] cons us into believing that we are participating when we are really simply performing as the responding "end" of a prefabricated system of external stimuli. . . . In a plebiscitary system, the views of the majority . . . swamp minority or unpopular views. Plebiscitism is compatible with authoritarian policies carried out under the guise of, or with the connivance of, majority views. The opinion can be registered by easily manipulated, ritualistic plebiscites, so there is no need for debate on substantive issues.

In the last few years, with the public's discovery of the Internet and the startling growth in use, electronic polling has become much more of a real possibility. Polls are a regular feature on the Internet, whether voting for Web-page layouts, songs, pinups-of-the-week, or presidential candidates. Of course, these polls are highly unscientific as there are no demographic controls, and they have little effect other than to provide marketing information, but there could potentially be a sufficient level of security in place to limit voting to registered voters. In this case, would it be used by governments, and if so, how and to what end?

One person in the forefront of the debate about electronic voting is Lorrie Cranor. One of her arguments in favor of electronic voting is that traditional voting methods, at least in North America, do not offer enough alternatives. Because one can only vote for one candidate, a concern exists about "wasting the vote" in a race involving more than two candidates. So in the 1992 election, it was claimed that "there were a lot of people who said that they were Perot supporters, but they felt that Perot didn't have a very good chance of winning. So as not to waste their vote, they voted for their second-choice candidate. And so at some point either the day before election or the week before or even the day of the election, they evaluated Perot's likelihood of being able to win and decided that they weren't going to vote for him."[50] Cranor has proposed an electronic system, Sensus, that guarantees privacy and security and permits the voter to express a "declared voting strategy"[51]:

> You express a statement of strategy which explains how you want to vote. So, for example, this statement of strategy would indicate whether you would prefer to vote for, say, your second choice candidate instead of your first choice candidate, if your first choice candidate didn't have very much chance of winning. And you wouldn't have to decide before the election whether or not your first choice candidate had enough chance of winning. This would be decided for you by the computer, basically optimizing your strategy so that you would cast the best vote to get the most possible value for your vote when the votes were actually counted.

The role of the computer in this system is to take into account each voter's strategy combined with the current vote tally and cycle through this process until everyone is as close to being satisfied as possible. Clearly, this approach encourages more candidates to run for office and is only possible with electronic voting. The extension of electronic voting to the legislative process seems to have very little support, especially from politicians, even if the many associated problems could be solved.

But it was the difficulties in both voting and counting the votes in Florida, during the year 2000 presidential election, that led to the undertaking of many studies to evaluate the prospects of online voting in the near future. One of the first such studies was carried out before the Florida election and reported early in 2001. It was sponsored by the National Science Foundation and was a joint effort of the Internet Policy Institute, the University of Maryland, and the Freedom Forum.[52] The study focused on three possible applications of the Internet, namely, poll-site Internet voting, kiosk voting, and remote Internet voting. The first category is rather straight forward, bringing the convenience of the Internet to the traditional poll site, where since voting is still under the control of election officials, and traditional security can be enforced.

The kiosk is a remote site, which could be located anywhere people congregate. It is possible for election officials to monitor and supervise the operation of these sites, and security could involve television cameras as well. Obviously such sites would pose more challenges than traditional polling sites, but it is expected that these could be met. The real challenge exists in the case of the most likely, convenient, and anticipated form of online voting[53]:

> *Remote Internet voting* seeks to maximize the convenience and access of the voters by enabling them to cast ballots from virtually any location that is Internet accessible. While the concept of voting from home or work is attractive and offers significant benefits (e.g., the ability to conduct online research on candidates prior to voting, and the empowerment of the disabled), it also poses substantial security risks and other concerns relative to

civic culture. Without official control of the voting platform and physical environment, there are many possible ways for people to intervene to affect the voting process and the election results. Current and near-term technologies are inadequate to address these risks.

The major findings of this prestigious study are given as follows[54]:

- Poll site Internet voting systems offer some benefits and could be responsibly fielded within the next several election cycles.
- Remote Internet voting systems pose significant risk to the integrity of the voting process, and should not be fielded for use in public elections until substantial technical and social science issues are addressed.
- Internet-based voter registration poses significant risk to the integrity of the voting process, and should not be implemented for the foreseeable future.

Finally, the report concludes with a number of recommendations for research to be undertaken in service of improving elections, perhaps by employing the Internet. Among the problems that will have to be solved are the following:

- Approaches to meeting the security, secrecy, scalability, and convenience requirements of elections. Particular emphasis should be placed on the development of secure voting platforms, and secure network architectures
- Development of methods to reduce the risk of insider fraud
- Development of reliable poll site and kiosk Internet voting systems that are not vulnerable to any single point of failure and cannot lose votes
- Development of new procedures for continuous testing and certification of election systems, as well as test methods for election systems
- Human factors design for electronic voting, including the development of appropriate guidelines for the design of human interfaces and electronic ballots, as well as approaches to addressing the needs of the disabled
- Protocols for preventing vote selling and reducing coercion
- The effects of Internet voting on participation in elections, both in general and with regard to various demographic groups—especially those with less access to or facility with computers
- The effects of Internet voting on elections, the public's confidence in the electoral process and on deliberative and representative democracy
- The implications of Internet voting for political campaigns
- Electronic authentication for kiosk and remote voting.

The crucial issues, which need to be solved, are emphasized here, namely, security at all levels, certification, elimination of fraud, and authentication for remote voting.

Another important and comprehensive study was released by the U.S. General Accounting Office in 2001, as a direct response to a wide range of concerns about voting across the U.S. Of the three major objectives, the last one involves issues associated with the use of the Internet for voting. An encapsulated conclusion follows[55]:

> The broad application of Internet voting in general faces several formidable social and technological challenges. These include providing adequate ballot secrecy and privacy safeguards; providing adequate security measures to ensure safeguards against intentional intrusions and inadvertent errors; providing equal access to all voters, including persons with disabilities, and making the technology easy to use; and ensuring that the technology is a cost-beneficial alternative to existing voting methods.

It is becoming clear that a realization of Internet voting is neither a given nor is it on the horizon. Many basic Internet security problems must be overcome, along with many specific voting security ones, as well as a number of social problems. In addition, there is much that can be done to improve the current system, short of implementing Internet voting prematurely. The voting process has problems that begin with registration and continue through vote projections and actual counting. A report issued jointly by the California Institute of Technology and the Massachusetts Institute of Technology addresses some of these problems. It notes that "between 4 and 6 million votes were lost in the 2000 election."[56] The report notes that the number of lost votes can be reduced by adopting the following measures:

- Upgrade voting technologies. Replace punch cards and lever machines with optical scanners. We estimate 1.5 million of these lost votes can be recovered with this step.
- Improve voter registration systems. We recommend improved database management, installing technological links to registration databases from polling places, and use of provisional ballots. We estimate this could save another 3 million lost votes. Aggressive use of provisional ballots alone might substantially reduce the number of votes lost due to registration problems.

Note that these are rather low-technology solutions. But for the future, the report makes the following three recommendations:

- We call for a new architecture for voting technology. This architecture will allow for greater security of electronic voting. It will allow for rapid improvement and deployment of user interfaces—that is, better ballots. It is a framework within which we can explode several myths about electronic voting.
- There must be significant investment by the federal government in research and development of voting equipment technologies and meaningful human testing of machines.

• The federal government should establish an independent agency to oversee testing and to collect and distribute information on the performance and cost of equipment.

Rebecca Mercuri, a long-time critic of advanced voting technologies, raises several important issues that are worth considering before concluding this discussion. In an article in 2002, she describes a fundamental difficulty in the use of electronic voting systems[57]:

These problems [in some currently available systems] result from an underlying fundamental conflict in the construction of electronic voting (e-voting) systems: the simultaneous need for privacy and auditability, which is the ability, when necessary, to recount the votes cast. Privacy is critical to a fair election, necessary to prevent voter coercion, intimidation, and ballot-selling. But maintaining the voter's privacy precludes the use by computer-based products of standard audit and control practices: logging transactions and identifying them from end to end. In other words, the privacy constraint directly conflicts with the ability to audit the ballot data.

For the system to work, there must be a way to backtrack vote totals from actual ballots that come from (and must be independently verified by) legitimate voters voting no more than once. In turn, the ballot must in no way identify or be traced back to the voter after it is cast. These constraints, many experts say, cannot be mutually satisfied by any fully automated system.

Such problems plague all electronic voting products, whether kiosk systems, where voters go to a polling station, or Internet-based, where voters can submit a ballot from their homes, offices, or any site connected to the global network. Unlike automated teller machines at banks, where video-cameras are used to deter theft, receipts are issued, cash provides a physical audit mechanism, and insurance covers losses, the privacy requirement means that analogous checks and balances cannot be employed to protect ballots in e-voting systems.

Internet voting is further flawed because authentication of the voter must be performed by the same system that records the ballots, and this compounds the auditability and privacy problems.

Who Won?

For many people, the most exciting and interesting part of the election process is election night, as the returns are presented to the nation over the television networks. In reporting the 1984 election, the networks for the first time used real-time computer graphics to display the results. Certain graphic information such as the candidates' pictures, maps of the states, and the forms of charts and graphs were prepared in advance. As the returns flooded in, the existing graphic information was combined with the new information and presented in a variety of colors and forms. A spokesman for CBS news noted, "In 1984, for the first time, we will be able to do true real-time, data-dependent images and animation."[58]

Computer models for predicting election outcomes on the basis of interviews with selected early voters have come under some criticism. In 1984, the landslide for President Reagan was anticipated quite early, and there was little surprise as most polls had predicted such a result. In the 1980 presidential election, however, many voters in the western part of the country apparently did not bother voting because the television networks declared President Reagan an early winner. While these lost votes probably did not affect the presidential election, they did have an effect on local and state elections. It has been suggested that early computer predictions should not be announced until the polls have closed everywhere. In Canada, voting results are not announced until the polls have closed, so that late voters on the West Coast will not be influenced by reports in the East. Staggered voting hours might be a solution. In any event, the power of computer models, as well as the early report of results, to affect the electoral process must be recognized and steps taken to minimize the impact.

SECURITY AND THE NATION'S DEFENSE

> Digitization of the battlefield is part of a major effort to reshape the Army and, thus, it is one of the Army's highest priorities. The Army hopes to identify how digitization will improve combat power and how to change its organizational structure, doctrine, and tactics to take advantage of digitization.[59]
>
> The nature of the terrorist threat makes it difficult to Identify and differentiate information that can provide an early indication of a terrorist threat from the mass of data available to those in positions of authority responsible for homeland security.[60]

A major responsibility of the federal government is to defend the nation from both internal and external enemies. Since September 11, 2001, an increased emphasis on Homeland Defense has emerged, coupled with the longstanding U.S. defense responsibilities elsewhere. Given the obvious dependence of the country on Information and Computer Technology (ICT), computer networks pose a prime target and, obviously, sufficient resources must be gathered to protect these vital systems. During 2002, many discussion papers, reports, and proposals were released, culminating in the Homeland Security Act of 2002.

Traditionally, the Department of Defense (DOD), with its vast resources, has taken the lead in the development of both computer hardware and software. Much of the early research in integrated circuits was funded by DOD for military purposes. Given the sheer size of the military establishment, problems of organization are serious. There is enormous difficulty in coordinating a worldwide enterprise consisting of millions of soldiers and civilian personnel and billions of dollars of equipment, while maintaining a high degree of military preparedness.

To maintain its large investment in advanced systems and to support new and risky projects, the Pentagon, in 1958, established an agency, DARPA (Defense Advanced Research Projects Agency), originally called ARPA, to fund research and development. This agency has had a major impact on semiconductors, computers, communication systems, applications, and artificial intelligence developments over the past 40 years or so. It has also exerted an enormous influence over the kind of research funded at U.S. universities and has thereby shaped the growth of computer science departments from their very inception.

The Computerized Battlefield

In the 1982 conflict between Britain and Argentina over the Falkland Islands, a single $200,000 computer-guided missile, the French Exocet, demolished the British destroyer Sheffield, a $50 million warship.[60a] The power of computer-age weapons was frighteningly revealed. The general class of weapons with microprocessors are called precision-guided munitions (PGMs). Probably the most publicized and sophisticated of the PGMs is the cruise missile. It is programmed to fly a ground-hugging route to its target to avoid most radar, and has a microcomputer aboard with detailed topographic information about its route. During flight, this computer can compare information received from its sensors with its programmed knowledge to keep the missile on course. Future versions are expected to be able to recognize their designated targets when they arrive, to reduce the possibility of being deceived by camouflage. After a 1,500-mile trip, the cruise missile can hit a ten-foot-square target.

With weapons this smart, how necessary are people? Perhaps the goal of the next stage of warfare planning will be to remove people from the battlefield. Wars of the future might be fought with computer-controlled aircraft in the sky and robots on the land. Robots with radio receivers and transmitters could lead troops into battle or into dangerous forays where the risk of death is high. Visions of the future battlefield go beyond even these possibilities to what *Time* has called "Cyberwar," waging "war by mouse, keyboard and computer virus."[61] It is only natural that the Information Age should spawn Information Warfare by means of "Info Attacks" plotted by "Cyberstrategists" with critical information technology, both private and public, as the targets.

Recent research on military robotics has produced some impressive results; consider the following[62]:

Today, more than 40 DARPA-backed companies and academic labs are developing robots. There are recon machines that can be air-dropped into enemy territory and relay back intelligence data in real time. There are 3-pound surveillance bots that frontline soldiers could lob through a window or around a corner to get an audio and video preview of conditions. There are robots that can negotiate harsh terrain, scurry up stairs, or rush into battle to rescue injured soldiers pinned down by heavy shelling or gunfire. Other machines in development can carry weapons, deliver jolts of electricity, sniff for biogerms, and see through walls. There's even a walking robot, which could lead soldiers around blind corners, drawing fire from potential snipers.

If warfare does break out, the foot soldier will be outfitted with a bewildering array of electronic aids, including helmets with night-vision sensors, voice activation for a computer built into the body armor, a transmitter/receiver to send information back to headquarters and to receive new intelligence; body armor to protect against chemical or biological hazards; and a weapon that can transmit still-frames to the high command and is connected to the helmet to aid in locating the enemy. More recently, advances in nanotechnology, the technology of the very small, have had an impact on military technology with such applications as "lightweight, bulletproof uniforms to wearable health-monitoring sensors . . . nanotechnology that can detect threats, better protect and conceal soldiers, lighten the load for foot soldiers and provide medical support."[63]

Beyond the individual soldier, the army itself is being dramatically altered by being faster and lighter, smarter, and better connected. For example, in terms of transportation, the first part of this goal is expected to be achieved by "transforming the army from a ponderous force built around the use of tanks and other heavy vehicles to one that is comprised of lighter, less heavily armored vehicles that can sprint across the battlefield at speeds of 60 mph and that can deliver the same dose of lethality as their bigger predecessors."[64] Other advances include the following[65]:

• Advances in sensor technologies, deployed in everything from Earth-orbiting satellites to unmanned aerial vehicles, or drones, now allow troops to "see over the hill" as never before. In future battles, says Keane, the Army will occupy strategic points "like pepperoni on a pizza, with sensors watching over the rest of the pie."

• Along with the lighter, faster vehicles of FCS must come a mobile network—think of it as a moving Internet. The network would travel with the vehicles as they progress across rough terrain, through forests and around hills. This technology is critical because it provides the "situational awareness," or knowledge of the enemy's location, that will compensate, along with speed, for an FCS vehicle's reduced armor. Unlike tanks, FCS vehicles won't be built to withstand withering fire. Their mission is to locate the enemy with sensors and then be first to fire.

The Strategic Defense Initiative

The possibility of nuclear war has been a fact of existence for almost all of us. It represents the terrifying vision of a technology that, once created and implemented, is inevitably loosed upon the world.

On March 23, 1983, President Reagan delivered his now famous "Star Wars" speech, launching the Strategic Defense Initiative (SDI). Its goal was the development of a comprehensive defense system to identify, intercept, and destroy all or most of an enemy's ballistic missiles. The debate over the feasibility of such a system and its impact on the current strategy of mutual deterrence has been raging ever since. Of course, since the breakup of the Soviet Union, the threat to world peace has decreased substantially and some have argued that SDI, or the threat of a functioning SDI, was a contributing factor to this momentous event. The financial costs of competing with the U.S. may have created such a strain within the economy of the Soviet Union that its political and military will may have faltered and finally crumbled. Nevertheless, the effort to achieve a working SDI has had an impact in a number of areas and is therefore worth recounting.

It was clear at the outset that enormous computational resources would necessarily be involved in the Star Wars project. Thus, it is not surprising that the computer science community was split by a debate over the practicality of such a project and the morality of participation in its development. The decision about whether or not to work on defense-related activities is of course not unique to computer scientists. The most obvious example is that of the many physicists who, after the dropping of nuclear bombs over Japan at the end of World War II, were reluctant to contribute to the development of hydrogen weapons. The role of scientists in service to the military is an old story, rife with tales of ambition and regret.

In discussing the various issues associated with the Strategic Defense Initiative (SDI), the emphasis will be mainly on computer software, rather than the very real and difficult physics problems also involved. Many critics of SDI have recognized that the most serious area of concern was software— the programs that are intended to direct the many computers in the wide variety of tasks necessary to make the system work. SDI will place unprecedented demands on software, to such a degree that many computer scientists have publicly expressed serious doubts about it ever working. And it must operate correctly the very first time it is used. Anyone familiar with writing even short programs knows that such an event is almost nonexistent: "Because of the extreme demands on the system and our inability to test it, we will never be able to believe, with confidence, that we have succeeded. Most of the money spent will be wasted."[66]

In 1988, the Office of Technology Assessment (OTA) of the U.S. Congress issued a comprehensive classified study together with an unclassified version, "to determine the technological feasibility and implications, and the ability to survive and function despite a preemptive attack by an aggressor possessing comparable technology, of the Strategic Defense Initiative Program. . . . This study shall include an analysis of the feasibility of meeting SDI software requirements."[67] (The OTA ceased operation in 1995.) Consider the following items from the principal findings of this important study:

Finding 1. After 30 years of BMD (Ballistic Missile Defense) research, including the first few years of the Strategic Defense Initiative (SDI), defense scientists and engineers have produced impressive technical achievements, but questions remain about the feasibility of meeting the goals of the SDI.

Finding 2. Given optimistic assumptions (e.g., extraordinarily fast rates of research, development, and production), the kind of first-phase system that SDIO [*Strategic Defense Initiative Organization*] is considering might be technically deployable in the 1995–2000 period. . . . Such a system might destroy anywhere from a few up to a modest fraction of attacking Soviet intercontinental ballistic missile (ICBM) warheads.

Finding 4. The precise degree of BMD system survivability is hard to anticipate.

Finding 7. The nature of software and experience with large, complex software systems indicate that there may always be irresolvable questions about how dependable BMD software would be and about the confidence the United States could place in dependability estimates. Existing large software systems, such as the long-distance telephone system, have become highly dependable only after extensive operational use and modification. In OTA's judgment, there would be a significant probability (i.e., one large enough to take seriously) that the first (and presumably only) time the BMD system were used in a real war, it would suffer a catastrophic failure. . . . The relatively slow rate of improvement in software engineering techniques makes it appear unlikely to OTA that the situation will be substantially alleviated in the foreseeable future.

Finding 8. No adequate models for the development, production, test, and maintenance of software for full-scale BMD systems exist. . . . Experts agree that new methods for producing and safely testing the system would be needed. Evolution would be the key to system development, requiring new methods of controlling and disseminating software changes and assuring that each change would not increase the potential for catastrophic failure. OTA has found little evidence of significant progress in these areas.

The inclusion of these extensive quotations is necessary and important in order to indicate the scope of the software engineering task facing the designers of SDI. SDIO seems to have recognized the enormous difficulty of its task: "If deployed, SDS (Strategic Defense System) will be more complex than any other system the world has seen."[68] The software manager, Colonel Charles W. Lillie, agreed that "the software development and testing practice lags up to 10 years behind the state of the art. But he asserted that the SDI office has recently taken several steps to shorten the lag."[69] In addition, it has been argued by SDI officials that previous military systems have been used without complete testing and they point to the Aegis ship defense system. OTA has also noted that computer simulations will be difficult to mount because of the lack of real-world data on nuclear explosions in outer space, multiple enemy missile launches, and unpredictable countermeasures by the enemy as well. In a bizarre example of military strategic thinking, indulged in by OTA, the following backhanded support of SDI is proposed: "But unless the Soviets had secretly deployed countermeasures, such as a software virus planted by a saboteur programmer, the Soviets could not be certain that a SDI software would *not* work, and therefore *might* be deterred from attack"[70] (emphasis added). Thus, expenditures of billions of dollars have already been made, and more will follow under a continuing renamed program, Ballistic Missile Defense System, to produce a system whose reliability is highly suspect, which cannot be adequately tested, and whose major impact has probably already been felt in the collapse of the Soviet Union.

On May 13, 1993, the Department of Defense declared that funding for SDI had ended and that the "Star Wars" program was dead. But one month later, having undergone a name change to "Ballistic Missile Defense Organization," it was alive and apparently well "and may cost taxpayers another $30 billion by the end of the century. The program has already cost $33 billion. . . . Clinton-Aspin [President Clinton and Secretary of Defense Les Aspin] request[s] for SDI-related programs is $3.8 billion."[71] In the 1996 Presidential campaign, Star Wars seemed to have become a political issue. Congressional Republicans were trying to pass the Defend America Act, which would include the old missile defense system of the Strategic Defense Initiative under a new name. Robert Dole argued: "If I ask most people what would you have the President do if there was an incoming missile, ballistic missile, you would say shoot it down. We can't because President Clinton opposes it. And we support it."[72] President Clinton supported a less costly version of this proposal.

Efforts to reinvent SDI continued during the Clinton administration, originally under the name of the American Missile Protection Act, which after several attempts passed and was signed by President Clinton on July 23, 1999, as the National Missile Defense Act. As his term ended, President Clinton deferred "the decision over whether to deploy the National Missile Defense system to his successor. 'I simply cannot conclude with the information I have today that we have enough confidence in the technology and the operational effectiveness of the entire [National Missile Defense] system to move forward to deployment'."[73] On September 17, 2002, the Bush administration released its National Security Strategy for 2002. It contains the following remarks, relevant to the current discussion[74]:

> "We must be prepared to stop rogue states and their terrorist clients before they are able to threaten or use weapons of mass destruction against the

United States and our allies and friends." Missile defense, the White House says, will still factor into the military strategy. "Our response must take full advantage of . . . modern technologies, including the development of an effective missile defense system."

Homeland Security and Cybersecurity After September 11, 2001

Concern about attacks on information systems, including the destruction or alteration of important data, have long been of concern. Indeed, such attacks against the U.S. Department of Defense (DOD) have already occurred[75]:

> Attacks on Defense computer systems are a serious and growing threat. The exact number cannot be readily determined because only a small portion are actually detected and reported. However, Defense Information Systems Agency (DISA) data implies that Defense may have experienced as many as 250,000 attacks last year. DISA information also shows that attacks are successful 65 percent of the time, and that the number of attacks is doubling each year, as Internet use increases along with the sophistication of "hackers" and their tools.

Many of these attacks are harmless, but some may be extremely dangerous and efforts are being taken by DOD to increase security—a difficult task. In the aftermath of September 11, a renewed concern about cybersecurity emerged. Actually, a number of events prior to this date had created an awareness of the vulnerabilities of information systems. For example, the concern with the arrival of the year 2000, the so-called Y2K disaster, advertised the degree to which the economy was dependent upon these systems. Early 2000 witnessed the devastating effects of distributed denial-of-service attacks against many large commercial Web sites, causing serious interruptions in operation and emphasizing how vulnerable even major commercial sites are. As part of the Homeland Security strategy, in October of 2001, President Bush "establishe[d] a federal critical infrastructure protection board, naming Clinton appointee Richard Clarke his special adviser for cyberspace security. The board is charged with making sure that state and local governments and non-governmental organizations are doing their respective parts to maintain effective warning systems and share information they receive about threats and attacks."[76]

This appointment followed the release of a draft proposal, "The White House's National Strategy to Secure Cyberspace." In recognition of both the importance of the Internet to the national economy and its historic vulnerability to hacker attacks, the White House attempted to produce a call to arms with this proposal. Among the highlights are the following[77]:

The overall national strategic goal is to empower all Americans to secure their portions of cyberspace. This strategic goal will be accomplished through six major tools for empowering people and organizations to do their part:

1. Awareness and Information: Educate and create awareness among users and owners of cyberspace of the risks and vulnerabilities of their system and the means to mitigate these risks.
2. Technology and Tools: Produce new and more secure technologies, implement those technologies more quickly, and produce current technologies in a more secure way.
3. Training and Education: Develop a large and well-qualified cybersecurity workforce to meet the needs of industry and government, and to innovate and advance the nation's security capabilities.
4. Roles and Partnerships: Foster responsibility of individuals, enterprises, and sectors for security at all levels through the use of market forces, education and volunteer efforts, public-private partnerships, and, in the last resort, through regulation or legislation.
5. Federal Leadership: Improve Federal cybersecurity to make it a model for other sectors by increasing accountability; implementing best practices; expanding the use of automated tools to continuously test, monitor, and update security practices; procuring secure and certified products and services; implementing leading-edge training and workforce development; and deterring and preventing cyber attacks.
6. Coordination and Crisis Management: Develop early warning and efficient sharing of information both within and between public and private sectors so that attacks are detected quickly and responded to efficiently.

Shortly after the release of this draft, the general consensus was that it did not mandate future conduct but rather called on industry and individuals to be more careful. The lack of enforcement provisions in the draft was of concern to some security experts. In February of the following year, the final report was released; excerpts are presented in Chapter 11.

On November 25, 2002, President Bush signed into law the Homeland Security Act, creating a new Cabinet-level Department of Homeland Security by January 24, 2003. The execution of this Act "is the largest reorganization of the federal government since World War II."[78] Other aspects of this massive change include the following[79]:

- The Cabinet-level intelligence clearinghouse will be dedicated to protecting the United States from terrorist attacks and will combine about 170,000 federal workers from 22 agencies.
- The department will bring together intelligence analysis and infrastructure protection, border protection and immigration, and a comprehensive response-and-recovery division.
- The department would be divided into four divisions: Border and Transportation Security; Emergency Preparedness and Response; Chemical,

Biological, Radiological and Nuclear Countermeasures, and Information Analysis and Infrastructure Protection.
  • While the new department would not become a domestic intelligence agency, it would analyze intelligence and "legally accessible information" from multiple sources such as the CIA, National Security Agency, FBI, Drug Enforcement Administration, Department of Energy, Customs Service, and Department of Transportation.

Of particular interest is the effort undertaken to build a secure computer system for this new department. Given the necessity to integrate existing systems from civilian, military, criminal, and investigatory databases, the designers face many challenges. Some of the concerns have been described as follows[80]:

  • There are a lot of disparate databases . . . law enforcement, immigration, bio-medical . . . and there are legal restrictions from sharing information between those databases.
  • The No. 1 goal is to balance the desire for privacy of individuals with the need for security. The administration immediately rejected the ideas of one giant "data warehouse" of information because of privacy concerns and of giving people chips to track their whereabouts.
  • Besides an e-mail system . . . the administration is working to create a secure videoconferencing system to connect state officials with the new department.
  • Further, the administration is working on creating a list of critical technologies for homeland security, such as data-mining equipment, authentication systems, biometrics devices, wireless services, and simulation and modeling technologies.

ISSUES AND PROBLEMS

The investments reported here have the potential to revolutionize the way the public interacts with government. This revolution can be achieved through the development and deployment of interactive, multimedia applications that are accessible through kiosks as well as other available delivery mechanisms, such as personal computers.[81]

Many issues could be discussed, but for the present the focus will be on an example of a fallible military technology, the responsibility of the federal government for the electronic dissemination of public information and services, and two issues related to the police use of information systems. Other issues such as the growing number of government databases and their impact on privacy will be examined in Chapter 9. Also to be discussed later in this book (Chapter 15) will be the very difficult questions associated with ethical and professional conduct. As noted previously, many scientists have long struggled with whether or not to engage in research that has direct or indirect military applications. Computer scientists have had to face similar questions in recent years.

A Terrible Accident

One important example that high technology is not infallible and that the consequences can be dreadful is the incident that occurred in July of 1988 in the Persian Gulf. At that time, the prime enemy was Iran, and the cruiser U.S.S. Vincennes, in the mistaken belief that it was under attack, shot down an Iranian airliner, killing 290 civilians. The Vincennes was equipped with the most advanced technology available, the $1 billion Aegis system, under which the captain issues commands from the Combat Information Center (CIS), a windowless room deep within the ship, connected to the outside world by radar and communications systems and relying on computers to process and display information rapidly. The information available to the captain was instantaneous and accurate and yet 290 people died. Why? The simple lesson is that too much data may overwhelm sound judgment, especially under battle conditions, exactly when such an advanced system is designed to make its major contribution.

Navy investigators, after studying the computer tapes, judged the data to be accurate but that two "key misperceptions led to the skipper's decision to shoot."[82] A radar operator reported that an F-14 fighter was headed directly towards the Vincennes, even though radar showed it climbing on a typical flight path. This report must be understood in the context of well-known previous events in the Gulf, specifically the attack on the frigate Stark by the Iraqis in 1987, which resulted in the loss of 37 sailors. The Stark captain's hesitant response in the face of a possible attack created a subsequent urgency not to let it happen again. Thus, a preconceived scenario was in place, and even when someone in the CIS announced that the radar blip might be a commercial airliner, it was noted but not really factored into the decision process. One recommendation was to improve computer displays to show an aircraft's altitude beside its radar track. The larger lesson is that human memories and emotions, heightened by stressful battle conditions, may compromise even the most sophisticated information technology system, with dire consequences for all.

Many of these concerns were forgotten in the aftermath of the Gulf War, fought during January and February of 1991. Considerable publicity was directed toward "smart weapons," such as the Tomahawk cruise missile and the Patriot antiballistic missile. In fact, computers were seen as a major factor in the surprisingly quick and thorough victory over Iraq. High technology received an enormous boost, and increased funding for a new generation of weapons was assured. At the same time, two points should be noted: the technology used had been developed in the 1970s and early 1980s, and a postwar analysis raised serious doubts about the actual effectiveness of computer-based weapons. In the next "Gulf War," in 2003, smart weapons again played a major role in combat, but the stabilization of Iraq would require more than weapons.

The Dissemination of Federal Information

The Federal government collects, processes, and distributes vast amounts of information used by all segments of the public. Up to fairly recently, most of this material was on hard copy, or ink on paper, frequently published by the General Printing Office or the National Technical Information System. Many types of information, however, such as technical, statistical, scientific, and reference, are best stored and disseminated by electronic means. For example, reference information such as Bureau of the Census statistics reports could be made available on optical disks. The crucial issues under discussion are how to maintain ready access to electronic media and the need to define the respective roles of the government and private information handlers in the electronic dissemination of information. Many of these questions were defined and discussed in a comprehensive report issued by the Office of Technology Assessment in 1988; some of the problems and challenges were given as follows[83]:

> • At a fundamental level, electronic technology is changing or even eliminating many distinctions between reports, publications, databases, records, and the like, in ways not anticipated by existing statutes and policies.
> • Electronic technology permits information dissemination on a decentralized basis that is cost-effective at low levels of demand.
> • Technology has outpaced the major government-wide statutes that apply to Federal information dissemination.
> • The advent of electronic dissemination raises new equity concerns since, to the extent that electronic formats have distinct advantages (e.g., in terms of timeliness, searchability), those without electronic access are disadvantaged.
> • *Technological advances complicate the Federal Government's relationships with the commercial information industry . . . the privatization of major Federal information dissemination activities has not yet been demonstrated to be either cost-effective or beneficial for important government functions.* [Emphasis added.]

There has been disagreement within the government over how much and how fast information dissemination should be privatized, not over whether or not it should be. Within the Office of Management of the Budget (OMB), officials argue that government agencies should only release information in bulk form, similar to the activity of wholesalers in consumer goods, while the private sector should act as retailers, packaging the information to meet market demands, the argument being that information companies are much more flexible and responsive than government bureaucracies. In opposition to this view, such groups as the American Civil Liberties Union and Computer Professionals for Social Responsibility claim that "information technology could greatly improve the public's ability to draw on government data. They call for new policies that would encourage the federal government to provide user-friendly access to its statistics and public records."[84] The battle is joined by these opponents and business supporters, largely on ideological and profit-motivated grounds. It appears that no comprehensive solution is in the offing, but rather a case-by-case approach is being applied in which the government is expected to provide services in those areas that are not economically viable for the private sector.

In the past few years, governments have taken advantage of the Internet as an efficient and relatively economic way to circulate information. Reports, studies, speeches, minutes of meetings, online conferences, and other types of information are made available shortly after they appear or even while they are taking place. The public, or at least that growing part of it with access to the Internet, now expects to find needed government information on demand. In a report to Congress, the Government Printing Office has made proposals about how to continue the process of making more information electronically available via the Federal Deposit Library Program (FDLP). The mission for the FDLP is "to provide equitable, efficient, timely and dependable no-fee public access to Federal Government information within the scope of the program."[85] Currently, a number of libraries across the country have been chosen to act as repositories for Federal information, providing ready access to all Americans. The report identifies four ways in which the GPO can bring electronic information into the FDLP[86]:

- GPO can identify, describe and link the public to the wealth of distributed Government information products maintained at Government electronic information services for free public use.
- GPO can establish reimbursable agreements with agencies that provide fee-based Government electronic information services in order to provide free public access to their information through the FDLP.
- GPO can "ride" agency requisitions and pay for depository copies of tangible electronic information products, such as CD-ROM discs, even if they are not produced or procured through GPO.
- GPO can obtain from agencies electronic source files for information the agencies do not wish to disseminate through their own Government electronic information services. These files can be made available through the *GPO Access* services or disseminated to depository libraries in CD-ROM or other tangible format.

The Police and Computers

Two applications will be discussed: the use of satellites and computers to track suspects and criminals, and the lack of adequate systems to enforce background checks for gun buyers. Global Positioning Systems (GPS) have found many applications, including tracking convicts on probation, who are required to remain near their homes for the period of their probation. A more recent use extends this application to track such people to determine if they were near crimes which occurred in their neighborhoods. In other situations, it can be determined if pedophiles have gone near schools or play grounds. It is interesting that the American Civil Liberties Union supports this program[87]:

> "To the extent that GPS surveillance is used as an alternative to incarceration for non-violent or first-time offenders, [it] is certainly a positive thing," said David Fathi, staff council for the organization's National Prison Project. "The ACLU welcomes any reasonable steps to reduce our country's over-reliance on incarceration, which has given [the United States] the highest incarceration rate in the world."

Certain designated classes of individuals, such as convicted felons, are not permitted to buy guns. However, the effectiveness of enforcing this restriction depends on the existence of readily accessible databases with up-to-date relevant background material. Unfortunately, many states have not implemented such databases. Just how bad the situation is has been reported by the Americans for Gun Safety Foundation. Some of their findings are given below:

- 25 states have automated less than 60% of their felony criminal conviction records, meaning that investigators must comb through paper records to determine the eligibility of hundreds of thousands of prospective gun buyers.
- 33 states cannot stop those who have been involuntarily committed to a mental health facility from buying a gun, because they do not supply any records to the state and federal databases used to deny firearms purchases.
- 13 states cannot stop those with domestic violence restraining orders from obtaining a gun, and 15 states cannot stop those with domestic violence misdemeanors, because they do not supply any records to the state and federal databases used to deny firearms purchases.
- In the 46 states that compile data, at least 9,976 convicted felons and other prohibited buyers obtained guns because of inadequate records. (That does not include those with domestic violence, illegal alien, or mental disability disqualifications in which there are often no records in the database.)

SUMMARY

Government is probably the largest single user of computers. These uses are incredibly varied and their impact is felt throughout society. The Federal Government has purchased and continues to purchase an enormous number of computers. It exerts considerable pressure on the market to conform to its requirements. Governments gather, store, and process vast amounts of information. The public may be concerned about how this information is safeguarded and how it is used. As the bureaucracy depends more heavily on computer systems, it may become less responsive to the needs of the public it is supposed to serve. It may hide behind the computer instead of providing human answers. The Congress has also benefited from the use of computers and communication networks in a variety of ways.

More recently, the electoral process has witnessed the introduction of computers for purposes of identifying targeted special-interest groups and funding. The television networks use computers to monitor the voting process and, more controversially, to predict the outcomes as early as possible. Voting and counting by computer is becoming more common with all the attendant risks of program error and even fraud. The Internet has begun to play a role in this area as candidates set up Web sites to disseminate their views, post press releases, and receive comments from their supporters and opponents. Because of well-advertised voting irregularities, renewed attention is being directed toward online voting, although this "solution" is also rife with problems.

The Department of Defense (DOD) is the largest user of computers within the Federal Government. The DOD has launched major programs to modernize its control and command structure and its weaponry, including advanced programs in artificial intelligence to equip airplanes and tanks with sophisticated computer systems. Major funding for AI has come from the DOD, in pursuit of improvements in battlefield capabilities. Important and expensive research and development efforts such as the Strategic Defense Initiative and the Strategic Computer Initiative have been launched, with a significant impact on computer science research and education. Given the important role of computers in the detection and recognition of large-scale military threats, some people have expressed a deep concern that accidental war may occur because computer systems will respond before humans can intervene. In spite of assurances by the government that humans will always retain ultimate responsibility, the ability to respond quickly is a high priority for military decision makers. The terrorist attacks of September 11, 2001, have resulted in a major rethinking of national defense with an increased emphasis on homeland security, in which computer technology is playing an increasing role.

Finally, there is considerable controversy over the role of the Federal Government in disseminating electronically stored information. The debate turns on the balance between the respective responsibilities of the private and public sectors in providing information, gathered by the government, to the public. The past few years have witnessed the sudden appearance of numerous Web sites to provide the public with up-to-date government reports and news releases, as well as the status of legislation, and the complete text of bills. The influence of the DOD in the growth of computer science has been well-documented. What is of concern is whether or not this influence has been, and will continue to be, of benefit to the field, its practitioners, and the country.

NOTES

1. Robert Wright, "Hyperdemocracy," *Time*, January 23, 1995, pp. 41–46.
2. *The Unpredictable Certainty: Information Infrastructure Through 2000*, NII Steering Committee, National Research Council, Washington, D C: National Academy Press, 1996. Available at http://www.nap.edu/nap/online/unpredictable/
3. "Paperwork Reduction: Burden Unlikely to be Met," U.S. General Accounting Office, GAO/T-GGD/RCED-96-186, July 5, 1996, Gaithersburg, MD: GAO Document Distribution Facility, p. 3. Available at http://www.access.gpo.gov/cgi-bin/waisgate.cgi?WAISdocID=6796319722+4+1+0&WAISaction=retrieve
4. "Budget of the United States Government: Analytical Perspectives," Fiscal Year 2003. 2002, Washington, DC: U.S. Government Printing Office. Available at http://www.whitehouse.gov/omb/budget/fy2003.pdf
5. Roy Mark. "Federal IT Spending to Reach $63.3 Billion," DC.internet.com, May 1, 2002. Available at http://dc.internet.com/news/article/0,,2101_1026231,00.html
6. *Op. cit.*, Budget of the United States Government, p. 391.
7. *Ibid.* pp 392–393.
8. "Paperwork Reduction: Mixed Efforts on Agency Decision Processes and Data Availability," U.S. General Accounting Office, GAO/PEMD-89-20, September 1989, p. 11. Available at http://archive.gao.gov/d26t7/139721.pdf
9. *Ibid.*
9a. *Ibid.*
10. "Managing Federal Information Resources, Seventh Annual Report Under the Paperwork Act of 1980," Washington, D C : Office of Management of the Budget, December 1989.
11. "Management of Federal Information Resources," Circular No. A-130 (Revised), February 8, 1996, Office of Management of the Budget. Available at http://www1.whitehouse.gov/WH/EOP/OMB/html/circulars/a130/a130.html
12. Paperwork Reduction: Burden Reduction Goal Unlikely to Be Met," Testimony before the Committee on Small Business, U.S. Senate, U.S. General Accounting Office, GAO/T-GGD/RCED-96-186, July 5, 1996. Available at

http://www.access.gpo.gov/cgi-bin/waisgate.cgi?WAISdocID=6796319722+
4+1+0& WAISaction=retrieve

13. Paperwork Reduction Act: Burden Increases and Violations Persist," Testimony
before the Subcommittee on Energy, Policy, Natural Resources, and Regulatory
Affairs, Committee on Government Reform, House of Representatives, GAO-
02-598T, April 11, 2002. Available at http://www.gao.gov/new.items/d02598t.
pdf

14. Dean Foust. "The IRS Is Badly Overtaxed," *Business Week*, April 15, 1996, p. 46.

15. "IRM/General Government Division Issue Area Plan, Fiscal Years 1994–1996,"
Accounting and Information Management Division, U.S. General Accounting
Office, GAO/ IAP-95-8, March 1995, Washington, D C: U.S. General
Accounting Office. Available at http://www.access.gpo.gov/cgi-bin/waisgate.
cgi?WAISdocID=696729821 +38+1+ 0&WAISaction=retrieve

16. Gary H. Anthes. "IRS to Require Electronic Filing," *Computerworld*, July 15,
1996, p. 28.

17. "Tax Administration: Continued Progress Modernizing IRS Depends on
Managing Risks," Testimony before Congressional Committees, GAO-02-715T,
May 14, 2002. Available at http://www.gao.gov/new.items/d02715t.pdf

18. *Ibid.*

19. "IRS's 2002 Tax Filing Season: Returns and Refunds Processed Smoothly;
Quality of Assistance Improved." Report to the Chairman, Subcommittee on
Oversight, Committee on Ways and Means, House of Representatives, GAO-
03-314, December 2002. Available at http://www.gao.gov/new.items/
d03314.pdf

20. Gary H. Anthes. "Air Traffic Takes Another Turn," *Computerworld*, April 25,
1994, p. 79.

21. Tim Ouellette and Steve Moore. "FAA's Reliance on Ancient Backup Systems
Raises Concern," *Computerworld*, July 31, 1995, p. 14.

22. Gary H. Anthes. "FAA Speeds Plan to Replace Traffic Control Systems,"
Computerworld, August 7, 1995, p. 16.

23. *Ibid.*

24. Gary H. Anthes. "Revamp Flies Off Course," *Computerworld*, August 5, 1996,
p. 28.

25. "Electronic Government: Proposal Addresses Critical Challenges," Statement
of Linda D. Koontz, General Accounting Office, GA-02-1083T, September 18,
2002. Available at http://www.gao.gov/new.items/d021083t.pdf

26. Alex Salkever and Olga Kharif. "The New Push for E-Government," Special
Report, *Business Week*, October 29, 2002. Available at http://www.business
week.com/technology/content/oct2002/tc20021029_2415.htm

27. "Creating a Performance-Based Electronic Government: Fiscal Year 2002
Progress," The Performance Institute, October 30, 2002. Available at http://
www.cio.gov/documents/egovernmentreport.pdf

28. *Ibid.*

29. "e-Government: The Next American Revolution," The Council for Excellence in
Government, 2001. Available at http://excelgov.org/usermedia/images/uploads/
PDFs/bpnt4c.pdf

30. *Ibid.*

31. "The Rise of the e-citizen: How People use Government Agencies' Web Sites," Pew Internet & American Life Project, April 3, 2002. Available at the Web site with URL: http://pew.internet.org/reports/pdfs/PIP_Govt_Website_Rpt.pdf
32. *Ibid.*
33. *Ibid.*
34. "Congress Online: Assessing and Improving Capitol Hill Web Site," Congressional Management Foundation, 2002. Available at http://www.congressonlineproject.org/congressonline2002.pdf
35. *Ibid.*
36. "The Electronic Government Act of 2002," Available at http://www.cdt.org/legislation/107th/e-gov/s803.pdf
37. "S. 803, E-Government Act of 2002, as Amended," Centre for Democracy and Technology, date unknown. Available at http:// www.cdt.org/legislation/107th/e-gov/020325s803analysis.pdf
38. *Op. cit.,* "The Rise of the e-citizen," p. 3.
39. "Digital Town Hall: How Local Officials Use the Internet and the Civic Benefits They Cite From Dealing with Constituents Online," Pew Internet & American Life Project, October 22, 2002. Available at http://www.pewinternet.org/reports/pdfs/PIP_Digital_Town_Hall.pdf
40. *Ibid.,* p. 7.
41. "Urban E-Government, 2002," Center for Public Policy, Brown University, Providence, RI, September, 2002. Available at http://www.InsidePolitics.org/egovt02city.pdf
42. "eGovernment Leadership—Realizing the Vision," Accenture, April 2002. Available at http://www.accenture.com. It will be necessary to supply personal information in order to register, prior to accessing the report.
43. *Ibid.*
44. *Ibid.,* pp. 8–9.
45. "Digital Technology: Working for Parliament and the Public," House of Commons Information Committee, First Report of Session 2001-2, July 15, 2002. Available at http://www.publications.parliament.uk/pa/cm200102/cmselect/cminform/1065/1065.pdf
46. Phil Noble. "Internet and Campaign 2002 Analysis," Politics Online, November 4, 2002. Available at http://www.politicsonline.com/pol2000/specialreports/campaign_analysis_2002.html
47. "The Internet's Role in Political Campaigns: Utilization by Incumbent United States Senators and Representatives in 2002," The Bivings Group, May 13, 2002. Available at http://www.bivings.com/campaignstudy/index.pdf
48. Nicholas Thompson. "Machined Politics," *The Washington Monthly*, May 2002. Available at http://www.washingtonmonthly.com/features/2001/0205.thompso.html
49. Elshtain, Jean Betheke. "Interactive TV—Democracy and the Qube Tube," *The Nation*, August 7–14, 1982, p. 108.
50. "Virtual Democracy: Is the Internet the Ultimate Voting Booth," An interview with Lorrie Cranor, *Off the Record*, February 6, 1996. Available at http:// www.mediapool.com/offtherecord/vot_tran.html
51. *Ibid.*

52. Report of the National Workshop on Internet Voting: Issues and Research Agenda," Internet Policy Institute, Sponsored by the National Science Foundation and conducted in cooperation with the University of Maryland and hosted by the Freedom Forum, March 2001. Available at http://www.net voting.org/Resources/InternetVotingReport1.pdf

53. *Ibid.*, pp. 1–2.

54. *Ibid.*, p. 2.

55. "Elections: Perspectives on Activities and Challenges Across the Nation," U.S. General Accounting Office, Report to Congressional Requestors, Report GAO-02-3, October 2001, p. 9. Available at http://www.gao.gov/new.items/d023.pdf

56. "Voting: What is, What Could Be," Caltech and MIT Voting Technology Project, July 2001, p. 3. Available at http://www.vote.caltech.edu/Reports/july01/July01_VTP_Voting_Report_Entire.pdf

57. Rebecca Mercuri. "A Better Ballot Box," IEEE Spectrum Online, October 2002. Available at http://www.ieee.spectrum.org/WEBONLY/publicfeature/oct02/evot.html

58. Tekla S. Perry. "TV Networks Vie for Viewer's Votes," *IEEE Spectrum*, October 1984, p. 68.

59. "Battlefield Automation: Army's Digital Battlefield Plan Lacks Specific Measurable Goals," Report to Congressional Committees, U.S. General Accounting Office, GAO/NSIAD-96-25, Gaithersburg, MD: U.S. General Accounting Office, November 1995, p. 4. Available at http://•www.access.gpo.gov/cgi-bin/useftp.cgi?IPaddress=wais.access.gpo.gov&filename=ns96025.pdf&directory=diskb/wais/data/gao

60. "National Preparedness: Integrating New and Existing Technology and Information Sharing Into an Effective Homeland Security Strategy," U.S. General Accounting Office, GAO-02-811T, June 7, 2002. Available at http://www.gao.gov/new.items/d02811t.pdf

60a. David Fairhall. "Destroyer Sheffield is Sunk, 30 Dead," Guardian Unlimited, May 5, 1982. Available at http://www.guardian.co.uk/falklands/story/0,11707,660281,00.html

61. Douglas Waller. "Onward Cyber Soldiers," *Time*, August 21, 1995, pp. 30–36.

62. Michael Behar. "The New Mobile Infantry," *Wired*, May 2002. Available at http://www.wired.com/wired/archive/10.05/robots_pr.html

63. Candace Stuart. "Army Chooses MIT To Help Create the New Nano-Equipped U.S. Soldier," *Small Times*, March 13, 2002. Available at http://www.small times.com/document_display.cfm?document_id=3264

64. Frank Vizard. "Future Combat: Part 1, The Army of the Future Will Be Lighter, Fleeter and Better Connected," *Scientific American*, January 13, 2003. Available at http://www.scientificamerican.com/print_version.cfm?articleID=000C031A-12A4-1E1E-8B3B809EC588EEDF

65. *Ibid.*

66. Professor David Parnas, a distinguished software engineer, in his statement of resignation from a nine-member Star Wars advisory panel on computing, as quoted in Philip Elmer-Dewitt, "Star Wars and Software," *Time*, July 22, 1985, p. 39. See Chapter 13 for more of Professor Parnas's views, especially with respect to professional responsibility.

67. *SDI: Technology Survivability and Software, Summary*, U.S. Congress, Office of Technology Assessment, OTA-ISC-354, Washington, D C, May 1988.

68. From a SDI report on the National Test Facility as quoted in John A. Adam, "Star Wars in Transition," *IEEE Spectrum*, March 1989, p. 37.

69. *Ibid.*

70. *Ibid.*, p. 38.

71. "Star Wars Still Alive," *Boston Globe*, June 21, 1993. Available at http://www.cpsr.org/cpsr/cpsr_21st_century_project/star_wars_alive

72. "Star Wars—The Sequel," Transcript of a *PBS Newshour* debate, June 4, 1996. Available at http://web-cr01.pbs.org/newshour/bb/military/star_wars_6-4.html

73. "Timeline: Missile Defense, 1944–2002," *Frontline*, Public Broadcasting System, 2002. Available at http://www.pbs.org/wgbh/pages/frontline/shows/missile/etc/cron.html

74. *Ibid.*

75. "Information Security: Computer Attacks at Department of Defense Pose Increasing Risks," Report to Congressional Requesters, U.S. General Accounting Office, GAO/AIMD-96-84. (Gaithersburg, MD: U.S. General Accounting Office, May 1996).

76. David McGuire. "Timeline: U.S. Government and Cybersecurity," *Washingtonpost.com*, June 26, 2002. Available with payment at http://www.washingtonpost.com/

77. "The White House's National Strategy to Secure Cyberspace," The President's Critical Infrastructure Protection Board, September 2002. Available at http://www.whitehouse.gov/pcipb/cyberstrategy-draft.pdf

78. "A Massive Federal Makeover," Fact Sheet, CNN.Com, November 25, 2002. Available at http://www.cnn.com/2002/US/11/20/facts.homeland/index.html

79. *Ibid.*

80. Bara Vaida. "Whitehouse Tech Officials Race to Build Security System," *GovExec.com*, January 9, 2003. Available at http://www.govexec.com/dailyfed/0103/010903td1.htm

81. "The Kiosk Network Solution: An Electronic Gateway to Government," Interagency Kiosk Committee, date unknown. Available at http://www.wings.usps.gov/kioskweb.html

82. David Griffiths. "When Man Can't Keep Up with the Machines of War," *Business Week*, September 12, 1988, p. 36. Russell Watson, John Barry, and Richard Sandza, "A Case of Human Error," *Newsweek*, August 15, 1988, pp. 18–20.

83. *Informing the Nation: Federal Information Dissemination in an Electronic Age*, U.S. Congress, Office of Technology Assessment, OTA-CIT-396, (Washington, D C: U.S. Government Printing Office, October 1988), pp. 8–9.

84. Henry H. Perritt, Jr. "Government Information Goes On-Line," *Technology Review*, November-December 1989, pp. 60–67.

85. *Study to Identify Measures Necessary for a Successful Transition to a More Electronic Federal Depository Library Program*, GPO Publication 500.11,

(Washington, D C: U.S. Government Printing Office, June 1996). Available at http://www.access.gpo.gov/su_docs/dpos/rep_cong/images/report.pdf
86. *Ibid.*, p. 26.
87. Julia Scheeres. "GPS: Keeping Cons Out of Jail," *Wired News*, October 15, 2002. Available at http://www.wired.com/news/privacy/0,1848,55740,-00.html

ADDITIONAL READINGS

Introduction

Making Government Work: Electronic Delivery of Federal Services. U.S. Congress, Office of Technology Assessment, OTA-TCT-578. (Gaithersburg, MD: U.S. Government Printing Office, November 1993). Available at http://www.ota.nap.edu/pdf/data/1993/9333.PDF

Information Processing: Complexity and Bureaucracies

Blodgett, Mindy and Sharon Gaudin. "Chasing Deadbeats Online," *Computerworld*, July 29, 1996, p. 29.

"Creating a Performance-Based Electronic Government," The Performance Institute, October 30, 2002. Available at http://www.cio.gov/documents/egovernmentreport.pdf

"Government Information Technology Services (GITS), Working Group Accomplishments Report," U. S. Department of the Treasury, June 1996. Available at URL:http://www.ustreas.gov/treasury/initiatives/work/final.html

"Improving the Flow of Information to Congress," Report to the Ranking Member, Committee on Labor and Human Resources, U.S. Senate, U.S. General Accounting Office, GAO/PEMD-95-1, January 1995, Gaithersburg, MD: U.S. General Accounting Office. Available at http://www.access.gpo.gov/cgi-bin/waisgate.cgi?WAISdocID=729222313 +1+0+0&WAISaction=retrieve

"Information Technology: Best Practices Can Improve Performance and Produce Results," Testimony before the Subcommittee on Government Management, Information Technology and Technology Committee on Government Reform and Oversight, U.S. House of Representatives, U.S. General Accounting Office, GAO/T-AIMD-96-46, February 26, 1996, Gaithersburg, MD: U.S. General Accounting Office. Available at http://www.access.gpo.gov/cgi-bin/waisgate.cgi?WAISdocID=696729821+35+ 1+0&WAISaction=retrieve

"Management Reform: Implementation of the National Performance Review's Recommendations," U.S. General Accounting Office, GAO/OCG-95-1, December 1994. Gaithersburg, MD: U.S. General Accounting Office. Available at http://www.access.gpo.gov/cgi-bin/waisgate.cgi?WAISdocID=725591777+1+0+0&WAISaction=retrieve

E-Governance and the Future

"Electronic Government: Success of the Office of Management and Budget's 25 Initiatives Depends on Effective management and Oversight," GAO, March 13, 2003. Available at http://www.gao.gov/new.items/d02495t.pdf

Goff, Leslie. "The Webbing of the President," *Computerworld*, September 2, 1996, pp. 79–80.

"The New E-Government Equation: Ease, Engagement, Privacy and Protection," Council for Excellence in Government, April 2003. Available at http://www.excel gov.org/usermedia/images/uploads/PDFs/egovpoll2003.pdf

Schwartz, Evan L. "Direct Democracy: Are You Ready for the Democracy Channel?" *Wired*, 2.01, January 1994, pp. 74–75. Available at http://www.eff.org/pub/Activism/ E-voting/democracy_online.article

"Telecommunications and Democracy," Communications Policy Briefing #4, The Benton Foundation, 1994. Available at http://cdinet.com/Benton/Catalog/Brief4/brief4.html

The Political Process

Cranor, Lorrie Faith. "Electronic Voting: *Computerized Polls May Save Money, Protect Privacy.*" Crossroads: The ACM Student Magazine, 2 (4), April 1996. Available at http://www.acm.org/crossroads/xrds2-4/voting.html

"Elections, A Framework for Evaluating Reform Proposal," GAO, October 2001. Available at http://www.gao.gov/new.items/ d0290.pdf

"An Overdue Reform: The Need for Statewide Computerized Voter Registration Systems," Demos, a Network for Ideas & Action, January 2002. Available at http://www.demos-usa.org/Pubs/Overdue/overdue_reform_final.pdf

"To Assure Pride and Confidence in the Electoral Process," The National Commission on Federal Election Reform, August 2001. Available at http://www.reformelections.org/data/reports/99_full_report.pdf

"Untuned Keyboards: Online Campaigners, Citizens, and Portals in the 2002 Elections," Pew Internet & American Life Project, March 21, 2003. Available at http://www.pewinternet.org/reports/pdfs/PIP_IPDI_Politics_Report.pdf

"Voting: What Is, What Could Be," Caltech & MIT Voting Technology Product, July 2001. Available at http://www.vote.caltech.edu/Reports/july01/July01_VTP_%20Voting_Report_Entire.pdf

Security and the Nation's Defense

Bellin, David and Chapman, Gary (Eds.). *Computers in Battle-Will They Work?* (New York: Harcourt Brace Jovanovich, 1987).

Broad, William J. *Teller's War: The Top-Secret Story Behind the Star Wars Deception.* (New York: Simon & Schuster, 1992).

Commercial Multimedia Technologies for the Twenty-First Century Army Battlefields: A Technology Management Strategy. National Research Council, 1995, Washington, D C: National Academy Press. Some of the material was accessed at http://www.nas.edu

Crock, Stan. "Star Wars Junior: Will It Fly?" *Business Week*, July 15, 1996, pp. 88–89.

"Electronic Warfare, Comprehensive Strategy Still Needed for Suppressing Enemy Air Defenses," GAO, November 2002. Available at http://www.gao.gov.new.items/d0351.pdf

Loeb, Vernon. "Bursts of Brilliance," *The Washington Post Magazine*, December 15, 2002, p. W06. Also available at http://www.washingtonpost.com/wp-dyn/articles/A36897-2002Dec10.htm

Molander, Roger C., Riddile, Andrew S., and Wilson, Peter A. *Strategic Information Warfare: A New Face of War*. National Defense Research Institute. Santa Monica, CA: RAND, 1996. Available at http://www.rand.org/publications/MR/MR661/MR661.pdf

"Strengthening National, Homeland, and Economic Security," Supplement to the President's Budget, July 2002. Available at http://www.nitrd.gov/pubs/blue03/03BB-final.pdf

Vizard, Frank. "Future Combat, Part 1," *Scientific American*, January 13, 2003. Available at http://www.scientificamerican.com/print_version.cfm?articleID=000C031A-12A4-1E1E-8B3B809EC588EEDF.cfm

Issues and Problems

Katz, Randy. "Professor Katz Goes to Washington." *Communications of the ACM* 39 (5), May 1996, pp. 13-17.

"Survey of Rural Information Infrastructure Technologies." National Telecommunications and Information Administration, U.S. Department of Commerce, NTIA Special Publication 95-3, September 1995. Accessed through the Institute for Telecommunications (ITS) home Web page at http://www.its.bldrdoc.gov

The Technological Reshaping of America. U.S. Congress, Office of Technology Assessment, OTA-ETI-643. Washington, D C: U.S. Government Printing Office, August 1995. Available at http://www.ota.nap.edu/pdf/data/1995/9541.PDF

Thomborson, Clark. "Role of Military Funding in Academic Computer Science." In Bellin, D. and Chapman, G. (Eds.). *Computers in Battle-Will They Work?* pp. 283–296.

— 8 —

FREE SPEECH ON THE INTERNET

Congress shall make no law respecting an establishment of religion, or prohibiting the free exercise thereof; or abridging the freedom of speech, or of the press, or the right of the people peaceably to assemble, and to petition the government for a redress of grievances.

First Amendment to the U.S. Constitution

INTRODUCTION

It has been said that the first use made of any new medium is sex. And not surprisingly the Internet has seemed to fulfill this observation. The most frequent charge leveled against the Internet by the popular press is that it is a cesspool of adult pornography, racism, child pornography, and fraud, hardly a safe place to visit. For example, a cover story in *Business Week* of September 2, 2002, reads,[1]

THE UNDERGROUND WEB

Drugs, Gambling, Terrorism, Child Pornography. How the Internet makes any illegal activity more accessible than ever.

The opening paragraph of this "Special Report" certainly sets the tone for the content to follow:

Warning: You are about to enter the dark side of the Internet. It's a place where crime is rampant and every twisted urge can be satisfied. Thousands of virtual streets are lined with casinos, porn shops, and drug dealers. Scam artists and terrorists skulk behind seemingly lawful Web sites. And cops wander through once in a while, mostly looking lost. It's the Strip in Las Vegas, the Red Light district in Amsterdam, and New York's Time Square at its worst, all rolled into one—and all easily accessible from your living room couch.

Protecting rights in this environment, both the rights of users, adults and children alike, as well as the rights of online companies, organizations, and individual Web site owners, is, to say the least, a challenge. The first part of that challenge, the protection of free speech, is the subject of this chapter.

Another popular misconception is that newer media are less deserving of protection than older, well-established ones. Thus newspapers, radio, television, and film have gradually come to be accepted as media deserving full protection. In part this view derives from a recognition, however self-serving, that they have been around long enough to behave responsibly and therefore, can be trusted. In contrast, the Internet and the Web represent an outlaw frontier, brash, irresponsible, untrustworthy, and incorporating few basic societal values. That little of this presentation is true seems to matter minimally, as the Internet is regularly described in terms similar to those above.

A given technological innovation will inevitably secure its place in society as the existing system of laws is expanded to accommodate it. What is remarkable about computer technology is how fast this process has occurred and how many interesting and important legal issues have arisen. Probably the issue that has generated the most publicity is the question of free speech and the concern with the unfettered flow of pornographic material over the Internet. The passage of the Telecommunications Act of 1996 was mainly directed at permitting such technologies as telephone, cable, and the broadcast media to compete under a weakened regulatory structure (more details will be provided in Chapter 12). But also included in the legislation was the Communications Decency Act, an attempt to prevent "indecent" material on the Internet and local bulletin boards from finding its way into the hands of children. The attempt to regulate content over the Internet has aroused vigorous opposition and once again, the sanctity of the First Amendment has become the major rallying cry.

Private networks such as CompuServe and America Online have dealt with court challenges to their status, either as broadcasters such as the television stations or networks, or as common carriers such as telephone companies, both local and long distance. This *distinction* between broadcasters and common carriers is crucial with respect to the responsibility, if any, that they have for the content of the material they carry. Around the world, some countries have also been concerned about the content of material carried on the Internet, and there have been attempts by governments at interceding and controlling unwanted information. Defenders of an unregulated world have argued that it is impossible to control the Internet, which itself was designed to operate under extreme physical disruptions and indeed to route transmissions around such impediments. Furthermore, it is argued that this unique means of global communication should not and cannot be subject to the laws of another era.

In spite of this claim, governments seek to deal with apparent problems by passing legislation that is intended to reflect the will of their constituents and to protect them and their children from dangers. U.S. legislative attempts to protect children from being exposed, or having ready access, to sexually explicit online material have not achieved much success up to now. We will trace the enactment and subsequent history of three major pieces of legislation, beginning with the Communications Decency Act of 1996, and followed by the Child Online Protection Act of 1998 and the Children's Internet Protection Act of 2000. A parallel process has accompanied the legislative one, and given the nature of the Internet it should not be surprising that it is a technological approach to dealing with the problem.

Over the past few years a technology has emerged, generally characterized by the word filters, that can be used to restrict access to selected or specifically characterized Web sites and content. At least, such are the claims. The filtering industry has been promoted as a way to protect children without government interference, although the last piece of legislation mentioned in the previous paragraph does mandate the use of filtering software under certain circumstances. The use of filtering programs has aroused considerable controversy, and this debate will be explored in this chapter.

Finally, the free speech issue in other countries will also be described. The U.S. is unique among democracies in its commitment to the protection of free speech. For example, racist speech, except under very special circumstances, is protected in the U.S. but generally restricted elsewhere. A few such countries will be chosen to compare with the U.S. The discussion of selected free speech issues will conclude this chapter.

EARLY FREE SPEECH ISSUES ON THE INTERNET

The Global Internet Liberty Campaign advocates[2]

- Prohibiting prior censorship of on-line communication.
- Requiring that laws restricting the content of on-line speech distinguish between the liability of content providers and the liability of data carriers.
- Insisting that on-line free expression not be restricted by indirect means such as excessively restrictive governmental or private controls over computer hardware or software, telecommunications infrastructure, or other essential components of the Internet.
- Including citizens in the Global Information Infrastructure (GII) development process from countries that are currently unstable economically, have insufficient infrastructure, or lack sophisticated technology.

- Prohibiting discrimination on the basis of race, color, sex, language, religion, political or other opinion, national or social origin, property, birth or other status.

- Ensuring that personal information generated on the GII for one purpose is not used for an unrelated purpose or disclosed without the person's informed consent, and enabling individuals to review personal information on the Internet and to correct inaccurate information.

- Allowing on-line users to encrypt their communications and information without restriction.

If anything has brought the Internet to the attention of the general public it is the flood of newspaper, magazine, and television stories on Internet pornography, on threats to children by sexual predators, on parents discovering that their children have been downloading images of group sex, and more. Perhaps nothing so typified this relentless attack on the Internet as a source of depravity than the infamous cover story of the July 3, 1995, issue of *Time*:

CYBERPORN
EXCLUSIVE: A new study shows how pervasive and wild it really is. Can we protect our kids—and free speech?

It should be obvious that freedoms guaranteed prior to the emergence of electronic means for distributing information should continue to receive the same protection and be subject to the same limitations. To elaborate on the truism that one of the earliest uses of any new communication technology has been to portray pornographic images, we note that the early movie industry was heavily censored, as was television. Now movies are classified and censored, broadcast television is censored, and cable pay television is classified because of their focus on sexual content. Local online bulletin boards, depending on location, may contain hard-core pornography. The Internet makes a considerable amount of pornography available, for free in newsgroups, and for a price on the sex Web sites. Accessibility to these Web sites requires proof of age and a credit card. It should also be pointed out that a number of steps must be taken to view potentially offensive images. Explicit sites or newsgroups must be selected, and since images are stored in a binary-coded form, appropriate decoders must be available. Thus, the average Internet user may never encounter pornography just as the average shopper may never encounter pornographic videos or magazines, unless he or she seeks them out. Of course, another source of pornography, often surprising to the average user, is spam, the unsolicited advertisements that flood the inbox of most Internet users. Increasingly, sexually explicit ads are appearing to entice new customers and to horrify new users, especially those with children.

Up to now, the word pornography has been used in a rather loose fashion to refer to material with a high or exclusive sexual content. But what should be made clear is that pornography is not a legal term; that is, a book or film can be characterized as pornographic without any legal implications. The fact that something is pornographic may be offensive to some people but only if it goes beyond excessive sexual content, in a way to be defined shortly, will it be against the law, and be characterized as obscene, a legal term. Therefore, creators of material found to be obscene by the courts cannot claim First Amendment protection. In spite of the injunction against laws limiting speech, Congress has passed many laws asserting that material exists that cannot claim protection, and furthermore, that compromises are necessary in order to protect the social good. Obscene material, child pornography, libelous or defamatory material, and certain kinds of threatening material are beyond the pale. In essence, therefore, the issue turns on interpretations and definitions. In this regard, consider one of the most famous quotations on obscenity, deriving from an opinion by Supreme Court Justice Potter Stewart, in which he states[3]

> that under the First and Fourteenth Amendments criminal laws in this area are constitutionally limited to hard-core pornography. I shall not today attempt further to define the kinds of material I understand to be embraced within that shorthand description; and perhaps I could never succeed in intelligibly doing so. But I know it when I see it, and the motion picture involved in this case is not that.

The current Supreme Court definition of obscenity, the *Miller* test,[4] requires that all of the following three conditions be met:

1. The average person, applying contemporary community standards, would find that the work, taken as a whole, appeals to the prurient interest (in sex); and
2. the work depicts or describes, in a patently offensive way, sexual conduct specifically defined by the applicable state (or federal) law; and
3. the work, taken as a whole, lacks serious literary, artistic, political, or scientific value.

Anyone found guilty of selling or transmitting such material found to be obscene is subject to criminal penalties. In the case of child pornography, purchasing or possessing is sufficient to incur criminal charges. To help sharpen the discussion, we will present a few examples that have aroused considerable publicity and that have contributed to a sense that perhaps Internet content should be regulated. These examples are taken from the earlier days of the popular Internet as a background to the more recent controversies. It should also be kept in mind that by its very nature, regulating a worldwide system such as the Internet is a non-trivial task—an impossible one in the opinion of many long-time Net aficionados.

The Jake Baker Case

Jake Baker was an undergraduate student at the University of Michigan when, in October of 1994, he began posting stories on a Usenet newsgroup, alt.sex.stories, of a particularly violent and pornographic nature. One story apparently referred to a woman that Baker knew from one of his classes. These stories were brought to the attention of university administrators, who had Public Safety officers search his room and computer account with his permission. It was discovered that Baker had been communicating by e-mail with an Arthur Gonda in Canada and that they were discussing the possibility of kidnapping someone, presumably to torture in a fashion described in the stories. Baker was suspended by University President Duderstadt and subsequently arrested by the FBI on February 9, 1995, and charged with violating 18 U.S.C. s 875(c): "Transmission in interstate or foreign commerce of a communication containing a threat to kidnap any person or any threat to injure the person or another."

This case has raised a host of issues, including the following[5]:

- Privacy of victim. Was Baker within his free speech/free press rights to use her name without her knowledge or permission?
- Threats. Does the story constitute a threat to Jane Doe? It is legally unclear whether a conversation regarding fiction between two other parties without her knowledge constitutes a threat.
- Therapy. Are Baker's stories a kind of psychological therapy? Baker claims that the stories help him to vent anger.
- Role Playing in Creative Writing. Was Baker role playing when he corresponded with Arthur Gonda? Was Baker writing about himself in his stories?
- Obscenity. Do Baker's stories have constitutional free speech/free press protection? Should they?
- Due Process. Did Baker receive due process from the University? Does Baker merit handling as a violent felon on the basis of his writing alone?
- The Internet. The Baker case would not merit much attention if it did not involve the Internet.
- Internet as a publishing medium. Did Baker abuse his posting privileges?
- Internet crossing jurisdictional boundaries. Was a crime committed by use of Internet media? How will this affect the future of the Internet?
- Obscenity standards on the Internet. Were Baker's stories inappropriate for the Internet?

This list covers just about all the issues that have arisen regarding Internet pornography over the past few years. Cases such as Baker's influenced the momentum toward regulating legislation, and the outcome of his case had an impact as well. On June 22, 1995, U.S. District Judge Avern Cohen "dismissed the charges, citing the government's lack of evidence that Baker planned to act on his writings." Judge Cohen noted that what the government failed to establish was the requirement stated in Kelner, 534 F.2d at

1027 of a "threat which on its face and in the circumstances in which it is made is so unequivocal, unconditional, immediate and specific as to the person threatened, as to convey a gravity of purpose and imminent prospect of execution."[6] This decision was widely hailed as a significant victory for the First Amendment on the Internet. On November 21, 1995, the government filed an appeal of dismissal. On June 30, 1997, the 6th U.S. Circuit Court of Appeals "upheld the dismissal of charges against Baker, ruling that Baker's email exchanges with a man in Canada did not constitute a credible threat against Jane Doe. A university officer is also quoted as saying Baker did not violate any university information technology policies."[7]

Time's Cover Story: The Marty Rimm Study

The *Time* cover story referred to above promised a great deal: "A research team at Carnegie Mellon University in Pittsburgh, Pennsylvania, has conducted an exhaustive study of online porn—what's available, who is downloading it, what turns them on—and the findings (to be published in the *Georgetown Law Journal*) are sure to pour fuel on an already explosive debate."[8] The *Time* editors were well aware that their story would be influential: "If you think things are crazy now, though, wait until the politicians get hold of a report coming out this week." Up to the appearance of the *Time* cover story, it might have been claimed that most Internet pornography pieces were not only sensational but anecdotal, with no real evidence of how pervasive or how hard core the images carried on the Internet are. With the appearance of an academic study, it would now be possible to formulate regulatory policy based on hard evidence, and its high profile in a major magazine would reinforce that process. Clearly, a lot was riding on the Carnegie-Mellon report, more commonly known as the Rimm study. The major findings as reported by *Time* are given as follows[9]:

- There's an awful lot of porn online. In an 18-month study, the team surveyed 917,410 sexually explicit pictures, descriptions, short stories and film clips. On those Usenet newsgroups where digitized images are stored, 83.5 percent of the pictures were pornographic.
- It is immensely popular. Trading in sexually explicit imagery, according to the report, is now "one of the largest (if not the largest) recreational applications of users of computer networks.". . .
- It is a big moneymaker. The great majority (71 percent) of the sexual images on the newsgroups surveyed originate from adult-oriented computer bulletin-board systems (BBS) whose operators are trying to lure customers to their private collections of X-rated material. There are thousands of these BBS services, which charge fees (typically $10 to $30 a month) and take credit cards; the five largest have annual revenues in excess of $1 million.
- It is ubiquitous. Using data obtained with permission from BBS operators, the Carnegie Mellon team identified (but did not publish the names of)

individual consumers in more than 2,000 cities in all 50 states and 40 countries, territories and provinces around the world.

• It is a guy thing. According to the BBS operators, 98.9 percent of the
consumers of online porn are men. . . .

• It is not just naked women. Perhaps because hard-core sex pictures are
so widely available elsewhere, the adult BBS market seems to be driven
largely by a demand for images that can't be found in the average magazine
rack: pedophilia (nude photos of children), hebephilia (youths) and what
the researchers call paraphilia—a grab bag of "deviant" material that
includes images of bondage, sadomasochism, urination, defecation, and
sex acts with a barnyard full of animals.

No sooner had the story appeared than controversy erupted. Attacks both
against *Time's* rush to publish an article based on a paper that had yet to
appear in an academic journal[10] (although it was shortly to be printed) and
against the paper itself were quickly mounted. The most important critique
was authored by two professors at Vanderbilt University, Donna L. Hoffman
and Thomas P. Novak. They produced criticisms of both the magazine article
and the journal paper.[11] When considering the *Time* story, they were concerned that, while the impression is made that there is a lot of pornography
online (i.e., on the Internet), the data is derived primarily from adult Bulletin
Board Systems (BBSs).[12] These are commercial enterprises that provide online
access to explicit images, and subsequently the Internet comes into play as
individuals post these images on newsgroups. The statement that there is "an
awful lot of pornography online" is thus misleading. In fact, the *Time* article
presents a far more accurate view but doesn't highlight it sufficiently, possibly
because it would weaken the "flood-of-pornography" theme. Thus, the article notes, "the Carnegie Mellon study is careful to point out, pornographic
image files, despite their evident popularity, represent only about 3 percent of
all the messages on the Usenet newsgroups, while the Usenet itself represents
only 11.5 percent of the traffic on the Internet."[13] The failure to make the
arithmetic explicit is somewhat irresponsible, in that pornography therefore
only represents about 1/3 of 1% of all Internet traffic. And within this very
small percentage, the amount of actual hard-core stuff is even smaller, because
the study's methodology included in the count material, such as text files with
comments by readers. Much more could be said, but the point is clear—for the
public at large and some of their government representatives, the Internet
must be cleaned up, even if government involvement is required.

Whose Community Standards? Amateur Action Bulletin Board

One last case will be reviewed that in and of itself is not significant, but it
could set a legal precedent that would reduce the content of the Internet to

a level acceptable by only the most restrictive community in the U.S. Amateur Action BBS (AABBS) had been operated by Robert and Carleen Thomas from their home in Milpitas, California, since February 1991. It provided typical services, including e-mail, chat lines, public messages, and a large database of explicit images that patrons could download. Most of the images were scanned from sexually explicit adult magazines purchased in public adult book stores. In July 1993, a complaint was received about AABBS by the United States Postal Office from a person living in western Tennessee. A U.S. Postal Inspector paid for a membership, accessed the BBS from Memphis after his account had been authorized by a phone call from Robert Thomas, and downloaded a number of GIF (Graphic Interchange Format) files, a common format for images, that later formed the basis for six of the 12 charges subsequently laid against the Thomases. They were tried in federal court in Memphis under a 12-count indictment that included conspiracy to violate federal obscenity laws and "six counts under 18 U.S.C. § 1465 for knowingly using and causing to be used a facility and means of interstate commerce—a combined computer/telephone system—for the purpose of transporting obscene, computer-generated materials (the GIF files) in interstate commerce."[14]

The decision was appealed and heard in the U.S. Court of Appeals for the Sixth Circuit, where the lower-court decision was upheld. This case has serious repercussions for the Internet with respect to content and accessibility. The defendants claimed that they should not have been tried in Tennessee because they did not cause the GIFs to be transmitted there. This claim was rejected because of a precedent that the court recognized as applying in this case, that " 'venue lies in any district in which the offense was committed,' and the Government is required to establish venue by a preponderance of the evidence."[15] The defendants further claimed that the community standards of their home location, Northern California, should apply in the determination of whether or not the GIFs in question were obscene. Recall that the first part of the Miller test contained the requirement that "the average person, applying contemporary *community* standards" must agree that the material under question is obscene. The Appeals Court found ample precedents that the relevant community could be " 'in any district from, through, or into which' the allegedly obscene material moves," that "prosecutions may be brought either in the district of dispatch or the district of receipt," and that "it is not unconstitutional to subject interstate distributors of obscenity to varying community standards."[16] Thus the notion of community standards seems to have been extended in a devastating manner. Purveyors of pornography could be held, and probably will be held, to the most restrictive standards anywhere in the U.S. and must be aware of those standards.

The defendants also claimed that the existence of computer networks required a correspondingly new definition of community standards, "one that is based on the broad-ranging connections among people in cyberspace rather than the geographic locale of the federal judicial district of the criminal trial. Without a more flexible definition, they argue, there will be an impermissible chill on protected speech because BBS operators cannot select who gets the materials they make available on their bulletin boards." This argument was also rejected. This case was appealed to the Supreme Court where the Circuit Court's decision was upheld. In the interim, attention has shifted to the federal government's attempt to implement control over content on the Internet by legislation.

Content Responsibility: CompuServe and Prodigy

What responsibility do private networks such as CompuServe and Prodigy have over content? The previous section dealt with free speech issues, but there are many things to be concerned about other than pornography. On October 31, 1991, U.S. District Judge Peter Leisure held that CompuServe was not liable for information carried on an online forum it had created; that is, statements that might be defamatory could not be blamed on the service provider. And in the trial, CompuServe readily support this point. Thus, this important ruling equated CompuServe and other similar networks to bookstores and newsstands, whose owners are not responsible for content unless they have knowledge beforehand.[17] In commenting on the importance of this decision, Caden and Lucas note that, "By labeling CompuServe as a distributor rather than a publisher, the court issued the first prominent legal decision concerning the culpability of on-line access providers. The decision encouraged growth within the Internet community by reducing the threat of liability to on-line access providers."[18]

In the case of Stratton Oakmont v. Prodigy Services, Stratton sued Prodigy for libel because of statements posted about its president on a Prodigy bulletin board. In its ruling against Prodigy, on May 24, 1995, the court found that Prodigy was acting as a publisher and was therefore responsible for content. It distinguished this case from the CompuServe one, on the grounds that Prodigy advertised itself as responsible for content: "Prodigy promulgated content guidelines, used a software screening program, utilized Board Leaders [with the ability to monitor and censor incoming messages], and had an emergency delete function."[19] Prodigy could not have it both ways: it could not monitor content and claim its commitment to family values and then attempt to absolve itself of responsibility when information on its system was found to be libelous. Later in October, Stratton decided not to challenge new evidence that Prodigy planned to bring forward, leaving it to the judge to decide. Prodigy apologized for the offensive statements but continued to insist that it was not a publisher. In any case, the passage of the Communications Decency Act, early in 1996, changed Prodigy's position, as the commentary taken from Blumenfeld & Cohen makes clear: " 'Good Samaritan' blocking of information that content providers or users find objectionable (on a purely subjective basis) is legalized, thus overturning a well-known case finding Prodigy liable for civil damages on account of a forum posting that defamed a company on the ground that Prodigy engaged in selective blocking of postings."[20]

LEGISLATIVE ATTEMPTS TO REGULATE SPEECH ON THE INTERNET

'(a) Whoever—
'(1) in interstate or foreign communications—

'(A) by means of a telecommunications device knowingly—
'(i) makes, creates, or solicits, and
'(ii) initiates the transmission of, any comment, request, suggestion, proposal, image, or other communication which is obscene, lewd, lascivious, filthy, or indecent, with intent to annoy, abuse, threaten, or harass another person;

'(B) by means of a telecommunications device knowingly—
'(i) makes, creates, or solicits, and
'(ii) initiates the transmission of, any comment, request, suggestion, proposal, image, or other communication which is obscene or indecent, knowing that the recipient of the communication is under 18 years of age, regardless of whether the maker of such communication placed the call or initiated the communication;

'(C) makes a telephone call or utilizes a telecommunications device, whether or not conversation or communication ensues, without disclosing his identity and with intent to annoy, abuse, threaten, or harass any person at the called number or who receives the communications;

'(D) makes or causes the telephone of another repeatedly or continuously to ring, with intent to harass any person at the called number; or

'(E) makes repeated telephone calls or repeatedly initiates communication with a telecommunications device, during which conversation or communication ensues, solely to harass any person at the called number or who receives the communication; or

'(2) knowingly permits any telecommunications facility under his control to be used for any activity prohibited by paragraph (1) with the intent that it be used for such activity,
shall be fined under title 18, United States Code, or imprisoned not more than two years, or both.'

TITLE V - Communications Decency Act of 1996, Section 502, Obscene or
Harassing Use of Telecommunications Facilities

The Communications Decency Act (CDA) of 1996

On February 1, Congress passed the Telecommunications Act of 1996 and
it was signed into law one week later by President Clinton. It was a far-
reaching attempt to deal with the new technologies that have dramatically
altered the telecommunications industry in the past few years. (More will be
said about the Act in Chapter 12.) The issue of interest, however, is Title V—
Obscenity and Violence, Subtitle A—Obscene, Harassing, and Wrongful
Utilization of Telecommunications Facilities, with the short title, the
Communications Decency Act of 1996. The quotation at the beginning of
this section provides the crucial words of the Act that have aroused so much
controversy.

Although the passage of the Act was expected, as it had been debated
for many months, there was a hope that the above provisions would be
weakened or even deleted. But such was not the case as it passed both
houses of Congress with overwhelming majorities. Within minutes of the
enactment, a suit was filed in federal court by the American Civil Liberties
Union and 19 other organizations to enjoin several sections of the Act.
Others in this group included the National Writers Union, Electronic
Frontier Foundation, and the Electronic Privacy Information Center. A
temporary restraining order was narrowly granted on the indecency pro-
visions. On February 26, another suit was launched by a group, the
Citizens Internet Empowerment Coalition (CIEC), led by the American
Library Association and including Apple, CompuServe, America Online,
Microsoft, the Association of American Publishers, and the Newspaper
Association of America. The suits were joined the following day and the
hearing began on March 21. In the interim, many sexually-oriented-
Web sites began displaying elaborate messages to forestall any legal
responsibility.[21]

If February 8 was a black day for free speech on the Internet for many,
then June 12 witnessed the sun breaking through. In a unanimous decision,
the three-judge panel in Philadelphia found for the plaintiffs and declared
the indecency provisions unconstitutional. What was encouraging to the
strong supporters of the First Amendment was the quality of the statements
made by the judges in support of their decision. Thus the following examples are indicative of the unanimous sentiments of the judges[22]:

- The Internet may fairly be regarded as a never-ending worldwide conversation. The government may not, through the CDA, interrupt that con-

versation. As the most participatory form of mass speech yet developed, the Internet deserves the highest protection from government intrusion. . .

- Any content-based regulation of the Internet, no matter how benign the purpose, could burn the global village to roast the pig.

- Internet communication, while unique, is more akin to telephone communication than to broadcasting because as with the telephone an Internet user must act affirmatively and deliberately to retrieve specific information online.

- Just as the strength of the Internet is chaos, so the strength of our liberty depends upon the chaos and cacophony of the unfettered speech the First Amendment protects.

- The CDA will, without doubt, undermine the substantive, speech-enhancing benefits that have flowed from the Internet. The diversity of the content will necessarily diminish as a result. The economic costs associated with compliance with the Act will drive from the Internet speakers whose content falls within the zone of possible prosecution.

One final point is that all the judges were impressed by the development of programs such as CyberSitter, SurfWatch, and NetNanny, which give parents the ability to prevent their children from accessing selected Web sites. Although government lawyers admitted that such programs could help and were being improved, they were not prepared to admit that parents acting responsibly meant that direct intervention by government was unnecessary. As expected, the government appealed and the case was decided in the Supreme Court.

The Supreme Court announced its decision on June 26, 1997, after having heard arguments on March 19. The Court's decision is described as follows by the Center for Democracy and Technology, an online civil liberties organization[23]:

> The Court struck down the Communications Decency Act (CDA), Congress' first attempt to censor speech online. Writing for the court, Justice John Paul Stevens held that "the CDA places an unacceptably heavy burden on protected speech" and found that all provisions of the CDA are unconstitutional as they apply to "indecent" or "patently offensive" speech. In a separate concurrence, Chief Justice William Rhenquist and Justice Sandra Day O'Connor agreed that the provisions of the CDA are all unconstitutional except in their narrow application to "communications between an adult and one or more minors."

This decision helped to legitimize the Internet as a medium deserving First Amendment protection. It demonstrated the deep commitment that the judiciary holds with respect to free speech, but Congress was not ready to give up its attempts to find a way to protect children from questionable material on the Internet.

The Child Online Protection Act (COPA) of 1998

To amend the Communications Act of 1934 to require persons who are engaged in the business of distributing, by means of the World Wide Web, material that is harmful to minors to restrict access to such material by minors, and for other purposes.[24]

COPA was passed by Congress and signed into law by President Clinton on October 21,1998. It is often referred to as Communications Decency Act II, or CDA II, in recognition of its role as the followup to the original CDA, the relevant sections of which were found unconstitutional. Not surprisingly, protecting children is an issue that merits the greatest attention of politicians. The central theme of this legislation is to provide protection for children against materials commercially distributed on the Web, that are "harmful to minors." During the debate on this legislation, the term "harmful to minors" received considerable attention. In the end, it is defined in the Act as follows[25]:

Part I of title II of the Communications Act of 1934 (47 U.S.C. 201 et seq.) is amended by adding at the end the following new section:

'SEC. 231. RESTRICTION OF ACCESS BY MINORS TO MATERIALS COMMERCIALLY DISTRIBUTED BY MEANS OF WORLD WIDE WEB THAT ARE HARMFUL TO MINORS.
....

'(e) DEFINITIONS—For purposes of this subsection, the following definitions shall apply:
'(1) BY MEANS OF THE WORLD WIDE WEB—The term 'by means of the World Wide Web' means by placement of material in a computer server-based file archive so that it is publicly accessible, over the Internet, using hypertext transfer protocol or any successor protocol.
....
'(6) MATERIAL THAT IS HARMFUL TO MINORS—The term 'material that is harmful to minors' means any communication, picture, image, graphic image file, article, recording, writing, or other matter of any kind that is obscene or that—

'(A) the average person, applying contemporary community standards, would find, taking the material as a whole and with respect to minors, is designed to appeal to, or is designed to pander to, the prurient interest;

'(B) depicts, describes, or represents, in a manner patently offensive with respect to minors, an actual or simulated sexual act or sexual contact, an actual or simulated normal or perverted sexual act, or a lewd exhibition of the genitals or post-pubescent female breast; and

'(C) taken as a whole, lacks serious literary, artistic, political, or scientific value for minors.

'(7) MINOR—The term 'minor' means any person under 17 years of age.'

Material that can be characterized as harmful to minors or satisfies two-thirds of the Miller test, community standards and lack of serious artistic or scientific value, is therefore obscene (see Miller test). Subsection (e) (6) (B) adds to the second part of the Miller test on depiction "in a manner patently offensive with respect to minors, an actual or simulated sexual act" more detail on unacceptable depictions for minors. Although various civil liberties groups were opposed to this Act, it should be noted that groups ostensibly in support of "family values" believed that it was necessary in order to protect children.

One set of criticisms of COPA derive from the work of the Electronic Privacy Information Center (EPIC), a leading Washington civil liberties lobby group. Their argument focuses on the burdens placed on Web content providers to meet their responsibilities under the Act and how free speech would be compromised. Consider the following[26]:

Although COPA contains a defense if Web speakers restrict access by requiring a credit card or adult access code, the evidence clearly established that either defense would burden free speech, for at least five reasons:
1. They deny access to all adults without credit cards
2. They require all interactive speech on the Web to be placed behind verification screens, even speech that is not "harmful to minors"
3. They deter adults from accessing protected speech because they impose costs on content that would be free, eliminate privacy, and stigmatize content
4. They allow hostile users to drive up costs to speakers
5. They impose financial burdens on speakers that will cause them to self-censor rather than incur those burdens.

On October 22, 1998, the ACLU and other groups filed a motion for a temporary restraining order against this bill.[27] Among other things, the memorandum pointed out that before COPA had been enacted, the Department of Justice had written "a seven-page letter to Congress outlining 'serious concerns' about the bill, and warning that it 'would likely be challenged on constitutional grounds'."[28] Given that COPA represents a second attempt to control access, it is surprising that serious constitutional problems remained. For example, in commenting on the requirements to verify age effectively, the memorandum notes,

Even if age or credit card verification were feasible, such a requirement would fundamentally alter the nature and values of the new computer communication medium, which is characterized by spontaneous, instantaneous, albeit often unpredictable, communication by hundreds of thousands of individual speakers around the globe, and which provides an affordable and often seamless means of accessing an enormous and diverse body of information, ideas and viewpoints. The COPA would thus prevent or deter hundreds of thousands of readers from accessing protected speech even if it were feasible for speakers to set up a system to verify age. Any age verification requirement would inevitably prevent readers who lack the necessary identification from accessing speech that would otherwise be available to them. Many adults do not have a credit card. Age verification would have an especially detrimental effect on foreign users, who are less likely than U.S.-based adults to have a credit card or other identification.

On February 1, 1999, Judge Lowell A. Reed Jr. of the U.S. District Court in Philadelphia found in favor of the plaintiffs and issued a preliminary injunction, blocking the enactment of COPA. The conclusion to Judge Reed's opinion is revealing in its expression of the dilemma for those who believe that children must be legally protected against certain kinds of material on the Internet, while at the same time not depriving adults of their free speech rights.[29]

The protection of children from access to harmful-to-minors materials on the Web, the compelling interest sought to be furthered by Congress in COPA, particularly resonates with the Court. This Court and many parents and grandparents would like to see the efforts of Congress to protect children from harmful materials on the Internet to ultimately succeed and the will of the majority of citizens in this country to be realized through the enforcement of an act of Congress. However, the Court is acutely cognizant of its charge under the law of this country not to protect the majoritarian will at the expense of stifling the rights embodied in the Constitution. Even at this preliminary stage of the case, I borrow from Justice Kennedy, who faced a similar dilemma when the Supreme Court struck down a statute that criminalized the burning of the American flag:

The case before us illustrates better than most that the judicial power is often difficult in its exercise. We cannot here ask another Branch to share responsibility, as when the argument is made that a statute is flawed or incomplete. For we are presented with a clear and simple statute to be judged against a pure command of the Constitution. The outcome can be laid at no door but ours.

The hard fact is that sometimes we must make decisions that we do not like. We make them because they are right, right in the sense that the law and the Constitution, as we see them, compel the result. And so great is our commitment to the process that, except in the rare case, we do not pause to express distaste for the result, perhaps for fear of undermining a valued principle that dictates the decision. This is one of those rare cases.

Texas v. Johnson, 491 U.S. 397, 420 (1989) (Kennedy, J., concurring).

Despite the Court's personal regret that this preliminary injunction will delay once again the careful protection of our children, I without hesitation acknowledge the duty imposed on the Court and the greater good such duty serves. Indeed, perhaps we do the minors of this country harm if First Amendment protections, which they will with age inherit fully, are chipped away in the name of their protection. [Boldness added for emphasis.]

Based on the foregoing analysis, the motion to dismiss the plaintiffs for a lack of standing will be denied.

Based on the foregoing findings and analysis, the Court concludes that the plaintiffs have established a likelihood of success on the merits, irreparable harm, and that the balance of interests, including the interest of the public, weighs in favor of enjoining the enforcement of this statute pending a trial on the merits, and the motion of plaintiffs for a preliminary injunction will be granted.

The paragraph highlighted above is revealing in portraying the conflict between a jurist carrying out his responsibility in a dedicated and conscientious manner and a citizen concerned with the welfare of the children in his country.

More than a year later, on June 22, 2000, the Third Circuit Court of Appeals upheld Judge Reed's ruling but on a different point. "Because of the peculiar geography-free nature of cyberspace, [COPA's] community standards test would essentially require every web communication to abide by the most restrictive community's standards."[30] Several months later, the Department of Justice petitioned the Supreme Court to overturn the decision of the Court of Appeals and arguments were heard on November 28, 2001. Finally, on May 14, 2002, the Supreme Court delivered a somewhat inconclusive decision.[31]

The Supreme Court rejected the lower court's decision but instead of making a ruling, it sent the case back for further examination but left the ban on enforcement of the Act in place. Some of the issues that were identified in the decision include the following[32]:

- The court ruled that the reliance of the Child Online Protection Act (COPA) on a notion of "community standards" to define what material in cyberspace is "harmful to minors" does not necessarily violate the First Amendment.

- "The most important message is that this law is unenforceable by the federal government," ACLU attorney Ann E. Beeson said.

- In a concurring opinion joined by Justices Ruth Bader Ginsburg and David H. Souter, Justice Anthony M. Kennedy noted a "very real likelihood" that COPA is unconstitutional on its face but argued that, given the fact that the law was enacted in response to the court's striking down of the CDA, "the Judiciary must proceed with caution and identify overbreadth with care before invalidating the Act."

Thus, after several years of trying, Congress was unable to pass legislation that protected children but did not limit First Amendment protection for adults on the Internet.

The COPA Commission

One provision in COPA called for the creation of a the COPA Commission, a federally mandated temporary panel to "identify technological or other methods that will help reduce access by minors to material that is harmful to minors on the Internet." The Commission held a series of meetings and hearings beginning with its first public meeting in March 2000. In addition, it advertised its interest in receiving research papers on Internet content regulation, filtering, and other means of controlling access. On October 20, 2000, it delivered its Final Report to Congress.[33] It made a number of recommendations, including increased public education about the availability and performance of technologies to protect children online, the allocation of resources to develop such technologies, increased law enforcement efforts to investigate and publicize Web sites that contain material harmful to children, and encouragement of ISPs to voluntarily initiate efforts to protect children. But what is most interesting is the brief conclusion.[34]

> The child-protective technologies and methods evaluated by the Commission provide an important but incomplete measure of protection from harmful-to-minors material online. The efforts recommended in this report, if implemented by industry, consumers, and government, will result in significant improvements in protection of children online.

The Children's Internet Protection Act (CIPA) of 2000

While COPA was making its way through the courts, supporters of an alternative approach to protecting children took another tack, while attempting to avoid constitutional issues. The kernel idea is based on the fact that the federal government provides funds for computer technology and Internet connections, on a voluntary basis, to libraries and schools across the country. The following funding sources are available[35]:

- School technology funds under the Elementary and Secondary Education Act
- Library technology funds under the Museum and Library Services Act
- "E-rate" service discounts for schools
- "E-rate" service discounts for libraries

The E-rate refers to a fund made available from telecommunication companies to enable schools and libraries to connect to the Internet. Thus, children in schools and libraries could be protected from material "harmful to minors" by requiring that any schools that accepted federal money from any of the programs listed above would be required to install filtering programs on all computers connected to the Internet. During 1999, various bills were proposed in Congress based on this approach, but it was with the Children's Internet Protection Act of 2000 (CIPA), passed by Congress and signed into law in December by President Clinton, that filtering became the battleground for free speech advocates.

CIPA was passed as Title XVII of the Departments of Labor, Health and Human Services, and Education, and Related Agencies Appropriations Act, 2001, an interesting context. Its enactment assumes that filtering software can do the job—a debatable proposition to be discussed in the next section. Three interesting features of CIPA follow[36]:

- CIPA's "harmful to minors" standard only applies to visual depictions of inappropriate content, and apparently not to text-based material of any kind, though CIPA does not proscribe efforts to filter additional material, and most filters block more than just pictures.
- Adults using library or school computers may ask to have filtering deactivated during their session only if they can demonstrate "bona fide research or other lawful purposes." Minors may or may not be able to have filtering deactivated, depending on the funding source involved.
- Finally, the bill also requires that communities adopt non-technological Internet policies [for example, responsible use policies], through a subtitle called the "Neighborhood Children's Internet Protection Act." That language lays out five topic areas for every Internet safety policy to address.

Of course, CIPA was challenged in the courts, beginning with a hearing before a special three-judge panel of the U.S. District Court of Philadelphia in March 2002. Not surprisingly, the petitioners include EPIC, the ACLU, and the American Library Association (ALA). The plaintiffs identified the following reasons for arguing that CIPA is unconstitutional[37]:

- It violates the First Amendment because it prevents citizens from communicating and accessing constitutionally protected speech, imposes a prior restraint on speech, is not narrowly tailored to limit speech in the least restrictive way possible...
- Web site blocking is erratic and ineffective.
- Web blocking is contrary to the mission of public libraries.

On March 31, 2002, the special panel struck down CIPA, declaring it unconstitutional.[38] Their concerns were strong and clear.

In sum, filtering products are currently unable to block only visual depictions that are obscene, child pornography, or harmful to minors (or, only content matching a filtering product's category definitions) while simultaneously allowing access to all protected speech (or, all content not matching the blocking product's category definitions). Any software filter that is reasonably effective in blocking access to Web pages that fall within its category definitions will necessarily erroneously block a substantial number of Web pages that do not fall within its category definitions. . .

Although software filters provide a relatively cheap and effective, albeit imperfect, means for public libraries to prevent patrons from accessing speech that falls within the filters' category definitions, we find that commercially available filtering programs erroneously block a huge amount of speech that is protected by the First Amendment.

In a by-now familiar process, the decision was appealed by the government, and on May 30, the three-judge panel of the U.S. Court of Appeals for the Third Circuit in Philadelphia upheld the lower-court decision, thereby striking down CIPA. Not surprisingly, the government appealed, and on November 12, 2002, the Supreme Court announced that it would hear the appeal.[39] Thus after six years, no effective (read constitutional) methods of dealing with controversial Internet content had been established, but the Supreme Court had yet to review COPA after its reexamination by the Appeals Court and it had not yet ruled on the constitutionality of CIPA.

On March 5, 2003, the Supreme Court heard arguments on the constitutionality of CIPA. Solicitor General Theodore Olson presented the government's case. The following paragraph is his opening argument[40]:

When libraries block Internet pornography from their computer terminals, they are simply declining to put onto their computer screens the same content they have traditionally excluded from their bookshelves. By offering Internet access without pornography, freedom of speech is expanded, not abridged. Under the Children's Internet Protection Act, or CIPA, no Internet speech is prohibited, inhibited, threatened, or chilled. Libraries are simply exercising their discretion as to the content that their libraries will contain, the historic discretion to exercise that—that authority, and to how their library resources will be used.

The ALA in its presentation made the following arguments[41]:

- The Internet is changing how we live, learn, work and interact with one another. As centers for lifelong learning, libraries are uniquely positioned to help deliver Internet safety education and teach the skills necessary to mine the best of the Web. The public library is their sole access point to a world of information online and in print for many people who cannot afford computers with Internet access.
- While the government argues that filtering the Internet is just like selecting which books to shelve, this only exposes their lack of understanding of librarians' work. Filters are blunt instruments that continue to fail in distinguishing Flesh Public Library or explicit health information from illegal and obscene materials online.

- Decisions about library collections should not be made by commercial entities with no public accountability, hidden censorship lists, and staff with no training in what constitutes "harmful to minors."

The decision was delivered on June 23. The Appeals Court decision was reversed and CIPA declared constitutional by a six to three majority. The Supreme Court had finally upheld an attempt by the government to regulate speech on the Internet. The Court claimed that the use of filtering software was no different than traditional collections policies used by libraries to guide their materials acquisitions. Furthermore, it stated that individuals—adults—who needed access to sites blocked by filtering programs could request that they be temporarily turned off, although this circumstance had been strongly criticized by opponents of CIPA because it violated a principle of librarians not to interfere in users' search activities. The ALA issued a press release expressing its unhappiness.[42]

> We are very disappointed in today's decision. Forcing Internet filters on all library computer users strikes at the heart of user choice in libraries and at the libraries' mission of providing the broadest range of materials to diverse users. Today's Supreme Court decision forces libraries to choose between federal funding for technology improvements and censorship. Millions of library users will lose.
>
> We are disappointed the Court did not understand the difference between adults and children using library resources. This flies in the face of library practice of age-appropriate materials and legal precedent that adults must have access to the full range of health, political and social information. The public library is the number one access point for online information for those who do not have Internet access at home or work. We believe they must have equal access to the Information Superhighway.

TECHNOLOGICAL APPROACHES TO REGULATE CONTENT

> Controlling access to the Internet by means of filtering software has become a growth industry in the U.S. and elsewhere. Its use has increased as the mandatory response to the current plagues of society, namely, pornography, violence, hate, and in general, anything seen to be unpleasant or threatening.[43]

The preferred technology for controlling access to the Internet has become known as filters—programs that are designed to restrict access to Web sites, newsgroups, and chat rooms by a variety of techniques. It is important to distinguish among different strategies for limiting access. The simplest approach is to compile a list of URLs and newsgroups that are to be blocked. Such a list must be continuously updated given the dynamic growth of the Internet. A substantial number of individuals must be employed to perform this function and must operate under an agreed upon and closely followed set of guidelines. Such filters require that users regularly download the updated banned site list and simply adopt it because of the near impossibility of evaluating its quality or determining whether or not it meets their concerns. For some filters, users can add newly discovered unacceptable sites to the banned list. The default strategy is to accept the judgment of others, namely, profit-making corporations subject to marketplace pressures in determining which sites are off-limits.

Another strategy is to compile a list of English keywords that characterize the material in Web sites that is judged unacceptable for viewing. This list can be regularly modified to reflect more precise descriptions or new concerns. Keywords, even Boolean combinations of keywords, are a rather poor representation of the meaning of texts and therefore may block otherwise acceptable sites. Their attraction is that they give the appearance of effectiveness because, for example, if it is desired to block access to sites containing documents and graphics dealing with naked women, such keywords and Boolean forms as nudity, naked, nudity AND women, and naked AND women, should be effective.

The last general category of blocking or filtering strategies is similar to systems used to rate music on CDs and cassettes, movies, and television shows. Simply put, Web sites would be expected to rate their content along several dimensions, including sexual explicitness, nudity, violent language, and violent graphics. The ratings, on simple numeric scales, can be combined into a profile that characterizes, for a given user, an envelope for acceptable sites. For example, if a site's ratings exceed the profile along even one dimension, that site will be blocked by the browser. Such a system requires, among other things, that sites rate themselves, that such ratings accurately reflect content—a non-trivial task subject to legitimate disagreements—and that disagreements on ratings be adjudicated by some impartial board. Also, it is necessary that sites rate themselves, for a default condition must be that non-rated sites are automatically blocked. Thus, perfectly acceptable sites may not be accessible, thereby depriving users of valuable information. These are just a few of the possible repercussions of self-rating systems.

In somewhat more detail, the American Library Association responds to the question "What is blocking/filtering software?" as follows[44]:

> Blocking/filtering software is a mechanism used to
> • Restrict access to Internet content, based on an internal database of the product, or
> • Restrict access to Internet content through a database maintained external to the product itself, or

- Restrict access to Internet content to certain ratings assigned to those sites by a third party, or
- Restrict access to Internet content by scanning content, based on a keyword, phrase or text string or
- Restrict access to Internet content based on the source of the information.

Many polls have shown that parents are deeply concerned about what their children may encounter on the Internet. One study reports results of mixed parental attitudes about the Internet[45]:

> Parents are nervous about two features of Web programming they haven't seen in broadcast or cable television: its wide-open nature and its interactivity. Parents fear the Web for its unprecedented openness—the easy access by anybody to sexuality, bad values, and commercialism. They also fear the Web for its unprecedented interactive nature—the potential for invading a family's privacy and for adults taking advantage of children. These fears are heightened among many parents because they don't believe they understand the technology well enough to make the best use of it. Yet they believe their children need it.

If the Internet is unsafe for kids, as many parents clearly believe, but the growth of E-commerce requires making it a safe place, then filtering as part of an overall business strategy makes sense. Furthermore, it has the distinct advantage of seeming to place the necessary power in the hands of parents and local officials, not in the federal government's, except for certain special cases such as child pornography. So whether it is the issue of personal privacy or Internet content, the predominant marketplace position is self-regulation. Nevertheless, as we have seen, the U.S. federal government has shown itself to be very interested in mandating the use of filters to protect children wherever federal money is involved in facilitating Internet access.

Problems With the Use of Filters

It has been suggested above that filters may not operate effectively because of a variety of problems. Some of these will be explored in this section, but it should be realized that what is viewed as a problem by critics of filters may be hailed as a virtue by supporters. For example, the National Coalition Against Censorship offers the following non-technical descriptions of some limitations of filters[46]:

- Oversimplification. How to distinguish "good" sex (or violence) from "bad"? Filters and labels assume that television programs and Internet sites can be reduced to a single letter or symbol, or a combination of these.

- Overbreadth. Ratings and filters often ignore context and, thus, inevitably exclude material that users might want to have, along with material they may not want.
- Feasibility. What about better descriptions of television programming and Internet sites? It sounds like a good idea, but it isn't feasible. There are thousands of television programs, content changes daily, and each new program would require a new description.
- Subjectivity. Any rating system that classifies or describes content is dependent on the subjective judgment of the rater.
- Full disclosure. Few Internet filters disclose what you lose by using them. The makers of these products claim that information is proprietary and its disclosure would provide a roadmap to objectionable material.
- Security. Filters and ratings give a false sense of security, by suggesting that all parents need to do to protect children is to block disturbing ideas and images.

Many specific examples could be given to illustrate these limitations. Searches of British regions such as Essex and Sussex are blocked because of the inclusion of "sex" within the search keywords. Of course many of these obvious errors can be addressed by what in computer science jargon is called hacks or patches. Other Web sites that should not be blocked because they provide necessary and useful education about sexual matters may be blocked because it is profitable to reach a large segment of the population that objects to sex education and therefore prefers this outcome. Context can sometimes be taken into account, but a system of keywords is fundamentally limited because just the occurrence of certain words or phrases rarely captures true meaning. Sites belonging to organizations that promote strong free speech viewpoints, such as the American Civil Liberties Union, have been blocked by more conservative organizations. Even objecting to the patterns of exclusion adopted by certain filtering companies may result in the critical source being added to the banned list. Thus, any sites on the Internet that host discussions that deal with free speech issues are very likely to be restricted because they will of necessity contain filter-sensitive words. The feasibility issue is paramount given the incredible growth curve of the Web and the fact the even existing Web sites change in unpredictable ways. Another issue is lack of consistency, in that employees of filtering companies who must evaluate sites for content may differ significantly from one another with respect to the criteria for acceptability.

Since as far back as 1996, the favored solution to limiting access to content on the Internet has been filtering software. It is a technology that is basically crude and unsophisticated but has the undeniable virtue that it produces results; it does restrict access to a considerable amount of material with sexual content. But it is also a technology that can be used to limit access according to an agenda that may or may not be known to users. The bottom line is that the price to pay for using filtering programs is too high in terms of limiting access to potentially interesting and useful sites because of the decisions made by some unknown group or individual. Finally, let me clearly state that if people wish to use filters, that is obviously their right; my concern, and others as well, is with the government mandating their use. That citizens in a democracy would be willing to rely on such an impoverished technology to limit their First Amendment rights should be of concern to all those who value free speech as the hallmark of that society.

OTHER ISSUES

Fundamental Freedoms
Everyone has the following fundamental freedoms:
a) freedom of conscience and religion;
b) freedom of thought, belief, opinion and expression, including freedom of
the press and other media of communication;
c) freedom of peaceful assembly; and
d) freedom of association.
—Canadian Charter of Rights and Freedoms (1982)

Sexual Harassment and Electronic Networks

A defense of free speech on electronic networks, the Internet to be more precise, has been made previously in this chapter, but there are certain consequences that must be addressed. What, if anything, should be done about people who download sexually explicit images on workstations in public areas at work, in libraries, and in universities and colleges? The concern arises because others in the area at nearby computers may find these images offensive and disturbing, resulting in an interference with normal work. Beginning in the early 1990s, many educational institutions concerned with this problem took steps to restrict student access to suspect newsgroups as a way of dealing with the problem. Thus, all newsgroups in the alt.sex hierarchy were cut off, including the so-called binaries, where most of the suspect coded images resided. However, this hierarchy contains many newsgroups that deal with sexual issues that in no way could be characterized as pornographic, even if a satisfactory definition of that term were possible. However, administrators at many institutions decided that censorship, although that term was rarely used in public, was the most effective way to deal with a burgeoning problem.

A detailed exploration of this situation was carried out by this author in 1993,[47] in order to argue that it should not be necessary to censor or suppress in order to achieve equitable environments. Having watchdog groups regularly monitoring Usenet to determine if any non-alt.sex newsgroups were problematic, or if any new newsgroups might be offensive with respect to racial, ethnic, or gender concerns, is not appropriate for educational institutions. Thus, this author proposed[48]

> "six basic principles . . . that adhere strongly to the principle of free speech, as a hallmark of an open and democratic society. . . . The first four principles are stated in the form of injunctions intended to serve administrative, pragmatic requirements while simultaneously serving free speech. The last two principles are an attempt to capture the benefits of electronic networks in a concise fashion, juxtaposed with the difficulties that organizations may have in enforcing the unenforceable."

Administrative Principles
1. Do not treat electronic media different from print media, or traditional bulletin boards merely because they can be more easily controlled
2. Do not censor potentially offensive material on networks; encourage the use of sexual harassment procedures, if appropriate
3. Be aware of your responsibility with respect to the uses and misuses of your facilities. However, do not use cost of services as an excuse to censor and limit access
4. Trust and educate people to be responsible

Social Principles
1. Issues will proliferate beyond the ability of organizations to control them by rigid policies
2. Occasional offensive postings do not detract from the benefits of electronic networks

It has been argued by some that "placing the burden on women to invoke sexual harassment procedures may compound an already difficult situation. Fellow students or workers may attempt to trivialize the events and criticize the complainant's lack of camaraderie and unwillingness to be one of the gang. The increasing number of women who participate in network communication and computing in general may change the culture sufficiently so that offensive displays will no longer be accepted or tolerated."[49]

Virtual Child Pornography

One area of sexually explicit material that is universally condemned is child pornography. No First Amendment defense exists. There have been several laws passed outlawing the creation, sale, and possession of this offensive material. The early laws attempted to deal with the coercion of children to appear in sexually explicit film and video productions as well as photographs and drawings. Subsequent laws were based on the belief and presumably evidence that material with children engaged in sexual conduct was used by pedophiles to attract other children and to encourage them to willingly participate in similar acts. In addition, it was feared that possession of child pornography would excite pedophiles to the point that they would be compelled to attack children, a terrible possibility.

Accusations have been made and evidence has shown that the Internet has become another distribution channel for this most despised material. Certainly Web sites exist that carry child pornography and this material is available for purchase or trade. There have been highly publicized police raids and a number of people have been arrested. In 1995, the U.S. Congress passed the Sex Crimes Against Children Prevention Act of 1995 (SCACPA), and required that the United States Sentencing Commission report on the adequacy of federal penalties. In its report, the Commission noted that penalties had been increased over the previous two years and were quite severe, but the report also examined the role of the Internet. In surveying computer use among defendants in pornography cases with respect to trafficking and receipt, computers were involved in 22 out of 66 cases. In nine of these, "defendants posted notices of interest in receiving child pornography, and in four cases defendants posted notices regarding the availability of child pornography."[50]

It is clear that although the numbers are small, Congress views computer and computer networks as a growth area and in fact, the legislative history of the SCACPA indicates that Congress has the following concerns[51]:

1. The wide dissemination and instantaneous transmission in computer-assisted trafficking of child pornography
2. The increased difficulty of investigation and prosecution by law enforcement officials
3. The increased likelihood that child pornography will be viewed by and harm children
4. The potential for pedophiles to lure children into sexual relationships through the computer.

In 1996, Congress passed the Child Pornography Prevention Act (CPPA) to deal with yet another problem made urgent by computer technology—virtual child pornography. Child pornography created virtually is described in the first paragraph of the opinion delivered by the Supreme Court, on April 16, 2002, on the constitutionality of CPPA.[51a]

> The Child Pornography Prevention Act of 1996 (CPPA) expands the federal prohibition on child pornography to include not only pornographic images made using actual children, 18 U.S.C. §2256 (8)(A), but also "any visual depiction, including any photograph, film, video, picture, or computer or computer-generated image or picture" that "is, or appears to be, of a minor engaging in sexually explicit conduct," §2256(8)(B), and any sexually

explicit image that is "advertised, promoted, presented, described, or distributed in such a manner that conveys the impression" it depicts "a minor engaging in sexually explicit conduct," §2256(8)(D). Thus, §2256(8)(B) bans a range of sexually explicit images, sometimes called "virtual child pornography," that appear to depict minors but were produced by means other than using real children, such as through the use of youthful-looking adults or computer-imaging technology. Section 2256(8)(D) is aimed at preventing the production or distribution of pornographic material pandered as child pornography. Fearing that the CPPA threatened their activities, respondents, an adult-entertainment trade association and others, filed this suit alleging that the "appears to be" and "conveys the impression" provisions are overbroad and vague, chilling production of works protected by the First Amendment.

The Supreme Court ruled that CPPA was unconstitutional for a number of reasons, including that it went too far, undermined First Amendment protection, and that the argument that even virtual child pornography should be banned because it stimulates molesters does not hold because "the mere tendency of speech to encourage unlawful acts is not a sufficient reason for barring it."[51b] Furthermore, "the law was unconstitutionally vague and far-reaching." President Bush and Congress vowed to reintroduce a new version of this Act, given the importance of the issue.

Racism and Hate[52]

What about racist speech, speech that denigrates, insults, even threatens members of an identifiable racial, ethnic, or religious group? It is not too difficult to find Web sites that proclaim such views, but this speech is for the most part protected in the U.S. However, in most other countries there are legal limits on racist speech. For example, Canada's Charter of Rights and Freedoms (1982), states that all Canadians have the following fundamental freedoms, among others: "freedom of thought, belief, opinion and expression, including freedom of the press and other media of communication."[53] But the constitution also contains this prior clause that permits Canada's Supreme Court to determine whether or not other factors may justify a limitation on speech: "1. The Canadian Charter of Rights and Freedoms guarantees the rights and freedoms set out in it subject only to such reasonable limits prescribed by law as can be demonstrably justified in a free and democratic society."

In Canada, as well as many other countries, it is believed that allowing racists to exercise their free speech rights in an extreme manner could cause serious harm. So Sections 38 and 39 of Canada's Criminal Code deal with hate propaganda, including inciting hatred and publicly advocating genocide. In Germany it is a crime to deny that the Holocaust occurred. In general, the U.S. is very tolerant of hate speech. Defenders of the rights guaranteed by the First Amendment often argue that if unpleasant and even disgusting speech is not protected, the First Amendment is worthless. But the question often arises with respect to whether or not a class of racist or hate speech exists that is in effect action, and therefore not protected. The answer, or at least an answer offered by the U.S. Supreme Court, is yes, there does exist such speech. Consider the following passage[54]:

> With respect to violence, the noted constitutional scholar, Cass Sunstein points out that the Supreme Court in the 1969 decision *Brandenburg v. Ohio* said, "the government could not take action against a member of the Ku Klux Klan, who said, among other things, 'We're not a revengent organization, but if our President, our Congress, our Supreme Court, continues to suppress the white, Caucasian race, it's possible that there might have to be some revengence taken.' The speaker did not explicitly advocate illegal acts or illegal violence."[55] Furthermore, the government was required to meet the following three criteria before it could regulate threatening speech: First, the speaker must promote not just any lawless action but "imminent lawless action. Second, the imminent lawless action must be 'likely' to occur. Third, the speaker must intend to produce imminent lawless action 'directed to inciting or producing imminent lawless action.'"
>
> Thus it should be clear that even in the U.S., the right to exercise free speech is not absolute despite the claim of certain advocates and it therefore follows that the Internet is not a domain of absolute free speech even though enforcement may be extremely difficult. With respect to violent speech, the Internet creates an environment in which any individual may reach millions with an incitement to commit an act of terror or to strike out at identifiable individuals. Professor Sunstein argues that the above criteria may not be workable in this new environment.

Two recent events, somewhat complementary, seem to provide an indication that there may be growing support for restricting hate speech by applying existing laws. In addition, there is also a growing perception that hate crimes are so heinous and so destructive of the basic fabric of a democratic society that special action is necessary.

E-Mail Threats

Richard Machado is believed to be the first person convicted in the U.S. of uttering threats over the Internet using e-mail. More precisely, he violated the civil rights of his targets as described below[56]:

> Richard Machado, who in February became the first man convicted of an Internet-related hate crime, was ordered in Federal court on Wednesday to spend four months in a halfway house after he failed to report to his probation officer. Machado, 21, of Los Angeles, was convicted in February of violating the civil rights of Asian students to whom he sent threatening

e-mail. The conviction related to a 1996 incident in which Machado, who had flunked out of the University of California at Irvine, sent a message to 59 students with Asian-sounding names that said, in part, 'I personally will make it my life career [sic] to find and kill everyone of you personally'.

The second case involved an Asian threatening Hispanics by e-mail.[57]

In the nation's second Federal case involving an alleged hate crime on the Internet, prosecutors in Los Angeles on Thursday filed civil rights charges against a 22-year-old man accused of sending death threats to 100 Hispanic people by e-mail. The man, Kingman Quon of Corona, Calif., faces seven Federal charges for the e-mail message, which was sent to about 100 people around the nation last March. The profanity-filled message included slurs against Hispanic people and expressed frustration with affirmative action, said Assistant United States Attorney Michael J. Gennaco. In the message, the prosecutor said, 'He says that Hispanics get unfair advantages, that they used affirmative action to get where they are. He says he is going to kill them all.'

Threats to Doctors Who Perform Abortions

In a 1999 court decision, the creators of the Nuremberg Files Web site were ordered by a jury in Portland, Oregon, to pay more than $107 million in damages to Planned Parenthood and a group of doctors. A report in the *New York Times* reads in part,[58]

In by far the largest judgment ever imposed on militant abortion opponents, a federal jury Tuesday ordered creators of Old West-style "wanted" posters and a World Wide Web site that lists the names of abortion providers to pay more than $107 million to Planned Parenthood and a group of doctors who contended that the material amounted to deadly threats. The plaintiffs hailed their victory as a major step in their fight to stop the "domestic terrorism" of some abortion foes, whose lists of "baby butchers" on the Web site, called "The Nuremberg Files," include the names, home addresses and license-plate numbers of many abortion doctors and the names of their spouses and children. When a doctor on the list is slain, as three have been, the Web site shows a line drawn through his name.

The decision was appealed and on March 21, 2001, the 9th U.S. Circuit Court of Appeals overturned the verdict. Basically, they argued that however offensive the information on the Web site was, the First Amendment provided protection, or in the words of the judges, "While pungent, even highly offensive, ACLA's [American Coalition of Life Advocates] statements carefully avoid threatening the doctors with harm in the sense that there are no quotable quotes calling for violence against the targeted providers."[59] So there is no language that can be interpreted as a call to violence. The reader may be interested in visiting the site, The Nuremberg Files,[60] but be warned that the language and graphics may be offensive to some.

A little more than a year later, the Appeals Court reversed itself in a 6-5 decision. It now ruled,[61]

> that comments posted on Web sites and anti-abortion "wanted" posters are not constitutionally protected speech under the First Amendment, but rather constitute a "true threat." The appeals court, however, sent the $108 million damages award back to a lower court for reconsideration.

Furthermore, the thrust of the case seemed to have changed.[62]

> The decision centered around the Freedom of Access to Clinics Entrances Act (FACE), a federal law that protects reproductive health services and its staff from violence or threats. A person who violates the law faces fines or imprisonment.
>
> "FACE itself requires that the threat of force be made with the intent to intimidate," Circuit Judge Pamela Ann Rymer wrote in her opinion. The defendant's "conduct amounted to a true threat and is not protected speech."

It is expected that the Supreme Court will hear this case in the near future.

Other Countries

Two more issues will be briefly introduced. If concern with free speech is a hotly debated topic in the U.S. and several other countries, for the majority of the world's countries, many other matters take precedence. In the U.S., whatever assaults exist against a full exercise of free speech, there are constitutional guarantees and a strong commitment to them; unfortunately, such is not the case in the rest of the world. The international organization Human Rights Watch issues reports that focus on the global attack on free speech on the Internet and elsewhere. In the summary of the 1996 report, the threat is clearly stated: "Governments around the world, claiming they want to protect children, thwart terrorists and silence racists and hate mongers, are rushing to eradicate freedom of expression on the Internet, the international 'network of networks,' touted as the Information Superhighway."[63] A few examples of these events follow[64]:

- China . . . requires users and Internet Service Providers (ISPs) to register with authorities
- Vietnam and Saudi Arabia . . . permit only a single, government-controlled gateway for Internet service

- [The] United States . . . has enacted new Internet-specific legislation that imposes more restrictive regulations on electronic expression than those currently applied to printed expression
- India . . . charges exorbitant rates for international access through the state-owned phone company
- Germany . . . has cut off access to particular host computers or Internet sites
- Singapore . . . has chosen to regulate the Internet as if it were a broadcast medium, and requires political and religious content providers to register with the state
- New Zealand . . . classifies computer disks as publications and has seized and restricted them accordingly.

Human Rights Watch recommends that international agreements enshrine freedom of expression as a basic principle for a Global Information Infrastructure. This would include "prohibiting prior censorship of on-line communication . . . promoting the wide dissemination of diverse ideas and viewpoints from a wide variety of information sources on the GII, and ensuring that the GII enable individuals to organize and form on-line associations freely and without interference."[64a]

Yahoo in France

One important case of a conflict in international laws regulating free speech is the suit launched in 2000 in France against Yahoo for permitting the sale of Nazi memorabilia on its auction site. Such advertisements and sales would be against French law but not against American law, however distasteful they might be. The French court issued an important ruling[65]:

> The case led to a landmark ruling in France, with a court ordering Yahoo to block Internet surfers in France from auctions selling Nazi memorabilia. French law bars the display or sale of racist material.
> Yahoo eventually banned Nazi material as it began charging users to make auction listings, saying it did not want to profit from such material.

Yahoo claimed its actions had nothing to do with this decision, but a second suit was launched in France with the courts in February 2003, throwing out "accusations by French human rights activists who said Yahoo should be held legally responsible for auctions that were once held on its website of Nazi paraphernalia. The court ruled that Yahoo and its former chief executive, Tim Koogle, never sought to 'justify war crimes and crimes against humanity' as they were accused of doing by human rights activists, including Holocaust survivors and their families."[66] However, the legal question of jurisdiction remained open with respect to whether or not decisions in one country could have any impact on Internet operations in another country, short of international agreements.

SUMMARY

It is said that the first issue that arises after the diffusion of a new communications technology is sex—how much, how explicit, and how harmful, especially to children? The Internet is no exception and in this chapter, some of the free speech issues related to the Internet were explored. Some examples of these issues, which arose in the early days of the popular Internet, were discussed, including the Jake Baker Case and the infamous *Time* magazine cover story that argued that the Web was replete with sexually explicit content.

The Internet has become the target of a number of attacks that threaten its openness and traditional frontier mentality. At the top of the list is the concern in the press, certain religious groups, law enforcement officials, and politicians that the Internet is rife with obscene material that must be controlled. The passage of the Communications Decency Act in 1996 was a clear demonstration by elected officials in an election year that they were serious about outlawing questionable material. However, the critical elements of this Act were found unconstitutional by the U.S. Supreme Court in 1997. Other legislation followed.

Parallel with the legislative approach, technology has been developed which purports to restrict access precisely to those sites which may be harmful to minors. Known as filtering software, the idea is to specify limitations on certain classes of search terms and Web sites so that they cannot be accessed. They have been hailed by supporters as the best way to protect children, and others, from viewing unpleasant content, and labeled as ineffective by critics. Legislation requiring their implementation on computers in libraries, which accept Federal government aid in connecting to the Internet, has been upheld by the Supreme Court in 2003.

Other issues of concern are racism, sexual harassment, virtual child pornography, and events in other countries. It should be noted that the hallmark of free speech protection in the U.S., the First Amendment, is unique in the world in terms of the strong protection it provides. However, the Internet, as a global technology, does not respect national boundaries, and therefore speech issues may arise in other countries that affect activities in the U.S.

NOTES

1. Ira Sager et al. "The Underground Web," Cover story, *Business Week*, September 2, 2002. Available at http://www.businessweek.com/print/magazine/content/02_35/b3797001.htm (Note that there is a cost associated with accessing this page.)

2. "Statement of Principles," Global Internet Liberty Campaign. (No date). Available at http://www.gilc.org/about/principles.html

3. "Exploring Constitutional Conflicts: Regulation of Obscenity and Nudity," University of Missouri—Kansas City Law Faculty. (No date). Available at http://www.law.umkc.edu/faculty/projects/ftrials/conlaw/obscenity.htm

4. Enunciated in *Miller v. California* (413 U.S. 15 [1973].

5. "What's the Big Deal Over Jake Baker?" The Jake Baker Information Page. Available at http://krusty.eecs.umich.edu/people/pjswan/Baker/big.deal.html Note that the Jake Baker Information Page will be moved to the MIT SAFE Archive at http://www.MIT.edu:8001/activities/safe/home.html

6. "United States v. Jake Baker and Arthur Gonda," U.S. District Court, Eastern District of Michigan, Southern Division. Available at http://ic.net/~sberaha/baker.html

7. "New Information Since 1/30/97," Jake Baker Information Page," January 30, 1997. Available at http://www.mit.edu/activities/safe/safe/cases/umich-baker-story/Baker/Jake Baker.html

8. Philip Elmer-DeWitt. "On a Screen Near You: Cyberporn," *Time*, July 3, 1995, p. 32.

9. *Ibid.*, p. 34.

10. Marty Rimm. "Marketing Pornography on the Information Superhighway: A Survey of 917,410 Images, Descriptions, Short Stories, and Animations Downloaded 8.5 Million Times by Consumers in Over 2000 Cities in Forty Countries, Provinces, and Territories," *Georgetown Law Journal*, 83, June 1995, pp. 1849–1934. Available at http://trfn.pgh.pa.us/guest/mrtext.html

11. Donna L. Hoffman and Thomas P. Novak. "A Detailed Analysis of the Conceptual, Logical, and Methodological Flaws in the Article: "'Marketing Pornography on the Information Superhighway'," July 2, 1995. Available at http://www2000.ogsm.vanderbilt.edu/rimm.cgi.

12. Donna L. Hoffman and Thomas P. Novak. "A Detailed Critique of the TIME Article: 'On a Screen Near You: Cyberporn (DeWitt, 7/3/95)' July 1, 1995 (version 1.01). Available at http://www2000.ogsm.vanderbilt.edu/dewitt.cgi.

13. *Op cit.*, Elmer-DeWitt.

14. "United States v. Thomas," 1996 FED App. 0032P (6th Cir.). Available at http://www.law.emory.edu/6circuit/jan96/96a0032p.06.html

15. *Ibid.*

16. *Ibid.*

17. "Cubby v. CompuServe." October 31, 1991. Available at http://www.eff.org/pub/CAF/law/cubby-v-compuserve.summary

18. Marc L. Caden and Stephanie E. Lucas. "Accidents on the Information Superhighway: On-Line Liability and Regulation," *University of Richmond Journal of Law & Technology*, 2 (1), 1996. Available at http://www.urich.edu/~jolt/v2i1/caden lucas.html.

19. *Ibid.*

20. "Overview of the Telecommunications Act of 1996," Blumenfeld & Cohen—Technology Law Group, February 1996. Available at http://www.technology law.com/techlaw/act_summary.html

21. "Bodacious Babes in Lingerie." Available at http://www.shout.net/~odin/tamali/ Here is the warning that appears on the site:

FIRST AMENDMENT PRIVACY CURTAIN. PLEASE READ THIS!

To protect the world from viewing adult-oriented material without their consent, and to protect the viewing of adult-oriented material by minors, we require all viewers to read and certify to the following:

By entering this site you are certifying that you are of legal adult age and are entering this website with full knowledge that it contains adult-oriented material.

Furthermore you are certifying that the viewing, reading, and downloading of the images in this website do not violate the community standards or the laws governing your street, village, city, town, county, state, province or country.

By continuing, you certify that you know your local laws and furthermore know that they do not prohibit the viewing of sexually explicit materials. Ignorance is not a valid defense.

You also certify that you are wholly liable for any false disclosures and responsible for any legal ramifications that may arise from viewing, reading, or downloading of images or material contained within this website and that the website creator and their affiliates cannot be held responsible for any legal ramifications that may arise as a result of fraudulent entry into or use of this website and/or material contained herein.

These pages are provided for adult entertainment and educational purposes, and are not designed to promote prurient interests. The website creator does not censor, or warrant the information presented here. Furthermore, a listing is not to be construed as any type of implied endorsement for the authors or services of the listed pages or the information contained thereon.

In addition to the above statements, you must also certify the following:

* I am at least 21 years of age
* The sexually explicit material I'm viewing is for my own personal use and isn't to be viewed by minors or anyone else but myself
* I am not a U.S. POSTAL OFFICIAL or LAW ENFORCEMENT AGENT or acting as an agent thereof, attempting to obtain any evidence for the prosecution of any individual or CORPORATION or for the purpose of entrapment
* I desire to receive and haven't notified the POSTAL SERVICE or any OTHER, GOVERNMENTAL AGENCY to intercept sexually explicit material
* I recognize I can stop receiving such material at any time by logging off and not returning
* I believe, that as an adult, I have the unalienable right to read and/or view any type of material that I choose
* The website creator has no editorial power over the pages contained herein and therefore cannot be held responsible for their contents
* That at no time will minors be subjected to said material of any kind
* By going to our home page and/or by looking at any of the pictures on this site you are agreeing that the pictures contained herein are not obscene or offensive in any way nor could ever be construed to be so, nor could any sexually explicit material of any kind ever be considered obscene or offensive. You also certifying that the material presented here is not illegal or considered obscene in your street, village, community, city, state, province or country. If you are unsure, do not continue.
* All of the above is understood and the following is true.

DISCLAIMER OF LIABILITY: The website creator is not liable to the users of this service or to its listed participants for the content, quality, performance or any other aspect of any information provided by the listed participants and transmitted by this service or for any errors in the transmission of said information. Nor is the website creator, responsible to any person for any damages arising in any manner out of the use of this service.

INDEMNIFICATION: The user and/or the listed participants shall indemnify and hold harmless the website creator, and their officers and employees, from and against any claims, liabilities, losses, costs, damages or expenses (including attorney's fees) arising from the user's use of or participation in this service or the information contained thereon.

I am at least 21 years of age. I consent to viewing any adult-oriented material that I may be exposed to as a result of following this link, and it is legal to view such material in my jurisdiction.

I certify that all statements on this page are true!

I can not, or do not agree with one or more of the above statements!

All models are at least 18 years old or older, depicting sexually attractive women. If you are not interested in such material please forget this address and remove it from your bookmark file.

22. "ACLU v. Reno," Full Text of Opinion, June 12, 1996. Available at http://www.epic.org
23. "An Overview of the Communications Decency Act," Center for Democracy and Technology. (No date). Available at http://www.cdt.org/speech/cda/
24. "The Child Online Protection Act," H.R. 3783, 105th Congress, 2nd Session 1998. Available at http://thomas.loc.gov/cgi-bin/query/C?c105:./temp/~c105 adcHe1
25. *Ibid.*
26. Ashcroft v. ACLU (formerly ACLU v. Reno II), The Legal Challenge to the Child Online Protection Act, The Electronic Privacy Information Center. Available at http://www.epic.org/free_speech/copa/
27. The material from this sentence until the end of the quotation from Judge Lowell A. Reed Jr. is taken from Richard S. Rosenberg, "Controlling Access to the Internet: The Role of Filtering," *Ethics and Information Technology*, Vol. 3, 2001, pp. 35–54, 48–49.
28. American Civil Liberties Union, et al. v. Janet Reno. Plaintiffs' Memorandum of law on Support of Their Motion for a Temporary Restraining Order and Preliminary Injunction, September 22, 1998. Available at http://www.aclu.org/court/acluvrenoII_tro.html
29. Conclusion to Judge Reed's Opinion in ACLU et al. v. Janet Reno, In the U.S. District Court for the Eastern District of Pennsylvania, February 1, 1999. Available at http://archive.aclu.org/court/acluvrenoII_pi_order.html
30. *Op. cit.*, Ashcroft v. ACLU.
31. Ashcroft, Attorney General v. American Civil Liberties Union et al. No. 00-1293. Available at http://a257.g.akamaitech.net/7/257/2422/29apr20021100/www.supremecourtus.gov/opinions/ot.pdf/00-1293.pdf

32. Charles Lane. "Justices Partially Back Cyber Pornography Law," *The Washington Post*, May 14, 2002, p. A03.
33. Commission on Child Online Protection, Report to Congress, October 2000. Available at http://www.copacommission.org/report/COPAreport.pdf
34. *Ibid.*
35. CDT Policy Post, Center for Democracy and Technology, Vol. 6, No. 22, December 18, 2000. Available at http://www.cdt.org/publications/pp_6.22. shtml
36. *Ibid.*
37. "Children's Internet Protection Act," Electronic Privacy Information Center, March 2001. Available at http://www.epic.org/free_speech/cipa.html
38. American Library Association, Civil Action Inc., et al. v. United States et al. No. 01-1303, March 31, 2002. Available at http://www.paed.uscourts.gov/docu-ments/ opinions/02D0415P.htm
39. Julia Scheeres. "Library Filtering Debate Heats Up," Wired News, November 13, 2002. Available at http://www.wired.com/news/politics/0,1283,56355,00. html
40. "In the Supreme Court of the United States, United States, et al., Petitioners v. American Library Association, Inc., et al.," Washington, DC, March 5, 2003. Available at http://supremecourtus.gov/oral_arguments/argument_transcripts/ 02-361.pdf
41. "Statement, American Library Association, Appellee, U.S. Government v. American Library Association," ALA, March 5, 2003. Available at http://www.ala.org/pio/presskits/cipa/cipa-statement.htm
42. "ALA Denounces Supreme Court Ruling on Children's Internet Protection Act," American Library Association, June 23, 2003. Available at http://www.ala.org/
43. *Op cit.* Richard S. Rosenberg, "Controlling Access to the Internet: The Role of Filtering." The discussion in this section will be taken from an earlier version of this paper, which appeared at the COPA Commission Web site. It is available at http://www.copacommission.org/papers/rosenberg.pdf
44. Statement on Library Use of Filtering Software. American Library Association, 1997. Available at http://www.ala.org/alaorg/oif/filt_stm.html
45. J. Turow. "The Internet and the Family: The View From Parents, The View From the Press." The Annenberg Public Policy Center of the University of Pennsylvania, 1999. Available at http://www.appcpenn.org/appc/reports/ rep27.pdf
46. Censorship's Tools Du Jour: V-Chips, TV Ratings, PICS, and Internet Filters. The National Coalition Against Censorship, March, 1998. Available at http://www.ncac.org/toolsdujour.html
47. Richard S. Rosenberg. "Free Speech, Pornography, Sexual Harassment, and Electronic Networks," *The Information Society*, 9 (4), October-December 1993, pp. 285–331.
48. *Ibid.*, p. 287.
49. *Ibid.*
50. "Sex Offenses Against Children: Findings and Recommendations Regarding Federal Penalties," United States Sentencing Commission, June 1996, p. 29. Available at http://www.ussc.gov/main/scac.pdf
51. *Ibid.*, p. 27.
51a. Ashcroft, Attorney General, et al. v. Free Speech Coalition et al." Argued October 30, 2001—Decided April 16, 2002. U.S. Supreme Court Decision is available at http://supremecourtus.gov/opinions/01pdf/00–795.pdf

51b. *Ibid.* p. 4.

52. Some of the material in this section is taken from Richard S. Rosenberg, "Who Will Censor? BC Tel and the Oliver "Hate" Web Site," *Intl. Inform & Libr. Rev,* Vol. 32, No. 3/4, September 2000, pp. 359–377.

53. Constitution Act, 1982 (79). Enacted as Schedule B to the Canada Act 1982 (UK) 1982, c. 11, which came into force on April 17, 1982. Available at http://canada.justice.gc.ca/Loireg/charte/const_en.html

54. Richard S. Rosenberg. Free Speech on the Internet: Controversy and Control. In L.J. Pourciau (Ed.) *Ethics and Electronic Information in the Twenty-first Century.* West Lafayette, Indiana, Purdue University Press, 1999, pp. 96–97.

55. Cass R. Sunstein. "Is Violent Speech a Right?" *The American Prospect,* No. 22 (Summer), 1995, 34–37. Available at http://epn.org/prospect/22/22suns.html

56. R.F. Raney. "More trouble for man in hate mail case," *The New York Times,* October 1, 1998. Available at http://www.nytimes.com/library/tech/98/10/cyber/articles/01email.html

57. R.F. Raney. "Charges filed in U.S. hate e-mail case," *The New York Times,* January 29, 1999. Available at http://www.nytimes.com/library/tech/99/01/cyber/articles/29mail.html

58. S.H. Verhovek. "Creators of anti-abortion Web site told to pay millions," *The New York Times,* February 3, 1999. Available at http://www.nytimes.com/library/tech/99/02/biztech/articles/03abortion.html

59. Dick Kelsey. "Appeals Court Backs Anti-Abortionists' Web Posyings," Newsbytes (The Washington Post Co.), March 28, 2001. Available at http://www.newsbytes.com/news/01/163787.html

60. Located at http://www.christiangallery.com/atrocity/

61. Gwendolyn Mariano. "Court Cracks Down on Anti-Abortion Site," Cnet News.com, May 17, 2002. Available at http://http://news.com.com/2100-1023-917077.html

62. *Ibid.*

63. "Silencing the Net: The Threat to Freedom of Expression On-line," Human Rights Watch, 8 (2), May 1996. Available at gopher://gopher.igc.apc.org:5000/00/int/hrw/general/27 Human Rights Watch is a nongovernmental organization established in 1978 to monitor and promote the observance of internationally recognized human rights in Africa, the Americas, Asia, the Middle East, and among the signatories of the Helsinki accords.

64. *Ibid.*

64a. *Ibid.*

65. "Court Clears Yahoo in Nazi Case," American Press, Wired.com, February 11, 2003. Available at http://www.wired.com/news/politics/0,1283,57633,00.html

66. *Ibid.*

ADDITIONAL READINGS

Early Free Speech Issues on the Internet

Alexander, Steve. "The Long Arm of the Law," *Computerworld,* May 6, 1996, pp. 99–100.

Cavazos, Edward A. and Morin, Gavino. *Cyberspace and the Law: Your Rights and Duties in the On-Line World.* (Cambridge, MA: The MIT Press, 1994).

Sinrod, Eric J. and Jolish, Barak D. "The Emerging Law of Privacy and Speech in Cyberspace," 1999 Stan. Tech. L. Rev. 1. Available at http://stlr.stanford.edu/STLR/Articles/99_STLR 1/

Legislative Attempts to Regulate Speech on the Internet

Dworkin, Ronald. *Freedom's Law: The Moral Reading of the U.S.* Constitution. (Cambridge, MA: Harvard University Press, 1996).

Lemley, Mark A. and Lessig, Lawrence. "Why CDA 2.0 Will Fail," Center for Democracy and Technology, October 13, 1998. Available at http://www.cdt.org/speech/copa/981013lemley_lessig.html

Reno, Attorney General of the United States, et al. v. American Civil Liberties Union et al., Appeal from the United States District Court for the Eastern District of Pennsylvania, Syllabus of Supreme Court Decision, June 27, 1997. Available at http://www.ciec.org/SC_appeal/syllabus.shtml

Technological Approaches to Regulate Content

Bell, Bernard W., "Filth, Filtering, and the First Amendment: Ruminations on Public Libraries' Use of Internet Filtering Software," *Federal Communications Law Journal* (53:2), 2001. Available at http://www.law.indiana.edu/fclj/pubs/v53/no2/bell.pdf

"Children's Internet Protection Act: Study of Technology Protection Measures in Section 1703," Department of Commerce, National Telecommunications and Information Administration, August 2003. Available at http://www.ntia.gov/ntihome/ntiageneral/cipa2003/CIPAreport08142003.pdf

National Research Council. *Youth, Pornography, and the Internet.* (Washington, DC: National Academy Press, 2002). Available at http://books.nap.edu/html/youth-internet/

Other Issues

Crews Jr., Clyde Wayne. "Why Canning 'Spam' Is a Bad Idea," Policy Analysis, The Cato Institute, No. 408, July 26, 2001. Available at http://www.cato.org/pubs/pas/pa408.pdf

Heins, Marjorie. "Violence and the Media: An Exploration of Cause, Effect and the First Amendment," First Amendment Center, 2001. Available at http://www.mediastudies.org/publications/first//violenceandmedia/violenceandthemedia.pdf

"Intel Corporation v. Kourosh Kenneth Hamidi," Supreme Court of California, June 30, 2003. Available at http://news.findlaw.com/wp/docs/intel/intelhamidi63003opn.pdf

"Marketing Violent Entertainment to Children: A Twenty-One Month Follow-Up Review of Industry Practices in the Motion Picture, Music Recording & Electronic Game Industries," A Report to Congress, Federal Trade Commission, June 20, 2002. Available at http://www.ftc.gov/reports/violence/mvecrpt0206.pdf

Reidenberg, Joel R. "The Yahoo! Case and the International Democratization of the Internet," Fordham University School of Law, Research Paper 11, April 2001. Available at http://papers.ssrn.com/paper.taf?abstract_id=267148

"State of the First Amendment 2002," First Amendment Center, 2002. Available at http://www.freedomforum.org/Publications/first/sofa/2002/SOFA-2002_report. pdf

9

PRIVACY PROTECTION

The makers of our Constitution undertook to secure conditions favorable to the pursuit of happiness. . . . They sought to protect Americans in their beliefs, their thoughts, their emotions and their sensations. They conferred, as against the Government the right to be let alone—the most comprehensive of rights and the right most valued by civilized men. To protect that right every unjustifiable intrusion by the Government upon the privacy of the individual, whatever the means employed, must be deemed a violation of the Fourth Amendment.

Justice Louis D. Brandeis, Dissenting, Olmstead v. United States, 277 U.S. 438, 1928

INTRODUCTION

The following are excerpts from magazine articles in the United States as well as Web pages:[1]

- The National Park Service will begin round-the-clock video surveillance at all major monuments on the Mall by October, moving aggressively in the wake of last year's terrorist attacks to tighten security around national symbols visited by millions of tourists each year. Closed-circuit television cameras will be installed for the first time to monitor public areas in and around the Washington Monument and the Jefferson, Lincoln, Franklin D. Roosevelt, Vietnam Veterans and Korean War memorials, according to John G. Parsons, associate regional director for the Park Service's National Capital Region. . . . Civil libertarian groups expressed concern that video monitoring might discourage demonstrators, who for decades have gathered at the Reflecting Pool and elsewhere on the Mall to protest government policy on issues ranging from veterans benefits to abortion, civil rights and the Vietnam War.[1]
- The clock is winding down for U.S. companies that exchange data with other businesses and subsidiaries in Canada to comply with a law providing broad privacy protections for Canadian citizens. Beginning Jan. 1, 2004, all companies that collect, use or disclose personal information about Canadian citizens during the course of commercial activities will

have to comply with Canada's Personal Information Protection and Electronic Documents Act. "Since Canada is our largest trading partner, a lot of companies will be affected by this," said Mark Rasch, former head of the U.S. Department of Justice's computer crimes unit and senior vice president at Solutionary Inc., a security consultancy in Omaha. The act is already in effect for banks, airlines, transportation companies and telecommunications firms. It requires businesses to offer Canadian citizens certain guarantees regarding the collection and use of personal data. It will be a violation to collect data in Canada and then transfer it out of the country, unless the transfer carries with it the same level of protection that's required in Canada, Rasch said.[2]

- As movies are increasingly broadcast and sold in digital format, Tinseltown execs are panicked that consumers will make infinite numbers of perfect digital copies and share them over the Internet. That's why the entertainment industry's honchos will once again journey to Capitol Hill when Congress convenes a new session later this month to ask lawmakers and the Federal Communications Commission for more protection. However, if Hollywood has its way, consumer privacy—not piracy—will pay a heavy price. Case in point: Hollywood wants a digital broadcast "flag" built into every new digital-TV receiver. This would allow content owners to track and/or designate which movies—or any programming, for that matter—could be copied, how often, and by whom.[3]

- The outrage over TIA [Total Information Awareness system] doesn't seem to have reached the President's ear, but it should. It's not too late for him to realize the folly of such a plan. Funded by the Defense Advanced Research Projects Agency (DARPA), the project would combine every American's bank records, tax filings, driver's license information, credit-card purchases, medical data, and phone and e-mail records into one giant centralized database. This would then be combed through for evidence of suspicious activity. . . . The DARPA plan shocked the media and individual citizens across the country. The program wouldn't catch terrorists, but it would terrorize ordinary citizens by logging their every movement in a federal government database. Why, many asked, would the Bush Administration stand behind such an intrusive plan? My question: Why ask why?[4]

- In May, three members of a Florida family were implanted with ID chips, sparking an international debate over the implications of the technology. The manufacturer insisted that the VeriChip would revolutionize the fields of security and health care by providing a tamper-proof form of identification. Privacy pundits, meanwhile, fretted over forcible chipping and biblical literalists warned that a microchip could be interpreted as the "Mark of the Beast."[5]

- Razor blades and medicines packaged with pinpoint-sized computer chips and tiny antennae that eventually could send retailers and manufacturers a wealth of information about the products—and those who buy them—will start appearing in grocery stores and pharmacies this year. Within two decades, the minuscule transmitters are expected to replace the familiar product bar codes, and retailers are already envisioning the conveniences the new technology, called "radio frequency identification," [RFID] will bring—even as others are raising privacy concerns. A grocery store clerk will know immediately when the milk on the shelf has expired, for example, and replace it before a customer can choose it. Stores could quickly pull from the shelves tainted and damaged products that are recalled or have expired, especially important in health care items. . . . "Simply stated, I don't think most people want their clothes spying on them," Rotenberg said [Executive Director, Electronic Privacy Information Center]. "It's also clear that there could be some very invasive uses of these techniques if merchants use the tracking technology to spy on their customers after purchase."[7]

- What makes librarians raise their voices above a whisper? Certain passages of the U.S.A. Patriot Act. Librarians are among the most vocal opponents of the law, taking particular exception to Section 215, which they claim makes it easier for the government to search library records. "A big part of the public library system was to sustain democracy so people could make up their own mind about things," says Carolyn Anthony, director of the Skokie Public Library near Chicago. "Aspects of the act compromise this." Before the Patriot Act, authorities could examine library records only after proving in open court that there was probable cause to suspect that a crime had been committed. The Patriot Act gave the government wider leeway by expanding the 1978 Foreign Intelligence Surveillance Act (FISA), legislation that created secret courts to review applications for domestic wiretaps and searches in the name of national security. Now the government needs merely to convince a FISA court that looking at book-borrowing histories or library Internet usage is relevant to an ongoing terrorist investigation, whether or not a crime has been committed. In addition, library employees are prohibited from revealing to anyone that a patron is under suspicion.[8]

Probably the single most frequent charge leveled against computers is that they rob us of our privacy. Banks of computers are envisioned in some back room, on which the intimate details of the lives of many people are stored. Government agencies, law enforcement officials, insurance companies, banks, e-commerce companies, schools, credit agencies, and many others have access to private information about most people in society. This situation was true before the arrival of computers, but somehow the computer has added a significant new element—whether it is due to the computer's ability to store and search rapidly through vast amounts of data, the image of the computer as a malevolent force, the economic benefits available to companies that are able to precisely target large segments of the population, or the general trend in society towards the accumulation of information that is made possible by computers.

Privacy Surveys

The national research firm Louis Harris & Associates has been conducting surveys on American attitudes toward privacy since 1970. It has frequently been assisted by Dr. Alan Westin of Columbia University. These surveys represent the most comprehensive attempt to gauge U.S. public opinion on the issue of personal privacy and technological impact, over an extended period of time.[9] Table 9.1 shows a rising concern of the public about threats to their personal privacy over the period 1970 to 1995. The rise between 1970 and 1978 probably reflects the post-Watergate and post-Vietnam disillusionment with government. The rise to near 80% during the conservative Republican administrations of Presidents Reagan and Bush is somewhat more difficult to explain. The surveys from 1990 on suggest a continuing distrust of institutions and a concern that control over personal information has been lost to credit bureaus, Web servers, and government. This distrust of large institutions of all kinds may be rooted in a realization that very little personal information remains private, that government seems to have an insatiable need to collect more and more information, that in the private sector, banks, credit bureaus, direct marketers, and e-commerce companies also seem driven to reap economic benefits from large, detailed databases on consumers, and that the technology permits, and indeed encourages, the collection and rapid processing of vast amounts of data.

In order to explore some of these issues more carefully, it will be helpful to look at a few of the results of five surveys, to monitor the changes in opinion between 1978 and 1995. One problem with this first set of surveys is that the targeted groups varied somewhat over the years so that strict comparisons are not possible. The arrival of the Web in 1993 certainly accelerated the movement toward the commercialization of the Internet and the problems of online privacy. Also, as the general public has become more aware of computers, primarily through direct exposure to personal computers, the level of sophistication has increased, especially among professionals. With these caveats consider Table 9.1, which reveals some of the fears and concerns of the general public during this period.

This table represents only a very small and carefully selected part of several quite extensive surveys. A few points are clear, however:

- The general public is clearly concerned about computers and their effect on privacy (see questions 1, 2, 3, and 4).
- It is surprising how many people accept the idea that technology has almost gotten out of control (see question 5).
- Note that in 1995, most people did not feel that their privacy rights were adequately protected (see question 3). Combined with the response to question 4, there is a clear perception that personal privacy is seriously

TABLE 9.1

RESPONSES TO QUESTIONS ON COMPUTERS AND PRIVACY FROM THE YEARS 1978, 1983, 1990, 1992, AND 1995

Questions	Responses	1978[a]	1983[b]	1990[c]	1992[d]	1995[e]
1. Do you feel that the present uses of computers are an actual threat to personal privacy in this country or not?	Yes	54%	51%	–	68%	–
	No	33%	42%		28%	
	Not sure	12%	6%		3%	
2. Consumers have lost all control over how personal information about them is circulated.	Agree			71%	76%	80%
	Disagree			27%	20%	19%
	Not Sure			3%	3%	2%
3. My rights to privacy are adequately protected today by law or business practice.	Agree			46%		45%
	Disagree			51%		54%
	Not Sure			3%		2%
4. In the year 2000, consumer privacy protection . . .	Will get better				12%	16%
	Will get worse				55%	41%
	Will remain same				32%	42%
5. Technology has almost gotten out of control	Agree	43%		45%		63%
	Disagree	41%		53%		36%
	Not sure	15%		2%		1%

Sources:
a. Louis Harris and Associates and Dr. Alan F. Westin, *The Dimensions of Privacy: A National Opinion Research Survey of Attitudes Toward Privacy* (for Sentry Insurance, New York: Garland Publishing, 1981).
b. Louis Harris and Associates, *The Road After 1984: The Impact of Technology on Society* (for Southern New England Telephone, December 1983).
c. A national opinion survey conducted for Equifax Inc. by Louis Harris & Associates and Dr. Alan F. Westin, Columbia University. Equifax Inc., 1600 Peachtree Street, Atlanta, Georgia.
d. Louis Harris & Associates and Dr. Alan F. Westin, *Harris-Equifax Consumer Privacy Survey 1992* (for Equifax Inc., 1991, 1992).
e. Louis Harris & Associates and Dr. Alan F. Westin, *Equifax-Harris Mid-Decade Consumer Privacy Survey 1995* (for Equifax Inc., 1995).

threatened and there is no relief in sight. One possibility is that government play a stronger role, but in the atmosphere of general distrust of government, this direction taken by many European countries is unlikely. (Much more on this topic will be provided later in the chapter.)

One important source of survey information on a host of Internet issues is the Pew Internet & American Life Project, which has been conducting detailed surveys on the Internet since early 2000; actually, it had begun including some questions on the Internet as early as 1995. We will refer to several of their surveys here and elsewhere; for the present purposes, consider a report which appeared in November 2000 on the activities and concerns of new Internet users. Carrying out commercial transactions on the Web requires a certain degree of trust, especially with respect to the use of credit cards. Findings with respect to this issue follow[10]:

- Internet users who have been on the Net for a year or less report lower levels of trust than users who have been online for two or more years.
- When asked whether most people can be trusted, 36% of Internet users online for two or more years answered "yes" versus 27% of users online for a year or less. In terms of using their credit card to purchase things on the telephone, veteran users are only slightly more likely to do this than new users.
- Seventy-three percent of all veteran Internet users have used their credit cards to make purchases over the telephone compared with 69% of users online for a year or less. Yet new users are much more likely to be concerned about credit card theft when making telephone purchases.
- Only 16% of veteran Internet users reported worrying "a lot" about credit card theft during phone purchases compared with 27% of veteran [credit card] users.

If the use of credit cards online is of concern to many, the availability of personal health records is of greater concern. People access health advice sites and typically provide personal health information. In addition, hospital and physicians are increasingly making patient records available online, ostensibly for professional purposes only. More on this important topic will be covered later in this chapter. In late 2000, the Pew Internet Project released a report on this topic; a few highlights are given as follows[11]:

- 89% of health seekers are concerned that a health-related Web site might sell or give away information about what they did online; 71% are "very concerned" about such privacy violations.
- 85% of health seekers are concerned that an insurance company might raise their rates or deny them coverage because of the health sites they have visited; 72% are "very concerned" about this possibility.

- 52% of health seekers are concerned that their employer might find out what health sites they have visited. This ranks comparatively low in part because most health seekers are getting their information online from home.
- 63% of health seekers and 60% all Internet users think that putting medical records online is a bad thing, even if the records are on a secure, password-protected site, because they worry about other people seeing their personal information. The rest think it's a good thing because they and their doctors would have easy access to patients' medical records.
- 81% of health seekers think people should be able to sue a health or medical company if it gave away or sold information about its Web site users after saying that it would not.

Two additional surveys will be examined. The first is a broad survey, reporting on a wide range of Internet issues. For the present purposes, we will consider only the privacy results included in the third year of this study, reported early in 2003. As such, the following results are of considerable interest[12]:

- Overall, 88.8 percent of all respondents age 16 or over in 2002 expressed some concern about the privacy of their personal information when or if they buy on the Internet—down from 94.6 percent in 2001.
- More specifically, 54.3 percent said they are very concerned or extremely concerned about the privacy of their personal information when buying online—a decline from 65.8 percent in 2001. Overall, the number of respondents who are not concerned at all increased to 11.2 percent, more than double the number in 2001 (5.5 percent).
- Comparing Internet purchasers to non-purchasers in 2002 shows much higher levels of non-purchasers than purchasers who are concerned about the privacy of their personal information when or if they buy online. Among purchasers, 32.8 percent are very concerned or extremely concerned, compared to more than half (58.3 percent) of non-purchasers.
- Comparing Internet non-users, new users, and the most experienced users shows that concerns about privacy of their personal information when or if they buy online decline as Internet use increases. Less than half of very experienced users are very concerned or extremely concerned about privacy of personal information when of if they buy online, compared to 64.6 percent of new users and 68.4 percent of nonusers.

With reference to the use of credit cards online, this report notes that, "For nearly one-quarter of the respondents (23.1 percent) who have some concerns about using their credit cards online, nothing will reduce their concerns about using a credit card online. Those who believe that their concerns can be reduced cite a variety of methods that will help, led by privacy or security guarantees provided by an independent company. Other methods include better technology, and increased education and consumer awareness."

We return to a survey carried out by Harris Interactive, once again with the consultation of Dr. Alan Westin president and publisher of Privacy and American Business. In examining the results, reported in March 2003, Harris Interactive divides the respondents into three groups[13]:

- Some people feel very strongly about privacy matters. They tend to feel that they have lost a lot of their privacy and are strongly resistant to any further erosion of it. We call them **privacy fundamentalists**, and they are currently about a quarter (26%) of all adults.
- At the other extreme there are people who have no real concerns about privacy and who have far less anxiety about how other people and organizations are using information about them. We call them **privacy unconcerned** and they are about ten percent of all adults.
- The third, and by far the largest group, now almost two-thirds of all adults (64%), are what we call **privacy pragmatists**, who have strong feelings about privacy and are very concerned to protect themselves from the abuse or misuse of their personal information by companies or government agencies.

Some of the results of this survey reinforce findings from earlier ones in the 1990s that privacy concerns are deep and pervasive among Internet users. The degree of concern has fluctuated over the years as have possible remedies. Later in this chapter, we will review some of these proposed remedies but for now consider the following concerns[14]:

- 69% of adults agree, "consumers have lost all control over how personal information is collected and used by companies." This is a decline of eleven points from 80% who felt this way in 1999.
- 54% of the public disagree that "most businesses handle the personal information they collect about consumers in a proper and confidential way." This is an increase of nineteen points from only 35% who felt this way in 1999.
- 53% of all adults disagree that "existing laws and organizational practices provide a reasonable level of protection for consumer privacy today." This is an increase of fifteen points from 38% in 1999. Several dimensions of privacy have become less important in recent years, even though most people still feel they are extremely important.
- Those who feel that being able to share a confidential matter with someone they trust is extremely important have fallen from 83% in 1994 to a still-high 76%.
- Those who feel that not having someone watch them or listen to them without their permission is extremely important have fallen from 79% in 1994 to a still high 73%.
- However, by far the largest decline in concern is found among those who feel that not being monitored at work is extremely important—they have fallen from 65% in 1994 to only 42% now. This, we believe, reflects

the fact that monitoring of telephone call center conversations is now so widespread and is, therefore, acceptable to many more people.

- One dimension of privacy has become much more important than it used to be. Those who think that not being disturbed at home is extremely important have increased from 49% in 1994 to 62% now—surely as a direct result of the growth of telemarketing calls.

One last survey, carried out by the Annenberg Public Policy Center at the University of Pennsylvania, carries the ominous title, "Americans and Online Privacy, The System is Broken." It reveals false assumptions and expectations of much of the online community. A few highlights follow[15]:

- 57% of U.S. adults who use the internet at home believe incorrectly that when a website has a privacy policy, it will not share their personal information with other websites or companies.
- 47% of U.S. adults who use the internet at home say website privacy policies are easy to understand. However, 66% of those who are confident about their understanding of privacy policies also believe (incorrectly) that sites with a privacy policy won't share data.
- 59% of adults who use the internet at home know that websites collect information about them even if they don't register. They do not, however, understand that data flows behind their screens invisibly connect seemingly unrelated bits about them.
- Among the 85% who did not accept the policy, one in two (52%) had earlier said they gave or would likely give the valued site their real name and email address—the very information a site needs to begin creating a personally identifiable dataset about them.
- Despite strong concerns about online information privacy, 64% of these online adults say they have never searched for information about how to protect their information on the web; 40% say that they know "almost nothing" about stopping sites from collecting information about them, and 26% say they know just "a little." Only 9% of American adults who use the internet at home say they know a lot.
- Overwhelmingly, however, they support policies that make learning what online companies know about them straightforward. 86% believe that laws that force website policies to have a standard format will be effective in helping them protect their information.
- Yet most Americans feel unsure or conflicted about whether key institutions will help them with their information privacy or take it away. Only 13% of American adults who use the web at home trust that the government will help them protect personal information online while not disclosing personal information about them without permission.
- Similarly, only 18% trust their banks and credit card companies and only 18% trust their internet service providers (ISPs) to act that way.

For those who believe that it is in the self-interest of the marketplace to protect individual privacy, that is, "Protecting privacy is good business," the results of this "cautionary tale" suggest that this belief might be reworded to read, "The appearance of protecting privacy is good business."

Clearly, there is a deep apprehension among most segments of society about the growing number of records being held in both private and government databases. The government records are needed for the various agencies to carry out their responsibilities. In the not too distant past, however, various departments did establish databases to collect information on individuals who were perceived as a possible threat to the stability of government. Such activities could inhibit the free exercise of constitutional rights. Such concerns have returned in the aftermath of September 11, as society, especially in the U.S., confronts the dilemma of achieving a proper balance between security measures necessary to protect the country and civil liberties, such as privacy rights, necessary to maintain an open and democratic way of life.

Privacy is a cultural, philosophical, legal, and political concept. If it is to be protected by legislation, an approach favored by many countries but weakly so by the U.S., the formulation of such legislation clearly depends on how privacy is viewed and valued. Concern with privacy did not begin with computers. As Edward Coke (1552–1634), an English writer on the law, put it, "For a man's house is his castle." The common person and the king should be equal with respect to the security of their home. The computer seems to have added several important new wrinkles to this principle. The collection, storage, and retrieval of large amounts of private information, by credit bureaus, for example, has become a major industry.

In response to a variety of problems associated with violations of privacy, legislation has been enacted in the United States to guarantee certain circumscribed rights. Such piecemeal legislation addresses some issues, but leaves others open. Given that there is a deep cultural component to the question of privacy, it is not surprising that different types of legislation exist in other countries. There also seems to be less distrust of government in Western Europe, Australia, New Zealand, Canada—that very close neighbor—and elsewhere, which helps explain why many counties have enacted comprehensive data protection laws administered by commissioners. As the Internet grows in importance and perhaps evolves into the Information Highway, enormous amounts of personal information will be gathered in commercial and other transactions. How will governments respond? This question has been extensively studied in North America and Europe and a variety of proposals and recommendations will be explored.

The term *freedom of information* is generally applied to the concept that governments must make the information they collect accessible to the public at large unless they can demonstrate a pressing need for secrecy. The explication of this idea requires a distinction between privacy and secrecy. In general, governments are reluctant to reveal their operations. Legislation was passed in 1966 and amended in 1996 in the United States to provide public access to government under a set of regulations, the Freedom of Information Act.

Finally, future privacy issues will arise in connection with new technological developments. Given varying national privacy laws, international agreements will have to be developed to deal with the flow of data across borders. It seems that everywhere one turns, someone or some group is asking questions and gathering information. How will it be used, who has access and for what purposes, and what rights do the people, about whom the information was gathered, have?

THE NATURE OF PRIVACY

> A man has a right to pass through this world, if he wills, without having his picture published, his business enterprises discussed, his successful experiments written up for the benefit of others, or his eccentricities commented upon, whether in handbills, circulars, catalogues, newspapers or periodicals.—Jurist Alton B. Parker, Decision, Robertson v. Rochester Folding Box Company, 1901.

Privacy as a social issue has long been a concern of social scientists, philosophers, and lawyers. The arrival of the computer has sharpened this concern and made concrete a number of threats to personal privacy. But what does the word privacy mean? Is privacy a right?

> Privacy is the claim of individuals, groups or institutions to determine for themselves when, how, and to what extent information about them is communicated to others.[16]

Alan Westin, the author of the above statement, has probably made the most important recent contributions to both the definition and scope of the meaning of privacy in the age of computers. In fact, the definition given above is arguably the most common one in current use. Westin's definition has been criticized because it formulates the definition in terms of a claim. The counter-argument is that privacy "is a situation or freedom about which claims may be made."[17] This dissension may appear to be the usual legal hairsplitting, but it seems to suggest that the Westin definition represents an activist view that privacy should be a right. Two other criticisms of the Westin definition are that it limits the concept of privacy to information control, and only information about the individual who makes the claim at that.

It is not surprising that information and its control feature so prominently. After all, the forthcoming "information age" will certainly catapult individual privacy to the forefront of civil liberty issues (if it has not done so already). Information is not the only thing that comes to mind when one thinks of privacy, however. Also important are being alone or alone with one's family, not being exposed to displays one considers offensive, and the right not to have one's behavior regulated (for example, the right to use contraceptives, or to have an abortion). These issues arise in connection with such privacy problems as surveillance by the use of wiretapping, electronic bugs, long-range microphones, and television cameras; possible censorship of the public media; and the tension between individual behavior and the demands of society.

The concept of privacy can be given three aspects: territorial privacy, privacy of the person, and privacy in the information context.[18] Territorial privacy refers to the very basic notion that there is a physical area surrounding a person that may not be violated without the acquiescence of the person. Laws referring to Peeping Toms, trespassers, and search warrants have been enacted to safeguard territorial privacy. The second category, in some sense, is concerned with protecting a person against undue interferences such as physical searches and information that violates his or her moral sense. The third category is the one most relevant here, as it deals with the gathering, compilation, and selective dissemination of information.

Privacy and Information

To live in contemporary society is to leave, stored in records held by institutions, a trail of the following kinds of information:

Vital statistics (birth, marriage, death)
Educational (school records)
Financial (bank records, stock portfolio, mortgages, loans, insurance)
Medical (health records, AIDS status, psychiatric reports)
Credit (credit cards, credit record, purchases)
City government (house taxes, improvements)
Employment (earnings, deductions, work record)
Internal revenue (taxation, deductions, earnings)
Customs and immigration (passports, visas, customs payments)
Police (arrests, convictions, warrants, bail, paroles, sentences)
Welfare (payments, history, dependents)
Stores (credit record, purchases)
Organizations (membership, activities)
Military (service record, discharge status)
Motor vehicles (ownership, registration, accident record)
Internet activity (search terms used, sites visited, purchases made)

This list represents only a sample of the kinds and sources of information being held about the average citizen. The computer has made it possible to store an enormous amount of information and to retrieve it in an efficient manner. Most of the above-listed records are held by government institutions at all levels. This fact is seen by some critics as evidence of the insatiable appetite of government to know more and more about its citizens. In the private domain there has been a corresponding increase in the amounts and uses of information, as anyone who has received unsolicited mail, both hard copy and online spam, samples, and charitable requests knows.

In recognition of this explosion in information, the concept of privacy has undergone some changes. Inevitably there will be disclosures of information—if not, why has it all been collected? But how can the rights of the affected person be protected? Perhaps the question to ask first is what should these rights be? A basic statement appeared in 1973, in an important U.S. government report, as follows[19]:

> An individual's personal privacy is directly affected by the kind of disclosure and use made of identifiable information about him in a record. A record containing information about an individual in identifiable form must, therefore, be governed by procedures that afford the individual a right to participate in deciding what the content of the record will be, and what disclosure and use will be made of the identifiable information in it. Any recording, disclosure, and use of identifiable personal information not governed by such procedures must be proscribed as an unfair information practice unless such recording, disclosure or use is specifically authorized by law.

This statement does not describe what information should be stored, or what the controls for its use should be, but it does argue for the legal establishment of privacy rights for the individual. Subsequent legislation did delineate and incorporate some of these rights by regulating the behavior of record keepers.

The general public in the United States is concerned about threats to personal privacy, and this worry is growing, as the results of surveys presented previously illustrate. Many people would claim that there is a basic human need for privacy. Not all basic human needs are defended in law, however. It has been recognized that individual privacy, in its many manifestations, is a basic prerequisite for the functioning of a democratic society. In this light, the recommendations made in the 1973 U.S. government report have served as a basis for subsequent legislation. In fact, they have almost assumed the status of a "Bill of Rights" for privacy and are known as the "fundamental principles of fair information practice."[20]

- There must be no personal-data record-keeping systems whose very existence is secret.
- There must be a way for an individual to find out what information about him is in a record and how it is used.

- There must be a way for an individual to prevent information about him that was obtained for one purpose from being used or made available for other purposes without his consent.
- There must be a way for an individual to correct or amend a record of identifiable information about him.
- Any organization creating, maintaining, using or disseminating records or identifiable personal data must assure the reliability of data for their intended use and must take precautions to prevent misuse of the data.

Records have been kept on individuals from time immemorial, but the use of computers has introduced a change in kind as well as in degree. Records can now be easily transmitted over long distances, searched efficiently, and merged if desired. Since the cost of storage is cheap, more data can be stored and so more is collected. As more information is collected, more uses are made of it, as if the availability drives the need. The appetite for information in both the private and public domains seems to grow without limit. Since these trends are likely to accelerate in the future, much is to be gained by trying to understand the various implications of contemporary threats to privacy.

Government Threats and Constitutional Protection

Individual privacy is threatened by the possible use of government databases for surveillance. Such use may inhibit the free exercise of constitutionally guaranteed rights, such as freedom of speech and petitioning the government for the redress of grievances. With private databases, such as those maintained by the large credit bureaus, the impact could also be quite serious. Without credit, a car, house and life insurance, and a mortgage are not available. A suspect credit rating may limit one's type of employment, housing, and one's children's educational possibilities. Quite clearly, the misuse of information by others could have a devastating effect on a person's life. With the increasing use of information systems to store personal records, the imbalance between the individual and the "system" has grown. It is therefore incumbent upon the record keeper to establish guidelines to insure the protection of individual privacy.

The Privacy Commission, set up after the passage of the Privacy Act of 1974, enunciated the three necessary objectives of a privacy protection policy as follows[21]:

Minimize Intrusiveness. This involves creating a balance between what is demanded of an individual and what is provided in return.

Maximize Fairness. This will make sure that information stored about an individual is not used unfairly.

Create Legitimate, Enforceable Expectations of Confidentiality. It is most important to guarantee that recorded information is subject to the most stringent security procedures.

Constitutional Guarantees

Some very complex privacy issues are highlighted by the First, Fourth, and Fifth Amendments to the Constitution. These amendments are concerned with the following rights and guarantees:

> *First Amendment.* Freedom of religion, speech, the press, peaceable assembly, and the right to petition for redress of grievances.
>
> *Fourth Amendment.* No unreasonable search and seizure by the federal government.
>
> *Fifth Amendment.* A person may not be compelled to testify against himself or be deprived of life, liberty, or property without due process.

By the collection of large amounts of data and surveillance of individuals and groups (as discussed earlier), the government could inhibit the freedoms of speech and assembly guaranteed in the First Amendment. Threats to these rights have occurred in the past, against both active and passive participants in political meetings and demonstrations. A basic challenge arises whenever threats to First Amendment rights surface: "What have you got to worry about if you haven't done anything wrong?" Unfortunately, the collection of data by the government, as well as surveillance, can be repressive in itself, in that it creates the impression that an activity is not proper and that participants ought to reconsider their actions. In some cases, information has been used directly to affect the employment of individuals. First Amendment rights are crucial to maintaining a democratic society, and any attempts to limit them must be forestalled.

The interrelation between information systems and the Fourth Amendment turns on such issues as the use of personal or statistical data as a reason for search and seizure, the information itself as the object of the search, and the use of the system to facilitate the search and seizure. With the use of criminal record information systems, police may carry out searches on the basis of instantaneous access to the database. Courts may be concerned about whether such information provides reasonable cause. Computer systems could be employed to monitor the shopping activity of individuals by accessing appropriate financial transactions systems. This activity would be much more intrusive than personal observation would be.

Possible Fifth Amendment violations may arise when data collected for one purpose is used by the government as evidence in an unrelated case. Another problem may occur in the use of criminal records in computer models to predict criminal behavior. In fact, a recent application, called racial profiling, has aroused considerable concern in its purported use to identify potential criminals who happen to be black. Clearly, individuals' rights could be denied on the basis of predictions, rather than actual unlawful actions. Since these records may include statements by the persons being modeled, self-incrimination is a definite possibility. More constitutional issues associated with databases and privacy will no doubt surface in the future.

Computer Matching

A final example of the possible misuse of the data that is collected and stored in government databases is particularly worrisome. It points out that the arrival of the computer has literally created new avenues for the exercise of bureaucratic power. The term *computer matching* probably reached public consciousness in late 1977, when Joseph A. Califano, Jr., the Secretary of Health, Education, and Welfare, announced a new program, "Project Match," to reduce welfare violations. The idea was to match computerized lists of federal employees against computerized lists of state welfare rolls. Any person whose name appeared on both lists, a so-called hit, would be a likely candidate for welfare fraud investigation.

The Privacy Act of 1974 (to be discussed later in this chapter) embodied the principle that information collected about individuals for certain purposes cannot be used without their consent for unrelated purposes. An individual's consent is not required if the information is to be used either in a manner consistent with the original purpose—the "routine use" provision— or for a criminal investigation. Computer matching has been justified by appeal to the routine use exception. In response to criticisms about the extensive use of computer matching, the Office of Management and Budget (OMB) drew up a set of guidelines in 1979. These have not satisfactorily addressed the critical issues, in the opinion of many critics.

In 1984, Richard P. Kusserow, Inspector General of the Department of Health and Human Services, argued that computer matching is just another necessary weapon in the government's arsenal against waste and fraud. Because the cost of such fraud is so enormous, the government is entitled to take whatever measures it deems necessary to protect the rights of innocent taxpayers. The Reagan Administration revised the OMB guidelines in 1982, in order, it was claimed, to "streamline paper-work requirements and reiterate requirements for privacy and security of records."[22] The government maintains that privacy safeguards are in place and that computer matching is not a threat to civil liberties. The critics argue that the safeguards are inadequate and that computer matching represents one more serious step in the erosion of personal privacy.

In 1986, the United States General Accounting Office (GAO) issued a report reviewing the activities of federal agencies in implementing the provisions of the Privacy Act of 1974. Although computer matching is not explicitly mentioned in the Act, the OMB revised guidelines were an attempt to address some of the concerns raised by increasing government use of this technique. In the conclusions to the report, GAO notes that[23]

Although computer matching is one of the most controversial activities generating privacy concerns, agencies (1) did not have current, complete data on the extent of matching programs, (2) did not always follow OMB's matching guidelines, and (3) differed in interpretation of the matching guidelines as to whether programs needed to be reported to OMB. In addition, two component agencies exempted their matching programs from OMB's guidelines. We found no evidence that OMB was previously aware of these discrepancies.

Without addressing the privacy concerns associated with computer matching, GAO makes the following bureaucratic recommendations to ensure that the OMB guidelines are effectively enforced[24]:

- Computer matching guidelines should specifically state that agencies are to annually report to OMB all participation in matching programs initiated in prior years but conducted on a recurring basis. This would contribute to more complete data in OMB's Annual Report to the Congress.
- Computer matching guidelines should provide for public notice of computer matching programs conducted by organizations not covered by the act when Privacy Act systems of records are disclosed by federal agencies.
- Computer matching guidelines should instruct agencies to notify OMB when like IRS [Internal Revenue Service] and OCSE [Office of Child Support Enforcement], they believe they are exempt from OMB guidelines. This would provide OMB with the opportunity to review and concur. [What about the possibility of refusal on occasion?]

Hearings were held on computer matching in the Senate in 1986 and in the House the following year. On October 18, 1986, the Computer Matching and Privacy Protection Act was enacted (which took effect in 1988). It will be discussed later in this chapter, in the section on Privacy Legislation.

In a major change, OMB revised its guidelines, OMB Circular No. A-130, in February 1996, in response to the passage of the Paper Reduction Act of 1995. The guidelines are quite detailed with respect to the requirements for computer matching activities. For example, here are two of the many requirements[25]:

3. For each matching program, an indication of whether the cost/benefit analysis performed resulted in a favorable ratio. The Data Integrity Board should explain why the agency proceeded with any matching program for which an unfavorable ratio was reached.
4. For each program for which the Board waived a cost/benefit analysis, the reasons for the waiver and the results of the match, if tabulated.

Finally, the OMB reiterated its existing guidelines in a memorandum issued in December, 2000.[26] One interesting announcement by the President is included in the section on additional guidance:

In the President's FY2001 budget, the President announced an initiative to make "privacy impact assessments," or "PIAs," a regular part of the development of new Government computer systems. A PIA is a plan to build privacy protection into new information systems, such as, for example, by asking systems personnel and program personnel to work through questions on data needs and data protection *before* the system is developed.

PRIVACY LEGISLATION

Section 602.

(b) It is the purpose of this title to require that consumer reporting agencies adopt reasonable procedures for meeting the needs of commerce for consumer credit, personnel, insurance and other information in a manner which is fair and equitable to the consumer, with regard to the confidentiality, accuracy, relevancy, and proper utilization of such information in accordance with the requirements of this title.[27]

Transactional Data Protection

Lawmakers frequently respond to public pressure by formulating legislation to deal with agreed-upon abuses. Since 1968, a series of laws have been passed that deal in the broad sense with credit protection where this term includes a variety of financial matters. Coupled with these financial activities is a concern with the privacy of the associated information, or the transactional data, and laws have been passed to protect this data from improper use. Among these laws are the ones shown in Table 9.2.

Space precludes the discussion of all these laws, so we will focus on one of the earliest, the Fair Credit Reporting Act of 1970, and briefly describe the Video Protection Act and the Gramm-Leach-Briley Act.

The Fair Credit Reporting Act of 1970

. . . to insure that consumer reporting agencies exercise their grave responsibilities with fairness, impartiality, and a respect for the consumer's right to privacy. (Fair Credit Reporting Act, 1970.)

In 1967, the first Congressional hearings were held to address threats to personal privacy by some credit bureaus: false records, biased records, outdated material, and errors in data entry. The Fair Credit Reporting Act (FCRA) was passed in 1970 and came into law in April 1971. Below is a brief overview of the main points of the Act[28]:

Accuracy of Information. Credit agencies must take all reasonable steps to guarantee the accuracy of reports in collection, storing, and processing.

TABLE 9.2

A Selection of Transactional-Data Protection Laws

Law (date enacted)	Purpose
1. *Consumer Credit Protection Act* (1968)	To state clearly the cost of borrowing
2. *Fair Credit Reporting Act* (1970)	To permit the correction of mistakes on credit records
3. *Currency and Foreign Transactions Reporting Act (Bank Secrecy Act)* (1970)	To keep certain records on individuals and to report certain types of financial transactions to the government
4. *The Right to Financial Privacy Act* (1978)	To limit some of the broad interpretations of the Bank Secrecy Act
5. *Tax Reform Act* (1976)	To restrict governmental use of tax information for other purposes
6. *Debt Collection Act* (1982)	To regulate the federal government's release of personal information on bad debts to credit companies
7. *Cable Communications Policy Act.* (1984)	To protect the privacy of subscribers to cable television
8. *Video Protection Privacy Act* (1988)	To protect records of individual borrowers held by video rental stores
9. *Telemarketing Consumer Protection Act* (1994)	To prevent fraudulent or harassing telemarketing practices
10. *The Gramm-Leach-Bliley Act* (1999) (or *Financial Services Modernization Act)*	To provide limited privacy protections against the sale of your private financial information.

Obsolete Information. Certain information must not be included after a number of years have elapsed: bankruptcies, 14 years; suits and judgments, 7 years; criminal arrest, 7 years.

Limited Uses of Information. This point specifies the conditions under which an agency may supply a report. Examples are credit, employment, licensing, legitimate business needs, court order, and with written instructions from the concerned individual.

Notices to Individuals. If the results of the report adversely affect the individual, he or she must be notified and supplied with the name and address of the relevant agency. If an investigation is to be undertaken, the affected individual must be notified.

Individual's Right of Access to Information. The individual has a right to be fully informed about all information held about him (except for medical records), and the sources and recipients of the information—for the previous 2 years for reasons of employment, and 6 months for others.

Individual's Right to Contest Information. An individual can dispute the information held on him, which may require a reinvestigation. If the disagreement is not resolved, the agency must permit the individual to include a brief statement in the file.

In 1976, FCRA was criticized by the federal district court judge in Minnesota in the case of Henry v. Forbes[29]:

> The Act does not provide a remedy for all illicit or abusive use of information about consumers . . . Individuals are not protected against the abuse of the credit reporting apparatus unless their circumstances are within the narrow bounds of coverage under the Act. . . . [The individual has] no remedy unless the information were used in violation of common law privacy rights (requiring highly public, outrageous conduct to make a cause of action).

Another set of criticisms can be summarized as follows: considerable vagueness exists with respect to who has access to the credit data. It permits disclosure to "anyone with a legitimate business need for the information in connection with a business transaction involving the consumer."[30] The FCRA only requires the credit agency to provide an inquiring consumer with "the nature and substance of all information," and does not permit him or her to inspect the file in person. The importance of the accuracy of the information collected, stored, and disseminated is not recognized in the Act. Finally, the Act is directed only at credit reporting agencies and not at other institutions that may request the information.

In September 1989, *Business Week's* cover story, "Is Nothing Private?" revealed what to many Americans was a confirmation of their worst fears. An editor signed up with two super credit bureaus, using the small lie that he needed to run credit checks on one or two prospective employees. For $20 apiece, one of the super bureaus produced credit reports based on just the names and addresses of two of his colleagues. It gets more interesting. For an initial fee of $500, the editor was able to access the super bureau's database from his home computer. He ran two names through the system— Representative Richard J. Durbin (D-Illinois) and Dan Quayle, then Vice

President of the United States. These requests did not set off alarms and reports were produced. Various innocuous tidbits about J. Danforth Quayle, with a Washington address, turned up, including that he has a big mortgage and that he charges more at Sears, Roebuck & Co. than at Brooks Brothers, and what his credit card number is. A spokesman for the Vice President said, "We find the invasion-of-privacy aspect of the credit situation disturbing. Further controls should be considered."[31]

In the early 1990s, unsuccessful attempts were made to update the Act, but differences among credit bureaus, direct marketers, and consumer and privacy advocacy groups could not be resolved. Linda Himmelstein reported on one proposal: "The Consumer Reporting Reform Act addresses access to, as well as accuracy and privacy of, consumer credit information. Among other things, the bill provides consumers with a free credit report annually and allows them to opt out of having their personal data used for marketing purposes."[32] There is no new privacy protection for consumers, even though they have made it clear that they require additional protection. In a survey of 4,000 Americans carried out by Yankelovich Partners, "45% of consumers strongly feel legislation is needed, compared with a 23% figure five years ago."[33] The study also found that, "66% feel it is a serious privacy violation for a firm to sell a mailing list without permission of the people listed. Moreover, 55% called unsolicited fundraising phone calls a privacy violation."

Finally, from a survey conducted in spring 1996, the following results are of interest[34]:

- Survey respondents were split fairly equally between being "greatly, somewhat, slightly or not at all" concerned about whether their name was on mailing lists.
- A whopping 83% of the survey participants said there should be a law requiring an opt-in procedure for names to be included on mailing lists.
- 50% of the general survey audience indicated that data on credit card ownership and credit limits should not be collected.
- 55% of the group's mail order buyers said they want their credit data to be off-limits.

In 1996, the "most comprehensive set of amendments" was added to the FCRA. These were "contained in the Consumer Credit Reporting Reform Act of 1996 (PL 104-208). The Amendments contained a number of improvements to the FCRA, but they also included provisions that allow affiliate sharing of credit reports, 'prescreening' of credit reports (unsolicited offers of credit made to certain consumers), and limited preemption of stronger state laws on credit."[35]

By the end of 2003, the FCRA will expire unless it is re-enacted. The federal role in this important area will be preempted by the states and for many industries, including direct marketers and of course credit reporting agencies, multiple systems of regulations will replace a uniform national system. In anticipation of new legislation, many organizations, industry groups, and privacy protection advocates have proposed modifications to the existing law. Space limitations preclude a comprehensive overview but the following, taken from recommendations made by the Electronic Privacy Information Center, the leading online privacy advocate, does include representative changes[35]:

- Consumers should receive notice whenever negative information is furnished to the CRA. This will put consumers in a better position to challenge inaccurate information before applying for credit.
- Consumers should have the right to receive a free credit report from each of the CRAs once a year. Currently, six states extend this right to their residents.
- When an adverse action is taken based on information within a credit report, the consumer should automatically receive a copy of the credit report.
- Consumers should receive notice whenever there is a change of an address or when inquiries are made based on an address that does not match the report.
- Consumers, at no cost, should have access to their credit score and to the underlying algorithm used to generate the score. Newly developed credit monitoring services should be provided at no charge to individuals.
- Congress should require CRAs to detail the purposes for which reports are obtained by users.
- There should be parity in obtaining access to a report: that is, businesses should have to provide the same amount and quality of information as consumers have to in order to obtain a report. Currently, in seeking a report, consumers must submit more personal information than business have to.
- Congress should eliminate the distinction between the "credit header" and the actual credit report. In effect, Congress should move the credit header "below the line," so that it can only be used for permissible purposes under the FCRA.
- There should be an opt-in standard for prescreening. Currently, consumers have to opt-out of this information sharing.
- There should be an opt-in standard for affiliate use of credit reports. Currently, there is only weak notice and opt-out choice protections.

Early in December 2003, President Bush signed the Fair and Accurate Transactions Act of 2003, that amends the Fair Credit Reporting Act.[36]

The Video Privacy Protection Act of 1988: The Bork Bill

In 1987, when Robert Bork had been nominated by President Reagan to the Supreme Court and was being considered by the U.S. Senate, a reporter obtained unauthorized access to the video rental list of his family. Presumably, the purpose was to uncover evidence that Mr. Bork, or his family, rented questionable (read pornographic) movies as a way of further discrediting his nomination. Congress acted quickly to protect the privacy of video renters. Individual laws of this kind, however well-motivated, are indications of the lack of a well-thought-out, comprehensive approach to consumer privacy protection in the United States.

The Gramm-Leach-Bliley Act of 1999

In this Act, also known as the *Financial Services Modernization Act of 1999*, the privacy provisions apply to financial institutions such as banks, stock brokers, investment, financial, and insurance companies. Some of its privacy provisions are as follows[37]:

- First, these financial institutions, whether they wish to disclose your personal information or not, must develop precautions to ensure the security and confidentiality of customer records and information, to protect against any anticipated threats or hazards to the security or integrity of such records, and to protect against unauthorized access to or use of such records or information which could result in substantial harm or inconvenience to any customer.
- Second, financial institutions are required to provide you with a notice of their information sharing policies when you first become a customer, and annually thereafter. That notice must inform the consumer of the financial institutions' policies on: disclosing nonpublic personal information (NPI) to affiliates and nonaffiliated third parties, disclosing NPI after the customer relationship is terminated, and protecting NPI.
- Third, the GLBA gives consumers the right to opt-out from a limited amount of NPI sharing. Specifically, a consumer can direct the financial institution to not share information with unaffiliated companies. Consumers have no right under the GLBA to stop sharing of NPI among affiliates. An affiliate is any company that controls, is controlled by, or is under common control with another company. The individual consumer has absolutely no control over this kind of "corporate family" trading of personal information.
- Fourth, financial institutions are prohibited from disclosing, other than to a consumer reporting agency, access codes or account numbers to any nonaffiliated third party for use in telemarketing, direct mail marketing, or other marketing through electronic mail. Thus, even if a consumer fails to "opt-out" of a financial institutions' transfers, your credit card numbers, pins or other access codes cannot be sold, as they had been in some previous cases.
- Fifth, certain types of "pretexting" were prohibited by the GLBA. Pretexting is the practice of collecting personal information under false pretenses. Pretexters pose as authority figures (law enforcement agents, social workers, potential employers, etc.) and manufacture seductive stories (that the victim is about to receive a sweepstakes award or insurance payment) in order to elicit personal information about the victim.

Privacy advocates are concerned that this Act is not effective in protecting the privacy rights of consumers. In the words of 37 state attorney generals,

"Current law does not adequately protect consumers' privacy."[38] Many financial institutions have not made the existence of opt-out provisions clear enough and have used confusing language in explaining consumer rights.

Government Personal Privacy Protection

Privacy is at the heart of liberty in a modern state and is essential for the well-being of the individual. For this reason alone, it is worthy of constitutional protection, but it also has profound significance for public order. The restraints imposed on government to pry into the lives of the citizen go to the essence of a democratic state.—R. v. Dyment (1988), 45 C.C.C. (3d) 245 at 254

Privacy Act of 1974

The passage of the Privacy Act of 1974 was the culmination of many studies and hearings, but the Watergate scandal was probably the major factor in its approval. The crucial elements of this Act, which applies to the departments, agencies, offices, and administrations of the federal government, are given below[39]:

The purpose of this Act is to provide certain safeguards for an individual against an invasion of personal privacy by requiring federal agencies, except as otherwise provided by law, to . . .

1. Permit an individual to determine what records pertaining to him are collected, maintained, used or disseminated by such agencies
2. Permit an individual to prevent records pertaining to him obtained by such agencies for a particular purpose from being used or made available for another purpose without his consent
3. Permit an individual to gain access to information pertaining to him in federal agency records, to have a copy made of all or any portion thereof, and to correct or amend such records
4. Collect, maintain, use, or disseminate any record of identifiable personal information in a manner that assures that such information is current and accurate for its intended use, and that adequate safeguards are provided to prevent misuse of such information
5. Permit exemptions from the requirements with respect to records provided in this Act only in those cases where there is an important public policy need for such exemptions as has been determined by specific statutory authority
6. Be subject to civil suit for any damages which occur as a result of willful or intentional action which violates any individual's rights under this Act.

With respect to subsection (5), records maintained by the CIA, any law enforcement agencies, prosecutors, courts, correctional institutions, or probation or parole authorities are exemptions as defined in the Act. Because police work depends so heavily on informers, these records must be excluded from general access. Also exempt are records involving national defense or foreign policy, specific statute exclusions, trade secrets, and the protection of the President. Many other categories are given in the Act. It also required the establishment of the Privacy Protection Study Commission, to conduct a study of the databases, automated data processing programs, and information systems of governmental, regional, and private organizations in order to determine the standards and procedures in force for the protection of personal information.[40]

Implicit in all the legislation discussed so far is an after-the-fact philosophy. The assumption is that computerized personal records systems are here to stay, and it is only necessary to regulate their use in order to limit the worst abuses. The law is employed to establish procedures and provide recourse for injured parties. The question of whether there is justification and need for a particular database has not been legally addressed. Any government agency can decide to set up a record-keeping system whenever it wishes. Most of the critical energy in the privacy issue has been directed toward the adequacy of procedures rather than the question of need, and this attitude has persisted into the privacy discussion with respect to the Internet. Given the vast amounts of personal information that are regularly captured in online transactions, the need to provide protection at the outset grows more urgent.

Family Educational Rights and Privacy Act

In contrast to the omnibus approach of the Privacy Act, the Family Educational Rights and Privacy Act (FERPA), passed in 1974, was directed at educational records. This law gives the parents of minors and students over 18 the "right to inspect and review, and request correction or amendment of, an education record."[41] Educational institutions must inform parents and students of their rights and must draw up appropriate procedures to conform with the regulations of the Act. Since there are over 60 million students in the U.S., this act covers a great number of people. A privacy law in this area was necessary, because in addition to grades, conduct, and attendance information, some schools keep track of the family life—its stability and economic and social level—and social life of the student, including relationships and membership in churches. The file may also contain psychological test data and teacher evaluations. The unauthorized use of this data could seriously affect the student's life both in and beyond school.

Schools tend to divulge personal information readily to other schools, law enforcement officials, and for research purposes to the government. Frequently, the interests of the student are secondary. The desire to collect more and more information seems to be increasing, because records are heavily used in decision making. This trend is especially strong in those institutions with large numbers of students. In many postsecondary institutions there is a history of cooperation with law enforcement officials, especially with respect to information about student radicals. It was this rather slipshod treatment of student records, with little access for students or their families, that motivated the passage of FERPA.

Privacy Protection Act of 1980

This Act defines regulations to be followed by law enforcement agencies in acquiring print media records, but it also provides "special protection against search and seizures of materials in the possession of the media and their representatives by federal, state, and local law enforcement agencies. Such materials are subject to seizure by law enforcement agencies *only* if the custodian of the materials is suspected of criminal activity or to prevent the death, serious bodily injury, or destruction of evidence."[42] Reporters may sue for damages if they feel that their right to privacy has been compromised.

Computer Security Act of 1987

This Act creates a means for establishing minimum acceptable security practices for federal computer systems. Responsibility was originally assigned to the National Bureau of Standards (now the National Institute of Standards and Technology, NIST) to develop standards and guidelines to guarantee the security and privacy of the federal computer system, with technical advice provided by the National Security Agency (NSA). The Office of Management of the Budget (OMB) has been working with NIST and NSA to assure the effective implementation of the Act. For example, in 1988, OMB issued guidance to agencies on computer security planning; it co-sponsored a workshop for federal employees on implementing the training and planning portions of the Act; in March of 1989, the inaugural meeting of the Computer System Security and Privacy Advisory Board established by the Act was held; and NIST and NSA reached an agreement that formalized their working relationship in computer security.[43]

Computer Matching and Privacy Protection Act of 1988

This Act amended the Privacy Act to require a biannual report by the President concerning the administration of the law. It was motivated by a concern with the increasing number of computer matches being carried out by various government agencies. In the opinion of Professor David Flaherty, a renowned privacy expert, the Act has a limited scope, "applying only to the 'computerized comparison of records for the purpose of (i) establishing or verifying eligibility for a Federal benefit program, or (ii) recouping payments or delinquent debts under such programs.' It does not apply to matches performed for statistical, research, law enforcement, foreign counterintelligence, security screening, and tax purposes."[44] The Act contains some measures to protect privacy, however. Agencies wishing to carry out matching programs must design written agreements describing how the resulting records will be used; citizens to be affected must be given prior notice in the *Federal Register*: "agencies cannot take steps to deny or cut off a benefit to a person on the basis of adverse data uncovered, unless they have validated their accuracy and offered the individual an opportunity to contest the findings [; and] agencies that conduct or participate in matches are required to create Data Integrity Boards, made up of an agency's own senior officials, to oversee and approve matches."[45] (See previous section on Computer Matching.)

Communication Privacy Protection

Electronic Communications Privacy Act of 1986

Title 111 of the Omnibus Crime Control and Safe Streets Act of 1968, usually called the Wiretap Act, amended the 1934 Communications Act so that government officials at all levels could legally use wiretaps and other forms of electronic surveillance. This was, in the spirit of the times, to provide law enforcement agents with wider powers to combat crime. Such technological developments as cellular telephones, citizen band radios, and electronically transmitted information in computer-readable form have created new forms of communication not anticipated in the 1968 Act. Thus, the 1986 Act was enacted to deal with these deficiencies and includes digital communications, data communications, video communications, and a separate chapter on e-mail (electronic mail). Of primary concern with respect to privacy is an amendment that permits the government to contract out the task of monitoring communications pursuant to a court order. The ramifications of this amendment are quite complicated and beyond the scope of the present discussion, but what is clear is that "the infringement of privacy rights will be multiplied by an incalculable factor because of the use of contracting parties. Rather than delegating the responsibility for conducting these privacy-sensitive interceptions, Congress should have added additional staff to the law enforcement agencies charged with conducting interceptions."[46]

Also of considerable interest, given its increasing use, are the provisions with respect to e-mail. It is a criminal offense, in the words of the legislation, to either "intentionally [access] without authorization a facility through which an electronic communication service is provided; or intentionally [exceed] an authorization to access that facility." A fine line must be drawn to permit bulletin boards to function while protecting e-mail. Thus, criminal liability applies only if the person who gains access to a system actually obtains, alters, or prevents another's access to electronic communication. One final provision is that the Act "prohibits an electronic communications service provider from knowingly divulging the contents of any stored electronic communication."[47]

Communications Assistance for Law Enforcement Act of 1994 ("FBI Digital Telephony Bill" or CALEA)

After much debate and considerable opposition from privacy advocates, this Act, also referred to as the "FBI Wiretap Bill" was signed into law by President Clinton on October 25, 1994. "This law requires telecommunications carriers, as defined in the Act, to ensure law enforcement's ability, pursuant to court order or other lawful authorization, to intercept communications notwithstanding advanced telecommunications technologies."[48] Original opposition to this bill focused on the apparently increased convenience and powers of the FBI to monitor conversations remotely on telephone systems, which will be required by the law, for the first time in history, to reserve part of the capacity for surveillance purposes. Besides the enormous costs of this requirement, the relatively easy availability of surveillance technology may prove attractive to overzealous or rogue investigators. Subsequent to the passage of the Act, "the FBI is claiming that compliance with CALEA requires that telephone companies and other service providers in some regions of the country build in enough surveillance capacity so that 'one percent' of all phone lines could be 'simultaneously' wiretapped, calls isolated, and forwarded to the FBI."[49] One additional, but important change, is that up to now, wiretap statistics have been based on the number authorized and intercepted, but the implementation of this Act will shift the discussion to "percentages of total communications activity." The apparent fear of illegal or subversive uses of telephone systems, over which much of the Internet operates, has resulted in this legislation as well as other attempts to control and limit potentially encrypted communications.

There seems to be a general consensus that privacy legislation should be concerned with three broad areas: (1) the setting up of databases and collection of data, (2) procedures for regulating the management of the information, that is, the right of access and data correction, and (3) monitoring and enforcement schemes. Different countries have chosen to emphasize these aspects to varying degrees. A major criticism of the U.S. system of privacy protection is the lack of regulation of private databases. There is nothing comparable to the systems of data protection boards and commissioners that exist in most European countries, as well as in Canada, Australia, and New Zealand.

The Children's Online Privacy Protection Act of 1998

The passage of this Act[50] is a prime example of the U.S. approach to privacy protection. It was discovered in the mid-1990s that some of the Web sites visited by children were able to gather personal information from them in return for gifts. Such behavior was deemed unacceptable and exploitative of young children; so Congress acted to protect their privacy. Among the requirements this Act (COPPA) places on operators (all the people that operate or maintain a website for profit) are the following[51]:

- First, COPPA requires an operator to post a clear and detailed privacy policy that states the names and addresses of the website operators, the type of information collected from children, the way such information will be used, and an indication of whether the information collected is disclosed to third parties. A link to a privacy policy must be posted in a visible place on every page where personal information is collected, and it should clearly imply that the use of the site is conditioned upon the acceptance of the privacy policy.
- Second, COPPA requires a website operator to obtain verifiable parental consent before collecting any personal information from children. COPPA did not specify an exact method for obtaining such consent; however, the FTC indicated several acceptable ways for compliance with this requirement. An operator can supply consent forms to be signed and mailed or faxed to the operator, require a parent to use a credit card, have a parent call a toll-free number, or accept an email accompanied by a digital signature.
- Third, a website operator must provide parents with the opportunity to review any information collected on their children by the website. The FTC issued a commentary explaining that the right of parental review can enable parents to delete certain information but not alter it.
- The fourth requirement prohibits website operators from conditioning a child's participation in online games and contests to disclosure of "unnecessary" personal information.
- Fifth, site operators must protect the confidentiality, security, and integrity of any personal information that is collected online from children. The FTC suggested use of passwords to access personal information on the website, installation of intrusion-detection software to monitor unauthorized access, and use of secure web servers and firewalls to ensure confidentiality.

Violations of COPPA are considered to be unfair or deceptive trade practices and fall under the purview of the Federal Trade Commission (FTC). The Act took effect in April 2000, after the FTC produced a set of regulations governing its enforcements.[52] The FTC has carried out a number of surveys, which show that children's websites have been complying with the Act.

OTHER PRIVACY ISSUES ON THE INTERNET

The NII promises enormous benefits. To name just a few, the NII offers the possibilities of greater citizen participation in deliberative democracy, advances in medical treatment and research, and quick verification of critical information such as a gun purchaser's criminal record. These benefits, however, do not come without a cost: the loss of privacy. Privacy in this context means "information privacy," an individual's claim to control the terms under which personal information—information identifiable to an individual—is acquired, disclosed, and used.[53]

A few years ago, it seemed that the media was rife with stories and feature pieces about the National Information Infrastructure (NII), the Information Highway, or the Information Superhighway. The NII represented a major initiative of the Clinton administration, nominally associated with then Vice President Al Gore. A number of government structures were created to stimulate, and assist in, the development of the NII, including the Advisory Council on the NII, the Information Infrastructure Task Force (IITF), and the National Telecommunications and Information Administration (NTIA). Let me briefly describe these. NTIA, an agency of the U.S. Department of Commerce, has a broad mandate with respect to such concerns as encouraging private investment, promoting and protecting competition, providing open access to the network, developing an international telecommunications policy, and promoting a minority telecommunications program. One of the specific programs is the Office of Policy Analysis and Development (OPAD). OPAD is concerned with universal service and open access, content regulation and the First Amendment, Electronic Commerce, and of interest for our present purposes, privacy. Thus the NTIA White Paper issued in February 1994 (Inquiry on Private Sector Use of Telecommunications-Related Personal Information) was developed by this office. Three committees of the IITF have been established—the Telecommunications Policy Committee, the Applications Committee, and the Information Policy Committee—which has created three Working Groups, the most relevant being the Working Group on Privacy. A year after the IITF began its work, it issued a progress report, with pertinent sections related to privacy and security concerns.[54]

It is important to be clear about the distinction between privacy and security. Privacy is a right and security is a means to ensure that right. In addition, confidentiality is a judgment that certain information is to be specially treated and not publicly available. Thus, once having determined that certain communications are to be private, encryption might be chosen as the appropriate technology. In storing information electronically, special passwords may be required to access it. These are important and necessary but lacking the prior commitment to ensure privacy, they represent an orthogonal concern. They will come into play after it has been decided, one hopes, that all communications on the Internet, or at least a clearly defined subset, are to be treated as private communications, subject to appropriate protection by means of comprehensive legislation or intrinsic protection resulting from the inexorable workings of the marketplace.

U.S. Government Privacy Recommendations

To determine possible directions for the U.S. to take in responding to its citizens' privacy concerns about the Internet, three sources will be briefly considered. The first is a pair of reports produced by the now terminated Congressional Office of Technology Assessment (OTA). These studies were commissioned by Congress to propose options for the legislative branch in dealing with privacy and security issues on "network environments."[55] In June 1995, the Privacy Working Group of the Information Infrastructure Task Force, a creation of the Clinton administration, released its final recommendations for privacy protection.[56] Finally, the National Telecommunications and Information Administration issued a final White Paper on privacy issues in the private sector in October 1995, after a year and a half of consultations.[57]

OTA Reports: Information Security and Privacy in Network Environments

The first OTA report recognizes that the privacy of networked information held by the government may not be adequately covered by the Privacy Act and further notes the lack of a tradition in the U.S. of comprehensive privacy legislation compared with Europe: "Although the United States does not comprehensively regulate the creation and use of such data in the private sector, foreign governments (particularly the European Union) do impose controls." Thus, in approaching the issue of privacy protection in the private sector for network environments, the report suggests that Congress might consider legislating standards comparable to existing OECD (Organization of Economic Cooperation and Development) guidelines or permit the "business community to advise the international community on its own of its interests in data protection policy." Another possibility is the creation of a Federal Privacy Commission, similar to data protection boards in Europe, to deal with privacy issues, but unlike the European model such a board is not intended to have any regulatory powers.

If created, a Federal Privacy Commission would not have the responsibility to approve the requests of public or private agencies to engage in the collection and storage of personal information. It would not be required to monitor the operating procedures of such agencies. It would basically have an advisory function rather than a regulatory one like the European model. Along with such a commission would be the development of privacy guidelines that would minimally satisfy the European Union's policy on data protection for the international flow of information. That is, the motivating force appears to be economic not social. The second OTA report, an update of the first, noted that the urgency to deal with the privacy problem had intensified. One comment, from a workshop whose results formed a major part of the report, is quite interesting: "Consumers are increasingly concerned with control of personal and transactional data and are seeking some protection from potential abuse of this information. Those participants who had been less inclined than most to trust the market on security issues found more comfortable ground on privacy, because few participants seemed to feel that the market will prioritize personal privacy."[58]

IITF Draft Principles for Providing and Using Personal Information

The IITF Working Group on Privacy notes that the National Information Infrastructure (NII), the Clinton Administration's term for the Information Highway, will by its very nature raise the privacy stakes beyond anything that has so far existed and therefore require more comprehensive privacy principles. Consider the following comments[59]:

A. No longer do governments alone obtain and use large amounts of personal information; the private sector now rivals the government in obtaining and using personal information. New principles would thus be incomplete unless they applied to both the governmental and private sectors.

B. The NII promises true interactivity. Individuals will become active participants who, by using the NII, will create volumes of data containing the content of communications as well as transactional data.

C. The transport vehicles for personal information—the networks—are vulnerable to abuse; thus, the security of the network itself is critical to the NII's future success.

Thus, although a set of updated privacy principles for the Information Highway are the goal of this report, the Working Group argues that they should not be implemented as legislation. In the report, it is stated that the purpose of these Principles is to provide a "guide" for any groups, institutions, or governments that need to design privacy regulations or laws but that these Principles do not have "the force of law." This position is certainly consistent with the long-standing attitude of the U.S. in opposition to broad and comprehensive privacy legislation and in favor of a piecemeal or sectoral approach, often resulting in legislation enacted under crisis situations or in response to a wellspring of public indignation. Thus the federal Privacy Act of 1974 seems to have been enacted as a result of the Watergate events with the basic intent to reassure the public that government would respect personal privacy if specific legislation were in place. The Fair Credit Reporting Act (1970) can be seen as a response to public opinion concerned with the accuracy and misuse of credit records by credit bureaus, banks, insurance companies, and other institutions that depend upon personal credit reports.

These two paragraphs are quite revealing:

> 9. Moreover, the Principles are intended to be in accord with current international guidelines regarding the use of personal information and thus should support the ongoing development of the Global Information Infrastructure.
> 10. Finally, adherence to the Principles will cultivate the trust between individuals and information users so crucial to the successful evolution of the NII.

Paragraph 9, above, states that the Principles are "intended to be in accord with current international guidelines . . ." but given that they do not have the force of law, it is not clear that a mix of voluntary guidelines will satisfy the countries of Europe that have adequate legislation in place. Paragraph 10 offers the plaintive hope that "adherence to the Principles will cultivate the trust between individuals and information users. . . ." What evidence is there that voluntary codes work? How will individuals know which voluntary code is in effect and how its provisions differ or are similar to other voluntary codes? What recourse will they have if they feel that their privacy has been compromised? The good will of the "information user"?

Privacy and the NII: Safeguarding Telecommunications-Related Personal Information

The White Paper extols the promise of the NII, especially the enormous quantity of commercial activity to be generated. All of this activity has as one of its side effects the creation of a "paper" trail of personal data and as discussed above, this data constitutes a wealth of extremely valuable marketing information. Existing applicable federal legislation is briefly reviewed with respect to privacy coverage and comments are solicited as to the adequacy of coverage for multimedia information and to the unrestricted use of secondary data. This position paper also points out that telephone transactions have become a rich source of data and that perhaps new regulatory policy is warranted. It is noted that the "United States currently has no omnibus privacy law that covers the private sector's acquisition, disclosure, and use of TRPI (Telecommunications-Related Personal Information)." But not surprisingly, its bottom line is not to recommend such legislation, at least not yet. Instead, the White Paper hopes for the following:

> NTIA's [National Telecommunications and Information Administration] proposed framework draws upon the IITF's Principles and has two fundamental elements—provider notice and customer consent. Under NTIA's proposed framework, each provider of telecommunications and information services would inform its customers about what TRPI it intends to collect and how that data will be used. A service provider would be free to use

the information collected for the stated purposes once it has obtained consent from the relevant customer. Affirmative consent would be required with respect to sensitive personal information. Tacit customer consent would be sufficient to authorize the use of all other information.

This approach, if embraced by industry, would allow service providers and their customers to establish the specific level of privacy protection offered in a marketplace transaction, *free from excessive government regulation*, so long as the minimum requirements of notice and consent are satisfied. For these reasons, NTIA believes that it is in the private sector's interest to adopt the privacy framework outlined in this paper, *without waiting for formal government action*. [Emphasis added.]

Formal government involvement in the marketplace regulation of privacy via appropriate legislation is not in the cards, even though Western Europe, Canada (to be discussed later in this chapter), and other countries have chosen this approach. The paper recommends a modified contractual approach to dealing with privacy concerns. Under a contractual approach, "companies would inform their customers about what sorts of personal information the firms intend to collect and the uses to which that information would be put. Consumers could then either accept a company's 'offer,' or reject it and shop around for a better deal." The modified contractual approach, favored by NTIA, "allows businesses and consumers to reach agreements concerning the collection, use, and dissemination of TRPI, subject to two fundamental requirements, provider notice and customer consent. Our recommended approach should adequately protect individuals' legitimate privacy interests without excessive government intervention in the marketplace." Finally, to reinforce its view, NTIA offers both the carrot and the stick. It recommends that the modified contractual framework be grounded in the "principles of fair information practices released by the IITF's Privacy Working Group in June 1995." NTIA expects the private sector to implement this framework voluntarily but "if such private sector action is not forthcoming, . . . that framework can and should form the basis for government-mandated privacy regulations or standards."

Although the efficacy of self-regulation or volunteerism has been previously discussed, it is worth remarking that information handlers readily propose and implement privacy policies in order to forestall possible government legislation. As remarked above, it has been difficult to update the Fair Credit Reporting Act of 1970, originally enacted because of the misuse of personal information, including inaccuracies in collection. The credit reporting agencies would certainly have preferred to operate within rules of their own making; for one thing, it would have been cheaper. Because of the current political atmosphere of apparent mistrust of government, it is likely that self-regulation will become the wave of the future and it is also likely that individual privacy will continue to be under attack. However, it is also possible that events in the European Community may spur North American governments to intervene in the personal information industries.

The European Privacy Directive

In June 1995, the European Union (EU), formerly known as the European Community, adopted the Privacy Directive, first drafted in 1992, that governs the handling of personal information both inside and outside the EU. This Directive provides broad protection for citizens in the member states of the European Union. The significant part of this Directive, for the present purposes, is Chapter IV, Transfer of Personal Data to Third Countries. Article 25, Principles, reads in part as follows[60]:

1. Member States shall provide that the transfer to a third country of personal data which are undergoing processing or are intended for processing after transfer may take place only if, without prejudice to compliance with the national provisions adopted pursuant to the other provisions of this Directive, the third country in question ensures an adequate level of protection.
2. The adequacy of the level of protection afforded by a third country shall be assessed in the light of all the circumstances surrounding a data transfer operation or set of data transfer operations; particular consideration shall be given to the nature of the data, the purpose and duration of the proposed processing operation or operations, the country of origin and country of final destination, the rules of law, both general and sectoral, in force in the third country in question and the professional rules and security measures which are complied with in those countries.

The simple version of point 1 is that no personal data can be transferred from any member state of the EU to a third country unless that country's level of protection is adequate, where adequate means equivalent to that offered in the EU. Since there are no comprehensive national privacy laws for the private sector in the U.S., it seemed to be the case that a confrontation would be looming. But the Directive allows the possibility that adequate "professional rules and security measures" may be sufficient, or that satisfactorily agreed-upon procedures that could be generalized may do as well. Thus, while it was possible that the Privacy Directive would serve to spur the development of federal privacy laws, what actually happened was that special arrangements were made between U.S. companies and the EC for the protection of personal information, the so-called Safe Harbor approach.

Safe Harbor

The agreement between the European Union and the United States, known as Safe Harbor, took effect in November of 2000. It provides companies in the U.S. that wish to carry on business with the member countries of the European Union with a set of regulations to which those companies must adhere. Companies must comply with the following seven Safe Harbor principles[61]:

- Notice: Organizations must notify individuals about the purposes for which they collect and use information about them. They must provide information about how individuals can contact the organization with any inquiries or complaints, the types of third parties to which it discloses the information and the choices and means the organization offers for limiting its use and disclosure.

- Choice: Organizations must give individuals the opportunity to choose (opt out) whether their personal information will be disclosed to a third party or used for a purpose incompatible with the purpose for which it was originally collected or subsequently authorized by the individual. For sensitive information, affirmative or explicit (opt in) choice must be given if the information is to be disclosed to a third party or used for a purpose other than its original purpose or the purpose authorized subsequently by the individual.

- Onward Transfer (Transfers to Third Parties): To disclose information to a third party, organizations must apply the notice and choice principles. Where an organization wishes to transfer information to a third party that is acting as an agent (1), it may do so if it makes sure that the third party subscribes to the safe harbor principles or is subject to the Directive or another adequacy finding. As an alternative, the organization can enter into a written agreement with such third party requiring that the third party provide at least the same level of privacy protection as is required by the relevant principles.

- Access: Individuals must have access to personal information about them that an organization holds and be able to correct, amend, or delete that information where it is inaccurate, except where the burden or expense of providing access would be disproportionate to the risks to the individual's privacy in the case in question, or where the rights of persons other than the individual would be violated.

- Security: Organizations must take reasonable precautions to protect personal information from loss, misuse and unauthorized access, disclosure, alteration and destruction.

- Data Integrity: Personal information must be relevant for the purposes for which it is to be used. An organization should take reasonable steps to ensure that data is reliable for its intended use, accurate, complete, and current.

- Enforcement: In order to ensure compliance with the safe harbor principles, there must be (a) readily available and affordable independent recourse mechanisms so that each individual's complaints and disputes can be investigated and resolved and damages awarded where the applicable law or private sector initiatives so provide; (b) procedures for verifying that the commitments companies make to adhere to the safe harbor principles have been implemented; and (c) obligations to remedy problems arising out of a failure to comply with the principles. Sanctions must be sufficiently rigorous to ensure compliance by the organization. Organizations that fail to provide annual self-certification letters will no longer appear in the list of participants and safe harbor benefits will no longer be assured.

Strangely enough, on the basis of these principles, Europeans doing business with some major U.S. companies receive far greater privacy protection than do Americans doing business with the same companies.

As of early 2003, some 295 companies, about "6% of the Fortune 500—representing $587 billion in annual revenues—have joined [Safe Harbor]."[62] Some interesting facts about these companies are the following[63]:

- Over one-fourth of the registrants—such as Axciom and DoubleClick—specialize in the collection and aggregation of personal information. Another 33%, including Microsoft, IBM and Intel, provide the products and services to manage and move that information. These are exactly the people we hope would understand the importance of data privacy.
- The reasons companies cite for joining the harbor also mirror this emphasis on cyberspace. Over 80% say their registrations cover their online data processes. By contrast, about half (41% to 54%) of the registrants signed up for the other possible choices: off-line data, manually processed data and human resources data.
- About three-fourths of the Safe Harbor members provide business-to-business services in the EU. Safe Harbor membership may be their way of saying, "You can trust us—we're not like the rest of those cowboys."
- The picture isn't all rosy, however. My analysis found that 11% of the Safe Harbor members don't even post their privacy policies on their public Web sites, and those policies that are online don't always reflect all seven Safe Harbor principles. Ten members have lapsed registrations. The biggest gap is the absence of the huge U.S. financial companies and telecommunications common carriers. That's because the U.S. and the EU haven't agreed on the terms by which these firms would join the harbor.

The Marketplace Versus the State

Simply put, the argument for letting the marketplace protect personal privacy is that it is in the best interests of business to be concerned about the privacy of its customers. Government, the argument goes, is too big, too bureaucratic, and not trustworthy, given a history of misuse of the personal information of its citizens. So protecting privacy is taken to be "good business" or as a more cynical view would have it, the appearance of privacy protection is good business. "It is also in the self interest of consumers to provide certain personal information in order to obtain products and services at more affordable costs. Such are the dimensions of the current privacy debate in the U.S."[64]

One curious aspect of the privacy debate is that many civil liberties and consumer groups seem to be suspicious of government involvement in the regulatory process, while at the same time they are highly critical of privacy violations in the private sector. The suspicion of government appears to be deep-seated and widespread across the political spectrum. The right points to Waco and other occasions of massive government intrusions into private lives; the left reminds us of the Nixon White House and all sides viewed with great suspicion attempts by the Clinton administration to impose a single encryption strategy with government as the keepers of the (private) keys. So, in some sense, it is hardly surprising that calls for improved privacy protection for personal information have been directed toward the companies and businesses that deal with such information.

It is generally acknowledged that serious concerns exist about privacy on the Internet. Internet users have expressed their growing apprehension about what happens to information acquired during visits to Web sites. Furthermore, they have voted with their wallets by not spending the amounts of money to shop online that were anticipated by many. Industry efforts to convince the Internet community and the public at large that the Internet is safe, convenient, and useful, have not been entirely successful. Press releases and statements by large corporations that they are trustworthy and mindful of the privacy rights of Internet users have not been received with open arms, if the polls are to be believed.

FREEDOM OF INFORMATION

I therefore call upon all Federal departments and agencies to renew their commitment to the Freedom of Information Act, to its underlying principles of government openness, and to its sound administration. This is an appropriate time for all agencies to take a fresh look at their administration of the Act, to reduce backlogs of Freedom of Information Act requests, and to conform agency practice to the new litigation guidance issued by the Attorney General, which is attached.

Further, I remind agencies that our commitment to openness requires more than merely responding to requests from the public. Each agency has a responsibility to distribute information on its own initiative, and to enhance public access through the use of electronic information systems. Taking these steps will ensure compliance with both the letter and spirit of the Act.

President William J. Clinton[65]

Freedom of information as a right exists in uneasy tension with the question of personal privacy in that the freedom of information concept is concerned with the rights of citizens to obtain access to information held by the government, but this desire may endanger the privacy of individuals about whom records are kept. Thus, the situation is such that the individual demands the right to know but at the same time wishes to guard his or her privacy. It is generally recognized that the vast amounts of information collected by the government are used to serve the public—for administrative purposes and for planning and research. Research uses—frequently by external agencies, research groups, and universities—involve statistical data in which information about individuals cannot be identified. Although there are some problems, it is generally agreed that information used for such statistical purposes usually protects privacy, and it is readily made available.

However, the following problem areas arise:

- There must be a reconciliation between the freedom to obtain information from the government when that information contains personal information about other people. Should there be absolute guarantees on the privacy of personal data or should the release of such information be discretionary?
- There are currently restrictions on individuals obtaining access to information about themselves.
- How does this relate to a freedom of information scheme?
- Various individual access procedures should be consistent with some overall freedom-of-information concept.

The Freedom of Information Act

The Federal Freedom of Information Act (FOIA) was passed in 1966, went into effect on July 4, 1967, and was subsequently amended in 1974 and 1976. Its basic principle is that any person may request access to government records and may make copies of the same. Certain records are exempt from disclosure. "Record" is taken to mean any document either in the possession of an agency or subject to its control. Some of the features of the FOIA are as follows[66]:

- Requests must be made to the agency that holds the record—that is, any "executive department, military department, Government corporation, Government-controlled corporation, or other establishments in the Executive Office of the President or any independent regulatory agency."
- If an agency refuses to provide the records within a ten-day period, appeal is possible, first to a higher level and then to a district court.
- A fee may be charged for searching, reviewing, and copying.
- Each agency is required to publish, in the *Federal Register,* information about its organization, access methods, rules of procedure, and so forth.

Not all agencies are required to respond to requests; in fact, there are nine exemptions. The first refers to national defense and foreign policy, and includes executive privilege as it relates to state secrets. A 1974 amendment directed the heads of agencies claiming this exemption to turn documents over to the courts for a final decision. Other exemptions include trade secrets and commercial information, internal personnel rules and practice, information limited by appropriate statutes, inter- and intra-agency memoranda, reports prepared in the course of regulating or supervising financial institutions, and geological and geophysical information. Two exemptions are particularly significant. Exemption (6) excludes[67]

> "personnel and medical files and similar files the disclosure of which would constitute a *clearly unwarranted invasion of personal privacy.*"
>
> ... under normal circumstances, intimate family relations, personal health, religious and philosophic beliefs and matters that would prove personally embarrassing to an individual of normal sensibilities should not be disclosed.

Exemption (7) deals with law enforcement records. The original wording in the act was criticized because it permitted the withholding of just about any file labeled "investigatory." Amendments introduced in 1974 defined this exemption more precisely. In part, they exclude access to investigatory files if such access "constitutes an unwarranted invasion of personal privacy." This differs from Exemption (6) only in that it omits the word "clearly." The courts have not held this difference to be significant. The FOIA does protect privacy, but the distinction must be made between an individual requesting information about a third party or about himself or herself. The latter case has been dealt with under the terms of the various privacy acts. With regard to the former, the absolutist position would be to restrict all access to personal information about another individual. However, there seems to be general agreement that on occasion the cause of open government must have higher claim than that of personal privacy. For example, it may be necessary to examine information about public officials to determine if they are exercising their responsibilities as required by law. There is a "balancing" test in Exemption (6): For each request for access, privacy and confidentiality must be balanced. Appeal to judicial review is possible, and case law will determine appropriate guidelines over time. Another approach might be to specify, in advance, records for which privacy must be maintained and to exempt them absolutely from disclosure. This approach may not be satisfactory in all cases, as it makes no provision for the public's right to know in special circumstances.

Technological innovations have also had an impact on the operation of the FOIA. With the increasing computerization of Federal record keeping, the question arises as to what constitutes a record under the FOIA. Vast amounts of information can be assembled from various distributed databases, organized under a variety of categories, and selectively printed. As Alan Westin has said, "It's as if you've created a great no man's land of information. Traditionally, thinking has been in terms of paper environments and without any sophistication about electronic information."[68] John Markoff, a writer on technology issues for *The New York Times* noted, "There are no explicit legal guidelines that agencies must follow when programming their computers to extract information asked for under the act. Nor are there guidelines on the form in which agencies must release the data. Some experts argue that unless issues involving computerized records can be resolved by the courts or by new laws, the lack of guidelines will become a common way for agencies to deny requests."[69] The interesting question is how much computing, if any, the government is required to do in order to respond to a request for information. On the other hand, the government could release enormous quantities of paper instead of using computers to produce a succinct, directed response. Thus, there is considerable interest in amending the FOIA to accommodate electronic information.

Since September 11, FOIA has again been brought to public attention as new directives have appeared in government to restrict the response to requests that might elicit information useful to terrorists. This judgment will be made by department heads and for the foreseeable future, it will be difficult to appeal them. What has become a frequent occurrence recently is the limitation on the exercise of long-established rights in the face of security needs. That these rights be restored as soon as feasible must be a wish of all concerned citizens.

ISSUES AND PROBLEMS: PRESENT AND FUTURE

The fundamental human right of privacy in Canada is under assault as never before. Unless the Government of Canada is quickly dissuaded from its present course by Parliamentary action and public insistence, we are on a path that may well lead to the permanent loss not only of privacy rights that we take for granted but also of important elements of freedom as we now know it. We face this risk because of the implications, both individual and cumulative, of a series of initiatives that the Government has mounted or is actively moving toward. These initiatives are set against the backdrop of September 11, and anti-terrorism is their purported rationale. But the aspects that present the greatest threat to privacy either have nothing at all to do with anti-terrorism, or they present no credible promise of effectively enhancing security. The Government is, quite simply, using September 11 as an excuse for new collections and uses of personal information about all of us Canadians that cannot be justified by the requirements of anti-terrorism and that, indeed, have no place in a free and democratic society.[70]

Privacy as an issue will not disappear. In fact, it is becoming more pronounced as the computer makes even greater inroads into the functioning of society. Future problems are inextricably linked to the increasing use of the Internet and the associated collection of vast amounts of personal information related to commerce, communication, and browsing. Although the Internet and its most popular service, the Web, have brought certain problems to the fore, the importance of privacy as a societal issue and its protection depends on a host of legal, political, and economic concerns. A few issues will be briefly reviewed to indicate the breadth of the ongoing assault on personal privacy.

In his annual report to the Canadian parliament for 2001-2002, the Privacy Commissioner suggested that the future for Canadians might not be very attractive, as the following scenarios illustrate[71]:

> • All our travels outside Canada will be systematically recorded, tracked and analyzed for signs of anything that the Government might find suspicious or undesirable. "Big Brother" dossiers of personal information about every law-abiding Canadian—initially travel information, but eventually supplemented by who knows what else—will be kept by the federal Government and will be available to virtually every federal department and agency, just in case they are ever handy to use against us.
>
> • Any time we travel within Canada, we will have to identify ourselves to police so that their computers can check whether we are wanted for anything or are otherwise of interest to the state.
>
> • Police and security will be able to access records of every e-mail we send and every cellular phone call we make. Information on what we read on the Internet, every Web site and page we visit, will likewise be readily available to government authorities.
>
> • We will all be fingerprinted or retina-scanned by the Government. This biometric information will be on compulsory national ID cards that will open the way to being stopped in the streets by police and required to identify ourselves on demand.
>
> • Our movements through the public streets will be relentlessly observed through proliferating police video surveillance cameras. Eventually, these cameras will likely be linked to biometric face-recognition technologies that will match our on-screen images to file photos—from such sources as drivers' licences, passports or ID cards—and enable the police to identify us by name and address as we go about our law-abiding business in the streets.

The U.S. will probably not be immune.

New Surveillance Technologies

Most of the discussion so far has been directed toward information stored in computer databases and gathered over the Internet, but other computer-facilitated technologies, some derived from military applications, have been diffusing into general use at a surprisingly fast rate. Familiarity is growing with "smart cards", which are very popular in Europe and are becoming more widely used in North America. Such a card contains a microchip and newer ones employ optical technology that permit the storage of medical records including X-ray images. An introduction to surveillance technology as of 1996 was provided by David Banisar of the Electronic Frontier Foundation[72]:

- Advanced microphones. The FBI has already developed a solid-state briefcase-size electronically steerable microphone array prototype, that can discreetly monitor conversations across open areas.
- Closed Circuit Television Cameras (CCTC). Technical developments have increased the capabilities and lowered the cost of video cameras, making them a regular feature in stores and public areas. In the UK, dozens of cities have centrally controlled, comprehensive citywide CCTC systems that can track individuals wherever they go, even if they enter buildings.
- Forward Looking Infrared (FLIR). Originally developed for use in fighter planes and helicopters to locate enemy aircraft, FLIR can detect a temperature differential as small as 18 degrees centigrade. Texas Instruments and others are marketing hand-held and automobile- and helicopter-mounted models that can essentially look through walls to determine activities inside buildings.
- Massive Millimeter Wave Detectors. Developed by Militech Corporation, these detectors use a form of radar to scan beneath clothing. By monitoring the millimeter wave portion of the electromagnetic spectrum emitted by the human body, the system can detect items such as guns and drugs from a range of 12 feet or more.
- Van Eck Monitoring. Every computer emits low levels of electromagnetic radiation from the monitor, processor, and attached devices. Although experts disagree whether the actual range is a only a few yards or up to a mile, these signals can be remotely recreated on another computer.
- Intelligent Transportation Systems. ITS refers to a number of traffic management technologies, including crash-avoidance systems, automated toll collection, satellite-based position location, and traffic-based toll pricing. To facilitate these services, the system tracks the movements of all people using public or private transportation. As currently proposed by TRW, a leading developer of the technologies involved, the data collected on travel will be available for both law enforcement and private uses such as direct marketing.
- Digital Cash. Potentially, digital cash will create one of the most comprehensive systems for the collection of information on individuals. Using computer software and smart cards to replace physical cash, consumers can spend virtual money for small transactions such as reading an electronic newspaper online, making phone calls from pay phones, paying electronic tolls, buying groceries, as well as for any transaction currently done through credit cards.

A few words about Closed Circuit Television Cameras (CCTC) may be helpful in appreciating the frequently conflicting aims of surveillance technology. Its use is more advanced in Britain, where some 1.5 million cameras have been installed for use in monitoring public areas. The employment of CCTV was motivated by Britain's infamous "soccer hooligans" in the 1960s and later by various kinds of social disorder, including race riots in 1984, union strikes in 1984-1985, 1989 riots in opposition to the government's poll tax, and ongoing terrorism by the IRA. To preserve order and to identify perpetrators, a massive introduction of CCTV has taken place. The claim is that crime has diminished, public spaces are much safer, business has improved, and the quality of street life has improved. Crime has in fact diminished in some cities but whether the use of CCTV is the crucial factor is not known. Most people seem to be willing to trade a certain measure of privacy, or at least public anonymity, for security. North America has generally been more cautious than Europe in adopting CCTC, but since September 11, there have been many calls to implement such systems in major cities. For example, Washington, DC, not surprisingly, has recently installed CCTV but not without some debate.

How can CCTV systems be evaluated for effectiveness? A major study, carried out for the European Commission, reports the following among its many findings[72a]:

- Although CCTV has been present in public space since its inception, its public presence exploded not only in the UK but in many European countries since the 1990s by utilising cameras against street crime. By this development CCTV as instrument of social control has "left" private and semi-private space to which it was confined from the 1970s till the mid-1980s.
- Standard evaluations of CCTV, usually carried out by operators of a system, highlight crime statistics in order to justify the efficiency of CCTV. They usually have a high authorial impact on the public and political decision-making processes. However, their scientific value is questionable. Not only is the explicit focus on changes in crime rates insufficient but the statistical procedure itself is often weak. The British criminologists Pawson and Tilley point out that most standard evaluations are "post hoc shoestring efforts by the untrained and self interested practitioner."
- The deployment of CCTV against street crime was initially advocated by conservative parties. But meanwhile it has been adopted as law and order strategy by parties of all political affiliations. In the UK Tony Blair's "New Labour" follows the course of John Major's Tory government and continues funding CCTV schemes. Thus, the rapid proliferation of CCTV is a common trend in private as well as public space all over Europe largely independent of the general political conditions.
- European politics shape CCTV by technical standardisation, market intervention and legal norms. . . . But although CCTV surveillance by public authorities needs a legal basis according to the Human Rights

Convention it is not affected by European data protection provisions. Its regulation remains the realm of national legislation. The same is true for private-operated systems without intermediate storage or with analogue image data storage without additional possibilities of evaluation.

• In recent years bodies of the European Parliament and the Council of Europe have discussed the issue and pointed out the need for further action and regulation. In particular, they stress discriminatory patterns of surveillance practice and the crucial development of automated algorithmic surveillance such as facial recognition or intelligent scene monitoring.

Unregulated Databases

Companies have fired workers from jobs without cause, doctors have refused to take new patients who are able to afford medical care, and apartment managers have refused to rent to prospective tenants with regular jobs and sufficient income. Many similar cases have been documented with the common denominator that the companies, doctors, and managers have all taken advantage of special-purpose commercial databases directed toward their concerns. Companies can turn to databases to determine if any of their workers have filed a worker compensation claim elsewhere, as well as the disposition of the case. Other databases will provide information to physicians about whether a prospective patient has ever sued a doctor for malpractice, or will provide information to an apartment manager if a prospective tenant has ever filed a claim for a violation of tenant's rights. The data for these lists is openly available in tenants' courts, small claims courts, worker compensation hearings, and civil court proceedings. All that is required is sufficient staff to extract relevant information from these records and then enter it into the database. By focusing on large population centers, companies with comprehensive databases find a ready market for their services. And it is all legal; the only possible danger for companies may result from inaccurate data. Credit bureaus, banks, cable companies, and video rental stores are all subject to a certain degree of regulation with respect to the privacy of their clients, but no uniform laws exist to protect the privacy of citizens in all their commercial activities.

The National Practitioner Databank

For years it has been difficult, if not impossible, to monitor the movements of health care professionals who, having been disciplined by one board, move to a new jurisdiction, leaving behind their flawed record and presenting themselves as competent professionals. In 1986, Congress passed a law to set up a national database, the National Practitioner Databank (NPDB), of disciplinary actions taken against physicians, dentists, nurses, therapists, and other licensed health professionals. The databank, accessible to hospitals, licensing agencies, and other medical groups, but not the general public, will supply such information as professional misconduct (including making sexual overtures to patients), misdiagnosis, and mistreatment, but not personal matters such as arrests, non-payment of taxes, or drug or alcohol abuse (except when professional performance is affected), and also malpractice payments, restrictions of privileges in hospitals and clinics, disciplinary actions by medical and dental societies, and state actions against hospitals and other health care institutions.

The data bank, popularly known as "docs in a box," opened for business on September 1, 1990. Doctors are permitted to inspect their own files and to enter explanatory statements, if they wish. The American Medical Association, which initially opposed the databank, now supports it but would like "nuisance suits," those that had little chance for success, to be left off. Hospitals will have to improve their verification of doctors' records and to rationalize their disciplinary procedures, because of the serious consequences of including such actions in the National Databank. Presumably the public will benefit in that incompetent health practitioners will no longer be able to find new places to work where their past record is unknown. Here is an important case in which the need of hospitals to know about their staff's background, in order to provide competent medical care and to reduce costly malpractice suits, outweighs any claim to privacy by members of that staff.

In 2000, the House held hearings to explore the possibility of opening up the NPDB to the general public. One presentation by the American Academy of Family Physicians, on behalf of its 90,000 members, made the following points[73]:

> • The Academy believes that the goal of the NPDB, to prevent sanctioned physicians from escaping sanction by moving across state lines, is a worthwhile one.
> • The Academy is concerned about proposals to open the NPDB to public inquiries. The Academy is concerned that its information often is misleading and will not serve any public good by being released. The databank contains reports on all medical tort claims paid out on behalf of a physician. However, there is no way to disaggregate the nuisance suits that ultimately are settled out of court.
> • Likewise, the President's Advisory Commission on Consumer Protection and Quality in the Health Care Industry, which met throughout 1998, considered and rejected the recommendation that the NPDB be opened to the public.
> • Opening the NPDB would be reflect [sic] incomplete and inaccurate information regarding the competency of any particular physician listed within. Further, states are responding to the growing public interest in knowledge about physicians through the timely creation of physician profiles. These profiles often track much more usable and relevant data for the general public and are easily accessible.

Electronic Mail

An important component of office automation, electronic mail, or e-mail, was discussed in Chapter 4. Although it has proven to be an extremely useful communication tool and facilitates cooperation throughout the company, an important privacy issue has emerged, one strongly related to a concern with workers' rights. (See Chapter 13.) The basic question is to what degree management can monitor its employees' e-mail, either on an occasional or regular basis. A class action suit launched in August 1990 against Epson America Inc. for "allegedly violating its employees' privacy by intercepting their e-mail," was dismissed in January 1991 in a Los Angeles County Superior Court because "the company did not violate a state penal code prohibiting electronic eavesdropping on private communications."[74] Another suit was filed against Nissan Motor Corp. in January 1991 by two employees, again in California, accusing the company of intercepting their electronic messages and violating their privacy. Some companies argue that they reserve the right to intercept messages, without prior warning, as a means of ensuring that employees do not abuse the system with personal communications. What does seem necessary is that companies issue clear guidelines, based on discussions with their employees about the use and misuse of e-mail, and that both employees and employers adhere to them.

However, even a clear statement of operating procedures may not help employees. In a case decided in Pennsylvania in early 1996, Michael A. Smyth sued The Pillsbury Company for being wrongfully discharged, based on information obtained from Mr. Smyth's supposedly protected e-mail in spite of the fact that the company "repeatedly assured its employees, including plaintiff, that all e-mail communications would remain confidential and privileged. . . . Defendant further assured its employees, including plaintiff, that e-mail communications could not be intercepted and used by defendant against its employees as grounds for termination or reprimand."[75] The judge found for the defendant and the final paragraph of his decision is quite revealing[76]:

> In the second instance, even if we found that an employee had a reasonable expectation of privacy in the contents of his e-mail communications over the company e-mail system, we do not find that a reasonable person would consider the defendant's interception of these communications to be a substantial and highly offensive invasion of his privacy. Again, we note that by intercepting such communications, the company is not, as in the case of urinalysis or personal property searches, requiring the employee to disclose any personal information about himself or invading the employee's person or personal effects. Moreover, the company's interest in preventing inappropriate and unprofessional comments or even illegal activity over its e-mail system outweighs any privacy interest the employee may have in those comments.

More on employee rights is covered in Chapter 13.

Cookies

This example has become the ubiquitous means by which personal information is given up to almost every site visited on the Internet. According to the Web browser, Netscape, "A cookie is a small bit of information used by some web sites. When you visit a site that uses cookies, the site might ask your browser to place one or more cookies on your hard disk. Later, when you return to the site, your browser sends back the cookies that belong to the site."[77] Netscape's Navigator is a Web browser, as is Microsoft Explorer, a software tool for locating Web sites, reading news, listening to music, watching movies, downloading information, and buying products. Existing software is able to determine several pieces of information about anyone who visits a Web site. Here is some of the information that was obtained from a visit to a demonstration Web site hosted by the Center for Democracy and Technology[78]:

> Your name is probably . . . and you can be reached at. . . .
> Your computer is a PowerMac.
> Your Internet browser is Netscape.
> You are coming from. . . .
> I see you've recently been visiting this page at
> www.cdt.org

Still more data could be obtained such as "your e-mail address, the exact files you viewed, and other detailed information gathered without your knowledge. . . . You reveal information to web site operators both directly and indirectly." Netscape describes the operation of cookies as, "When your browser displays a Web page—for example, each time you click a link or type a URL, or when a Web page is displayed in an email message—it gives certain kinds of information to the site. This information may include (but is not limited to) your operating environment [such as your browser type and operating system], your internet address [also known as the IP address], and the page you're coming from [This allows the site to know which site referred you]."[78a]

Cookies are an overly clever name for "client-side persistent information," itself a euphemism for the following process: we gather information about your shopping habits and make it available for subsequent perusal by us, by downloading it without your knowledge onto your hard drive. Of course the official Netscape line is that "cookies are beneficial to the Web . . . shopping done via the Web could be gradually gathered in the cookies file, and then paid for (as if at a supermarket checkout) when the user enters the appropriate page. The concept can also be used to create a permanently customized view of a site—if you regularly have specific needs from a search engine, for example."[79] Thus the major motivation is convenience—it saves the user from having to re-enter information that may be required for successive visits to a Web site, but there are drawbacks[80]:

John Yang, a research assistant in the geology department at Florida International University in Miami, said a Cookie program can be built to track the user's every move while connected to a particular server. This information can then be fed into a database to keep statistics on site usage so Webmasters can tailor a site to a particular user's interests.

Combine Cookie with JavaScript and a site's administrator could launch a very effective direct mail campaign without ever having asked the user for permission, Yang observed.

In more malevolent hands, these new tools can do far worse. For example, a Webmaster could pretend to be a particular site in order to retrieve a user's Cookie data without authorization. "If you use a server that does not encrypt its information, there is a real problem," Yang said.

In response to the concerns expressed about possible invasions of privacy, Frank Chen, security product manager of Netscape, responded that steps were being taken to deal with the situation by first fixing security bugs in JavaScript and then dealing with making Cookies more secure. "He added that Netscape is looking at adding a feature that will either disable Cookie and JavaScript support or alert the user to their presence. 'You've got to be able to store some information on the client side in order to build robust client-server applications, but we also have to inform users of the types of information they will receive,'" Chen said.[81] Note that the emphasis on security issues finesses the justified privacy concern about why so much information must be gathered in the first place, without most users being aware of this process.

This last point should be emphasized. Most new users are unaware that cookies exist or how they work. The default conditions are set without informing users. It is necessary to go to the Preferences tab of Edit on the Netscape toolbar or the Internet Options tab of Tools on the Explorer toolbar. But having discovered that certain aspects of online privacy can be controlled, it is still necessary to understand what settings to choose. If you want to be notified when cookie requests are made, you will discover that certain sites, and the number is growing, cannot be visited unless all cookies are automatically accepted. For commercial sites, and others as well, cookies are a valuable resource, as discussed above. Knowing the past behavior of potential and current customers is a marketer's dream.

Medical Privacy: Health Insurance Portability and Accountability Act of 1996 (HIPAA)

The need for the protection of medical records is motivated by the following concerns: administrative errors that "misclassify, release, or lose information . . . computerization [of medical records means remote access and rapid dissemination of information]. . . . Access by unrelated parties [including] insurance companies, drug companies; [and often unknown to patients] when her or his records have been subpoenaed."[82] Typically, to receive medical treatment it is necessary to sign a waiver that allows "the health care provider to release your medical information to government agencies, insurance companies, employers and others."[83] Such requirements that violated basic health privacy rights led to the passage of HIPPA.

Although HIPAA was passed in 1996, it took several years for a set of privacy regulations to be released by the Department of Health and Human Services, as required by the Act. Indeed, it was not until the last few days of the Clinton administration, on December 20, 2000, that the President released the final version. The Bush administration began its review of the regulations and took into account extensive comments in finally releasing its version of the regulations, late in 2002, a document of 450 pages.[84] A highly condensed statement of what the regulations, or health privacy rules, are intended to accomplish is given below[85]:

> The health privacy rule gives patients the right to access and copy their medical records, limits the use and disclosure of personal health information without a patient's written authorization, and requires health plans and health care providers to provide patients with a written notice describing the types of permissible uses and disclosures of their medical information. It also restricts most disclosures of health information to the minimum needed for the intended purpose, and establishes new financial penalties for improper use or disclosure of personal health information.

On April 15, 2003, the HIPAA rule took effect. For the next two years, no enforcement will take place, as investigators will follow up on customer complaints in order to produce a final rule based on two years of working experience. Some of the issues and penalties are described in the following passage[86]:

> HIPAA regulations are intended to give people more control over how their medical information is used. They affect anyone who works with or has access to medical information, from huge scientific research centers and big city hospitals to rural one-physician practices or any business that offers health insurance to employees. Under the new rules, failure to properly protect medical information could result in fines of up to $250,000 and prison terms up to 10 years. Technical support people and systems administrators who have to ensure that medical data is gathered, stored and transmitted securely said they were hit hardest by the demands of HIPAA.

SOME PRIVACY IMPLICATIONS OF SEPTEMBER 11

Last January, an FBI agent entered a branch of the St. Louis Public Library and requested a list of all the sign-up sheets showing names of people who used library computers on Dec. 28, 2002. Even though the FBI agent did not have a warrant or subpoena, the library quickly surrendered the list of all users. The FBI acted because someone phoned in a tip that they "smelled something strange" about a library patron of Middle Eastern descent. . . . The Justice Department isn't the only agency taking aim at American liberties. The Department of Transportation has compiled secret "no fly" lists of passengers suspected of terrorist ties—or at least those critical of the administration. In one instance, two dozen members of a peace group, students chaperoned by a priest and nun, were detained en route to a teach-in thus missing their flight.[87]

Not surprisingly, in the aftermath of September 11, major steps were undertaken to reinforce security both within the U.S. and overseas. Part of this ongoing process has meant a renewed assault on personal privacy in an attempt to facilitate investigative procedures aimed at identifying potential terrorists and terrorist groups, thereby forestalling further tragic events. While Americans seem to be willing to give up some measure of freedom to increase security, there is a limit, both in degree and in time. Too great a loss of traditional freedoms, including personal privacy, and for too long a time, may not be acceptable. The purpose of this chapter is to briefly survey and evaluate a few notable examples of these ongoing threats.

Biometric Information

At a conference on the future of biometrics, the following technologies were included:[88]

Fingerprints	Thermal (Face)
Voice	Vein Patterns (Hand)
Facial	Finger Geometry
Iris	Stride Recognition
Retina	DNA
Signature Dynamics	Keystroke Dynamics
Hand Geometry	Body Odor
Skin Spectroscopy	

The following needs for such technologies were listed:

- Significant Population Increase
- Fewer Human Safeguards
- E-Commerce, PC Banking
- Increased "Identity Theft"
- Increased Fraud
- Too Many PINS & Passwords
- Need for Improved Physical / Logical Access Control

These technologies have been in great demand since September 11, especially at airports and other transportation facilities, government buildings, and a myriad of safety-critical sites. Major research programs have been initiated by the government to accelerate the development of systems with high rates of accuracy. The effort in face recognition has been longstanding with many difficulties to be overcome. An evaluation of progress in this area, as of the end of 2002, was made by the U.S. National Institute of Standards and Technology (NIST) in its report, Face Recognition Vendor Test 2002 (FRVT 2000). The conclusions to this report are given as follows[89]:

> FRVT 2002 is the most thorough and comprehensive evaluation of automatic face recognition technology to date. The evaluation has examined many long-standing questions and raised several new questions for further study.
> • Indoor face recognition performance has substantially improved since FRVT 2000.
> • Face recognition performance decreases approximately linearly with elapsed time database and new images.
> • Better face recognition systems do not appear to be sensitive to normal indoor lighting changes.
> • Three-dimensional morphable models substantially improve the ability to recognize non-frontal faces.
> • On FRVT 2002 imagery, recognition from video sequences was not better than from still images.
> • Males are easier to recognize than females.
> • Younger people are harder to recognize than older people.
> • Outdoor face recognition performance needs improvement.
> • For identification and watch list tasks, performance decreases linearly in the logarithm of the database or watch list size.

Total Information Awareness (TIA) System

TIA is a new research program under the direction of the Pentagon's Defense Advanced Research Project Agency (DARPA), which has aroused considerable controversy since it came to the public attention of Congress as well as the public at large. This is how DARPA describes its objective[90]:

> The Total Information Awareness (TIA) program is a FY03 new-start program. The goal of the Total Information Awareness (TIA) program is to revolutionize the ability of the United States to detect, classify and identify foreign terrorists—and decipher their plans—and thereby enable the U.S. to take timely action to successfully preempt and defeat terrorist acts. To that end, the TIA program objective is to create a counter-terrorism information system that: (1) increases information coverage by an order of magnitude, and affords easy future scaling; (2) provides focused warnings within an hour after a triggering event occurs or an evidence threshold is passed; (3) can

automatically queue analysts based on partial pattern matches and has patterns that cover 90% of all previously known foreign terrorist attacks; and (4) supports collaboration, analytical reasoning and information sharing so that analysts can hypothesize, test and propose theories and mitigating strategies about possible futures, so decision-makers can effectively evaluate the impact of current or future policies and prospective courses of action.

When the TIA project came to public attention, it seemed that a system was being proposed that would destroy basic human rights by integrating personal information across a wide variety of databases in order to determine possibly suspicious behavior. Data mining, the process of interest, has become a tool used by marketers to better target customers. It involves the extraction of useful nuggets of information through the processing of large amounts of data. Congress became concerned and demanded to be kept closely informed about research results. Led by Senators Ron Wyden, Democrat of Oregon, and Chuck Grassley, Republican of Iowa, relevant legislation was passed[91]:

> Washington, DC—U.S. Senator Ron Wyden (D-Ore.) today announced that his legislation to protect the privacy and civil liberties of law-abiding Americans from the Defense Department's "Total Information Awareness" (TIA) Program will become law as part of the FY2003 omnibus spending bill. Wyden's amendment to the bill makes research funding for the program, which is designed to sift through information on citizens' financial transactions, travel, medical records and other activities, dependent upon a report to Congress on TIA's privacy and civil liberties implications. It also requires Congressional approval for the deployment of any technology related to the program.

A final comment from a conservative columnist of the *New York Times* is relevant,[92]

> In the name of combating terrorism, it would scoop up your lifetime paper trail—bank records, medical files, credit card purchases, academic records, etc.—and marry them to every nosy neighbor's gossip to the F.B.I. about you. The combination of intrusive commercial "data mining" and new law enforcement tapping into the private lives of innocent Americans was described here "a supersnoop's dream."

On May 20, 2003, DARPA released a report to Congress on the Terrorist Information Awareness Program (formerly the Total Information Awareness Program). The reason for the name change was because the "program created in some minds the impression that TIA was a system to be used for developing dossiers on US citizens. That is not DoD's [Department of Defense] intent in pursuing this program. Rather, DoD's purpose in pursuing these efforts is to protect citizens by detecting and defeating foreign terrorist threats before an attack. To make this objective absolutely clear, DARPA has changed the program name to Terrorism Information Awareness."[93]

Lawful Access

Although this issue arose in Canada as well as Europe, its relevance to the U.S. was sufficiently clear that the Electronic Freedom Foundation (EFF), an important online civil liberties organization, combined with its Canadian counterpart, Electronic Foundation Canada (EFC), with which it has no formal relationship, to issue a response to the Canadian Government.[94] On August 25, 2002, the Canadian Department of Justice issued a discussion paper, soliciting opinions on how law enforcement officials would be able to access the Internet traffic of specific clients of Internet Service Providers (ISP).[95] The Canadian government document defined "lawful access" as, " an important and well-established technique used by law enforcement and national security agencies to conduct investigations. In the context of telecommunications in Canada, it consists of the interception of communications and search and seizure of information carried out pursuant to legal authority."

Selected portions from the submitted comments of EFC and EFF follow:

- EFC and EFF oppose the Proposal as a vague and unjustified plan for intrusive covert surveillance of private communications that clearly threatens the fundamental values and fabric of Canadian society.
- First, the Proposal radically expands surveillance powers over private communications, including Internet communications. The Internet is not merely a one-to-one medium of communication: it is a valuable yet inexpensive publication medium as well as a virtual assembly hall for political, religious and cultural association.
- Second, we seriously question the Proposal's general approach to communications privacy, which essentially contemplates making fine distinctions among telecommunications and data associated with telecommunications according to the mechanics of their transmission or use. From the individual's perspective, communications are communications, whether telephone conversations or e-mail.
- Third, the Proposal cannot be evaluated in isolation; it must be viewed in light of other proposed erosions of privacy and freedom.
- Fourth, we reject the Proposal's implicit assumption that Canada's participation in international instruments like the Council of Europe Convention on Cybercrime can justify the Proposal. Insofar as Canada has not yet ratified the Convention, the Proposal is clearly premature.

Canada's exercise in exploring new powers for lawful access should serve as a cautionary tale for the U.S.

National ID Card Proposal

Shortly after September 11, many Americans called for the institution of a national identity card, or an ID card, as a means of improving the accuracy of individual identification. Many countries, including European democracies, have required ID cards for years, but in the U.S. the idea has never made much headway. However, with the fear of terrorism rampant, advances in technology have made the possibility of instituting a card with biometric information somewhat more attractive, or so it was believed by proponents. Even the proposal to transform state drivers' licenses into *de facto* national ID cards has not succeeded. Americans seem to be convinced that ID cards will be more of a threat to personal freedoms than they will be a tool to identify terrorists. The image derived from many spy movies of a person being confronted by a policeman demanding, "Your papers, please," in a heavy East European accent, seems to have had a lasting impact.

Canada has also never had an ID card but early in 2003, the Minister for Citizenship and Immigration asked Canadians to consider the benefits that an ID card would provide for Canadians, namely, to identify terrorists, to combat identity theft, and to facilitate travel to the U.S. Hearings were held across the country and comments were solicited from individuals and groups. One submission, representing Electronic Frontier Canada, raised the following points[96]:

> It must be emphasized that in principle ID cards can be dangerous devices inimical to the basic tenets of a democratic society. They contribute to the loss of anonymity because they will encourage law enforcement officials to demand their presentation any where and anytime. It is also inevitable that their purposes and applications will expand, so-called "function creep," not because it is necessary but because it is possible. Witness the history of the Social Insurance Number (SIN) in Canada [comparable to the SSN in the U.S.]. The availability of an apparent unique identifier resulted in a host of mundane uses beyond any initial expectations and Parliament seemed to be unable or unwilling to curtail such extraneous applications.

Privacy Issues in Peer-to-Peer (P2P) Systems

Although there are many examples of threats to privacy on the Internet, just a few more will be mentioned here. The Center for Democracy and Technology reported on the following privacy issues related to the use of peer-to-peer (P2P) systems; such systems have received considerable attention in their use for downloading music and videos, while bypassing central servers.[97]

- Peer-to-peer file sharing systems provide Internet users with the ability to share files on their computers with thousands or millions of other peo-

ple. In doing so they make it possible, and in some cases too easy, for people to share even very personal files, sometimes by accident.

• Recent studies have found dozens of examples of Kazaa [the most
commonly used P2P system for sharing music files] users who have made
available for download sensitive documents on their computers like their
tax returns, e-mail inboxes, or check registers—almost certainly by mistake. Once available, these sensitive files could be used to commit fraud,
invade privacy, or even commit identity theft.

• Many file-sharing programs contain "spyware" that collects information about a user's online activities, then communicates that information
back to a third party, typically without the user's knowledge or consent.
While often used primarily for sending ads, spyware can be used for more
invasive collection of information. These programs can be difficult for users
to detect or even remove, and may seriously affect the stability and security
of a user's computer.

• CDT strongly believes that developers of file-sharing software, like any
developer that includes spyware, should observe fair information practices.
They should give users clear notice about the type of information being collected about them, meaningful choices about whether to participate, and
access to personal information being collected and retained.

An Example of a Federal Privacy Law: Canada's PIPED Act

The word "privacy" does not appear in the Bill of Rights nor does it appear
in Canada's Charter of Rights. The major thrust of legislation has been to
control, not to forbid, the collection and use of private information.
Information about any individual is not always in that individual's control.
Rather it can be gathered, stored, and disseminated by both private and public agencies. The law has provided protection, and one must continue to turn
to the law for future protection. The distinguished jurist, William O.
Douglas, referred to the police in the following quotation, but he might just
as well have been concerned with other institutions and groups in society[98]:

> The free state offers what a police state denies—the privacy of the home,
> the dignity and peace of mind of the individual. That precious right to be
> let alone is violated once the police enter our conversations.

Canada was concerned that with the European Data Protection Directive
taking effect in 1998, it would be necessary for Canada to have legislation
in place that provided essentially equivalent protection. As discussed earlier,
the U.S. response to this situation was the development of "Safe Harbor"
regulations, a non-governmental approach to assuring adequate protection.
Led by the federal government department, Industry Canada (roughly equivalent to the U.S. Department of Commerce), legislation was introduced and
passed in April 2000. It was based on a voluntary code, the Canadian
Standards Association Model Code for the Protection of Personal

Information, which had been adopted in 1995 by a committee composed of industry, government, legal, and civil liberties organization representatives. It should be noted that this Model Code was intended to be a voluntary set of privacy procedures available for adoption by businesses to represent their commitment to protect the privacy of their customers.

Canada's Personal Information Protection and Electronic Documents Act (PIPEDA)[99] was implemented in three stages:

- Stage 1. As of January 1, 2001, the Act applies to every organization which operates as a federal work, undertaking or business.
- Stage 2. On January 1, 2002, the Act will apply to personal health information.
- Stage 3. From January 1, 2004, the Act will apply to every organization that collects, uses or discloses personal information in the course of commercial activity within a province.

Personal information includes any factual or subjective information, recorded or not, about an identifiable individual. This includes information in any form, such as[100]:

- Name, age, weight, height
- Medical records
- Income, purchases and spending habits
- Race, ethnic origin and colour
- Blood type, DNA code, fingerprints
- Marital status and religion
- Education
- Home address and phone number

The legislation provides the following rights for Canadians:

- Expect an organization to collect, use or disclose your personal information reasonably and appropriately, and not use the information for any purpose other than that to which you have consented*
- Know who in the organization is responsible for protecting your personal information
- Know why an organization collects, uses or discloses your personal information*
- Expect an organization to protect your personal information by taking appropriate security measures
- Expect the personal information an organization holds about you to be accurate, complete and up-to-date
- Obtain access to your personal information and ask for corrections*
- Complain about how an organization handles your personal information.

Note that the "*" indicates exceptions may apply to the full exercize of the specified right. There are of course legal obligations on organizations that collect personal information, as well. The Act is administered by the Privacy Commissioner of Canada, who has powers to investigate complaints and issue opinions, which have legal force. There is more, but space limitations preclude additional discussion. What is important is that all Canadians have legal protection with respect to the collection, storage, and use of their personal information by all organizations, both public and private. How well it will work has yet to be determined.

SUMMARY

The impact of computers on privacy is one of the major concerns voiced by the public at large. Although most people agree that computers have improved the quality of life, there is a definite apprehension that some form of an Orwellian 1984 society is not far off. Privacy is an important but difficult right to maintain when so much information about individuals is gathered and stored by both public and private agencies. Personal information must be safeguarded and only used for the purpose for which it was originally collected.

One of the fears of legitimate groups is that databases built up by government surveillance will be used to harass lawful activities. The increasing use of computer matching is of concern to civil libertarians, because the searching of computer records in order to turn up possible violations seems to be an action contrary to the presumption of innocence. Credit bureaus play a major role in the marketing of information. Because credit ratings are so important in almost every aspect of life, it is necessary to guarantee that such data is as accurate as possible and that individuals be informed as to their use.

In response to public concern, a number of acts have been passed by the federal government to deal with the most serious violations, the so-called sectoral approach. In contrast, the European approach in the private sector is to establish government agencies to license and regulate companies that operate databases. The Internet provides new challenges to personal privacy as an increasing number of users carry out commercial transactions. The much-discussed Information Highway will also gather enormous quantities of information about individuals. There seems to be little willingness in the U.S. to have government pass broad-based legislation to protect personal privacy, presumably because of a general mistrust of government. However, the passage of the European Privacy Directive has required that companies in the U.S. wanting to do business in Europe must subscribe to a set of principles known as "Safe Harbor."

Freedom of information occasionally conflicts with privacy rights, but balances must be struck to ensure that the public is able to obtain information about the actions of government, taking into account that private information is protected—an often difficult task.

The terrorist actions of September 11, 2001, have introduced new challenges to protect personal privacy, while at the same time maintaining national security. Indeed, a number of measures and laws have been introduced in the name of security that threaten individual privacy, the hallmark of a free and open society. Other countries such as Canada have recently enacted legislation to protect individual privacy in the private sector.

NOTES

1. Spenser S. Hsu. "Video Surveillance Planned on Mall," *The Washington Post*, March 22, 2002, Page A01.
2. Jaikumar Vijayan. "Canadian Privacy Law Deadline Approaching," *Computerworld*, May 5, 2003. Available at http://www.computerworld.com/printthis/2003/0,4814,80949,00.html
3. Jane Black. "Will Your TV Become a SPY?" *BusinessWeek*, January 3, 2003. Available at http://www.businessweek.com/technology/content/jan2003/tc2003013_2538.htm
4. Jane Black. "Snooping in all the Wrong Places," *BusinessWeek*, December 18, 2002. Available at http://www.businessweek.com/technology/content/dec2002/tc20021218_8515.htm
5. Julia Scheeres. "No Cyborg Nation Without FDA's OK," *Wired News*, October 8, 2002. Available at http://www.wired.com/news/print/0,1294,55626,00.html
6. "Packages May Soon Send Data on Consumers," Associated Press, *The New York Times*, July 9, 2003. Available at http://www.nytimes.com/aponline/technology/AP/Beamed-Bar-Codes.html
7. Michele Orecklin, "Checking What You Check Out," *Time*, May 12, 2003, p. 42. Available at http://www.time.com/time/magazine/0,9263,1101030512,00.html
8. Louis Harris & Associates and Dr. Alan F. Westin. *The Dimensions of Privacy: A National Opinion Research Survey of Attitudes Toward Privacy* (for Sentry Insurance, New York: Garland Publishing, 1981). The poll was conducted between November 30 and December 10, 1978 and between November 27, 1978 and January 4, 1979.

   Louis Harris & Associates. *The Road After 1984: The Impact of Technology on Society* (for Southern New England Telephone, December, 1983). The poll was conducted between September 1 and September 11 and between September 7 and September 23, 1983.

   Louis Harris & Associates and Dr. Alan F. Westin. *The Equifax Report on Consumers in the Information Age* (for Equifax Inc., 1990). This poll was conducted between January 11 and February 11 and between April 20 and April 30, 1990.

Louis Harris & Associates and Dr. Alan F. Westin. *Harris-Equifax Consumer Privacy Survey 1991* (for Equifax Inc., 1991). This poll was conducted between January 1 and July 8, 1991.

Louis Harris & Associates and Dr. Alan F. Westin, *Harris-Equifax Consumer Privacy Survey 1992* (for Equifax Inc., 1991, 1992). This poll was conducted between June 9 and June 18, 1992.

Louis Harris & Associates and Dr. Alan F. Westin, *Harris-Equifax Health Information Privacy Survey 1993* (for Equifax Inc., 1993). This poll was conducted between July 26 and August 26, 1993.

Louis Harris & Associates and Dr. Alan F. Westin, *Equifax-Harris Consumer Privacy Survey 1994* (for Equifax Inc., 1994). This poll was conducted between August 17 and September 4, 1994.

Louis Harris & Associates and Dr. Alan F. Westin, *Equifax-Harris Mid-Decade Consumer Privacy Survey 1995* (for Equifax Inc., 1995). This poll was conducted between July 5 and July 17, 1995.

9. "New Internet Users: What They Do Online, What They Don't, and Implications for the 'Net's Future," Pew Internet & American Life Project, September 25, 2000. Available at http://www.pewinternet.org/reports/pdfs/New_User_Report.pdf

10. "The Online Health Care Revolution: How the Web Helps Americans Take Better Care of Themselves," Pew Internet & American Life Project, November 26, 2000. Available at http://www.pewinternet.org/reports/pdfs/PIP_Health_Report.pdf

11. "The UCLA Internet Report: Surveying the Digital Future, Year Three," UCLA Center for Communication Policy, February 2003. Available at http://ccp.ucla.edu/pdf/UCLA-Internet-Report-Year-Three.pdf

12. "Most People Are 'Privacy Pragmatists' Who, While Concerned about Privacy, Will Sometimes Trade It Off, for Other Benefits," The Harris Poll #17, March 19, 2003. Available at http://www.harrisinteractive.com/harris_poll/index.asp?PID=365

13. *Ibid.*

14. Joseph Turow. "Americans & Online Privacy, The System is Broken," The Annenberg Public Policy Center, University of Pennsylvania, June 2003. Available at http://www.asc.upenn.edu/usr/jturow/internet-privacy-report/36-page-turow-version-9.pdf

15. Alan F. Westin. *Privacy and Freedom* (New York: Atheneum Publishers, 1967), p. 7.

16. Kent Greenwalt. "Privacy and Its Legal Protections," *Hastings Center Studies*, September 1974, p. 45.

17. *Privacy and Computers*, Department of Communications/Department of Justice, Canada (Ottawa: Information Canada, 1972), p. 13.

18. *Records, Computers, and the Rights of Citizens*, U.S. Dept. of Health, Report to the Secretary's Advisory Committee on Automated Personal Data Systems (Washington, DC, 1973), pp. 40–41.

19. *Ibid.*, p. 41.

20. *Personal Privacy in an Information Society*, Report of the Privacy Protection Study Commission (Washington, DC, 1977), pp. 14–15.

21. Richard D. Kusserow. "The Government Needs Computer Matching to Root Out Waste and Fraud," *Communications of the ACM,* 27 (6), June 1984, p. 543.

22. *Privacy Act: Federal Agencies' Implementation Can Be Improved,* United States General Accounting Office, GAO/ GGD-86-107, (Washington, DC, August 1986), p. 47.

23. *Ibid.,* p. 49.

24. "Management of Federal Information Resources," Circular No. A-130, Revised, Office of the Management of the Budget, Whitehouse, February 8, 1996. Available at http://www1.whitehouse.gov/WH/EOP/OMB/html/circulars/a130/ a130.html

25. "Memorandum for Heads of Executive Departments and Agencies," Office of Management and Budget, December 20, 2000. Available at http://www.whitehouse.gov/omb/memoranda/m01-05.html

26. Fair Credit Reporting Act, as amended, January 7, 2002. Available at http://www.ftc.gov/os/statutes/fcra.htm

27. *Op cit., Records, Computers, and the Rights of Citizens,* pp. 66–69.

28. As quoted in Warren Freedman, *The Right of Privacy in the Computer Age,* (New York: Quorum Books, 1987), p. 14.

29. Richard F. Hixson. *Privacy in a Public Society: Human Rights in Conflict* (New York: Oxford University Press, 1987), p. 220.

30. Jeffrey Rothfeder, Stephen Philips, Dean Foust, Wanda Cantrell, Paula Dwyer, and Michael Galen. "Is Nothing Private?" *Business Week,* September 4, 1989, p. 74.

31. Linda Himmelstein. "Attack of the Cyber Snoopers," *Business Week,* June 1994, pp. 134, 136, 138.

32. "Survey Shows Growing Concern Over Privacy Issue," *Direct Marketing Technology,* October 20, 1995. Available at http://www.mediacentral.com/Magazines/Direct/Archive/10209501.htm

33. "Consumers Nervous About Privacy: DIRECT poll," *Direct Newsline,* June 17, 1996. Available at http://www.mediacentral.com/Magazines/DirectNewsline/OldArchives/199606/1996061701.html

34. "The Fair Credit Reporting Act (FCRA) and the Privacy of Your Credit Report," Electronic Privacy Information Center, (no date). Available at http://www.epic.org/privacy/fcra/

35. *Ibid.*

36. A brief description of the Fair and Accurate Transaction Act is available at http://www.washingtonpost.com/ac2/wp-dyn/20A35173-2003Dec4.htm. The Act itself is available at http://frwebgate.access.gpo.gov/cgi-bin/getdoc.cgi?dbname=108_congbills&docid=f:h262enr.txt.pdf

37. *"The Gramm-Leach-Bliley Act,"* Electronic Privacy Information Center, (no date). Available at http://www.epic.org/privacy/glba/

38. Joanna Glasner. "Opt-Out Is a Copt-Out," *Wired News,* May 7, 2002. Available at http://www.wired.com/news/print/0,1294,52328,00.html

39. Section s.2(b) of the Privacy Act of 1974, 5 U. S. C., s.552a, passed as part of Pub. L. 93-579.

40. *Op cit., Personal Privacy in an Information Society,* p. xv.

41. *Ibid.* p. 413.

42. *Op cit.*, Freedman, *The Right of Privacy in the Computer Age* (1987), p. 15.
43. *Managing Federal Information Resources*, Seventh Annual Report Under the Paperwork Reduction Act of 1980, Office of the Management of the Budget (Washington, DC, 1989), pp. 35–36.
44. David H. Flaherty. *Protecting Privacy in Surveillance Societies: The Federal Republic of Germany, Sweden, France, Canada, and the United States* (Chapel Hill. The University of North Carolina Press, 1989), pp. 357–358.
45. *Ibid.*
46. Russell S. Burnside. "The Electronic Communications Privacy Act of 1986: The Challenge of Applying Ambiguous Statutory Languages to Intricate Telecommunication Technologies," *Rutgers Computer & Technology Law Journal*, 13 (2), 1987, p. 508.
47. *Ibid.*, p. 512.
48. "Federal Bureau of Investigation (FBI) Implementation of the Communications Assistance for Law Enforcement Act," Federal Register, Vol. 60, No. 36, February 23, 1995. Available at http://cpsr.org/cpsr/privacy/epic/wiretap/fed_reg_notice.txt
49. "Oppose the FBI National Wiretap Plan!" Electronic Privacy Information Center (EPIC), February 14, 1996. Available at http://www.epic.org/privacy/wiretap/oppose_wiretap.html
50. *The Children's Online Privacy Protection Act of 1998.* Available at http://www4.law.cornell.edu/uscode/15/6501.html
51. "The Children's Online Privacy Protection Act," The Electronic Privacy Information Center, (no date). Available at http://www.epic.org/privacy/kids/
52. FTC's COPPA Regulations, 64 Fed. Reg. 212. Available at http://www.ftc.gov/os/1999/9910/64fr59888.pdf
53. *Privacy and the National Information Infrastructure: Principles for Providing and Using Personal Information, Final Version*, Privacy Working Group, Information Policy Committee, Information Infrastructure Task Force, June 6, 1995. Available at http://ntiaunix1.ntia.doc.gov:70/0/papers/documents/niiprivprin_final.txt
54. *The National Information Infrastructure Progress Report, September 1993-1994.* Information Infrastructure Task Force, September 1994. Available on NII Virtual Library WWW site at http://iitf/doc.gov
55. *Information Security and Privacy in Network Environments.* U.S. Congress, Office of Technology Assessment, Washington, DC: U.S. Government Printing Office, September 1994. Available at http://www.wws.princeton.edu/~ota/*Issue Update on Information Security and Privacy in Network Environments.* U.S. Congress, Office of Technology Assessment, Washington, DC: U.S. Government Printing Office, June 1995. Available at Web site above.
56. *Privacy and the National Information Infrastructure: Principles for Providing and Using Personal Information.* Information Infrastructure Task Force Working Group on Privacy, January 19, 1995. Available on IITF Web site at http://iitf.doc.gov
57. *Privacy and the NII: Safeguarding Telecommunications-Related Personal Information.* NTIA, Office of Policy Analysis and Development, Washington, DC. Available at gopher://www.ntia.doc.gov:70/HO/policy/privwhitepaper.html

58. *Op. cit., Issue Update on Information Security and Privacy in Networked Environments*, p. 71.

59. *Op. cit., Privacy and the National Information Infrastructure: Principles for Providing and Using Personal Information.*

60. "Directive 95 on the Protection of Individuals With Regard to the Processing of Personal Data and on the Free Movement of Such Data," The European Parliament and the Council of Europe, June 15, 1995. Available at http://www2.echo.lu/legal/en/dataprot/directiv/directiv.html An addendum to the Directive, referred to as the Recitals, is available at the same Web page, except for the last part, . . ./recitals.html.

61. "Safe Harbor Overview," Export Portal, U.S. Department of Commerce, (no date). Available at http://www.export.gov/safeharbor/sh_overview.html

62. Jay Cline. "Safe Harbor: A Success," *Computerworld*, February 19, 2003. Available at http://www.computerworld.com/printthis/2003/0,4814,78641,00.html

63. *Ibid.*

64. Richard S. Rosenberg. "Privacy Protection on the Internet: The Marketplace Versus the State." *Wiring the World: The Impact of Information Technology on Society*, IEEE Society on Social Implications of Technology, Indiana University South Bend, June 12-13, 1998, pp. 138–147. Also available at http://www.ntia.doc.gov/ntiahome/privacy/files/5com.txt. Most of this section is taken from this paper.

65. "Memorandum for Heads of Departments and Agencies, Subject: The Freedom of Information Act," The White House, Office of the Press Secretary, October 4, 1993. Available at http://cpsr.org/cpsr/foia/white_house_foia_policy.txt

66. *Public Government for Private People, Volume 2*, The Report of the Commission on Freedom and Individual Privacy, Province of Ontario, Canada (Toronto, 1980), pp. 455–457.

67. *Ibid.*, p. 114.

68. As quoted in John Markoff, "Freedom of Information Act Facing a Stiff Challenge in Computer Age," *The New York Times*, June 18, 1989, p. Y 13.

69. *Ibid.*

70. "Annual Report to Parliament, 2001-2002," The Privacy Commissioner of Canada, January 2003. Available at http://www.privcom.gc.ca/information/ar/02_04_10_e.asp

71. *Ibid.*

72. David Banisar. "Big Brother Goes High-Tech," *Covert Action Quarterly*, Spring 1996. Available at http://www.media-awareness.ca/english/resources/articles/privacy/big_brother.cfm

72a. Leon Hempel and Erich Töpfer. "Inception Report. Working Paper No. 1, Technical University of Berlin, January 2002. Available at http://www.urbaneye.net/results/ue.wp1.pdf

73. "Statement Concerning Proposals to Open the National Practitioner Data Bank to the Public," American Academy of Family Physicians, March 15, 2000. Available at http://www.aafp.org/x987.xml

74. Jim Nash and Maureen J. Harrington. "Who Can Open E-mail?" *Computerworld*, January 14, 1991, pp. 1, 88.

75. "Michael A. Smyth v. The Pillsbury Company," C.A. NO. 95-5712, United States District Court for the Eastern District of Pennsylvania, January 18, 1996. Available at http://www.epic.org/privacy/internet/smyth_v_pillsbury. html

76. *Ibid.*

77. "What Are Cookies, and How Do They Work?" Netscape 7.0 Help, June 18, 2002.

78. "Who's Watching You and What Are You Telling Them?" Center for Democracy and Technology. Available at http://www.13x.com/cgi-bin/cdt/snoop.pl

78a. "Using Privacy Features," Netscape, June 22, 2002. Available at http://www.thamizha.com/developer/english/privacy_help.html

79. "Netscape's Cookies Crumble," *Australian Personal Computer Online—News*, April 1996. Available at http://www.com.au/apc/9604/thenet/onnews.htm

80. James Staten. "Netscape Tricks Raise Security Concerns," *MacWeek*, March 13, 1996. Available at http://www.zdnet.com/macweek/mw_1011/gw_net_tricks.html on May 13, 1996.

81. *Ibid.*

82. Taken from "Threats to Medical Record Privacy." Electronic Privacy Information Center (EPIC), 1995. Available at http://www.epic.org/privacy/medical/threats.html

83. "How Private is My Medical Information," Privacy Rights Clearinghouse, Fact Sheet #8, March 1993. Available at http://www.vortex.com/privacy/prc.med-8.Z

84. "Standards for Privacy of Individually Identifiable Health Information," U.S. Department of Health and Human Services, August 8, 2002. Available at http://www.hhs.gov/ocr/hippa/020808finalprivacymods.doc

85. "Medical Records Privacy: Questions and Answers on the HIPAA Final Rule," Congressional Research Service, The Library of Congress, Order Code RS20500, Updated January 3, 2003. Available at http://www.epic.org/privacy/medical/RS20500.pdf

86. Michelle Delio. "Techs Tangle With Privacy Regs," *Wired News*, April 15, 2003. Available at http://www.wired.com/news/medtech/0,1286,58468,00.html

87. James Bovard. "Surveillance State," *The American Conservative*, May 19, 2003. Available at http://www.amconmag.com/05_19_03/cover.html

88. Paul Collier. "The Future of Biometrics," Beyond the Technology: The Law and Policy Implications of Increased Biometrics Use, New York City, November 5-6, 2002. Available at http://www.search.org/policy/bio_conf/PaulCollier.ppt

89. "Face Recognition Vendor Test 2002," Overview and Summary, The National Institute of Standards and Technology, March 2003, Available at http://sequoyah.nist.gov/pub/nist_internal_reports/ir_6965/FRVT_2002_Overview_and_Summary.pdf

90. "Total Information Awareness (TIA) System," Defense Advanced Research Projects Agency, (no date). Available at http://www.darpa.mil/iao/TIASystems.htm

91. "Wyden Wins Fight to Curb Government Snooping," News Release, February 13, 2003, Senator Ron Wyden. Available at http://wyden.senate.gov/media/2003/02132003_tia.html

92. William Safire. "Privacy Invasion Curtailed," *The New York Times*, February 13, 2003, Section A, p. 41.
93. "Terrorism Information Awareness Program," Guide to the Report to Congress, Defense Advanced Research Projects Agency, May 20, 2003. Available at http://www.darpa.mil/body/tia/terrorism_info_aware.htm
94. "Comments of Electronic Frontier Canada and Electronic Frontier Foundation," Electronic Frontier Foundation, December 17, 2002. Available at http://www.eff.org/Privacy/Foreign_and_local/Canada/20021219-EFC-EFF-comments.rtf
95. "Lawful Access—Consultation Document," Department of Justice, Government of Canada, August 25, 2002. Available at http://www.justice.gc.ca/en/cons/la_al/law_accesss.pdf
96. Richard S. Rosenberg. "Re: National Identity Card," Appearance Before the Standing Committee on Citizenship and Immigration," Electronic Frontier Canada, February 19, 2003, Vancouver, BC. Available at http://www.efc.ca/pages/privacy/ParlPresFeb19.pdf
97. CDT Policy Post, Volume 9, Number 11, May 19, 2003. Available at http://www.cdt.org/publications/pp_9.11.shtml
98. William O. Douglas. Address to the American Law Institute, 1953.
99. *The Personal Information Protection and Electronic Documents Act.* Available at http://www.privcom.gc.ca/legislation/02_06_01_01_e.asp
100. "A Guide for Canadians," Office of the Privacy Commissioner of Canada, February 2001. Available at http://www.privcom.gc.ca/information/02_05_d_08_e.asp

ADDITIONAL READINGS

The Nature of Privacy

Agre, Philip E. and Rotenberg, Marc (Eds.). *Technology and Privacy: The New Landscape.* (Cambridge, MA: The MIT Press, 1998).

Bennett, Colin J. and Grant, Rebecca (Eds.). *Visions of Privacy: Policy Choices for the Digital Age.* (Toronto, Ontario, Canada: University of Toronto Press, 1999).

Branscomb, Anne Wells. *Who Owns Information? From Privacy to Public Access* (New York: Basic Books, 1993).

Burnham, David. *The Rise of the Computer State* (New York: Random House, 1983).

Privacy Legislation

Bennett, Colin. *Regulating Privacy: Data Protection and Public Policy in Europe and the United States.* Ithaca, NY: Cornell University Press, 1992.

Cavoukian, Ann and Tapscott, Don. *Who Knows: Safeguarding Your Privacy in a Networked World.* (Toronto, Ontario, Canada: Random House of Canada Limited, 1995).

Electronic Surveillance in a Digital Age. U.S. Congress, Office of Technology Assessment, OTA-BP-ITC-149. Washington, DC: U.S. Government Printing Office, July 1995. Available at http://www.ota.nap.edu/pdf/data/1995/9513.PDF

Privacy: The Key Issues of the 90's. A Direct Marketer's Guide to Effective Self-Regulatory Action in the Use of Information, Washington, DC: Direct Marketing Association, Inc., October 1993.

Rothfeder, Jeffrey. *Privacy for Sale: How Computerization Has Made Everyone's Private Life an Open Secret.* New York: Simon & Schuster, 1992.

Other Privacy Issues on the Internet

Baig, Edward. "How to Practice Safe Surfing," *Business Week*, September 9, 1996, pp. 120–121.

Blackman, Joshua D. "A Proposal for Federal Legislation Protecting Informational Privacy Across the Private Sector," *Santa Clara Computer and High Technology Law Journal,* 9 (2), November 1993, pp. 431–468.

"A Matter of Trust: What Users Want From Web Sites," Results of a National Survey of Internet Users for Consumer WebWatch, Princeton Survey Research Associates, January 2002. Available at http://www.consumerwebwatch.org/news/report1.pdf

Rosenberg, Richard S. and Prosser, Susan. "Health Information in Canada: Can Privacy be Protected?" *CEPE 2001* IT and the Body (Computer Ethics: Philosophical Enquiry), Lancaster University, UK, December 14–16, 2001, pp. 184–203.

Freedom of Information

"Access to Information: Making It Work for All Canadians," Report of the Access to Information Review Task Force, Government of Canada, June 2002. Available at http://www.atirtf-geai.gc.ca/accessReport-e.pdf

Glasner, Joanna. "Fretting About the State of FOIA," *Wired News*, March 14, 2003. Available at http://www.wired.com/news/business/0,1367,58039,00.html

Kline, Greg. "Information at Risk," News-Gazette Online, January 20, 2002. Available at http://www.news-gazette.com/story.cfm?Number=10892

"Summary of Annual FOIA Reports for Fiscal Year 2001," United States Department of Justice, Office of Information and Privacy, 2002. Available at http://www.usdoj.gov/foiapost/2002foiapost27htm

Issues and Problems: Present and Future

"The Anonymizer FAQ." Accessed from the Web site with URL:http://www.anonymizer.com/on June 1, 1996.

"Considering Consumer Privacy: A Resource for Policymakers and Practitioners," Center for Democracy and Technology, March 2003. Available at http://www.cdt.org/ccp/ccp.pdf

"Crime Prevention Effects of Closed Circuit Television: A Systemic Review," Home Office Research Study, United Kingdom, August 2002. Available at http://www.homeoffice.gov.uk/rds/pdfs2/hors252.pdf

Frook, John Evan. "IA Scoop: Netscape Embraces Cookie in Launch of Personal Workspace," *Interactive Age Daily Media and Marketing Report*, April 4, 1996. Available at http://techweb.cmp.com/ia/marketapr96/2apr4.htm

"Letter to Representative Bob Franks regarding H.R. 3508." Center for Democracy and Technology, June 4, 1996. Available at http://www.cdt.org/privacy/children/Franks_let.html

Markey (D-MA), Representative Edward J. "Electronic Privacy and Children's Privacy," Statement before the Federal Trade Commission, June 5, 1996. Available at http://www.cdt.org/privacy/children/960605_Markey_stmnt.html

Smith, Robert Ellis. "The True Terror Is in the Card," *The New York Times Magazine*, September 8, 1996, pp. 68–59.

Some Privacy Implications of September 11

"Annual Report to Parliament, 2001-2002," The Privacy Commissioner of Canada, January 2003. Available at http://www.privcom.gc.ca/information/ar/02_04_10_e.pdf

"Medical Privacy—National Standards to Protect the Privacy of Personal Health Information," Office for Civil Rights—HIPAA. (No date). Available at http://www.hhs.gov/ocr/hipaa/

"Public Attitudes Towards the Uses of Biometric Identification Technologies by Government and the Privacy Sector," ORC International, August 2002. Available at http://www.search.org/policy/bio_conf/Biometricsurveyfindings.pdf

Steinhardt, Barry. "Privacy and Biometric Technologies," Beyond the Technology: The Law and Policy Implications of Increased Biometrics Use, New York City, November 5–6, 2002. Available at the conference site, http://www.search.org/policy/bio_conf/02_bio_conf_1.asp

"Using Biometrics for Border Security," United States General Accounting Office, November 2002. Available at http://www.gao.gov/new.items/d03174.pdf

Viscusi, W. Kip and Zeckhauser, Richard J. "Sacrificing Civil Liberties to Reduce Terrorism Risks," John M. Olin Center for Law, Economics, and Business, Harvard University, Discussion Paper No. 401, January 2003. Available at http://www.law.harvard.edu/programs/papers/pdf/olin_center/401.pdf

10

INTELLECTUAL PROPERTY RIGHTS

Congress shall have Power . . . to promote the Progress of Science and useful Arts, by securing for limited Times to Authors and Inventors the exclusive Right to their respective Writings and Discoveries.

The Constitution of the United States, Article 1, Section 8, 1788.

INTRODUCTION

First a disclaimer: This chapter should not be viewed as providing legal advice in the area of intellectual property (IP). The goal is to describe, in a rather condensed fashion, some of the major Internet issues related to IP. The downloading of music and movies has come to be seen by millions of users as an inalienable right, regardless of the fact that such works have copyright protection. In the "real world," it is necessary to buy something in order to own it, but the online transfer of files seems to be immune from IP protection, at least in the minds of millions of users worldwide. In addition, music or videos represented as bits can be copied indefinitely and relatively quickly, without degradation, which facilitates sharing in spite of existing laws. In addition, the discovery of effective compression techniques and the use of broadband connections make it feasible to download very large video files. All of these technological advances have converged over the past few years to create a challenge to traditional IP laws that has yet to be resolved.

We will explore two major areas of concern, digital media and software piracy. The first, it is claimed, involves enormous amounts of money lost to record companies and movie studios, while the second threatens the livelihood of many software developers and erodes the technological cutting edge of many countries, especially the U.S. In some cases, the claims made by industry advocates have fallen on deaf ears because of the general perception that wealthy companies are just crying wolf. Indeed, when Microsoft complains about software piracy, few are likely to feel any sympathy for this extraordinarily wealthy and powerful corporation. The crux of the matter seems to be that millions of people feel they have a right—not entirely legal perhaps, they might admit—to build up their music and video collections and to copy needed software. If challenged, their likely response might be that sampling music on the Internet is just a prelude to purchasing desirable compact discs (CDs), and also that they are not really stealing software, just trying it out in order to decide which is the best to buy. However self-serving these responses might be, there is also a lingering sense of community that supports a local ethic in the midst of illegal activities. Simply put, if so many people are doing it, surely it can't be wrong; or if all else fails, they can't catch all of us.

A few statistics and survey results may be helpful in order to appreciate the magnitude of the situation and the relevant concerns. Given that college students are a major segment of Internet users and a particularly competent and adventuresome one, it is hardly surprising that these "Internet users are twice as likely to have ever downloaded music files when compared to all Internet users: 60% of college Internet users have done so compared to 28% of the overall population."[1] In April of 2001, the results of an extensive survey revealed that some 37 million Americans have downloaded music. The following findings are interesting[2]:

> • In all, 29% of adult Internet users say they have downloaded music, a proportion that has grown from the 22% of Internet users who told us they had downloaded music as of the summer of 2000. More than half (51%) of those between ages 18 and 29 who have Internet access have downloaded music files.
> • Moreover, 53% of youth between the ages of 12 and 17 have also downloaded music files—that is more than 7 million youth who have retrieved music files to their computers' hard drives. This online activity is especially popular with older teenage boys. Almost three quarters of boys ages 15–17 with Internet access have downloaded music files.
> • In the six months between August 2000 and February 2001, music downloading became an increasingly regular activity for Internet users. The number of adult American Internet users downloading music on any given day doubled to more than 6 million. That is twice the number of Internet users buying retail products online on any given day and equal to the number seeking health information on the Web or looking for travel information.
> • The striking growth of the music downloading population occurred across virtually every demographic group and level of online experience. It was pronounced among the very freshest newcomers to the Internet as well as the most experienced online veterans. The increase in the number of music downloaders also occurred among online men and women, the well-

to-do and those in modest economic circumstances, and in different racial and ethnic groups, particularly among Hispanics.

All expectations are confirmed. The people downloading movies are not just a bunch of boys—adults, women, and minorities are all interested in participating in this vast enterprise. Additional details may be helpful in understanding and appreciating the scope of this phenomenon, and there seems to be no shortage of surveys available. For instance, consider the following findings from a survey conducted during May of 2002[3]:

- Music downloading and CD burning have become a mainstream phenomenon in America. According to our study, about one-third of Americans between the ages of 12 and 44 have downloaded music files from the Internet. This means approximately 89 million Americans between the ages of 12 and 44 are downloaders. About one-third of 12 to 44-year-old Americans have burned their own CDs.
- The number of Americans who have "dropped out" of music purchasing continues to rise. The number of drop-outs between the ages of 16 and 40 increased 38% and now comprises 7.6% of this age group. 7.3% of 12–44s are music purchasing "drop-outs". Multiplied against the U.S. 12–44 population, that computes to an estimated 10 million consumers in this age group who have left the ranks of music purchasers.
- About half of American teenagers have burned someone else's copy of a CD instead of buying it. About 30% of 12 to 44-year-olds and 48% of teens have burned instead of bought. While there is no way to know if people would have bought the music they burned, there's no doubt that this adds up to a significant amount of lost sales for the record industry.
- Many consumers, particularly young consumers, have lost the connection between music and monetary value. Three in four teenagers don't think there is anything morally wrong about downloading music for free from the Internet. Also, one in five 12 to 44-year-old Americans say they no longer have to buy CDs because they can download music for free from the Internet.
- Teens say they would be more likely to avoid buying a copy-protected CD than older age groups. About a third of 12 to 17-year-olds said they wouldn't buy a copy-protected CD. Also, just over 50% of Americans 12 to 44 who have burned their own CDs would not purchase a copy-protected CD.
- Many downloaders have gone on to buy an artist's CD after downloading a track for free from the Internet. Some good news about downloading: about half of the downloaders in our sample reported making at least one purchase after first sampling a track for free from the Internet.
- The majority of music downloaders do have "some reservations" about artists and labels not being compensated but download music for free anyway. The music industry is dangerously close to losing 12–24s, many of whom feel that music is and should be free. However, when the issue is framed in terms of artists and labels deserving compensation for their work, attitudes do modify a bit.

- When it comes to download compensation, teens and young adults are more sympathetic to the plight of musicians than they are toward their record labels. Also, just over 50% of Americans 12 to 44 years old said that music downloading sites should be allowed to operate only if musicians are compensated for their work.

The ethical positions exhibited by various age groups is revealing and pose serious problems for content providers, especially music and video companies. These attitudes translate into large monetary losses worldwide. As reported by the International Federation of the Phonographic Industry (IFPI)[4]:

- World sales of recorded music fell by 7% in value and by 8% in units in 2002. Mass downloading from unauthorised file sharing on the internet and the massive proliferation of CD burning continues to be a major cause of the fall in CD sales globally, combined with competition from other entertainment sectors and economic uncertainty on consumer spending.
- Recorded music sales worldwide fell to US$32 billion in 2002. Compared to 2001, sales of CD albums fell globally by 6%, and there were continued declines in sales of singles (−16%) and cassettes (−36%). Music videos however saw a growth in value of 9%, driven by strong growth in DVD.
- The US saw a third consecutive year of decline, with album sales down 10% in units, mainly due to falling sales from major album releases affected by sales substitution from internet sources.

The other main IP concern is the rampant copying of computer software, often referred to as software piracy. The attempt to characterize software in order to design appropriate legal protection has been a long and torturous process that is by no means complete. Computers themselves are readily protected under patent law, as they are certainly inventions. But problems have arisen even here because of the difficulty in determining how to safeguard the masks used to produce integrated circuits. The major concern, however, lies with computer software, more specifically with applications programs. Congress has passed legislation that includes penalties against those who infringe upon the safeguards granted by patents or copyrights. There is the protection afforded by case law that covers trade secrets, and there is also the law of contracts. Each is applied differently and has different advantages and disadvantages.

One of the problems in protecting programs is a basic question of definition. As Michael Gemignani, an IP lawyer, pointed out several years ago, a program may be viewed as[5]

a particular form of expression of a flowchart or algorithm, a process for controlling or bringing about a desired result inside a computer, a machine part or completion of an incomplete machine, a circuit diagram of an incomplete machine, a circuit diagram or blueprint for a circuit board, a data compilation, a code writing.

The list does not end there. All the key terms in the constitutional mandate—limited time, author, inventor, and discovery—must be interpreted in the present context.

The growing debate over software protection is a part of the larger issue of protecting intellectual property rights. The big stakes in this area are of course related to technology, a clear indication of its importance. For example, some important cases of the 1980s are given below[6]:

- 1985: The Polaroid challenge against Kodak over violations of the patent for instant cameras is successful, and damages of $909.5 million were awarded on October 12, 1990, considerably less than the anticipated award of $10 billion.
- 1987: Corning Glass Works wins a patent suit against Sumitomo over the design of optical fibers.
- 1988: Fujitsu agrees to pay IBM over $1 billion over copyrights for mainframe operating systems but gains access to newer versions of this software.
- 1989: A five-year suit between NEC and Intel ends when a judge rules that microprocessors can be copyrighted (and Intel lost its claim because it neglected to print the copyright symbol) but that the functions of a chip can be duplicated without a violation.

The 1990s witnessed similar suits, and within the computer industry, the area of "look and feel" of computer interfaces in general and application program interfaces in particular dominated the first half of the 1990s. Actions were taken by Apple against Hewlett-Packard and Microsoft, by Xerox against Apple, by Lotus Development Corp. against Paperware Software International and Mosaic Software (Lotus won this case in June 1990), and by Lotus against Borland International. These cases will be discussed in a following section. It is clear that the once relatively dormant area of patent and copyright law has become energized as developments in the computer industry continue to accelerate. However, the new arena for litigation is obviously the Internet and World Wide Web as issues of protection for digital forms of information are emerging. The economic stakes are very high.

The Business Software Alliance's (BSA) Piracy Study reported that estimated worldwide software piracy in 2001 totaled $10.97 billion, a decline of 6.7% from 2000.[7] "Software piracy is measured in this study as the amount of business application software installed in 2001 without a license." The BSA uses the term piracy rate to mean the percentage of total sales represented by the piracy number. So that even though there was a decline in estimated dollar loss, the piracy rate rose from 37% in 2000 to 40% in 2001, worldwide. Apparently the worst offenders in terms of dollar losses were

Asia/Pacific (over \$4.7 billion), Western Europe (\$2.75 billion), North America (\$2.0 billion), Latin America (nearly \$1 billion), and Eastern Europe (a little less than 0.5 billion). However, the piracy rate is almost the inverse of this list, namely, Eastern Europe (67%), Latin America (57%), Asia/Pacific (54%), Middle East and Africa (52%), Western Europe (37%), and North America (26%). Some general comments on trends are given as follows[8]:

- The results from the annual BSA Global Piracy Study for 2001 indicate that software piracy continued to pose challenges for the software industry. For the first time in the study's history, the world piracy rate increased in two consecutive years, 2000 and 2001. The 2001 piracy rate of 40% is a marked increase from 37% in 2000. Both years were up from the low set in 1999 at 36%.
- Since the study began in 1994, we have seen a steady decrease in the rate of software piracy. Unfortunately, this downward trend in piracy rates has not been evident in the past two years. In 2000, we started to notice stability in the level of piracy for developed countries, rather than the downward trend we expected. We speculated that after the reduction of casual piracy, we were seeing a core level of piracy that would be more persistent. In 2001, we saw the effects of a worldwide economic slowdown that hit technology spending particularly hard. The results of this year's study indicate that software piracy rose in response to the pressure of the curtailed spending of the economic downturn.

This introduction will be followed by a brief overview of the development of intellectual property law, and more specifically the special issues that have arisen with respect to digital information and the response of governments locally and internationally. Finally, examples of cases and problems will be reviewed for both music and videos, and software piracy.

HISTORY, DEFINITIONS, AND INTELLECTUAL PROPERTY LAWS

All of the people that create music rely on a fair reward for their creativity, their time and their hard work to keep doing what they do. In the case of those involved in creating commercially produced music, their fair reward depends on people buying rather than stealing music—the latest form of which involves mass copying and transmission of music over the internet without the permission of those who created it.[9]

The story of copyright is not very old, actually just less than 300 years. Until printing was well-established as the dominant means to produce copies of created works, few claims could be made for ownership and associated rights. The following is a brief version of this early history[10]:

> The history of American copyright law originated with the introduction of the printing press to England in the late fifteenth century. As the number of presses grew, authorities sought to control the publication of books by granting printers a near monopoly on publishing in England. The Licensing Act of 1662 confirmed that monopoly and established a register of licensed books to be administered by the Stationers' Company, a group of printers with the authority to censor publications. The 1662 act lapsed in 1695 leading to a relaxation of government censorship, and in 1710 Parliament enacted the Statute of Anne to address the concerns of English booksellers and printers. The 1710 act established the principles of authors' ownership of copyright and a fixed term of protection of copyrighted works (fourteen years, and renewable for fourteen more if the author was alive upon expiration). The statute prevented a monopoly on the part of the booksellers and created a "public domain" for literature by limiting terms of copyright and by ensuring that once a work was purchased the copyright owner no longer had control over its use. While the statute did provide for an author's copyright, the benefit was minimal because in order to be paid for a work an author had to assign it to a bookseller or publisher.

Thus certain author's rights were established, but over the years a host of issues arose, including the removal of printers from IP consideration and their replacement by publishers; the gradual increase in the length of the copyright enforcement period both during and after the life of the creator; the effect of new technologies on coverage and enforcement; the growing power of the media; and most recently, the creation of digital media and the Internet. The reproducibility of digital media and relative ease of transmission have permitted the crisis described above to develop.

The U.S. Constitution recognized the rights and obligations of authors and inventors and shortly after its creation, Congress passed the Copyright Act of 1790 to implement these rights in legislation. This Act was based on the British Statute of Anne. Other legislation followed over the years in response to new issues and new technologies. Some hundred years later, it was becoming clear that IP was an international issue, not just a national one, and that these rights required international agreements for realistic protection. Thus, the Berne Convention for the Protection of Literary and Artistic Works was passed in 1886 and "abolished the requirement to register foreign works and introduced an exclusive right to import or produce translations."[11] While the United Kingdom ratified the Berne Convention in 1887, the U.S. did not sign until 1988. It is interesting that a byproduct for the U.S. of signing the Berne Convention was that it was no longer necessary to include the copyright notice on a work in order to receive copyright protection.

In 1976, a major revision of the U.S. Copyright Act took place, motivated by the following concerns[12]:

> • First, technological developments and their impact on what might be copyrighted, how works might be copied, and what constituted an infringement needed to be addressed.
> • Second, the revision was undertaken in anticipation of Berne Convention adherence by the U.S. It was felt that the statute needed to be amended to bring the U.S. into accord with international copyright law, practices, and policies.
> • The 1976 act preempted all previous copyright law and extended the term of protection to life of the author plus 50 years (works for hire were protected for 75 years).
> • The act covered the following areas: scope and subject matter of works covered, exclusive rights, copyright term, copyright notice and copyright registration, copyright infringement, fair use and defenses and remedies to infringement.
> • With this revision, for the first time the fair use and first sale doctrines were codified, and copyright was extended to unpublished works. In addition, a new section was added, section 108, that allowed library photocopying without permission for purposes of scholarship, preservation, and interlibrary loan under certain circumstances.

An additional comment about "fair use" may be useful. Authors frequently quote other authors to support their arguments, to provide a contrary opinion, to introduce a novel or interesting idea, or for many other reasons. For the first time, an attempt was made to characterize how much could be quoted without infringing on the rights of the copyright holder. Even so, there remains considerable leeway in the following characterization of fair use[13]:

> In determining whether the use made of a work in any particular case is a fair use the factors to be considered shall include—
> 1. The purpose and character of the use, including whether such use is of a commercial nature or is for nonprofit educational purposes
> 2. The nature of the copyrighted work
> 3. The amount and substantiality of the portion used in relation to the copyrighted work as a whole
> 4. The effect of the use upon the potential market for or value of the copyrighted work.

For the present purposes, the most important piece of IP legislation is the Digital Millenium Copyright Act of 1998 (DMCA). The DMCA is divided into five titles[14]:

> • Title I, the "WIPO Copyright and Performances and Phonograms Treaties Implementation Act of 1998," implements the WIPO treaties.

- Title II, the "Online Copyright Infringement Liability Limitation Act," creates limitations on the liability of online service providers for copyright infringement when engaging in certain types of activities.
- Title III, the "Computer Maintenance Competition Assurance Act," creates an exemption for making a copy of a computer program by activating a computer for purposes of maintenance or repair.
- Title IV contains six miscellaneous provisions, relating to the functions of the Copyright Office, distance education, the exceptions in the Copyright Act for libraries and for making ephemeral recordings, "webcasting" of sound recordings on the Internet, and the applicability of collective bargaining agreement obligations in the case of transfers of rights in motion pictures.
- Title V, the "Vessel Hull Design Protection Act," creates a new form of protection for the design of vessel hulls.

Under Title I, section 120 has been the most controversial since the DMCA Act took effect. It prohibits attempts to circumvent existing technological measures implemented to protect access for purposes of copying. The actual law is far more complicated than this brief description. Later in this chapter, we will describe in more detail how controversial this section has become. It should be noted that a tension exists between the claim of the owner to exercise fair use rights and the need to prevent unauthorized copying. The major forms of providing IP protection to authors, inventors, and others will be described next.

Patents

Obtaining a patent is a long and involved process, but it does confer considerable advantages—a monopoly on use, as well as considerable tax benefits. Are computer programs patentable? The relevant portion of the U.S. Code, section 101, states: "Whoever invents or discovers any new and useful process, machine, manufacture, or composition of matter, or any new and useful improvement thereof, may obtain a patent therefore, subject to the conditions and requirements of this title."[15] Thus, a program would have to be considered a programmable process or a programmed machine. The statute further confers "the right to exclude others from making, using, or selling" the invention. As the U.S. Patent and Trademark Office comments, "What is granted is not the right to make, use, or sell, but the right to exclude others from making, using, or selling the invention."[16] The history of attempts to patent programs is rife with controversy, confusion, and a basic inability to define the nature of a relatively new technology.

Companies and individuals wishing to patent their software are confronted by a tangled situation. The Patent Office has consistently rejected most patent applications. The Court of Customs and Patent Appeals has generally supported attempts to patent software. The Supreme Court has usually overturned decisions by the Court of Customs and Patent Appeals and has not clarified the question of the patentability of software. And finally, Congress has so far not passed necessary and appropriate legislation. In 1968, the Patent Office made an official statement: "Computer programs per se ... shall not be patentable."[17] In the following year, the Court of Customs and Patent Appeals, in hearing a patent appeal, set aside this opinion.[18] Since then a series of cases have proceeded to the Supreme Court, which consistently rejected patent claims until the case of Diamond v. Diehr in 1981. In this case, Diehr applied for a patent for a process for molding raw uncured synthetic rubber into cured products. This process involved measuring temperatures, using a computer to determine cure times, and opening a press accordingly. The Patent Office rejected the claim, and the Court of Customs and Patent Appeals reversed the rejection, arguing that the mathematical formula was embodied in a useful process. The Supreme Court upheld this opinion in a five-to-four decision. Three basic points of law emerged from the Court's opinion.[19] First, the mere inclusion of a mathematical formula, or programmed computer, does not invalidate a claim. Second, in this claim it was stated, "the respondents [did] not seek to patent a mathematical formula." Third, the claims sought "only to foreclose from others, the use of that equation in conjunction with the other steps in their claimed process." Before the Diehr decision, out of about 100,000 patent applications filed each year only about 450 were for program patents. However, patent applications for software increased considerably in the 1980s.[20]

The battle to obtain software patents continued, with many applications first rejected, then appealed, then accepted, then rejected yet again. Given that the basic objection to software patents is that because programs are very close to mathematical formulae and these are not patentable, neither are programs, creative applications have argued for software embedded in a machine, device, or process. This strategy has worked in that 4,569 software-related patents were granted in 1994 in such areas as networking (623), operating systems (558), graphical user interfaces (223), and databases (173).[21] However, many complaints about the process, heightened by the events associated with the 1994 case *In re Alappat*, involving a series of disallowals, approvals, and appeals,[22] resulted in the U.S. Patent and Trademark Office (PTO), issuing new "Examination Guidelines for Computer-Related Inventions."[23] The crucial issues resulting in a change of approach by the PTO are given as follows[24]:

> A patent may be granted for a claim directed to software technology if the claim, as a whole, is directed to a machine that carries out a function that the patent laws were designed to protect. Decisions issued after Alappat suggest that patent protection of software technology may be extended to "electronic structures" and to machines having a memory device containing a specified data type. Consistent with these recent cases, Patent

Examination Guidelines proposed by the Patent Office appear to permit the issuance of patents claiming a computer program stored in a storage medium, such as a floppy disk. An "electronic structure" represents patentable subject matter.

There are a number of advantages and disadvantages to the patent process with respect to software protection. Patent protection is broad and long-term (17 years). Independent development is no defense against an infringement charge. However, there are some serious disadvantages. Obtaining a patent is a long and costly process. Protecting a patent may also be quite costly. One important concern about patent applications is whether or not the entire program must be included to meet disclosure requirements. The simple answer is that flow charts or block diagrams, sufficiently detailed and complete, will suffice, but in the new guidelines mentioned above, the emphasis on utility requires that the office personnel should[24a]

- Determine what the programmed computer does when it performs the processes dictated by the software (i.e., the functionality of the programmed computer)
- Determine how the computer is to be configured to provide that functionality (i.e., what elements constitute the programmed computer and how those elements are configured and interrelated to provide the specified functionality); and
- If applicable, determine the relationship of the programmed computer to other subject matter outside the computer that constitutes the invention (e.g., machines, devices, materials, or process steps other than those that are part of or performed by the programmed computer).

Copyright

A new Copyright Act was enacted in 1976 and became effective in 1978. The new law was not meant to apply to computer software issues until a report was issued by the National Commission on New Technological Uses of Copyrighted Works (CONTU). On the basis of CONTU's recommendations, the Computer Software Copyright Act of 1980 was enacted. It contained the following definition[25]:

A "computer program" is a set of statements or instructions to be used directly or indirectly in order to bring about a certain result.

(The noted author John Hersey, a member of CONTU, objected strenuously to the recommendation to provide copyright protection to programs. He argued that a program is not a "writing" in the Constitutional sense.) Permission was granted to an individual user to make copies or changes in a copyrighted program, for backup purposes. In Section 102(a) of the Copyright Act the definition of what can be copyrighted is as follows:

> Copyright protection subsists . . . in original works of authorship fixed in any tangible medium of expression, now known or later developed, from which they can be perceived, reproduced, or otherwise communicated, either directly or with the aid of a machine or device.

A number of cases since 1978 have clarified some of the issues of copyright protection. Its advantages are (a) it is easy to obtain—inexpensive and quick; (b) it is appropriate for works which have wide circulation; (c) it endures during the author's lifetime plus 50 years; and (d) preliminary injunctions may possibly be much more easily obtainable than for possible patent violations. Nevertheless, there are some serious drawbacks. There are still some open questions about what is actually covered. For example, are object programs embodied in ROMs? What about the source program on tape? The scope of protection may be uncertain. For example, can one reproduce copyrighted subject matter in order to develop an object that cannot be copyrighted? Since software is widely proliferated, it will be difficult to enforce copyrights. Can the masks used to produce integrated circuits be copyrighted?

This last question can be answered: yes. In 1984, Congress passed the Semiconductor Chip Protection Act to protect the technology embodied in chips and the associated masks. Congress was concerned that chips and masks, representing one of the major achievements of American ingenuity, were vulnerable to copying and decided to explicitly create a new form of intellectual property protection to help stimulate continued investment in new chip design. While the copying of chips is prohibited, the reverse engineering of masks is permitted. Both chips and mask works are defined and the requirements for protection of masks delineated.[26]

Proving that infringement has occurred, under the Computer Software Copyright Act, may be extremely difficult. It is necessary to demonstrate that copying has taken place and that this constitutes an improper appropriation. The Act does permit a user to copy a program for private use. Improper use must be determined by a lay person, not a technical expert. The most critical issue arises from a statement issued by the Supreme Court in 1954: "Protection is given only to the expression of an idea—not the idea itself." Several important cases will be considered to illustrate the nature of the issues associated with software copyright cases.

Trade Secrets

The most favored method of protection, at least up to fairly recently before the surge in copyright cases, has been under trade secret laws. As there is no federal trade secrecy legislation, the relevant laws have been established, not in a uniform manner, in the individual states. One definition of a trade secret is "any formula, pattern, device or compilation of information which is used in one's business and which gives him an opportunity to obtain an advantage over competitors who do not know how to use it."[27] Three conditions are necessary to legally protect a trade secret: novelty, secrecy, and value in business. Trade secret law appears to cover computer programs as "processes comprising inventions, with documentation protectable as ancillary 'know-how'."[28] Databases and documentation could also receive protection as information of value. An attempt has been made to establish uniform laws on trade secrecy—the "Uniform Trade Secrets Acts" were drawn up in 1979, approved by the American Bar Association in 1980, and adopted by Minnesota and Arkansas in 1981.

The main advantages of trade secrecy laws are that preliminary injunctions are readily obtained, the applicability over a wide range of subjects is relatively clear, protection applies to both ideas and expressions, the waiting period is brief, and the application remains in force for a long period, even one of perpetual duration. Among the disadvantages are the lack of uniformity across the United States, the stress on secrecy as a bar to progress, the lack of protection against independent development, the difficulty in maintaining long-term secrecy—especially for widely proliferated software—and possible preemption by the Copyright Act.

Other Methods

To protect software, an employer may make a contract with the relevant employees as part of the terms of employment, which may include such stipulations as no unauthorized copies and no public discussion of programs under development. Whatever the specific terms of a contract, an employee is expected to respect confidentiality. Associated with the sales or licensing of software, there may also be contractual arrangements controlling disclosure. In such a rapidly evolving industry, employees tend to move readily among companies. Contractual arrangements are a reasonable way to maintain software protection, but the restrictions must not be too severe or they will not be upheld by the courts.

Finally, to protect secrecy it is certainly advisable to improve the effectiveness of security procedures. Also, technology may be employed to increase the difficulty of making unauthorized use of programs. The copying of disks may be made quite difficult by special built-in protection. For example, the software may be restricted to run only on certain machines. Additional methods of foiling would-be violators have been and could be devised.

INTELLECTUAL PROPERTY CASES FOR COMPUTERS AND SOFTWARE

Important Copyright Cases

Whelan Associates, Inc. v. Jaslow Dental Laboratories

This is the first of two cases relevant to the impassioned debate on the "look and feel of computer user interfaces." Although not really a user interface case at all, Whelan is important because of the scope of its judicial decision. Jaslow hired Whelan to write a program to computerize Jaslow's office procedures, with a view to marketing it to other labs. Jaslow would pay development costs, Whelan would own the rights, and Jaslow would get a royalty on sales. Jaslow aided in the design, even to tailoring the interface to his own methods. The program, Dentalab, written in an obsolete language to run on an IBM mainframe, was delivered in 1979. A few years later, Jaslow wrote his own version of the program called Dentacom, in BASIC, to run on PCs, without studying Whelan's code. When he began marketing his PC program, Whelan sued for copyright infringement.[29]

Although Whelan seemed to be concerned only that Jaslow had copied the underlying structure of her program, the similarity in interfaces became an important issue. In 1985, the court found for Whelan on all issues. With respect to copyright infringement, the court found that "the Dentacom system [Jaslow's program], although written in another computer language from the Dentalab, and although not a direct transliteration of Dentalab, was substantially similar to Dentalab because its structure and overall organization were substantially similar."[30] The decision was appealed and Whelan's victory upheld but the appellate court decision introduced a measure of confusion in that it ruled that screen displays that were similar were indications that the programs were also similar. The results of this case were evaluated by Pamela Samuelson, a professor of law, as follows[31]:

> The structure of the program was expression [of the idea] because it wasn't part of the general purpose or function of the program and because there were other ways for Jaslow [the defendant] to have structured such a program besides the way that Whelan had structured hers, so it was an infringement for Jaslow to have used a similar structure to Whelan's.

Broderbund Software v. Unison World

In another important case settled just a few months after Whelan, in 1986, Broderbund Software prevailed over Unison World in a decision that established that " 'the overall structure, sequencing and arrangement of screens' in the user interface of a program are protected by copyright, or—broader yet—that a test of the 'look and feel' to an ordinary observer is applicable to software cases generally."[32] This raises the question, however, of what is required of a user interface that it be capable of existing independently of the working parts of a program. Answers are slowly being proposed in current cases, of which the most stunning decision is that in Lotus Development Corp. v. Paperback Software International and Mosaic Software.

Lotus Development Corp. v. Paperback Software International and Mosaic Software

This case was brought in February 1987 by Lotus, the very successful developer of the leading spreadsheet for IBM PCs and compatibles, Lotus 1-2-3. Paperback and Mosaic also produce spreadsheets but their software sells for $99 each compared to Lotus at $495. Lotus charged that the two companies had copied its screen format, a grid-like image, as well as its keystroke sequences, or macros. In his ruling in favor of Lotus, on June 28, 1990, federal judge Keeton stated, "I conclude that a menu command structure is capable of being expressed in many if not an unlimited number of ways, and that the command structure of 1-2-3 is an original and non-obvious way of expressing a command structure."[33] The immediate implication of this verdict is that once a program becomes a *de facto* industry standard, it will be extremely difficult for new products to challenge its dominance, if they are unable to employ a compatible interface. In the middle of October 1990, Paperback Software announced that it would "stop marketing its VP Planner product line by December 1 and pay Lotus Development Corp. $500,000 for violating its 1-2-3 spreadsheet copyrights. . . . [Paperback] also agreed not to appeal a June federal court ruling."[34] Following up on its courtroom success, Lotus launched a suit against Borland International, the maker of the spreadsheet Quattro Pro, also selling for $99; however, the issue was that Quattro had as an option the 1-2-3 menus and commands as an alternative to its own interface. The eventual result of this case would be to end the "look-and-feel" debate, but not in the way that Lotus had anticipated. Before describing the outcome of this case, it may be helpful to explore the implications of the debate itself

The Interface Debate

Considerable debate had erupted within the industry and elsewhere about the merits of copyright protection of interfaces, as once guaranteed by the courts. Simply put, those supporting copyright protection argue that the original designers must have their work protected in order to earn a reasonable return on their investment, to encourage the design of new and innovative systems, and to attract and keep bright designers. Those in opposition might argue that copyright protection impedes innovation by freezing designs which may not be optimal, unfairly rewards those who happen to be first but not best, and discourages the free exchange of ideas for the benefit of all. Pamela Samuelson's response to the Lotus decision was expressed in a characteristically blunt fashion[35]:

> I am a lawyer. I interpret cases for a living. I have read Judge Keeton's opinion carefully and I have worked very hard to figure out what it means. I would tell you what it means if I could understand it, but I cannot. And neither can anyone else. So anyone who says he or she is sure the Lotus decision is a very narrow one and only makes copying the whole of someone else's interface illegal is giving his opinion and making a prediction

A considerably more radical position was taken by a founder of The League for Programming Freedom, Richard Stallman, a renowned MIT programmer and recipient of a MacArthur Foundation fellowship.[36] Stallman argued that software should not be copyrighted but should be freely available to everyone. This is based on the notion of a community of programmers, all of whose tools and products are shared resources. One fear of copyright can be seen by drawing an analogy with typewriters. If the typewriter interface, i.e., the specific keyboard layout, could be copyrighted, each manufacturer would be required to produce a different layout. For computers, interface copyright will inevitably lead to greater incompatibility.

Apple Computer, Inc. v. Microsoft Corp. and Hewlett-Packard Co.

A preliminary decision in Apple Computer's suit against Microsoft and Hewlett-Packard for copyright infringement of its interface was won by Apple in March of 1991, much to the displeasure of Stallman. However, Apple ultimately lost its suit in 1994 and ironically the seeds of this loss were sown in 1985, when an agreement between Apple and Microsoft ended an earlier Apple suit over Windows 1.0. Apple "granted Microsoft a license to use the visual displays in Windows 1.0 in future programs. Microsoft, in turn, granted Apple a license to use any new visual displays created by Microsoft. The programs in suit are based on a desktop metaphor with windows, icons, and pull-down menus that can be manipulated on the screen with a device called a mouse."[37] Thus Judge Rymer, of the Court of Appeals for the Ninth Circuit, ruling against Apple, said, "to the extent that later versions of Windows and HP's NewWave programs use the visual displays in Windows 1.0 (which came from Apple), that such use is authorized . . . and cannot infringe."[38] Despite strenuous objections, Apple's arguments were dismissed. Indeed, Judge Rymer claimed that Apple's basic ideas, "the graphical user interface in a desktop metaphor, use of windows to display multiple images and facilitate user interaction, iconic representation of familiar objects from an office environment, manipulation of icons to convey instructions and control operations, use of menus to store information or computer functions, and opening and closing of objects to retrieve or transfer data," are not protectable. Of course, Apple appealed to the Supreme Court and in February 1995, the Court refused to overturn the Court of Appeals decision. Thus a serious blow was dealt to protection in the "look-and-feel" debate.

Lotus Development Corp. v. Borland International, Inc.

Lotus first filed suit in 1990 against Borland, charging that Quattro Pro infringed on its copyright, and won in a federal court some three years later. Borland appealed and the case was heard in the U.S. Court of Appeals for the First Circuit in October 1994; the ruling came down on March 9, 1995, overturning the lower-court decision. The Appeals Court's decision reversed the district court,[39]

> holding that the menu command hierarchy was a "method of operation" that is excluded from copyright protection under 17 U.S.C. § 102(b), because "[t]he Lotus holding that the menu command hierarchy was a "method of operation" that is menu command hierarchy provides the means by which users control and operate Lotus 1-2-3." . . . The court defined "'method of operation,' as that term is used in § 102(b) [as] the means by which a person operates something, whether it be a car, a food processor, or a computer." ... Even to the extent that the menu command hierarchy included expression, the court denied that expression any copyright protection: "Accepting the district court's finding that the Lotus developers made some expressive choices in choosing and arranging the Lotus command terms, we nonetheless hold that expression is not copyrightable because it is part of Lotus 1-2-3's 'method of operation.'"

The court used an analogy based on VCRs (video cassette recorders) to explain its reasoning "in finding that the Lotus 1-2-3 command menu hierarchy was a 'method of operation'" by likening it "to the buttons on a VCR." The buttons on the VCR are themselves the "method of operation" of the VCR—their arrangement and labeling does not make them a "literary work" "nor does it make them an 'expression' of the abstract 'method of operating' a VCR. . . . Lotus 1-2-3 depends for its operation on use of precise command terms that make up the Lotus menu command hierarchy. . . the arrangement of buttons on a VCR would not be copyrightable because the buttons are an uncopyrightable 'method of operation.' Similarly, the 'buttons' of a computer program are also an uncopyrightable method of operation."[40]

Lotus appealed to the Supreme Court, which heard the case on January 8, 1996, and issued the following opinion on January 16:

> The judgment of the United States Court of Appeals for the First Circuit is affirmed by an equally divided Court.

In other words, Lotus lost because the Supreme Court in a 4–4 tied vote (Justice Stevens took no part in the decision) let the decision of the First Circuit stand. Lotus petitioned for a rehearing and this was denied on March 4, 1996. The lack of an opinion by the Supreme Court leaves many issues undecided, but for the present there is no look-and-feel basis for attempting to copyright user interfaces.

INTELLECTUAL PROPERTY CASES AND EVENTS FOR INTERNET MUSIC AND VIDEOS

> Make no mistake: the implications of the peer-to-peer file-sharing movement that Napster pioneered go way beyond pop music. There are already Napster-like services for videos and full-length feature films. Books, blueprints, vintage comics and stock photos may be next in line. Even newspapers and magazines are worried.[40a]

Intellectual Property Rights Protection

Given that the preceding section has dealt, in considerable detail, with copyright and patent issues, it should be interesting to continue the discussion in the context of the Internet. In September 1995, the U.S. federal government's Information Infrastructure Task Force released a lengthy report, a White Paper (incorporating detailed government proposals); the following selection is taken from the introduction[41]:

> This Report represents the Working Group's examination and analysis of each of the major areas of intellectual property law, focusing primarily on copyright law and its application and effectiveness in the context of the NII [National Information Infrastructure]. The approach of this Report is to discuss the application of the existing copyright law and to recommend only those changes that are essential to adapt the law to the needs of the global information society. By providing a generalized legal framework, based on the extensive analysis and discussion of the way in which the law has been and should be interpreted, we can lay the groundwork for the rapid and efficient development of the NII.

The report states that only a few minor changes in current copyright legislation will be necessary to provide for the new medium of the Internet, but these "minor changes" have aroused considerable criticism. It should be noted that the report contained a legislative proposal, the NII Copyright Protection Act of 1996, "to amend Title 17 to adapt the copyright law," that in fact was introduced into both the House and Senate. To its defenders, including film studios, and book and magazine publishers, the proposals are indeed minor and just clean up a few loose ends to ensure that copyright holders receive full value over the new media where it is so easy to download, store, and retransmit information. Perhaps the most vocal critic first of the White Paper and then of the legislation is Pamela Samuelson, a professor at the University of California at Berkeley, with a joint appointment in Law and the School of Information Management and Systems. She wrote a highly critical article in *Wired* that attacked the proposed legislation in a vigorous and impassioned manner. For example, here is her interpretation of what she labels as the White Paper's "maximalist agenda," namely, the attempt to control all aspects of a copyrighted work's transmission and use in order to obtain as much financial return as possible.[42]

In her view, the proposed legislation would

- Give copyright owners control over every use of copyrighted works in digital form by interpreting existing law as being violated whenever users make even temporary reproductions of works in the random access memory of their computers
- Give copyright owners control over every transmission of works in digital form by amending the copyright statute so that digital transmissions will be regarded as distributions of copies to the public
- Eliminate "fair use" rights whenever a use might be licensed (The copyright maximalists assert that there is no piece of a copyrighted work small enough that they are uninterested in charging for its use, and no use private enough that they aren't willing to track it down and charge for it. In this vision of the future, a user who has copied even a paragraph from an electronic journal to share with a friend will be as much a criminal as the person who tampers with an electrical meter at a friend's house in order to siphon off free electricity. If a few users have to go to jail for copyright offenses, well, that's a small price to pay to ensure that the population learns new patterns of behavior in the digital age)
- Deprive the public of the "first sale" rights it has long enjoyed in the print world (the rights that permit you to redistribute your own copy of a work after the publisher's first sale of it to you), because the white paper treats electronic forwarding as a violation of both the reproduction and distribution rights of copyright law
- Attach copyright management information to digital copies of a work, ensuring that publishers can track every use made of digital copies and trace where each copy resides on the network and what is being done with it at any time
- Protect every digital copy of every work technologically (by encryption, for example) and make illegal any attempt to circumvent that protection
- Force online service providers to become copyright police . . . responsible not only for cutting off service to scofflaws but also for reporting copyright crime to the criminal justice authorities
- Teach the new copyright rules of the road to children throughout their years at school.

Of course, there are defenders, especially publishers, who formed the Creative Incentive Coalition (CIC) to promote acceptance of the new copyright legislation. Among the members of CIC are publishers, television stations, motion picture producers, software producers, computer companies (including IBM and Microsoft), McGraw-Hill, Time Warner, and Turner Broadcasting.[43] Their claim is that minor changes in existing copyright law are necessary to protect creators, but since CIC's members are corporations, it is clear who they are concerned about. The issue of who is responsible for content is a recurring theme for many Internet legal issues. For the typical online user, the potential threat that every byte viewed or downloaded will have to be paid for, is a vision of the future definitely not worth the wait.

Napster and Friends

It is very likely the case that most readers of this book know far more about the topic of downloading music files than does the author; nevertheless, a brief history and overview of some of the issues will be presented. The development of efficient compression techniques for digital files made possible the sequence of events that has aroused such passion in the online community. That compact disk-(CD) quality music could be quickly downloaded, especially over high-speed connections, stimulated the unexpected development and distribution of very effective programs to locate and download music and other files. The format of choice for music is the by now familiar MP3 format, Motion Picture Experts Group, Audio Layer 3. This format produces a file one-tenth the size of CD music files with equivalent sound quality.

May 1999 is a noteworthy month in the history of the Internet for it is during this month that Napster, the music sharing program, made its appearance and grew in use in an extraordinary fashion. The developers are Shawn Fanning and Sean Parker, then 19 and 20 respectively, and students at Northeastern University.

People have been able to share music files for a long time but it was the genius of Fanning and Parker to provide a central resource for searching for distributed files. So to find a particular song, one would enter the title into Napster's search engine and a list of computers around the world, on the Internet, running the software that has the desired song is returned. It is up to you to select the computer from which you wish to download the song, presumably based on speed of connection. Furthermore, other computers that have songs that seem to match your interests can be located. In short order, large collections of copyrighted music can be acquired for little cost except for an Internet connection. Selections of songs can then be downloaded, or burned, onto CDs, reflecting individual tastes and preferences. In response to questions and charges about acquiring music in this way, most people have ignored copyright issues and claimed a natural right. Roughly a year after its introduction, Napster claimed about 20 million registered users, which grew to almost 60 million by early 2001.

Almost as soon as it became popular, Napster aroused the interest of the Recording Industry Association of America (RIAA). The following timeline highlights some of the major events in Napster's brief but exciting life[44]:

- **December 7, 1999:** The RIAA, on behalf of the record labels it represents, sues Napster in the U.S. District Court in San Francisco on grounds of copyright infringement.
- **May 5, 2000:** In federal court in San Francisco, Judge Patel rules that Napster is in violation of the Digital Millennium Copyright Act of 1998. . . making it illegal to disseminate products or devices that enable people to hack through technologies that are used to keep digitized film, music and books from being freely copied and distributed over the Internet.
- **July 26, 2000:** Patel grants the RIAA's request for a preliminary injunction and orders Napster to shut down. Patel said it seemed clear that Napster users were not simply engaging in swapping their personal favorite songs, and the song-swapping service was encouraging "wholesale infringing" against the music industry.
- **February 12, 2001:** The 9th Circuit Court of Appeals rules that Napster users are illegally copying and distributing copyrighted commercial songs. It orders Napster to stop its users from trading and distributing copyrighted material. However, the ruling allows Napster to continue operating until Patel's injunction is modified to comply with the appeal court's decision.
- **March 2, 2001:** Judge Patel issues an injunction, placing the burden of providing the exact file names of the copyrighted material on the record companies. For each song the record companies want removed from Napster, they are required to detail the name of the artist and the name of the work, one or more file names of the work, and proof of ownership of the song
- **March 5, 2001:** Napster voluntarily begins to block access to copyrighted songs on its system. Napster begins with the albums and songs on the *Billboard 200* album and the *Billboard Hot 100* singles charts.
- **March 27, 2001:** The RIAA files a brief with the U.S. District Court claiming Napster has not complied with the injunction set forth by Patel to remove copyrighted material from its service.
- **June 22, 2001:** The 9th Circuit Court of Appeals upholds its ruling that Napster contributes to copyright infringement and must remove copyrighted material from its service. The ruling leaves the U.S. Supreme Court as the only legal venue left for Napster to argue its case.
- **September 3, 2002:** Judge Peter J. Walsh blocks the sale of Napster to Bertelsmann [one of the world's largest publishers]. The ruling effectively douses Napster's hopes of reviving its song-swapping service. The majority of the staff is let go—including co-founder Shawn Fanning—and plans for a Chapter 7 bankruptcy liquidation of the company's assets begins.

And then there were Aimster, Audiogalaxy, Freenet, Gnutella, Grokster, Kazaa, Morpheus, Scour, Streamcast, and others. Napster may have led the way but a host of systems followed. As Napster rose and fell, other programs, performing similar and new functions, were created and released. The most successful has been Kazaa, in existence since late 2000. In May 2003, it was announced that Kazaa was on the verge of becoming the most popular free program on the Web, with over 230 million downloads. Kazaa, or Kazaa Media Desktop (KMD), is based on peer-to-peer (P2P) technology and differs from Napster in that there is no central server necessary. The software automatically seeks out other KMD users and makes the necessary connection, permitting the transfer of files of widely varying content. One feature of Kazaa that makes it efficient is that for each user it keeps track of "supernodes" nearby with high speed connections, so that the nearest supernodes are searched first.[45]

Not surprisingly, Kazaa has been sued by RIAA and in January 2003, Kazaa, or its owner Sharman Networks, sued major record labels and Hollywood studios, claiming that, "major entertainment companies have colluded to drive potential online rivals out of business. The conduct should preclude the industry from being able to defend its copyrights in court, at least until the behavior is corrected."[46] Suits, countersuits, bankruptcies, loss of CD sales, and rampant lawlessness have characterized the past few years as the record industry has been slow in adapting to the new technologies. Free downloading is a habit difficult to curtail and the search for viable online business models for this industry goes on.

In April 2003, a surprising decision was delivered in a suit against Grokster and Streamcast, the parent company of Morpheus[47]:

> "Defendants distribute and support software, the users of which can and do choose to employ it for both lawful and unlawful ends," Wilson [federal judge Stephen Wilson in Los Angeles] wrote in his opinion, released Friday. "Grokster and StreamCast are not significantly different from companies that sell home video recorders or copy machines, both of which can be and are used to infringe copyrights."

Earlier, a similar decision in the Netherlands had been delivered in favor of Kazaa. Surely more decisions will follow as the courts around the world grapple with the problem of reconciling the massive worldwide downloading of copyrighted material with the legal rights of the copyright holders. Kazaa itself is a model of international cooperation. The original program was written by Jaan Tallinn, Ahti Heinla and Priit Kasesalu. "The three young men who developed the software hail from Estonia. They were commissioned to do the work by a company in the Netherlands. That company has since sold the software to another based in the Pacific island nation of Vanuatu, whose executives work in Australia."[48]

In an attempt to influence the behavior of U.S. college students, the RIAA sued four students on charges that they have,[49]

> According to the complaints . . . "taken a network created for higher learning and academic pursuits and converted it into an emporium of music piracy." In a news release, the recording industry alleges that the students were engaging in copyright infringement, each offering from 27,000 to more than a million songs to other students.

The dollar penalties are enormous: $150,000 per song title listed in the complaints, for a grand total of $97.8 million. Given that students at universities and colleges are a major segment of the music downloading population, such a massive assault is clearly meant to dissuade both students and the administrations of their colleges and universities to halt such activities. Whether this strategy will work is an open question, but many more suits have followed.

RECENT INTELLECTUAL PROPERTY CASES FOR COMPUTER SOFTWARE

> "It feels a bit like the tide is turning in these copyright cases," said Cindy Cohn, an attorney with the Electronic Frontier Foundation. "It really feels like there is some sanity creeping in." The EFF and others have been concerned that digital copyright law hampers legitimate research into encryption and other technological matters and stifles consumers' rights.[50]

It is not just music and movies that are problematic given the technologies available on the Internet. The software that has been designed to protect digital files against copying has itself been compromised on occasion and some of these cases have come to the attention of the courts. The root issue in the cases to be discussed is the application of the Digital Millennium Copyright Act (DMCA) in a number of interesting situations.

The Felten Case

Edward Felten, a professor at Princeton University, led a team of researchers that had broken a security code for digital music and was prepared to present the results at the International Information Hiding Workshop to be held during April 2001. He was threatened with legal action by the Secure Digital Music Initiative Foundation connected to the Recording Industry Association of America if he went ahead with his presentation. Professor Felten decided not to present his paper and criticized his opponents for using the courts to limit his free speech rights. Felten launched a suit in order to permit him and his colleagues to present their updated results at a forthcoming conference. Independently, the Electronic Frontier Foundation (EFF), a leading online civil liberties organization, initiated its own suit arguing on behalf of Felten's rights. This suit included a challenge to the constitutionality of the DMCA.

In November, the Felten suit was dismissed but his position seemed to be upheld, in part[51]:

> "Based on these and other statements from the government and the recording industry [that scientists attempting to study access control technologies are not subject to the DMCA] the judge dismissed our case," noted Princeton Professor Ed Felten. "Although we would have preferred an enforceable court ruling, our research team decided to take the government and industry at their word that they will never again threaten publishers of scientific research that exposes vulnerabilities in security systems for copyrighted works."

Thus case law was beginning to acknowledge that the practical exceptions in the DMCA to the injunction against attempts to break the safety encryption on digital files did have some force.

Dmitry Sklyarov and the ElcomSoft Case

Dmitry Sklyarov was a programmer for the Russian software company ElcomSoft. He was arrested in July 2001, while in the U.S. to present a talk at Defcon, a "hacker" convention, for the following reason[52]:

> From the federal government's point of view, it's merely enforcing a law enacted by Congress in October 1998 that punishes anyone who distributes "any technology, product, service, device, component or part" that, like Sklyarov's software, bypasses copy-protection mechanisms. Sklyarov is facing a five-year prison term and a fine of $500,000.

More precisely, what Sklyarov was doing is described as follows[53]:

> Dmitry helped create the Advanced eBook Processor (AEBPR) software for his Russian employer Elcomsoft. According to the company's website, the software permits eBook owners to translate from Adobe's secure eBook format into the more common Portable Document Format (PDF). The software only works on legitimately purchased eBooks. It has been used by blind people to read otherwise-inaccessible PDF user's manuals, and by people who want to move an eBook from one computer to another (just like anyone can move a music CD from the home player to a portable or car).

The DMCA was of course the 1998 law referred to above. The prosecution was an attempt to enforce this law, the use of which was being opposed by the online civil liberties community as well as many IP lawyers. Of great concern was the limitation on fair use, the argument being that one could modify one's purchase in order to make its use more convenient.

On December 17, 2002, "in a U.S. District Court in San Jose, Calif., a jury acquitted Elcomsoft of all criminal charges. (Sklyarov himself was not on trial because he had cut a deal to testify against his former employer, after quitting, in exchange for immunity.) Cyberlibertarians rejoiced, proclaiming that the decision would make it much harder to prosecute criminal cases under the DMCA."[54] This result was seen as an important victory against a strict interpretation of the DMCA, but more case law will be required if the DMCA use in this area is to be curtailed.

Jon Johansen and the DeCSS case

This case, a trial in Oslo, Norway, is concerned with the development and distribution of software to defeat the copy protection software in place on DVDs, Digital Video Disks. In more detail,[55]

- The movie industry has a protection system on DVDs called Content Scrambling System (CSS) which stops people from using DVD players that are not offically licenced. It also makes DVD region encoding possible.
- The programme gets rid of that protection, opening them for copying and playing.
- The Norwegian authorities claim Johansen put the software on the internet in October 1999, and that it was downloaded 5,000 times in just three months.
- In the US the DeCSS programme has been the subject of at least three lawsuits.

Mr. Johansen was a 15-year-old teenager when he wrote the DeCSS software; he faced charges which could result in a prison term of up to two years. The claim by Johansen is that he wrote the software to permit him to view his own copy-protected movies on his computer, running under the Linux operating system. The intent of the copy protection software was not to permit the viewing of movies on any other system but a DVD player. The decision in the trial came down on January 7, 2003, in a Norwegian court, as follows[56]:

On Tuesday a panel of judges ruled that Mr. Johansen did not violate Norway's laws when, in order to use a Linux computer to play a DVD he'd purchased, he broke protections on the disc. That ruling—coupled with a U.S. federal jury verdict that ElcomSoft didn't violate criminal copyright charges by selling cracking software—points to increased sophistication on the part of the legal system when dealing with such matters, activists say.

The thrust of this decision seems to be that ownership of a DVD permits the owner to view it in any manner he or she wishes, independent of the expectations or desires of the movie studios. However, Mr. Johansen's trials are not yet over as the Norwegian police appealed the acquittal on January 17.

A Different Point of View

Creative Commons

There has been a growing trend to extend the period of control of copyrighted material beyond the death of the creator as well as for the companies that have acquired control. The model of the creator, publisher, or production company reaping benefits for a limited period of time before the work enters the public domain, where it is available for free from that point on, seems to be ending. Digital technologies offer great benefits to owners of copyrighted material as well as buyers and users but, as seen above, they also offer more comprehensive control than previously available. Lawrence Lessig, a prominent Internet lawyer and Stanford law professor, has proposed, with others, a new vision for IP protection, called the Creative Commons. A brief description follows[57]:

> Creative Commons is a non-profit corporation founded on the notion that some people may not want to exercise all of the intellectual property rights the law affords them. We believe there is an unmet demand for an easy yet reliable way to tell the world "Some rights reserved" or even "No rights reserved." Many people have long since concluded that all-out copyright doesn't help them gain the exposure and widespread distribution they want. Many entrepreneurs and artists have come to prefer relying on innovative business models rather than full-fledged copyright to secure a return on their creative investment. Still others get fulfillment from contributing to and participating in an intellectual commons. For whatever reasons, it is clear that many citizens of the Internet want to share their work—and the power to reuse, modify, and distribute their work—with others on generous terms. Creative Commons intends to help people express this preference for sharing by offering the world a set of licenses on our Website, at no charge.

Free Software Movement

For many years, Richard Stallman, a one-time programmer at MIT, has been traveling around the world to gain support for his vision of the status of software. It is a vision that resonates with the development of software as a global cooperative project, in direct opposition to the business model best exemplified by Microsoft. Opposed to the commercialization of the Unix operating system in spite of the voluntary contributions of many programmers around the world, Stallman initiated the GNU Project about 20 years ago.[58]

The GNU Project was launched in 1984 to develop a complete Unix-like operating system which is free software: the GNU system. (GNU is a recursive acronym for "GNU's Not Unix"; it is pronounced "guh-NEW".) Variants of the GNU operating system, which use the kernel Linux, are now widely used; though these systems are often referred to as "Linux", they are more accurately called GNU/Linux systems.

As it has turned out, the efforts of Linus Torvald, the creator of Linux, have been more successful in the growth and distribution of the Linux operating system.

The final word on new models for software ownership goes to Richard Stallman, whose philosophy goes beyond operating systems, which he has enunciated in his notion of Free Software. Consider the following, brief description:[59]

"Free software" is a matter of liberty, not price. To understand the concept, you should think of "free" as in "free speech," not as in "free beer."

Free software is a matter of the users' freedom to run, copy, distribute, study, change and improve the software. More precisely, it refers to four kinds of freedom, for the users of the software:

- The freedom to run the program, for any purpose (freedom 0).
- The freedom to study how the program works, and adapt it to your needs (freedom 1). Access to the source code is a precondition for this.
- The freedom to redistribute copies so you can help your neighbor (freedom 2).
- The freedom to improve the program, and release your improvements to the public, so that the whole community benefits (freedom 3). Access to the source code is a precondition for this.

A program is free software if users have all of these freedoms. Thus, you should be free to redistribute copies, either with or without modifications, either gratis or charging a fee for distribution, to anyone anywhere. Being free to do these things means (among other things) that you do not have to ask or pay for permission.

You should also have the freedom to make modifications and use them privately in your own work or play, without even mentioning that they exist. If you do publish your changes, you should not be required to notify anyone in particular, or in any particular way.

SUMMARY

The development of software and computers must be protected against illegal copying to ensure that developers are properly rewarded for their work and to encourage others to enter the marketplace. Traditional means of protecting intellectual property are patents and copyrights. Patent protection for programs was first recognized in a 1981 Supreme Court decision but it has taken several years for the Patent Office to be receptive to software applications. First in 1980 and then in 1984, the Software Copyright Act extended copyright protection to computer programs. Also in 1984, Congress passed the Semiconductor Chip Protection Act to protect chips and the masks used to produce them. Of recent concern has been the attempt by some software and hardware companies to protect the "look-and-feel" of their user interfaces. In 1990, Lotus Development, the developer of the 1-2-3 spreadsheet program won an important suit to copyright its interface and command structure, but subsequently, this decision was overturned.

In 1998, a major piece of IP legislation was passed, the Digital Millennium Copyright Act. It has been described by its critics as a major blow against fair use and a limitation against the scientific study of existing encryption strategies. In a number of cases, suits have been launched against individuals for the supposed violations of these provisions, with limited success.

Clearly, the most significant and widespread recent IP issue is the uploading and trading of digital music and movie files. The names Napster and Kazaa have achieved worldwide fame as millions of people trade copyrighted material. In the U.S., the Recording Industry Association of America has recently taken aggressive steps to launch suits against individuals trading hundreds of thousands of songs online. New business models are being implemented to facilitate the purchase of music.

NOTES

1. "The Internet Goes to College," Pew Internet & American Life Project, September 15, 2002. Available at http://www.pewinternet.org/reports/pdf/PIP_College_Report.pdf
2. "The Music Downloading Deluge," Pew Internet & American Life Project, April 24, 2001. Available at http://www.pewinternet.org/reports/pdfs/PIP_More_Music_Report.pdf
3. "The National Record Buyers Survey II," Edison Media Research, (no date). Available at http://www.edisonresearch.com/MicrosoftWord-RecordBuyers2.pdf
4. "Global Sales of Recorded Music Down 7% in 2002," International Federation of the Phonographic Industry, April 9, 2003. Available at http://www.ifpi.org/
5. Michael C. Gemignani. Law and the Computer. (Boston: CBI, 1981), p. 84.
6. Paula Dwyer, et al. "The Battle Being Raged Over 'Intellectual Property'," Business Week, May 22, 1989, p. 89. Keith H. Hammond. "What Will Polaroid Do With All That Moolah?" Business Week, October 29, 1990, p. 38.
7. "Seventh Annual BSA Global Software Piracy Study," Business Software Alliance, June 2002. Available at http://bsa.org/usa/policyres/admin/2002-06-10.130.pdf
8. Ibid.

9. "Copyright Use and Security Guide for Academic Institutions," International Federation of the Recording Industry, March 25, 2003. Available at http://www.ifpi.org/site-content/library/academic-brochure-english.pdf

10. "Timeline: A History of Copyright in the United States," Association of Research Libraries, Washington, DC, November 22, 2002. Available at http://arl.cni.org/info/frn/copy/ytimeline.html

11. "A History of Copyright," UK Intellectual Property on the Internet, (no date). Available at http://www.intellectual-property.gov.uk/std/resources/copyright/history.htm

12. *Op. cit.*, "Timeline: A History of Copyright in the United States."

13. "Section 107—Limitations On Exclusive Rights: Fair Use," Legal Information Institute, U.S. Code Collection, (No date). Available at http://www4.law.cornell.edu/uscode/17/107.html

14. "The Digital Millennium Copyright Act of 1998," U.S. Copyright Office Summary, December 1998. Available at http://www.loc.gov/copyright/legislation/dmca.pdf

15. David Bender. *Computer Law: Evidence and Procedure* (New York: M. Bender, 1982), p. 4A-2.

16. "What is a Patent?" U.S. Patent and Trademark Office. Available at http://www.uspto.gov/web/patinfo/what_is_a_patent.html

17. As quoted in Gemignani, *Law and the Computer*, p. 102.

18. *Ibid.*

19. As quoted in Bender, *Computer Law*, pp. 4A-7–4A-8.

20. J. Michael Jukes and E. Robert Yoches. "Basic Principles of Patent Protection for Computer Software," *Communications of the ACM*, 32 (8), August 1989, pp. 922–924.

21. Mitch Betts. "Feds to Ease Software Patent Guidelines," *Computerworld*, April 17, 1995, p. 20.

22. Curtis L. Harrington. "Computer Program Patentability Update," (No date) Available at http://www.wweb.net/comart/curt/update.html

23. "Examination Guidelines for Computer-Related Inventions," U.S. Patent and Trademark Office, 1995. Available at http://www.uspto.gov/web/software/files/guides.doc

24. W. Scott Petty. "Yes Virginia, the U.S. Patent Office Grants Software Patents!" *Georgia Computer Law Section Newsletter*, Winter 1996. Available at http://www.kuesterlaw.com/comp4g.htm

24a. "Examination Guidelines for Computer-Related Inventions—Final Version," Patent and Trademark Office (no date). Available at http://www.uspto.gov/web/offices/com/hearings/software/analysis/files/guides.doc

25. *Op cit.*, Bender, p. 4A–31.

26. Frederick L. Cooper III. *Law and the Software Marketer* (Englewood Cliffs, NJ: Prentice-Hall, 1988), pp. 91–96.

27. Bender. *Computer Law*, p. 4A–78.

28. *Ibid.*, p. 4A–79.

29. Pamela Samuelson. "Why the Look and Feel of Software Interfaces Should Not Be Protected by Copyright Law," *Communications of the ACM*, 32 (5), May 1989, pp. 563–572.

30. Paul R. Lamoree. "Expanding Copyright in Software: The Struggle to Define 'Expression" Begins,' *Computer & High Technology Law Journal*, 4 (1), January 1988, p. 62.

31. *Op cit.*, Samuelson, p. 567.

32. *Op cit.*, Lamoree, p. 78.

33. As quoted in John Markoff, "Lotus Wins Copyright Decision," *The New York Times*, June 29, 1990, p. C 3.

34. Patricia Keefe. "Paperback Pulls Spreadsheet, Won't Appeal Lotus Victory," *Computerworld*, October 22, 1990, p. 7.

35. Pamela Samuelson. "How to Interpret the Lotus Decision (And How Not to)," *Communications of the ACM*, 33 (11), November 1990, p. 32.

36. Prepared by Richard Stallman and Simson Garfinkel for the League for Programming Freedom. "Against User Interface Copyright," *Communications of the ACM*, 33 (11), November 1990, pp. 15–18.

37. Neil Boorstyn. "An Analysis of Apple Computer, Inc. v. Microsoft Corp. and Hewlett-Packard Co., 35 F3d 1435 (1994, CA 9)," Reprint of article contained in *The Copyright Law Journal*. Available at the McCutchen on-line Web site http://www.mccutchen.com/IP/IP_2105.HTM

38. "Apple Computer, Inc. V. Microsoft Corp., 35F.3d1435 (9th Cir. 1994)." Available at http://www.home.earthlink.net/~mjohnsen/Technology/Lawsuits/appvsms.htm

39. Jesse M. Feder. "Lotus v. Borlund 3/9/95 1st Cir. Decision," Available at http://www.panix.com/~jesse/lotus.html

40. *Ibid.*, Id. at 26–27.

41. *Intellectual Property and the National Information Infrastructure*. The Report of the Working Group on Intellectual Property Rights, Information Infrastructure Task Force, Washington, DC: U.S. Patent and Trademark Office, September 1995. Available at www.uspto.gov

41a. Adam Cohen. "Napster the Revolution," CNN.com, September 25, 2000. Available at http://www.cnn.com/ALLPOLITICS/time/2000/10/02/revolution.html

42. Pamela Samuelson. "The Copyright Grab," *Wired*, 4.01, January 1996, p. 136. Available at http://www.hotwired.com/wired/whitepaper.html

43. "Coalition Supports Digital Update of Copyright Laws," Creative Incentive Coalition, 1996. Available at http://www.cic.org/hears.html

44. "A Napster Timeline," Grammy.com June 3, 2002. Available at http://www.grammys.com/features/0130_naptimeline.html

45. "Supernodes," Kazaa, (no date). Available at http://www.kazaa.com/us/help/glossary/supernodes.htm

46. John Borland. "Kazaa Strikes Back at Hollywood, Labels," Cnet.com, January 27, 2003. Available at http://news.com.com/2100-1023-982344.html

47. John Borland. "Judge: File-Swapping Tools Are Legal," Cnet.com, April 25, 2003. Available at http://news.com.com/2100-1027-998363.html

48. Ariana Eunjung Cha. "File Swapper Eluding Pursuers," *The Washington Post*, December 21, 2002, page A01.

49. Scott Carlson. "Recording Industry Sues Four Students for Allegedly Trading Songs Within College Networks," *The Chronicle of Higher Education*, April 4, 2003. Available at http://chronicle.com/free/2003/04/2003040401t.htm

50. Lisa Bowman. "Norway Piracy Case Brings Activists Hope," ZDNetUK, January 9, 2003. Available at http://news.zdnet.co.uk/story/0,,t269-s21283 90,00.html

51. "Security Researchers Drop Scientific Censorship Case," Press Release, Electronic Frontier Foundation, February 6, 2002. Available at http://www.eff.org/IP/DMCA/Felton_v_RIAA/20020206_eff_felten_pr.html

52. Declan McCullagh. "Hacker Arrest Stirs Protest," Wired.com, July 19, 2001. Available at http://www.wired.com/news/print/0,1294,45342,00.htm

53. "Background & Status," FreeSklyarov, December 2002. Available at http://www.freesklyarov.org/

54. Alex Salkever. "Digital Copyright: A Law Defanged?" *Business Week*, December 19, 2002. Available at http://www.businessweek.com/technology/content/dec 2002/tc20021219_4518.htm

55. "DVD Teenager Hit by Court Charge," BBC News, January 17, 2002. Available at http://news.bbc.co.uk/1/hi/entertainment/new_media/1754708.stm

56. *Op. cit.*, "Norway Privacy Case Brings Activists Hope."

57. Creative Commons Web Site, (No date). Available at http://www.creative commons.org/

58. "GNU's Not Unix!" May 25, 2003. Available at http://www.gnu.org/

59. "The Free Software Definition," GNU.org, February 7, 2003. Available at http://www.gnu.org/philosophy/free-sw.html

ADDITIONAL READINGS

History, Definitions, and Intellectual Property Laws

Baker, Jonathan D. and Oblon, Michael A. "Intellectual Property and the National Information Infrastructure (The White Paper)," 1996. Available at http://roscoe.law.harvard.edu/courses/techseminar96/course/sessions/whitepaper/whitepaper. html

"Conference on the Public Domain," Duke Law School, November 9–11, 2001. Papers available at http://www.law.duke.edu/pd/papers.html

"Eight Myths About the NII Copyright Protection Act." Creative Incentive Coalition, 1996. Available at http://www.cic.org/myths.html

Gordon, Wendy J. Draft of Chapter 7, "Intellectual Property," *Oxford Handbook of Legal Studies, 2003*. Available at http://www.bu.edu/law/faculty/papers/pdf_files/GordonW051203.pdf

Litman, Jessica. Digital Copyright. (Amherst, NY: Prometheus Books, 2001).

Okerson, Ann. "Who Owns Digital Works? Computer Networks Challenge Copyright Law, But Some Proposed Cures May Be as Bad as the Disease," *Scientific American*, July 1996. Available at http://www.sciam.com/0796issue/0796okerson.html

"The Property of the Mind," *The Economist*, July 27, 1996. Available at http://www.economist.com/issue/27-07-96/ wbsf1.html

Samuelson, Pamela. "The NII Intellectual Property Report." *Communications of the ACM*, 37 (12), December 1994, pp. 21–27. Available at http://alberti.mit.edu/arch/4.207/texts/samuelson.html

Samuelson, Pamela. "Regulation of Technologies to Protect Copyrighted Works." *Communications of the ACM*, 39 (7), July 1996, pp. 17–22.

Intellectual Property Cases for Computers and Software

"Expanding Global Economies: The Benefits of Reducing Software Piracy, Business Software Alliance, April 2, 2003. Available at http://bsa.org/idcstudy/pdfs/White_Paper.pdf

"Piracy Study: Trends in Software Piracy, 1994–2002," Eighth Annual BSA Global Software Study, June 2003. Available at http://www.bsa.org/globalstudy/2003_GSPS.pdf

Intellectual Property Cases and Events for Internet Music and Videos

"Copyright Use and Security Guide for Academic Institutions," IFPI—Representing the Recording Industry Worldwide, (no date). Available at http://www.ifpi.org/site-content/library/academic-brochure-english.pdf

"Intellectual Property on the Internet: A Survey of Issues," World Intellectual Property Organization, Geneva, December 2002. Available at http://ecom-merce.wipo.int/survey/pdf/survey.pdf

Lessig, Lawrence. *Code and Other Laws of Cyberspace.* (New York: Basic Books, 1999).

Lessig, Lawrence. *The Future of Ideas: The Fate of the Commons in a Connected World.* (New York: Random House, 2001).

National Research Council. *The Digital Dilemma: Intellectual Property in the Information Age.* (Washington, DC: National Academy Press, 2000).

Recent Intellectual Property Cases for Computer Software

"The Digital Millennium Copyright Act of 1998," U.S. Copyright Office Summary, December 1998. Available at http://www.loc.gov/copyright/legislation/dmca.pdf

"Unintended Consequences: Three Years Under the DMCA," Electronic Frontier Foundation, May 3, 2002. Available at http://www.eff.org/IP/DMCA/20020503_dmca_consequences.pdf

Vaidhyanathan, Siva. "Copyright as Cudgel," *The Chronicle of Higher Education*, August 2, 2002. Available at http://chronicle.com/free/v48/i47/47b00701.htm

— 11 —

COMPUTER CRIME AND SECURITY

Another important pattern that has emerged from IFCC [Internet Fraud Complaint Center] data is the increasing prevalence of non-fraudulent activity that is being reported. The adoption of technology as an invaluable tool, for both commerce and communication, has resulted in a proliferation of problems that range from online harassment to computer intrusions. Outreach efforts must focus on keeping all online users safe from harm, whether that harm is fraudulent or non-fraudulent in nature.[1]

INTRODUCTION

A given technological innovation will inevitably secure its place in society as the existing system of laws is expanded to accommodate it. What is remarkable about computer technology is how fast this process has occurred and how many interesting and important legal issues have arisen. Computer professionals and legal professionals share at least one thing: they both have an extensive and impenetrable jargon. In a very short time a new sub discipline has come into being, usually called computer law. One lawyer (Thomas Christo) has argued that it is wrong to speak of computer law when in fact there is just the *Law*.[2] Nevertheless, a number of universities do offer courses in computer law and there are several journals in this area. What, then, are some of the issues that currently fall within the purview of computer law?

There are several major areas of concern, some of which have been discussed previously. For the present purposes, the term computer crime involves the use of the computer, with or without the Internet, to steal or embezzle money. In addition, there are also such crimes as stealing computer time, unlawful access to files, the acquisition of privileged information, and the corruption or actual destruction of computer files. This last activity has probably become the most highly publicized, as such terms as "virus," "worm," "hacker," "denial of service," and "Cyberterror," have penetrated the public consciousness. While much computer crime has traditionally been perpetrated in banks, small and large companies, and government bureaucracies, viruses and worms have had a direct impact on the ordinary citizen at home. Computer viruses seem to be arriving more frequently than biological ones and with devastating effects as well.

The growth of the Internet, with its many vulnerabilities, has offered a ready target for malicious hackers, political activists, and apparently terrorists. Another factor is the increasing use of high-speed connections, which means that home computers are rarely turned off and therefore pose an easy target for malicious programmers, whose programs troll the Internet looking for ready targets. The enormous increase in the use of e-mail around the world has been accompanied by the devastating impact of viruses and worms, embedded in attachments. Without adequate detection programs including firewalls to limit the entry of unknown programs, the average home computer is vulnerable to attacks. Indeed, the early years of this decade have witnessed the rapid spread of several damaging viruses and worms.

Other crimes that have received public attention are identity theft, auction frauds, and the Nigerian (or 419) scam. The use of computers to commit crimes is not the only way they are associated with unlawful activities. Sabotage can be directed towards the computer installation itself in order to uncover information useful to crack various security codes. The computer can be the target of people who object—for political, social, and economic reasons—to the growing influence of computers in everyday life. The attack might be directed toward the communication network in which the computer is embedded—for example, phone lines might be tapped and Internet communications monitored. These possibilities have stimulated an ongoing concern with computer security exacerbated by the potential of cyberterrorism. Since September 11, 2001, government and private sector resources have been directed toward preventing, detecting, and dealing with terrorism that threatens the operation of the Internet. As world economies become ever more dependent on E-commerce, the Internet will receive increased attention as a vital pillar and hence an attractive target for those interested in creating havoc. Security measures already taken and proposed will therefore be examined here.

VIRUSES, WORMS, AND HACKERS

Again, we are having to deal with destructive attacks that are reportedly costing billions. In the past 2 months, organizations and individuals have had to contend with several particularly vexing attacks. The most notable, of course, is Code Red but potentially more damaging are Code Red II and SirCam. Together, these attacks have infected millions of computer users, shut down Web sites, slowed Internet service, and disrupted business and government operations. They have already caused billions of dollars of damage and their full effects have yet to be completely assessed.

Keith A. Rhodes, Chief Technologist, Center for Technology and Engineering, U.S. General Accounting Office[3]

One of the more glamorous products of the new technology is the crime story. Hardly a day passes without a report that yet another computer system has been broken into and money has been taken, or that a new virus from the East will begin destroying files in PCs in two weeks; discussions of computer security and new anti-viral programs abound. The glamor factor used to arise because computers seemed to be so formidable that any breakdown in their security was clearly noteworthy. Now, with so many computers in homes and small businesses, a new virus has enormous economic and social impact. From stories dealing with violations of large computer networks, a "David and Goliath" image emerged of the lonely, clever computer programmer, or hacker, cracking the all-powerful system, thought to be invincible up to now. Many people were quite sympathetic to the human-versus-machine success story, even if a crime had been committed, at least up to a few years ago when the scale grew so large that millions were affected. Given that crimes are indeed being perpetrated, however, measures must be taken to prevent them; security must be improved; and both professionals and the public at large must be educated about the dangers of such crimes.

A Few Definitions

It will be helpful to clarify a number of terms used in the discussion of viruses and worms. The following definitions represent a compromise between technical details and general understandability. One cautionary note is to be careful about definitions that push biological analogies too far.

Virus. Simply put, a virus is a program that can insert executable copies of itself into other programs. In more detail, a computer virus must satisfy the following properties[4]:

1. It must be capable of modifying software not belonging to the virus by attaching its program structure to the other program.
2. It must be capable of executing this modification on a number of programs.
3. It must have the capability of recognizing this modification in other programs.

4. It must have the ability to prevent further modification of the same program upon recognition of previous modification.
5. Modified software produced by the virus must have attributes 1–4.

Bacterium. This is a program designed to cause a system to crash, that is, to cease operation without warning, thereby causing the loss of data. A bacterium does not attach itself to other programs but replicates itself to the limit of system capacity, preventing other legitimate programs from running.

Worm. A worm searches a computer system for idle resources and then disables them, not by replication of its own code, as do viruses and bacteria, but by systematically erasing various locations in memory. Thus the system is unable to function as designed.

Trojan Horse. This appears to be a useful program but it contains within it hidden code that may have a destructive function. Viruses are typically spread by Trojan Horses. On the other hand, a programmer may include a "trap door" in the Trojan Horse to permit subsequent tampering, for example, a way to get into the system around the security envelope. (More detail is given later in this section.)

Time Bomb. Also called a logic bomb, this is one of the above infections modified to become operative on a given date or after its host program has run a certain number of times. Note that the Burleson program described in the next section is a time bomb.

Hacker. This is a term with multiple meanings that have changed over time. Consider the following descriptions of a hacker:
1. A programmer who works long hours and seems to be strongly motivated by, and infatuated with, programming; or
2. A compulsive programmer who is driven to find solutions to problems, claimed to be extremely difficult or even impossible; or
3. A programmer who produces programs that are not particularly elegant and represent a collection of patches, or hacks, rather than a coherent whole; such programs are difficult to maintain, modify, or verify; or
4. A programmer who breaks into systems to prove that it is possible, and that no system can resist his, or her, efforts; such a hacker is sometimes called a cracker; or
5. A programmer who is a variant of 4 but in addition feels that society benefits by his, or her, actions in that hidden information is brought to light or proprietary software is made available to the entire community of programmers.

Perhaps it is more instructive to let this particular Internet subcommunity define itself[5]:

- Hackers are the "wizards" of the computer community; people with a deep understanding of how their computers work, and can do things with them that seem "magical".
- Crackers are the real-world analogs of the "console cowboys" of cyberpunk fiction; they break in to other people's computer systems, without their permission, for illicit gain or simply for the pleasure of exercising their skill.
- Phreaks are those who do a similar thing with the telephone system, coming up with ways to circumvent phone companies' calling charges and doing clever things with the phone network. All three groups are using emerging computer and telecommunications technology to satisfy their individualist goals.
- Cypherpunks: . . . think a good way to bollix "The System" is through cryptography and cryptosystems. They believe widespread use of extremely hard-to-break coding schemes will create "regions of privacy" that "The System" cannot invade.

One attorney, who specializes in computer and communications law, prefers to use the term "rogue programs" to cover all these types of deviant programs and the term "computer rogues" to describe all individuals who devise, implement, and implant such programs as well as those who commit other crimes by using computers.[6] Donn Parker, an expert on computer crime, prefers to use the term computer abuse. He defines it as follows: "any incident involving an intentional act where a victim suffered or could have suffered a loss, and a perpetrator made or could have made a gain . . . associated with computers."[7]

The Scope of the Problem

Since 1996, the Computer Security Institute, based in San Francisco, has produced a survey on computer crime in cooperation with the FBI, which is interested in investigating "violations of Computer Fraud and Abuse Act of 1986, including intrusions to public switched networks, major computer network intrusions, privacy violations, industrial espionage, pirated computer software and other crimes where the computer is a major factor in committing the criminal offense." The 2002 survey received responses from "503 computer security practitioners in U.S. corporations, government agencies, financial institutions, medical institutions and universities," and included the following highlights[8]:

- Ninety percent of respondents (primarily large corporations and government agencies) detected computer security breaches within the last twelve months.

- Eighty percent acknowledged financial losses due to computer breaches.
- Forty-four percent (223 respondents) were willing and/or able to quantify their financial losses. These 223 respondents reported $455,848,000 in financial losses.
- As in previous years, the most serious financial losses occurred through theft of proprietary information (41 respondents reported $170,827,000) and financial fraud (40 respondents reported $115,753,000).
- For the fifth year in a row, more respondents (74%) cited their Internet connection as a frequent point of attack than cited their internal systems as a frequent point of attack (33%).
- Forty percent detected denial of service attacks.
- Eighty-five percent detected computer viruses.

Some Early Examples

It is not an easy task to count viruses and worms, given that many are slight variations of existing versions, but attempts continue. Consider the following estimates of numbers since 1990[9]:

> In 1990, estimates ranged from 200 to 500; then in 1991 estimates ranged from 600 to 1,000 different viruses. In late 1992, estimates were ranging from 1,000 to 2,300 viruses. In mid 1994, the numbers vary from 4,500 to over 7,500 viruses. In 1996 the number climbed over 10,000. 1998 saw 20,000 and 2000 topped 50,000. It's easy to say there are more now.

Here, then, are a few examples of some classic computer crimes presented for purely academic interest, of course:

The Burleson Revenge. In September 1985, Donald Gene Burleson, a programmer at a Fort Worth, Texas, brokerage house, inserted a special program into the company's computer that later caused 168,000 sales commission records to be suddenly deleted. Mr. Burleson had been dismissed three days before this event. He was charged and later "convicted of computer abuse under the Texas Penal Code which permits a felony charge to be filed if the damage exceeds $2,500 from altering, damaging, destroying data, causing a computer to malfunction or interrupting normal operations."[10] He was fined $11,800 and sentenced to seven years' probation.

The Pakistani Brain. During the period of early 1986 to late 1987, shoppers, mostly American, purchased such brand-name software as Lotus 1-2-3 and Word Star at prices as low as $1.50 per disk at Brain Computer Services in Lahore, Pakistan. The brothers Alvi, owners of the store, also included, for free and of course unknown to the purchasers, a piece of hidden software, a virus, on each disk, which destroyed data and left behind the message, "WELCOME TO THE DUNGEON—Amjad and Basit Alvi." The copying of Pakistani disks was so extensive that before long, about 100,000 disks were so infected. Only disks bought by Americans were infected and Basit offered the reason, "Because you are pirating, you must be punished."[11] On a purely technical level, the virus designer, Amjad, is widely recognized as highly skilled and the virus as very elegant.

Breach of a Classified System. San Francisco, January 17, 1990—"Federal authorities today charged three men in California with engaging in a widespread pattern of breaking into Government and telephone company computers and obtaining classified information from a military computer. The prosecutor said the case might represent the first intrusion into a classified military computer by trespassers."[12]

Computergate. On September 7, 1990, John Kohler, executive director of the New Jersey Republican General Assembly staff, resigned, admitting, contrary to previous denials, that he knew about "improper access to Democrat staff computer records."[13] Apparently the actual culprit was fired earlier in the year.

Two Important Cases

Two cases that generated considerable publicity in the early stages of the Internet's growth will be discussed in more detail than the previous group, because of their importance and significance for current and future security practices.

The INTERNET Worm

The most publicized and most discussed case of computer crime in the early years of the public Internet is known as the INTERNET worm, although all the early reports referred to it as a virus. Its importance goes beyond the event itself in November 1988, to include possible legal repercussions, as lawmakers attempted to formulate comprehensive legislation to deal with present and future threats to computers and networks. On September 26, 1988, *Time's* cover story was on computer viruses, and on August 1, 1988, *Business Week's* cover asked the question, "Is Your Computer Secure?" and mentioned hackers, viruses, and other threats.[14]

Curiously enough, within a rather short period, on November 4, 1988, a front-page story in *The New York Times* announced "'Virus' in Military Computers Disrupts Systems Nationwide."[15] Over the next few weeks, stories appeared on a regular basis in many newspapers and magazines, and on television. Consider the following headlines on front-page pieces by John Markoff of *The New York Times*:

- November 5: Author of Computer 'Virus' is Son of U.S. Electronic Security Expert: Cornell Graduate Student Described as 'Brilliant'
- November 6: How a Need for a Challenge Seduced Computer Expert
- November 8: Loving Those Whiz Kids: Mischief Like the Computer 'Virus' Release Comes from Group That Is Indispensable
- November 9: The Computer Jam: How It Came About

The initiator of the INTERNET worm was Robert T. Morris, a graduate student in computer science at Cornell University in Ithaca, New York. On the evening of November 2, 1988, the first of about 6,200 computers allegedly affected, on a network of about 60,000, gradually slowed down or ground to a halt, as an unknown program began seizing computer resources. The activity began initially on ARPANET, a computer network created for academic users by the Defense Advanced Research Projects Agency (DARPA). It then spread to the MILNET, an unclassified network of the Department of Defense, and finally to the global INTERNET. All of these networks and others are connected by gateways across North America and indeed the world. Some local systems broke connections with the network as word of the unprecedented disaster spread and thereby avoided being infected. Within about 48 hours, life was back to normal everywhere.

The impact was so wide-ranging—NASA Ames Laboratory, Lawrence Livermore National Laboratory, The Massachusetts Institute of Technology, Stanford University, the Rand Corporation, among others, were affected—that the uproar in the research communities was deafening. The costs of containing the damage, clearing out the memories, and checking all programs for signs of the rogue program were estimated at $96 million, then $186 million, then $1 billion. Final estimates were considerably more sober, closer to $1 million and 2000 computers affected.[16]

On November 4, the culprit was identified as Robert T. Morris, the son of one of the government's leading experts on computer security, chief scientist at the National Computer Center in Bethesda, Maryland, a branch of the National Security Agency. One of the flaws in the system's security was in the basic electronic mail handling program, *sendmail,* which permits computers on the networks to communicate with one another. Another was a utility program, *fingerd,* which is called to identify users at a given location; this was the virus' most successful means of migration. The last method was to guess passwords in order to gain access to trusted hosts where it might be able to migrate. What was disturbing to many of the users was that these flaws were generally known but were not exploited because that would have been a violation of collegiality, a breakdown in a system of trust shared by a large community.

Mr. Morris was indicted on July 26, 1989, by a federal grand jury in Syracuse, New York, and accused under the Computer Fraud and Abuse Act of 1986 (see discussion later in this chapter) of gaining access to federal interest computers, preventing authorized access by others, and causing damage in excess of $1,000. The fact that there was a delay of more than six months between the date of the incident and the indictment suggests that government lawyers were in some disagreement over how to frame the charges. This uncertainty is probably the major legal legacy of the INTERNET worm, as the government has considered amending current legislation to be more comprehensive and relevant. The trial began on January 16, 1990, and on January 23, a federal jury found Mr. Morris guilty of intentionally disrupting a nationwide computer network, the first jury conviction under the 1986 Act.[17] On May 5, 1990, a federal judge fined Mr. Morris $10,000, placed him on three years' probation, and ordered him to perform 400 hours of community service. The judge stated that prison punishment did not fit the crime, although the Act provided for up to five years in prison. An appeal was heard on December 4, 1990.[18] "On March 7, 1991, the U.S. Court of Appeals for the second circuit court upheld Robert's conviction. In the autumn of 1991, the Supreme Court refused to hear the case."[19]

Kevin Mitnick: A True Compulsive or a Gifted Hacker

In early January 1989, Kevin Mitnick was arraigned in Los Angeles, held without bail, and charged with such crimes as illegally accessing computers at Digital Equipment Corp. and at the University of Leeds, in England, and stealing computer programs and long-distance telephone services. His trouble with computers and the law had actually begun in 1981 when he and friends had physically broken into a Pacific Bell phone center. He was even able to change the credit rating of the judge in the 1989 case, which explains, in part, why he was denied bail and prohibited from making telephone calls. He was charged and convicted under the Federal Computer Fraud and Abuse Act of 1986, one of the first so treated, and sentenced to 12 months in jail, six months in a residential treatment program, and three years of probation.[20] Given that he did not even own a computer, he was not fined. As you might have guessed, his career was not over.

In September 1992, Mitnick was being investigated by the FBI for possible illegal access to a commercial database and two months later a warrant was issued for "his arrest for having violated the terms of his 1989 probation. There were two charges: illegally accessing a phone company computer, and associating with one of the people with whom he'd originally been arrested in 1981."[21] Mitnick eluded arrest and while on the run managed, among other actions, "to wiretap the telephones of the FBI agents who were searching for him."[22] On Christmas Day in 1994, a computer at the home of security expert Tsutomu Shimomura in San Diego was broken into and files removed. Mitnick left taunting messages on Shimomura's answering machine and used some of the files taken from his computer to break into other systems. Some of these files turned up about a month later in the account of another well-known computer person, Bruce Koball, on the WELL, a Sausolito, California network. Koball got in touch with John

Markoff of the *New York Times* and Shimomura, who within about two weeks was able to trace Mitnick to a Raleigh, North Carolina, location where he was arrested by the FBI.

On March 16, 1999, he pled guilty to seven counts of wire and computer fraud and was released from prison less than a year later but required, as terms of probation, to avoid Internet access for three years. "On January 21, 2003, Mitnick logs on to the Net for the first time in eight years—and launches a career as a security consultant."[23]

One serious concern arising out of Mitnick's adventures is the ease with which he was able to penetrate a variety of Web sites and accounts on supposedly secure systems. He was a master of what has been called "social engineering," the ability to convince people to behave in ways that were beneficial to him but not necessarily to the organizations which employed them. Names of key security officials, passwords to secure accounts, safety-critical files, and other information was obtained during his exploits, nullifying the need to develop clever techniques to penetrate systems remotely.

In his new role as a consultant, Mitnick offers the following advice to deal with social-engineering attacks[24]:

- Verify the Call. If an employee you don't know calls asking for proprietary information or computer files, put the person on hold and call the extension to make sure the call is genuine.
- Establish the Need to Know. Don't send sensitive company info to anyone without checking with higher-ups to make sure the requester is authorized to have it.
- Beware of Surveys. Do not participate in phone surveys. Social engineers often call, posing as tech suppliers in need of data about their customers.
- Watch Your E-Mail. Hackers use social engineering in e-mail, by using friendly subject lines and making it look as if the message is from someone you know. Do not click on links or delete lines. You may be opening the door to a virus or a hacker.
- Be Smart. Do not post sensitive information such as passwords in your work area. Deliverymen and other visitors may be hackers in disguise.

A Final Comment About Hackers

It must be acknowledged, however, that there does exist a small community, simplistically described as hackers, who maintain their *right* to enter any system for any purpose they deem appropriate. In an electronic forum held over a nationwide bulletin board in early 1990, hackers expressed a variety of opinions on breaking into systems, perusing files, and the "virtues" of privacy.[25] Among the opinions expressed was a version of the "means justify the end" for hackers; that is, breaking into a system is warranted if the purpose is useful, a position countered by the analogy of entering an unoccupied house if there is something inside it of use to the perpetrator. Many hackers argue that the very concept of secret information is offensive and that if it were not collected, there would be no need to protect it. Thus, they claim that their role must be to "liberate" the data, to defeat the notion of secure systems, and thereby to inhibit the open-ended collection of information.

Despite the hackers' seemingly democratic principle of information for the people, their self-indulgence emerges, loud and clear: we define the issues, we say what is right and wrong, and by virtue of our skills, we reserve the right to act in whatever way we wish. How representative are these opinions? It is impossible to know, but even if they come from a very small minority, it is a highly skilled and a highly motivated one.

The Computer Fraud and Abuse Act of 1986

The original act, the Counterfeit Access Device and Computer Fraud and Abuse Act of 1984, was signed into law by President Reagan in October 1984 as part of the Comprehensive Crime Control Act of 1984. In 1986, it was amended with the Computer Fraud and Abuse Act. The 1986 Act prohibits six types of computer abuse and provides for three types of felonies. The following computer abuses are defined as criminal conduct {§1030(a)(1)-(6)}[25a]:

1. Knowingly accessing a computer without authorization and obtaining restricted information with the intent to use that information to the detriment of the United States.
2. Intentionally accessing a computer without authorization and obtaining information in the financial record of a financial institution.
3. Intentionally, without authorization to access any computer of a department or agency of the United States, access[ing] such a computer of that department or agency that is exclusively for the use of the Government of the United States or, in the case of a computer not exclusively for such use, is used by or for the Government of the United States and such conduct affects the use of the Government's operation of such computer.
4. Knowingly, and with intent to defraud, accessing a Federal interest computer and obtaining something of value, unless the value so obtained is limited to the use of computer time.
5. Intentionally accessing a Federal interest computer without authorization, and by means of one or more instances of such conduct altering, damaging, or destroying information in any such Federal interest computer, or preventing authorized use of any such computer or information and thereby causing damage in excess of $1,000 or damaging records.
6. Knowingly, and with intent to defraud, trafficking in computer passwords.

Number 5 is the section under which Morris was charged and convicted. Although the number of computer-related crimes seems to have increased significantly, only a few convictions have taken place under this Act. There seems to be a number of limitations, both in the language of the Act and in the very nature of computer crime, which make such crimes difficult to prosecute. In the first instance, the Act focuses on computers used and owned by government departments without acknowledging the vast number of corporate computers equally likely to be abused. Access alone is not a crime, unless information is obtained, and neither is browsing, or the looking at files without causing damages.[26] Viruses or worms were not anticipated in the Act. Since many technical issues arise, prosecutors may have difficulty in dealing with such cases. Gathering evidence may also be difficult without violating the privacy of individuals whose files are on the system under investigation. One final point is that the Act does not require that intent to defraud or cause damage be proven; thus any unauthorized access to a government computer system could leave the perpetrator subject to criminal charges.

Worms and Viruses Galore

Since 1999, with some degree of regularity, a series of worms/viruses has swept around the world, crashing and infecting both commercial and home systems. A system of warnings and corrective patches to download have been put in place and reporting sites have also proliferated. It seemed to begin with the Melissa virus in March of 1999, followed by BubbleBoy in November. May of 2000 witnessed the spread of the I Love You worm, which had twice the impact of Melissa; the worm sent a copy of itself to everyone in the Outlook address book. But 2001 witnessed a bumper crop: Code Red (July), SirCam (July), Nimda A (September), and Nimda E (November). Table 11.1[27] below describes in more detail the characteristics of some of these viruses and worms. In 2002, the dominant infection was called Klez, which began in mid-April but continued through July, overtaking SirCam as the most active computer pest in history. The worm, Sapphire.Slammer, began its life in late August 2003 and spread more quickly than other worms.

Occasionally, the creators of destructive worms and viruses are caught and punished. For example, David Smith, the creator of the Melissa worm, "was sentenced in the US to a 20-month custodial sentence and fines totaling $7,500."[28]

OTHER CRIMES AND ISSUES

The prevalence of identity theft appears to be growing. Moreover, identity theft is not typically a stand-alone crime; rather, identity theft is usually a component of one or more white-collar or financial crimes, such as bank fraud, credit card or access device fraud, or the use of counterfeit financial

TABLE 11.1

HIGH-LEVEL COMPARISON OF THE ATTACKS

	What is it?	How does it spread?	Who is at risk?	What damage can it do?
Code Red	Code Red is a worm, which is a computer attack that propagates through networks without user intervention. This particular worm makes use of a vulnerability in Microsoft's Internet Information Services (IIS) Web server software—specifically, a buffer overflow.	The worm scans the Internet, identifies vulnerable systems, and infects these systems by installing itself. Each newly installed worm joins all the others, causing the rate of scanning to grow rapidly.	Users with Microsoft IIS server installed with Windows NT version 4.0 or Windows 2000.	The program can deface Web sites, and was designed to perform a DoS attack against the www.whitehouse.gov Web site. It can also decrease the speed of the Internet.
Code Red II	Code Red II is also a worm that exploits the same IIS vulnerability. However, the worm also opens a backdoor on an infected server that allows any follow-on	Code Red II spreads like Code Red: however, in doing so, it selects Internet addresses that are in the same network range as the infected computer to increase the likelihood of	Users with Microsoft IIS Web server software installed with Windows 2000.	Like Code Red, Code Red II can decrease the speed of the Internet. Unlike Code Red, it also leaves the infected system open to any attacker who can alter

Continued

TABLE 11.1—cont'd

HIGH-LEVEL COMPARISON OF THE ATTACKS

	What is it?	How does it spread?	Who is at risk?	What damage can it do?
	remote attacker to execute arbitrary commands.	finding susceptible victims.		or destroy files and create a denial of service. It does not deface Web pages.
SirCam	SirCam is a malicious computer virus that spreads through E-mail and potentially through unprotected network connections. Once the malicious code has been executed on a system, it may reveal or delete sensitive information.	This mass-mailing virus attempts to send itself to E-mail addresses found in the Windows Address Book and addresses found in cached browser files. It also attempts to copy itself to specific Windows networked computers.	Any E-mail user or user of a computer with unprotected Windows network connections to the infected computer.	SirCam can publicly release sensitive information and delete files and folders. It can also fill the remaining free space on the computer's hard drive. Furthermore, it can lead to a decrease in the speed of the Internet.

instruments. Since 1998, the Congress and most states have enacted laws that criminalize identity theft. The passage of federal and state identity theft legislation indicates that this type of crime has been widely recognized as a serious problem across the nation.[29]

Statement by Richard M. Stana, Director, Justice Issues, General Accounting Office, before the Subcommittee on Crime, Terrorism and Homeland Security and the Subcommittee on Immigration, Border Security, and Claims, Committee of the Judiciary, House of Representatives

The National White Collar Crime Center and the Federal Bureau of Investigation issued their second annual report on Internet fraud covering the period, January 1 to December 31, 2002. Some of the highlights follow[30]:

- As has been the case since IFCC [Internet Fraud Complaint Center] began operation in 2000, Internet auction fraud was by far the most reported offense, comprising 46% of referred complaints. Non-delivery of merchandise and payment account for 31% of complaints, and credit/debit card fraud made up nearly 12% of complaints. Investment fraud, business fraud, confidence fraud, and identity theft round out the top seven categories of complaints referred to law enforcement during the year (all at 1.0% or more). Among those individuals who reported a dollar loss, the highest median dollar losses were found among Nigerian Letter fraud ($3,864), identity theft ($2,000), and check fraud ($1,100) complainants.
- Among complainants, 71% are male, half are between the ages of 30 and 50 (the average age is 39.4), and over one-third reside in one of the following four states: California, Florida, Texas, and New York. While most complainants are from the United States, IFCC has received a number of complaints from Canada, Australia, Great Britain, Germany, and Japan.
- The amount lost by complainants tends to be related to a number of factors. Males tend to lose more than females. This may be a function of both online purchasing differences by gender, and the type of fraud the individual finds himself or herself involved with. While there isn't a strong relationship between age and loss, the proportion of individuals losing at least $5,000 is higher for those 60 years and older than it is for any other age category.
- Electronic mail (E-mail) and Web pages are the two primary mechanisms by which the fraudulent contact took place. In all, 66% of complainants reported they had e-mail contact with the perpetrator and 18.7% had contact through a Web page.
- Only one in four complainants had contacted a law enforcement agency about the incident prior to filing a complaint with IFCC. These individuals had a higher median dollar loss ($500) than the total complainant population.

Auction fraud, non-delivery of goods and payment, and credit/debit card fraud comprise most of the Internet fraud and are relatively straightforward. The focus in the remainder of this section is on the more Internet-related frauds as well as other crimes that have received attention.

Denial of Service Attacks

Early in 2000, a few of the most frequently visited Web sites, including Yahoo, E-bay, CNN, and Amazon, were unable to function for several hours because of concerted distributed denial of service attacks (DDSA). In somewhat more detail,[31]

> The kind of attack—known as a "distributed denial of service" attack—does not involve actually breaking into the target computer system. It more closely resembles piling trash up in front of the door so that others can't get in. The standard denial of service strike, which has been used by hackers against smaller web sites for several years, involves flooding the target computer with requests for information, blocking access for other users. The new twist—distributing the attack over tens or even hundreds of other computers to make the same calls in a coordinated torrent, like the mini-broomsticks in the "Sorcerer's Apprentice"—has proved effective at bringing down sites that most observers would have believed to be big enough to handle any amount of traffic.

Charged and convicted for this DDSA was a Canadian teenager, known as "Mafiaboy," fourteen years old when the crime was committed. He was tried in January 2001 on two charges of "mischief" against the CNN site. He was "sentenced to eight months in a youth detention centre."[32]

Nigerian Scam (or 419 Fraud)

It is almost impossible to be an Internet regular and not receive an e-mail similar to the following one[33]:

> ATTN: SIR/MADAM
> I am Barr. Peter Briggs esq., principal partner at Briggs, Adams & Udoka Chambers. Our client Mr. Peter Mayer, and his family met their demise on the 27th of January 2002 in the Lagos bomb blast explosion. Mr. Brian Hush, was before his death an expatriate staff of Shell Exploration and Production Company in Nigeria (SEPCO) and had secured huge sum of money and choice properties in Nigeria.
>   Our firm has tried unsuccessfully to locate any member of his family to act as his next of kin for the purpose of entitlement to take under statutory distribution of intestate's estate.

By the law his money, property and other investments will become inaccessible after a specified period. We have already received notices from the bank where the deceased had an account valued at US$11.755M (Eleven Million Seven Hundred and Fifty Five Thousand United States dollars), and his stock brokers where he has a portfolio worth several millions, to provide the next of kin or have his account and stocks confiscated, respectively.

For this reason I write to your goodself, seeking your consent to present you as the next of kin of the deceased, so that his money and investment can be transferred to you. I have necessary legal documents to back up any claim we make.

All I require is your honest cooperation to enable us to conclude this deal. I guarantee that this will be executed under a legitimate arrangement, thus protecting you from any breach of law.

Please contact me immediately so that we can discuss further about this issue.

Yours sincerely,

Barr. Peter Briggs (Esq.)

The basic pattern is simple; one way or another, a substantial amount of money is sitting in a bank account somewhere and you are being solicited to help move the money to an account in your bank, for which you will be paid a tempting percentage. At this point it is necessary for you to make contact. This first contact will require you to put up some of your own money to show good faith and in some cases, many thousands of dollars are lost in this fraud. By the way, the 419 is the section of the criminal code in Nigeria that makes this activity illegal.[34]

The Image of the Web

With all the crimes and misdemeanors discussed so far, it is not surprising that the reputation of the Web is suspect. In addition, the media are quick to portray the online world as murky, threatening, dangerous, and rife with all forms of criminal acts. Consider the September 2, 2002, cover story of *Business Week*, titled "The Underground Web" and depicting a fast-talking huckster offering drugs, gambling, and child pornography with the further promise, "How the Internet makes any illegal activity more accessible than ever."[35] The cover story article begins with the following warning[36]:

Warning: You are about to enter the dark side of the Internet. It's a place where crime is rampant and every twisted urge can be satisfied. Thousands of virtual streets are lined with casinos, porn shops, and drug dealers. Scam artists and terrorists skulk behind seemingly lawful Web sites. And cops wander through once in a while, mostly looking lost. It's the Strip in Las Vegas, the Red Light district in Amsterdam, and New York's Times Square at its worst, all rolled into one—and all easily accessible from your living room couch. Indeed, the very nature of the Web is what makes it such a playground for hoodlums. Its instant, affordable, far-flung reach has fostered frictionless commerce and frictionless crime. Fraudsters can tap into an international audience from anyplace in the world and—thanks to the Net's anonymity—hide their activities for months, years, forever. And they can do it for less than it costs in the physical world: $200 buys an e-mail list with the names of thousands of potential dupes.

For several more pages, the tenor is bad stuff abounds, the worst instincts are catered to, and that criminals and terrorists have found a wonderful new home to ply their trades. But of course, the Internet is much more than this characterization, as this book describes.

SECURITY: CRIME AND TERRORISM

In the past few years, threats in cyberspace have risen dramatically. The policy of the United States is to protect against the debilitating disruption of the operation of information systems for critical infrastructures and, thereby, help to protect the people, economy, and national security of the United States. We must act to reduce our vulnerabilities to these threats before they can be exploited to damage the cyber systems supporting our Nation's critical infrastructures and ensure that such disruptions of cyberspace are infrequent, of minimal duration, manageable, and cause the least damage possible.

President George W. Bush, February 2003[37]

As in many other areas of life, prevention is far better than detection, indictment, and possible conviction. What steps can administrators of computing facilities take to ensure the physical security of the system itself, and the security of the communications network?

Physical security involves the computer itself, the peripheral equipment, and the rooms and buildings, including furniture, storage media, and terminals. Obvious care must be taken with respect to fire, water, earthquakes, explosions, and other natural causes. Special care must he taken to control access by people in order to safeguard the equipment and physical surroundings. It is necessary to require identification badges for those individuals who work in restricted areas. There must be alternative power supplies as well as backup systems to be used in case of damage. An entire subindustry has grown up to advise companies in physical security and to supply security equipment. As the dependency of society on computers increases, it becomes a basic necessity to take steps to guarantee physical security.

System security involves the basic operation of the computer itself. The issue is access—to the computer, the associated files, sensitive production programs, and even the operating system. The basic controls used to restrict access are computer identification numbers (IDs) and passwords. Within this system there may be privileged function levels, including user and program access control. An ID is typically issued by the computing center; it is the user's responsibility to choose a password as a second level of security. The operating system of the computer will permit access only to identifiable IDs and passwords. Once on a system, the ordinary user is restricted to his or her own files and system programs, including programming languages and library functions. Individual users may provide other users with access to their files, where access may mean reading the file, writing into it, or both. The operating system must ensure individual user security as well as protect itself from unauthorized access. There are a number of by-now-traditional means of cracking system security, which depend upon whether the goals are to cause damage or extract information, or both.

Anti-Crime Security Measures

The release of fast-spreading and damaging viruses and worms as well as hacker-initiated distributed denial of service attacks have resulted in increased demands for improved security measures to be installed and for security to be taken much more seriously in Information Technology (IT) budgeting. In its Global Information Security Survey of 2002, the major consulting firm Ernst & Young reported the following highlights[38]:

- Only 40% of organizations are confident that they would detect a systems attack.
- 40% of organizations do not investigate information security incidents.
- Critical business systems are increasingly interrupted—over 75% of organizations experienced unexpected unavailability.
- Business continuity plans exist at only 53% of organizations.
- Only 41% of organizations are concerned about internal attacks on systems, despite overwhelming evidence of the high number of attacks within organizations.
- Less than 50% of organizations have information security training and awareness programs.

Of particular interest are the current and planned uses of security technologies. The following lists these technologies and policies (the first number indicating the percent currently deployed, and the second the percent expected to deploy)[39]:

- Standard vendor-supplied security hardware (59, 13)
- Defined security standards (57, 10)
- Privacy statements (45, 10)
- Virtual Private Network (44, 19)

- Intrusion Detection System (36, 24)
- Ethical Hacking (28, 22)
- Vulnerability management services (27, 15)
- Public Key Infrastructure (26, 19)
- Smart Cards (21, 12)
- Wireless security products (20, 10)
- Cyberseals (15, 6)
- Biometrics (11, 5)

Security is difficult because the threats are a moving target in computer systems and networks. What works now may not work next year or next month. As noted in a report in the *Economist*, "Digital Security,"[40]

> Total computer security is impossible. No matter how much money you spend on fancy technology, how many training courses your staff attend or how many consultants you employ, you will still be vulnerable. Spending more, and spending wisely, can reduce your exposure, but it can never eliminate it altogether. So how much money and time does it make sense to spend on security? And what is the best way to spend them? There are no simple answers. It is all a matter of striking an appropriate balance between cost and risk—and what is appropriate for one organization might be wrong for another. Computer security, when you get down to it, is really about risk management. Before you can take any decisions about security spending, policy or management, the first thing you have to do is make a hard-headed risk assessment.

Nevertheless, spending on security is increasing at the expense of other IT costs, and there is no reason for this trend to change in the near future, especially with the growing threat of terrorism.

Cyber-Terrorism

Since September 11, a new and potentially devastating threat has appeared. It is argued by some in government and law enforcement that the Internet has facilitated planning and communications among terrorists. Furthermore, because so much of many countries' economic infrastructure is beginning to depend on the Internet, it has grown in importance as a terrorist target, especially in the U.S. In response, a variety of proposals and planning documents have appeared, outlining measures to identify and apprehend terrorists and to protect vulnerable but valuable sites. Probably the first important document to be released by the U.S. Department of Homeland Security (DHS), which came into existence on November 25, 2002, was *The National Strategy to Secure Cyberspace*. The strategic objectives are to "prevent cyber attacks against America's critical infrastructures," to "reduce national vulnerability to cyber attacks," and to "minimize damage and recovery time from cyber attacks that do occur."[41] Furthermore, the *Strategy* promotes five national priorities[42]:

- A National Cyberspace Security Response System
- A National Cyberspace Security Threat and Vulnerability Reduction Program
- A National Cyberspace Security Awareness and Training Program
- Securing Governments' Cyberspace
- National Security and International Cyberspace Security Cooperation

The first priority focuses on improving our response to cyber incidents and reducing the potential damage from such events. The second, third, and fourth priorities aim to reduce threats from, and our vulnerabilities to, cyber attacks. The fifth priority is to prevent cyber attacks that could impact national security assets and to improve the international management of and response to such attacks.

The *Strategy* is very detailed and apparently comprehensive. As a final excerpt, consider the major actions and initiatives proposed for security response[43]:

1. Establish a public-private architecture for responding to national-level cyber incidents
2. Provide for the development of tactical and strategic analysis of cyber attacks and vulnerability assessments
3. Encourage the development of a private sector capability to share a synoptic view of the health of cyberspace
4. Expand the Cyber Warning and Information Network to support the role of DHS in coordinating crisis management for cyberspace security
5. Improve national incident management
6. Coordinate processes for voluntary participation in the development of national public-private continuity and contingency plans
7. Exercise cybersecurity continuity plans for federal systems
8. Improve and enhance public-private information sharing involving cyber attacks, threats, and vulnerabilities.

A number of questions arise with respect to money (who will provide resources and how much will be available?), expertise (is there enough and how will the best people be identified?), determination of actual threats (what is the evidence of real threats and how dangerous are they?), and what will be the impact on non-terrorist threats?

Proposals for security were also made by the leading scientific and technical organizations in the U.S., namely, the National Academy of Sciences, National Academy of Engineering, Institute of Medicine, and National Research Council, which launched their own study, shortly after September 11. Although acknowledging the global nature of the problem and recognizing its multidimensionality, including "diplomacy, military actions, intelligence, and an understanding of the origin and sustenance of terrorism," a major effort was launched, which resulted in an important study, published by the National Academy Press. This book included proposals to deal with a wide range of possible terrorist actions such as radioactive threats, bioterrorism, toxic chemicals, threats to energy plants and the electric power grid, and much more. A few of the most important technical initiatives recommended in the study follow[44]:

Immediate Applications of Existing Technologies
1. Develop and utilize robust systems for protection, control, and accounting of nuclear weapons and special nuclear materials at their sources.
2. Ensure production and distribution of known treatments and preventatives for pathogens.
3. Design, test, and install coherent layered security systems for all transportation modes, particularly shipping containers and vehicles that contain large quantities of toxic or flammable materials.
4. Protect energy distribution services by improving security for supervisory control and data acquisition (SCADA) systems and providing physical protection for key elements of the electric-power grid.
5. Reduce the vulnerability and improve the effectiveness of air filtration in ventilation systems.
6. Deploy known technologies and standards for allowing emergency responders to reliably communicate with each other.
7. Ensure that trusted spokespersons will be able to inform the public promptly and with technical authority whenever the technical aspects of an emergency are dominant in the public's concerns.

Urgent Research Opportunities
1. Develop effective treatments and preventatives for known pathogens for which current responses are unavailable and for potential emerging pathogens.
2. Develop, test, and implement an intelligent, adaptive electric-power grid.
3. Advance the practical utility of data fusion and data mining for intelligence analysis, and enhance information security against cyberattacks.
4. Develop new and better technologies (e.g., protective gear, sensors, communications) for emergency responders.
5. Advance engineering design technologies and fire-rating standards for blast- and fire-resistant buildings.
6. Develop sensor and surveillance systems (for a wide range of targets) that create useful information for emergency officials and decision makers.
7. Develop new methods and standards for filtering air against both chemicals and pathogens as well as better methods and standards for decontamination.

It was clear, to reiterate the obvious, that after September 11, 2001, nothing would be the same and that technology would be expected to play an important role both in the detection of potential terrorist activities and to protect core IT infrastructure. (For additional discussion on threats to the Information Society, see Chapter 14.)

SUMMARY

For any person on the Internet, the concern about viruses and worms rises and falls as warnings fill the media. The regular release of "patches" by Microsoft is indicative of the fragile nature of computer security for the many millions around the world. In this chapter, definitions were provided for some of the commonly used terms, although it must be admitted that over time the distinctions have become quite blurred. Examples of early viruses and hackers were presented including the noteworthy hacker, and now celebrated security guru, Kevin Mitnick.

It does appear, however, that recently, attacks have become more severe and more prevalent. Major Web sites and portals have been subject to massive denial of service attacks and the computers of many individuals have been infected with the destruction of valuable files. In addition to such attacks, there has been a parallel increase in the number of e-mail messages, or spam, offering "once-in-a-lifetime" deals. The very common Nigerian (or 419) scam has been attracting gullible users lured by promises of multi-million-dollar gains. Such events have reinforced the image of the Internet, or Web, as a dangerous place.

To compound all these threats, the terrible terrorist attacks of September 11 have now added "cyber-terrorism" to the equation. Concern with security now goes beyond traditional viruses and worms to include attempts to initiate attacks that will devastate the Internet and thereby seriously damage the economy. As a byproduct of security measures, it is possible that individual civil liberties may be compromised. Tradeoffs will have to be carefully reviewed by all affected parties.

NOTES

1. "IFCC 2002 Internet Fraud Report, January 1, 2002–December 31, 2002," The National White Collar Crime Center and the Federal Bureau of Investigation, 2003. Available at http://www1.ifccfbi.gov/strategy/2002_IFCCReport.pdf
2. Thomas K. Christo. "The Law and DP: A Clash of Egos," *Datamation*, September 1982, pp. 264–265, 267–268.
3. Keith A. Rhodes. "Code Red, Code Red II, and SirCam Attacks Highlight Need for Proactive Measures," Testimony before a Hearing of the Subcommittee on Government Efficiency, Financial Management and Intergovernmental

Relations of the House Committee on Government Reform, August 29, 2001. Available at http:/ /www.gao.gov/new.items/d011073t.pdf

4. R. Burger. *Computer Viruses: A High-Tech Disease*, Second Edition, Grand Rapids, MI: Abacus, 1988, p.15. As referenced in James Tramontana, "Computer Viruses: Is There a Legal 'Antibiotic'?" *Rutgers Computer & Technology Journal*, 16 (1), 1990, note 26, p. 255.

5. "alt.cyberpunk Faq list." Available at http:/ /www.faqs.org/faqs/cyberpunk-faq/

6. Anne W. Branscomb. "Rogue Computer Programs and Computer Rogues: Tailoring the Punishment to Fit the Crime," *Rutgers Computer & Technology Law Journal*, 16 (1), 1990, p. 4.

7. Donn Parker. *Crime by Computer* (New York: Scribner's, 1976), p. 169.

8. "Computer Security Issues and Trends: 2002 CSI/FBI Computer Crime and Security Survey," Computer Security Institute, Spring 2002. Available at http://www.gocsi.com/pdfs/fbi/FBI2002.pdf

9. "Number of Viruses," C-Systems Virus Tutorial, (No date). Available at http://www3.sk.sympatico.ca/petej/v/vtnumber.htm

10. *Op cit.*, Branscomb, p. 18.

11. Philip Elmer-DeWitt. "You Must Be Punished," *Time*, September 26, 1988, p. 54.

12. Andrew Pollock. "3 Men Accused of Violating Computer and Phone Systems," *The New York Times*, January 18, 1990, pp. A1, A17.

13. "Computergate Hits New Jersey," Computerworld, September 17, 1990, p. 147.

14. Katherine M. Hafner et al. "Is Your Computer Secure?" *Business Week*, August 1, 1988, pp. 64–67, 70–72, and Philip Elmer-DeWitt, "Invasion of the Data Snatchers," *Time*, September 26, 1988, pp. 50–55.

15. John Markoff. " 'Virus' in Military Systems," *The New York Times*, November 4, 1988, pp. 1, 13.

16. *Op cit.*, Branscomb, p. 7.

17. John Markoff. "Jury Convicts Student Whose Program Jammed Computers," *The New York Times*, January 23, 1990, p. A13.

18. John Markoff. "Computer Intruder Gets Probation and Fine But Avoids Prison Term," *The New York Times*, May 5, 1990, pp. 1, 8. "Morris Appeal Due," *Computerworld*, November 12, 1990, p. 8.

19. Katie Hafner and John Markoff. *Cyberpunk: Outlaws and Hackers on the Computer Frontier* (New York: Simon & Schuster, A Touchstone Book, 1992), p. 346. This book contains considerable detail about the INTERNET worm case as well as the activities of Kevin Mitnick in the 1980s.

20. *Op cit.*, Branscomb, pp. 18–21 and "Drop the Phone," *Time*, January 9, 1989, p. 15.

21. Taken from an excerpt from Tsutomo Shimomura interview with John Markoff, *Takedown: The Pursuit and Capture of Kevin Mitnick, America's Most Wanted Computer Outlaw by the Man Who Did It* (New York: Hyperion, 1996). The excerpt was accessed at http://www.takedown.com/bio/mitnick.html

22. John Markoff. "Cyberspace's Most Wanted: Hacker Eludes F.B.I. Pursuit," *The New York Times*, July 4, 1994. Available at http://www.takedown.com/coverage/most-wanted.html

23. "Catch Him If You Can," *Business Week*, June 9, 2003. Available at http://businessweek.com/magazine/content/03_23/b3836101_mz063.htm

24. "Don't Be Duped," *Business Week*, June 9, 2003. Available at http://business-week.com/magazine/content/03_23 b3836099_mz063.htm

25. "Is Computer Hacking a Crime?" *Harper's Magazine*, March 1990, pp. 45–57. A transcript of selections of a nationwide forum held on a computer bulletin board over an eleven-day period, including a variety of perspectives.

25a. "18 U.S.C. 1030. Fraud and Related Activity in Connection with Computers," (no date) U.S. Department of Justice. Available at http://www.usdoj.gov/criminalcybercrime/1030_new.html

26. Christopher D. Chen. "Computer Crime and the Computer Fraud and Abuse Act of 1986," *Computer/Law Journal* X (1) Winter 1990, pp. 71–86.

27. *Op. cit.*, Keith A. Rhodes, "Code Red, Code Red II, and SirCam Attacks Highlight Need for Proactive Measures."

28. "Klez Worm Is the Most Prolific of the Year," Sophos, December 4, 2002. Available at http://www.sophos.com/pressoffice/pressrel/uk/20021204yeartop ten.html

29. Richard M. Stana. "Identity Theft: Prevalence and Links to Alien Illegal Activities," General Accounting Office, June 25, 2002. Available at http://www.gao.gov/new.items/d02830t.pdf

30. "IFCC Internet Fraud Report, January 1, 2002 – December 31, 2002," the National White Collar Crime Center and the Federal Bureau of Investigation, 2003. Available at http://www1.ifccfbi.gov/strategy/2002_IFCCReport.pdf

31. John Schwartz and Ariana Eunjung Cha. "Hackers Strike Again," The *Washington Post*, February 9, 2000.

32. "'Mafiaboy' Hacker Jailed," BBC News, September 13, 2001. Available at http://news.bbc.co.uk/1/hi/sci/tech/1541252.stm

33. Received by the author as one of almost 300 similar messages during the first six months of 2003. Other supposed originating countries are Angola, Burkina Faso, Congo, Cote D'Ivoire, Dubai, Ethiopia, Ghana, Hong Kong, Kenya, Liberia, Philippines, Sierra Leone, South Africa, South Korea, Spain, Taiwan, Togo, Zaire, and Zimbabwe.

34. "Welcome to NigerianFraudWatch," NigerianFraudWatch.org, (No date). Available at http://www.nigerianfraudwatch.org/

35. Ira Sager, Ben Elgin, Peter Ellstrom, Faith Keenan, and Pallavi Gogoi. "The Underground Web," September 2, 2002. Available at http://www.business-week.com/print/magazine/content/02-35/b3797001.htm with a Business Week online account.

36. *Ibid.*

37. "The National Strategy to Secure Cyberspace," Department of Homeland Security, February 2003. Available at http://www.dhs.gov/interweb/assetlibrary /National_Cyberspace_Strategy.pdf

38. "Global Information Security Survey 2002," Ernst & Young, 2002. Available at http://www.ey.com/global/vault.nsf /Global_Info_Security_Survey_2002.pdf

39. *Ibid.*

40. "Digital Security, Putting it All Together" *Economist*, October 24, 2002. Available at http://www.economist.com/surveys/displayStory.cfm?Story_id= 1389499&CFID=9039138&CFTOKEN=265ddd7-ab5fbb31-d282-4b10-9149-5bf9cc131137

41. *Op. cit.* "The National Strategy to Secure Cyberspace."

42. *Ibid.*

43. *Ibid.*

44. *Making the Nation Safer: The Role of Science and Technology in Countering Terrorism.* Committee on Science and Technology for Countering Terrorism, National Research Council. (Washington, DC: National Academy Press, 2002). Available at http://www.nap.edu/catalog/10415.html?onpi_newsdoc062402

ADDITIONAL READINGS

Viruses, Worms, and Hackers

Freedman, David H. and Mann, Charles C. *At Large: The Strange Case of the World's Biggest Internet Invasion.* (New York: Simon & Schuster, 1997).

Salkever, Alex. "As the Worm Turns: Lessons from Blaster," *Business Week*, August 19, 2003. Available at http://www.businessweek.com/print/technology/content/aug2003 /tc20030819_2562_tc047.htm

Weintraub, Arlene and Kerstetter, Jim. "Cyber Alert: Portrait of an Ex-Hacker," *Business Week*, June9, 2003. Available at http://www.businessweek.com/print/magazine/content/03_23 /b3836097_mz063.htm

Other Crimes and Issues

"ID Theft: When Bad Things Happen to Your Good Name," Federal Trade Commission, February 2001. Available at http:/ /www.ftc.gov/bcp/conline/pubs/credit/idtheft.pdf

"IFCC 2002 Internet Fraud Report: January 1, 2002–December 31, 2002," The Internet Fraud Complaint Center, Prepared by the National White Collar Crime Center and the Federal Bureau of Investigation, 2003. Available at http:/ /www1.ifccfbi.gov/strategy/2002_IFCCReport.pdf

"Strengthening Antistalking Statutes," U.S. Department of Justice, Office of Justice Programs, January 2002. Available at http://www.ojp.usdoj.gov/ovc/publications/bulletins/legalseries/bulletin1/ncj188192.pdf

Security: Crime and Terrorism

"An Analysis of International Initiatives on High-Tech Crime: A Review of Implications for the Canadian Policy Environment," Prepared for Industry Canada by Zero Knowledge Systems Inc., December 2001. Available at http://www.lexinformatica.org/cybercrime/pub/Perrin.pdf

Arquilla, John and Ronfeldt, David (Eds.) *Networks and Netwars: The Future of Terror, Crime, and Militancy.* (Santa Monica, CA: Rand, 2001). Available at http://www.rand.org/publications/MR/MR1382/

Schneier, Bruce. *Secrets & Lies: Digital Security in a Networked World.* (New York: Wiley, 2000).

— 12 —

THE ROLE OF GOVERNMENT IN THE NEW MARKET PLACE

The business of America is business.

Calvin Coolidge, Address to the Society of American Newspaper Editors, January 17,1925

INTRODUCTION

In Chapter 4, a variety of applications of computers in the business world presented and discussed. In Chapter 7, a similar exercise was carried out for the role of computers in government. The primary purpose in each of these cases was to focus on specific innovative uses within a given domain. Of course, many information-processing problems do not respect arbitrary boundaries. Several issues naturally reside in the sometimes murky area between government and business.

The relationship between business and government has been long and complex. Most companies wish to pursue their activities with minimal interference from government, except perhaps when guaranteed loans are required on occasion or when foreign companies are felt to have an unfair advantage. In a capitalist system, the government has a variety of responsibilities, among them the creation of a climate in which companies may compete openly and the protection of its citizens' welfare. To these ends, governments have to pass antitrust and consumer protection legislation. In countries where the state owns and manages most of the major companies, the goals of these companies and the people are taken to be indistinguishable. Even in a free enterprise system, government has found it necessary, over the years, to intervene in the marketplace in order to ensure that all companies have a fair chance to compete, a level playing field. The following is a list of relevant issues that illustrate some of these interventions:

Antitrust Cases. The U.S. government charged IBM with antitrust violations in a suit that lasted 13 years until it was finally dropped in January of 1982. Microsoft was charged with unfair practices to maintain a monopoly position since the mid-1980s. The case was settled in July 1995, with rather minor restrictions imposed on Microsoft, but a new major antitrust case was initiated on May 18, 1998, and was almost concluded late in 2002.

Regulation of the Telephone Industry. Up until about 20 years ago, long-distance telephone lines were a monopoly run by AT&T (American Telephone and Telegraph). In January of 1982, AT&T agreed to separate itself from a number of local telephone companies under an agreement arranged by the federal courts. The agreement took effect on January 1, 1984.

Industry Standards. The government plays an important role in helping to set standards in the computer and communication industries (and other areas as well).

Auctioning the Airwaves. The Federal Communications Commission (FCC) auctions segments of the radio spectrum to provide a variety of services.

Legal Protection of Software and Hardware. The government protects programs by such means as copyright and patent laws (as discussed in Chapter 10).

Protection of Privacy. Issues arising from the growth in the use of computer-based information systems have led to problems and legislation (as discussed in Chapter 9).

Electronic Financial Transactions Systems. Future regulation of the banking and financial industries must take into account the increasing use of computer and communication systems for banking services.

International Trade Agreements. The U.S. government has negotiated specific high-technology trade agreements with Japan, for example, a 1996 agreement on computer semiconductors.

Transborder Data Flows. As information becomes a major resource, governments must develop policies to control the flow of information across national borders. This process is complicated by differing national policies on privacy and freedom of information.

Technology Transfer. Individual countries are concerned with protecting their technological developments. In the United States this concern covers both economic competitors such as Japan and political ones such as the Soviet Union. In the United States, open discussion of technical issues is a way of life, and restrictions will be resisted. In fact, restrictions on the export of strong encryption programs have long been debated in the U.S.

Thus, the federal government must intrude into the marketplace from time to time. In general, its policy is to set rules for the players, monitor the resulting performance, and take specific actions only if violations occur. This is the usual procedure for competitive industries such as computers, automobiles, and household appliances. In regulated monopolies such as the telephone system and radio, television, and cable systems, the government has traditionally exerted control by the issuance of licenses, their renewals, and the setting of rates. There has been much debate about the proper role of government, which acts from a variety of motives ranging from the accommodation of public opinion to the exercising of a particular political philosophy.[1]

The computer industry has grown very rapidly since 1945 and no hardware/software/services company has been more successful than International Business Machines (IBM), at least up to fairly recently. In fact, as of 2002, IBM was the 11th leading U.S. company in sales at almost $86 billion, and sixth in profits at $7.75 billion. As a further indication of its dynamism and flexibility, IBM leads all other companies worldwide in Information Technology (IT) revenue and is third in profits behind Microsoft and SBC Communications. In one of the final acts of the Johnson administration, in early 1969, IBM was charged with a variety of antitrust violations. After much expense on both sides, the charges were finally dropped 13 years later. How IBM's domination of the computer market was achieved and maintained was an important issue in the government's suit.

The other major government suit of the late 1970s and early 1980s was directed against AT&T. "Ma Bell," as it was sometimes called, had been a gigantic company composed of a number of local telephone companies, a long-distance service, a manufacturing division, Western Electric, and a world-famous research facility, Bell Labs. During the 1970s, AT&T's monopoly over long-distance service was challenged, and the result was a consent agreement between the company and the federal courts that required AT&T to divest itself of its local telephone companies. The subsequent growth of these companies, continued challenges in the long-distance market, new challenges from cable companies, and the phenomenal growth of the Internet and the World Wide Web, finally prompted Congress to pass a new Telecommunications Act in 1996 to deal with the impact of the new telecommunications technologies.

Since money plays such an important role in our lives, the new technological developments in banking and bill paying will have an important impact. Already, automatic teller machines (ATMs) are everywhere and are changing long-established banking habits. Additional changes taking place now include: point-of-sale terminals (POS terminals), debit cards, smart cards, home banking, and regional, national, and global banking networks. Several social issues naturally arise with the growth in electronic banking. Among these are privacy, new possibilities for large-scale theft and sabotage, system reliability, reduced competition, and consumer protection. The rise in popularity of the Internet and its promise for the future has opened up a host of legal, social, and regulatory issues. In previous chapters, we have examined such issues as privacy, free speech, and intellectual property rights as they relate to the Internet and in this and the next chapter, additional and equally important concerns will be addressed.

Another important area of the economy in which some degree of government involvement has taken place are the nation's stock exchanges and brokerage companies. Computers have made possible the trading of enormous quantities of securities very rapidly and have contributed to a certain degree of instability. Many individuals have been attracted to stock trading over the Internet, creating a host of day traders whose influence on the stock market has been significant. Furthermore, the flow of information around the world via communication networks has become an important factor in the conduct of international business. This development coincides with the growth in multinational corporations and their increasing dependence on the rapid and efficient transmission of information. Of course, international regulation is a much more difficult task than regulation within a single country.

Of major concern to governments is the competitiveness of their industries in response to worldwide challenges. The United States is currently locked in technological combat primarily with Japan and Europe. Japan has made enormous advances since World War II, in becoming a major economic force and technological leader. It has invested heavily in new technology and now challenges the United States across a broad range of products and services, especially computers and microelectronics. In response, the U.S. government, in the process of meeting its defense requirements, has sponsored research and development in many areas of high technology. Many economists and politicians have urged the development of a national plan to maintain economic superiority. The centerpiece of most proposals is a national resolve to continue world leadership in computer hardware and software. Except in times of war or major terrorist threats, national mobilization has not been a hallmark of U.S. society. To deal with current threats, IT has become an important tool, requiring cooperation between the government and industry.

INDUSTRY REGULATION

What is good for the country is good for General Motors and what's good for General Motors is good for the country.

Charles E. Wilson, former president of General Motors, in testimony before the Senate Armed Forces Committee, 1952

The U.S. government has recognized at least two major forms of environments in which businesses can operate. One is the typical free marketplace situation in which companies compete against one another under a set of rules enunciated as laws and regulations. The other is a monopoly situation, in which the government permits a single company to operate without competition, under an agreement that its rates will be regulated. Up to fairly recently the telephone industry was the prime example of a regulated monopoly. An intermediate form is represented by the radio, television, and cable industries. Individual stations must apply for licenses, which are renewed at regular intervals if no violations have occurred. Governments have seen fit to try to ensure that the competition in the open marketplace is as unrestricted as possible. For example, in 1890 Congress passed the Sherman Antitrust Act in response to the activities of large railway and industrial trusts. In later years, various companies—such as Alcoa Aluminum, American Tobacco, and Hughes Tool—were charged with antitrust violations. The longest antitrust case to date involved IBM.

IBM and the Computer Industry

Our industry is healthy and competitive, and IBM has not violated the antitrust laws.—John Opel, president of IBM, 1982[2]

On January 17, 1969, the last possible day it could take action, the Justice Department of the Johnson administration launched an antitrust suit against IBM. Almost 13 years later, on January 8, 1982, the Justice Department of the Reagan administration dropped the longest antitrust suit in history. In the interim, many millions of dollars were spent in legal fees, 66 million pages of documents were collected, and IBM was somewhat restrained in its activities. The government originally charged IBM with monopolizing the computer industry. In general, industries dominated by a few large companies are certainly more stable but perhaps less innovative, although in the personal computer market, including software, competition and innovation are the hallmark, so far. Those who favor minimal government involvement in business point to the computer industry as an example of a successful and innovative field, neglecting to consider the influential role of the Department of Defense, the National Aeronautics and Space Administration, and the National Science Foundation. Nevertheless, even with the IBM giant, there has been room for Silicon Valley and Route 128 (near Boston).

Since it was the undisputed leader in the industry from the 1960s to the 1980s, IBM's every move, announced or predicted, was carefully watched and evaluated. This situation had given IBM extraordinary power in manipulating the market to suit its own needs. The government's antitrust case depended, in part, on proving that certain practices of IBM in controlling the computer industry were illegal. For example, when competitors began marketing new models that were faster and cheaper than the current IBM versions, IBM might announce a price cut or its own new models. Generally customers were forced to wait until the details of IBM's new machines were released. Making inroads into IBM's domination was not easy under the best of conditions. In order to convince an IBM customer to switch, a price reduction in equipment would not be sufficient. It was necessary to guarantee that existing programs would continue to run properly on the new computer. Nevertheless, IBM's share of the market did slowly diminish. In response to the government's charges, IBM argued that its practices were commonly accepted in other businesses, that it did not really control the market, and that in such a technically active field no single company could ever maintain control for very long. Little did IBM know how true its words would turn out to be.

IBM seemed to assume a much less competitive stance during the years of the trial, to avoid the possibility of further charges. While IBM appeared to be dormant, though, there was considerable ferment below the surface. The best example of the "new" IBM was its stunning achievement in the personal computer market. From its introduction of the PC (Personal Computer) in 1981, IBM took the lead in dollar value of personal computers sold in 1983. The IBM name once again demonstrated its worth in this early personal computer era. First-time buyers found comfort in dealing with a company that had a proven track record and was not likely to go out of business. Because of its belief in the primacy of hardware and the urgent need to develop an operating system for its PCs, IBM entered into negotiations with a small software company called Microsoft. The introduction of DOS was a major boost in persuading businesses that the PC was more than a toy. If Apple, with its Macintosh introduced in 1984, promoted the idea of fun and ease of use, then IBM's PCs, and a host of clones, countered with arguments intended to appeal to the business community.

Although IBM legitimized the PC, it did not anticipate that competing in this market would be substantially different from its traditional "big iron" experience. Furthermore, the incredibly rapid and sustained growth in this market favored smaller, more agile companies to the detriment of the older giants of the industry. For example, Digital Equipment was unable to compete in the PC market and its leadership in minicomputers suffered, as did the company itself, as more powerful PCs put considerable pressure on this segment of the industry. Subsequently, Digital Equipment was taken over by the once successful PC maker, Compaq, itself later absorbed by Hewlett-Packard, a venerable Silicon Valley company. IBM itself ran into serious difficulties in the early 1990s as profits evaporated and losses mounted. In 1990, IBM's profits were slightly over $6 billion and it seemed that a return to the very profitable years of the mid 1980s was in the offing. But the following year IBM reported a loss of over $2.8 billion; 1992 was worse with a loss of $6.87 billion and in 1993 losses reached an incredible $8.1 billion, to which massive layoffs (about one-fifth of all employees in 1993) were a major contributor.

IBM's stock value fell substantially as well, and terms such as dinosaur, out-of-touch, lost cause, and stumbling giant were applied with increasing frequency. IBM's problems reverberated throughout the computer industry because so many companies depended on filling software and hardware niches. In March 1993, Lou Gerstner assumed control of IBM and the turnaround began, albeit slowly. Although losses in 1993 were $8.1 billion, in the following year profits were $2.88 billion, a turnaround of almost $11 billion! Growth was sustained in 1995 as profits reached almost $4.2 billion, hardly a performance to be expected from a company sounding the death rattle. Mr. Gerstner left IBM in March 2002 and there was no doubt that IBM, "has transformed itself from a company dependent on mainframe computers and other hardware to an enterprise whose future is tied to supplying services and software for corporate customers. Those two businesses now represent about 80 percent of I.B.M.'s operating profits."[3] It is of some interest that IBM's success in the services area was made possible because one other piece of judicial action removed a restriction from the early days of the computer industry. In January of 1996, a federal judge "terminated much of the 1956 consent decree against IBM, intended at the time to level the playing field between Big Blue and its competitors."[4]

Mr. Gerstner was replaced by Sam Palmisano, who became chairman on October 29, 2002. His vision for the near future focused on what IBM calls "on-demand computing"[5]:

> Mr. Palmisano told the business executives and industry analysts in attendance that on-demand computing would allow corporate customers to purchase computing resources as needed as a utility-style service, almost like electricity. Beyond cost savings, Mr. Palmisano explained that the utility model would help companies become more flexible and fast-moving by integrating more closely internal operations like procurement, marketing and manufacturing. The company also expects it to improve communications with partners, suppliers and customers.

No longer the behemoth of computing, IBM has managed to survive amidst recent difficult times for IT, to post regular profits, and to flexibly transform its activities into new growth areas. The true impact of the antitrust suit is difficult to ascertain but for IBM, it seems to have resulted in a more agile company than it might have been otherwise.

One other major company that has been viewed with some concern by its competitors and the U.S. Justice Department because of its aggressive marketing activities and its monopolization of the operating system market for PCs is, not surprisingly, Microsoft, the world's largest independent software company.

Microsoft: The Software Industry and the Internet

An Early Investigation

Microsoft's phenomenal growth and dominance in the software industry could not help but attract the interest of the Federal Trade Commission (FTC) and the U.S. Department of Justice (DOJ), spurred on by the vocal complaints of competitors and some consumer groups. In November 1989, the FTC launched an antitrust investigation of Microsoft that resulted in a deadlock at the FTC when votes were taken on February 5 and July 21, 1993, on whether to file a complaint. When the FTC ended its inquiry on August 20, 1993, DOJ began its own investigation.[6] As reported in 1994, the government's concerns were as follows[7]:

- Whether Microsoft favored its applications division by providing information on undocumented application programming interfaces (API) in Windows, thus putting rivals such as Lotus Development Corp., WordPerfect Corp. and Borland International, Inc. at a disadvantage.
- Whether Microsoft's policy of requiring PC vendors to pay for DOS and Windows licenses for every processor they ship has the practical effect of excluding operating system vendors such as Novell and IBM.
- Whether Microsoft used its dominance in operating systems to coerce PC vendors into bundling its own applications with machines, thereby freezing out competitors.

It was crucial to the government's case to show that users were harmed by Microsoft's business practices, "because the U.S. Supreme Court has ruled that antitrust laws were designed to protect competition and consumer interests not to settle feuds between competitors."[8]

On July 15, 1994, Microsoft and the government came to an agreement to end the investigation, thereby placing Microsoft in the company of IBM and AT&T as "having been officially declared a monopolist by the U.S. government."[9] The official charges filed by the Justice Department's Antitrust Division are as follows[10]:

- Per-processor contracts with PC makers that forced them to pay royalties for MS-DOS and Windows on every processor they shipped, even if the machine did not ship with that software. This forced PC makers selling non-Microsoft operating systems to pay two royalties one to Microsoft and one to its competition potentially making a rival system more expensive.
- Unreasonably long contracts with PC makers typically three to five years that included minimum commitments that effectively excluded rival operating systems from the market.
- Overly restrictive nondisclosure agreements to prevent third parties that test beta products such as Chicago from working on rival system software.

In essence, the Justice Department alleged that Microsoft has used these unfair practices to maintain a monopoly power in the operating systems market since at least the mid-1980s, with market share consistently in excess of 70%.

The proposed settlement was to apply to all Microsoft products except Windows NT Workstation or Windows NT Advanced Server under the following terms[11]:

- The proposed settlement prohibits Microsoft from using per-processor licenses and minimum purchase terms. Licenses are limited to one or two years.
- Nondisclosure agreements are limited to one year and may not prevent programmers from working on rival operating systems as long as Microsoft's proprietary information is not disclosed.
- Furthermore, Microsoft cannot require PC makers to purchase another Microsoft product as a condition for licensing a Microsoft operating system.
- The settlement will last for six and a half years after it is signed by the presiding judge. Microsoft agreed to abide by the settlement terms immediately.

There was considerable disagreement among rival companies, informed commentators, and the general public about who had won and whether Microsoft would really change its practices. Many felt that given a generally weak case, the government had done as well as it could, while others, mainly small competitors, were angered by their perception that nothing had changed. In an editorial, *Business Week* complimented the Department of Justice (DOJ) because it "was able to use antitrust policy as a scalpel rather than a bludgeon."[12] Furthermore, the Clinton administration was lauded and encouraged "to aggressively investigate allegations of monopolies and other activities that squelch competition."[13]

In January 1996, U.S. District Court Judge Stanley Sporkin, a former enforcement director at the Securities and Exchange Commission, entered the proceedings because he believed that the settlement was not justified, and a month later he rejected the agreed-upon consent degree, resulting in the unlikely alliance of Microsoft and the DOJ expressing anger and disbelief at his actions. A number of Microsoft's rivals made presentations that were accepted by Judge Sporkin. Among these were that the settlement was too narrow, insufficiently documented, minimally enforceable, and that "the government and Microsoft 'have been unable and unwilling to adequately address certain anticompetitive practices' the company has vowed to keep using."[14]

While Judge Sporkin was continuing his investigation, Microsoft was attempting to purchase Intuit, Inc., the maker of Quicken financial software, for $2 billion, in a hostile takeover. This deal was opposed by the Justice Department, which launched an antitrust lawsuit. Major banks were also opposed to the acquisition, because of their concern with a company as aggressive and skilled as Microsoft using Quicken over its proposed Microsoft Network to dominate home banking.[15] On May 20, 1995, Microsoft called off the proposed Intuit takeover. At this point, Judge Sporkin's rejection of the almost one-year-old antitrust settlement agreement between the government and Microsoft was being reviewed by the U.S. Court of Appeals in Washington, and the Justice Department was considering the possibility of further antitrust charges related to "The Microsoft Network and/or other Windows 95 bundling practices."[16] The first of these was settled on June 16, 1995, when a federal appeals court reversed Judge Sporkin, removed him from the case, and approved the 1994 settlement. Two months later, U.S. District Judge Thomas Penfield Jackson approved the consent decree.

A Major Antitrust Case: U.S. v. Microsoft

Early in August 1996, Netscape Communications asked the DOJ "to investigate Microsoft Corp.'s Web server sales practices. Netscape claims that licensing and technical restrictions in how users may run World Wide Web server software on Microsoft's Windows NT operating system violate antitrust laws and give Microsoft an unfair advantage over Netscape and other rivals."[17] The following year, in October,[18]

> The Justice Department files a complaint demanding a $1-million-a-day fine against Microsoft for its alleged violation of the 1995 consent decree. The complaint claims that Microsoft overstepped its bounds by demanding PC manufacturers bundle the Internet Explorer Web browser with their hardware products before being able to obtain a Windows 95 license.

More than five years later, the major decisions were made but the case continued to linger on. We will briefly trace the key points in the trial, the key decisions, the appeals, the major outcomes, and what it might all mean.

The case began on December 5, 1997, with Judge Jackson hearing opening arguments, and within a week, he issued a preliminary injunction preventing Microsoft from requiring PC makers to bundle Internet Explorer with Windows 95. It was this concern that had motivated the early legal actions against Microsoft. Microsoft claimed that Explorer was an integral part of its operating system and could not easily be separated. Courtroom demonstrations took place with even Judge Jackson uninstalling the Internet Explorer icon. In January 1998, Microsoft, facing contempt charges, agreed to permit computer makers to install Windows 95 without having to show the Explorer icon. In the end, this was a Pyrrhic victory because currently Explorer controls close to 95% of the personal browser market, while Netscape Navigator has less than 2.5%.

On May 18, 1998, twenty states joined the Justice Department to file an antitrust suit against Microsoft. Key features of this complaint read as follows[19]:

5. To protect its valuable Windows monopoly against such potential competitive threats, and to extend its operating system monopoly into other software markets, Microsoft has engaged in a series of anticompetitive activities. Microsoft's conduct includes agreements tying other Microsoft software products to Microsoft's Windows operating system; exclusionary agreements precluding companies from distributing, promoting, buying, or using products of Microsoft's software competitors or potential competitors; and exclusionary agreements restricting the right of companies to provide services or resources to Microsoft's software competitors or potential competitors.

7. Internet browsers pose a competitive threat to Microsoft's operating system monopoly in two basic ways. First, as discussed above, one of the most important barriers to the entry and expansion of potential competitors to Microsoft in supplying PC operating systems is the large number of software applications that will run on the Windows operating system (and not on other operating systems). If application programs could be written to run on multiple operating systems, competition in the market for operating systems could be revitalized. The combination of browser technology and a new programming language known as "Java" hold out this promise. Java is designed in part to permit applications written in it to be run on different operating systems. As such, it threatens to reduce or eliminate one of the key barriers to entry protecting Microsoft's operating system monopoly.

13. Microsoft's conduct with respect to browsers is a prominent and immediate example of the pattern of anticompetitive practices undertaken by Microsoft with the purpose and effect of maintaining its PC operating system monopoly and extending that monopoly to other related markets.

15. Having failed simply to stop competition by agreement, Microsoft set about to exclude Netscape and other browser rivals from access to the distribution, promotion, and resources they needed to offer their browser products to OEMs and PC users pervasively enough to facilitate the widespread distribution of Java or to facilitate their browsers becoming an attractive programming platform in their own right.

In antitrust proceedings the key concern is whether or not the defendant has misused its powers in an illegal manner. Having a monopoly or near monopoly control of some segment of the economy is not in itself a violation of antitrust laws.

The antitrust trial began on October 18, 1998, with the CEO of Netscape, Jim Barksdale, the opening witness. Just a month previously, Internet Explorer had overtaken Navigator in the browser market. The sequence of events in this long trial proceeded as follows: The government completed its case on January 12, 1999, with a surprise concession, "the government's top economic witness admits that Microsoft has done nothing so far that would harm consumers";[20] Microsoft rested its case on February 27 and rebuttal arguments began on June 1; closing arguments concluded on September 21; and on November 5, Judge Jackson delivered his initial findings of fact, a preliminary ruling indicative of the final decision. This rather long document of more than 200 pages represented a scathing indictment of Microsoft's business practices, in Judge Jackson's view of course, and was a strong indication of his final verdict. A brief excerpt follows to indicate the tenor of his concerns[21]:

409. To the detriment of consumers, however, Microsoft has done much more than develop innovative browsing software of commendable quality and offer it bundled with Windows at no additional charge. As has been shown, Microsoft also engaged in a concerted series of actions designed to protect the applications barrier to entry, and hence its monopoly power, from a variety of middleware threats, including Netscape's Web browser and Sun's implementation of Java. Many of these actions have harmed consumers in ways that are immediate and easily discernible. They have also caused less direct, but nevertheless serious and far- reaching, consumer harm by distorting competition.

410. By refusing to offer those OEMs [Original Equipment Manufacturers] who requested it a version of Windows without Web browsing software, and by preventing OEMs from removing Internet Explorer—or even the most obvious means of invoking it—prior to shipment, Microsoft forced OEMs to ignore consumer demand for a browserless version of Windows. The same actions forced OEMs either to ignore consumer preferences for Navigator or to give them a Hobson's choice of both browser products at the cost of increased confusion, degraded system performance, and restricted memory. By ensuring that Internet Explorer would launch in certain circumstances in Windows 98 even if Navigator were set as the default, and even if the consumer had removed all conspicuous means of invoking Internet Explorer, Microsoft created confusion and frustration for consumers, and increased technical support costs for business customers... By constraining the freedom of OEMs to implement certain software programs in the Windows boot sequence, Microsoft foreclosed an opportunity for OEMs to make Windows PC systems less confusing and more user-friendly, as consumers desired. By taking the actions listed above, and by enticing firms into exclusivity arrangements with valuable inducements that only Microsoft could offer and that the firms reasonably believed they could not do without, Microsoft forced those consumers who otherwise would have elected Navigator as their browser to either pay a substantial price (in the forms of downloading, installation, confusion, degraded system performance, and diminished memory capacity) or content themselves with Internet Explorer. . . .

411. Many of the tactics that Microsoft has employed have also harmed consumers indirectly by unjustifiably distorting competition. The actions that Microsoft took against Navigator hobbled a form of innovation that had shown the potential to depress the applications barrier to entry sufficiently to enable other firms to compete effectively against Microsoft in the market for Intel-compatible PC operating systems. That competition would have conduced to consumer choice and nurtured innovation. The campaign against Navigator also retarded widespread acceptance of Sun's Java implementation. This campaign, together with actions that Microsoft took with the sole purpose of making it difficult for developers to write Java applications with technologies that would allow them to be ported between Windows and other platforms, impeded another form of innovation that bore the potential to diminish the applications barrier to entry. There is insufficient evidence to find that, absent Microsoft's actions, Navigator and Java already would have ignited genuine competition in the market for Intel-compatible PC operating systems. It is clear, however, that Microsoft has retarded, and perhaps altogether extinguished, the process by which these two middleware technologies could have facilitated the introduction of competition into an important market.

Based on these Findings of Fact, the plaintiffs issued a Joint Proposed Conclusions of Law on December 6, just after Judge Jackson appointed Richard Posner, chief judge of the 7th U.S. Circuit Court of Appeals, as a mediator. Four violations of the Sherman Act were identified[22]:

I. Microsoft violated Section 2 of the Sherman Act by unlawfully maintaining its monopoly in operating systems for Intel-compatible personal computers.
II. Microsoft violated Section 1 of the Sherman Act by unlawfully tying a Web browser to its operating system.
III. Microsoft violated Section 1 of the Sherman Act by entering into numerous unlawful exclusionary agreements.
IV. Microsoft attempted to monopolize the browser market.

Mediation efforts ended in failure on April 1, 2000, and on April 3, 2000, Judge Jackson issued his verdict. Given the nature of the Conclusions of Law document, his verdict was not surprising. Microsoft was found guilty of violating the Sherman Act's restrictions on anticompetitive behavior by misusing its market dominance in several situations. The penalty phase began with government officials filing their proposed remedies. As expected, proposals to break up Microsoft were forthcoming, the exact formula to be determined by Microsoft in order to satisfy the government's requirements. Simply put, two independent companies should result, one marketing operating systems and one applications.

Microsoft's response to the government resulted in a Revised Proposed Final Judgment by the plaintiffs and more jockeying by the litigants until June 7, when Judge Jackson issued his final ruling. The following is a typical description of the key points in this ruling by the media[23]:

> U.S. District Judge Thomas Penfield Jackson decided that Microsoft could retain its operating systems for PCs, TV set-top boxes, handheld computers and other devices. But the company would be forced to create a separate firm for its other software and Web products—such as Outlook, Internet Explorer, BackOffice and the Microsoft Network (MSN)—resulting in sweeping changes from corporate offices and homes to the entire Internet.
>
> In addition to the breakup, Jackson imposed restrictions on Microsoft's business practices that go into effect in 90 days unless an appeals court blocks the action. Microsoft said it will immediately appeal the ruling.
>
> As part of a strongly worded decision, Jackson said the court "has reluctantly come to the conclusion . . . that a structural remedy has become imperative: Microsoft as it is presently organized and led is unwilling to accept the notion that it broke the law or accede to an order amending its conduct."
>
> He added that Microsoft "continues to do business as it has in the past and may yet do to other markets what it has already done to the PC operating system and browser markets."

Microsoft appealed directly to the Supreme Court but was turned down as the Court refused to hear the case before the Court of Appeals had acted. But before the Appeals Court could hear arguments, it held a hearing to review the conduct of Judge Jackson. Apparently, after he delivered his verdict, Judge Jackson publicly expressed his disdain toward Microsoft in a manner that angered the company and raised concerns with his fellow judges about his conduct.

The U.S. Court of Appeals for the District of Columbia heard Microsoft's appeal on February 27, 2001. The following day, it reversed Judge Jackson's decision to split Microsoft, chastised him for his conduct outside the courtroom, and assigned the case to a new judge, Colleen Kollar-Kotelly. However, it did find merit in the case and upheld the finding that Microsoft had abused its near monopoly power. Microsoft again appealed to the Supreme Court, arguing that Judge Jackson's conduct should have precluded the Appeals Court from upholding his findings. However, on September 6, in a major but not unsurprising shift in position, the Department of Justice said that it no longer sought the breakup of Microsoft. Presumably, the change in administration in Washington from the Clinton to Bush presidency signaled that a more pro-business attitude had also arrived.

Much happened over the next year but in the end, the expected outcome was announced by Judge Kollar-Kotelly on November 1, 2002. The proposed settlement does not include a major change in the structure of

Microsoft—the earlier proposed breakup had long ago vanished as a possible punishment—but a collection of rebukes and minor changes. For example, a few of the penalties are given as follows[24]:

> [T]he consent decree does contain provisions for Microsoft to open up its code.
>
> The settlement also prohibits the software firm from retaliating against original equipment manufacturers (OEMs), software vendors or hardware vendors that use software that competes with Microsoft's products. In addition, the company cannot take action against OEMs that ship computers containing both a Microsoft and a non-Microsoft operating system.
>
> Kollar-Kotelly approved these provisions but noted that she would have liked to restrict not just retaliation, but also threats of retaliation. "Given the power Microsoft wields as a monopolist, it would be appropriate to prohibit Microsoft from stifling competition with threats of bad treatment," she wrote.

A few comments taken from the conclusion of Judge Kollar-Kotelly's Memorandum of Opinion are of interest[25]:

> In conclusion, the Court is compelled to comment more generally on the terms of the proposed remedy. First, the Court commends the parties for their intense efforts at reaching a settlement and their willingness to try to do so in the face of previous failures. Second, and more importantly, praise is due based solely on the quality of the fruits of their collaborative labors. While the proposed final judgment, in general, is appropriately crafted to address the anticompetitive conduct, as well as conduct related thereto, the Court regards the document as laudable not for these traits alone, but for the clear, consistent, and coherent manner in which it accomplishes its task. Far from an amalgam of scattered rules and regulations pieced and patched together to restrict Microsoft's anticompetitive business conduct, the proposed final judgment adopts a clear and consistent philosophy such that the provisions form a tightly woven fabric. The proposed final judgment takes account of the theory of liability advanced by Plaintiffs, the actual liability imposed by the appellate court, the concerns of the Plaintiffs with regard to future technologies, and the relevant policy considerations. The product, although not precisely the judgment the Court would have crafted, with the exception of the reservation of jurisdiction, does not stray from the realm of the public interest.

The final sentence does not appear to be a ringing endorsement of the merits of this agreement. Various loose ends remain and almost every day there is an announcement of a further step that must be taken or another complaint that has recently surfaced. For example, on May 29, 2003, Microsoft agreed to pay $750 million to America Online to settle an antitrust suit launched on January 23, 2002.

After years of litigation and many millions of dollars in lawyers' fees, what has changed in the software industry? Probably very little is the answer most would offer. Microsoft remains the dominant company, and except for a yet-to-be-realized challenge by Linux, it will remain so. It may be chastened but only its behavior in the years to come will provide adequate witness. (The consent decree will be in effect for five years.)

AT&T and the Telephone Industry

Mr. Watson, come here; I want you.[26]

The American Telephone and Telegraph used to be referred to as the largest company on earth, and it was not an exaggeration. On January 1, 1984, AT&T underwent the first and most momentous of a series of dramatic changes, which have had a significant impact on U.S. society. The role of telephone systems has become crucial in the growth of computer networks both national and global, especially the Internet. Given the size and importance of AT&T, it is useful to trace its history, albeit briefly, in order to better understand the way in which telephone systems have become so important.

Alexander Graham Bell invented the telephone in 1876.[27] Bell Telephone Company, the predecessor of AT&T, was founded on July 8, 1877. Under the leadership of Theodore Vail, a shrewd and visionary businessman, AT&T was formed in 1885, after an early battle with Western Union. AT&T had purchased Western Electric as its manufacturing division and forced Western Union to withdraw completely from the telephone business. It then underwent a period of rapid growth, stringing telephone lines across the country, fighting off competitors, and purchasing independent telephone companies. By 1910, it had even achieved control of Western Union. In 1913, under the threat of antitrust action, an understanding with the Justice Department was reached, the Kingsbury Commitment, by which AT&T promised to sell its Western Union stock, desist from purchasing any additional competitors, and permit interconnection with independent companies. It seems inevitable that companies that come to dominate their industries will probably have used methods that violate antitrust legislation, or are at least borderline.

After the passage in 1921 of the Willis-Graham Act, which excluded telephone mergers from antitrust charges (if they were approved by the regulatory agencies), AT&T launched a new wave of acquisitions until by 1932 its market share had reached 79%. In order to protect its position, AT&T strongly advocated regulation, arguing that where there was no serious competition, public control should be in force. It prospered under the regulatory system, which after the passage of the Communications Act of 1934 included the Federal Communications Commission (FCC). In practice, regulation precluded the entrance of competitors and protected AT&T's

monopoly. In 1956, after several years of dealing with a new antitrust suit filed in 1949, AT&T and the Justice Department agreed to a Consent Decree that generally accepted AT&T's position that the basic issues of the suit should be resolved by Congress. Existing arrangements were to continue, except that AT&T was not permitted to engage in any business other than the furnishing of common carrier communications services. Thus, AT&T and its subsidiary, Western Electric, could only be involved in regulated services. This seemed to confirm AT&T's mandate, but the new age of computer communications was fast approaching and AT&T seemed to be excluded.

Challenges to AT&T's control of the telephone equipment market began to appear. In addition to the telephone, there are other kinds of terminal equipment: modems for connecting computers to communication networks, key telephone sets for small businesses with several lines, and Private Branch Exchanges (PBXs) for large businesses with internal switching centers. Telephone companies permitted only their own equipment to be connected to telephone lines. In 1966, the FCC ruled that though the telephone companies could set standards, they could not prohibit devices manufactured by other companies from being attached to their networks. Both PBXs and key telephone sets entered the competitive market. This was an important development because PBXs were soon to become the basic infrastructure of the office and its interface to the existing telephone system.

Perhaps the most significant assault on the existing telephone system was initiated by Microwave Communications Incorporated (MCI), which applied in 1963 for the right to build a microwave system between St. Louis and Chicago. MCI planned to offer such services as voice, data, and facsimile (Fax) transmissions, in direct competition with AT&T. After initial approval by the FCC in 1966 and final approval in 1969, a court challenge by AT&T was instituted and withdrawn in 1971 after MCI was authorized to compete with AT&T in the domestic private line, more than seven years after the date of MCI's original application. The telephone companies correctly anticipated that the MCI application would have immense repercussions far beyond its modest beginnings. Other companies entered the field and MCI itself soon expanded to a nationwide network, primarily providing private-line service. A dial-up call would use a telephone company's local lines to reach the nearest MCI office, then go over the MCI network to the destination city's MCI office, and finally over local telephone lines to the destination telephone. AT&T appealed to the FCC and won, but eventually the case went to the courts. In May 1978, the Supreme Court supported a lower-court ruling that overturned the FCC decision. Thus, after almost 100 years of operating as a monopoly, AT&T faced serious competition in the long-distance market.

Another challenge to AT&T's monopoly was the development of satellite-based communications systems and the blurring of the boundary between computer and communications technologies. Computer manufacturers began to compete with communications companies in the production of a range of products. The FCC had permitted a policy of free market competition in the satellite communication industry in 1972. AT&T was permitted to use domestic satellites for its public long-distance service but was not allowed to compete for three years in the private satellite market. In November 1974, convinced that new technology had made the Consent Decree of 1956 obsolete, the Justice Department initiated the largest antitrust suit ever against AT&T. The suit argued that AT&T should be broken up into separate companies: Western Electric for Telephone equipment, Long Line for long-distance service, and the Bell operating companies (BOCs) for local service. Finally, on January 8, 1982, an agreement was reached between AT&T and the Justice Department along the lines suggested in the original suit.[28]

> An historic agreement has been reached: AT&T agreed to a consent order divesting the company of all facilities used to provide local telephone service, and the Department of Justice dropped its antitrust case against the company.

After divesting itself of its local telephone companies, AT&T was organized in two main divisions, as follows[29]:
- AT&T Communications
  Long-distance. 1984 sales: $35 billion
- AT&T Technologies. 1984 sales: $17 billion
  AT&T Bell Laboratories: Research and development
  AT&T Network Systems: Telephone equipment, manufacturing, and sales
  AT&T Technology Systems: Manufacturing and sales of components, e.g., chips
  AT&T International: Overseas marketing of equipment and services; foreign partnerships
  AT&T Information Systems: Computers and business systems.

On January 1, 1985, AT&T Information Systems—set up as an arms-length, deregulated subsidiary by the government—was reorganized along three lines of business: computers, large business systems, and small business systems. The remaining parts of the AT&T empire—the 22 local operating companies, about two-thirds of its assets—were reorganized into 7 independent regional Bell operating companies, the Baby Bells: Pacific Telesis, U.S. West, BellSouth, NYNEX, Bell Atlantic, Southwestern Bell, and Ameritech, and the Central Services Organization, a research and development division jointly owned by these companies and now called Bell Communications Research (Bellcore). In the communication switching equipment area, AT&T competed initially with such companies as Northern Telecom (Canada), Rolm (U.S.), and L. M. Ericsson, Philips, and Plessey (Europe), and in the long-distance carrier market its major competitors were MCI and Sprint. It had been expected that the major confrontation would be with IBM: "The stage is set for a bout of worldwide dimensions: never before have two private corporations brought such resources and so many years of preparation into a head-on competition."[30] However, no major confrontation occurred, although each company unsuccessfully attempted to move into the other's domain; in the end, each company was left to deal with challenges within its own industry.

Telecommunications in an Era of Rapid Change

The idea of a natural monopoly was introduced earlier in this chapter, and much of the discussion of the history of telephone companies turned on regulatory issues, but with the introduction of powerful new technologies at such an incredible pace, natural monopolies no longer exist in the telephone industry, which is better described as an oligopoly, i.e., a market controlled by a small number of major players. The recent history of AT&T is witness to this observation.

Ups and Downs of AT&T and the Baby Bells

During the latter half of the 1980s and the first half of the 1990s, AT&T took a number of steps to improve its competitive position. In 1991, it took over the computer company NCR, in yet another attempt to gain a foothold in the computer industry. Once again this attempt proved unsuccessful, as in 1996, AT&T sold NCR; it also sold the former Bell Labs unit, the telephone equipment manufacturer, renamed Lucent Technologies, leaving AT&T as basically a long-distance service provider. But more moves were soon to follow. In 1999, in a major move into the cable market, it acquired TCI and its 33 million subscribers for $48 billion. The following year it added another major cable company, MediaOne, for $44 billion. Even these ventures did not last very long, as on December 19, 2001, AT&T announced the sale of its cable unit, largely consisting of TCI and MediaOne, to Comcast. While AT&T was attempting to restructure itself, the RBOCs were not standing still.

Over the years, the original seven Baby Bells have been reduced to four through mergers and acquisitions.[31]

In 1997, two Bells purchased two other Bells, making a new total of five companies.
- Bell Atlantic & NYNEX—All NYNEX states were renamed Bell Atlantic
- SBC Communications (formerly Southwestern Bell) & Pacific Telesis
In the law few years, there have been even more changes:
- SBC Communications purchased SNET [New England Telephone] and Ameritech
- Bell Atlantic and NYNEX changed their name to Verizon, and purchased GTE
- US West became Qwest

And BellSouth remained BellSouth. On a regular basis, these companies complained about AT&T's activities and petitioned state and federal regulators for permission to pursue new ventures. AT&T also argued that it was artificially constrained and limited in its ability to compete nationally as well as globally. Finally, in February 1996, congress passed the first comprehensive telecommunication legislation in 60 years.

The Telecommunications Act of 1996

The Act was signed into law by President Clinton on February 8, 1996. We have already discussed the most publicized part, the Communications Decency Act, but although its attempt to regulate content on the Internet has been overturned, in part, by the Supreme Court and rightly so, it is also important to review if the rest of the Act, which will launch major changes in the U.S. telecommunications system. First, here is a brief overview of the Act itself, taken from the analysis of the law firm, Blumenfeld & Cohen[32]:

- Telephone Service. The Act overrules all state restrictions on competition in local and long-distance telephone service. The Baby Bells are freed to provide long-distance service outside their regions immediately, and inside their regions once completing a series of steps to remove entry barriers for local telephone competition.
- Telecommunications Equipment Manufacturing. The Act allows the Baby Bells to manufacture telephone equipment once the FCC approves their application for out-of-region long-distance.
- Cable Television. Telephone companies are permitted to offer either cable television services or to carry video programming for other entities via "open video systems." The Act substantially relaxes the rules governing cable television systems under the 1992 Cable Act.
- Radio and Television Broadcasting. The Act relaxes the FCC's media concentration rules. . . Television equipment manufacturers are required to equip all new TVs with a so-called "V-chip" ("V" for violence) allowing parental blocking of violent, sexually explicit or indecent programming.

A complementary view was expressed in the popular media, as *Newsweek* described the impact of the Act on the general public as follows[33]:

- Long-Distance Phone Service. The Baby Bells can now battle AT&T, MCI and Sprint for customers. Calls to Aunt Molly may cost less.
- Local Phone Service. Cable and long-distance companies can compete in local markets. Business customers are likely to feel the effects first.
- Television. Television makers will be required to install chips in TV sets that will allow viewers to block out violent and sexual programs.
- Cable. Customers in big metro areas could see higher bills when rate regulations are lifted. Smaller-city subscribers might be affected sooner.

- Internet. People who make indecent material available to minors will now face criminal penalties.

The motivation for this legislation originated from several sources. The Republican-controlled Congress was interested in lessening government regulation of industries that were taking advantage of such advanced technologies that distinctions among telephone, broadcasting, and cable systems had nearly vanished. That is, voice, music, images, and movies are all transmitted by bits moving over copper wires, fiber optics, coaxial cable, or through the air as satellite signals. Thus, distinct regulatory strategies for telephone, broadcast, and cable do not seem viable or supportable. The telephone companies, both local and long-distance, want to compete independently of the distance the call covers and they want to carry all sorts of information and not be restricted in any way. In fact, they are developing technical methods for expanding the usable bandwidth of copper wire in order to carry movies and other information-intensive communications. Cable companies are interested in carrying telephone communications, having regulations over their pricing formulae reduced or eliminated, and providing Internet access over high-speed cable modems, which will require the provision of two-way data flow. Broadcast media want to reduce regulations over ownership both vertical and horizontal. All can find in the Act possibilities to further their interests. Some even want the FCC removed, or at least its powers diminished, to permit the unfettered marketplace to decide the winners and losers.

On August 1, 1996, the FCC issued its first rules on local competition in the telephone industry in the wake of the Telecommunications Act. This is only the first step in developing the ground rules for local competition. The next two parts will deal with access charge reform and universal service reform. There is some consensus that in this round the long-distance carriers achieved an advantage. With respect to reseller discounts, for example, "local phone companies must offer long-distance companies a discount of 17 to 25 percent off the retail price of any network service, so that these rivals could resell the service under their own brand names."[34] Long-distance companies will be able to purchase individual services and equipment from local providers rather than complete packages that the locals would have preferred to provide. However, current access charges that the long-distance companies must pay will be kept in place for the time being.

It will take many years until the winners and losers in the corporate world are determined, to say nothing of the population at large. There is some hope that telephone rates both local and long-distance will decrease after decade-long increases. Encouraging competition by removing restrictions against who can enter which market should result in lower rates for consumers. Combined with advances in telecommunications technologies, the average citizen should be able to take advantage of many of the new services. However, nothing is a given and the stakes are very high. In an overview of issues that must be confronted by the Federal Communications Commission, the following points are highlighted[35]:

> Over the next few months, a single federal agency will begin to fundamentally alter the nation's communications and mass-media landscape, rewriting a broad swath of rules that affect the choices consumers have for getting online and the variety of television and radio programming they watch and hear.
>
> The rules in question govern how much telephone companies need to open their lines to competitors for local phone and high-speed Internet service. . . .
>
> Opponents of the proposed rules fear that, taken together, they ultimately could lead to a few powerful conglomerates controlling the flow of electronic information, from programming of television and radio news and entertainment to owning the pipes that connect people to the Internet.
>
> The FCC is considering changes in the rules specifying which parts of the network the Bells must make available. The changes also might preempt the states' rate-setting authority, in light of court decisions that have questioned the fairness of, among other things, rates varying from area to area.

So the next few years will witness global competition, global arrangements, and cooperation, taking place at an unprecedented pace. The Internet is only one stage in the establishment and continuous growth in worldwide communications.

ELECTRONIC BANKING AND FINANCIAL TRANSACTIONS

> During the past decade, consumers, businesses, and governments have continued to increase their use of electronic payments. At the same time, advances in computer processing, telecommunications, and data storage have contributed to a range of payments system innovations. Although only a limited number of these innovations have enjoyed commercial success so far, there has been some movement toward expanding the range of options and techniques for making electronic payments in the United States and increasing the overall efficiency of the payments system.[36]

Financial transactions are such a common occurrence in everyday life that it is not surprising that computers have found eager acceptance in the banking community. The sheer mass of numerical computations required to record, to update, and to process banking records has made the industry a major purchaser of equipment and employer of information-processing professionals. Early applications involved the use of keypunches to prepare financial information that was then read into the computer. Accounts were then updated and financial statements produced. As software and hardware became increasingly sophisticated, banks have modernized their method of operation. Tellers could enter transaction information into a local computer via terminals at the counter. For independent banks, this information would be useful directly; for branch banks, the local computer would send the information over a communication system to the central computer. The merging of computers and communication systems is a marriage made in heaven, for financial institutions. Up to fairly recently, the common term used to refer to a host of services facilitated by computers and electronic networks is EFTS (Electronic Funds Transfer Systems). It is less commonly used currently. The next step has been to permit customers access to their accounts directly or via the Internet.

Banking in America

In 1983, Stephen T. McLin, strategic planning chief for Bank of America, in commenting on how banks could reduce costs, noted that, "the central challenge in retail banking . . . is 'to migrate customers from the brick and mortar system to electronic delivery systems.'"[37] This challenge is being met, as we shall see, but first a brief review of the development of retail banking. Banks can be chartered by both the federal government and the states. The history of banking reflects the tension between the desire of rural, frontier America for local control over banks and the seeming expansionist tendencies of the international banks. This confrontation has turned on the issue of branch banking—which banks can set up branches and what constitutes a branch bank. "By 1988, 45 states had passed some type of legislation permitting regional or nationwide branching. Many states allowed for the formation of regional compacts designed to give regional banks enough time to prevent themselves from being absorbed by the money center banks."[38]

Dimensions of Electronic Banking

Included under this heading is a multitude of processes, services, and mechanisms that depend on computers and communication systems for their operation. Some components have been in existence for quite a while, others have been introduced recently, and still others are in the planning stage. The full array will certainly change the way we shop, bank, and generally carry out our financial transactions. The impact on society will be in such areas as employment, privacy, social relations and patterns of interaction, centralization of control, financial transactions, and possible major consolidations of financial institutions.

Preauthorizations and Automated Banking

The following were probably the first procedures that could legitimately be referred to as instances of electronic banking:

Direct deposits of regular payments: paychecks, royalties
Direct payments of recurrent expenses: mortgages, loans
Direct regular contributions: charity
Payment of bills by telephone.

Once a person authorizes deposits or payments, these are made automatically without further interaction. Typically, large companies would deliver tapes of employees' salaries to banks for disbursement into appropriate accounts. Such tapes are of course generated by the companies' computers. Since these procedures do not require sophisticated computer techniques, they were instituted quite early in the course of electronic banking. Now such information is transmitted over secure electronic networks.

The use of Automated Teller Machines (ATMs) for depositing and withdrawing money, transfers between accounts, and other services—and the authorization of credit and checks—have become a way of life for many people. They have proven to be convenient, easy to use, and extremely popular because of their availability at all hours of the day and night. For their part, the banks find that ATMs, which can operate 24 hours a day, save them a considerable amount of money because employees are not needed. The banks are encouraging the use of ATMs during regular banking hours as well, by reducing their staff size and reserving the remaining staff for special problems. Although ATMs permit a variety of banking functions, they are mostly used for cash withdrawals. The direct economic benefits of ATMs are obvious: a much lower cost per transaction compared with a teller transaction.

Another part of electronic banking is the use of terminals to perform credit checks. Before authorizing a purchase, a store is able to verify electronically that a customer has sufficient funds on hand or that the balance available on a credit card is sufficiently large. This kind of checking can also be carried out by telephone with only slightly more difficulty, but the communications networks necessary for electronic banking discourage the use of the telephone in this context.

POS (Point-of-Sale) Operations

The common feature of POS operations is that the electronic financial transactions are made directly at the time of purchase. Thus, instead of using cash, a check, or a credit card, the customer will have a debit card that, when placed in a POS terminal, transfers money from the customer's bank account to the store's. The card used in ATMs is really a debit card, since its use may result in instantaneous transfers into and out of bank accounts. If the customer has insufficient funds or lacks a line of credit, the purchase will not be completed.

The widespread use of the debit card may be a major step along the way to the cashless society. Another important implication is the loss of the "float period" between the time a purchase is made and the time it must be paid for. The float period is not desirable for the banks, because it gives the customer use of the bank's money interest-free. In periods of high interest rates, substantial amounts of money are involved. With the debit card, the float period is effectively eliminated and at the same time payment to the vendor is guaranteed.

What benefits do debit cards have for consumers? Consider the following list proposed by Jane Bryant Quinn[39]:

1. For the prudent, debit cards are pure discipline. You don't spend more money than you have in the bank.
2. The cards can be easier to use than personal checks, especially in places where you're not known.
3. For couples with joint checking, debit cards eliminate the need to juggle two checkbooks or carry loose checks.
4. If you use a debit card for small purchases, you run no risk of paying interest on them. With a credit card, by contrast, interest might be due even if you pay off the bill at the end of the month. (That usually happens when you roll over debt or when your card has no grace period.)

Debit cards are quite widely used currently, and there is a variation—the prepaid card, issued by businesses, banks, and other companies, used to pay for a wide range of goods and services. The initial value of the card is coded on a magnetic strip and subsequent payments result in a corresponding reduction in its value.

Automated Clearinghouse

A major part of the cost of processing a check is the physical movement of the check itself from the merchant, to a local bank, to a central clearinghouse, to the customer's bank, and eventually back to the customer, with perhaps additional stages involved. The replacement of all this paper processing by an electronic system is well under way. Such networks have been in existence for some time to facilitate the movement of money among financial institutions. Large networks of ATMs and POS services are being built. Banks are getting larger through mergers, acquisitions, and the formation of networks to permit customers access to banking services on a regional basis. Such growth is necessary if the costs of constructing both regional and national systems are to be financed.

Current Banking Technologies

One bank that made history was a rather small bank in Pineville, Kentucky, the Security First Network Bank, that on October 18, 1995, became the first Internet bank, approved by the government. How does the bank try to sell itself?[40]

- You'll save money. Our regular Internet checking accounts have no monthly fees or minimum balance requirements. You get 20 free electronic payments each month, unlimited check-writing privileges, and a free ATM or Debit card.
- You'll make money. Our Money Market and CD rates are some of the highest in the country. Our costs are lower, so we pass the benefits on to you.
- You'll save time. Paying your bills will take minutes, not hours. Who else lets you open a bank account from the convenience of your home, in less than five minutes?
- Peace of mind. All your transactions are protected by military grade security in use by the U.S. Department of Defense and top intelligence agencies.
- SFNB's wide range of services. Have your electronic payments sent to anyone.
- No software to buy . . . ever. You can use your SFNB account any time, from any computer with Internet access, worldwide.
- No manuals to sift through. SFNB is so easy to use that one "walk" through our demo and you are ready to go. And SFNB interfaces with popular personal finance software, so you don't have to change your habits.
- Forget banker's hours and holidays. Our customer service reps are here 24 hours a day, 365 days a year at no charge to you.

From the point of view of the consumer, electronic banking offers many conveniences. A survey by the Pew Internet & American Life Project revealed the following[41]:

- In March 2000, when we first asked about certain "convenience" activities like banking or making travel reservations online, not many Internet users had sampled them. Seventeen percent of Internet users (about 14 million Americans) had ever done any banking online. Thirty-six percent of Internet users (about 31 million Americans) had ever made a travel purchase online. We now [2002] find that 32% of Internet users (about 37 million Americans [an increase of 164%]) have now done their banking online and 50% of Internet users (about 59 million Americans) have made a travel purchase online.
- Of all seventy activities we track, none have seen as much growth as online banking and online travel purchases. When it comes to a "typical day" online, online banking has evolved into a fairly common task, nearly equal to instant messaging in its popularity.
- On a typical day in March 2000, 5% of Internet users conducted bank business online. On a typical day in September 2002, 10% of Internet users conducted bank business online.

• The rise in the popularity of online banking builds on the Federal Reserve's recent report about a drop in the number of paper checks written by consumers. In 1995, the Fed processed 49.5 billion checks. In 2000, the Fed processed 42.5 billion checks—a 14% drop.

Some additional interesting results, which certainly explain why banks have invested so heavily in providing a wide range of online services to their customers, are the following[42]:

Percent of e-bankers who say this was a "very important" factor in their decision to bank online:

• I can do my banking when it is convenient for me	79%
• Banking online saves me time	71%
• Banking online gives me better control over my finances	52%
• I can do my banking in private, without having to talk to anybody	41%
• There is more banking information available to me online	36%
• Banking online saves me money	30%
• There are more bank services available to me online	25%

It is worthwhile to examine first the "big picture" for electronic financing, the term used by the World Bank for the host of services and infrastructure emerging locally and globally, as well. In a discussion paper released by the World Bank, the changes being wrought by computers, networks, and the Internet, are presented as follows[43]:

• E-finance will lead to much lower costs and greater competition in financial services through both new entry from outside today's financial sector and greater competition among incumbent financial service providers.

• Internet and related technologies are more than just new delivery channels, they are a completely different way of providing financial services. Using data mining techniques, for example, providers can tailor products without much human input and at very low cost.

• Technological advances are also changing the face of the financial services industry. New providers are emerging within and across countries, including online banks, online brokerages, and companies that allow consumers to compare financial services such as mortgage loans and insurance policies. Nonfinancial entities are also entering the market, including telecommunications and utility companies that offer payment and other services.

• Trading systems for equities, fixed income, and foreign exchange are consolidating and going global. Trading is moving toward electronic platforms not tied to any location. Electronic trading and communication networks have lowered the costs of trading and allow for better price determination.

- The Internet and other technological advances have shrunk economies of scale in the production of financial services. Lower scale economies have increased competition, particularly among financial services that can easily be unbundled and commoditized through automation including bill payment services, mortgage loans, insurance, and even trade technology.

Some of the goals of banks that deal with the general public at the community level are expressed in a detailed survey conducted by the American Bankers Association of community banks. Most of the survey is concerned with very specific banking information but for the purposes of this review, the following results are both relevant and interesting. All states are represented and the banks that responded had an average asset size of $178.8 million. Some of these results are given as follows[44]:

- Virtually all banks with over $200 million in assets have websites.
- 46.4% (up 92% in one year) have special Web services for small business customers. For example, Balances (91.2%), Wire transfers (74.7%), Cash management (74.1%), View postings (65.3%), and Check images (52.9%).
- In response to the question: What is the primary reason for offering online banking? The answers are Customers want it (47.7%), Competition offers it (29.6%), To attract new customers (14.8%), Eventually, it will be a profit source (5.8%), and To save money for banks (2.2%).

For a slightly different environment, Canada, the growth of online activities has even affected the relatively recent technology of banking machines. Online banking has doubled between 2000 and 2002 from 8% of banking activity to 16%, while ABMs (Automatic Banking Machines) have decreased from 45% to 40%, and telephone use has decreased from 10% to 8%.[45]

Problem Areas

One of the byproducts of electronic banking is an increase in financial information. For example, the use of a POS terminal results in a record indicating that an individual spent a particular amount of money at a particular time and place. Because these records are created electronically and stored in computer databases, they are relatively straightforward to retrieve. Since electronic banking operates online and in real time (i.e., transactions take effect instantaneously) such systems could be used to locate individuals whenever they initiate a transaction. Furthermore, more institutions will have access to an individual's financial records. In 1978, Congress passed the Right to Financial Privacy Act, limiting the government's access to financial records. The Act outlines the procedures necessary to obtain such financial records as the following[45a]:

Customer authorization
Administrative subpoena or summons

Search warrant
Judicial subpoena
Formal written request, a copy of which is filed in court.

The government must notify individuals that their financial records are being requested and advise them that they may under law have the right to attempt to keep those records from the requesting agency. Records obtained by one agency cannot be provided to any other government department or agency. Such legislation represents legitimate concerns about the increasing availability of private information, in this case financial, even though the Act is primarily concerned with specifying the conditions under which the government *can* have access. Some 20 years later, the Gramm-Leach-Bliley Act of 1999 (Financial Services Modernization Act) was passed to deal in part with privacy issues related to financial information. (See the discussion in Chapter 9.)

Stock Market Regulation

Sometimes called Black Monday, this event described below set off a flurry of accusations and was seen as yet another crime committed by Wall Street insiders and traders against the small investor[46]:

> From the close of trading on Friday, October 16, to its lowest point on Tuesday, October 20, a period of just 10 trading hours, the S & P 500 Index fell 22%. During the same 10 hours, the S & P Futures Index fell 36%. This precipitous drop in prices on October 19 and 20, 1987, and the events that surrounded it, are now known as the Crash of 1987. The 1987 stock market plunge was the worst ever.

In the wake of the crash, studies were initiated by several authorities, including the Presidential Task Force (the Brady Commission), the Commodity Futures Trading Commission (CFTC), the Securities Exchange Commission (SEC), the General Accounting Office (GAO), the New York Stock Exchange (NYSE), and the Chicago Mercantile Exchange (CME). All these reports addressed two major questions: What caused the crash? Were financial institutions flawed? The answers are surprising, especially in the light of the instant analyses following the crash. The SEC report does not answer the "what" and indeed says that the precise combination of causes may never be known. It was, indirectly, critical of computerized strategies involving the simultaneous buying and selling of stocks and stock index futures.[47] (This practice will be discussed later in this section). The Brady Commission report notes (p. x), "The precipitous market decline . . . was 'triggered' by specific events: an unexpectedly high merchandise trade deficit which pushed interest rates to new high levels, and proposed tax legislation which led to the collapse of the stocks of a number of takeover candidates."[48] Note that nothing is said about the internal workings of the stock exchanges themselves. After analyzing all of the above reports, the author of the opening quotation of this section, Franklin Edwards of Columbia University, attempts to capture the common opinion: "a combination of speculative euphoria in world stock markets and serious underlying macroeconomic disequilibria set the stage for a crisis of confidence that inevitably would have, and finally did, precipitate a market break."[49]

In the early reactions to the crash, a likely major candidate for blame was the computer in two respects, first as initiating and responding to trades in a manner that produced a frenzied, uncontrollable cycle of selling, and second as an inadequate record keeper and monitor of the overheated market. These charges were not supported by the subsequent studies. Nevertheless, immediately following the crash, the New York Stock Exchange suspended program trading ("Program trading exacerbated the decline"[50]), an act that falsely suggested a major contributing role for computers. Perhaps three definitions would be helpful at this point[51]:

Program Trading. Prior to the entry of computers, program trading involved the purchase or sale of a portfolio, or "basket" of stocks, as if the portfolio were a single stock. With the advent of computers, the term "computerized trading" is frequently used and the image evokes huge blocks of stock bought or sold with a single keystroke.

Stock-Index Arbitrage. Arbitrage is the simultaneous purchase and sale of similar securities on different markets in the hope of achieving a gain based on small differences in prices on the two markets. In the most popular form of arbitrage, called stock-index arbitrage, a portfolio of stocks is traded instead of a single stock. Traders prepare a basket of stocks that mirrors the Standard & Poors (S&P) stock index and monitors the value of that index on the Chicago Mercantile Exchange, which deals in futures, that is, in contracts to deliver a fixed quantity of stocks at a fixed price and a fixed time. Simultaneously, the value of the basket is monitored on the New York Stock Exchange, where the sum of the current values of each stock determines the overall value. Because of discrepancies that arise between these two markets and last only a few minutes, it is possible for a trader, by instantaneously issuing buy or sell orders for large baskets at values, for example, between 10 and $100 million, to profit by moves of the two markets in opposite directions. It has been possible for vast amounts of money to be made by this process.

Portfolio Insurance. One way for an investor to hedge against losses is to program his or her own computer to monitor the instantaneous behavior of the portfolio. If it falls below a certain value, a warning can be triggered and the investor can issue a sell, with a few keystrokes, or if it rises, the investor can issue a buy order. The computer program can issue such orders automatically if the conditions are well-defined. Portfolio insurance is commonly used by corporations, pension funds, endowments, and mutual funds.

Index arbitrage and portfolio insurance played some role in the crash of 1987, although they probably did not initiate it. The question for regulatory authorities, such as the internal ones run by the Exchanges, and especially SEC, the federal agency responsible for the operation of all the nation's exchanges, is to ensure that all investors, large and small, have equal opportunity. The destabilizing impact of computers, if any, must be eliminated or reduced. Among the recommendations in the SEC study that are relevant to the use of computers are the following[52]:

- Program trading information should be publicly disseminated, and the NYSE's DOT (designated order turnaround) system should be enhanced.
- Better market-surveillance systems are needed.
- Various improvements should be made to increase the efficiency of the automated settlement systems used by clearing associations.

The creative use of computers to manipulate stocks in ways not previously anticipated will require regulators to exercise constant vigilance. To this end, the New York Stock Exchange (NYSE), the National Association of Securities Dealers (NASD), and the American Stock Exchange (AMEX) have invested in sophisticated computer programs to identify suspicious abnormal trading. Given the enormous number of daily transactions, it requires considerable computing power to detect such suspicious activities. The NYSE has a system with more than one million records on individuals who might have access to private information and therefore could be involved in a stock purchase or leveraged buyout. It also has a system for monitoring every transaction, which is first alerted by some unusual activity, the exact nature of which is not publicly available for obvious reasons. The second level is then triggered by analysis and comparison with normal behavior. The company is alerted and newspapers are consulted to uncover any information to explain the unusual occurrence. If no satisfactory explanation is discovered, a full investigation is initiated by the NYSE's surveillance staff.[53]

Day Trading

"Day traders rapidly buy and sell stocks throughout the day in the hope that their stocks will continue climbing or falling in value for the seconds to minutes they own the stock, allowing them to lock in quick profits. Day traders usually buy on borrowed money, hoping that they will reap higher profits through leverage, but running the risk of higher losses too."[54] Of course the Internet has facilitated the rapid increase in the number of these individuals. Day trading is neither illegal nor unethical; it is just fraught with risk as the Securities & Exchange Commission notes[55]:

- Be prepared to suffer severe financial losses

Day traders typically suffer severe financial losses in their first months of trading, and many never graduate to profit-making status.

- Day traders do not "invest"

Day traders sit in front of computer screens and look for a stock that is either moving up or down in value. They want to ride the momentum of the stock and get out of the stock before it changes course.

- Day trading is an extremely stressful and expensive full-time job

Day traders must watch the market continuously during the day at their computer terminals. It's extremely difficult and demands great concentration to watch dozens of ticker quotes and price fluctuations to spot market trends.

- Day traders depend heavily on borrowing money or buying stocks on margin

Borrowing money to trade in stocks is always a risky business. Day trading strategies demand using the leverage of borrowed money to make profits. This is why many day traders lose all their money and may end up in debt as well.

- Don't believe claims of easy profits

Don't believe advertising claims that promise quick and sure profits from day trading. Before you start trading with a firm, make sure you know how many clients have lost money and how many have made profits.

Jonathan Lebed: You're Never Too Young

Mr. Lebed, "a 15-year-old high-school student," is "the first minor ever to face proceedings for stock market fraud."[56] Indeed, although he is not unique in employing the Internet for fraudulent activities, his youth does draw attention, at least to reinforce the observation that on the Internet, age is clearly no barrier to innovation. The charges against Mr. Lebed read as follows[57]:

> On eleven separate occasions between August 23, 1999, and February 4, 2000, Lebed engaged in a scheme on the Internet in which he purchased large blocks of thinly traded microcap stocks and, within hours of making such purchases, sent numerous false and/or misleading messages, or "spam," over the Internet touting the stocks he had just purchased. Lebed then sold all of these shares, usually within 24 hours, profiting from the increased price his messages had caused. During the course of the scheme, Lebed realized a total net profit of $272,826.

The SEC ordered Mr. Lebed to cease and desist his illegal activities and within seven days to pay the U.S. Treasury the sum of $272,826 plus prejudgment interest of $12,174.

Advice for Online Investors

One useful source of advice for online investors is given as follows[58]:

The North American Securities Administrators Association (NASAA), which represents state and provincial securities regulators in the U.S., Canada and Mexico, developed the "10 Tips for Online Investors" to educate investors and help them to think carefully about making an investment online.

When You Invest Online, Be Sure To

1. Receive full disclosure, prior to opening your account, about the alternatives for buying and selling securities and how to obtain account information if you cannot access the firm's Web site.
2. Understand that most likely you are not linked directly to the market, and that the click of your mouse does not instantly execute the trade.
3. Receive information from the firm to substantiate any advertised claims concerning the ease and speed of online trading.
4. Receive information from the firm about significant Web site outages, delays and other interruptions to securities trading and account access.
5. Obtain information before trading about entering and canceling orders (market, limit and stop loss), and the details and risks of margin accounts (borrowing to buy stocks).
6. Determine whether you are receiving delayed or real-time stock quotes and when your account information was last updated.
7. Review the firm's privacy and Web site security policies and whether your name may be used for mailing lists or other promotional activities by the firm or any other party.
8. Receive clear information about sales commissions and fees and conditions that apply to any advertised discount on commissions.
9. Know how to, and if necessary, contact a customer service representative with your concerns and request prompt attention and fair consideration.
10. Contact your state or provincial securities agency to (1) verify the registration/licensing status and disciplinary history of the online brokerage firm, or (2) file a complaint, if appropriate.

OTHER ONLINE REGULATORY ISSUES

While the use of encryption technologies is not a panacea for all information security problems, we believe that adoption of our recommendations would lead to enhanced protection and privacy for individuals and businesses in many areas, ranging from cellular and other wireless phone conversations to electronic transmission of sensitive business or financial documents. It is true that the spread of encryption technologies will add to the burden of those in government who are charged with carrying out certain law enforcement and intelligence activities. But the many benefits to society of widespread commercial and private use of cryptography outweigh the disadvantages.

Kenneth W. Dam, Chair, Committee to Study National Cryptography Policy, Computer Science and Telecommunications Board, National

Research Council, National Academy of Sciences and National Academy of
Engineering, May 30, 1996[59]

The issues to be explored relate to a variety of attempts by governments to
influence or control material carried on the Internet or the methods used or
proposed to ensure the security of Internet transmissions, namely encryption, and also relate to perceived government-imposed restrictions on business and organizations. These topics include the so-called Clipper Chip
debate (a restriction on access to preferred encryption choices by business
and individuals), restriction on the export of computer technologies (including encryption software), terrorism concerns, gambling, taxes, and the regulation of radio, telephone, and television on the Internet.

The Clipper Chip

A state-of-the-art microcircuit called the "Clipper Chip" has been developed by government engineers. The chip represents a new approach to
encryption technology. It can be used in new, relatively inexpensive encryption devices that can be attached to an ordinary telephone. It scrambles telephone communications using an encryption algorithm that is more
powerful than many in commercial use today.[60]

The issue is encryption—the need to transform communications into a
secure form so that sender and receiver are assured that no third party has
access and can determine the content. It is important for commerce that payments are secure, that money transfers are guaranteed, and that confidentiality is respected at all costs. Individuals want the same assurance for their
private communications.

An Introduction to Cryptography

There will be no mathematics in this discussion; many fine books exist on
the subject. The point is to provide just enough background to make the
presentation meaningful. First a few definitions are in order.[61]

Encryption is the transformation of data into some unreadable form. Its
purpose is to ensure privacy by keeping the information hidden from anyone for whom it is not intended, even those who can see the encrypted data.

Decryption is the reverse of encryption; it is the transformation of
encrypted data back into some intelligible form.

Encryption and decryption require the use of some secret information,
usually referred to as a *key*. Depending on the encryption mechanism used,
the same key might be used for both encryption and decryption, while for
other mechanisms, the keys used for encryption and decryption might be
different.

Most of the concern with cryptography, the process of creating and using cypher systems, has been to ensure secrecy and verification, or authentication—a necessity for government security in many of its operations, including military, criminal, and espionage. With the rise of telecommunication networks as the preferred means for exchanging information, commercial and otherwise, these concerns have assumed prime importance in the private sector as well. In the quotation above, the term *key* is used and an elaboration of this concept follows.

The basic process of traditional cryptography is to encrypt the original document, or plaintext, by a well-defined method such as permutation of a fixed amount, the key, into the cyphertext, which was then sent, or carried, to the intended receiver, who would have to know the key, how many characters to permute the cyphertext, in order to recover the plaintext. Obviously, this kind of encryption, sometimes called weak encryption, is too simple and too easy to decrypt to guarantee secure transmission. More recently, strong cryptographic systems have come into use. In such systems, the strength lies not in the algorithm, such as permutation, but in the secrecy of the key. Thus the algorithm can be made public without affecting the security of the system, but only if the effort to compute the key is extraordinarily great. Private key cryptography involves a unique key for each pair of users and the security of the system depends upon both parties protecting the key. In 1977, the then National Bureau of Standards issued the Data Encryption Standard (DES) as a Federal Information Processing Standard and it is still in use.[62] The other modern approach is public key cryptography[63]:

> Private key (sometimes called asymmetric key or two key) systems use two keys: a public key and a private key. Within a group of users who exchange— for example, within a computer network—each user has both a public key and a private key. A user must keep his private key a secret, but the public key is publicly known; public keys may even be listed in directories of electronic mail addresses. If you encrypt a message with your private key, the recipient of the message can decrypt it with your public key. When you receive an encrypted message, you, and only you, can decrypt it with your private key.

RSA is the best known public key encryption system. It was invented by Ron Rivest, Adi Shamir, and Leonard Adelman in 1977 and is probably the most widely used authentication scheme. One more definition is required, of the key escrow system. Under such a system, some or all of the keys are kept "in escrow" by third parties: "The keys are released only under proper authority to allow some person other than the original sender or receiver to read the message. The U.S. government is strongly supporting key escrow as a way to balance the needs for secrecy between communicating persons against the needs of law enforcement and national security agencies to sometimes read these encrypted communications (with proper legal authority)."[64]

The U.S. Government's Clipper Chip

Although the government's proposals in cryptography have been referred to as the Clipper Chip, the actual situation is somewhat more complicated. Clipper is strictly speaking one component of the Capstone project, which consists of four components in total: "Clipper (for bulk data encryption), a digital signature algorithm, a key exchange algorithm, and a hash function." So Clipper, in intent, is comparable to DES and incorporates in hardware an algorithm named Skipjack to be used for low-speed data/voice transmission. Thus the intent of the government is that the Clipper Chip be installed in telephones and would therefore meet the demands of business and consumers for secure communications. But the very controversial part of its program is that the government would manage the key escrow system and would be able to decrypt selected communications if it could convince the courts that its need was justified because of national security requirements or the necessity to combat crime. One model for this proposal is the wiretap laws governing the use of such devices by law enforcement officials.

It was not surprising that many individuals and companies were opposed to the Clipper Chip or that many did not trust the government to manage a key escrow system, but the strength and breadth of the opposition and the duration of its existence has been surprising. Nothing has united Internet users across the country (except perhaps for opposition to the Communications Decency Act) as opposition to the Clipper Chip. Opposition united "almost all communications and computer industries, many members of Congress and political columnists of all stripes. The anti-Clipper aggregation is an equal opportunity club, uniting the American Civil Liberties Union and Rush Limbaugh."[65] In writer Steven Levy's estimation,[66]

> By adding Clipper chips to telephones, we could have a system that assures communications will be private—from everybody but the Government. And that is what rankles Clipper's many critics. Why, they ask, should people accused of no crime have to give Government the keys to their private communications? Why shouldn't the market rather than Government determine what sort of cryptosystem wins favor?

On the other hand, Dr. Dorothy Denning of Georgetown University, a leading expert on cryptography and data security, supported the government's initiatives. In a debate with John Perry Barlow, a founder of the Electronic Frontier Foundation, she made the following argument: "The government needs a new encryption standard to replace DES. They came up with a very strong algorithm called SKIPJACK. In making that available, they didn't want to do it in a way that could ultimately prove harmful to society. So they came up with the idea of key escrow so that if SKIPJACK were used to conceal criminal activity, they would be able to get access to the communications."[67] John Perry Barlow's argument against Clipper was different than the one stated by Steven Levy. Barlow believes that, independent of the access to content that the government's system makes possible, what is of equal concern "is . . . the functional nature of the chip . . . to greatly enhance the ability of government to observe who we are calling, when, and from where, all fairly automatically and centrally."[68]

The American Civil Liberties Union raised constitutional issues in a letter it sent to the Computer System Security and Privacy Advisory Board on May 13, 1993. One of its arguments was that by holding the keys in a public key escrow system, First Amendment issues on restriction of free speech are raised: "Such a prohibition on encrypted speech is a direct restriction on speech and we do not believe that the government may, in effect, ban all encrypted speech, because encrypted speech that is evidence of crime may be unobtainable."[69] There are also Fourth and Fifth Amendment issues with respect to "requiring disclosure of the key to the government in advance of there being probable cause sufficient to entitle the government to seize an encrypted communication and to search and seize the key to such communication."[70]

Since April 1993, during the Clinton administration, the government tried to modify its original proposal in ways that might mollify its critics and still meet its ultimate aims, but with little success. On May 30, 1996, the National Research Council (NRC) released a report, requested by Congress, on the government's cryptographic policies. After extolling the virtues of cryptography for business applications, the NRC committee made the following strong recommendations[71]:

> The committee said that the government should explore "escrowed" encryption for its own use, but should not continue to aggressively promote this unproven technology to the private sector. In escrowed encryption, the decoding key would be held by a trusted third-party organization or institution. This is attractive to law enforcement agencies because with a court order, they could obtain the key and unlock even the most unbreakable code. However, many companies don't like the idea of giving a third party the key to all their secrets, even if the third party is considered trustworthy.
>
> The U.S. government's current support of escrowed encryption as a technical pillar of its cryptography policy is inappropriate now, the report says, because there are many unresolved questions about this approach, such as the liability of third-party encryption. Even when these problems are resolved, adoption of escrowed encryption or of any other specific technology or standard by the commercial sector should be voluntary and based on business needs, not government pressure.

The impact on U.S. companies goes beyond the concern with government access to encrypted communication; it also involves business, the export of high-technology products.

This long battle, the "Crypto Wars," effectively came to an end in May 1999, when an appeals court upheld a judgment against the U.S. government, which had sought to prevent Daniel Bernstein from distributing encryption software. Consider the following opinion[72]:

> B. FLETCHER, Circuit Judge:
> The government defendants appeal the grant of summary judgment to the plaintiff, Professor Daniel J. Bernstein ("Bernstein"), enjoining the enforcement of certain Export Administration Regulations ("EAR") that limit Bernstein's ability to distribute encryption software. We find that the EAR regulations (1) operate as a prepublication licensing scheme that burdens scientific expression, (2) vest boundless discretion in government officials, and (3) lack adequate procedural safeguards. Consequently, we hold that the challenged regulations constitute a prior restraint on speech that offends the First Amendment. Although we employ a somewhat narrower rationale than did the district court, its judgment is accordingly affirmed.

The failures of the Clinton administration in regard to establishing acceptable guidelines for the use of strong encryption by individuals resulted, since this decision, in a period of relative calm. In retrospect, it is viewed by some as a triumph of the Internet community over the repressive forces of government regulators. However, the events of September 11 reignited a concern with the use of the Internet to plan terrorist actions by maintaining secure communication. Therefore, a renewed motivation has emerged to identify online terrorists and to discover the content of their messages. So it is expected that the debate over cryptography will reappear, but this time national security needs may alter the previous outcome.

ITAR (International Traffic in Arms Regulations)

The U.S. government regulates the export of arms that employ advanced technologies that could harm the country. Included in the list of restricted exports are advanced computers and strong cryptosystems, implemented in either software or hardware. Encryption materials are included in Category XIII and require a license for export that must be approved by the Departments of State and Commerce, with input from the National Security Agency. What makes the problem of such great concern to business is that, "Export restrictions also apply to all products that contain cryptography, such as electronic mail, databases and data-compression products."[73] There is also a general perception that if a cryptosystem does receive an export license, it probably can be easily decrypted and is therefore not of much interest. What underlies this government policy is that U.S. military, police, and espionage officials want to be able to access communications around the world, as well as in the U.S.

The authors of the NRC report, referred to earlier, also noted that "current federal restriction on the export of encryption technologies allow only the export of relatively weak cryptography. This is done to protect the nation's ability to gather foreign intelligence. However, these export laws not only inhibit U.S. companies from selling their best cryptographic technology overseas, but they also limit what is available in this country. Even though there are no legal limits on the kinds of encryption that can be sold in the United States, many companies find it impractical to develop and market different products for both U.S. and overseas markets."[74] A group of members of Congress wrote a letter to the President in May 1996 arguing against the export restrictions. They referred to the section of the Computer Systems Policy Project that reads, "unless the U.S. relaxes out-of-date export controls, the U.S. technology industry will lose $60 billion in revenues and 200,000 jobs by the year 2000."[75]

One curious byproduct of bureaucratic decision making is the special dispensation allowed to individuals traveling overseas with their portables in hand when these portables have strong encryption software aboard. Under the condition that such software is for personal use only, no license requirement is necessary.[76] Finally, a White House Fact Sheet on Anti-Terrorism Proposals revealed that the government's commitment to control strong cryptographic systems has not wavered[77]:

> We will seek legislation to strengthen our ability to prevent terrorists from coming into possession of the technology to encrypt their communications and data so that they are beyond the reach of law enforcement. We oppose legislation that would eliminate current export barriers and encourage the proliferation of encryption which blocks appropriate access to protect public safety and the national security.

Terrorism

Among the many charges directed at the Internet is that it could be used by terrorist groups to plan their activities. Of course, similar accusations could be laid against telephone companies that carry conversations among known or suspected terrorists. Police forces have cautioned that bomb-making instructions are available on the Internet and that (more) restrictions are required to remove these or to impose severe penalties on those who post them and those who access them. It is forgotten or conveniently ignored that libraries have such information as well and yet who (except for the FBI perhaps) would suggest that librarians monitor borrowers to determine who is interested in weapons manufacture. Nevertheless, at a July 1996 meeting, the G7 (Group of Seven leading industrialized nations) adopted a set of measures to combat international terrorism. Among these, one was directed at the Internet: "6. Note the risk of terrorists using electronic or wire communications systems and networks to carry out criminal acts and the need to find means, consistent with national law, to prevent such criminality."[78] This rather cryptic pronouncement is devoid of any hint of practical measures that might be undertaken and therefore serves to inflame popular sentiment against the Internet as a home for terrorists, to say nothing of pornographers and child molesters.[79]

Although it might seem an obvious step to reinvestigate the earlier attempts to control encryption software, even threats of terrorism directly following actual terrorist acts have not caused the government to attempt to implement previously unsuccessful policies. It may be remembered that, "a plan proposed by Clinton . . . which would have required all American makers of encryption software to install a back door accessible by U.S. intelligence agencies acting with court approval, was abandoned, in part because of the argument that the requirement would not apply to foreign software makers, who are now perfectly capable of equaling the most sophisticated American-made commercial encryption software."[80] Even in the days following the terrorist attacks of September 11, as Congress was engaged in passing the USA Patriot act, this Clinton plan was remembered and for some it seemed that the time was now ripe to make it work, but[81]

> an effort in the Senate to revive that plan and include it in the anti-terrorism bill that was signed into law October 26 received little support and was withdrawn, and on much the same grounds—that however powerful an intelligence tool code breaking was during its golden age, in World War II and the Cold War, the technical reality is that those days are gone. Code breaking simply cannot work the magic it once did.

Gambling

Everyone likes to place bets, informally or at race tracks, gambling casinos, bingo parlors, or state lotteries. Legal bets can only be placed locally, as the Federal Interstate Wire Act "prohibits anyone in the gambling business from taking bets over a network—including the Internet—that crosses state or international borders."[82] Enter the Internet. It operates worldwide, it transmits information instantaneously, and sites can be established in one country and accessed from another. Thus a gambling facility could be established in the Caribbean, in Southeast Asia, or elsewhere and Americans could place bets after having set up an account. One operation has been set up in Belize and requires that $1,000 first be wired to a bank located there. "Then, for $100, you must purchase a start-up kit, including special software, a card reader that attaches to your PC, and a smart card that holds your security and account information."[83] Kerry Rogers, the chief technical director, claimed that 4,000 people have registered, half from the U.S. It is unlikely that state governments will sit back and do nothing; one should probably expect a licensing process whereby betting-on-demand on the Internet will be established, and considerable tax money will flow to governments or attempts will be made to limit, or even prevent, online gambling.

In a report released by the General Accounting Office (GAO) in December 2002, Internet gambling is simply defined as "any activity that takes place over the Internet and that includes placing a bet or wager." The current estimates of the size of the gambling market are given below.[84]

> Since the mid-1990s, Internet gambling operators have established approximately 1,800 e-gaming Web sites in locations outside the United States, and global revenues from Internet gaming in 2003 are projected to be $5.0 billion dollars.

The GAO report was carried out for Congress to explore a number of issues related to Internet gambling, including the U.S. payments system, especially credit cards, for use in online gaming, the views of the credit card industry with respect to the use of credit cards in paying for gambling, and the views of law enforcement officials with respect to the use of online gambling for money laundering. The following is one result of this study[85]:

> Representatives of law enforcement agencies told us that Internet gambling could be used to launder money, but others viewed the threat as less serious. Law enforcement representatives said that the anonymity and jurisdictional issues characteristic of Internet gambling make on-line gaming a potentially powerful tool for money launderers. They noted that few money laundering cases involving Internet gambling had been prosecuted but attributed the small number of cases primarily to a lack of regulation and oversight. However, regulatory agencies and officials from the credit card and gaming industries did not believe that Internet gambling was any more susceptible to money laundering than other forms of e-commerce.

The report was somewhat unusual in that it did not include recommendations for Congress. Nevertheless, a half-year later Congress overwhelmingly passed the "Unlawful Internet Gambling Funding Prohibition Act," on June 10, 2003, but not before dealing with a number of special-purpose amendments. One of the major concerns motivating passage was terrorism, as Michael Oxley, chairman of the Financial Services Committee said, "Internet gambling services [are] a haven for money launderers. . . . Offshore Internet gambling sites can be a haven for terrorists to launder money."[86] Because the bill does not regulate "any lawful transaction with a business licensed or authorized by" a state government, betting on horse races and dog races is permitted.

Internet Taxes

As E-commerce has become a fact of life, the question of taxation has become more urgent, especially for local and state governments. As the Internet became a preferred location to purchase books, records, computers and accessories, software, and many other items, state and city officials were concerned that tax revenues would be lost because Web sites had no fixed geographic location. They argued that Internet purchases should be taxed to compensate for the loss of local taxes. Spokespeople for the new Web sites argued that a tax moratorium was necessary in order to encourage Web commerce and to gain experience in determining the nature of such commerce. Furthermore, there were issues that required study related to how to collect and disburse taxes appropriately. In 1998, Congress passed a law, the Internet Tax Freedom Act, creating a tax moratorium on Web purchases until October 2001, unless extended. The law was extended for two more years until November 1, 2003, in spite of the concerns of state and local officials.

In 2003, the debate has continued over whether or not the moratorium should again be extended. However, over the past two years, many states have taken measures to recover taxes under special circumstances, which may or may not survive legal challenges. For example, the following steps have been taken[87]:

- Tax authorities in Alabama, Florida and Kentucky are assessing sales taxes on the amount consumers pay for high-speed digital subscriber line Internet service, commonly referred to as DSL.
- Maryland, Virginia, and 13 other states have passed laws that require Internet access to be taxed when it is "bundled" with other taxable services by a single provider, such as a telephone company. Another six states are poised to enact similar legislation.
- Classifying DSL broadband service as a telecommunications service, not as Internet access, is one step states are taking to get around the Internet tax moratorium.
- This week, Atlanta-based EarthLink, the nation's third-largest Internet service provider (ISP), said its DSL subscribers will see an up to 9 percent increase in their monthly bills because of taxes it now has to pay on the purchase of bandwidth.

Early in 2003, before talks began about another extension of the prohibition on Internet taxation, an agreement was reached among many large retailers and 38 states and the District of Columbia. The agreement is briefly described as follows[88]:

Some of the nation's largest retailers this week started voluntarily collecting taxes on all of their online sales. The companies are among the first in the nation to collect sales taxes from online shoppers across the country, not just shoppers who live in the states where the companies maintain actual stores or distribution centers. In return, 38 states and the District of Columbia agreed to absolve the retailers from any liability for taxes not previously collected on Internet sales. . . . Under current federal law, Internet merchants must charge applicable sales taxes if the buyer is located in the same state as the company. But the new deal effectively applies the same sales tax laws to retailers online and bricks-and-mortar operations.

Online units are often chartered as separate entities and maintain physical locations in only a handful of places, thus exempting customers from most states from paying sales taxes.

One last story about Internet taxes originates in Massachusetts, where the Revenue Commissioner announced early in January 2003 that the income tax form would include a line inviting taxpayers to pay sales tax, which they have avoided, on all appropriate items that they have purchased outside the state. This tax includes purchases made over the telephone, by catalogue, and of course over the Internet. Residents are supposed to pay the difference between the Massachusetts sales tax, 5%, and the out-of-state sales tax, if it is less.[89] It is not known how successful this appeal to individual honesty has been.

Spam

If there is one thing that unites almost all Internet users, it is our hatred of spam, the relentless bombardment of e-mail messages attempting to sell sexual aids, medicinal drugs, vacation getaways, fast university degrees, invitations to purchase pornography, and much, much more. How do they find us? Don't we have the right to be let alone? If we opt out when they offer us the possibility, won't that help? Why doesn't the government do anything about it? When will it stop? Spam raises issues of free speech, privacy, and business regulation. Should government interfere with the private sector's right to advertise? Can my e-mail address be hijacked for commercial purposes? There are lots of questions and few answers, and as the sheer volume of spam has increased, the anger has grown as well. Congress attempted to craft legislation during 2003 to limit spam without interfering with legal rights to advertise.

Although the term is widely used, what constitutes spam? A report from a conservative think tank proposes the following possibilities[90]:

> There are several competing definitions of spam, none of which is entirely satisfactory.
> • One common definition is *unsolicited commercial email* (UCE). This definition excludes unsolicited political messages and some types of fraudulent messages, which most people think of as spam. And it arguably includes such things as résumés sent to potential employers, which are not generally considered spam. "Commercial" is surprisingly tricky to define; one economics professor who had developed a new statistical method send unsolicited email to his colleagues at other universities letting them know about his methods and offering his text for sale; was this "commercial" or scholarly content?
> • Another common definition is *unsolicited bulk email* (UBE). This definition is troubling because it suggests that all bulk email should be solicited; but it does not follow necessarily that all unsolicited email is unwanted, or that all bulk email is problematic.
> • Yet another is *unsolicited commercial bulk email* (UCBE).

- Still others are concerned that the email is *unwanted* or somehow *deceptive* in content or header information.

It is the difficulty in defining spam that makes the task of determining satisfactory methods of control so problematic. Many Internet Service Providers have taken steps, in response to complaints from their customers, to limit the distribution of mass unsolicited e-mail. Not surprisingly, the net has often been cast too widely and desired, expected, or needed e-mail has been intercepted. The report just referred to discusses the merits of legislation and cautions that the crucial issue is adequate enforcement.[91]

- For end users, the best solutions are the new Bayesian content filters, which can be tailored to individual preferences.
- ISPs, the most seriously affected, have limited and constrained the spam problem successfully using filters, litigation, and contractual solutions.
- Spammers have been largely forced off of legitimate ISPs onto foreign relays and hijacked ISPs.
- Many (not all) provisions of the new laws proposed thus far are too broad, but none would be helpful without vigorous enforcement.
- Significantly stepped up enforcement levels would be necessary for any law to have a deterrent effect.

Note that one technical solution receiving considerable attention is non-legislative and individual, namely the use of a filtering program that adapts to each user's specific needs and interests. The technical name is a Bayesian content filter, a statistical approach to adapting to individual Internet style. However, most people believe that government intervention is necessary, perhaps based on a legitimate and effective list of Internet users who do not wish to receive unsolicited e-mail. Currently, responding to an offer in spam that supposedly removes your name from some list, just confirms that your e-mail address is active and worth pursuing. Indeed, the simple result of replying is that your address is probably marketed to new lists, which will generate more spam. In June 2003, the Senate Commerce committee "unanimously approved a bill to make it illegal for anyone to use fraudulent or deceptive return e-mail addresses, fake e-mail headers or use false subject lines. The bill would allow marketers to send an initial unsolicited e-mail message, but require that the message contain a clear way for consumers to opt out of receiving further messages."[92] Finally, on December 15, 2003, the President signed into law the CAN-SPAM Act, which places limitations on those sending unsolicited, commercial e-mail.[92a]

OTHER ISSUES

The Internet is essentially a network of networks and computers which have agreed to use a common protocol with which to communicate. These protocols can operate over a number of media, including copper wire, fiber optic cable and electromagnetic spectrum. Furthermore, the Internet's protocols operate independently of whether ASCII text, voice, video, graphical or other data is being carried within its packet-based mode of transmission. Thus, the Internet is a multi-media, transmission-technology independent form of communication.

Regulation should not be used to inhibit the further development of technology. It is in the public interest to allow the integration of voice, video, graphics and text applications.[93]

Radio, Telephone, and TV on the Internet

These broadcast media and the telephone are available now on the Internet, the quality is improving, and the use of limited bandwidth is becoming more efficient. The long-distance telephone companies certainly feel threatened as their trade association, the America's Carriers Telecommunication Association (ACTA), petitioned the Federal Communications Commission (FCC) on March 4, 1996, "to order the Respondents to immediately stop their unauthorized provisioning of telecommunications services."[94] ACTA expressed the following concerns[95]:

> This petition concerns a new technology: a computer software product that enables a computer with Internet access to be used as a long distance telephone, carrying voice transmissions, at virtually no charge for the call.
>
> ACTA submits that the providers of this software are telecommunications carriers and, as such, should be subject to FCC regulation like all telecommunications carriers. ACTA also submits that the FCC has the authority to regulate the Internet.
>
> ACTA submits that it is not in the public interest to permit long distance service to be given away, depriving those who must maintain the telecommunications infrastructure of the revenue to do so, and nor is it in the public interest for these select telecommunications carriers to operate outside the regulatory requirements applicable to all other carriers.

The Federation of American Research Networks (FARNET), representing a variety of both not-for-profit and for-profit organizations such as Internet service providers, network service providers, interexchange companies, Regional Bell operating companies, universities and supercomputer centers, urged the FCC to deny ACTA's petition. In part, it argued against singling out "for regulation one particular type of communication that is now taking place over the Internet. Besides being administratively burdensome, and perhaps even technically impossible, such an action would severely prohibit the future development of the Internet as a multi-media communications tool."[96] There were more arguments: "Regulation should not be used to inhibit the further development of technology" and "The commission has a clear mandate from the Telecommunications Act of 1996 to make pro-competitive, deregulatory decisions in the public interest."[97] It is worth mentioning that more recently, a model for telephone over the Internet has emerged called Voice over IP (VoIP).

Similar arguments and counterarguments are being raised about radio and television on the Internet, and as technological developments squeeze more bandwidth out of existing hardware, the Internet may evolve more rapidly than expected into the Information Highway. Given that the Telecommunications Act of 1996 calls for less regulation and more competition, the government may be unwilling to restrict the use of the Internet for specific modes of communication previously carried elsewhere. The future seems to be wide open.

Uniform Computer Information Transactions Act (UCITA)

During the 1990s, attempts were undertaken by the National Conference of Commissioners on Uniform State Laws (NCCUSL) to amend the Uniform Commercial Code (UCC) to accommodate the challenges presented by computers and their applications. This effort culminated in 1999 with the first UCITA proposal, which was greeted with considerable concern from both legal and computer users quarters. Early in 2003, even the American Bar Association decided not to support UCITA.[98] Currently, only two states, Virginia and Maryland, have adopted it. Some of the arguments leveled against UCITA are given as follows[99]:

- **It replaces the public law of copyright with the private law of contract.** Under the public law of copyright, a vendor sells copies of information such as books or software. UCITA would allow for the "licensing" of information. Rather than owning a copy, you are granted permission to use the copy within limits dictated by the "license." When you purchase a license to use a piece of software for instance, you agree to a contract, that you are unable to read in advance or negotiate, governing everything from how the software is to be used to whether or nor you are allowed to publicly criticize the product. The public law of copyright comes with certain privileges such as fair use, the private law of contract does not.
- **The scope of UCITA is overly broad.** As stated above, the definition of computer information would cover nearly all things digital. Moreover, the UCITA framework would allow those items not covered by the original draft to "opt-in" or be governed by the UCITA.
- **UCITA enables "mass-market" or shrink-wrap/click-on licenses.** When you buy a piece of software or other information products, you buy the product without the capability to read the license. In some cases, the act of opening the box or "breaking the plastic wrapping" is consent to the terms of the license. This is a fundamentally unfair position because the licensee has no idea ahead of time concerning the terms and conditions laid-

out in the license. UCITA would enable a vendor, such as a computer software company, to restrict a consumer's right to sue for a product defect, to donate the product to charity, to use the product, or even to publicly discuss or criticize the product or information contained in it.

• **UCITA would undercut fair use, preservation, and the unhindered use of works in the public domain.** Click-on/shrink-wrap licenses would supersede the traditional copyright balances that insure access to information, a key principle for the function of libraries.

• **UCITA would prevent reverse-engineering even in cases of interoperability.** Reverse-engineering allows software developers to make better products. Without this capacity, there is no guarantee that new programs will work together.

Despite this opposition, the NCCUSL intends to pursue the adoption of UCITA in a number of states. However, in order to become a national law, it must be adopted by most states, currently an unlikely prospect.

SUMMARY

Relations between government and business in the United States have been involved, torturous, occasionally acrimonious, sometimes beneficial, usually controversial, and always unpredictable. In this chapter, we have focused on certain industries—computers, communications, and financial transactions—and certain problem areas—antitrust, taxation, and gambling. The development and significance of electronic banking has been discussed, with special emphasis on the dimensions of electronic banking and the potential problem areas. Other concerns are stock market regulation, especially online trading, as well as cryptography, spam, and the Internet as a medium for radio, telephone, and TV.

Although committed to the free enterprise system, the U.S. government has at times found it necessary to challenge the activities of certain large companies. On January 8, 1982, the Justice Department dropped a 13-year antitrust suit against IBM. On the same day, it also dropped an antitrust suit against AT&T, after AT&T agreed to divest itself of the local telephone companies.

IBM, freed of the antitrust suit, launched an aggressive challenge on all fronts to extend its domination of computer-related business. For example, within three years after the personal computer, the PC, was introduced in 1981, it held the lead in sales. AT&T's first steps after divestiture were somewhat more tentative. It was also challenged in the profitable long-distance market by a number of companies. The major antitrust activity over the past few years, however, has been the government's efforts against Microsoft, by far the dominant company in operating systems and Internet browsers.

In a major change fostered by technological innovation, the banking system is being transformed by the introduction of electronic funds transfer systems. Examples of this process are the appearance of automatic teller machines, point-of-sales terminals, and electronic banking via home computers. Concerns about electronic banking include security of financial records, potential increased frequency of electronic crime, impact on competition, and impact on consumers' privacy.

Other areas in which the government must play a role with respect to business activities are the regulation of stock exchanges, especially problems arising from the use of computers and computer networks, and the use of the Internet to carry telephone and broadcast transmissions. The Internet has made offshore gambling easy to access and therefore a concern for the difficulty of regulating such activities. Online taxation, or actually the lack thereof, has become a serious concern of many states and cities, which argue that the Internet no longer requires special treatment as a new technology.

NOTES

1. "IT 100/200 Scoreboard," *Business Week* Online, 2002. Available at http://bwnt.businessweek.com/it100/
2. John Opel, president of IBM, as quoted in Bro Uttal, "Life After Litigation at IBM and AT&T," *Fortune*, February 8, 1982, p. 59.
3. Steve Lohr. "Results at I.B.M. Defy the Slump in Technology," *The New York Times*, October 17, 2002, Late Edition—Final, Section C, Page 1.
4. "IBM Decree-Lifting is an Incomplete Success," Edupage, July 25, 1996. Available at http://www.educause.edu/pub/edupage/archives/96/edupage-0125.html#anchorz
5. Steve Lohr. "The New Leader of I.B.M. Explains His Strategic Course, "*The New York Times*, October 31, 2002, Late Edition—Final, Section C, Page 5.
6. Stuart J. Johnston and Ed Scannell. "Microsoft Holds Steady Under Probe," *Computerworld*, April 18, 1994, p. 30.
7. Stuart J. Johnston and Ed Scannell. "Users Hold Key to Antitrust Battle," *Computerworld*, April 18, 1994, pp. 1, 30. Available at http://www.computerworld.com/search/AT-html/9404/940418SL15doj1.html
8. *Ibid.*, p. 30.
9. Mitch Betts. "A Step-by-Step Look at the Microsoft Case," *Datamation*, July 25, 1994, p. 14. Available at http://www.computerworld.com/news/1994/story/0,11280,7014,00.html
10. *Ibid.*
11. *Ibid.*
12. "Antitrust, the Smart Way," Editorial, *Business Week*, August 1, 1994, p. 88.
13. *Ibid.*
14. Richard Brandt, Catherine Yang, and Amy Cortese. "Sorry, Bill, the Deal Is Off," *Business Week*, February 27, 1995, pp. 38–40.

15. Terence P. Paré. "Why the Banks Line Up Against Gates," *Fortune*, May 29, 1995, p. 18.
16. Mitch Betts, Ellis Booker, and Stuart J. Johnson. "Microsoft Opponents Go for Blood," *Computerworld*, May 29, 1995, p. 4.
17. Kim S. Nash, "Netscape Takes Action Against Microsoft's Web Practices," *Computerworld*, August 7, 1996. Available at http://www.computerworld.com/search/AT-html/briefs/9608/960807net.html
18. "U.S. v. Microsoft: Timeline," *Wired News*, November 4, 2002. Available at http://www.wired.com/news/antitrust/0,1551,35212,00.html
19. "United States of America v. Microsoft Corporation," Civil Action No. 98-1232 (Antitrust) Complaint, May 18, 1998. Available at http://www.usdoj.gov/atr/cases/f1700/1763.htm
20. *Op. cit.*, "U.S. v. Microsoft: Timeline."
21. "Court's Findings of Facts," Civil Actions No. 98-1232 (TPJ) and No. 98-1233 (TPJ), Judge Thomas Penfield Jackson, November 5, 1999. Available at http://www.usdoj.gov/atr/cases/f3800/msjudgex.htm
22. "Plaintiffs' Joint Proposed Conclusions of Law," Civil Actions No. 98-1232 (TPJ) and No. 98-1233 (TPJ), December 6, 1999. Available at http://www.usdoj.gov/atr/cases/f3900/3932.htm
23. Joe Wilcox and Scott Ard. "Judge: Microsoft Must Be Broken in Two," News.com, June 7, 2000. Available at http://news.com.com/2100-1001-241578.html
24. Joanna Glasner. "The MS Decision: Is It Over Yet?" *Wired News*, November 2, 2002. Available at http://www.wired.com/news/business/0,1367,56157,00.html
25. "Memorandum Opinion," Civil Action No. 98-1232 (CKK), Colleen Kollar-Kotelly, United States District Judge, November 1, 2002. Available at http://dcd.uscourts.gov/PunIntDeterm11-1.pdf
26. Alexander Graham Bell, first complete sentence transmitted by telephone, March 10, 1876.
27. "Telecom Industry History," Blumenfeld & Cohen Law Company, 1992. Available at http://www.technologylaw.com/techlaw/telephony.htm
28. Charles L. Brown, chairman of AT&T, as quoted in a full-page advertisement in the *New York Times*, January 10, 1982, p. 9.
29. Jeremy Main. "Waking up AT&T: There's Life After Culture Shock," *Fortune*, December 24, 1984, pp. 66–68, 70, 72, 74.
30. Frederic Withington. "Sizing Each Other up," *Datamation*, July 20, 1982, p. 8.
31. "History of the Bells," TeleTruth, December 2001. Available at http://www.teletruth.org/History/bbells/bb_history.html
32. "Overview of the Telecommunications Act of 1996," Blumenfeld & Cohen, 1996. Available at http://www.technologylaw.com/techlaw/act_summary.html
33. Steven Levy. "Now for the Free-for-All," *Newsweek*, February 12, 1996, p. 42.
34. Mark Landler, "Sigh of Relief Greets New Telephone Rules," *The New York Times*, August 2, 1996, pp. C 1, C 6.
35. Jonathan Krim. "FCC Preparing to Overhaul Telecom, Media Rules," *The Washington Post*, January 3, 2003, p. E01.
36. "The Future of Retail Electronic Payments Systems: Industry Interviews and Analysis," Staff Study 175, Board of Governors of the Federal Reserve System,

December 2002. Available at http://www.federalreserve.gov/pubs/staffstudies/2000-present/ss175.pdf

37. As quoted in Orin Kramer. "Winning Strategies for Interstate Banking," *Fortune*, September 19, 1983, p. 118.

38. Thomas D. Steiner and Diogo B. Teixeira. *Technology in Banking: Creating Value and Destroying Profits* (Homewood, IL: Dow Jones-Irwin, 1990), p. 10.

39. Jane Bryant Quinn. "The Era of Debit Cards," *Newsweek*, January 2, 1989. p. 51.

40. "Why Security First National Bank?" Security First National Bank, 1996. Available at http://www.sfnb.com/whyus/

41. "Pew Internet Project Data Memo: Online Banking," Pew Internet & American Life Project, November 2002. Available at http://www.pewinternet. org/reports/pdfs/PIP_Online_Banking.pdf

42. *Ibid.*

43. Stijn Claessens, Thomas Glaessner, and Daniela Klingebtei. "Electronic Finance: A New Approach to Financial Sector Development?" World Bank Discussion Paper No. 431, March 2002. Available at http://www-wds.worldbank. org/servlet/WDS ContentServer/WDSP/IB/2002/04/05/000094946_02032604542947/Rendered/PDF/multi0page.pdf

44. "Web Concensus 2003," Community Bank Competitiveness Survey, American Bankers Association, *ABA Banking Journal*, March 2003. Available at http://www.aba.com/aba/pdf/webconcensus.pdf

45. "Technology and Banking: A Survey of Canadian Attitudes," Canadian Bankers Association, 2002. Available at http://www.cba.ca/eng/Events/National_Findings. pdf

45a. "Chapter 35—Right to Financial Privacy," 1978. Available at http://www4.law. cornell.edu/uscode/ch35.html

46. Franklin R. Edwards. "The Crash: A Report on the Reports," from Henry C. Lucas, Jr. and Robert A. Schwartz (Eds.), *The Challenge of Information Technology for the Securities Markets: Liquidity, Volatility, and Global Trading* (Homewood, IL: Business One Irwin, 1989), p. 86.

47. *Ibid.*, p. 87.

48. As quoted in *ibid.*, pp. 87–88.

49. *Ibid.*, p. 88.

50. New York Stock Exchange Chairman John J. Phelan as quoted in Gary Weiss, "Two Key Questions: Was Program Trading to Blame . . . [?]" *Business Week*, November 2, 1987, p. 51.

51. M. Mitchell Waldorp. "Computers Amplify Black Monday," *Science*, October 30, 1987, pp. 602–604.

52. Edwards, *op cit.*, pp. 98–99.

53. David Stamps. "The IS Eye on Insider Trading," *Datamation*, April 15, 1990, pp. 35–36, 38, 43.

54. "Day Trading: Your Dollars at Risk," U.S. Securities & Exchange Commission, January 8, 2003. Available at http://www.sec.gov/investor/pubs/daytips.htm

55. *Ibid.*

56. Michael Lewis. "Jonathan Lebed's Extracurricular Activities," *The New York Times*, February 25, 2001, Late Edition—Final, Section 6, Page 26.

57. "United States of America Before the Securities and Exchange Commission, In the matter of Jonathan Lebed, File No. 3-10291, September 20, 2000. Available at http://www.sec.gov/litigation/admin/33-7891.htm

58. "Investor Education Press Release," North American Securities Administrators Association, May 25, 2000. Available at http://www.nasaa.org/nasaa/scripts/ prel_display.asp?rcid=71

59. "U.S. Policies Should Foster Broad Use of Encryption Technologies," Press Release, National Research Council, May 30, 1996. Available at http://epic. org/crypto/ reports/nrc_release.html The Overview and Recommendations of the National Research Council report are available at http:// www2.nas.edu/ cstbweb/2646.html

60. Taken from a Statement by the Press Secretary, Office of the Press Secretary, The White House, April 16, 1993. Available at http://www.scimitar.com/revolution/by_topic/express/ techno/clipper/announce.html

61. *Answers to Frequently Asked Questions About Today's Cryptography, Version 3.0*, RSA Laboratories, 1996. Available at http://www.rsa.com/PUBS/labs_ faq.pdf

62. Susan Landau, Stephen Kent, Clint Brooks, Scott Charney, Dorothy Denning, Whitfield Diffie, Anthony Luck, Douglas Miller, Peter Neumann, and David Sobel. "Cryptography in Public: A Brief History," in Lance J. Hoffman (Ed.), *Building in Big Brother: The Cryptographic Policy Debate* (New York: Springer-Verlag, 1995), pp. 41–42.

63. Deborah Russell and G. T. Gangemi, Sr. "Encryption." In Hoffman (Ed.), *Building in Big Brother*, pp. 19–20.

64. Lance J. Hoffman. "Key Escrow Systems, Keeping Secrets Secret Except When . . ." In Hoffman (Ed.), *Building in Big Brother*, p. 109.

65. Stephen Levy. "Battle of the Clipper Chip," *The New York Times Magazine*, June 12, 1994, p. 46.

66. *Ibid.*

67. "The Denning-Barlow Clipper Chip Debate," *Time* Online, March 10, 1994. Available at http://ftp.eff.org/papers/barlow-denning.html

68. *Ibid.*

69. "Cryptographic Issue Statements: Letter to the Computer System Security and Privacy Advisory Board," American Civil Liberties Union, May 13, 1993. In Hoffman (Ed.), *Building in Big Brother*, pp. 409–412.

70. *Ibid.*

71. *Op cit.*, "U.S. Policies Should Foster Broad Use of Encryption Technologies."

72. Bernstein v. USDOJ, U.S. Court of Appeals for the Ninth Circuit, Case Number 97-16686, May 6, 1999. Available at http://www.ca9.uscourts. gov/ca9/newopinions. nsf/04485f8dcbd4e1ea882569520074e698/491e916afa78729088256958006 caee4?OpenDocument

73. David S. Bernstein. "Encryption's International Labyrinth. In Hoffman (Ed.), *Building in Big Brother*, pp. 456–459.

74. *Op cit.*, "U.S. Policies Should Foster Broad Use of Encryption Technologies."

75. "Letter to the President," 27 U.S. Representatives, May 15, 1996. Available at http://www.epic.org/crypto/key_escrow/house_letter_5_15_96.html

76. "Answers to Frequently Asked Questions About Cryptography Export Laws," RSA Data Security, Inc., 1996. Available at http://www.rsa.com/PUBS/exp_faq. pdf

77. "Fact Sheet on Administration Anti-Terrorism Proposals," The White House, July 29, 1996. Available at http://www.epic.org/privacy/terrorism/fact_sheet_ july96.html

78. G7/P8 Ministerial Conference on Terrorism," Paris, July 30, 1996. Available at http://www.epic.org/privacy/terrorism/g7_resolutions.html

79. See reports of the first World Congress Against Sexual Exploitation of Children held in Stockholm, Sweden, during August 1996. For example, Paul Knox, "Child Porn Flood Swells," *The Globe and Mail* (Toronto, Canada), August 27, 1996, pp. A1, A7.

80. Stephen Budiansky. "Losing the Code War," *The Atlantic Monthly*, February 2002. Available at http://www.theatlantic.com/issues/2002/02/budiansky.htm

81. *Ibid.*

82. *Ibid.*, p. 136.

83. *Ibid.*, p. 137.

84. "Internet Gambling: An Overview of the Issues," United States General Accounting Office, GAO-03-89, December 2002. Available at http://www.gao.gov/new.items/d0389.pdf

85. *Ibid.*

86. Declan McCullagh. "House Votes to Restrict Net Gambling," News.com, June 10, 2003. Available at http://news.com.com/2100-1028-1015475.html

87. Brian Krebs. "States Skirt Internet Tax Ban," *The Washington Post*, June 9, 2003. Available at http://www.washingtonpost.com/ac2/wp-dyn/A33787-2003 June9.html

88. Brian Krebs. "Major Dot-Com Retailers Begin Levying Sales Tax," *The Washington Post*, February 6, 2003. Available at http://www.washingtonpost. com/ac2/wp-dyn/A31210-2003Feb5.html

89. "Tax Due on Some Out-of-State Purchases," TheBostonChannel, January 23, 2003. Available at http://www.thebostonchannel.com/news/1932599/detail. html

90. Hanah Metchis and Solveig Singleton. "Spam, That Ill O' The ISP: A Reality Check for Legislators," Competitive Enterprise Institute, May 21, 2003. Available at http://www.cei.org/pdf/3482.pdf

91. *Ibid.*

92. Jennifer S. Lee. "Senate Once Again Backs Stringent Penalties for Spam Senders," *The New York Times*," June 20, 2003. Available at http://www.nytimes. com/2003/06/20/technology/20SPAM.html?8bl

92a. "CAN-SPAM Act of 2003." Available at http://thomas.loc.gov/cgi-bin/query/ F?c108:6:./temp/~C108500KL:e669:

93. "RE: RM No. 8775, ACTA petition relating to 'Internet Phone' Software and Hardware," Sent to the Federal Communications Commission by the Federation of American Research Networks, May 6, 1996. Available at http://www. farnet.org/acta.htm

94. "Before the Federal Communications Commission," Washington, DC, March 4, 1996. Available at http://www.fcc.gov/Bureaus/Common_Carrier/Other/actapet. html

95. *Ibid.*

96. *Op cit.*, "RE: RM No. 8775, ACTA petition relating to 'Internet Phone' Software and Hardware."

97. *Ibid.*

98. Patrick Thibodeau. "UCITA backers Lose Political Information," *Computerworld*, February 17, 2003. Available at http://www.idg.net/english/crd_ document_1314038.html

99. "The Digital Future Coalition Discusses the Controversies of UCITA, Fall 1999," Association of Research Libraries, December 6, 1999. Available at http://www.arl.org/info/frn/copy/controv.html

ADDITIONAL READINGS

Industry Regulation

"Government and the Internet," a Survey, *The Economist*, June 22, 2000. Available at http://www.economist.com/surveys/showsurvey. cfm?issue=20000624&CFID= 13476755&CFTOKEN=4dfc3fe-b7cade24-9ee4-4fcc-948c-e784c90aa94e

"The IT Industry," a Survey, *The Economist*, May 8, 2003. Available at http://www.economist.com/surveys/showsurvey.cfm?issue=20030510&CFID= 13476755&CFTOKEN=4dfc3fe-b7cade24-9ee4-4fcc-948c-e784c90aa94e

"Joint Status Report on Microsoft's Compliance With the Final Judgments," In the United States District Court for the District of Columbia, July 3, 2003. Available at http://www.usdoj.gov/atr/cases/f201100/201135.pdf

Kushnick, Bruce. *The Unauthorized Biography of the Baby Bells & Info-Scandal*, New Networks Institute, 1998. Available at http://www.teletruth.org/docs/unau-thbiocomplete.pdf

"Microsoft Ruling," *PBS NewsHour*, November 1, 2002. Available at http://www.pbs.org/newshour/bb/business/july-dec02/microsoft_11-01.pdf

"Telecommunications," a Survey. *The Economist*, October 7, 1999. Available at http://www.economist.com/surveys/showsurvey.cfm?issue=19991009&CFID= 13476755&CFTOKEN=4dfc3fe-b7cade24-9ee4-4fcc-948c-e784c90aa94e

The Telecommunications Act of 1996. Available at http://www.technologylaw.com/techlaw/act.html

Wallace, James, and Erickson, Jim. *Hard Drive: Bill Gates and the Making of the Microsoft Empire*, New York: Harper Business, 1993.

World Telecommunication Development Report, International Telecommunication Union, 1995. Available at http://www.itu.ch/WTDR95/

Electronic Banking and Financial Transactions

Chaum, David. "Achieving Electronic Privacy," *Scientific American*, August 1992, pp. 96–101. Accessed from the Web page with URL:http://www.digicash.com/publish/sciam.html on May 26, 1996.

"Electronic Activities," Department of the Treasury, Office of the Comptroller of the Currency, May 8, 2002. Available at http://www.occ.treas.gov/ftp/release/2002-44a.pdf

Fancher, Carol H. "Smart Cards," *Scientific American*, August 1996, pp. 40–45.

"The Future of Retail Electronic Payments Systems: Industry Interviews and Analysis," Board of Governors of the Federal Reserve System, Staff Study 175, December 2002. Available at http://www.federalreserve.gov/pubs/staffstudies/2000-present/ss175.pdf

Furst, Karen, Lang, William W., and Nolle, Daniel E. "Internet Banking: Developments and Prospects," Program on Information Resources Policy, Harvard University, April 2002. Available at http://www.occ.treas.gov/netbank/ebankingdpapr02.pdf

Levy, Stephen. "The End of Money?" *Newsweek*, October 30, 1995, pp. 62–65." Update on Actions Taken to Address Day Trading Concerns," United States General Accounting Office, November 2001. Available at http://www.gao.gov/new.items/d0220.pdf

Other Online Regulatory Issues

Denning, Dorothy. "The Future of Cryptography," *Internet Security Review*, October 1995. A revised version, January 1996, was accessed at the Web page with URL:http://www.cosc.georgetown.edu/~denning/crypto/Future.html on August 28, 1996.

Denning, Dorothy. "A Taxonomy for Key Escrow Encryption Systems," *Communications of the ACM* 39 (3), March 1996, pp. 34–40.

Jolish, Barak. "The Encrypted Jihad," Salon.com, February 4, 2002. Available at http://www.salon.com/tech/feature/2002/02/04/ terror_encryption/index.html

Mann, Charles C. "Homeland Insecurity," *The Atlantic Monthly*, September 2002. Available at http://www.theatlantic.com/issues/2002/09/mann.htm

McConnell, Bruce W., and Appel, Edward J. Draft Paper: "Enabling Privacy, Commerce, Security and Public Safety in the Global Information Infrastructure," Executive Office of the President, Office of Management and Budget, May 20, 1996. Accessed from the Web page with URL:http://www.epic.org/crypto/key_escrow/white_paper.html on June 1, 1996.

"More Thorough Analysis Needed to Justify Changes in High Performance Computer Control," United States General Accounting Office, August 2002. Available at http://www.gao.gov/new.items/d02891.pdf

Schneier, Bruce. "Testimony and Statement for Record," Hearing on "Overview of the Cyber Problem—A Nation Dependent and Dealing With Risk, Subcommittee on Cybersecurity, Science, and Research Development, Committee on Homeland Security, U.S. House of Representatives, June 25, 2003. Available at http://hsc.house.gov/files/Testimony_Schneier.pdf

Other Issues

Foster, Ed. "The Fate of UCITA," InfoWorld, January 31, 2003. Available at http://www.infoworld.com/article/03/01/31/05gripe_1.html

"UCITA Timeline," Americans for Fair Electronic Commerce Transactions, February 4, 2003. Available at http://www.4cite.org/pdf/UCITATimeline.pdf

"Video on the Internet, Webbed." *The Economist*, January 20, 1996, pp. 82–83. Available at http://www.internetworld.com/June96/phones.html

— 13 —

EMPLOYMENT AND UNEMPLOYMENT

Any kind of machinery used for shortening labour—except used in a cooperative society like ours—must tend to less wages, and to deprive working men of employment, and finally, either to starve them, force them into some other employment (and then reduce wages in that also), or compel them to emigrate. Now, if the working classes would socially and peacefully unite to adopt our system, no power or party could prevent their success.

Manifesto, Cooperative Community, Ralahine, County Clare, Ireland, 1883 (on the introduction of the reaping machine)

INTRODUCTION

The most serious and complex problem associated with the impact of computers on society has to do with work. The basic and almost simplistic expression of this concern is the question, does technological change create or destroy jobs? In the present context, technological change refers to innovations in computer and communications technology. Definitive answers are scarce; by way of focusing the debate, the arguments may be briefly stated as follows. Yes, the introduction of new technology may reduce the number of jobs in the directly affected industry. On the other hand, it may actually increase the number, because increased productivity resulting from the new technology will increase demand, and more workers will be necessary to satisfy it. Even if there is a net loss of jobs in a specific industry, it is argued, new jobs will be created in support areas for the new technology, in whole new industries resulting from unpredictable technologies, and in the service and white collar areas. For example, the introduction of robots will create a robot support industry to install, service, and monitor performance, to say nothing of design and manufacture. Jobs are eliminated in those industries that benefit from robots but are created in the robot support companies. The common term for this effect is *job displacement*. The question about technology and jobs can be restated in terms of the economy as a whole, to take job displacement into account.

Assuming that new jobs will be created, will there be a sufficient number of these to take up the slack of previously lost jobs? It is likely that in factories that manufacture robots, robots themselves will be a major factor in production. The technology associated with computers is qualitatively different from previous technologies. It brings not only ways to do things more efficiently, but also the likelihood of doing many things with very few workers. The possibility that many of society's needs could be satisfied with a significantly reduced work force is of concern to many people.

What about the theory that an unending chain of inventions and discoveries will always be part of our future, creating new products and new jobs? In our time such inventions and processes as Xeroxing, Polaroid cameras, video cassette recorders, personal computers, and more recently, Web pages have certainly created new industries and jobs in design, manufacturing, marketing, sales, and service. In the past 200 years, since the beginning of the Industrial Revolution in England, enough jobs have been created, it has been claimed, to accommodate growth in population, increasing urbanization and reduction of farm labor, and a rapidly accelerating chain of inventions. These observations apply mainly to the industrialized countries, but increasingly to the rest of the world.

Prior to the Industrial Revolution, most of the population was engaged in agriculture. With advances in farming machinery, fertilizers, and disease-resistant and weather-conditioned crops, productivity on the farm has soared. Thus many non-competitive family farms failed or were sold. Currently in the United States, less than 2% of the work force produces enough food for the entire country, as well as enormous quantities for export. Where did all the farm workers go? Most of them became blue collar workers in the rapidly growing industrial plants. Recently, the percentage of the work force in blue collar jobs has also been decreasing. Most American workers are now employed in service and white collar jobs—that is, they do not produce things but work with people, paper, and information.

The expectation now is that as society moves from an industrial to an information base, the major source of new jobs will be in the office; in service areas such as restaurants, hotels, and entertainment; in the financial domain; and in government. The model of the future has a much-reduced labor force in production and an expanded number of people in the service and information areas. There is a serious problem with this view—the increasing rate of automation in the office. The introduction of computers, office networks, telecommunication systems, and fax machines has as its goal a major improvement in office productivity, but as a byproduct there will be fewer

jobs. Of these, even fewer will be the kind of low-skill jobs that have traditionally served as an entry point for many hundreds of thousands of workers.

Another major concern is with the changing nature of work. The Industrial
Revolution spawned a number of responses from workers whose livelihood
was threatened by the use of machines. Probably the most well-known were the
Luddites, who flourished in the beginning of the 18ᵗʰ century. They are best
known for having smashed newly introduced machines—in supposed blind
opposition to progress, according to the conventional view. However, the well-
known British historian E. P. Thompson has argued as follows[1]:

> At issue was the "freedom" of the capitalist to destroy the customs of the
> trade, whether by new machinery, by the factory-system, or by unrestricted
> competition, beating down wages, undercutting his rivals, and undermining
> the standards of craftsmanship.

Since that time there has been an uneasy relationship between the worker
and new technology. While welcoming the relief from drudgery and dangerous work that machines have provided, the worker has been concerned first
with becoming merely an adjunct to the machine and then being replaced by
it. In many cases the machines themselves were dangerous.

This fear has grown, especially in the factory, as work has become organized under such principles as scientific management (Frederick Taylor) and
the assembly line (Henry Ford). The reduction of production to a series of
small, repeatable actions encouraged a belief that the worker was easily
replaceable, that his or her skill could be extracted, and that he or she would
perform a boring, routine task efficiently for many years of working life. The
computer can be seen as merely the most recent phase of technology or as a
new force that gives management a powerful tool for extending its control,
whether in factory or office. Computers and communications systems may
reproduce the factory model in the office—at least this is the fear of many
workers. The relatively open social system in the office may be replaced by
a rigid, highly structured environment in which the performance of the
worker at the computer may be closely monitored.

Within a month of each other in 1994, two of the major business magazines in the U.S. had very similar covers:

THE END OF THE JOB
No longer the best way to organize work, the traditional job is becoming
a social artifact. Its decline creates unfamiliar risks—and opportunities.[2]

The Economy is Changing.
Jobs are Changing.
The Workforce is Changing. Is America Ready?
RETHINKING WORK[3]

Almost ten years later another magazine cover story on jobs appeared[4]:

The New Global Job Shift
The next round of globalization is sending
upscale jobs offshore. They include basic
research, chip design, engineering—even
financial analysis. Can America lose these
jobs and still prosper? Who wins? Who loses?

As we set out in the 21st century, there is a sense that work of the future will be organized quite differently than it is currently. "The job is a social artifact, though it is so deeply embedded in our consciousness that most of us have forgotten its artificiality or the fact that most societies since the beginning of time have done just fine without jobs."[5] Thus as they move toward the future, companies will put more emphasis on the work to be done and less on the individual job labels of the workers. As jobs vanish, the role of managers will require redefinition or may even disappear. The idea is that workers will be very flexible, open to new experiences, eager to learn, and willing to take risks for themselves and the company, and that the company will depend much less on individual workers and much more on constantly shifting contractual arrangements. The role of computer technology is crucial in this shift but how it is used is not predetermined; rather, it depends on a number of economic and social concerns of management.

EXPERIENCES OF WORKERS

There is no substitute for hard work.

Thomas Edison

Computers will make their presence felt in several ways in both factory and office. Computers have been used to automate various decision-making processes so that workers who formerly monitored ongoing production now must watch video terminals to see what is happening. The most dramatic innovation in the factory is the introduction of robots into the assembly line. In both factory and office, there may be problems in integrating people and machines in an efficient, safe, and productive manner, especially if the goals of management do not include concern about anything but profits and immediate return on investment.

Workers Voice Their Concerns

The men and women who do the hard work of the world have learned from him [Ruskin] and Morris that they have a right to pleasure in their toil, and that when justice is done them they will have it.—William Dean Howells, *Criticism and Fiction*, 1891.

It is useful and important to characterize the nature of the workplace as seen through the eyes of the workers themselves. The opinions of satisfied or indifferent workers, probably a majority, are sometimes neglected in favor of the angry or frustrated ones. Our interest is in real and potential problems, difficulties, and alienation, but how representative these angry voices are is a real question. It is also true that in times when unemployment rates are high, workers are less likely to complain openly.

What aspects of work are likely to be most affected by computers? In the words of a spot welder in the early 1970s in an automobile assembly plant,[6]

> I don't understand how come more guys don't flip. Because you're nothing more than a machine when you hit this type of thing. They give better care to that machine than they will to you. They'll have more respect, give more attention to that machine. And you know this. Somehow you get the feeling that the machine is better than you are. (Laughs.)

The theme of the machine receiving preferred treatment is likely to become more common. The machine referred to above is in fact part of traditional assembly line equipment, which differs significantly from the new generation of equipment. Robots are a form of flexible automation that can be programmed to perform a variety of tasks. The relationship of the worker to such new machines will be different. Will workers perceive themselves as mere caretakers, or as surviving only until the next generation of even more sophisticated machines arrives? Their concern derives from a real awareness of their place in the production process.[7]

> You really begin to wonder. What price do they put on me? Look at the price they put on the machine. If that machine breaks down, there's somebody out there to fix it right away. If I break down, I'm just pushed over to the other side till another man takes my place. The only thing they have on their mind is to keep that line running.

There is nothing unique about the American experience in this regard, of course. Witness the following account describing work in a Japanese automobile factory[8]:

> I have really been fooled by the seeming slowness of the conveyor belt. No one can understand how it works without experiencing it. Almost as soon as I begin, I am dripping with sweat. Somehow, I learn the order of the work motions, but I'm totally unable to keep up with the speed of the line. My work gloves make it difficult to grab as many tiny bolts as I need, and how many precious seconds do I waste doing just that? . . . If a different model transmission comes along, it's simply beyond my capacity. Some skill

is needed, and a new hand like me can't do it alone, I'm thirsty as hell, but workers can neither smoke nor drink water. Going to the toilet is out of the question. Who could have invented a system like this? It's designed to make workers do nothing but work and to prevent any kind of rest.

One of the issues that is of increasing concern to many workers is job security. There is an increasing trend toward what has come to be called downsizing, the reduction of the workforce to reduce labor costs by taking advantage of technological innovations. Part of the process may be different contractual arrangements with workers. For example, consider the following remarks of an employee "laid off from her job as a bankruptcy collection agent, then taken on again as a contractor,"[9] who says,

> I'm grateful to have work, and I'm happy with what I'm doing. I do a good job for them because I feel an obligation as a contractor. But I don't feel loyalty, not the old fashioned sense of loyalty we used to have. It's the realization that it's just not going to be the same ever again.

Some Historical Issues

The history of technological innovation and its effect on the workplace is complex. To begin with, it is almost impossible to discuss the history of work without assuming a particular political viewpoint. In its starkest form, the capitalist or free enterprise position argues that the constant pressure to increase productivity, in order to meet competition, results in increased investment in capital equipment. The worker is gradually relieved of a dangerous environment, decision-making responsibility, and the power to disrupt the production process. From a Marxist point of view, the basic goals of capitalist management are simply to extract skills from workers and to achieve sufficient return on investment by reducing the cost of labor. Management also wants complete control over its workers—to use them as it wishes, independently of their needs and desires as human beings. Free enterprise spokesmen point out that industrialization has permitted workers to substantially improve their standard of living. Marxists argue that the price has been high—loss of autonomy, loss of skills, and loss of respect. Technological optimists predict that the age of computers will accelerate benefits, with more and cheaper goods available, less work necessary to maintain income levels (not in the cards for the foreseeable future, however), and improved living conditions for the Third World. A closer examination of the industrialization process reveals a rather disturbing long-term trend: Workers have been losing control, initiative, and skills.

An important examination of this process was carried out by Harry Braverman several years ago. Written from a Marxist point of view, his book *Labor and Monopoly Capital: The Degradation of Work in the Twentieth*

Century, has been recognized even by non-Marxist economists and sociologists as a valuable contribution to the history of labor studies.[10] In his view, the most important implication of the Industrial Revolution for the worker was loss of control. In the evolution from the craftsman working on his or her own to the worker on the factory floor, the distinguishing feature is loss of control—over pace of work, the individual steps, and the quality of the product. From this loss—this sale of one's labor—many consequences follow. The worker and the work process have been endlessly studied in order to improve efficiency, reduce costs, and (in Marxist terms) squeeze out the last drop of surplus labor.

Scientific Management

As enterprises grew larger, the problems of organization became paramount. Near the end of the 19th century, serious attempts were made to apply new techniques to the management of large and varied companies. Initiated by Frederick Winslow Taylor, this principled effort was called scientific management.[11] He bluntly stated that it was management's sole responsibility and duty to control every facet of labor's activity. Although previous thought and practice had recognized this domination, Taylor set out to demonstrate in painstaking detail how management could translate its power into the closely controlled supervision of the labor process. He based all his subsequent research on the notion of "a fair day's work"— apparently, the maximum amount of work a worker could do on a regular basis throughout his lifetime without damaging his health. In the eyes of management, when workers slow their pace, loaf, or talk, they fail to fulfill their potential, and here scientific management comes into play. The worker attempts to conceal from management how fast the work can actually be done; so management is paying a salary that does not correlate with the realities of the situation. Supervision and discipline that are vague and general will not be adequate as long as the workers themselves control the labor process. From first-hand experience, and a series of experiments that took 26 years, Taylor derived a precise formulation by which workers could be carefully instructed in each movement of their prescribed tasks.

His contributions can be summed up in terms of three principles, as follows[12]:

1. Dissociation of the labor process from the skills of the workers. Management should organize the labor process independently of the workers' knowledge and craft.
2. Separation of conception from execution. Basically, the task of the worker is to perform a series of prescribed actions that do not involve planning or decision making. The worker must not introduce his or her ideas into the labor process because this compromises management's control.

3. The use of the monopoly over knowledge to control each step of the labor process and its mode of execution.

The implementation of these principles involves the systematic planning of each production step and the careful instruction of workers in its proper execution. Scientific management and its successor theories became a dominant force in the growth of large industrial enterprises.

The Modern Assembly Line

At the turn of the century, the production of automobiles was essentially a craft. Individual mechanics would move around a stationary work site until the assembly of the automobile was complete. After Henry Ford introduced the Model T in 1908, the demand was so enormous that new production techniques were needed. In 1914, the first continuous assembly line was introduced at his Highland Park plant near Detroit. The improvements in productivity were astounding. Within three months an automobile could be assembled in about one-tenth the time, and "by 1925 an organization had been created which produced almost as many cars in a single day as had been produced, early in the history of the Model T, in an entire year."[13] The pay structure was flattened, and bonuses and incentives were done away with. They were no longer necessary to stimulate productivity, because the combination of the division of labor and the moving assembly line meant that management could precisely control the rate of production. The assembly line principle quickly spread to other industries and served as a foundation for industrial growth.

Worker reaction was decisive and negative: they left in large numbers as other work was available. In 1913, the turnover rate was 380% and a major unionization drive began. In response, Ford increased pay to $5.00 per day, considerably above the going rate. This measure slowed the exodus of workers and introduced another feature to the industrial scene—the use of higher wages to limit possible disruptions. This strategy has also been one of the responses appropriated by labor unions as they confront potential and actual loss of jobs resulting from the introduction of computers.

COMPUTERS AND EMPLOYMENT

They talk of the dignity of work. Bosh. The dignity is in leisure.

Herman Melville, *Redburn*

Before examining computers and employment, it will be useful to consider the broader perspective of technology in general.

Technology and Employment

When large numbers of men are unable to find work, unemployment results.—Calvin Coolidge, the 30th President of the United States, 1923–1929

In a study by the National Academies of Sciences and Engineering and the Institute of Medicine on technology and employment in the U.S., published in 1987 but still very timely, the following principal finding was given[14]:

> Technological change is an essential component of a dynamic, expanding economy. The modern U.S. economic system, in which international trade plays an increasingly important role, must generate and adopt advanced technologies rapidly, in both the manufacturing and nonmanufacturing sectors, if growth in employment and wages is to be maintained. Recent and prospective levels of technological change will not produce significant increases in total unemployment, although individuals will face painful and costly adjustments. Rather than producing mass unemployment, technological change will make its maximum contribution to higher living standards, wages, and employment levels if appropriate public and private policies are adopted to support the adjustment to new technologies.

In this carefully worded statement, the obvious is juxtaposed with the speculative. Yes, technology is important, no significant levels of unemployment will result, but "individuals" beware, and all will be fine if government and business cooperate. In the mid-1990s, this endorsement would likely ring hollow in the ears of the many employees "dehired" by several very profitable high-tech companies.

It is clear that changes in technology can be disruptive, making some jobs obsolete and reducing opportunities for others. But perhaps, a definition of technology itself would be helpful at this point. It certainly includes tools, devices, machines, and all manner of equipment, but it also includes a body of knowledge incorporated in processes, skills, routines, and organization of work and social groupings. This latter component is frequently overlooked when the impact of new hardware is evaluated. It is also important to understand the dependent concept of productivity. There are several definitions but labor productivity is typically defined as the goods or services produced per employee-hour. This measure depends crucially on capital investment in technology to reduce the labor component and thereby increase labor productivity. That is, with more equipment or improved processes, fewer people may be needed to produce the same or greater amounts of products or services. One striking example may suffice: in 1950, some 244,000 operators were required to handle over 175 million long-distance calls; in 1980, about 128,000 operators handled over 2.64 billion calls, an increase in productivity of almost 60-fold. Of course, such a dramatic increase was only possible with improved switching equipment, which resulted in a steep increase in the number of direct long-distance dialings. So in fact operators are probably not handling many more calls themselves, an observation that points out the weakness of the definition of labor productivity.

As part of a comprehensive analysis of the relationship between technology and structural unemployment, the Office of Technology Assessment (OTA) of the U.S. Congress was concerned with the problems of re-employing workers displaced by technology.[15] The OTA report points out that labor productivity is only one factor in overall productivity and efficiency. Others include "good labor management relations, well-trained employees, improved design so that products can be made more easily and perform better, and higher quality, in the sense of meeting design specifications more closely."[16] If the relationship between technology and productivity is complicated, then the relationship between productivity and employment is equally complicated. In addition to technology, employment depends on international trade, domestic competition, changes in consumer preference, international relations, inflation, fiscal policy, and a host of other factors. Nevertheless, technology is a major factor and a country cannot hope to be competitive without employing advanced technology in its manufacturing and service industries. The impact of technology is evident in the long-term shifts in the distribution of jobs by major occupational groups. For example, farm labor, which constituted over 70% of the labor force in 1820, was reduced to less than 50% by 1880, less than 40% by 1900, and is currently running at a little more than 1% of the labor force, because of mechanization, fertilizers, and new crop varieties. Table 13.1 shows these changes for the major occupational groups.

The number of production workers has also declined, though not as sharply since the Second World War. Operatives, most of whom are semi-skilled manufacturing workers, reached a peak of 20.4% in 1950 and then

TABLE 13.1

PERCENTAGES OF TOTAL U.S. EMPLOYMENT ACCOUNTED FOR BY MAJOR OCCUPATIONAL GROUPS, FROM 1900 TO 1980

Occupational Group	1900	1920	1940	1960	1980
Professional and technical services	4.3	5.4	7.5	10.8	16.1
Managers and administrators	5.8	6.6	7.3	8.1	11.2
Salesworkers	4.5	4.9	6.7	7.1	6.3
Clerical workers	3.0	8.0	9.6	14.1	18.6
Craft and kindred workers	10.5	13.0	12.0	13.6	12.9
Operatives	12.8	15.6	18.4	18.9	14.2
Nonfarm laborers	12.5	11.6	9.4	5.2	4.6
Service workers	9.0	7.8	11.7	11.2	13.3
Farmworkers	37.5	27.0	17.4	6.0	2.8

Source: Technology and Structural Unemployment: Reemploying Displaced Adults. U.S. Congress, Office of Technology Assessment, OTA-ITE-250 (Washington, DC, 1986), p. 331.

decreased to 14.2% in 1980. Furthermore the proportion of production workers within manufacturing has decreased substantially; in absolute terms, between 1979 and 1985, 1.7 million manufacturing jobs were lost. This decline has continued as fewer and fewer workers together with increasingly sophisticated technology and organizational structures, and overseas production of many products, manufacture all the goods required. In 2000, the percentage of production workers had decreased to 9%, with a projected decrease to 8.2% by the year 2010. The increase in clerical workers and professional and technical workers should also be noted.[17]

Future Jobs

Given the previous discussion, can anything be said about what the jobs of the future will be? One important question is whether or not high technology will be a major contributing factor to job growth. The Bureau of Labor Statistics, part of the Department of Labor, regularly issues job projections every two years, based on a sophisticated model. Tables 13.2 and 13.3 show the fastest growing occupations, in terms of percentage growth, between 1988 and 2000 and between 2000 and 2010, respectively. Some observations from these projections follow:

• For the 1988–2000 projection more than one-half of the 17 fastest growing jobs are health service occupations, reflecting an aging population with in-home and technological needs.
• Notice that for the 2000–2010 projection as well, more than half of the 30 categories are in the health and human services occupations.
• There is a rapid growth for occupations related to computer technology for both projections. Curiously, the 1988–2000 includes only the occupations of computer systems analysts and computer programmers. Not surprisingly, as the field has grown, it has generated an increased number of specialized occupations. Consider that the 2000–2010 projection includes software engineers, applications; support specialists; software engineers, systems software, network and computer systems administrators; systems analysts; and computer and information systems managers.
• The occupations in both projections are mostly in the service areas.
• Given that the first projection ends in 2000 and the second begins in 2000, could the accuracy of the model be tested by considering how well the first has projected the occupations in the year 2000? Without a major analysis, it can be said that five of the 17 occupation are among those chosen for fast growth but their actual numbers are, on the whole, not very close to the predicted ones.

Tables 13.4 and 13.5 show those occupations with the largest predicted job growth in terms of absolute numbers. Some observations from these projections follow:

TABLE 13.2

Fastest Growing Occupations, 1988–2000, Moderate Alternative Projection
(Numbers in Thousands)

| | Employment | | 1988–2000 | |
Occupation	1988	2000	Numerical change	Percent change
Paralegals	83	145	62	75.3
Medical assistants	149	253	104	70.0
Home health aides	236	397	160	67.9
Radiologic technologists and technicians	132	218	87	66.0
Data processing equipment repairers	71	115	44	61.2
Medical records technicians	47	75	28	59.9
Medical secretaries	207	327	120	58.0
Physical therapists	68	107	39	57.0
Surgical technologists	35	55	20	56.4
Operations research analysts	55	85	30	55.4
Securities and financial services sales workers	200	309	109	54.8
Travel agents	142	219	77	54.1
Computer systems analysts	403	617	214	53.3
Physical and corrective therapy assistants	39	60	21	52.5
Social welfare service aides	91	138	47	51.5
Occupational therapists	33	48	16	48.8
Computer programmers	519	769	250	48.1

Source: Monthly Labor Review, U.S. Department of Labor, Bureau of Labor Statistics,
November 1989, p. 60.

1988–2000 projection (Table 13.4)

- Retail growth—salespersons, retail will have the largest growth.
- Food-related jobs are among the fastest growing—waiters and waitresses, food counter, fountain and related, and food preparation.
- Health services are also growing very fast—registered nurses, nursing aides, orderlies, and attendants.
- It is interesting that only one high-tech occupation, computer programmer, is included.

2000–2010 projection (Table 13.5)

- Service areas—cashiers, waiters, nurses, guards, teachers, teacher aides, receptionists, child care, workers, etc. will predominate in job growth.
- Health service areas will also contribute in a major way to job growth.
- Among high-tech occupations, computer support specialists, software engineers (applications), software engineers (systems software), systems analysts, and network and computer systems administrators, are included.

TABLE 13.3

FASTEST GROWING OCCUPATIONS, 2000–2010 (NUMBERS IN THOUSANDS)

	Employment		Change		Quartile rank by 2000 median annual earnings[1]	Most significant source of education or training
	2000	2010	Number of jobs added	percent		
Computer software engineers, applications	380	760	380	100	1	Bachelor's degree
Computer support specialists	506	996	490	97	2	Associate degree
Computer software engineers, systems software	317	601	284	90	1	Bachelor's degree
Network and computer systems administrators	229	416	187	82	1	Bachelor's degree
Network systems and data communications analysts	119	211	92	77	1	Bachelor's degree
Desktop publishers	38	63	25	67	2	Postsecondary. voc. award
Database administrators	106	176	70	66	1	Bachelor's degree
Personal and home care aides	414	672	258	62	4	Short-term on-job training
Computer systems analysts	431	689	258	60	1	Bachelor's degree
Medical assistants	329	516	187	57	3	Moderate-term on-job train.
Social and human services assistants	271	418	147	54	3	Moderate-term on-job train.
Physician assistants	58	89	31	53	1	Bachelor's degree
Medical records and health information technicians	136	202	66	49	3	Associate degree
Computer and information systems managers	313	463	150	48	1	Bachelor's or higher degree plus work experience

Continues

TABLE 13.3—Continued

FASTEST GROWING OCCUPATIONS, 2000–2010 (NUMBERS IN THOUSANDS)

	Employment		Change		Quartile rank by 2000 median annual earnings[1]	Most significant source of education or training
	2000	2010	Number of jobs added	per-cent		
Home health aides	615	907	291	47	4	Short-term on-job training
Physical therapist aides	36	53	17	46	3	Short-term on-job training
Occupational therapist aides	9	12	4	45	3	Short-term on-job training
Physical therapist assistants	44	64	20	45	2	Associate degree
Audiologists	13	19	6	45	1	Master's degree
Fitness trainers and aerobics instructors	158	222	64	40	3	Postsecondary voc. award
Computer and information scientists, research	28	39	11	40	1	Doctoral degree
Veterinary assistants and laboratory animal caretakers	55	77	22	40	4	Short-term on-job training
Occupational therapist assistants	17	23	7	40	2	Associate degree
Veterinary technologists and technicians	49	69	19	39	3	Associate degree
Speech-language pathologists	88	122	34	39	1	Master's degree
Mental health and substance abuse social workers	83	116	33	39	2	Master's degree
Dental assistants	247	339	92	37	2	Moderate-term on-job train.
Dental hygienists	147	201	54	37	1	Associate degree

TABLE 13.3

FASTEST GROWING OCCUPATIONS, 2000–2010 (NUMBERS IN THOUSANDS)

	Employment		Change		Quartile rank by 2000 median annual earnings[1]	Most significant source of education or training
	2000	2010	Number of jobs added	percent		
Special education teachers, preschool, kindergarten, and elementary school	234	320	86	37	1	Bachelor's degree
Pharmacy technicians	190	259	69	36	3	Moderate-term on-job train.

[1] The quartile rankings of Occupational Employment Statistics annual earnings data are presented in the following categories: 1=very high ($39,700 and over), 2=high ($25,760 to $39,660), 3=low ($18,500 to $25,760), and 4=very low (up to $18,490). The rankings were based on quartiles using one-fourth of total employment to define each quartile. Earnings are for wage and salary workers.

Source: Daniel E. Hecker, "Employment Outlook: 2000–2010, Occupational Employment Projections to 2010," *Monthly Labor Review*, November 2001, p. 79. Available at http://www.bls.gov/opub/mlr/2001/11/art4full.pdf

General Comments

From the point of view of high technology's contribution to employment, it can be seen from Table 13.4 that most of the new jobs in 2000 were predicted to be traditional, low-skilled service jobs: salespersons, janitors and cleaners, waiters and waitresses, general office clerks, secretaries, nursing aides and orderlies, home health aides, truck drivers, receptionists, cashiers, guards, and food counter and food preparation workers. Computer programmers and computer systems analysts are also included, but both make rather small contributions compared to the other occupation groups. Among the fastest-growing occupations are paralegals, medical assistants, home health aides, medical records technicians, medical secretaries, and travel agents—again, not exactly technology-rich jobs.

Clearly, the manufacturing sector will not provide the majority of new jobs in the economy and has not done so for some time. As shown, although high-technology industries are growing very fast, they will not provide many new jobs, in comparison to the more mundane areas. There are three reasons: the high-technology sector is relatively small, its productivity is growing faster than many other manufacturing sectors, and many jobs created by U.S. companies are actually off-shore, in the Far East, typically. The

TABLE 13.4

OCCUPATIONS WITH THE LARGEST JOB GROWTH, 1988-2000, MODERATE ALTERNATIVE
PROJECTION (NUMBERS IN THOUSANDS)

	Employment		1988–2000	
	1988	2000	Numerical Change	Percent Change
Salespersons, retail	3,834	4,564	730	19.0
Registered nurses	1,577	2,190	613	38.8
Janitors and cleaners, including maids and housekeeping cleaners	2,895	3,450	556	19.2
Waiters and waitresses	1,786	2,337	551	30.9
General managers and top executives	3,030	3,509	479	15.8
General office clerks	2,519	2,974	455	18.1
Secretaries, except legal and medical	2,903	3,288	385	13.2
Nursing aides, orderlies, and attendants	1,184	1,562	378	31.9
Truck drivers, light and heavy	2,399	2,768	369	15.4
Receptionists and information clerks	833	1,164	331	39.8
Cashiers	2,310	2,614	304	13.2
Guards	795	1,050	256	32.2
Computer programmers	519	769	250	48.1
Food counter, fountain, and related workers	1,626	1,866	240	14.7
Food preparation workers	1,027	1,260	234	22.8
Licensed practical nurses	626	855	229	36.6

Source: Monthly Labor Review, U.S. Department of Labor, Bureau of Labor Statistics,
November 1989, p. 60.

products of high technology, computers, microprocessors, communication
equipment, robots and advanced manufacturing equipment, software, and
computer peripherals, will improve productivity in application areas and so
will have a deleterious effect on other manufacturing employment. The
recession of the early 1980s resulted in the loss of some three million manufacturing jobs. Most of these will never be replaced.

As mentioned above, in the early 1980s, recessions led to large-scale job
losses, especially in manufacturing. Displaced workers were defined as those
who, through no fault of their own, lost their jobs as well as their investment
in training. However, in the last few years the focus of displacement has
shifted from manufacturing workers to "the firing of middle managers,
financial industry employees, and, with increasing automation in office
equipment, clerical workers."[18] A survey carried out in 1988 revealed that

TABLE 13.5

OCCUPATIONS WITH THE LARGEST JOB GROWTH, 2000–2010,
(NUMBERS IN THOUSANDS OF JOBS)

Occupation	Employment		Change		Quartile rank by 2000 median annual earnings[1]	Most significant source of education or training
	2000	2010	Number	percent		
Combined food preparation and serving workers, including fast food	2,206	2,879	673	30	4	Short-term on-the-job training
Customer service representatives	1,946	2,577	631	32	3	Moderate-term on-job training
Registered nurses	2,194	2,755	561	26	1	Associate degree
Retail salespersons	4,109	4,619	510	12	4	Short-term on-the-job training
Computer support specialists	506	996	490	97	2	Associate degree
Cashiers, except gaming	3,325	3,799	474	14	4	Short-term on-the-job training
Office clerks, general	2,705	3,135	430	16	3	Short-term on-the-job training
Security guards	1,106	1,497	391	35	4	Short-term on-the-job training
Computer software engineers, applications	380	760	380	100	1	Bachelor's degree
Waiters and waitresses	1,983	2,347	364	18	4	Short-term on-the-job training
General and operations managers	2,398	2,761	363	15	1	Bachelor's or higher degree, plus work experience

Continues

TABLE 13.5—Continued

Occupations with the Largest Job Growth, 2000–2010,
(Numbers in Thousands of Jobs)

Occupation	Employment		Change		Quartile rank by 2000 median annual earnings[1]	Most significant source of education or training
	2000	2010	Number	percent		
Truck drivers, heavy and tractor-trailer	1,749	2,095	346	20	2	Moderate-term on-job training
Nursing aides, orderlies, and attendants	1,373	1,697	323	24	3	Short-term on-the-job training
Janitors and cleaners, except maids and house-keeping cleaners	2,348	2,665	317	13	4	Short-term on-the-job training
Postsecondary teachers	1,344	1,659	315	23	1	Doctoral degree
Teacher assistants	1,262	1,562	301	24	4	Short-term on-the-job training
Home health aides	615	907	291	47	4	Short-term on-the-job training
Laborers and freight, stock, and material movers, hand	2,084	2,373	289	14	3	Short-term on-the-job training
Computer software engineers, systems software	317	601	284	90	1	Bachelor's degree
Landscaping and groundskeeping workers	894	1,154	260	29	4	Short-term on-the-job training
Personal and home care aides	414	672	258	62	4	Short-term on-the-job training
Computer systems analysts	431	689	258	60	1	Bachelor's degree

TABLE 13.5—Continued

OCCUPATIONS WITH THE LARGEST JOB GROWTH, 2000–2010,
(NUMBERS IN THOUSANDS OF JOBS)

Occupation	Employment		Change		Quartile rank by 2000 median annual earnings[1]	Most significant source of education or training
	2000	2010	Number	percent		
Receptionists and information clerks	1,078	1,334	256	24	3	Short-term on-the-job training
Truck drivers, light or delivery services	1,117	1,331	215	19	3	Short-term on-the-job training
Packers and packagers, hand	1,091	1,300	210	19	4	Short-term on-the-job training
Elementary school teachers, except special education	1,532	1,734	202	13	1	Bachelor's degree
Medical assistants	329	516	187	57	3	Moderate-term on-job training
Network and computer systems administrators	229	416	187	82	1	Bachelor's degree
Secondary school teachers, except special and vocational education	1,004	1,190	187	19	1	Bachelor's degree
Accountants and auditors	976	1,157	181	19	1	Bachelor's degree

[1] The quartile rankings of Occupational Employment Statistics annual earnings data are presented in the following categories: 1=very high ($39,700 and over), 2=high ($25,760 to $39,660), 3=low ($18,500 to $25,760), and 4=very low (up to $18,490). The rankings were based on quartiles using one-fourth of total employment to define each quartile. Earnings are for wage and salary workers.

Source: Daniel E. Hecker, "Employment Outlook: 2000–2010, Occupational Employment Projections to 2010," *Monthly Labor Review*, November 2001, p. 80. Available at http://www.bls.gov/opub/mlr/2001/11/art4full.pdf

between 1983 and 1988, 4.6 million workers over age 20 were displaced. This is a considerable number given that during this period total employment rose substantially. The most significant fact about this group of displaced workers is that the jobs they lost were less likely to have been in manufacturing industries. Thus we may be witnessing the first indication that information processing technology is having an impact on office employment. If this is indeed the case, then it may now be the turn of a segment of white-collar workers to enter a long period of decline.

A somewhat more restrictive definition of displaced workers was used in 1994[19]: "Displaced workers are persons 20 years and older who were released from jobs because their plant or company closed or moved, there was insufficient work for them to do, or their position or shift was abolished." A more recent survey reported that 4.0 million workers were displaced from the jobs that they had held for at least three years between January 1999 and December 2001.[20] "Another 6.0 million persons were displaced from jobs they had held for less than 3 years (referred to as short-tenured). Combining the short- and long-tenured groups, the number of displaced workers totaled 9.9 million, up from 7.6 million in the prior survey [January 1997 through December 1998]." Some of the other findings of this survey are of particular interest[21]:

- Nearly two-thirds of the long-tenured displaced workers were reemployed at the time of the survey.
- Nearly half of the long-tenured displaced workers cited plant or company closings or moves as the reason for their displacement.
- Forty-three percent of displaced workers who had worked for their employer for 3 or more years had received written advance notification that their jobs would be terminated. Those who had received advance notice, however, were no more likely to be reemployed in January 2002 than were those who had not received advance notice.
- One-third of long-tenured displaced workers lost jobs in manufacturing. This proportion continued to be much larger than the industry's share of long-tenured employees. (Long-tenured employment is defined as the number of persons employed for 3 years or more as measured by the CPS supplement on job tenure.)
- Just over half of long-tenured workers who were displaced from full-time wage and salary jobs and who were reemployed in such jobs had earnings that were lower than those on the lost job. Among this group of reemployed full-time workers, about 3 in 10 experienced earnings losses of 20 percent or more.

In summary, part of the cause of the unemployment, or displacement, discussed above, is the increasing tendency toward industrial automation as a means to improve manufacturing productivity and toward office automation as a means to improve white-collar productivity. Note that the loss of manufacturing jobs is disproportionably large given manufacturing's share of long-term employees. For example, Japan—the world's leading country in

the introduction of robots—has presented a serious challenge to other industrialized nations, although this challenge has diminished considerably
recently. The message is quite clear: increase productivity or cease to compete on the world scene, with an accompanying loss of jobs and a lowering
of the standard of living. In some sense, while Japan may be seen to be
exporting unemployment as well as VCRs, cameras, and television sets, the
dilemma of industrialized countries may be seen as follows:

- Automate rapidly (thereby increasing unemployment, only temporarily
it is hoped) in order to compete internationally and perhaps restore the
immediate loss in jobs with an increase in total production or in a lowering
of service costs.
- Don't automate aggressively, in order to save jobs in the short run.
However, because cheaper goods may be produced elsewhere, or cheaper services may be available elsewhere, domestic jobs will eventually be in jeopardy.

So it is clear that the bulk of future jobs will not be produced in manufacturing but in the service area, especially in the sectors that include relatively low-
paying jobs. Are we heading toward a society in which a relatively small
percentage of the labor force produces sufficient food and manufactured goods
and performs professionally in such areas as education, medicine, engineering,
science, finance, computers, and government, while most workers are involved
in health services, food preparation and serving, custodial work, sales clerking,
leisure, clerical work, and other relatively low-skilled and low-paying jobs?

Both Tables 13.3 and 13.5 have two additional columns not present in
Tables 13.2 and 13.4. The first provides information about earning levels for
the occupations, and the second the most significant source of required education and training. The following summation is taken from the Bureau of
Labor Statistics' report on its results.[22]

> The economy will continue generating jobs for workers at all levels of edu-
> cation and training, although growth rates are projected to be faster, on aver-
> age, for occupations generally requiring a postsecondary award (a vocational
> certificate or other award or an associate or higher degree), than for occupa-
> tions requiring less education or training. Most new jobs, however, will arise
> in occupations that require only work-related training (on-the-job training or
> work experience in a related occupation), even though these occupations are
> projected to grow more slowly, on average. This reflects the fact that these
> occupations accounted for about 7 out of 10 jobs in 2000.

Part-Time, Contingent, and Contract Workers

Another indication of the major changes that the labor force has undergone in recent years, and a trend that is very likely to continue, is the
decrease in the number of regular employees and the increase in the number of part-time, contract, or contingent employees. The Bureau of Labor

Statistics has been interested in this trend as well and conducted a major survey in February 1995. A simple working definition for contingent jobs is given as "jobs which are structured to last only a limited period of time." Other alternative work arrangements were also considered, namely, "those working as independent contractors and on-call workers, as well as those working through temporary help agencies or contract companies."[23] Results show that "between 2.7 and 6.0 million workers— a range of 2.2 to 4.9 percent of total employment—were in contingent jobs." The last figure includes both wage and salary workers and those workers who had no expectation of long-term employment. There were many other findings, including the following: "8.3 million workers (6.7 percent of the total employed) said they were independent contractors, 2.0 million (1.7 percent) worked 'on call,' 1.2 million (1.0 percent) worked for temporary help agencies, and 652,000 (0.5 percent) worked for contract firms that provided the worker's services to one customer at that customer's worksite."[24]

Another study followed some four years later. "Using three alternative measures, contingent workers accounted for 1.7 percent to 4.0 percent of total employment in February 2001, compared with 1.9 percent to 4.3 percent in February 1999."[25] The figure of 4.0 percent is considerably below the 4.9 percent of February 1995. Again, in comparison to the results of 1995, the survey found the following[26]:

- 8.6 million independent contractors (6.4 percent of total employment)
- 2.1 million on-call workers (1.6 percent of total employment)
- 1.2 million temporary help agency workers (0.9 percent of the employed)
- 633,000 contract company workers (0.5 percent of total employment).
- The proportions of workers employed in all four alternative arrangements were about unchanged since February 1999.
- With the exception of independent contractors, for whom there was a slight decline, these rates were little changed from those of the first survey in February 1995.

There had been an expectation during the 1990s that the number of contingent and limited contract workers would steadily increase as computers and networks became more prevalent and workers would find the flexibility of alternative work arrangements more attractive.

Clearly, weakening the contractual relations between workers and their employers should weaken worker loyalty and commitment. Although somewhat dated, the following two quotations are indicative of a growing dismissal by management of the importance of a well-motivated, committed, and loyal workforce[27]:

- Workers are expensive. They can justify their employment if they can truly contribute to the value-added flow of the enterprise.

• In places like the U.S., you hire people who have the knowledge to go with the new technology, and you fire those who don't.

Another point of view argues that current trends are not unique or indicative of a disturbing direction in employer–employee relations. Economist Steven J. Davis found, "That over a typical 12-month period, one in ten U.S. manufacturing jobs disappears—and does not open up again at the same location within the following two years. Other jobs, however, are being created at the same time. The phenomenon of large-scale job destruction and creation has been part and parcel of the U.S. economy and other market economies for as long as we have data."[28] However the process works, most people (64%) believe "that Congress can do something about it," and the figure rises to 78% for those "already hard-hit by a layoff."[29]

The Computer and the Office

There are at least two possibilities for the office of the future. The promising model includes an increase in productivity, more jobs, improved skills for office workers, and increased opportunities for executives. The pessimistic version suggests that the industrial model will be reproduced in the office, with rows of women at desks and terminals, automatically monitored by the computer system, with a major reduction of the traditional social intercourse of the office. The clerical work force is heavily dominated by women: 62% in 1970, but 80% in 1980. Although the office and the typewriter have been a major source of employment for women, the next stage of technological innovation may not be so kind. In 1978, Siemens, a West German company, estimated that office automation could result in a reduction of the labor force by 25 to 30%. Occupations such as file clerk, bookkeeper, typist, and bank teller, which are predominantly filled by women, are the leading candidates for automation.

Interestingly enough, the term *word processing* was first introduced by IBM in the early 1960s to sell dictation equipment. In 1967, IBM also used it as part of an advertising campaign for its magnetic tape Selective typewriters. The goal for the future office is clearly stated in an encyclopedia entry for word processing (WP): "WP represents a further stage in modern society's application of automation, reaching beyond manufacturing and production lines into the office."[30]

Those who look forward to increased office automation, especially (but not exclusively) equipment manufacturers and software developers, have an optimistic view. In the long run the routine and ordinary will be automated, and the number of employees with higher technical skills will increase. Office work will be more satisfying as the drudgery is relegated to machines. The level of human interaction will rise among those employees who need to communicate and who have sufficient time. Besides word processing, office automation includes communication networks, electronic mail, scheduling of meetings, information retrieval, and other applications. The complete package will arrive in stages because of high capital costs as well as associated technical problems. Productivity improvements will not be spectacular and in fact may not initially appear to justify the expense and effort. Over the next few years the office will undergo a transformation that will affect work in many ways. The shape of the future is difficult to predict. A concerned and informed public can help to humanize the new technology.

The High-Tech Sector

This sector is expected to be the engine of growth for the leading economies of the world. However, it is important to recognize that at least for the foreseeable future, this sector is subject to the usual economic forces. Consider two successive reports issued by the Information Technology Association of America, the trade association for high-tech industries. The reports present the state of the Information Technology (IT) workforce for 2002 and 2003, respectively. The major findings for 2002 are as follows[31]:

- The 10.4 million-member IT workforce that ITAA measured in 2001 fell by 5% to 9.9 million workers in early 2002. In aggregate terms the U.S. IT workforce experienced a net loss of 528,496 workers over a 12-month period. Companies hired 2.1 million IT workers during the year, but also dismissed 2.6 million IT workers.
- IT firms lost 15% of IT workers, while non-IT companies dropped 4% during the same period.
- Reductions were spread evenly across the United States, with all regions of the country losing five percent of their IT workforce, however, the South led in reductions as a percentage of the total, with 34%, or 181,928 IT workers lost. The South also has the largest number of IT workers, home to 3,406,519 of them.
- Ninety-two percent of IT workers work for non-IT companies.
- Software programmers and engineers are the single largest category of IT worker, constituting almost 21% of the total workforce, and the United States is home to 2,039,880 programmers. However, it was technical support workers who were most likely to be let go within the last year.

The workforce loss corresponds to the dot-com crash that was devastating for E-commerce and that is only slowly coming to an end. In a positive tone, the report also states that,[32]

"Companies are optimistic about future hirings over the next twelve months. They project an aggregate demand for IT workers of 1,148,639 in 2002, of which they expect 578,711 positions to go unfilled due to a lack of qualified workers, referred to as the 'gap' in IT workers. While demand is up 27% over 2001, it is only 71% of the level measured in 2000. Over the three years demand and gap have been counted by ITAA, gap remains consistently around 50% of total demand."

The 2003 IT workforce survey summarized the situation very simply in that it "finds that future demand for IT workers continues to drop even as companies lay off fewer workers and the overall size of the IT workforce stabilizes."[33] The problems in the economy are clearly reflected in the IT workforce results[34]:

- The U.S. economy begins 2003 with 10.3 million IT workers, up 4.2 percent from the start of 2002 (but less than one percent from last quarter).
- Gains have been made not so much in response to companies adding new workers but to a slowdown in the rate at which workers have been let go.
- Data collected through 2002 and for this survey indicate that demand for IT workers is down dramatically. Hiring managers say they will seek to fill just 493,431 IT jobs over the next 12 months—down from 1.6 million at the start of 2000.

The dilemma of IT and employment can be summed up very simply in the following[35]:

The good news, according to Gartner Inc. prognosticators, is that technology is going to continue to help companies become more efficient. The bad news is that it could cost you your job. Gartner said it expects successful companies buoyed by a stronger economy and continued advances in technology to lay off millions of employees starting within the next two years ... IT systems that further automate existing manual operations will "substantially lower the labor load of business," said Carl Claunch, director of research at Gartner. Claunch added that IT productivity is likely to outpace corporate revenue growth on an average basis, providing an additional impetus for the downsizing of many workforces.

The Computer and the Factory

A brief overview of the application of robotics will be presented here, followed by the more inclusive area of industrial automation. The context is the impact of such advanced technology on both employment and work itself in the manufacturing plant. The focus is on robots because of their growing importance but of course computers and computer networks have had, and will continue to have, a major impact.

What is a Robot?

The major application of robots in the foreseeable future will be in the industrial environment, although a small but steadily growing number of application areas include service robots for cleaning and vacuuming, and retrieving and delivering parcels and mail; telerobotics for use in dangerous environments such as mines, radioactive and chemically toxic areas, and in space and undersea situations; and medical robots for precise work in operations. Industrial robots are used for materials handling, spot and arc welding, assembly (mounting, screwing, bonding, sealing, gluing, and soldering), painting, casting, plastic molding, and numerical control. The industrial robots, after being appropriately programmed, operate in an autonomous fashion, while most of the other applications require a human operator in more or less continuous control. Based on the industrial model, the following "semi-official" definition was adopted by the Robot Institute of America in 1979 and the International Federation for Robots in 1981[36]:

> A Robot is a reprogrammable multi-functional manipulator designed to move materials, parts, tools, or other specialized devices, through variable programmed motions for the performance of a variety of tasks.

A more recent definition adopted by the same organizations is somewhat simpler[37]:

> IFR members use the definition of the term 'robot' contained in International Standard ISO 8373 when compiling statistics of manipulating industrial robots installed in particular countries. Such a robot is defined to be an 'automatically controlled, reprogrammable multipurpose manipulator programmable in three or more axes'.

These don't sound very much like C3PO, R2D2, or the Terminator, but it should be remembered that industrial robots are designed for specific tasks in the factory. Before science fact meets science fiction, considerable research and development will be required.

Worldwide Distribution

Although the first robot patent was granted in the U.S., and the first robot was manufactured in the U.S. in 1961 by a company called Unimation, which no longer exists, the world leader in the manufacture and use of industrial robots is Japan. The lead is substantial no matter how robots are counted, whether by the definitions given above or by a simpler notion of pick-and-place machines. For example, at the end of 1994, the U.S. base of installed robots was about 53,000 compared with "more than seven times as many in use" in Japan.[38] In the U.S., there has been a considerable fluctuation in predictions of new robots coming online and the actual numbers produced and sold. The early 1980s promised a period of sustained growth, but 1987 witnessed such a fall off that only one U.S. robot maker, Adept Technology, survived. Sales began to pick up again in the early 1990s so that by 1995, more than 10,000 robots were shipped at a value of nearly $900 million, "a jump of 34% in units and 30% in dollars over 1994's record-setting pace. Robot shipments are up more than 128% since 1991, when the robotics industry began surging forward.[38a]

The United Nations Economic Commission for Europe, in its annual World Robotics Survey, reports the following interesting results for 2001[39]:

- Worldwide at least 760,000 units (possibly the real stock could be over one million units), of which 360,000 in Japan, 220,000 in the European Union and just under 100,000 in North America. In Europe, Germany is in the lead with just under 100,000 units, followed by Italy with 44,000, France with 23,000, Spain 16,000 and the United Kingdom with 13,000.
- Worldwide sales of multipurpose industrial robots, admitting the fact that the figures for Japan and the Republic of Korea include all types of industrial robots, peaked in 1990 when they reached over 80,000 units (see table 1 and figure 1). Following the recession in 1991–1993, worldwide sales of industrial robots fell to about 53,000 units in 1993. The world robot market then started a period of strong recovery, which peaked in 1997 when it reached a level of 82,000 units. In 1998, however, sales plunged by 15% to just under 69,000 units. The market recovered sharply in 1999 with sales of nearly 80,000 units, an increase of almost 15% over 1998. In 2000, growth accelerated to 24%, attaining a record of almost 99,000 units. In 2001, however, the world market fell by 21%, reaching 78,100 units.
- Robot business was booming in Japan in the 1980s and early 1990s. The optimism was unlimited. It seemed as if everything that could be robotized was robotized. Since the middle of the 1990s, the momentum in the robot business has moved to Europe and North America but also to countries like Brazil. While the robot stock continuously increases in Europe and North America (8% and 10%, respectively, in 2001) it has been steadily falling in Japan since 1998. However, *as from* 2004 it is expected to start to increase again.
- From 1995 to 2000 the robot market in the United States was booming every second year and, in the years between, it was flat or falling. In 1995, 1997 and 1999 it increased by 32%, 28% and 37%, respectively. By contrast, in 1996 and 1998, the market dropped by 5% and 13%, respectively, while in 2000 it was almost flat (+1%). However, the highest sale of multipurpose industrial robots, in their strict definition, ever recorded was in 2000 when it reached nearly 13,000 units. In 2001, the market fell by nearly 17% to 10,800 units.

Why Use Robots? Work and Productivity

Robots have not been introduced into the workplace as rapidly as proponents had hoped or expected. Factors were reliability deficiencies in the available technology, high costs, high interest rates, and perhaps that their flexibility and efficiency were oversold. However, in reaction to the massive onslaught of "Japan Inc.," North America and Europe had come to view the robot as the key to restoring their lost economic superiority, at least with respect to manufacturing. Especially in the industry that had suffered the most—the U.S. automobile industry—hopes for increased productivity have focused more and more on a large investment in improved industrial automation, including robots. Robots can affect the industrial process in the following ways:

Improvement of Productivity. Increased plant operating time because of fewer shutdowns, ease of retooling, automation of small-batch production.

Stability and Improvement in Product Quality. Reduced quality variation, 24-hour working days with elimination of changeover problems.

Improvement in Production Management. Reduction of manpower allocation problems, benefits of durability and accuracy of robots, overcoming of skilled manpower shortages.

Humanization of Working Life. Release of people from dangerous, unhealthy, and monotonous work.

Resource Conservation. Saving of materials by efficient robots, saving of energy by robots working in environment with reduced lighting, air conditioning, and so forth.

The United Nations report, referred to above, includes a number of arguments for the use of robots as well as possible repercussions of their use; these include the following[40]:

- **Why invest in robots?** In the last decade the performance of robots has increased enormously while at the same time prices have been plummeting. A robot sold in 2001 would have cost less than a fifth of what a robot with the same performance would have cost in 1990. In the last few years the price decrease of robots has, however, started to level off. Profitability studies have shown that it is not unusual for robots to have a pay-back period as short as 1–2 years.
- **And not hire people?** In Germany, for instance, the prices of robots relative to labour costs have fallen from 100 in 1990 [where 100 is taken as a base level in order to compare performances in other years] to 35 in 2001 and to less than 20 when taking into account the radically improved performance of robots. In North America, the relative price dropped to 20 and to about 10 if quality improvements are taken into consideration.
- **If robots are so profitable why is there not an even stronger rush to invest?** Robots are not products to be acquired "over the counter". In order to reap the benefits of robots, potential user companies must have sufficient

in-house technological know-how as well as a thorough comprehension of their production processes.

• **Are robots a threat to employment?** Yes, certain types of employment will continue to be replaced by robots, in particular those which have very bad working conditions: heavy lifting, repetitive tasks or hazardous workplaces involving smoke, heat, chemicals, etc. Robots are never installed suddenly on a massive scale but rather in a step-wise manner, which leaves room for adjustment in employment. In the long run, 10–20 years from now, the robot population will, however, have grown very substantially while in the same time demographic conditions will have resulted in a sharp decrease in the working population. Robots will then to a larger extent help the active working population in supporting the "dependency burden", that is, an increasing share of the population that is not in the labour market, primarily because of the ageing of the population.

The very large, sustained budget deficits and trade imbalances in the U.S., and the fluctuations in productivity over the past 20 years (less so recently, however) have given rise to a serious concern about America's future, especially in manufacturing. Many studies and books have appeared debating the weaknesses and strengths of the U.S. economy, challenging the very idea of a post-industrial society, and arguing that manufacturing is fundamental to threatened U.S. world economic leadership. The discussion frequently centers on the issue of productivity, that it must be increased, and how that goal is to be achieved. For many industries, a major infusion of capital investment is required and robots, computers, and factory automation have become the symbols of the new manufacturing. Not unexpectedly, considerable debate exists regarding the definition of productivity itself, especially in the service sector, and also about what it will take to improve it.

More on Productivity

Two kinds of productivity are usually considered: labor productivity and multifactor productivity. Labor productivity is expressed in terms of dollars of output (necessarily adjusted for inflation) per hours worked. Thus one can compare productivity within different industries in one country, or the same industry across different countries, or one can even compare productivity among countries by taking the total output of the economy, the gross national, or gross domestic, product and dividing it by the total number of hours worked by all contributing workers. However, even though the phrase labor productivity is used, it is actually productivity that is being measured. The Bureau of Labor Statistics (BLS) in one of its regular reports on productivity notes that,[41]

> These productivity measures describe the relationship between real output and the labor time involved in its production. They show the changes from period to period in the amount of goods and services produced per hour.

Although these measures relate output to hours at work of all persons engaged in a sector, they do not measure the specific contribution of labor, capital, or any other factor of production. Rather, they reflect the joint effects of many influences, including changes in technology; capital investment; level of output; utilization of capacity, energy, and materials; the organization of production; managerial skill; and the characteristics and effort of the work force.

Thus the definition supplied by the BLS is really appropriate for multifactor productivity, "a composite measure of how efficiently an economy makes use of both labor and capital inputs. Growth in multifactor productivity reflects such factors as the introduction of new technology, improvements in skill and motivation of the work force, and better techniques of management and organization."[42] Other factors may be interest rates, the quality of the educational system, and the financial support for research and development by both government and industry. A two-year study by the McKinsey Global Institute (MGI), released in November 2002, set forth "perspectives on IT and labor productivity" that include the following[42a]:

- Robust but mixed productivity performance in the US, France, and Germany. The US, France, and Germany all experienced fairly robust productivity growth during the 1990s. Uniquely, the US productivity growth rate accelerated after 1995. In all three countries, performance varied widely across sectors. The IT-producing sectors contributed disproportionately to US growth, and more external/regulatory barriers to innovation and growth remain in France and Germany than in the US.
- No simple, positive correlation between IT and productivity. IT is not a silver bullet able to singlehandedly drive productivity improvement. At the economy-wide level, MGI found no correlation between jumps in productivity, and jumps in IT intensity. Moreover, our sector studies revealed specific instances where IT failed to raise productivity.
- Business and technology innovation are the key drivers of productivity growth. MGI's case studies of 20 industries in the US, France, and Germany reveal that business and technology innovations have been the engine of productivity growth in all three countries. IT frequently played a critical enabling role by providing creative management teams with a powerful tool they could use to innovate and leverage economies of scale. The rate at which innovations diffuse, and the extent to which they are fully leveraged to scale, both within and across sectors, help explain productivity performance.
- Effective IT applications share three characteristics. IT applications have their greatest impact when they are tailored to sector-specific business processes, deployed in a sequence that builds capabilities over time, and co-evolved with managerial and technical innovation incrementally.

One survey asked individuals to rate the impact of the Internet on their work productivity. Over the years 2000, 2001, and 2002, the sum of those answering "somewhat more productive" and "much more productive" rose from 56.7% to 60.9% to 64.5%.[43]

Industrial Automation

A number of key terms are used to describe the various important areas of computerized manufacturing technology.[44]

Computer-Aided Design (CAD). CAD serves as an electronic drawing board for design engineers and draftsmen, with applications in aircraft design, automobiles, and integrated circuits. Included in this heading are *computer-aided drafting* and *computer-aided engineering* (CAE). CAE is concerned with interactive design and analysis.

Computer-Aided Manufacturing (CAM). CAM includes those types of manufacturing automation used primarily on the factory floor to help produce products. Some of the important subfields are *robots, numerically controlled* (NC) machine tools, and (of increasing importance) *flexible manufacturing systems* (FMS). Two other areas included in CAM are *automated materials handling* (AMH) and *automated storage and retrieval systems* (AS/RS).

Management Tools and Strategies. These include, most importantly, *computer-integrated manufacturing* (CIM) and *management information systems* (MIS) (see Chapter 4). CIM involves the integration and coordination of design, manufacturing, and management using computer-based systems. It is currently an approach to factory organization and management.

Robots are only part of the manufacturing process. The factory of the future is expected to be organized around (a) computers and sophisticated graphics systems at the design stage (CAD) and (b) computers, numerically controlled machines, routing systems, and robots at the manufacturing stage (CAM). CAD/CAM is not a well-defined production strategy, but rather a developing set of systems and strategies that are being applied to various aspects of the design and manufacturing process. It has taken off in recent years as both substantial improvements in hardware technology and research developments in graphics, computational geometry, and AI have provided enormous power at reasonable costs.

An exact definition of CIM is not possible, as most commentators characterize it as a concept or approach rather than a well-established manufacturing system. Still it can be characterized in a variety of ways, by referring to two orthogonal organizing schemes: vertical and horizontal. Vertical integrated manufacturing, the most commonly understood reference to CIM, involves the use of CAD to design a product and a CAM system to produce it directly from the CAD instructions. The entire process, including inventory, shipping strategies, and production schedules, and other procedures that depend on Management Information Systems and CAP (computer-aided planning) systems, is controlled and regulated by CIM. The horizontal approach, on the other hand, is concerned only with systematizing the manufacturing process itself—the computer control and coordination of equipment on the factory floor. This latter approach is also subsumed under the term flexible manufacturing systems (FMS). As with robotics, one major objective is minimizing direct labor costs.

Social Concerns

The work of Frederick Taylor has already been introduced and discussed; its influence has persisted to the present day. Indeed, the terms Taylorism and Fordism have come to stand for a style of management, predominantly American, which seeks to reduce substantially the worker's role in manufacturing. More recently, two new terms have come into use, mainly in Europe, which have been employed to differentiate two approaches to the application of automated systems in the factory, namely, human-centered and technocentric. Although these approaches rarely appear in a pure form, of all countries in the world, the U.S. is the most technocentric. The following characterizes the technocentric style[45]:

> It denotes an attempt to gradually reduce human intervention in the production process to a minimum and to design systems flexible enough to react rapidly to changing market demand for high quality products. Workers and technicians on the shop-floor are sometimes seen as unpredictable, troublesome and unreliable elements capable of disturbing the production and information flow which is best controlled centrally through computers. The "unmanned factory" is the ultimate goal. It represents the division of labor carried to its extreme whereby subdivided and simplified tasks executed by a mass of low-skilled labour are progressively taken over by increasingly flexible intelligent and versatile industrial robots and machines communicating among each other via networks and computers.

There are some serious questions about whether this goal is at all viable. Experience seems to show that to make flexible manufacturing systems work, highly skilled and motivated workers must be involved, able to deal quickly and effectively with breakdowns and other problems. Advocates of the technocentric approach might argue that it is only a matter of time until the technology is sufficiently well-refined to achieve the goals set for it.

The human-centered approach depends on the purposeful integration of people into the entire manufacturing process, from planning and design to execution, problem solving, and re-design. Machines are valued for their role in replacing workers in dangerous and uncomfortable situations and in those involving endless repetitive actions, as well as for enhancing human abilities. People are valued for their creativity, adaptability, and special abilities to respond quickly to unforeseen events as well as their motivation, pride, and intelligence. Given that humans do make mistakes, that they do forget aspects of their jobs, that they do become irritated, and that they do lose concentration, is the answer to replace them with machines, when this becomes possible? The question is badly formed, not just because people are invaluable, but because even with advanced technology, it is a well-trained and well-motivated work force that provides the essential ingredient to make technology work.

Finally, we turn briefly to explore the question: What is the impact of robots on the quality of work and on the work environment? The answers are neither new nor surprising, especially given the Japanese experience. Almost every commentator on these issues has stressed one point: advanced planning and consultation with labor is necessary. It has been maintained that success often depends on paying special attention to the problems of displaced workers, gaining line management support for the change, and educating employees in the use of the equipment before installation. Unions would like to be informed early in the planning process, to be able to help their displaced members be assimilated into new jobs. It also seems to be ordinary common sense that the workers who are actually going to be involved with the new machines should be consulted about the selection of these machines. Many companies—including Ford, Westinghouse, IBM, and GM—have taken pains to consult with those workers who will be most affected by robots. This responsibility should be extended, however, to include retraining and compensation.

The Organization of Work

The contributions of Frederick Taylor to the organization of the productive process concern scientific management, time studies, and the assembly line. His goal was to separate the planning process from the execution process. Management's prerogative is to decide how a product is to be manufactured and then assign workers specific tasks to perform. Because of this division of labor and the separation of thought and action, work on assembly lines has been characterized as boring, mind numbing, and alienating. The trade-off of job security and good wages for mediocre working conditions has been justified by many commentators on the labor scene. However, with the rise of Japan as well as Western Europe as major world competitors, it has become clear to many observers that the traditional means of production still dominant in the United States could not compete successfully, or at least this seemed to be the story in the early 1990s. The sudden emergence and early success of dot.com companies demonstrated that innovativeness was still a hallmark of the U.S. economy. In this high-tech world, very skilled people work very hard, motivated by stock options and profit sharing.

Many reasons have been offered for the Japanese success story, which peaked in the mid-1990s: American aid; a modern industrial plant; a special relationship among government, business, and labor; new management techniques; a premium on quality control; the use of advanced technology such as robots; and the encouragement of worker participation in industrial decision making. Much has been written about this last point. Workers are organized into groups for specific tasks and are permitted to carry out these tasks as they wish, as long as production goals are met. On a regular basis, workers meet with management to suggest improvements in production. This system reverses the Taylor maxim. It must be working, or management would not continue to operate under such a system. In addition, management makes a long-term commitment to its workers—to train them appropriately and find alternative work if market conditions change.

Many of the above methods actually originated in the United States and were imported into Japan, where they were enthusiastically accepted and widely used. In an interesting turn of events, the same methods were being accepted in the United States after having proven their value elsewhere. Unfortunately, the economic recession of the early 1980s and the slowdown in the early 2000s has limited to a considerable degree the willingness of many companies to experiment. In fact, certain industries took advantage of high unemployment rates to renegotiate major changes in work rules with their unions. For example, in the steel, automobile, and airline industries, crews have been reduced in size and jobs enlarged with new duties. In fact, one of the casualties of the events of September 11, 2001, was the airline industry, as fear of terrorism inhibited many from flying, resulting in near bankruptcy situations. In some cases, due to high unemployment, management has gained more power to schedule work and required workers to give up relief periods.

Finally, what direct impact will computers have on the organization of work? In direct contradistinction to the problems associated with computers and workers, current approaches to the enhancement of work, sometimes referred to as computer-facilitated cooperative work, especially in the Scandinavian countries and Germany, offer a workplace in which the computer, with appropriate software, provides the necessary resources to encourage workers to realize their full potential. The goal is to provide computer and communication facilities to enable people to perform their jobs better by cooperating with their fellow workers, wherever they may be located. Management must be prepared to surrender part of its autonomy in the belief that a well-trained, well-motivated work force, operating with work-enhancing tools, will produce better products and provide better services. Thus computer technology, in the view of supporters of the cooperative approach, can indeed be a liberating force in the work place, freeing people from the drudgery of routine work, and permitting them to produce quality work in a creative fashion.

Whether management will be sufficiently enlightened to recognize this potential is questionable, for it will require a break with long-held beliefs and the exercise of a measure of trust that computers, as a new technology, are indeed different and that their potential is unlimited. The major component of this necessary trust is actually in the workers, in their desire to excel, in their interest to explore the possibilities of the new technology, in other words, a return to workers of some degree of control over the work process. Experiments are in progress in many countries of the world to develop both software and hardware to realize some of these aims. However, in the real world, computers for the most part are not at all liberating. They are management's current tools to reinforce control, to extract knowledge, and to ultimately reduce the labor component, in order to increase profits and minimize potential work disruption.

The Service Sector

> A McDonald's outlet is a machine that produces, with the help of unskilled machine attendants, a highly polished product.[46]

The impact of computer technology in manufacturing and in the office has received most of the attention when a concern with employment and the changing nature of the work place is discussed. However, the service sector can benefit greatly from technology and given its overwhelming importance in the economy, serious attention must be paid to understanding something about its operation. First, the definition of services is usually given as that sector of the economy "whose output is not a physical product or construction, is generally consumed at the time it is produced and provides added value in forms (such as convenience, amusement, timeliness, comfort or health) that are essentially intangible concerns of its purchaser."[47] Note that services go beyond fast food and football, and include finance, communications, education, health care, transportation, legal assistance, entertainment, and travel. Most employment growth over the next few years is expected to be in the professional and related occupations and the service occupations: Over the 2000–2010 period, total employment is projected to increase by 15.2% percent or by 22.2 million, from 145.6 million in 2000 to 167.8 million in 2010. Professional and related occupations will grow from 26.8 million to 33.7 million, or 26%, and service-occupations will grow from 26.1 million to 31.2 million, or 19.5%.[48]

Although capital investment in services has been growing rapidly, one of the concerns about such investment is that the desired payoff in terms of increased productivity has not generally been achieved. It is difficult to define productivity for services in general; nevertheless, carefully constructed measures can be produced for individual segments. In some of these areas, productivity has clearly increased (recall the example of long-distance calls) and in others it has not—if complaints about the limited return of office automation are to be believed.

The real question, however, concerns not just job numbers but job quality. As the Bureau of Labor Statistics has noted in its employment projections,[49]

> Employment is projected to grow in occupations in every education and training category. Nearly 8 million new jobs are expected in occupations usually requiring short-term on-the-job training; another 4 million will be in occupations that usually require a bachelor's degree. The remaining 10 million jobs are spread among other education and training categories, but most are in occupations that usually require less than a bachelor's degree for entry.

Furthermore, few of these areas are likely to benefit from computer technology in any way that will improve job availability, wages, or quality of work. In addition, these are areas with an increasing frequency of part-time or contingency workers, which means that the jobs lack many of the benefits that provide a safety net in difficult times. Of course, those parts of the service sector in such areas as communications, finance, insurance, and transportation will obviously benefit from increased capitalization in technology. Salaries will be higher, work will probably be more interesting, and advancement more possible, but in terms of the service sector as a whole, these areas do not provide a large percentage of the jobs.

TELECOMMUTING AND REMOTE WORK

Telecommuting costs often absorbed by employees can include:

1. Buying a larger house to create office space
2. Purchase of office furniture and supplies
3. Installation of extra phone lines
4. Photocopiers, fax machines, printers
5. Heating and air conditioning caused by the home being occupied more hours per day
6. Business phone charges not refunded (long distance, 3-way calling, voice mail, etc.)
7. Equipment repairs
8. Insurance
9. Interior decoration
10. Extra phone handsets and answering machines[50]

Telecommuting: Electronic Cottage Industry

The phrase "electronic cottage,"[51] apparently first used by Alvin Toffler, conjures up visions of people working at home by means of computers and the Internet. The cottage part is a pre-industrial vision of workers at home, performing piece work that they return upon completion to central locations where they then pick up new supplies. There are remnants of this mode of labor in the Western world today. In northern Scotland, tweed fabrics are woven on home looms. In late 1984, the U.S. Labor Department permitted home knitters to sell their work for profit. (They are still required to observe minimum wage and child labor laws. Much of this work is done in New England and had been illegal since 1942.)[52] Two commonly used terms are defined as follows[53]:

- *Telework*, organizational work performed outside of the normal organizational confines of space and time, augmented by computer and communications technology
- *Telecommuting*, the use of computer and communications technology to transport work to the worker as a substitute for physical transportation of the worker to the location of the work.

From the point of view of the U.S. Bureau of Labor Statistics, the following factors are relevant in the discussion and analysis of telecommuting[54]:

- Work Status. To qualify as a telecommuter, an employee must receive pay for work done at an alternate site. This excludes two groups from the ranks of telecommuters: the self-employed and employees who take work home without extra pay.
- Worksite. Alternate worksites for telecommuters include the home, satellite offices, and just about anyplace else.
- Extent. Most telecommuters telecommute 1 or 2 days per week.
- Telecommunication. Telecommuters use similar technologies to accomplish work at primary and alternate worksites. However, these technologies have greater importance while telecommuters are working at alternate sites.
- Formality. Some employers establish telecommuting programs with formal policies and procedures. In other organizations, telecommuting occurs informally.

A number of companies have chosen to encourage part of their staff to remain at home while performing their information-processing activities. Other companies, not particularly in favor of this mode of work for reasons to be discussed, have nevertheless permitted telecommuting as a way of hiring and utilizing information systems staff in a highly competitive market. An estimate of the number of teleworkers is not easy to determine because definitions vary and are not universally accepted. Link Resources surveyed households with respect to telecommuting issues; it estimated that, "7.6 million people are telecommuting this year [1995] in one form or another, and the number is growing at 15 percent per year, though telecommuters with formal arrangements amount to only 1.6 percent of U.S. workers."[55] This number represents company employees but Link also provides these numbers: "Additionally, there are 24.3 million self-employed home-based workers and 9.2 million after-hours home office workers, bringing the total of work-at-home residents to 41.1 million."[56] To appreciate the magnitude of the change, consider the following projections: "15 million telecommuters in 2002—about 10.5 percent of the workforce or 17.5 percent of information workers. This is a gain of 650 percent over the next 10 years [1992 to 2002], with half of the growth occurring in the last 3 years."[57]

More recently, the International Telework Association and Council, "a non-profit organization dedicated to advancing the growth and success of work independent location," produced the following estimates, "23.6 million teleworkers in the US as of October 2000 compared to 19.6 million a year earlier. These numbers include occasional teleworkers, day extenders, retirees and homemakers."[58] However, two estimates released in early 2002 seem to show that the growth of telecommuting is weakening.[59]

> New research from IDC in Framingham, Mass., and Cahners In-Stat/MDR in Scottsdale, Ariz., show its [telework's] growth is slowing.
> • In a report to be released later this month, IDC puts the number of teleworkers this year at 9.1 million, just a bit higher than the 8.9 million in 2001. Based on an annual growth rate of 2.1%, IDC predicts 9.9 million teleworkers by 2006.
> • Released last month, the Cahners report puts the number of teleworkers in firms with more than 100 workers at 11.8 million in 2001 and predicts that an 8.4% annual increase will bring that number to 17.6 million by 2005.

Part of the reason for the decline may be the general slowdown of the economy, especially the problems in the wake of the dot.com crash.

Advantages and Disadvantages

Proponents of remote office work, or telecommuting, claim that an increasing number of employees will be working at home because it makes economic sense. Commuting is eliminated, which means savings in fuel costs, automobile pollution, time, and a general reduction in the stress associated with driving. Employees have an increased flexibility for arranging their working hours around their family responsibilities. People will be able to choose where they live independently of the need to be close to a job. There must also be advantages for the employer, or new working arrangements will not be implemented. Productivity improvements are supposedly a major reason for physically decentralizing work. One difficulty in measuring productivity is that more work may be accomplished by home workers because more time is being spent, rather than because the worker is more efficient.

From management's point of view, employees may be easier to attract if flexible work arrangements are possible. If the number of staff at a central location is reduced, the building rental costs can also be reduced—a saving somewhat offset by increased telephone charges. However, for many women who want a career, there can be problems with staying at home. It may appear to be convenient to work at home, but mothers who do so may not be taken seriously, even if child care can be adequately arranged. The problem is a general one for remote workers—if they are out of sight, will they be out of mind at promotion time?

In summary, a list of advantages, including some of those mentioned above, consists of the following[60]: Telecommuting conserves energy (vehicle, highway, and office-related), reduces pollution, reduces land requirements for roads and parking lots, promotes safety, improves health by reducing driving-related stress, increases time spent with family, and permits choice of desired home location. It should be clear that some of the benefits claimed for telecommuting disproportionally accrue to the employer. For example, see the quotation at the beginning of this section. Furthermore, the growth in telework has placed a real burden on the IT departments of those companies which need to supply the necessary technology.[61]

> While the teleworking phenomenon may be benefiting the corporate bottom line, it isn't so easy on the IT department, which has to enable these millions of workers to be just as efficient and just as connected as if they were working right down the hall.
>
> • [G]etting the right technology in place is the biggest obstacle to successfully moving workers offsite, plotting out extra security, erecting more VPNs [Virtual Private Networks], and making company information, like vacation time and work policies, available online.
>
> • It also means making sure that every teleworker has three or four means of communication—email, instant messaging, telephone lines, online meeting software and collaboration software.
>
> • "Do they have necessary remote access and security? Can employees call in through VPNs from hotels or from home? With more managers and professionals moving from desktops to laptops, have you thought through support issues, like asset management and increased security? Do you have 24/7 support capability so when a problem hits for someone on the road, they're not hearing that there won't be anyone in support until 9 the next morning?" [Mike Bell, Gartner Group]

Social Concerns

A few years ago, one informed critic of telecommuting, Tom Forester, the author and editor of several books on technology and society, proposed the following reasons that telecommuting, as discussed in the late 1980s, would not necessarily grow as fast as proponents suggested[62]:

1. Not many people are or will be in a position to work at home in future because of space constraints and the nature of their occupations.
2. Of those who could work at home, not many will choose to do so, because homeworking suits only some people and not others. Even fewer people can cope with the psychological problems on a long-term basis.
3. We are thus most unlikely to see a major increase in homeworking (or the 'mass return home after the industrial revolution' envisioned by the electronic cottage theorists).
4. We may, however, see a small but steady increase in the number of people doing some rather than all of their work at home, as flexible working patterns become more widespread and more people seek to 'get the best of both worlds'.

Even now, it is not clear whether or not these predictions have any substance. More people are working at home as employees of corporations but the patterns are so diverse that it is difficult to identify specific trends. Nevertheless, a number of studies do identify current areas of concern for both employees and employers. For example, an industry study on the role of broadband access, obviously a technology that enhances remote work, comments on the burdens placed on workers, as follows[63]:

> No single ingredient will be a more potent catalyst to change than workers themselves. To gain the quality of life benefits and commuting cost savings of e-work, employees must be willing to explore and consider changes to the status quo. Through open and honest communication, employers and employees must determine whether e-work provides a realistic option for a given employment situation. E-workers must understand that the roles and responsibilities of the job do not change because it is conducted remotely. This extends to the protection of valuable intellectual property; the safeguarding of company infrastructure, including computers, data and networks; and the need to agree on such basics as hours of work, tasks to be performed, schedules to be met and similar criteria. E-workers must be willing to innovate and determine how available technology solutions, including broadband, can be used to improve job performance, team collaboration and over all knowledge management for the enterprise.

The U.S. General Accounting Office explored the potential barriers, including tax, regulatory, and liability ones, facing employers who wished to introduce telecommuting. Among these barriers are the following[64]:

- Employer concerns: management views about supervising remote work, security/privacy, and impact on profits

- Uncertainties about how state tax laws may apply to interstate telecommuting (could increase corporate and individual taxes and sales tax collection duties)
- Concerns over application of workplace health and safety rules to home offices
- Other issues (federal tax matters, wage and hour laws, and workers' compensation).

As with any technological innovation, the impact on the social lives of affected individuals is not easy to discern and may require considerable time for trends to become apparent, at which point it may be impossible to ameliorate the situation, even if it is recognized as being unsatisfactory. Perhaps it is possible to limit potential problems; if so, the following advice may be helpful[65]:

- Be more intentional about addressing off-site work issues. Develop an off-site plan as part of a workforce strategy.
- Treat the differences in work arrangements as one aspect of workforce diversity. Seek to understand and draw on the differences so as to allow each employee to make an optimal contribution.
- Offer training on managing off-site workers. The survey findings suggest that this may be the single most important and high-impact action companies can take to make off-site arrangements even more successful.
- Expand technology planning beyond the technical and cost aspects to focus on enhancing communication and connectedness between people, the business, and customers. Develop a technology plan that fosters connectedness, not just connectivity.
- Finally, consciously replace the office-centered model of work with a mental model of an omni-site extended network, in which distinctions of on- and off-site disappear—and no one is considered remote.

THE RESPONSE OF UNIONS

With all their faults, trade unions have done more for humanity than any other organization of men that ever existed. They have done more for decency, for honesty, for education, for the betterment of the race, for the developing of character in man, than any other association of men.

Clarence Darrow[66]

Labor unions are the worst thing that ever struck the earth because they take away a man's independence.

Henry Ford[67]

Unions may have their supporters and their detractors, but they are concerned about the welfare of a large but diminishing segment of the workforce. Their activities are an attempt to protect the workers they represent from threats to job security and loss of benefits. How they perceive the challenge of technology is indicative of the feelings of the workers themselves as opposed to the intentions of management.

The unions have been caught in a difficult position. Faced with the loss of jobs during the recession of the early 1980s, unions have negotiated contracts in which hard-won concessions gained over the years have been given up. They have tried to protect current jobs for a reduced work force. In this context, technological change has not been in the forefront of most unions' bargaining positions. For some unions, however, the handwriting has been on the wall for quite a while. Some years ago, after a series of bitter strikes, the printers' union in New York settled for a contract that essentially meant the end of the industry, as it had existed, and therefore of the union, as well. Typographers and printers have fallen victim to computerized composition and typesetting. At most newspapers, reporters can enter their stories directly into a computer, where they can be edited and subsequently formatted for the final layout. In a significant technological innovation, the computer-stored information can be sent across the country, and indeed such papers as the *New York Times* and *USA Today* can be printed simultaneously in many parts of the country. Equally significant, if not more so, is the electronic distribution of newspapers over the Internet, a process that permits access from anywhere at any time.

Bureau of Labor Statistics figures show that, "In 2002, 13.2 percent of wage and salary workers were union members, down from 13.4 percent (as revised) in 2001. . . . The number of persons belonging to a union fell by 280,000 over the year to 16.1 million in 2002. The union membership rate has steadily declined from a high of 20.1 percent in 1983, the first year for which comparable union data are available."[68] The distribution of union membership is not uniform across occupations or industries. A few highlights relevant to this section follow:

- In 2002, workers in the public sector had a union membership rate over four times that of private-sector employees, 37.5 percent compared with 8.5 percent. The unionization rate for government workers has held steady since 1983.
- The rate for private industry workers has fallen by nearly half over the same time period.
- In 2002, full-time wage and salary workers who were union members had median usual weekly earnings of $740, compared with a median of $587 for wage and salary workers who were not represented by unions.

Not surprisingly, as union membership has declined among blue-collar workers, it has increased among workers in the service sector as this sector has grown in its overall proportion of the workforce. Thus unions have had to move away from their industrial roots and attempt to organize the growing numbers of service and white-collar workers. This effort has created tensions within the union movement between blue-collar and white-collar workers, between private and public-sector workers, and between a traditionally white, male-dominated institution and the large numbers of women, blacks, and Hispanics in the new labor force.

Union membership in Europe is considerably higher than in the U.S.: For example, in Britain it stood at about 30% in 1997 (down from 38% in 1990), while in Sweden it was over 86% (82% in 1990), in Germany 33% (38.5% in 1990), and in the Netherlands 29% (29.5% in 1990).[69] Although these numbers are considerably larger than the U.S. numbers, they represent a decline except for a few countries. One interpretation of the decline in U.S. union membership is that the unions have been too successful, that the gap between union pay and non-union pay has become so large that unionized companies are no longer competitive and companies have substantially increased their efforts to combat unionism.[70] Thus the advice to unions from some supporters is to forego wages as their main focus in negotiations and move to other areas such as job security and benefits. In addition, unions must come to terms with the increased numbers of part-time workers and their different needs as well as new compensation programs such as profit sharing, employee stock option plans, and even joint ownership and management. Other reasons for the loss of union membership may be a reduction in average plant size—it is easier to organize workers in one large plant than in several smaller ones—and perhaps a general mistrust of all institutions.

Given that the major impact of technology is in the information-intensive industries, the question that emerges is, will unions succeed in representing professionals whose work has been affected by computers, and if so, when. Up to now, no major professional organization has adopted collective bargaining, except for the American Nurses Association. Engineering societies seem to be too diverse and fragmented to fall under a single umbrella organization and also a large percentage, about one-third, are management. Professionalism also remains an obstacle given the common perceptions that unions are only suitable for factory workers.[71] With the dot.com crash and its aftermath, it appeared that opportunities might exist for unions in heretofore barren ground. Consider the following comments from both a union representative and management, made during the early days of 2001:

- "When the dot-coms were flying high, and it looked like options were going to make employees wealthy, there was no reason to think organizing would bring them anything," Jeff Miller, spokesperson for the Communications Workers of America (CWA), told the *E-Commerce Times*. "But as things kind of went south, employees started getting together to figure out how to have more say and power in dealing with the employer," Miller said. "That's a natural reaction."[72]

- "Unions fight for higher wages, more job security, better benefits, as they should," Challenger [chief executive officer of job outplacement firm Challenger, Gray & Christmas] said. "But in a startup, companies are trying to hold those to a minimum, and that's a risk that employees going into startups need to take into account." Challenger added: "Attempts at unionizing in dot-coms are unrealistic. There are many areas in the economy that are much better targets for unionizing."[73]

- Organized labor leaders view the high-tech work force as an opportunity to revitalize union representation as a whole, which has declined steadily in the United States as its advantages in white-collar businesses have remained unclear. The result, if successful, could be an entirely different kind of labor union for the 21st century, one that is more appropriate for office workers seeking child care rather than coal miners fighting black-lung disease.[74]

About one year later, the optimism of union organizers had significantly faded as attempts to organize Amazon's Seattle service center, the online grocer Webvan, and the online electronics reviewer Etown.com, all failed as Amazon shut down its operations in Seattle and Webvan and Etown went out of business. The obituary for the death of union efforts might read as follows[75]:

> The failure of unions to crack the tech industry, in good times and bad, is somewhat odd considering that New Economy workers deal with many issues that unions fight against: erratic work schedules, benefits and pay equity. While highly paid and highly skilled tech workers may not be union-minded, organizers had hoped for a better response from lower-paid workers such as truck drivers and stock clerks. But tech companies successfully rebuffed most unionizing efforts by offering stock options as incentives for employees to work long hours and make other sacrifices in the name of the company. They argued that unions would inhibit flexibility, a necessary trait for a competitive high-tech company to succeed—and to have its stock soar.

However, one issue that may yet mobilize union organizing in high-tech industries is the threat to jobs posed by both the special immigration of foreign workers to fill vacant positions in the U.S. by use of H-1B and L-1 visas, and the export of technical jobs to countries with lower standards of living. A survey in June 2003 reported that, "In an exclusive Search400.com survey, 44% of respondents said they did not believe forming an IT union was the answer to stopping the visa and outsourcing abuses. However, 39% said unionization was the only way to slow the mass exodus of IT jobs."[76]

One final statement about work and life, from a union, may be an appropriate way to end this section.[77]

Work, and not just income, is an essential condition of well-being in society. Through the activity of human work in all its forms, people should be able to realize their human dignity and self-expression, participate in social and economic life, secure decent personal and familial incomes, and contribute to the building of a more just world.

WOMEN, COMPUTERS, AND WORK

One area in need of greater focus is the responsiveness of workplace practices to the needs of working women. A large scale survey of working women published by the Women's Bureau of the Department of Labor in October 1994 reported that, while most women are breadwinners and many are the sole support of their households, "they are not getting the pay and benefits commensurate with the work they do, the level of responsibility they hold, or the societal contribution they make."[78]

The widespread use of computers and the Internet has provided, and is expected to provide, many jobs for women. The impact of computers on employment is also expected to affect women significantly, given their high representation in office work. Do computers represent new opportunities for women or will they merely reinforce the old inequities? An increasing number of women have been choosing careers in computer science and engineering. Society has tended to discourage women in the sciences, and how the schools react to the challenge will be very important to girls and women. Of equal if not more importance is whether or not the workplace climate has improved and women can now achieve success based on their proven abilities.

Indications of the situation in elementary and secondary schools are not encouraging. Girls are being excluded, either overtly or subtly, from many computer-related activities, or so it is said. Arguments are formulated that girls are just not suited for computers, that their minds are not logical, and that if computer time is in short supply, boys should be given priority. Whether girls think differently from boys—girls (supposedly) intuitively, boys (supposedly) logically—is neither proven nor relevant, but actions based on this assumption, whether acknowledged or not, must be regularly examined and challenged. In almost every area of computer use—video games, computer courses at school, computer games—boys are in the majority and in effect define the associated culture. One feature of this culture is the excitement of shared expertise. It is argued by some that if the environment were made more cooperative and less aggressive, more girls could be encouraged to participate.

Another somewhat discouraging observation is that the percentage of women earning Ph.D.s in computer science is so low compared to other science and engineering disciplines. Consider Table 13.6, which indicates the

TABLE 13.6

Doctrates Awarded to Women, by Field of Study and Year of Doctorate: 1992–2001

Field of study	1992	1993	1994	1995	1996	1997	1998	1999	2000	2001	Percent women 1992	Percent women 2001
Science and engineering, total	7,080	7,652	7,921	8,287	8,651	8,936	9,347	9,086	9,384	9,303	28.7	36.5
Engineering, total	506	522	635	696	777	750	774	789	837	925	9.3	16.8
Sciences, total	6,574	7,130	7,286	7,591	7,874	8,186	8,573	8,297	8,547	8,378	34.2	41.9
Computer sciences, total	120	138	137	186	139	150	159	156	141	155	13.8	18.8
Biological sciences, total	1,831	2,050	2,109	2,217	2,415	2,495	2,536	2,394	2,618	2,545	38.2	44.8
Psychology, total	1,928	2,088	2,101	2,181	2,331	2,365	2,455	2,453	2,410	2,296	59.1	66.9

Source: "Science and Engineering Doctorate Awards: 2001," National Science Foundation, NSF 03-300, taken from Table 2, 2002. Available at http://www.nsf.gov/sbe/srs/nsf03300/pdf/secta.pdf

percentage of women awarded doctorates between 1992 and 2001. Even though the percentage of women earning doctorates rose from 13.8% in 1992 to 18.8% in 2001, the percentage in 2001 is considerably below that in the sciences, and more specifically in the biological sciences and psychology. It is, however, slightly higher than that in engineering, suggesting that computer science is perhaps more like engineering than science for women.

Consistent with these statistics is the current representation of women in bachelors' degree programs in computer science. Over the previous 10 years, up to 2001/02, the percentage of women who have earned a computer science/computer engineering (CS/CE) degree has hovered around 18%, in spite of the demand for computer scientists, according to the Taulbee surveys.[79] The percentage of women earning MS degrees has increased over the same period from just under 20% to 25%.

How do these statistics translate into faculty positions for women in computer science and computer engineering? According to the Taulbee survey, which includes major universities in the U.S. and Canada, women as of 2001/02 make up 15% of the assistant professors (up from just under 10% in 1989/90), 13% of associate professors (7% in 1989/90), and just under 7% of full professors (3% in 1989/90). One slightly encouraging trend for women is that newly-hired, tenure-track faculty are at 17%, just about the same as 1994/95.[80] Thus important role models for women students—women faculty—remain a rather small percentage of the overall faculty.

The non-academic workplace has not been hospitable to women with technical skills either. Consider the following results obtained from an analysis of Bureau of Labor statistics for 2002 by the Information Technology Association of America in 2003[81]:

- Women comprised 46.6% of the U.S. workforce in 2002.
- Percentage of women in the overall IT workforce fell from 41% to 34.9% between 1996 and 2002 [overall IT workforce of 4,158,000]
- Women earned only 22% of computer science and engineering undergraduate degrees in 2000.
- By removing the Data Entry Keyers and the Computer Operator positions from the 2002 data set entirely, the percentage of women IT Professionals drops to 25.3% of the 3,563,000 IT workers. This figure is up slightly from 1996, when women comprised 25% of the IT workforce when Data Entry and Computer Operator fields were removed.

Is the situation for women in leadership roles as problematic? A report produced by the American Association of University Women (AAUW) raises the following issues and makes the following recommendations:

- Women are more educated, more employed, and employed at higher levels today than ever before, but they are still largely pigeonholed in "pink-collar" jobs.

• The report highlights the need for advanced education for women in computer and information fields and reiterates that without better education in high-tech fields, the technological gender gap will continue to grow.
• The study also found that by staying out of the higher-echelon technology jobs, working women were less likely than men to have access to such family-friendly benefits as flexible schedules, job sharing and telecommuting.

Among the report's recommendations for change:
• Increase educational access and opportunity for women and girls in underrepresented racial-ethnic communities.
• Promote the benefits of education in computer science, engineering, mathematics, and technology to women and girls, and create opportunities and incentives for women and girls to pursue these fields.
• Enhance women's education and training in financial management and economic self-sufficiency, particularly for single working mothers.
• Promote equitable access to flexible work arrangements and additional research on work-family policies and programs.

Professional women, as noted, continue to face an unfair struggle for career advancement and adequate recognition of advanced degrees. There seems to be an unstated reluctance to choose equally qualified women over men for management positions. The explanation frequently offered, that men simply feel more comfortable working with men, does not do justice to the depth of the problem. Men tend to patronize women at a professional level. Women have only recently increased their representation in professional ranks and lack the widespread "old-boys" network that has traditionally provided contacts, support, and information for successful men. This situation is changing, as several professional women's organizations in the sciences are now in operation: the Association of Women in Computing, the Society of Women Engineers, and the Aerospace Women's Committee, among others. These societies work to keep women informed of educational and professional opportunities, provide support in stressful situations, and actively promote the visibility of their members.

One group of workers connected to the computer industry has generally been overlooked in the discussions of women in technology—Asian women who work in sweatshop conditions to produce microprocessors and peripherals. For example, wafers containing chips manufactured in the U.S. are sent to Third-World countries such as Thailand and Malaysia, where they are separated, have their leads soldered, and are then returned for incorporation into products. The work pays a pittance by Western standards and causes considerable eye strain. Another example is the assembly of compact disk drives. One of the most successful companies in this area is Seagate Technology, Inc., with 1990 sales estimated at about $2.5 billion. Of its 40,000 employees in 1990, 27,000 were in Southeast Asia, about half in Singapore, and most of these were women. As Seagate chairman Alan

Shugart says "In Thailand, there is a lot of close work under microscopes. It is pretty tough to find people in the U.S. to do that kind of work."[82] The pay in Singapore in the early 1990s was about $2 per hour while in Thailand it started at 50 cents. Here is a description of one of the factories: "At one location, the employees, nearly all women, piece together drives while facing each other across three-by-three-foot tables. They rarely speak, rarely look up. One American Seagate manager described them as 'mini-robots' and then was cautioned by an aide to display more sensitivity."[83] Advances in technology clearly rest on a foundation of human blood, sweat, and tears.

Job Safety: VDTs and Other Problems

The video or visual display terminal (VDT) or unit (VDU), or the pre-plasma computer monitor, is the most common piece of evidence of the increasingly widespread distribution of computers in the workplace and at home. Estimates vary but there are probably more than 50 million VDTs in use in the workplace today and the number is growing. Large numbers of workers, many of them women, have been spending 6-8 hours per day front of VDT screens. Over the years, a number of fears have been expressed about possible threats to health from long-term interaction with VDTs and keyboards. These concerns can be grouped into four main categories: visual, physical, psychological, and most controversial, radiation-related. The greatest fears have been aroused because of potential genetic defects. A number of incidents have been reported of what appeared to be unexpectedly high rates of miscarriages and birth defects among women working with VDTs. During a one-year period between 1979 and 1980, at a Sears Computer center in Dallas, there were seven miscarriages and one premature infant death, in 12 pregnancies in one year. In the same period, four of seven babies born to VDT operators at the *Toronto Star* newspaper had birth defects.

Subsequent investigations have revealed that screens do not emit sufficient ionizing radiation to cause any damage, but questions are being asked about the effects of electromagnetic fields (EMFs). Similar radiation is produced by electric blankets, electric razors, hair dryers, and other electric appliances, power lines, and the human body itself. There is some debate in the scientific community about the dangers of low-level radiation and the experimental evidence is at present, inconclusive. The current medical opinion about the impact of magnetic radiation emitted by VDTs on pregnancy is, "that most of the epidemiological studies suggest that VDT work is not associated with an increased risk of adverse pregnancy outcome. A few studies showed an excess of some adverse outcomes, but the effects of recall bias could not be excluded in these studies."[84] A problem still exists, however, because even though modern VDTs generally emit low levels of radiation, older units do not, and what constitutes safe levels is not generally agreed upon.

More recent findings downplay the negative health risks of VDT radiation; as such, consider the following results:

- Another issue of concern for the VDT operator is whether the emissions from radiation, such as X-ray or electromagnetic fields in the radiofrequency and extreme low frequency ranges, pose a health risk. Some workers, including pregnant women, are concerned that their health could be affected by electromagnetic fields emitted from VDTs. The threat from X-ray exposures is largely discounted because of the very low emission levels. The radio frequency and extreme low-frequency electromagnetic fields are still at issue despite the low emission levels. To date, however, there is no conclusive evidence that the low levels of radiation emitted from VDTs pose a health risk to VDT operators. Some workplace designs, however, have incorporated changes—such as increasing the distance between the operator and the terminal and between work stations—to reduce potential exposures to electromagnetic fields.[85]

- Most of the large epidemiological studies of pregnancy outcomes among office workers have not shown a relationship between VDT use and spontaneous abortion. Of the ten studies of spontaneous abortion, eight have shown no relationship to VDT use. One study that did collect data on job stress and ergonomic work load found that neither factor was correlated significantly with spontaneous abortion. [the other study that did report an increased risk was counterbalanced by two additional ones that did not]. Two studies have been conducted that made measurements of electromagnetic fields produced by the VDT. In one study that measured the electromagnetic fields in the workplace of both VDT users and nonusers, no increased risk of spontaneous abortion was found.[86]

- Although concern about on-the-job hazards related to VDT use during pregnancy has increased as more women of childbearing age are in the workforce, there is insufficient evidence available to support the assumption that exposure to VDT electromagnetic fields may cause birth defects and miscarriages. A study conducted by the National Institute for Occupational Safety and Health (NIOSH) and the American Cancer Society found no increase in the risk of spontaneous abortion (miscarriage) associated with the occupational use of VDTs. The conventional scientific opinion is that VDT use alone is not a hazard to the pregnant worker, but that the poor work postures and job stresses often associated with prolonged or intense VDT work are hazards.[87]

In late 1989, IBM began shipping VDTs with reduced electromagnetic emissions, while strenuously maintaining that existing VDTs posed no safety hazards. Careful statistical analysis of the clusters of birth defects, mentioned above, indicate that such clusters are bound to occur by chance alone and do not demonstrate that there is a connection between birth defects and VDT work. Just to be safe, the following advice seems entirely prudent[88]:

- Don't sit too close to your computer display. Keep at least an arm's length away from the screen, but remember that at this distance you will still be within the magnetic field. Computer monitors vary greatly in the strength of the magnetic fields which they emit, so you should check yours with an ELF and VLF meter.
- Rearrange your office work area so that you and your co-workers are not exposed to EMF from the sides and backs of each other's VDTs.
- Turn off your VDT when you are not using it.
- Consider purchasing a low radiation VDT which contains an active compensating coil, or a zero radiation display based on shielded LCD technology.

Although reproductive issues have received considerable attention, there are many other important health-related issues. Other problems are eye strain (even the formation of cataracts has been claimed), back, neck, arm, hand, and finger trauma. In some cases a solution is achieved by better background lighting, reduction of glare, proper height of tables and chairs, regular breaks, and the elimination of stress attributable to excessive use of the monitor. The vision problems that arise from extended work with VDTs include eye strain, fatigue, blurring, and double vision similar to those associated with other visually demanding work. There are other problems related to screen flicker and cursor blinking, which can cause headaches. The term *ergonomics* is used to describe the field of study concerned with the design of working environments to facilitate ease and safety of use (ergos: work, and nomos: study of). Most organizations have adopted a set of procedures to prevent or alleviate physical and psychological problems that may arise from the extended use of computers. For example, the following guidelines were prepared by the Health and Safety Branch of the National Institutes of Health:[89] select eyeglasses for correct focal length, use anti-glare screen, keep eye-to-screen distance between 16 and 27 inches, take periodic stretch breaks, adjust chair back height and tension for lumbar support, adjust chair height so that thighs rest horizontally, adjust VDT angle and/or lighting to reduce neck/eye strain, and adjust keyboard height to 28-30 inches above floor.

Physical problems associated with long-term use of the keyboard are known under a variety of terms, namely, repetitive stress injuries, cumulative trauma disorder, VDT disease, and upper-limb disorders (ULD). A more general term currently in use is MSDs (musculoskeletal disorders): "injuries and disorders of the soft tissues (muscles, tendons, ligaments, joints, and cartilage) and nervous systems."[90] Apparently, MSDs can cause carpal tunnel syndrome, a painful condition that may debilitate the hands and arms. In 1989, out of 284,000 occupational illnesses, 147,000 were repetitive-motion disorders, up 28% over the previous year, making it the fastest growing occupational complaint.[91] In general, ULD may involve damage to muscles, nerves, and tendons, as well as swelling and inflammation. It is important to recognize the onset of these disorders as they may be difficult to alleviate. Much more research needs to be undertaken but for the present, careful attention to furniture design, keyboard height and location, arm and wrist angles, and frequent breaks must be observed.

Recently, as might be expected, a reaction has set in to the widespread diagnosis of repetitive-stress injuries as the underlying disorder associated with computer use. In 2001, "a study out of the Mayo Clinic in Rochester, Minn . . . that found that heavy computer use—up to seven hours a day— was not associated with an increased risk of carpal tunnel syndrome. 'For 15 years, we've thought that RSI equals carpal tunnel,' says study author Dr. J. Clarke Stevens, a neurologist at Mayo. But there's no convincing evidence to date for a link, he maintains."[92] He does admit there is a 10% possibility of developing carpal tunnel in one's lifetime. Others continue to argue that MSDs are related to computer use.

On April 5, 2002, in a reversal of proposed Clinton administration policy, the Bush administration announced "its long-awaited plan to reduce repetitive-stress injuries in the workplace, which calls for *voluntary* industry guidelines rather than requiring employers to take corrective actions."[93] (emphasis added) The current experimental word on carpal tunnel syndrome (CTS) is the result of a major followup study at 3500 workplaces in Denmark, published in the Journal of the American Medical Association. The conclusion of this study is simple and apparently unequivocal: "The occurrence of possible CTS in the right hand was low. The study emphasizes that computer use does not pose a severe occupational hazard for developing symptoms of CTS."[94]

THE CHANGING NATURE OF WORK

> The man whose whole life is spent performing a few simple operations, of which the effects are perhaps always the same, or very nearly the same, has no occasion to exert his understanding or to exercise his invention in finding out expedients for removing difficulties which never occur. He naturally loses, therefore, the habit of such exertion, and generally becomes as stupid and ignorant as it is possible for a human creature to become.[95]

The importance of work in our lives can hardly be overestimated and therefore anything that affects the many hours we spend working has an impact well beyond the work place. The physical and psychological challenges to the well-being of workers both in the office and the factory raise many important social issues. For all the talk about the potential liberating power of the new technology, there may be a price to pay, especially for women and especially in the office. More specifically, there is a growing concern with threats to worker autonomy and self-respect posed by various kinds of technology, including drug testing, television and telephone surveillance, and sophisticated body searches. Of course, careful attention must be paid to computer-based technology such as computer monitoring, which is only the most recent version of the process of determining base-line work levels and adherence to pre-established work regimens. Such monitoring is physically unobtrusive although the employee is constantly aware that every few milliseconds his or her activities are being measured. The result is usually an increase in stress level with detrimental psychological side effects.

Somewhat more abstract but obviously of concern is the growing uncomfortable relationship between people and machines, especially when these machines may pose a challenge to human dignity. Thus it is all the more important that the introduction of sophisticated computers into the workplace be accompanied by proper training that stresses the long-term benefits of computer-aided work and assures employees of their ongoing value. Part of employees' fear is that they will ultimately be replaced by the computer. Even though there is little likelihood of this occurring in the short run, sufficient evidence exists to warrant some apprehension. A more realistic concern is that an increasing number and variety of jobs will be deskilled—they will consist of nothing more than "tending" machines.

Deskilling

Does the introduction of new technology—computer systems, to be specific—raise or lower the overall skills of employees? The pessimistic viewpoint is that the new technology, for example, office automation, will certainly raise the skills of some of the workers, but most of the office staff will have a reduced range of responsibilities. Their work will be narrowly constrained to data entry—that is, sitting at a terminal all day, rapidly typing rows and columns of numbers. At least this was the view a few years ago before the increasing use of the Internet for the electronic transfer of information. Under the old scenario, skills would have been reduced for many of these employees, most of whom were likely to be women. As jobs are deskilled, they are also reclassified and downgraded in terms of wage scales. Thus, entry-level jobs will pay less and be less secure, more routine, and monotonous. Consistent with this view is the assumption that office managers are always interested in maximizing volume and speed in data processing. The only restraints are such side effects as absenteeism, high turnover, poor work quality, or even sabotage. This view justifies the fears of many critics that management wishes to reproduce the factory model in the office.

Many women are concerned that the new automation will reinforce gender segregation in the office. With more women employed in routine jobs, their path for advancement will be much longer and more difficult. In fact, most women will have no opportunity for advancement because there will be no opportunity to improve their skills. On the factory floor, many workers see their future as adjuncts to powerful, computerized machines. Here also deskilling is an issue. Fewer workers will be able to exercise a broad range of skills, and most workers will be narrowly constrained. From a historical point of view, the process of separating the actions of the worker from the planning and organization of these actions will culminate in the computerized factory, where very few workers are required. An alternate scheme is to incorporate workers into the planning process in order to make use of their skills at the manufacturing level.

A number of government reports have appeared in the last few years that attempt to directly address this issue of the impact of technological change ~he workplace and the worker. Consider the following presentation of ~ debate[96]:

> Two opposing points of view are prominent
> - Technological change leads to upgrading of skills, making for better jobs but also requiring more training or education, so that less skilled people may have trouble finding jobs
> - Or, on the contrary, that advanced technology de-skills jobs, making them narrower, more repetitive and perfunctory, and leaving workers as nothing but machine tenders at relatively low pay.
>
> A third view has also emerged:
> [T]echnological changes are increasing the quality and number of some higher level jobs while eliminating or downgrading middle-level positions, thus creating a skills gap between lower and higher level jobs.

It is also important and necessary to point out that it is not just technology that affects the nature of jobs. The technology is implemented in a matrix of economic, historic, and social forces that present a variety of decisions for management and labor. To succumb to a belief in technological determinism is to abrogate responsibility; certainly the range of decisions may be constrained, but there are decisions to be made and both management and workers must co-operate, if possible, to produce a humane work place. A few years ago, the following advice on how to use their equipment and deal with their workers was recommended to factory managers[97]:

> If skills can be progressively built into machines, then workers need not be especially skilled themselves. . . . [G]ear up for long production runs, buffer yourself with enough inventory to keep the lines moving, inspect for defects—if at all—at the end of those lines, treat workers primarily as a reservoir of costs that can be bled out under pressure as the need arises, and you will boost your market share, your profits, your stockholder's good disposition, your bond ratings, your own compensation, and the Nation's industrial health.

The International Labor Organization (ILO) is the global organization whose mandate is to represent the needs of workers everywhere. ILO is well aware of the dramatic changes in the workplace since the introduction of computer-based technologies, including, of course, the Internet. The simple version of ILO's concern is stated as, "A critical challenge that faces human society at the start of the twenty-first century is to attain full employment and sustained economic growth in the global economy and social inclusivity."[98] Some of the ILO's conclusions concerning human resources training and development are given as follows[99]:

2. Technological changes, changes in financial markets, the emergence of global markets for products and services, international competition, dramatic increases in foreign direct investment, new business strategies, new management practices, new forms of business organization and of the organization of work are among the more significant developments that are transforming the world of work. . . . For some workers these developments have resulted in career opportunities or successful self-employment, improved living standards and prosperity but for other workers they have resulted in job insecurity or unemployment, declining living standards and poverty.

3. Education and training cannot alone address this challenge, but should go hand-in-hand with economic, employment and other policies to establish, in an equitable manner, the new knowledge and skills-based society in the global economy. Education and training have distinct but converging outcomes as society is changing. They have both a dual rationale: develop skills and knowledge that will help countries, enterprises and individuals utilize the new opportunities and enhance the employability, productivity and income-earning capacity of many population groups that have been adversely affected by globalization and changes in society at large.

4. Human resources training and development are fundamental, but are by themselves insufficient to ensure sustainable economic and social development, or resolve the aggregate employment challenge. They should be coherent and form an integrated part of comprehensive economic, labour market and social policies and programmes that promote economic and employment growth.

5. It is the task of basic education to ensure to each individual the full development of the human personality and citizenship; and to lay the foundation for employability. Initial training develops further his or her employability by providing general core work skills, and the underpinning knowledge, and industry-based and professional competencies which are portable and facilitate the transition into the world of work. Lifelong learning ensures that the individual's skills and competencies are maintained and improved as work, technology and skill requirements change; ensures the personal and career development of workers; results in increases in aggregate productivity and income; and improves social equity.

6. Education and training of high quality are major instruments to improve overall socio-economic conditions and to prevent and combat social exclusion and discrimination, particularly in employment. In order to be effective they must cover everyone, including disadvantaged groups. Therefore, they must be carefully targeted at women and persons with special needs, including rural workers; people with disabilities; older workers; the long-term unemployed, including low-skilled workers; young people; migrant workers; and workers laid off as a result of economic reform programmes, or industrial and enterprise restructuring.

11. The cost of education and training should be seen as an investment. Increasing this investment can be fostered by recognizing that investing in education and training can be a shared responsibility of both the public and private sector.

In a study commissioned by the U.S. Department of Labor's Office of the American Workplace (and carried out by researchers at Harvard and Wharton Business Schools together with Ernst & Young), it was reported that, "Lifting workers' skills while simultaneously implementing innovative workplace management solutions pays off in profits and competitiveness."[100] Important findings from this report, with respect to upgrading worker skills, are worth noting[101]:

- Integrating business process and technology improvements with high performance work practices are the key to maximizing their benefits. Process practices, such as Just-In-Time inventory management, are most effective when implemented in conjunction with employee training and empowerment programs.
- Companies investing in employee development enjoy significantly higher market values, on average, than their industry peers.
- Companies with "above average" and early implementation of TQM [Total Quality Management] programs that included an element of employee empowerment were rewarded with significant share price increases.
- Companies which have adopted aggressive employee development and involvement practices—such as skills training and team-based management—make significantly larger productivity gains than those which do not.

It is clearly worth the investment by management to upgrade the skills of its employees in order to remain competitive and profitable.

Surveillance and Monitoring

The rights of workers in the workplace are not clearly defined. By providing jobs, management would seem to have power over its workers that threatens their basic civil liberties. For example, drug tests, polygraph tests, and psychological evaluation may be required to qualify for a job and to keep one. On the job, employees may be subject to television surveillance, telephone and computer monitoring, and even regular body searches. Professed reasons are to deter and detect criminal activities, to measure performance in order to establish basic rates of work, and to maintain such rates. Management maintains its right to control the labor process by whatever means it deems necessary. Workers argue that monitoring creates an atmosphere of suspicion and recrimination resulting in decreased productivity and unacceptable levels of stress.

Table 13.7 shows the kinds of monitoring and testing that have increased concern about the challenges to privacy and civil liberties in the workplace. It is taken from an Office of Technology report called "The Electronic Supervisor."[102] The first three categories seem to be directed toward measuring work performance and are sometimes called work monitoring or work measurement; they are of primary concern in the present context. Others investigate more personal issues both in and outside the workplace and are beyond the scope of this discussion. A review of some of the following findings in the above report reveals the depth of concern that this issue has raised (the numbers are as given in the report)[103]:

2. Computer-based systems offer opportunities for organizing work in new ways, as well as means of monitoring it more intensively. Electronic monitoring is most likely to raise opposition among workers when it is imposed without worker participation, when standards are perceived as unfair, or when performance records are used punitively. Worker involvement in design and implementation of monitoring programs can result in greater acceptance by workers, but despite activities of labor

TABLE 13.7

SOME CATEGORIES OF BEHAVIOR SUBJECT TO MONITORING, MEASUREMENT, OR TESTING

Monitoring, Measurement, Testing	Performance	Behaviors	Personal Characteristics
Output: Keystrokes, etc.	x		
Use of Resources: Computer time, phone	x	x	
Communications contents: "eavesdropping"	x	x	
Location: Cards, beepers, TV cameras		x	x
Concentration, mental activity: brainwave		x	x
Predisposition to error: drug testing		x	x
Predisposition to health risk: genetic screening			x
Truthfulness: polygraph, brainwave			x

Source: *The Electronic Supervisor: New Technology, New Tensions* (Washington, DC: U.S. Congress, Office of Technology Assessment, OTA-CIT-333, September 1987).

unions in some industries and recent progress in labor-management cooperation in others, most firms do not have mechanisms to do this.

3. There is reason to believe that electronically monitoring the quantity or speed of work contributes to stress and stress-related illness, although there is still little research separating the effects of monitoring from job design, equipment design, lighting, machine pacing, and other potentially stressful aspects of computer-based office work.

4. Monitoring the content of messages raises a different set of issues. Some employers say that service observation (listening to or recording the content of employees' telephone conversations with customers) helps assure quality and correctness of information and the protection of all parties in case of dispute. However, service observation also impacts the privacy of the customer, and workers and labor organizations have argued that it contributes to stress of the employee, and creates an atmosphere of distrust. Monitoring the content of electronic mail messages or personal computer (PC) diskettes also raises privacy issues.

It is obviously very difficult to obtain accurate statistics about how much monitoring goes on and who gets monitored. Typically, routinized work, and low-level work such as simple data collection are likely candidates for monitoring. Thus many word processors, data-entry clerks, telephone operators, customer service workers, telemarketing workers, and insurance claims clerks are subject to monitoring, but certainly not all. Alan Westin, who produced a report used in "The Electronic Supervisor," estimated that the great majority of clerical workers are not monitored (65 to 80%) and that most professional, technical, and managerial workers are not (95% or more). But note that if 20 to 35% of clerical workers are monitored, this amounts to 4 to 6 million workers.[104]

In a survey reported in April 1996, some 84 of 300 Fortune 500 corporations responded to a series of questions with respect to their workplace privacy policies. Among the highlights of the findings are the following[105]:

Disclosures of Personal Employment Data

Seventy percent of the corporations have a policy concerning which records are routinely disclosed to inquiries from government agencies. As a result, the employees of 3 out of 10 corporations are left without such guidance. Also, 7 out of 10 (70%) disclose personal information to credit grantors; almost one-half (47%) disclose it to landlords; and one out of 5 (19%) give the data to charitable organizations.

Informing the Individual

Over half of the corporations inform personnel of the types of records maintained (62%), and how they are used (56). Nearly half (49%) of the corporations responding find it necessary to collect information without informing the individual.

Three out of four (75) organizations check, verify, or supplement background information collected directly from personnel.

Authorizing Personal Data Collection

Nine out of ten (93%) companies obtain written permission from the individual when seeking information about him/her from a third party.

When written permission is not obtained, only 3 out of 10 (32%) corporations have a policy of informing an individual of the types of information sought; one of 4 (25%) tell them the techniques used to collect it; and 3 of 10 (29%) disclose the sources.

Use of Investigative Firms

Two-thirds (67%) of the organizations responding retain the services of an investigative firm to collect information concerning personnel. A quarter (25%) of these corporations do not review the operating policies and practices of the investigative firm.

The American Management Association has conducted surveys of monitoring in the workplace for several years. The 2001 survey included tracking Internet activity. The various types of monitoring and surveillance covered in the study and the percentage of respondents that practiced this form included: "Telephone use (time spent, numbers called) [43.3%], recording and review of telephone conversations [11.9%], storage and review of voice mail messages [7.8%], storage and review of computer files [36.1%], storage and review of e-mail messages [46.5%], video recording of employee job performance [15.2%], computer use (time logged on, keystroke counts, etc.) [18.9%], video surveillance for security purposes [37.7%], and monitoring Internet connections [62.8%]."[106] 77.7% of a sample of 1,627 companies surveyed carried out active monitoring of communications and performance and 82.2% participated in all forms of electronic monitoring and/or surveillance.

The typical office in a medium to large company has in place a wide variety of systems to monitor performance and activities. Workers in offices are overseen to a degree unimaginable elsewhere. From management's point of view, their actions are a consequence of quite legitimate and indeed necessary requirements such as potential legal liabilities for actions of their employees, security concerns, productivity measurements, legal compliance, and performance review.[107] In a review of the OTA report, discussed above, written some 10 years later, the following conclusion appears[108]:

> Congress was presented with three options to consider based on the findings of the report. And Congress took no actions. Ten years later more monitoring technologies have appeared, some of which have been discussed in this paper. The trends are clear. With no general legal protection of workers' privacy, no actual protection exists. The courts have found little reason to challenge the determination, and actual activities, of management to employ every means at its disposal to monitor the work, stationary and otherwise, of its workforce. Key strokes are efficiently counted, absences from the computer computed, e-mail read when desired, Internet activities captured and measured, location regularly monitored, back-

ground checks carried out over the Internet, and visits to the washroom checked. All these have been added to the existing arsenal of drug and alcohol testing, psychological and stress testing, and new and improved genetic testing. The workplace on the verge of the 21st century may be exciting for some but for most workers, it would not be too much of an exaggeration to characterize the situation as grim and getting grimmer. The best advice to those entering the workforce, especially those with little social conscience, might be: Get promoted quickly to management or be prepared to suffer an ongoing assault on most aspects of your private life.

Given that an increasing amount of communication in offices is taking place via electronic mail (e-mail), it behooves organizations to have well-defined policies in place. The following set of e-mail principles was proposed by the then Information and Privacy Commissioner of Ontario, Tom Wright, who administered the Freedom of Information and Protection of Privacy Act and the Municipal Freedom of Information and Protection of Privacy Act of the province of Ontario[109]:

1. The privacy of e-mail users should be respected and protected.
2. Each organization should create an explicit policy on the use of e-mail which addresses the privacy of the users.
3. Each organization should make its e-mail policy known to users and inform users of their rights and obligations in regard to the confidentiality of messages on the system.
4. Users should receive proper training in regard to e-mail and the security/privacy issues surrounding its use.
5. E-mail systems should not be used for the purposes of collecting, using and disclosing personal information, without adequate safeguards to protect privacy.
6. Providers of e-mail systems should explore technical means to protect privacy.
7. Organizations should develop appropriate security procedures to protect e-mail messages.

These principles should form the basis of an e-mail privacy statement for most public and private organizations.

SUMMARY

Of all the issues associated with technology, especially computers, the most important is work—how much, and what kind. The subject of jobs and computers will be with us for a very long time, and everyone will be affected.

The relationship between technology and work is a complex one. Historically, except for periods of worldwide economic dislocations, technological innovation has not decreased the number of jobs. The open question is whether or not computers are a fundamentally different kind of technology. The contributions of Frederick Taylor and Henry Ford were key to the development of the assembly line. The separation of actual work from its planning has serious consequences for workers. The process continues, with the introduction of robots into the factory and computer networks into the office. The voices of the workers themselves should be listened to. What workers really want, whether or not they are dissatisfied, and the role of computers in their lives are issues of concern to society at large.

Which jobs will be most affected by computers and how? Granted that many jobs will be lost, where will the new jobs come from? Will there be enough? The number of blue-collar jobs is decreasing. The number of service and information jobs is increasing. Agricultural jobs are now only about 2% of the total. Fewer people are producing the products and food for the entire country.

How does office automation affect the social organization of the office? Computer networks have opened up new possibilities for distributing work and reducing the size of central offices. There are advantages to employers to having some part of their staff working at home, but the advantages to employees are somewhat more debatable.

Unions are dedicated to the welfare of their members. Unfortunately, in recent, difficult economic times, job security has overridden considerations of working conditions, wages, and other benefits. However, some unions have attempted to include technological issues as bargaining issues in their contracts.

Women are affected in many important ways by computers because of their large representation in the office. Problems of job advancement, equal pay for equal work, and discrimination in the workplace and in academia exist. Serious questions have been raised about the physical, psychological, and long-term genetic effects of video display terminals, including their potential effects on pregnant women. Other ergonomic concerns, such as glare, background lighting, and seating are more amenable to correction.

Some of the changes in the lives of workers and in the nature of their jobs as a result of the introduction of computers into the workplace have not been for the better. Considerable debate exists over whether or not the skill level of both workers and jobs has increased or decreased—the so-called deskilling issue. Also very serious is the increasing use of computer systems to monitor performance in ways that threatens individual privacy.

NOTES

1. E. P. Thompson, *The Making of the English Working Class* (Middlesex, England: Penguin, 1980), p. 600.
2. William Bridges, "The End of the Job," *Fortune*, September 19, 1994, pp. 62–64, 68, 72, 74.

3. Keith H. Hammonds. Kevin Kelly, and Karen Thurston. "Rethinking Work," Special Report, *Business Week*, October 7, 1994, pp. 74–77, 80–81, 84–87.
4. Pete Engardio et al. "The New Global Job Shift," Cover Story, *Business Week*, February 3, 2003. Available at http: //www.businessweek.com/magazine/content/03_05/b3818001.htm
5. *Op cit.*, Bridges, p. 64.
6. Phil Stallings, as quoted in Studs Terkel, *Working* (New York: Avon paperback 1975), p. 223.
7. *Ibid.*
8. Described in Satoshi Kamata, *Japan in the Passing Lane* (New York: Pantheon Paperback), 1983, p. 22.
9. Joan Young, Cantonsville, MD, as quoted in Hammonds et al., p. 85.
10. Harry Braverman. *Labor and Monopoly Capital: The Degradation of Work in the Twentieth Century* (New York: Monthly Review Press, 1974).
11. Frederick Winslow Taylor, *The Principles of Scientific Management.* (New York: Norton Library, 1967.). Originally published in 1911.
12. *Op cit.*, Braverman, p. 147.
13. *Ibid.*, p. 147.
14. Richard M. Cyert and David C. Mowery (Eds.). *Technology and Employment: Innovation and Growth in the U.S. Economy*, Panel on Technology and Employment; Committee on Science, Engineering, and Public Policy; National Academy of Sciences, National Academy of Engineering, and Institute of Medicine (Washington, DC: National Academy Press, 1987), p. 168.
15. *Technology and Structural Unemployment: Reemploying Displaced Adults*, U.S. Congress, Office of Technology Assessment, OTA-ITE-250 (Washington, DC, February 1986), pp. 321–367.
16. *Ibid.*, p. 321.
17. Daniel E. Hecker. "Employment Outlook: 2000-2010, Occupational Employment Projections to 2010." *Monthly Labor Review*, November 2001, p. 60. Available at http:/ /www.bls.gov/opub/mlr/2001/11/art4full.pdf
18. Diane E. Herz. "Worker Displacement in a Period of Rapid Job Expansion: 1983–87," *Monthly Labor Review*, May 1990, p. 21.
19. "Worker Displacement During the Early 1990s," Bureau of Labor Statistics, September 14, 1994. Available at ftp:/ /stats.bls.gov/pub/news.release/disp.txt
20. "Displaced Workers Summary," Bureau of Labor Statistics, United States Department of Labor, August 21, 2002. Available at http://www.bls.gov/news.release/disp.nr0.htm
21. *Ibid.*
22. *Op. cit.*, Daniel Hecker, p. 57.
23. "New Data on Contingent and Alternative Employment Examined by BLS," Bureau of Labor Statistics, USDL 95-318, August 17, 1995. Available at ftp://stats.bls.gov/pub/news.release/conemp.txt
24. *Ibid.*
25. "Contingent and Alternative Employment Arrangements, February 2001," Bureau of Labor Statistics, May 24, 2001. Available at http://www.bls.gov/news.release/conemp.nr0.htm
26. *Ibid.*

27. The first quotation is by Stephen Roach, Chief economist, Morgan Stanley and the second, by Luc Soete, Maastricht Economic Research Institute on Innovation and Technology. Both are taken from Bill Barol, "Staying Afloat," *Time Digital, Time's Technology Supplement,* April 15, 1996, TD 24–TD 30, TD 32.

28. As described and quoted in Rob Norton, "Job Destruction/Job Creation," *Fortune,* April 1, 1996, p. 55.

29. From a poll conducted in late 1995 and reported in Elizabeth Kolbert and Adam Clymer, "The Politics of Layoffs: In Search of a Message," Sixth of seven articles on The Downsizing of America, *The New York Times,* March 8, 1996, p. A13.

30. Edward W. Gore, Jr. in *McGraw-Hill Encyclopedia of Science and Technology,* Volume 14, Fifth Edition (New York: McGraw-Hill, 1982), p. 708.

31. "Bouncing Back: Jobs, Skills and Continuing Demand for IT Workers." Information Technology Association of America, May 2002. Available at http://www.itaa.org/workforce/studies/02execsumm.pdf

32. *Ibid.*

33. "2003 Workforce Survey," Information Technology Association of America, May 2003. Available at http://www.itaa.org/workforce/studies/03execsumm. pdf

34. *Ibid.*

35. Thomas Hoffman, "IT Advances to Drive Lots of Job Cuts." *Computerworld,* October 7, 2002. Available at http://www.computerworld.com/management topics/management/story/0,10801,74951,00.html

36. "Robot Institute of America Worldwide Robotics Survey and Directory," Robot Institute of America (Dearborn, MI, 1982), p. 1.

37. "International Robot Standards," International Federation of Robotics, June 20, 2003. Available at http://www.ifr.org/

38. "Demand for U.S. Industrial Robots Surging," *Industry Flash, 1*(4), December 5, 1994. Available at http://www.hitex.com/FAQ/robotics/7.html

38a. "Robot Sales Soar to New Records in 1995," Robotics Industries Association, February 21, 1996. Available at http://www.robotics.org/whatshot.html

39. "2002 World Robotics Survey," United Nations Economic Commission for Europe, Press Release, October 3, 2002. Available at http://www.unece.org/press/pr2002/02stat01e.pdf

40. *Ibid.*

41. "Productivity and Costs," Bureau of Labor Statistics, U.S. Department of Labor, News Release, June 4, 2003. Available at http://www.bls.gov/news. release/archives/prod2_06042003.pdf

42. Michael L. Dertouzos, Richard K. Lester, Robert M. Solow, and the MIT Commission on Industrial Productivity. *Made in America: Regaining the Productive Edge* (Cambridge, MA: MIT Press, 1989), pp. 26–27.

42a. "Whatever Happened to the New Economy?" McKinsey Global Institute, November 2002. Available at http://www.mckinsey.com/knowledge/mgi/reports/pdfs/new_economy/whatever_happened_new_economy.pdf (Registration is required.)

43. "Surveying the Digital Future," The UCLA Internet Report, Year Three, UCLA Center for Communication Policy, February 2003. Available at http://ccp. ucla.edu/pdf/UCLA-Internet-Report-Year-Three.pdf

44. *Computerized Manufacturing Automation: Employment, Education, and the Workplace*, U.S. Congress, Office of Technology Assessment, OTA-CIT-235 (Washington, DC, April 1984), pp. 32–98.

45. Karl-H. Abel. *Computer-Integrated Manufacturing: The Social Approach* (Geneva: International Labour Office, 1990), p. 6.

46. George Cohon, CEO of McDonald's Restaurants of Canada Ltd., as quoted in Report on Business Magazine, *Globe and Mail*, Toronto, Canada, April 1988, p. 14.

47. James Brian Quinn, Jordan J. Baruch, and Penny Cushman Paquette. "Technology in Services," *Scientific American*, December 1987, p. 50.

48. *Op. cit.*, Daniel E. Hecker, p. 60.

49. "Charting the Projections: 2000–10," *Occupational Outlook Quarterly*, Winter 2001–02, p. 3. Available at http://www.bls.gov.opub.ooq2001/art01.pdf

50. Source unknown, but taken from a collection at http://www.teleworker.com/quotes.html

51. Alvin Toffler. *The Third Wave* (New York: Bantam, 1981).

52. "Home Work," *Fortune*, December 10, 1984, pp. 10–11.

53. Margrethe H. Olson. "Organizational Barriers to Professional Telework," in Eileen Boris and Cynthia R. Daniels (Eds.), *Homework: Historical and Contemporary Perspectives on Paid Labor at Home* (Urbana and Chicago: University of Illinois Press, 1989), pp. 215–216.

54. Matthew Mariani. "Telecommuters," *Occupational Outlook Quarterly*, Fall 2000. Available at http://www.bls.goc/opub/ooq/Fall/art02.pdf

55. As quoted in "On Telecommuting: A PS Enterprises Research Paper, PS Enterprises, 1995. Available at http://www.well.com/user/pse/telecom.htm

56. As quoted in the Home Office Facts and Figures Web Page, Home Office Association of America, 1995. Available at http://www.hoaa.com/hostats.htm

57. A projection of the U.S. Department of Transportation as quoted in *Saving Energy in U.S. Transportation*, U.S. Congress, Office of Technological Assessment (Washington, DC: U.S. Government Printing Office), July 15, 1994. Available at http://www.ota.nap.edu

58. "Telecommuting (or Telework): Alive and Fading Away?" International Telework Association and Council, June 2001. Available at http://www.telecommute.org/aboutitac/alive.shtm

59. Toni Kistner. "Reports: Growth in Telecommuting Slows," *Computerworld*, February 11, 2002. Available at http://www.computerworld.com/mobiletopics/mobile/story/0,10801,68188,00.html

60. Richard P. Johnson. "Ten Advantages to Telecommuting," September 1994. Available at http://128.165.144.22/Group /tsa10/rick_johnson/telebenefits.html

61. Sharon Gaudin. "Teleworking Boom Causing IT Headaches," Jupermedia, January 21, 2003. Available at http://itmanagement.earthweb.com/netsys/article.php/1572431

62. Tom Forester. "The Myth of the Electronic Cottage," *Futures, 2* (3), June 1988, p. 232.

63. "Any Time, Any Place, Anywhere: Broadband and the Changing Face of Work," Positively Broadband Campaign, August 2002. Available at http://www.positivelybroadband.org/library/downloads/17505_final_whitepaper. pdf

64. "Telecommuting: Overview of Potential Barriers Facing Employers," U. S. General Accounting Office, July 2001. Available at http://www.gao.gov/new.items/d01926.pdf

65. Amy Richman, Karen Noble, and Arlene Johnson. "When the Workplace Is many Places: The Extent and nature of Off-Site Work Today," Executive Summary, American Business Collaboration for Quality Dependent Care, 2001–2002. Available at http://www.abcdependentcare.com/docs/ABC_Executive_Summary_final.pdf

66. Clarence Darrow. *The Railroad Trainmen*, November 1909. Available at http://carpentersunionbc.com/Pages/postersvintage.html

67. Henry Ford (booklet distributed to Ford employees during CIO drive), as quoted in *Time*, August 20, 1945.

68. "Union Members Summary," Bureau of Library Statistics, February 25, 2003. Available at http://www.bls.gov /news.release/union2.nr0.htm

69. Jeremy Waddington and Reiner Hoffmann. "Trade Unions in Europe: Reform, Reorganization, and Restructuring," Chapter 1 in Waddington and Hoffmann (Eds.), *Trade Unions in Europe: Facing Challenges and Searching for Solutions* (Brussels: ETUI, 2000). Available at http://www.etuc.org/ETUI/Publications/Books/Challenges/ChallChap1.pdf

70. "Workers of the World Disunite," *The Economist*, August 18, 1990, p. 57.

71. Sar A. Levitan and Frank Gallo. "Collective Bargaining and Private Sector Professionals," *Monthly Labor Review*, September 1989, pp. 24–33.

72. Michael Mahoney. "Are Unions Strangling E-Commerce?" *E-Commerce Times*, February 16, 2001. Available at http://www.ecommercetimes.com/perl/printer/7562.htm

73. *Ibid.*

74. Troy Wolverton. "Will High Tech Chaos Finally Give Birth to Unions," News.com, January 16, 2001. Available at http://news.cnet.com/news/0-1007-201-4385393-0.htm

75. Alorie Gilbert. "Unions a Casualty of Dot-com Shakeouts," News.com, January 11, 2002. Available at http://news.cnet.com/news/0-1007-200-8437119.html

76. Kate Evans-Correia. "Debate Rages Over Need for IT Union," Search400.com, June 27, 2003. Available at http://search400.techtarget.com/originalContent/0,289142,sid3_gci912197,00.html

77. From "The Facts," published by the Canadian Union of Public Employees, and reprinted in *The Globe and Mail*, Toronto, Canada, March 2, 1988, p. B10.

78. "Report of The Commission on the Future of Worker-Management Relations," The Dunlop Commission, U.S. Departments of Commerce and Labor, Section 3, 1995. Available at URL:http://www.ilr.cornell.edu/lib/e_archive/Dunlop

79. "CRA Taulbee Trends: Women Students & Faculty," Computing Research Associates, June 26, 2003. Available at http://www.cra.org/info/taulbee/women.data.html

80. *Ibid.*

81. "Report of the ITAA Blue Ribbon Panel on IT Diversity," Information Technology Association of America, May 5, 2003. Available at http://www.itaa.org/workforce/docs/03divreport.pdf

82. As quoted in Evelyn Richards, "Asia's Taskmaster: How One U.S. Company Drives Employees," *The Vancouver Sun* (Canada), June 30, 1990, p. D10. Originally published in *The Washington Post*.

83. *Ibid.*

84. "General EMF Health Effects. Video Display Terminal Magnetic Fields and Pregnancy Outcomes." *BENER Digest Update*, June 17, 1996. Available at URL:http://infoventures.microserve.com/emf/currlit/bu12482.html

85. "Working Safely With Video Display Terminals," U.S. Department of Labor, Occupational Safety and Health Administration, OSHA 3092, 1997 (Revised). Available at http://www.osha.gov/Publications/osha3092.pdf

86. "NIOSH Publications on Video Display terminals," Third Edition, U.S. Department of Health and Human Services, National Institute for Occupational Safety and Health, September 1999. Available at http://www.cdc.gov/ niosh/pdfs/99-135a.pdf

87. "Health and Safety Guidelines for Video Display Terminals in the Workplace," Department of Consumer and Business Services, Oregon Occupational Safety & Health Division, December 2002. Available at http://www.cbs.state.or.us/osha/pdf/pubs/1863.pdf

88. *Ibid.*

89. "Safety and Health Program for Video Display Terminal (VDT) Operators," Health and Safety Branch, National Institutes of Health, Safety Notes, Number 11, July 25, 1996. Available at http://www.niehs.nih.gov/odhsb/notes/note11.htm

90. "Ergonomics: The Study of Work," U.S. Department of Labor, Occupational Safety and Health Administration, 2000 (Revised). Available at http://www.washingtonpost.com/wp-srv/business/legacy/pdf/ergonomic_study_of_work.pdf

91. Mitch Betts. "Repetitive Stress Claims Soar," *Computerworld*, November 19, 1990, p. 1.

92. Jacqueline Stenson. "RSI Revisited; Controversy Over Computer's Role," MSNBC, August 21, 2001. Available at http://www.msnbc.com/news/610809.asp?cp1=1

93. Caroline E. Mayer. "Guidelines, Not Rules, on Ergonomics," *The Washington Post*, April 6, 2002, Page E01.

94. John Hviid Andersen et al. "Computer Use and Carpal Tunnel Syndrome," Abstract, *JAMA.* 2003;289:2963-2969, June 11. Available at http://jama.ama-assn.org/cgi/content/abstract/289/22/2963.html

95. Adam Smith. *The Wealth of Nations* (London: Everyman's Library, J. M. Dent & Sons Ltd., 1947), vol. II, p. 278.

96. *Op cit.*, *Technology and Structural Unemployment*, p. 336.

97. W. Abernathy, K. Clark, and A. Kantrow. *Industrial Renaissance: Producing a Competitive Future for America* (New York: Basic Books, 1983).

98. "Annex 2: Resolution Concerning Human Resources Training and Development," General Conference of the International Labor Organization, meeting in its 88th Session, June 14, 2000 (Updated March 21, 2002). Available at http://www.ilo.org/public/english/employment/skills/recomm/report/annex2.htm#conc1

99. *Ibid.*
100. "Study Finds Competitive Gains From Innovative Workplace Practices," Ernst & Young, June 5, 1995. Available at http://www.ey.com/us/work.htm
101. *Ibid.*
102. *The Electronic Supervisor: New Technology, New Tensions*, U.S. Congress, Office of Technology Assessment, OTA-CIT-333, (Washington, DC, September, 1987).
103. *Ibid.*, pp. 9–12.
104. *Ibid.*, p. 32.
105. David F. Linowes. "A Research Survey of Privacy in the Workplace," Institute of Government and Public Affairs, University of Illinois at Urbana—Champaign, April 1996. Available at http://www.securitymanagement.com/library/000149.html
106. "2001 AMA Survey, Workplace Monitoring & Surveillance: Policies and Practices," Summary of Key Findings, 2001. Available at http://www.amanet.org/research/pdfs/emstu_short.pdf
107. *Ibid.*
108. Richard S. Rosenberg. "The Workplace on the Verge of the 21st Century," *J. Bus. Ethics*, (22:11), October 11, 1999, pp. 3–14.
109. "Privacy Protection Principles for Electronic Mail Systems," Information and Privacy Commissioner/Ontario, Toronto, Canada, February 1994. Available at www.ipc.on.ca/scripts/index_.asp?action=31&N_ID=1&P_ID=11399&IJ_ID=0

ADDITIONAL READINGS

Introduction

"The Downsizing of America," a Seven-Part Series, *The New York Times*, March 3, 1996 to March 9, 1996.

Thompson, Paul. *The Nature of Work, 2nd Edition* (London: Macmillan Education Ltd., 1989).

Zuboff, Shoshana. *In the Age of the Smart Machine: The Future of Work and Power* (New York: Basic Books, 1988).

Experiences of Workers

Aronowitz, Stanley. *False Promises* (New York: McGraw-Hill, 1974).

Doray, Bernard. *From Taylorism to Fordism: A Rational Madness* (London: Free Association Books, 1988).

Garson, Barbara. *All the Livelong Day* (Middlesex, England: Penguin, 1977).

Littler, Craig R. (Ed.). *The Experience of Work* (Aldershot, Hants, England: Gower, 1985).

O'Toole, James. *Work and the Quality of Life* (Cambridge, MA: MIT Press, 1974).

Computers and Employment

"2003 Workforce Survey," Information Technology Association of America, May 23, 2003. Available at http://www.itaa.org/workforce/studies/03execsumm.pdf

Bjerknes, Gro, Ehn, Pelle, and Kyng, Morten (Eds.) *Computers and Democracy* (Aldershot, Hants, England: Avebury [Gower], 1987).

Greenbaum, Joan. *Windows on the Workplace.* (New York: Monthly Review Press [Cornerstone Books], 1995).

Hipple, Steven and Kosanovich, Karen. "Computer and Internet Use at Work in 2001," *Monthly Labor Review*, February 2003, pp. 26–35.

Human Resource Practices for Implementing Advanced Manufacturing Technology. Committee on the Effective Implementation of Advanced Manufacturing Technology, Manufacturing Studies Board, Commission on Engineering and Technical Systems (Washington, DC: National Academic Press, 1986). Available at http://www.ul.cs.cmu.edu/books/human_resource/hum001.htm

Leontief, Wassily and Duchin, Faye. *The Future Impact of Automation on Workers* (New York: Oxford University Press, 1986).

Olson. Margrethe H. *Technological Support for Work Group Collaboration* (Hillsdale, NJ: Erlbaum, 1989).

Toosi, Mitra. "A Century of Change: The U.S. Labor Force, 1950–2050," *Monthly Labor Review*, May 2002, pp. 15–28. Available at http://www.bls.gov/opub/mlr/2002/05/art2full.pdf

Telecommuting and Remote Work

Di Marino, Vittorio. *Promoting Decent Work: The High Road to Teleworking* (Geneva: The International Labour Organization, 2001.) Available at http://www.ilo.org/public/english/protection/safework/telework/hrdptl.pdf

"The Future of Telecommuting." *Wired.* 3.10, October 1995, p. 68. Available at http://www.hotwired.com/wired/3.10/departments/reality.check.html

Kugelmass, Joel. *Telecommuting: A Manager's Guide to Flexible Work Arrangements* (New York: Lexington Books, 1995).

Pacific Bell Telecommuting Guide. (No date.). Available at http://www.pacbell.com/products/business/general/telecommuting/tcguide/tcguide.pdf

Richman, Amy, Noble, Karen, and Johnson, Arlene. "When the Workplace Is Many Places: The Extent and Nature of Off-Site Work Today," American Business Collaboration, Executive Summary, 2002. Available at http://www.abcdependentcare.com/docs/ABC_Executive_Summary_final.pdf

The Response of Unions

"Commission on the Future of Worker-Management Relations, Final Report," U.S. Departments of Commerce and Labor, December 1994, Available at http://www. ilr.cornell.edu/library/e_archive/Dunlop/dunlop.contents.htm

Heckscher, Charles C. *The New Unionism: Employee Involvement in the Changing Corporation* (New York: Basic Books, 1988).

Montgomery, David. *Workers' Control in America: Studies in the History of Work, Technology, and Labor Struggles* (New York: Cambridge University Press, 1979).

Computers, Women, and Work

Applewhite, Ashton. "Why So Few Women?" *IEEE Spectrum*, May 2002. Available at http://www.Spectrum.ieee.org/WEBONLY/resource/may02/care.html

Brodeur, Paul. "The Magnetic-Field Menace," *MacWorld*, July 1990, pp. 136–144.

Grajewski, Barbara, et al. "Work With Video Display Terminals and the Risk of Reduced Birthweight and Preterm Birth," *American Journal of Industrial Medicine*, Vol. 32, 1997, pp. 681–688.

Hemenway, Kathleen. "Human Nature and the Glass Ceiling in Industry," *Communications of the ACM, 38* (1), January 1995, pp. 55–62.

Looker, Dianne and Thiessen, Victor. "The Digital Divide in Canadian Schools: Factors Affecting Student Access to and Use of Information Technology," Statistics Canada, June 2003. Available at http://www.statcan.ca/english/research/81-597-XIE/81-597-XIE.pdf

Pearl, Amy et al. "Becoming a Computer Scientist," A Report by the ACM Committee on the Status of Women in Computer Science, *Communications of the ACM 33* (11) November 1990, pp. 47–57.

"The Uphill Struggle: No Rose Garden for Women in Engineering," *IEEE Spectrum*, May 1995, pp. 40–50.

"Women in Technology Leadership," Prepared for Deloitte & Touche by Roper Starch Worldwide, June 2001. Available at http://www.roper.com/Newsroom/Report-final.pdf

The Changing Nature of Work

"Building a Digital Workforce: Confronting the Crisis," National Policy Association, Digital Economic Opportunity Committee, June 2002. Available at http://www.npa1.org/DigitalDivide/book3insidepages1.pdf [See also . . ./report1. pdf and . . ./book2insidepages.pdf]

Building a Workforce for the Information Economy, Computer Science and Telecommunications Board (Washington, DC: National Academies Press, 2001). Available at http://www.nap.edu/books/0309069939/html/

Garson, Barbara. *The Electronic Sweatshop: How Computers Are Transforming the Office of the Future Into the Factory of the Past* (New York: Simon & Schuster, 1988).

Grudin, Jonathan, "Computer-Supported Cooperative Work: History and Focus," *IEEE Computer*, May 1994, pp. 19–26.

"Representations of Work," Special Issue of *Communications of the ACM, 38* (9), September 1995.

Research Recommendations to Facilitate Distributed Work. National Research Council (Washington, DC: National Academy Press, 1994). Available at http://www.nap.edu/nap/online/distr_work

14

THE INFORMATION SOCIETY

In 1982, a cascade of computers beeped and blipped their way into the American Office, the American school, the American home. The "information revolution" that futurists have long predicted has arrived, bringing with it the promise of dramatic changes in the way people live and work, perhaps even in the way they think. America will never be the same.

Time, January 3, 1983

INTRODUCTION

Time declared the computer "Machine of the Year" for 1982. In the form of the personal computer, it had truly arrived as a major factor in the national consciousness. On television and in magazines, a Charlie Chaplin look-alike demonstrated how a personal computer, the IBM PC, would save your small business. The once almost mystical mainframe had emerged from the cloistered computing center, transformed into a keyboard and a monitor. Other companies were also heavily engaged in trying to convince American families to purchase a computer. Such names as Dell, Gateway, Apple, Compaq, and Texas Instruments have become quite familiar. The competition is fierce, and there have been and will continue to be many casualties.

Some 20 years later, a similar story is being told, but now the theme is networks, the Internet, the Web, and the importance of being connected. The computer is seen by some as a means of getting online, of exploring a new frontier, making new (unseen) friends, playing new games (of all kinds), downloading music (unconcerned about copyright), and generally cruising cyberspace. It sounds exciting and millions around the world have taken the plunge, as of course have the many thousands of companies that have established Web sites in hopes of doing business. This movement from a freestanding, general-purpose computer to an active window on the world has come about remarkably quickly, with consequences that are difficult, if not impossible, to predict. This transition will be briefly explored and the nature of the current online world described, or at least many of its features. For the present, note that a number of measures indicate that the creation, storage, and movement of information is becoming cheaper, as befits the creation of an Information Society. In addition, the growth of broadband access to the Internet facilitates the expectation of further growth of E-commerce and much more.

The proponents of the revolutionary aspects of cyberspace have expressed extravagant claims that a new realm of experience has emerged, one in which the bounds of the physical world are no longer in force. It is possible to interact with others anonymously, currently with typed text and images but spoken language is on the way. It is possible to create a persona that then interacts with other personae over the Internet in chat rooms, list serves, via ICQ or Instant Messaging, or e-mail. Such interactions are open-ended in that gender can be concealed or switched, appearance enhanced, experiences manufactured and altered to suit circumstances. You can become anything you desire and can reveal only what may serve current needs. If all the world's a stage, then cyberspace has become the stage of choice for many. Thus, it has become a *de facto* test bed for exploring gender switching, anonymity, role-playing, as well as the creation of communities for a number of purposes. Online communities, composed of people who will probably never meet, have been formed for political, sexual, ecological, religious, and many other purposes. These are certainly not communities in the traditional sense where people meet face-to-face to share ideas, engage in activities, and establish relations based on years of personal relationships.

Enormous amounts of information are now available for free—after one has paid for a computer, software, and Internet Service Provider, of course. This information is provided on a growing number of Web sites set up by governments, libraries, companies, unions, consumer groups, universities, political organizations, religious groups, and individuals. In fact, the Web may be seen as a giant vanity press—anyone can publish and advertise, if willing to pay the costs of maintaining a Web site. And anyone can access this vast, diverse, distributed, and multi-owned database, if they have the skills and resources. What about the large segments of the U.S. population and elsewhere that do not have computers or even telephones? Will they again be marginalized, the so-called digital divide? How can their interests be served in a society that is not inclined to use government to provide services that are not absolutely necessary? Will libraries, community centers, senior citizen centers, and of course, the schools, be able to provide access services? There is an implicit assumption that information will continue to be free, or available at very low costs, but the future may be different. Governments may decide that for the large amounts of information they provide, the costs necessary to produce it should be recovered. Others providing free information may want users to subscribe formally and pay for what they use. The question of how to provide adequate access to the Internet will not be answered any time soon nor will the answers please everyone.

Given that the Internet was the sole preserve of a relatively small number of people just a few years ago and that the Web seems to have been born yesterday (mid-2003 was its 10th anniversary), it is almost impossible to predict future directions with any chance of accuracy. Nevertheless, business and governments must take steps to plan, to invest, to build infrastructures to take advantage of business opportunities, and to better serve the public. Recognizing and anticipating technological limitations and developments is a necessary step. An overview of some of the expectations and goals of Information Highway proponents is therefore a useful exercise. In addition, the issue of information as a commodity, to be produced, stored, and distributed, must be addressed.

Finally, the increasing dependency on technology to provide a vast array of information and services may also mean an increased risk of harm both physically and financially. The more society depends on information, the more it is subject to the risks of inaccuracies, blunders, misuses, and criminal activities. Information must be protected against unauthorized use, which raises serious issues with respect to security. If the promise of the Information Society is increased wealth with less physical labor for many, then one of the costs is increased security for all and increased risk for some.

THE MAKING OF THE ONLINE WORLD

The open society, the unrestricted access to knowledge, the unplanned and uninhibited association of men for its furtherance—these are what may make a vast, complex, ever growing, ever changing, ever more specialized and expert technological world, nevertheless a world of human community.

J. Robert Oppenheimer, 1953.

The Home/Personal Computer

When the home computer first appeared, it was possible to distinguish it from the personal computer in the office mainly by price, internal memory, and manufacturer. Although there was no clear dividing line, the home computer was generally considered to be under $1,000, usually under $500. In the early 1980s, the most popular of these computers were the enormously successful Commodore 20 and 64. The basic model was a keyboard with internal memory varying from 4K to 64K bytes and requiring a hookup to a television set, resulting in a picture less sharp than on a dedicated monitor.

For all but the simplest tasks, peripheral devices were necessary—such as cassette recorders, floppy disk drives, and modems, as well as more memory. Dot-matrix printers, varying in price from $200 to $1000, were also a necessity. Thus what began as a rather modest investment quickly accelerated to a substantial amount, to say nothing of open-ended expenditures for software. Of course, compared to currently available computers, these early models seem to be nothing more than toys. One rough rule of thumb has emerged over the years: the price remains almost constant when a new system is purchased every two to three years or so, while the power, in speed and memory, increases by a factor of four to five.

The Home

For most of the 1980s, the selling of the home computer represented a triumph of American marketing ingenuity more than a fulfillment of a genuine need. The home computer was a machine in search of a purpose. Consumers were assaulted by advertisements that used the following strategies:

Induce Guilt. Parents will be denying their children "a piece of the future" if they do not immediately buy a computer.

Promise Immediate Solutions. You can save your bakery or hat factory by organizing production with a personal computer.

Urge Additional Purchases. The computer itself is only a small part of the story. It is also necessary to buy more software, a disk drive, a printer, and a modem.

Argue for the Complete Package. For very little you can buy the whole thing.

Remind the Customer of Video Games. Although computers are useful, a wide range of exciting video games will be sure to please the whole family.

But in 1990, for a number of reasons, IBM decided that the time was right to return to the home market, and a short time later Apple repackaged its Macintosh into a competitive product, the Macintosh Classic. IBM executives learned that 20% of its PS/2 computers were being used at home and that the home PC market had grown substantially, to 3.7 million units in 1989. At the end of June, IBM announced the PS/1, a specially tailored computer for the home market, designed to avoid the earlier mistakes.

As computer technology has advanced, including much more sophisticated software, the home computer became much more useful. In a 1990 survey, the following reasons were given for purchasing a computer (with the percentage of respondents in parentheses): bringing work home from the office or running a home business (57), doing school work (47), and writing letters, budgeting, and other personal chores (19). (Some respondents bought a computer for more than one reason.) The first reason was obviously a major factor in IBM's decision to market the PS/1, especially since almost 35 million Americans operated a full- or part-time business at home in 1990. (This number increased to over 40 million in 1993.) Very few intended to use their PCs to play games—actually less than 3% compared with more than 30% in 1985—even with the overwhelming popularity of Nintendo and other new generation video games. The current generation of improved software and faster hardware has greatly simplified computer use and has made it much easier for first-time users to feel comfortable with computers. The leader in this direction has been Apple with its graphics user interface (GUI) for the Macintosh. In 1990, Microsoft introduced its Windows software, with much success, to provide a GUI for IBM PCs and compatibles. If the early story of the home computer is more appearance than substance, the situation changed in the 1990s as witnessed by such success stories as Compaq (early in its history), Dell, HP, Gateway, and NEC, to say nothing of IBM and Apple. And of course, Microsoft has become the dominant software company in the world.

A comparison between the computer and the automobile in their early stages of development offers an interesting lesson: the car would never have become so popular had the consumer been required to learn the skills of a mechanic to use it. The computer is being sold as a powerful device, immediately useful without much knowledge of its inner workings. However, the parallel between cars and computers breaks down in a fundamental way. A car has a straightforward, but narrowly defined purpose, and knowledge of how to operate it enables the driver to use it. A computer can do so many things that a knowledge of programming could give great power to the user. In its current state, however, programming is not particularly easy, and most likely will never be easy; so most users depend on others to program for them, hence the enormous market in such application programs as spreadsheets, databases, word processors, and more recently, Internet connect software and Internet browsers and search engines.

Finally, the growth in PC sales, in the U.S. and indeed worldwide, for both home and commercial markets has been substantial except for a downturn in 2001, paralleling a general economic decline. In the U.S., sales of PCs for home use increased from 12.1 million units in 1998 to 18.8 million in 2000, and declined to 15 million in 2001. It is estimated that sales will recover to 17.5 million in 2003. For comparison, worldwide sales of PCs for home use in 1998 were 26.6 million, growing to 49.2 million in 2000 and falling to 43.4 million in 2001, with estimated sales of 50.3 million in 2003 (compared to estimated worldwide sales of PCs for commercial purposes of 88.9 million).[1]

At Large

With a computer connected to the Internet, via a modem to the telephone line or the cable system, the user has access to a growing number of services and information sources. Now the excitement centers around being connected—at home, at school, at work or at the library—having access, getting in touch, and making friends, maybe. For schools, having access has changed the way assignments are given and communications are undertaken. Planning trips, buying books, paying bills and other banking tasks, checking for breaking news stories, and keeping in touch with relatives and friends, has changed forever.

The Internet originated as a network to link researchers at universities, private institutions, and government laboratories, who carried out research funded by the Defense Advanced Research Project Agency (DARPA) of the U.S. Department of Defense. This network encouraged researchers to exchange information prior to publication in journals and to reduce travel costs in the process. Although face-to-face interaction is invaluable, interaction over a network can also play an important role in facilitating the exchange of ideas and the writing of scientific papers. In the beginning, only text-based information was circulated and it was of some importance that very few messages failed to reach their destination. It would have been impossible to guess that from these humble beginnings, such a worldwide phenomenon would have emerged. As the Internet was growing in the research environment, experiments were in progress in the private sector to create access for consumers to products over two-way, television-like systems, called videotex.

From Videotex to the Internet

> . . . an interactive service which, through appropriate access by standardized procedures allows users of Videotex terminals to communicate with databases via telecommunication networks.[2]

What if a two-way communications network linked the homes of the nation via regional computer centers to a large number of businesses and services? From the comfort of one's home, a vast array of transactions could be carried out, using a personal computer or a specially equipped television monitor with keyboard. This was the vision of the early 1980s as the first steps were taken toward interactive television. The following services were envisioned for videotex, some of which are currently commonplace:

• *Information Retrieval*. Probably the most basic service, it includes electronic newspapers and specialized databases and directories, including stock market, entertainment, sports, community, and health services information.

• *Commercial Transactions*. Making reservations for entertainment, sporting events, and travel, and paying bills and teleshopping.

• *Messaging*. A "switchboard" to store and forward messages from one user to another, electronic mail, electronic bulletin board (one-to-many communication), and computer conferencing.

- *Computing.* Access to games and financial analysis programs, as well as more sophisticated software.

- *Telemonitoring.* Provision of home security by the remote sensing of fire or intruders with alarms triggered at security agencies; the control of systems within the home for energy management.

- *Working at Home.* Accelerating current trends, stockbrokers, information systems professionals, designers, architects, real estate agents, travel agents, secretaries, editors, and so forth can do some or all of their work at home.

- *Services for the Disabled.* Disabled people can be monitored at home and communication with them facilitated by the use of Bliss symbols, Braille printers, and voice synthesizers.

- *Education at Home.* Extension of current television education courses can be carried out as part of the regular curricula and continuing education.

What is interesting about this list is how similar it is to current advertisements for the Internet. Thus, while the vision was realistic, the technology at the time was somewhat deficient, but there was a more serious problem. The real obstacles seemed to be two-fold: the need for sufficiently large numbers of interested information providers and most importantly, a public convinced that videotex was something worth paying for. In fact, there seemed to be something of a chicken-and-egg dilemma: many people were not interested in the few videotex services available, because they did not provide a sufficiently broad range of useful or interesting possibilities; potential information providers were not interested because the number of current users was too small. A few commercial systems were actually marketed in the U.S., although many previous experiments had failed. Of all the developed countries, France has had the most success in this area, although major investments have taken place in England, Germany, Canada, and Japan.

The Failure of Videotex

Three forms of information services marketed in the 1980s may be distinguished as follows:

Information Retrieval Via Online Databases. Large databases storing many different kinds of information could be accessed on personal computers via telephone lines by paying a fee for services. Examples were newspaper indexes, financial information, and computer hardware and software specifications. The user must access a database, formulate a query, and interrogate the database.

Teletext. This system provided a continuous stream of information that was available over television channels. The information could be repeatedly broadcast in the "blanking interval" between frames on a television channel or the normal channel itself could be used. Using a special keypad, the viewer types in a number to designate a teletext frame, that is, a screen image, and the decoder freezes it for viewing. The amount of information available and the time needed to cycle through it determine how long the user must wait until the frames of interest appear.

Videotex. (The t is usually dropped at the end of this word, probably to lend it a high-tech gloss). This term is used for a two-way information system. Typically, telephone lines are used to connect the central computer of the system to each individual user. The home user, by means of a special keypad or a home computer with appropriate software, requests information after viewing a "menu" of possibilities. The computer retrieves information from its own databases (or from others to which it has access) and transmits it. This information consists of text as well as graphics and can appear in color. Two national systems and U.S. experiences will be briefly reviewed as a background to today's systems and those on the horizon.

Canada: Telidon

Canada's version of videotex was announced in 1978 after almost 10 years of development. Telidon operated with menus and direct page numbers in the usual manner, but was more advanced than European systems in the quality of its graphics. The European systems—Oracle, Prestel, and Antiope, sometimes called first-generation videotex—employed a method of pictorial representation called alphamosaic. Pictures are built up from a pattern of blocks in which both color and intensity can be controlled. The resolution leaves much to be desired, as straight diagonal lines look like staircases.

Telidon is a more advanced, second-generation system, employing a graphics method called alphageometric. A system of points, line, arcs, and polygons are used to produce a much more sophisticated image. Underlying the picture transmission is a communication protocol, the Picture Description Instructions (PDIs). For example, using PDIs, a line is described by its endpoints. A microprocessor in the Telidon terminal decodes the description of a picture, which has been transmitted in terms of PDIs, and then displays it on the screen. The description is independent of the display characteristics so that on a high-resolution monitor, finer increments could be used and greater fidelity achieved. Telidon appeared to be well-suited to the representation of detailed graphics such as architectural plans, circuit diagrams, and weather maps, and such cursive alphabets as Arabic and Chinese.

Telidon was developed under the leadership of Canada's Department of Communication and unlike the situation in the U.S., considerable government financial support was made available. As in Britain, forecasts of market growth were wildly over-optimistic, with 3 to 4.3 million units predicted for 1990. By the end of 1981, there were 2,000 Telidon terminals in use in several experimental projects such as an information system for farmers containing farm management information, market reports, weather reports, financial news, and crop data. U.S. trials were undertaken, as well as one in Venezuela. The North American Presentation-level Protocol Standards incorporated a substantial portion of the Telidon specifications, which seemed to indicate an important role for Telidon. By 1985, when its direct financial support ended, the Canadian government had spent $50 million (and the private sector $200 million) for research, development, and marketing.

France: Télétel

This system is more commonly known by the name Minitel, which is actually the name of the videotex terminal. In the late 1970s, a number of French laboratories were involved in the design of the representation of visual images for videotex (the Antiope standards), of the decentralized architecture of the computer system and databases, and of the videotex terminal. The French Telecommunications Administration made a very important decision at this time to adopt a program to convert the telephone directory to an electronic form (the Electronic Directory) by distributing to all phone subscribers a free-of-charge terminal. Thus a potential market of up to 30 million terminals was possible in the 1990s and by the end of 1988, there were 3.6 million in use compared to only 12,000 by the end of 1982.[3] This captive market of users encouraged information providers to participate. The growth in the number of services available was also quite rapid, from 146 at the end of 1981 to some 9000 in 1987. The major categories of services in terms of the number of hours connected to Minitel in 1987, was as follows (with percentage of total use in parentheses)[4]: Professional applications, like stock market reports (23%); Messaging, chatting (22%); Electronic telephone directory (18%); Games (14%); Practical services, like train reservations, home shopping (10%); Banking, finance (9%); General information, like weather reports (4%).

One of the more popular services is known as Kiosque, a bulletin board, which provides "the user with anonymity as they [sic] can enter into date relationships with strangers."[5] Apparently, such interactions have frequently been sexual in nature, bringing considerable notoriety to Minitel as well as the government's attention, in the form of an increased sales tax. What does not seem to be happening is the use of the system as an electronic newspaper, that is, as a source of general and broad-based information. It is clear that users want customized services, appealing to special interests. France's Telecom expected to give away about 8 million terminals reaching about 25 million subscribers and hoped to pay off its investment by 1993. Surely the key step in this enormous venture has been the decision to give away the terminals in order to create a mass market for services. No other country has taken this step, or is likely to do so. Other reasons for the success of France's

Minitel are as follows: a specially-designed portable video monitor without the inconveniences of ordinary television sets; the immediate availability of a service, the Electronic Directory (lacking in other videotex programs); preliminary social experiments were undertaken to test the service including the communication hardware and the information sources; and the charging mechanism was designed to encourage use.

One might have thought that with the arrival of the Internet, Minitel would have disappeared from France, but this is not the case. It is thriving and although its life expectancy is short, it is making excellent profits.[6]

> Minitel is estimated to have 16 million regular users in France, compared to about 8 million for the Internet. The 9 million Minitel terminals in homes and offices are typically accessed to buy train or movie tickets, check stocks, publish small ads, search databases, use chat rooms or send faxes and e-mails to other Minitel or Internet users. . . . Nevertheless, even its most ardent proponents recognize that Minitel can't hold out forever against the onslaught of the Internet. The momentum behind the Net is simply too great for this enduring symbol of *l'exception française* to survive in the long term. But analysts still give Minitel a two-to-five-year window for survival.

The United States

During much of the early development of videotex, the United States was content to wait and watch as developments unfolded in Britain, Germany, Japan, France, and Canada. Meanwhile, commercial online information retrieval systems were being developed by such companies as Mead Data Central, Dow-Jones News/Retrieval, and Lockheed's Dialog Information Service, once the world's largest electronic information retrieval company (sold to Knight-Ridder for some $353 million in 1988). With the appearance of the foreign videotex systems, a number of U.S. companies began their own field trials. The earliest interactive system, QUBE, was implemented over cable by Warner Amex in 1977 in Columbus, Ohio. (See Chapter 7 for more detail.) Some 32,000 potential QUBE subscribers could have participated in a meeting of the town planning commission in 1978. No more than 2,500 actually tuned in and cast non-binding votes. Although our concern here is not interactive participatory democracy, this application of two-way systems obviously has significant impact in the future. In January 1984, Warner Amex ended the interactive QUBE experiment because of its inability to attract larger audiences.

One of the most important videotex ventures was the Viewtron system, launched in October 1983 by Knight-Ridder Newspapers. Their long-term aim was to sign up 150,000 subscribers in the Miami-Fort Lauderdale area. Pre-launch expenditures were $26 million. Customers were required to purchase a special terminal, manufactured by AT&T, for $600 (later to rise to $900), and pay a monthly fee of $12 along with an estimated telephone bill of $14 per month. The service sold no more than 1000 terminals, and even the introduction of a leasing arrangement did not help much, nor did the opening up of the system to personal computers, equipped with specialized software. The resolution of the monitor was quite poor compared to ordinary television, the color choices were limited, figures appeared to be constructed out of Lego blocks, and transmission rates were slow. Viewtron was terminated in 1986 after total expenditures of about $50 million. Other experiments also failed. Thus a *Business Week* article, in January 1985, seemed to say it all: "For Videotex, the Big Time Is Still a Long Way Off."[7] Potential customers have not been willing to buy expensive terminals—or pay hefty monthly fees to lease them—because they did not see any services they particularly needed that they could not find elsewhere for less. And service providers with no ready audience have been slow to develop new offerings. It took about another 10 years for the Internet to attract public attention and use, motivated by the technology of the Web.

The Internet and the World Wide Web

It was noted in Chapter 3 that as of January 2003, a survey determined there were over 171 million Internet hosts, but it is not clear that this number is meaningful. As the authors of the survey note, the definition of host is ambiguous: "A host used to be a single machine on the net. However, the definition of a host has changed in recent years due to virtual hosting, where a single machine acts like multiple systems (and has multiple domain names and IP addresses). Ideally, a virtual host will act and look exactly like a regular host, so we count them equally."[8] The reason for the concern is that there is some correlation between the number of hosts and the number of users but it is not well-defined. Up to a few years ago, the Internet doubled in size every year or so; more recently, growth has been slowing down, to about 16 percent between January 2002 and January 2003. The final comment should be appreciated regarding how many users there are: "In summary, it is not possible to determine the exact size of the Internet, where hosts are located, or how many users there are."[9] Thus, while commercial information service providers are having problems, the Internet is thriving, although it may be facing some technical limitations as the number of users grows and the volume of traffic increases because of the increased number of sound and image files.

Although the terms are overused, the wired world or cyberspace is becoming a reality to many and the signs are clear. The number of Internet users in the U.S. and Canada, defined as those who have used the Internet at least once in the past year, was estimated by Nielsen/Commercenet in late 1995 as 23 million, probably too high compared to other surveys.[10] Even higher was the result produced by Adnet, which did a survey of surveys, and came up with a worldwide number of 50 million, of which 35 million were in the U.S., as of mid-1996. (The term user was not defined, however.)[11] By late 2002, estimates had increased to over 605 million, worldwide. (See Chapter 3 for more detail.) What is evident is that increasing numbers of businesses, schools, libraries, community centers, and homes are connected to the Internet by local Internet Service Providers (ISPs), long-distance telephone companies (AT&T), local telephone companies, online information service providers (America Online), and others.

On February 8, 1996, one day after President Clinton signed into law the Communications Decency Act of 1996, parts of which were subsequently overturned by the Supreme Court, John Perry Barlow, a founding member of the Electronic Freedom Foundation, a leading online civil liberties organization, published, online of course, "A Declaration of the Independence of Cyberspace." It captures much of the strong feeling that the early founders and aficionados of the Internet had about that new technology. For example, consider the following opening lines[12]:

> Governments of the Industrial World, you weary giants of flesh and steel, I come from Cyberspace, the new home of Mind. On behalf of the future, I ask you of the past to leave us alone. You are not welcome among us. You have no sovereignty where we gather.
>
> We have no elected government, nor are we likely to have one, so I address you with no greater authority than that with which liberty itself always speaks. I declare the global social space we are building to be naturally independent of the tyrannies you seek to impose on us. You have no moral right to rule us nor do you possess any methods of enforcement we have true reason to fear.
>
> Governments derive their just powers from the consent of the governed. You have neither solicited nor received ours. We did not invite you. You do not know us, nor do you know our world. Cyberspace does not lie within your borders. Do not think that you can build it, as though it were a public construction project. You cannot. It is an act of nature and it grows itself through our collective actions.

Its basic message is that the Internet, i.e., Cyberspace, must be let alone, that those who do not understand its true nature and promise must refrain from attempting to extend earth's archaic laws to this new future. This message was used several years later as the lead quotation in a magazine survey in *The Economist*, titled "The Internet Society." The reference was not entirely favorable[13]:

> It is hard to believe today, but Mr. Barlow's musings struck a chord at the time, spreading rapidly through the internet. The declaration encapsulated the exhilaration and wonder of millions of people as they logged on to the world wide web for the first time. It really did seem possible that the internet had launched a spontaneous revolution that might lead to a brave new borderless world.
>
> Seven years later, Mr. Barlow's claims sound absurd: just another example of the 1990s hype that produced the dotcom boom and bust. The internet, it seems, has turned out to be simply another appliance, a useful new medium like radio or television, not something likely to usher in a "civilization of the mind". Cyber gurus like Mr. Barlow have also lost heart, and now issue

equally exaggerated warnings about the internet's strangulation by government and corporate interests. With the help of governments, big entertainment companies are trying to "control everything that we know", Mr. Barlow says. "The fight about this will, in my view, determine the future of humanity."

In an earlier survey of the Internet, *The Economist* referred to it as "The Accidental Superhighway," and contrasted its success with the failures of the giant telecommunications and cable companies to achieve similar results. "The Internet's builders laid no cables and dug no trenches; they simply leased existing telephone lines. When the Internet linked up with public and commercial networks in the mid-1980s, its growth accelerated."[14] It is *The Economist's* view that the wonders of the Internet occurred because it was "left to its own devices and filled unmet needs," not because large corporations thought that money could be made from certain technological advances or because governments made plans for systems that would benefit the general public. With the dawn of the World Wide Web, the stakes were raised substantially as the power of the Internet began to become clear. Again, *The Economist's* description is well worth considering[15]:

> Suddenly the light dawned. The Internet was not just a way to send e-mail and download the occasional file. It could be a place to visit, full of people and ideas: "cyberspace". It was a new medium, based on broadcasting and publishing but with another dimension added: interactivity. Internet veterans had known this for years; they could see the potential behind the screens of plain text and baffling computer commands. But thanks to the friendly, multimedia side of the Net, called the World Wide Web, a much broader audience started to catch on to it.

COMMUNICATING ONLINE

E-mail among computers, as we think of it today, came into being in 1971 when Ray Tomlinson at Bolt Beranek and Newman became the first person to send a message from a computer on one network to a computer on another network. It's not entirely accurate to say that Tomlinson created e-mail, because many other people were involved at the time and were working on the same problems. However, Tomlinson is the undisputed source for the way we write e-mail addresses. Limited by a caps-only printing terminal, Tomlinson decided on the now-ubiquitous @ symbol (shift 2) to separate the user name from the computer name and to indicate that the address was outside the local network. "The @ sign seemed to make sense," Tomlinson later recalled. "I used the @ sign to indicate that the user was 'at' some other host, rather than being local."[16]

Two major functions spurred the early growth of the Internet: electronic mail and newsgroups. Electronic mail is the first technological step in connecting people asynchronously, independently of time. The Internet's reliability in completing transmissions successfully even though parts of the system were non-functioning encouraged the growth and confidence in this new technology. Messages, large or small, were separated into packets and routed by an incremental process and then reassembled at the destination. It worked so well that its use increased rapidly and other applications soon followed.

What seemed to trigger the metaphor and indeed the reality of cyberspace was the creation of discussion groups called newsgroups or bulletin boards that permitted the participation of anyone with an Internet account anywhere in the world. While electronic mail is typically a one-to-one or a one-to-a-few process, newsgroups involve one-to-many; that is, one person posting a message that is accessible to anyone who subscribes to the newsgroup. The idea of a newsgroup arose from the use of small discussion groups in research environments, created for the purpose of sharing technical information. The topics then moved into less technically-oriented directions—political, social, religious, cultural, sexual, etc. In the process, a fiercely independent, vociferous, anarchic, and worldwide group of advocates developed for whom the Internet became a new way of life. They are committed to defending a set of values they believe has been lost in the real world, namely independence, free speech, privacy, irreverence, and audacity.

Although newsgroups still exist and are still growing in number and diversity, other forms of communication have evolved such as listservs, chat rooms, ICQ, Instant Messaging (IM), and most recently, Blogs (Biographical logs). Once a message is posted on a newsgroup, anyone can visit the newsgroup and read it and all other messages as well. But a listserv operates by forwarding individual messages, as e-mail, to all members. Thus there is no billboard of messages to be read at any time by anyone. Chat rooms involve two or more people communicating with each other synchronously. ICQ and IM are different systems that make possible the operation of online chat rooms. Blogs are a form of one-to-many communication in which individuals essentially make public their daily diaries. Discussions about the views expressed can then follow. Underlying the readily available millions of Web pages is an active, global system of conversions, dialogues, diatribes, and talk. Not just text files are exchanged, of course, as the technology has developed to permit sound files, images, and even video to be transmitted. But even more surprising at first blush is the increasing use of IM in the business world to keep in touch with employees, clients, suppliers, and others.

Electronic Mail: New Ways of Keeping in Touch

One of the most important aspects of the "office of the future," described in Chapter 4, was electronic mail, the computer facility by which messages could be distributed simultaneously within an organization and to geographically remote points. In-house networks have been interconnected via telephone lines and satellite communication systems spanning countries and continents. The telephone conference call is a familiar event but by using computers, conferences can be established over networks that operate independently of time and space. Another important use of networks is the electronic bulletin board, a system by which individuals can post messages, announcements, and opinions to make them available simultaneously to many other participants. Bulletin boards can be operated from homes and serve a small community of local users, or they can be nationwide and serve thousands. Over the past decade, networks have spread across most countries, instantaneously linking interested people eager to share information. During the terrible events in 1989, in Tiananmen Square, in Beijing, electronic mail was used to keep people in the West informed.

For computer-generated documents, electronic mail has become an efficient means for distributing information. Within organizations, meetings can be announced by "broadcasting" time, place, and agenda to the relevant parties. Individuals can use electronic mail to avoid "telephone tag"; that is, a message is sent over the Internet and is therefore available whenever the receiving party signs on and checks the incoming mail. The number of networks linking the U.S. and indeed the world is large and growing. There are gateways between many of these networks so that users can send messages to almost anyone on some network. Almost every company, large and small, has an in-house electronic mail system so that employees can easily exchange information and so that management can reach employees quickly and efficiently. Large, worldwide companies employ intercontinental networks to facilitate interaction among employees, who are separated by long distances. The earliest users of electronic mail were universities and research institutions, which had developed the necessary software. It is now inconceivable to imagine a research environment or any business, large or small, for that matter, without electronic mail. Preliminary versions of papers, early research results, and tentative proposals are circulated among researchers for immediate comment and analysis.

A major report from Rand, a large research organization, a few years ago, discussed the social implications of a universal system of e-mail. The report defines an electronic mail system as follows[17]:

1. Permits the asynchronous electronic interchange of information between persons, groups of persons, and functional units of an organization
2. Provides mechanisms supporting the creation, distribution, consumption, processing, and storage of this information

By universal access, the authors assume that it is available "at modest individual effort and expense to (almost) everyone in the United States in a form that does not require highly specialized skills, or accessible in a manner analogous to the level, cost, and ease of use of telephone service or the U.S.

Postal Service."[18] This notion of a ubiquitous service has some very interesting consequences as the report makes clear. Efficiency is an important goal, and one of the reasons for adopting universal e-mail is to replace the archaic postal service, which is so much slower than e-mail. But what is more interesting than the efficiency argument is the transforming argument: "The hypothesis is made that electronic mail makes possible more egalitarian, deliberative, and reflective dialogs among individuals and groups.... It might therefore lead to new social and political linkages within U.S. society, reduce the feelings of alienation that many individuals in the United States feel and give them a new sense of 'community,' revitalize the involvement of the common citizen in the political process, etc., and in general strengthen the cohesion of U.S. society."[19]

An interesting coding system has arisen among users of electronic mail to replace the missing vocal, facial, and body signals that usually accompany face-to-face conversations. These symbols, or *emoticons*, are scattered throughout the message to "flesh out" the bare words appearing on the monitor. The following are a few of the more commonly used ones, that are more easily appreciated if the head is tilted to the left[20]:

: -)	smile	; -)	wink	: - 0	bored	: - !	foot in the mouth
: -D	laughter	: - (	frown	: - x	angry	:-#	my lips are sealed
: - /	skeptical	: - e	disappointed	: - 7	wry	:-@	screaming

and some weird and obtuse ones:

: - F	buck-toothed vampire with one tooth missing	*: o)	clown
+-: -)	holds religious office	@ = pro-nuclear	@ : -) wears a turban
: @)	Babe the pig	@@@@@@ : -) Marge Simpson	%-) brain dead

In addition to these symbols, documents are also filled with acronyms (to reduce the typing burden) such as the following: IMHO (In My Humble/Honest Opinion), BTW (By The Way), TIA (Thanks In Anticipation), CUL8R (See You Later), AAMOF (As A Matter Of Fact), and ROTFLOL (Rolling On The Floor Laughing Out Loud).[21]

Another communication medium that has become popular is the Fax, so popular that it has challenged e-mail as a way of quickly distributing material, especially original hard copies, over long distances. Fax is not really a new technology but it is an example of how the microprocessor has transformed and indeed created a vital new industry. Every office has a Fax machine, as do many individuals, and an enormous amount of information is now Faxed worldwide. Fax boards can be inserted into personal computers so that computer-generated documents are immediately available for transmission and reception. The volume of information transmitted over the new electronic media continues to expand, and technological innovations contribute to more ways to transmit information—a direct reflection of the ever-increasing importance of information to advanced societies.

Newsgroups: Bulletin Boards

Near laundromats, supermarkets, and community centers, people post notices on public bulletin boards advertising coming attractions, wanting to buy and sell furniture, rent apartments, sell airline tickets, and meet new friends. Bulletin boards are a common feature of most communities, serving to reinforce community ties and indicative of community vitality. In 1977, the first electronic bulletin board in the U.S., the Community Memory Project, was founded in Berkeley, California. Terminals were not placed in retail stores and community centers until 1984, a long delay because of the voluntary nature of the project and the difficulty in acquiring necessary software. People were encouraged "to speak [their] mind, check the city council's agenda, find toxic hot spots in the neighborhood and locate used cars and housing."[22] Other such bulletin boards appeared all over the country, organized by community groups, clubs, and individuals. From the comfort of one's home a person could connect with like-minded individuals to sell, buy, inform, advertise, commiserate, rejoice, and complain. Furthermore, distance is no obstacle as electronic bulletin boards are nationwide, and even worldwide.

Legal issues quickly arose as to the responsibility of the bulletin board operator, or systems operator, the "sysop", with respect to the behavior of subscribers. If somebody posted an identification code and password for a proprietary computer system, is the sysop at fault? The law is not entirely clear, but "people have been prosecuted for using the bulletin boards to post stolen credit card numbers, pirated software or, in one case, information traded among members of a pedophile ring."[23] These bulletin boards usually served local communities and had to respond to local or community values. When we turn to the newsgroups carried over Usenet, different issues arise. As described previously, newsgroups began as discussion groups for technical issues such as novel software developments and new hardware products. The move toward other topics created some dissension among the managers of the early Internet, but inevitably the range of topics covered, the organizational structure of Usenet, and the number of newsgroups grew rapidly and fostered an enormous number of regular users. It is almost impossible to determine how many generally accessible newsgroups exist, discounting the untold numbers of local ones, but over 50,000 is the estimate for 2003. One of the problems with keeping track is that newsgroups are created and disappear on a regular basis.

It is interesting to participate in a variety of newsgroups, or at least observe some of the interaction (as a lurker—a pejorative tag, used because only by posting messages is one's presence known). The number of newsgroups reflects the incredibly diverse interests of contemporary society. It is only necessary to search and in all likelihood an appropriate newsgroup for the moment will be found or one can be created. Typically, discussions are interwoven with individual threads representing separate themes. Some threads go on for weeks as arguments and counterarguments are posted. Then new threads appear and old ones finally die. The vitality of a newsgroup ebbs and flows as new members join and old ones move on. It is these newsgroups, especially the binary ones, or binaries, that attracted the early attention of Congress and its regulating zeal. A binary newsgroup is one that primarily carries postings in a coded form and the postings of interest, when decoded, are frequently of a sexual nature, and occasionally are even obscene. However, in terms of the volume of information carried over the Usenet, itself a small part of the total Internet traffic, there is probably very little that actually violates criminal law. Nevertheless, the Internet is frequently characterized by the media as a cesspool, as a threat to common decency, and as having minimal useful or lasting content.

Listservs, Chat Rooms, ICQ, and Instant Messaging

All of these systems move beyond the newsgroup model in different ways. A variety of groups and organizations have set up listservs to share ideas, keep in touch, debate policies, and strengthen ties. Membership is controlled so that the participants can "speak" openly among themselves. All in all, listervs offer a relatively safe environment, which cannot usually be said for the other forms of online communication. Chat rooms have a much different reputation, as hotbeds of sexually explicit interactions and worse, but first a little history and background may be useful.

ICQ (I seek you) was created in 1996 by four young Israeli computer users[24]:

> These guys realized that millions of people were connecting to the Internet to use the World Wide Web, but these users were not interconnected. They created a technology which would enable Internet users to locate each other online on the Internet, and to create peer-to-peer communication channels easily. They called their technology ICQ (I seek you), and released it in November of 1996. Within 6 months, by "word of mouse", 850,000 users had been registered by Mirabilis. By June of 1997, Mirabilis was able to handle 100,000 concurrent users and had become the largest Internet communications network. Success of this magnitude with a new communication technology did not go unnoticed, and Mirabilis and ICQ were acquired by America Online in June of 1998 for $287 million. AOL had also created its own Instant Messenger system.

A patent for ICQ was granted to the inventors in late 2002 for instant messaging over the Internet as well as over cellular networks. Of course, America Online, which had purchased ICQ, could attempt to enforce its rights against both Yahoo and Microsoft but probably will not for fear of alienating millions of Internet users, because it might be viewed as attempting to dominate and control the Internet.[25]

What makes instant messaging so attractive is that it "allows you to maintain a list of people that you wish to interact with. You can send messages to any of the people in your list, often called a buddy list or contact list, as long as that person is online. Sending a message opens up a small window where you and your friend can type in messages that both of you can see.[26] Most messaging systems, such as AOL Instant Messenger, ICQ, MSN Messenger, and Yahoo! Messenger, provide such features as the following[27]:

- Instant messages—Send notes back and forth with a friend who is online
- Chat—Create your own custom chat room with friends or co-workers
- Web links—Share links to your favorite Web sites
- Images—Look at an image stored on your friend's computer
- Sounds—Play sounds for your friends
- Files—Share files by sending them directly to your friends
- Talk—Use the Internet instead of a phone to actually talk with friends
- Streaming content—Real-time or near-real-time stock quotes and news

Blogs

blog (n.) Short for *Web log*, a blog is a Web page that serves as a publicly-accessible personal journal for an individual. Typically updated daily, blogs often reflect the personality of the author.
(v.) To author a Web log.[28]

It is obviously difficult to determine how many blogs exist, how many are active, and how they are distributed around the world. Anyone can set up a Web site and make available to the world his or her priceless prose on any subject. In addition, journalists, news media, and virtually any organization can set up blogs to augment their published views in a less formal manner. With respect to numbers, some estimates are given as follows:

- Blogcount estimates that there are roughly 2.4 million to 2.9 million active as of June 2003.[29]
- Of this figure, Blogcount attributes more than 1.6 million active users to the top three centrally hosted services. Smaller hosts, intranet blogs, and standalone tools account for the remainder.
- Of the 655,631 Weblogs currently indexed by The National Institute for Technology and Liberal Education (NITL) BlogCensus, the overwhelming majority are published in the English language [350,000].
- Roughly 2 percent of the online community has created a blog, according to Jupiter Research.
- Blogs seem to be read mostly by men (60 percent vs. 40 percent women), in homes where the total income is more than $60,000 per year (61 percent).

- [T]he majority (73 percent) of blog readers have been online for more than 5 years.

Although they had not come to public attention before 2002, most blogs had been around for at least four years previously. Clearly, they are a well-established phenomenon and serve the growing needs of the online community.

Some Problems

Flaming

Not all the postings to newsgroups, listservs, or chat rooms are nice. Not all people are nice. The Internet can be an unfriendly place, a place for the thick-skinned or the thick-headed. If you are new to the Net (a newbie), any blunders you make will not be treated lightly by some, and in fact asking for help or apologizing for mistakes will only inflame those who view their participation on the Internet as a license to be obnoxious, insulting, and downright crazy. The act of posting rude and outrageous messages directed at individuals or groups or whole countries for that matter, is known as "flaming." Since quantifying flaming is not precise, it is impossible to determine how common it is. Suffice it to say that for the novice, the tone of discourse is much higher pitched than in other media, although talk radio is not for the timid. It is almost as if there is so much noise on the Internet that to be heard, it is necessary to shout and shout and shout.

Jack Kapica, the writer of a weekly newspaper column on cyberspace, explored the issue of flaming and offered a number of interesting observations[30]:

- Cyberspace blurs notions of public and private.
- The Net does not transmit subtle emotions, hence the need for "emoticons"—smileys—to ensure those whose prose is weak that their comments are taken in the intended manner.
- Our culture abhors extreme emotional displays; flamers compose a message in which all the fury lies in the prose, and none in the physical presence.
- The very ephemerality of cyberspace is what starts so many flame wars.
- If they are in any way objectionable, people forget the public nature of these postings and take them personally.

In a paper written in 1985, the authors suggested a number of guidelines to deal with the problem of heightened emotions on the Internet, as part of a program for electronic mail etiquette (later called netiquette when extended to the full range of Internet activities). Among these are the following helpful suggestions[31]:

- Sometimes just the annotation "Flame! Flame!" alerts the reader to the fact that the writer knows he or she is being emotional. The intent is that the reader should take that into account and not assume this is a careful reasoned statement. . . .
- Resist the temptation to fire off a response. Go ahead and write the response, but file it away instead, and wait 24 hours. Reconsider the response later, in the light of a new day. . . .
- Use alternative media to break the cycle of message-and-response. A telephone call or personal conversation can do wonders, when body language, eye contact, and all the other cues we've developed can take effect.

Although these are all reasonable and well-intentioned suggestions, therein lies the problem, for those who would most benefit from adherence to them are least likely to either pay attention or to follow the advice.

Spamming

An Internet user has the freedom to send a message to any one of the more than 50,000 newsgroups in existence. Given that the message may be of interest to more than one newsgroup it can be cross-posted to as many newsgroups as appropriate by including the names of the newsgroups in the destination information. While 5, 10, or even 20 newsgroups may be appropriate, what about 2,000 or 5,000 newsgroups? Clearly enormous amounts of memory in hundreds of thousands of computers will be used to store all these messages, resulting in a possible degradation of service and inconvenience to many. Who would want to send the same message to thousands of newsgroups (or on occasion, the same message to the same newsgroup, many times)?

The first major incident occurred in January 1994, when "Clarence Thomas IV of Andrews University posted a message, warning of Jesus' immanent return, to all the newsgroups Andrews University receives—over six thousand."[32] The response of the Usenet community was one of outrage, as it had just experienced the full force of a major spam. Since then, there have been many occasions of spamming. The origin of this term is not clear but there are at least two possible sources: the word spam was used in a Monty Python skit in which it was repeated endlessly, and "the term may also have come from someone's low opinion of the food product with the same name, which is generally perceived as a generic content-free waste of resources."[33]

If the Usenet community values anything beyond a few basic freedoms, it is bandwidth, the maximum amount of information (bits/second) that can be carried over a channel, because without available bandwidth—and excessive spamming consumes considerable bandwith—communication degrades and the *raison d'etre* of the Internet disappears.

It should be noted that cross-posting a message is not wasteful of space because only a single copy exists at a host machine and newsreading software will not display the same message more than once to a given user. Spamming, however, can fill up hosts with multiple copies, especially if more than one incident occurs. It is seen as the worst violation of the understood principles governing acceptable Internet behavior. Probably no incident received as much publicity within the Internet community, and among the public at large, as the infamous Canter and Siegel spam on April 12, 1994. Lawrence A. Canter and Martha S. Siegel are lawyers who sent out a message to more than 6,000 newsgroups: "Green Card Lottery 1994 May be the Last One!! Sign up now!!"[34] As immigration lawyers, Canter and Siegel were attempting to drum up business by falsely claiming that the annual Green Card Lottery permitting foreigners to work legally in the U.S. was coming to a sudden end. There were so many angry messages sent to their Internet Service Provider that service was disrupted and their account was cancelled. Canter and Siegel wrote a book about their experience and advised others to ignore netiquette if they were interested in making money. This event heightened the ongoing dichotomy on the Internet between the growing influence of the world of commerce and the purist attitude of the veteran user community.

Even with this early history of spamming, very few would have predicted the degree to which spamming has emerged as a major problem on the Internet. Governments, regulatory agencies, consumer groups, and much of the large Internet community is concerned about the increasing frequency of unwanted e-mail messages. Also of concern is the explicit sexual imagery contained in many messages. (See Chapters 4 and 12 for additional comments.)

Online Seduction

Earlier this year, a 14-year-old female from Oregon met a 30-year-old male, who claimed to be 17 years old, over the internet. After corresponding for about a year, the victim agreed to come and visit the suspect on Oahu. The suspect called the victim's father, posing as the father of the victim's friend. The victim was allowed to come. The parents notified the Honolulu Police Department when they couldn1t contact their daughter. She was located unharmed at a residence in Kailihi. The man, not a 17-year-old boy, had spent time picking out his prey from a chat room. Luckily for that teen and her family, she was recovered before any serious injury occurred.[35]

It is difficult to determine how frequent such chat room seductions are or how many children are in actual danger, compared to those involved in more traditional forms of encounters. Certainly, the danger exists, as do other threats to the well-being of children, and parents and guardians do have a responsibility to supervise their children's online behavior. Advice comes from many quarters about how this responsibility should be exercised in an effective manner. Consider the following guidelines for parents, taken from the New York State Criminal Justice Services[36]:

Learn everything you can about computers and the Internet, including:
- Hardware, software and terminology
- Misuse and risks
- Blocking, filtering and ratings
- "Good" web sites

Develop and increase proficiency through use. Make "surfing the net" a family experience.
- Share places of interest.
- Ask your children to demonstrate use.

Talk with your children about what they can and cannot do online.
- Be reasonable and set reasonable expectations.
- Try to understand their needs, interests and curiosity.

Place the computer in a central area of your home, not a child's bedroom or a secluded area.

Know your child's password and screen name.

Set reasonable time limits on use and ensure that your expectations are respected.

Periodically review Internet site "bookmarks", "history" and "cookies" files.

Internet service provider (ISP) accounts should always be established and maintained by a parent.
- This ensures that a parent can legally maintain control of use and can access records, if necessary.

You should also realize that children may be accessing the Internet from outside of the home. Places include: friends' homes, stores, work, "Internet coffee cafes", libraries and schools.

Be open with your children and encourage them to come to you if they encounter a problem online.
- If they tell you about someone or something that they encountered, your first response should not be to blame them or take away their Internet privileges.
- Work with them to help them avoid problems in the future.

Other helpful measures include considering the use of filtering and blocking programs to limit access to potentially dangerous sites, with the caveat that useful and interesting sites may also inadvertently be blocked. Paying attention to rating services for Web sites is also useful. However, since children are particularly eager participants in instant messaging, it will be difficult to monitor their behavior effectively.

VIRTUAL COMMUNITIES

Principle 7: Anonymity

In order to ensure protection against online surveillance and to enhance the free expression of information and ideas, member states should respect the will of users of the Internet not to disclose their identity. This does not prevent member states from taking measures and co-operating in order to trace those responsible for criminal acts, in accordance with national law, the Convention for the Protection of Human Rights and Fundamental Freedoms and other international agreements in the fields of justice and the police.[37]

Mention has been made of the power of the Internet (or cyberspace, or the connected world) to foster the creation of relationships varying from intense one-on-one encounters to informal groups of people interested in gardening. Aside from the commercial applications, currently being heavily promoted, what makes the Internet so exciting for so many people around the world, is the possibility of establishing contact, exchanging views, presenting one-self in different ways to different people, recreating a persona on demand, or in a less glamorous mode, combining with others to form political, social, cultural, or gay and lesbian groups. Underlying many of these relationships is the ability to assume whatever identity one wishes in order to hide one's true identity, that is, to maintain anonymity. If no one knows who you are, you can be anything you wish. There are obvious criticisms that can be directed against those who employ anonymity: They must have something to hide, they are doing or saying things that they are ashamed of, or they want to deceive others maliciously or playfully. On the other hand, reasons are proposed for the use of anonymous postings: political suppression, whistle-blowing, recovering from abuse, or fear for one's safety.

Therefore, it is not surprising that the Internet has provided means for individuals to maintain their anonymity, nor that some would feel that the use of these means permitted harassment, racism, and traffic in child pornography. The use of anonymous remailers has become a growth indus-try and many thousands of Internet regulars are clients. Anonymity supports the growth of many kinds of virtual communities that will be described later in this chapter. The lobbying power of political, environmental, and social groups has become commonplace on the Internet. Whether protesting against the U.S. government's invasion of Iraq, against the indecency provi-sions of the Telecommunications Act of 1996, or for or against the use of fil-tering software in libraries, a large core of Internet supporters can be counted on to stand up and have their messages counted. Supporters of environmental causes can be instantaneously rallied to confront threats directed against any forest or lake or river anywhere in the world. Political prisoners can have their cases placed on the world stage, requiring govern-ments to answer for their actions rather than their preferred choice of hid-den business as usual.

Anonymity

> The 'Net is viewed as many things—a marketing channel for consumer sales, a place to have opinions with anonymity, a new way to file your income taxes, and . . . —Steve Spanoudis, An Internet Philosophy, http://www.theotherpages.org/index2.html

The purpose here is not to engage in a philosophical or psychological explo-ration into the nature of anonymity but rather to discuss how it is main-tained on the Internet, to what degree, and most importantly, to what end.

As discussed above, anonymity as a democratic right has engendered considerable debate. For law enforcement officials, it is seen as a serious impediment to identifying criminals; for free speech advocates, it is seen as a legitimate exercise of a basic democratic right. On the Internet, these arguments have assumed a new urgency since September 11, as those who use the Internet for planning terrorist acts are a new target for police. A concise legal view of the problems that anonymity raises is given as follows[38]:

> Anonymity, often considered a cornerstone of democracy and a First Amendment guarantee, is easier to attain than ever before due to the recent emergence of cyberspace. Cyberspace enables anyone to communicate, via text, sound, or video, to hundreds or thousands of other people, nearly instantaneously and at little or no cost. . . . Due to the nature of the technology, identities in cyberspace are easily cloaked in anonymity. Once a message sender's identity is anonymous, cyberspace provides to the masses the means to perpetrate widespread criminal activity with little chance of apprehension. . . . Despite the fact that no one sovereign controls cyberspace, it is not an ungoverned and lawless frontier; many actions in cyberspace have consequences in the real world. . . . The question of whether a state or the federal government can create a narrowly tailored restriction on cyberspace anonymity without violating the First Amendment remains unresolved, however. The Supreme Court has not directly addressed the issue, but it may soon consider the constitutionality of criminalizing certain kinds of cyber-anonymity in light of the unique nature of cyberspace.

Anonymous Remailers

In the real world, it is very difficult to conceal one's identity, because proof is demanded for most commercial, educational, legal, and political transactions. To obtain a computer account, typically, proof of identity must be provided, and in using the account to send e-mail, the user's name is attached to the message or can be relatively easily recovered. Because of the perceived need to protect one's identity on the Internet for a number of justified reasons (at least in the minds of some), the void was filled by the creation of anonymous remailers. An anonymous remailer is a computer service that privatizes your e-mail. A remailer allows you to send electronic mail to a Usenet newsgroup or to a person without the recipient knowing your name or your e-mail address.[39] In response to the question, "How does a remailer work?" the Anonymous Remailer FAQ describes the operation of what was the most famous of all anonymous (or more precisely, psuedo-anonymous) remailers, anon.penet.fi, maintained by Johan Helsingius in Finland[40]:

> His "an@anon.penet.fi" addresses are common in controversial news groups. Suppose you read a post from a battered woman <an123@anon.penet.fi> crying out for help. You can write her at <an123@anon.penet.fi>. Helsingius'

computer will STRIP AWAY your real name and address (the header at the top of our e-mail), replace this data with a dummy address, and forward your message to the battered woman. Helsingius' computer will notify you of your new anonymous address; e.g., <an345@anon.penet.fi>. You can use Helsingius' free service to forward letters to anyone, even to persons who do not use his service. His computer sends each user detailed instructions about his system.

More technically, this server is psuedo-anonymous because, although no one on the Internet knows the identity of an345@anon.penet.fi, Johan Helsingius does. However, there are truly anonymous remailers; one example is a Cypherpunk remailer[41]:

> If you want to mail messages without even an anonymized return address on it, then you should use a cypherpunk remailer. You can encrypt the messages sent to the remailer, and the remailer will decrypt them and send them on to the recipient, whose address is hidden inside the encrypted message. This means that someone who monitors your outgoing mail can't see who you are sending anonymous mail to. For even more security, you can also chain remailers, in other words use more than one remailer to send your message. Now not even the remailers you use know who is sending mail to who. Some remailers even allow you to post to Usenet.

As of August 1996, Helsingius' anonymous server had more that 500,000 clients and was by far the most popular such server on the Internet. At the end of August, he shut down his system and therein lies an instructive tale, still worth telling as the Internet evolves.

anon.penet.fi and alt.religion.scientology

Here is a short version of this very complicated and unclear story. The Church of Scientology was engaged in a long-term, vituperative debate about the operations of the church in the newsgroup alt.religion.scientology. Apparently, one or more ex-members downloaded secret documents from Church computers (no doubt a criminal act) and posted them on alt.scientology anonymously via anon.penet.fi. The Church protested that stolen and copyrighted material was being used without their permission. In addition, anti-scientology messages began to be mysteriously cancelled. Many newsreaders have cancellation software that can be used by posters who wish to cancel a message recently sent, but canceling someone else's message is a serious violation of netiquette and even of U.S. law. A variety of dirty tricks followed, culminating in police raids at the homes of two prominent anti-scientology activists, but the event of interest was a raid in Helsinki, Finland, at Helsingius' office, in February 1995. Apparently, the Finnish police demanded to have the name of the anonymous poster to alt.religion.scientology or else they would confiscate the entire system. Helsingius agreed and subsequently posted a description of the events and offered to delete the names of any of his clients, if asked to do so. Thus, an anonymous remailer had been breached and interestingly enough, only a handful of people requested that their names be removed.

The Closing of anon.penet.fi

On Friday, August 30, 1996, the following message was made available on the Internet[42]:

> Hello all,
>
> I just got off the phone with Johan Helsingius who runs the anon.penet.fi anonymous e-mail service.
> 1. He has decided to close the service.
> 2. This is not related to the article in *The Observer*. It is, in fact, due to a decision of a lower Finnish court on petition from the Church of Scientology. Penet went to court last week and made the decision today. The implication of the decision (rather than Penet's to shut the server) is that e-mail over the Internet is not protect by the usual Finnish privacy laws.
> 3. The server is currently down while Julf re-writes the software. Once it runs again, it will be phased out for private use, but groups such as the Samaritans and human rights agencies should be able to use it.
> 4. They are appealing against the decision.
> 5. Julf expects that revisions in Finnish law to provide a safe legal status for anonymous remailers will be in place at the earliest in Spring next year.
> 6. Once again: this is unrelated to *The Observer*'s scandalous reporting.
>
> Your faithful furry friend,
> Azeem

An important institution was closing down, the victim of threats and lack of legal safeguards. The reference to "the article in *The Observer*" should be clarified. The Sunday, August 25, 1996, issue of the British newspaper, *The Observer*, had the following headline: "The peddlers of child abuse: We know who they are. Yet no one is stopping them."[43] The two people named and pictured are Clive Feather, a director of the Internet Service Provider, Demon Internet, and Johan Helsingius, described as follows: "Johan Helsingius is the man US police experts charge with being at the hub of 90 per cent of the child pornography on the Internet. Perverts can log on to and participate in 'live' and 'interactive' filmed sessions that involve the rape of infants."[44] This is the kind of outrageous, unsubstantiated charge that has created the image of the Internet as rife with pornography, of children and of adults. In a statement released by Helsingius, the following is included[45]:

Police sergeant Kaj Malmberg from the Helsinki Police Crime Squad is specialized in investigating computer crimes. He confirms that already a year ago Johan Helsingius restricted the operations of his remailer so that it cannot transmit pictures. . . ."The true amount of child pornography in Internet is difficult to assess, but one thing is clear: We have not found any cases where child porn pictures were transmitted from Finland," Kaj Malmberg says.

Final Comments on Anonymity

The question remains: Is anonymity on the Internet a necessary evil or is there a basic right to be anonymous? As might be expected, there is considerable disagreement. The newsgroup alt.sexual.abuse.recovery (asar) provided a forum for people who have been sexually abused to share their experiences, including the events themselves and subsequent therapy and memories. Usually postings to this newsgroup contain warnings (SPOILER!!!) of a perhaps unpleasant recounting to follow. Should people who find comfort in both telling their stories and hearing from others be required to use their real name or not post at all? How could such a community exist or provide support in the absence of anonymity? There is an organization in England called the Samaritans, which provides help to people in need and offers help by posting messages. Some of these are anonymous and some of the Samaritans offering help are anonymous. How else could it operate?

One new development related to the "sharing" of copyrighted music files is the introduction of systems for peer-to-peer (P2P) communication that make it difficult to determine the identity of the participants. For example, a music-swapping service, Blubster, operates with a new Internet data transfer protocol described as follows[46]:

> Blubster uses an Internet data transfer protocol known as UDP for content look-up and transfer negotiating. Unlike the TCP protocol that serves this function in other file-sharing networks, UDP is a so-called "connectionless" method that doesn't reveal links between nodes or acknowledge transmission in an identifiable manner. Because UDP transfer logs don't reveal detailed information about which user at which IP address is accessing what content at what time, they are considered less vulnerable to legal discovery than TCP logs.

Concealing, or making it more difficult to determine, one's identity for the purpose of preventing discovery for the execution of possibly illegal acts is one of the major concerns about anonymity on the Internet. Fraudulent activities could become commonplace on the Internet in commercial transactions if money could be moved anonymously. What about raising money for political donations if donors of large sums can remain anonymous? How will the political process be affected? Although it was argued above that many interactions on the Internet depend on anonymous participants, others would argue that communities built on deceit have little value and are in no way comparable to real-world communities. In the real world, anonymous letters to newspapers and magazines are rarely printed; however, a letter writer may request that his or her name be withheld if the letter is published. Thus, responsibility is assured and public anonymity is guaranteed. Perhaps an equivalent model can be designed for the Internet.

Gender and Identity

This is one way of looking at the identity issue on the Internet or in cyberspace: "We are moving from modernist calculation toward post modernist simulation, where the self is a multiple, distributed system."[47] In the past few years, a number of writers and scholars from such diverse disciplines as architecture, literature, psychology, computer science, philosophy, sociology, anthropology, and the visual arts have found in the Internet and cyberspace a metaphor for a disembodied world of minds and ideas, where self is a work in progress over time and space. In this section, an introduction will be made into some aspects of these concepts and in the next, a somewhat more mundane exploration of the notion of virtual communities as online versions of their real-world counterparts will be presented.

Mark Slouka, currently a professor at Columbia University, has written a book with the provocative and carefully chosen title, *The War of the Worlds*,[48] in recognition of the H. G. Wells classic novel. In Wells' book, an alien invasion threatens the existence of Earth's people and in Slouka's book, an alien world, roughly comparable to virtual reality, threatens our world, the real reality. The threat is pervasive, increasing, and supported by several spokespersons, whose quoted remarks are simultaneously outrageous and ridiculous. Slouka leaves the impression that what is predicted is actually on the verge of being achieved, even though he warns that[49]

> My quarrel is with a relatively small but disproportionately influential group of self-described 'Net religionists' and 'wannabe gods' who believe that the physical world can (and should) be 'downloaded' into a computer, who believe that the future of mankind is not in RL (real life) but in some form of VL (virtual reality); who are working very hard (and spending enormous amounts of both federal and private money) to engineer their very own version of the apocalypse.

It is impossible to appreciate the large, tempting target confronting Slouka without a few choice quotations that make it difficult to believe that we are not being subjected to a colossal put-on; consider the following representative remarks:

In cyberspace, Nicole Stenger promised, multiplied versions of the self would 'blossom up everywhere.' These multiplied selves would be 'ideal, ironical, statistical.' It would be 'a springtime for schizophrenia!'[50]

When virtual reality came on-line, Allucquere Rosanne Stone predicted, cyberspace would become 'a toolkit for reconfiguring consciousness'; it would make it possible for a man to be 'seen, and perhaps touched, as a woman and vice versa—or as anything else.'[51]

"The only thing wrong with the universe is that it is currently running someone else's program." (Ken Karakotsios)[52]

"When the scales fall from our eyes, we will see that our 'origins are to be found in both the animal and the mechanical kingdoms, with the animal and the mechanical qualities together incorporated in the definition of human nature." (Bruce Mazlish)[53]

"'As we wire ourselves up into a hivish network . . . many things will emerge that we, as mere neurons in the network, don't expect, don't understand, can't control, or don't even perceive.' But this, he explains patiently, is 'the price for any emergent hive mind.'" (Kevin Kelly)[54]

Slouka is not particularly concerned with the Information or Post-industrialist Society; rather it is the post-flesh, post- touching, post-human one that he fears. It is an easy vision to attack, and a frightening one for anyone with the slightest modicum of humanity. To trivialize human existence and its many thousands of years of development is to make mockery of everything that makes us human, and Slouka readily expresses his bewilderment and disgust at this unthinking and yes, unthinkable, vision of the future. Kelly's portrayal of the hive with its mass of worker bees creates images of the Nuremberg rallies in Slouka's mind, with their masses of humans as drones, unthinkingly serving a single-minded goal.

One well-known story of gender-switching and deceit will be briefly described. A number of users of a CompuServe chat service as far back as 1983 encountered a woman named Joan, a neuropsychologist, who apparently had been seriously injured in an automobile accident, confining her to a wheelchair and rendering her mute. Given a computer, modem, and a connection to CompuServe, she soon found her voice and began long-term relationships with women from the spring of 1983 to the spring of 1985. She was witty, sympathetic, and supportive in times of need. But as it turned out, she wasn't a woman either; Joan was a prominent New York psychiatrist in his early fifties, "who was engaged in a bizarre, all-consuming experiment to see what it felt like to be female, and to experience the intimacy of female friendship."[55] In keeping with the electronic context, his activities have been called "mind rape." Indeed one woman had a real affair with him, after he was introduced to her by Joan. All the women who had conversed with him felt betrayed, after having volunteered intimate details of their lives. Current online interactions are more sophisticated, in terms of the technology, but one wonders how many similar deceptions are being perpetrated and how many more people are being betrayed.

From a major online resource, *The Psychology of Cyberspace*, constructed by John Suler, we have the following revealing remarks on "Identity Management"[56]:

> A single person's identity embodies multiplicity. You possess many sectors within your personality and play numerous roles in your life—such as child, parent, student, employee, neighbor, friend. Cyberspace offers a niche for each of these specific facets of selfhood. Some people even talk about how we can "deconstruct" ourselves online. We don't have to present ourselves in toto— how we look, talk, move, our history, thoughts, feelings, and personality, all in one big package. In different environments, we can divvy up and present our characteristics in packets of various sizes and content. Thanks to thousands of online groups each devoted to a distinct professional, vocational, or personal topic, we can express, highlight, and develop specific interests and life experiences while setting aside others. You don't have to mention to your stock trading e-mail list that you also hang out at the "I Dream of Jeannie" fan club site. When you join an online community, you often have a choice about how much, if any, personal information you place into the members' profile database. Online communication tools even give you the choice about whether you want people to see how you look or hear your voice. The desire to remain anonymous reflects the need to eliminate those critical features of your identity that you do NOT want to display in that particular environment or group. The desire to lurk—to hide completely—indicates the person's need to split off his entire personal identity from his observing of those around him: he wants to look, but not be seen.

This concept of presentation of self in cyberspace seems very calculated, as if we can recognize and enumerate the multitude of attitudes and views that define or characterize us as individuals and then determine which ones will be presented or revealed. Could we carry out such a program consciously in the real world? When we meet a new person, the process of getting to know that person is initiated. It is a long, involved, fragmentary journey that has many dead ends, surprises, and sudden flashes of insight. We never arrive at a point of knowing in any concrete sense; the discovery of others is a process, not an event, as is the discovery of self. What does cyberspace offer? Probably an illusion that we are in control of this process both for ourselves and for others. Finally, more attention should be paid to our evolution as humans in human societies.

MUDS, MOOS, and . . .

One simple and early form of computer play for several players was invented in England in 1978 but soon spread around the world. It was called an MUD by its inventor, for "Multi-User Dungeon." The FAQ on MUDs and MUDding provides the following definition[57]:

A MUD (Multiple User Dimension, Multiple User Dungeon, or Multiple User Dialogue) is a computer program which users can log into and explore. Each user takes control of a computerized persona/avatar/incarnation/character. You can walk around, chat with other characters, explore dangerous monster-infested areas, solve puzzles, and even create your very own rooms, descriptions and items.

A MOO is an object-oriented MUD, that is, a MUD implemented in an object-oriented language which permits richer environments to be created. And the names roll on: LambdaMOO, "an offshoot of MOO. Added more functionality, many new features, and a great deal more stability, in a general rewrite of the code."[58] There has been an evolution of MUDs in many directions from their primarily wizard and warriors origins; one of these is into a class of MUDs called TinyMUDs, which are more social and provide an environment for individuals to meet and chat. Clearly, there are many varieties of MUDs available on the Internet and to become a player or participant, it is necessary to access the MUD's Internet protocol port. (This is as technical as the discussion will become.)

What is of interest in these online games or social groupings are the motivations of the players or participants, the group dynamics, and the benefits derived. One way to gain an understanding of MUDs is to examine the different classes of identities that players can assume. One information document describes three dimensions of this process[59]:

- **Name**—[Y]ou could take the name of your favourite movie star and be a 007. You can take any word that is in your mind or create something new that either makes a good sound or makes it impossible for anyone to pronounce as a word. Unique to MUDs is the possibility to change your name as often as you want. [Of course, changing your name means that others may or may not believe you are still the same person.]
- **Gender**—Have you ever wanted to change to the other sex? Now there is a chance to do so and you may be surprised by the results. A lot of guys act as female characters to get special attention—female players are rare on MUDs. As a result the few real world females are male inside MUDs to avoid special attention! So you can never really be sure who your partner is.
- **Description**—The two main areas to consider in the creation of a character, namely physical appearance and history/background. In terms of physical appearance some MUDs will issue a list of characteristics that have to be filled in, while others leave it up to the individual to pad out their character. Such aspect as 'what colour are your eyes?', 'how tall are you?' 'what colour hair do you have?' The history and background of the character should include such aspects as where the characters was born, what the parents did for a living, and what kind of childhood they had.

Players can of course participate in more than one group and adopt more than one persona, with the attendant problems of keeping track of diverse characters. One point to ponder is why so many men adopt female identities. It has been argued that the point of playing is to be accepted into a group on the basis of one's creativity as manifested in an interesting, exciting, and dynamic character. As difficult as this process is in real life, in the virtual world it is a necessary requirement. But what is one to make of such communities, whose existence depends on the acceptance of deception as a fundamental basis upon which to explore relationships?

Why do males want to be females in virtual worlds? A few suggestions are given as follows[60]:

- Due to the pressure of cultural stereotypes, it may be difficult for some men to explore within themselves what society labels as "feminine" characteristics. These males may rely on the anonymity of cyberspace to express their "feminine" side which they feel they must otherwise hide. Some of these males may strongly identify with women.
- Adopting a feminine role in cyberspace may be a way to draw more attention to themselves. Getting noticed and responded to in cyberspace is not always easy, especially in such distracting, "noisy" environments as the visual chat habitats. Donning a female name and/or avatar, especially a sexy one, will almost instantly draw reactions. The gender-switched male may even like the feeling of power and control over other males that goes along with this switch.
- Some males may adopt a feminine identity to investigate male/female relationships. They may be testing out various ways of interacting with males in order to learn, first hand, what it's like being on the woman's side. Hopefully, they use that knowledge to enhance their relationships with females. Some, however, may be looking for ways to gain power and control.
- In some online games where participants assume imaginary identities (e.g., MUDs), being a female may be advantageous. Sometimes males lend more assistance to females, so they progress faster in the game.
- Disguised as a female, a male looking for intimacy, romance, and/or cybersex from another male may be acting upon conscious or unconscious homosexual feelings.
- Transsexuals (people who feel, psychologically, that they are the opposite sex rather than their given biological gender) and/or transvestites (people who cross-dress for sexual arousal or as an identification with females) may be drawn to virtual gender-switching. In rare cases, gender-switching could be a sign of what would be diagnosed as "gender confusion"—i.e., a psychological disturbance where one's identity as a male or female has not fully developed.

What is cybersex? Is it like phone sex? "Virtual sex is a generic term for erotic interaction between individuals whose bodies may never touch, who may never even see each other's faces or exchange real names. This can include phone sex, exchanges of electronic e-mail encounters on chatlines, Bulletin Board Systems (BBSs), and other on-line virtual communities."[61] An informal survey reveals the following two, not surprising views: "A lot of people find virtual sex to be a disembodied, alienating and ultimately meaningless experience. Others, however, have discovered that it can be as involving, intense and transformative as the best kinds of embodied erotic encounters, and that furthermore, its virtuosity enhances rather than detracts from the experience."[62]

One of the foremost commentators on these and other activities is Sherry Turkle, a psychologist at the Massachusetts Institute of Technology and a well-known author. In an interview in 1995, she promotes the benefits of multiple personalities on the Internet, a matter of choice, as opposed to multiple personalities in the real world: "people who assume online personas are aware of the lives they have created on the screen. They are playing different aspects of themselves and move fluidly and knowledgeably among them. They are having an experience that encourages them to challenge traditional ways of thinking about healthy selves as single and unitary."[63] The interviewer points out that Ms. Turkle has recounted the story of a young man, "who tells you that for him, real life—RL, as he calls it—doesn't have any special status. It's just another window, along with the ones where he plays roles in a number of virtual communities." She agrees and comments that for this person, "RL is usually not even his best window." She goes on to note, "It's not uncommon. But for me, his case is important because it demonstrates how a bright young man who is doing well in school and who has real-life friends can easily go through a period when things are more interesting on the Net than off."[64]

If nothing else, virtual worlds will force us to rethink many of the ideas that we have long held about the unity of self, the notion of presentation, honesty, playfulness, and relationships. It is ironic that this artificial medium, made possible only because of machinery—computers and telecommunications networks—has raised serious questions about what makes us human and how such social animals, as we are, form relationships and communities. Nevertheless, there do exist dangers, in that dependency on artificial worlds for human relationships may be destructive of real relationships in the real world, which after all is not *just* another chat room, another MUD, or another window on a computer screen. What is most striking is how the body is ignored, as if it were an impediment in the way of really connecting. It is felt by some of the most vociferous virtual world or cyberspace proponents that freedom and perhaps even the next stage of evolution will free the mind, the true self, from the constraints of the body. How hundreds of thousands of years of evolution can be ignored, or swept aside, by virtue of a few years of a new, and in the long run, rather primitive technology, is perhaps a tribute to the power of the human mind in projecting speculation into fact and ignoring history and biology, if necessary.

In mid-2003, Sherry Turkle offered the following responses to questions posed to her about the benefits of online interactions; not surprisingly, her enthusiasm and optimism remain undiminished[65]:

- **Has society been changed by our interactions with the Internet?** Definitely. The ability to join online communities, or being able to play out aspects of self that are different than what your physical self permits, has profoundly changed what is available to the human psyche. One of my students formed a friendship on the Internet with a person who turned out to be profoundly physically impaired. Certain aspects of that person's self— the vivaciousness, the sense of exploration, of risk-taking—would not have had an opportunity to express themselves without the sociability the Internet provides.

- **Do you worry about the potential for dishonesty on the Internet?** It's a place where people experiment with identity. Medieval times had festivals and fairs for that kind of play. As long as we know that it's a space for that kind of play—that somebody calling themselves "fabulous hot babe," might be an 80-year-old guy in a nursing home in Miami—it's good. Now, you don't want that on the site where your American Express card is processed. As long as we keep these spaces separate, I think that the Internet as a place for identity play is good.

- **Have you ever adopted an alternative identity online?** I've experimented with being a man and saw how people responded to me differently. I found it quite a fascinating exercise. One of the things that a lot of women notice in virtual communities is that if you're a man, people stop offering to help you—especially when there is a lot of technical stuff to do.

Social and Political Activity

In recent years, there has been concern about the social impact of the Internet on several levels. One major worry was that use of the Internet would prompt people to withdraw from social engagement and become isolated, depressed, and alienated. A related fear was that Internet users might abandon contact with their local communities as they discovered how easy it is to go online to communicate with those in other parts of the world and get information from every point on the planet.[66]

Some findings included in a Pew Internet survey of online communities are given as follows[67]:

90 million Americans have participated in online groups
- 84% of Internet users, or about 90 million Americans, say they have used the Internet to contact or get information from a group. We call them "Cyber Groupies."
- 79% of Cyber Groupies identify at least one particular group with which they stay in regular contact.
- 49% of Cyber Groupies say the Internet has helped them connect with groups or people who share their interests.
- Cyber Groupies try out different groups; the average Cyber Groupie has contacted four online groups at one time or another.

28 million have used the Internet to deepen their ties to their local communities
- 26% of Internet users have employed the Internet to get information about local groups. That comes to 28 million people.

Online communities foster chatter and connection
- 60% of Cyber Groupies say they use email to communicate with the group; of these emailers 43% email the group several times a week.
- 33% of the 28 million Local Groupies who use email send email to their main local organization several times a week.

More contact with different people
- 50% of Cyber Groupies say that participation in an online community has helped them get to know people they otherwise would not have met.
- 35% of Local Groupies say that participation in an online community has helped them get to know people they otherwise would not have met. This lower number relative to Cyber Groupies may be due to the fact that Local Groupies probably were acquainted already with members of the online group.
- 37% of Cyber Groupies say the Internet has helped them connect with people of different ages or generations.
- 27% of Cyber Groupies say the Internet has helped them connect with people from different racial, ethnic, or economic backgrounds.

The virtual worlds just discussed seem to be characterized by individuals trying to understand themselves by entering environments in which they have some degree of control over what information, about themselves, is presented to others. By playing with different and even contrasting personae they hope to discover more about their interests, desires, and sexuality. But there are many other ways in which the Internet's global and asynchronous properties can be used to form communities, in which individuals reach out to others to form lobbying groups, to exchange information and support for a host of medical and psychological problems, and to mount worldwide campaigns against political oppression, child exploitation, and looming environmental disasters. Some of these groups and their missions are listed in the Appendix. Many groups use listservs to inform members and exchange views. Joining and quitting is usually done automatically by posting an appropriate message, but some listservs have qualifications that prospective members must meet.

One of the oldest online communities is the Well, established in the San Francisco/Berkeley area in 1985 and later acquired by the online magazine, *Salon*, in 1999. The Well had a number of discussion groups, called conferences, on such diverse topics as parenting, health, politics, housing, and of course, Internet rights. The founders of the Well did not permit anonymity because they wanted to establish a community of individuals known to one another and responsible for their words and actions. Furthermore, it was intended that once posted, messages could not be changed—the historical record would be maintained. The Well is an example of a local community network in which many participants would also meet and interact offline.

It was also characterized as a vigorous and vociferous community, with lively debates, name–calling, and explicit language, definitely not for the faint-at-heart.[68]

Online groups offer members a number of advantages, including instantaneous delivery of announcements—a definite boon for organizational reasons—Web links to important information that is always available, accessibility from home and work, access for the disabled, a communication channel that is less inhibiting than face-to-face confrontations, and a forum that never closes. The downside, even for these communities, is that posted material must be taken at face value and those seeking reliable information face a real dilemma, especially when medical conditions are at risk. Since both the source and quality of the information are generally unknown, the prevailing marketplace cautionary dictum continues to be appropriate, *caveat emptor*.[69] On the other hand, so many people of diverse backgrounds are part of help and self-help groups that errors and bad advice are usually noticed and corrected before any damage can be done.

Many of the online communities parallel their real-world counterparts while others are unique to the Internet. Existing self-help, political, environmental, and religious organizations can facilitate many of their efforts using computer networks. Thus, Greenpeace is able to mobilize opposition to a logging operation anywhere in the world, and Amnesty International can use the Internet to rally support for political prisoners at a moment's notice. Some groups such as the Electronic Privacy Information Center exist on the Internet, providing both archival and fast-breaking information for its supporters, encouraging them to lobby their members of Congress, mounting online petitions, and testifying before Congress on matters of vital interest. In May 1996, Human Rights Watch issued a report titled, "Silencing the Net: The Threat to Freedom of Expression On-line." Whereas in the U.S., extraordinary effort in defending free speech seems to be generated on behalf of those who create and post pornography, in many other parts of the world, the basic right to criticize and campaign against governments or ruling parties continues to be at risk. The report notes the following[70]:

> Governments around the world, claiming they want to protect children, thwart terrorists and silence racists and hate mongers, are rushing to eradicate freedom of expression on the Internet, the international "network of networks," touted as the Information Superhighway. . . . Authoritarian regimes are attempting to reconcile their eagerness to reap the economic benefits of Internet access with maintaining control over the flow low of information inside their borders. Censorship efforts in the U.S. and Germany lend support to those in China, Singapore, and Iran, where censors target not only sexually explicit material and hate speech but also pro-democracy discussions and human rights education. . . . Because the Internet knows no national boundaries, on-line censorship laws, in addition to trampling on the free expression rights of a nation's own citizens, threaten to chill expression globally and to

impede the development of the Global Information Infrastructure (GII) before it becomes a truly global phenomenon.

Without freedom of expression guaranteed, the existence of activist social and legal groups is threatened, and as noted above, the promise of a Global Information Infrastructure will not be realized, certainly not in a form that improves human existence worldwide.

More recently, the organization Reporters Without Borders released a report surveying attacks against the unrestricted flow of information on the Internet. A selection from the preface, written by Vinton Cerf, a prominent Internet pioneer, follows[71]:

> Despite its great promise, the Internet is not, in and of itself, a guarantor of the free flow of information. George Soros, the well-known financier, takes pains to remind us that the freedom offered by the Internet can be taken away. Indeed, what you will read in the pages that follow illustrates exactly this point. Many governments do want to limit the information its citizens can reach. In some cases the motivations are understandable and even laudable. I can see no redeeming value in child pornography for example and I support efforts to expunge it from the Internet. But those of us living in free societies have been warned repeatedly that censorship is a slippery slope and must be treated with the greatest care.

ACCESS

> The new universal service policy should:
> * Recognize the cost of not getting all citizens connected.
> * Allow users to control usage costs as available evidence suggests that usage costs are as important, if not more important, than access costs for achieving universal service goals.
> * Allow users to identify the set of services that enables the user to be served by a communication service with adequate facilities.
> * Provide citizens with affordable, quality customer premises equipment such as phones, modems and computers.
> * Provide ongoing consumer education so that individuals and organizations are aware of the options available to them, are able to make informed decisions about these options, understand the pricing of the services, and know how to get assistance if they have difficulties with service reliability, bills, privacy, marketing tactics, and/or other problems.[72]

In the Information Society, everyone can be a publisher as well as a consumer of information. The issues to be explored revolve around the questions of who will be able to gain access to the vast stores of information being made available over computer networks and at what costs. It is not a new question;

the telephone, radio, and television are all technologies whose introduction and growth raised questions of access. One model is the public library, an institution that is deemed so important that access is free and costs are borne by all citizens. The telephone has come to be accepted as virtually indispensable and for a long time, local rates were kept artificially low, subsidized in part by long-distance charges. With deregulation of this latter market, local rates rose, but a variety of charging strategies were introduced to enable low-income customers to have a basic, if typically inadequate, level of service. Television cable service is also structured to provide levels of service to accommodate viewers at different income levels and viewing habits, although access to television is not usually regarded as a right. The Internet is certainly not currently viewed as either a necessity or a right, but the Information Highway has been hailed as bringing a host of necessary services to all. And so we return to the questions raised above: if access to the Information Highway is so important, how will it be provided, given that a certain amount of capital investment in technology must be in place and ongoing charges related to connect time must be also be made? In addition, people will require adequate training and ongoing access to technical support. Thus, one possibility is government subsidies to ensure a basic level of service—not likely in the current atmosphere of antipathy toward government involvement in the affairs of its citizens; another is industry willingness to provide an effective rate structure for different income levels, leaving the question of capital costs open. Other possibilities may exist, including free access at public facilities such as libraries and community centers.

Technological Factors

First, it is necessary to gain an appreciation of the shape and scope of digital information as it has been evolving over the past few years. Some of these features have been presented in bits and pieces so far and at this point we turn to what is currently available in the working environment, taking the World Wide Web as a model.

Digital Information

On Web sites around the world, enormous amounts of information are readily available, for those with appropriate computers, modems, software, and Internet accounts or gateway access. What makes the Web so interesting is the ease with which it is possible to access, as well as present, information in a semi-structured fashion and that the information exists as text, sound, and images, both single and multiple frame. Everything is stored digitally that is accessible at the single byte level. Thus, all forms of information are at root structured collections of bytes—many bytes. The Internet carried "U.S. traffic equivalent to perhaps 1/1000 of the voice

telephone network (20 trillion bytes per month in spring 1995)."[73] The
Internet is currently doubling in size every year, and Web traffic is growing
even faster so that the Web is now the largest source of packets (basic units
of data transmitted across a network). In a study of the production of
information of all kinds around the world, some interesting statistics were
produced, with the caveat that in many cases, estimates have been
employed. An example of the big picture is that in 1999, "the world's total
yearly production of print, film, optical, and magnetic content would
require roughly 1.5 billion gigabytes of storage. This is the equivalent of
250 megabytes per person for each man, woman, and child on earth."[74]
The four major storage media are taken to be paper, film, optical, and
magnetic with the last including PC disk drives, departmental servers,
enterprise servers, and camcorder tape. Magnetic media account for about
85% of all information storage and the overwhelmingly preferred storage
format is digital. A few more interesting statistics follow[75]:

• In 2000 the World Wide Web consisted of about 21 terabytes of static
HTML pages, and is growing at a rate of 100% per year. Many Web pages
are generated on-the-fly from data in databases, so the total size of the
"deep Web" is considerably larger.

• Although the social impact of the Web has been phenomenal, about
500 times as much email is being produced per year as the stock of Web
pages. It appears that about 610 billion emails are sent per year, compared
to 2.1 billion static Web pages.

• There are two groups of Web content. One, which we would call the
"surface" Web, is what everybody knows as the "Web," a group that consists of static, publicly available Web pages, and which is a relatively small
portion of the entire Web. Another group is called the "deep" Web, and it
consists of specialized Web-accessible databases and dynamic Web sites,
which are not widely known by "average" surfers, even though the information available on the "deep" Web is 400 to 550 times larger than the
information on the "surface."

• The "surface" Web consists of approximately 2.5 billion documents,
up from 1 billion pages at the beginning of the year, with a rate of growth
of 7.3 million pages per day. Estimates of the average "surface" page size
vary in the range from 10 kbytes per page to 20 kbytes per page. So, the
total amount of information on the "surface" Web varies somewhere from
25 to 50 terabytes of information [HTML-included basis].

• If we take into account all web-accessible information, such as web-
connected databases, dynamic pages, intranet sites, etc., collectively known
as "deep" Web, there are **550 billion web-connected documents**, with an
average page size of 14 kbytes, and 95% of this information is publicly
accessible. [*original emphasis*]

All this information would be useless if it could not be readily searched and
accessed, viewed and even downloaded.

Browsers and Search Engines

2003 marked the 10th anniversary of the first Web browser, Mosaic, developed at the University of Illinois' National Center for Supercomputer Applications. It seemed clear at the time that software was needed to permit non-specialists to access the vast amounts of information available on the Internet. It would have been impossible to predict the following impact of the browser[76]:

> The unassuming piece of software revolutionized high technology akin to the way the remote control reinvented television, but in manifold more dimensions with universal consequences. In roughly six months of 1995, Mosaic transformed the Internet from the esoteric province of researchers and technophiles to a household appliance, creating a multibillion-dollar industry and changing the way society works, communicates and even falls in love—in short, affecting nearly every facet of life.

One of the early success stories of the Web was that of Netscape's Navigator, once the most commonly used browser. However, after a heated competition with Microsoft's Internet Explorer, Netscape's market share has been substantially reduced so that Explorer now holds more than 90% of the browser market. It may be recalled that Microsoft's methods to compete in the browser market resulted in part in the antitrust suit launched by the Department of Justice. From rather humble beginnings, a browser has become an indispensable tool to the point that serious consideration is being given to a special-purpose Internet computer that is nothing more than a Web browser, that is, a device for linking to Web sites and exploring the resources available. Browsers have been augmented to send and receive e-mail, to post and view messages on Usenet newsgroups, and to play music and view videos. That is, in a real sense, browsers have become the operating systems for Web exploration, and for many people this is all they require of their computers.

Indeed, browser technology may be approaching a level of maturity that invites new innovations and the development of new markets. For example, the following products have already been introduced or are on the verge of entering the marketplace[77]:

> It's not surprising . . . that the role of the browser is being pared back to the essential but none-too-exciting function of reading HTML code. During the heady years of the browser wars, Netscape and Microsoft competed partly by trying to offer browsers that did everything, from e-mail to coding. The result was bulky, confusing applications that didn't handle the basics properly.
> - [A]pplications such as GuruNet, a Web-based program, allows PC users to click on any word in an active document and get relevant information such as a definition of the word or background on a business. Bob Rosenschein, the inventor of GuruNet and CEO of parent company

Atomica, said he developed the software when it became clear that search
engines might not be the ideal way to retrieve the quick bits of information
often sought through the PC.

• Stephen Klein, CEO of software maker ActiveBuddy, saw similar limitations in the browser. His solution was to develop "interactive agents" for
expanding the functions of instant messaging software. Using such tools,
for instance, you can type "weather" into the window of an IM program
and instantly get a brief forecast for your hometown. At work, you can type
in "vacation days," and a business version of the software quickly shows
how much paid time off you have available.

• Macromedia, creator of widespread browser add-ons such as the Flash
and Shockwave animation players, is one application maker no longer content to toil in the background and is seeking "first-class citizen" status for
its products. The company recently announced plans for software that will
allow Flash applications to run on their own.

Accessing Web sites, while the basic function of browsers, is not enough
when faced with millions of Web sites and the problem of determining which
ones contain information that might be useful at the moment. Almost immediately after browsers appeared, a class of programs, called search engines,
were introduced to meet the needs of dealing with an enormous amount of
possibly useful information. Many of these names have become familiar to
Web dwellers—Yahoo, Infoseek, Web Crawler, Lycos, Excite, Magellan,
AltaVista, HotBot, and of course, the most familiar one, Google. Many of
these search engines actually survey Web sites on a continuous basis, indexing keywords in new documents and adding this new information to the
existing base. So one can think of autonomous programs, intelligent agents,
or Web robots (webbots) scurrying about the Web, itself a biological
metaphor, scrounging for information and bringing it home. Thus, Google
can be given a search query, consisting of a structured expression containing
key words that characterize the topic of interest, and within a few seconds
it will return with links to hundreds, or hundreds of thousands, of potential
"hits." Now the problem is how to refine the search so that among the hits
there is a higher frequency of good outcomes and in addition, fewer good
outcomes are overlooked.

As with much else on the Internet, advertising plays a necessary facilitating role. That advertisements should appear on the output produced by
search engines is not surprising, but that advertisers should influence the
order in which the results are presented is unacceptable, as the Federal Trade
Commission said in June 2002 in response to a complaint brought by
Commercial Alert of Portland, Oregon.[78]

Your complaint alleges that when search engines include Web sites in search
results lists, on the basis of "paid placement" and "paid inclusion," such
search results are advertisements. Your complaint contends that "without

clear and conspicuous disclosure that the ads are ads," such "concealment may mislead search engine users to believe that search results are based on relevancy alone, not marketing ploys." After careful review, the staff of the Bureau of Consumer Protection has determined not to recommend that the Commission take formal action against the search engine companies listed in your complaint at this time. That determination should not, however, be construed as a determination by either the Bureau of Consumer Protection or the Commission as to whether or not the practices described in your complaint violate the FTC Act or any other statute enforced by the Commission.

Although the staff is not recommending Commission action at this time, we are sending letters to search engine companies outlining the need for clear and conspicuous disclosures of paid placement, and in some instances paid inclusion, so that businesses may avoid possible future Commission action. In addition, this response to your complaint will be placed on the Commission's public record and on the FTC's Web site.

Thus, an infrastructure is in place for creating Web sites containing structured information, varying from advertisements, reports, studies, books, songs, pictures, videos, and arbitrary mixtures of these. In addition, and necessarily so, there is an array of relatively easy-to-use programs for searching the range of Web documents, using rather simplistic keywords for characterizing subjects of interest, and a means for displaying, playing, and viewing retrieved objects. Recent innovations include the downloading of small, self-contained programs, written in Java, that run on the user's computer and produce animated visual displays. One can expect improvements in search efficiency and accuracy, but the problem of intelligent searches will be challenging for years to come. Given the technology that has been described, the discussion can turn to the fundamental question of access to information in a democratic society.

Government Policies and Universal Access

The Telecommunications Act of 1996 was discussed in Chapter 8 with respect to one section, the Communications Decency Act and its attempt to limit free expression on the Internet. Other sections dealing with deregulation of the telephone and cable industries were reviewed in Chapter 12. For the present, the concern is with what role governments will play in ensuring that their citizens have access to the Internet and ultimately the Information Highway, and this is where the Telecommunications Act comes into the picture. The Act places the following responsibilities on the Federal Communications Commission (FCC)[79]:

- Promote the availability of quality services at just, reasonable, and affordable rates
- Increase access to advanced telecommunications services throughout the Nation

   • Advance the availability of such services to all consumers, including
those in low-income, rural, insular, and high-cost areas at rates that are reasonably comparable to those charged in urban areas.

The private sector also has responsibilities with respect to universal service.
In this regard, the Act states that[80]

   • All providers of telecommunications services should contribute to
Federal universal service in some equitable and nondiscriminatory manner
   • There should be specific, predictable, and sufficient Federal and State
mechanisms to preserve and advance universal service
   • All schools, classrooms, health care providers, and libraries should,
generally, have access to advanced telecommunications services
   • And finally, that the Federal-State Joint Board and the Commission
should determine those other principles that, consistent with the 1996 Act,
are necessary to protect the pubic interest.

The practical means to provide access for schools and libraries across the
country, mandated by the 1996 Act, is the E-rate, or, more precisely, the
Schools and Libraries Universal Service Support Mechanism, a fund based
on taxes levied on telephone bills, reaching about $2.25 billion per year. In
2003, a survey was conducted by a consortium of organizations, the
Education and Library Networks Coalition (EdLiNC), to report on
the impact of six years of operation of the E-rate program. Not surprisingly,
the survey reports that the E-rate program has been a great success; the concise version of the findings is given as[81]

   1. The e-rate is an important tool for economic empowerment in unde-
      served communities
   2. The e-rate is beginning to bring new learning opportunities to special
      education students
   3. E-rate is transforming education in rural America
   4. E-rate technology is helping schools improve student achievement and
      comply with NCLB [No Child Left Behind Act]
   5. Schools and libraries are devoting significant resources and exercising
      great care in completing e-rate applications.

The Pew Internet & American Life Project reported in April 2003 on a survey it had conducted on "Internet access and the digital divide." This survey
was of considerable interest because it was concerned with why people were
not using the Internet, including those who had previously been online.
Among the findings are the following[82]:

   The online population is fluid and shifting. While 42% of Americans say
   they don't use the Internet, many of them either have been Internet users at

one time or have a once-removed relationship with the Internet through family or household members.

Internet access has grown across-the-board, but clear demographic gaps remain

Still, there remain a variety of factors that separate Internet users from nonusers. On the demographic side:

• Younger Americans are much more wired than older Americans.

• Well-to-do Americans are more wired that less well-off Americans, and the employed are far more wired than the unemployed.

• White Americans are more wired than African-Americans and Hispanics.

• Well-educated Americans are more wired than those who only completed high school.

• Suburban and urban residents are more wired than rural residents.

• Parents of children living at home are more wired than non-parents.

There are also social differences between Internet users and non-users

Our survey explored other dimensions of the social world of Americans with respect to Internet use. The research indicates:

• Those who are socially content—who trust others, have lots of people to draw on for support, and who believe that others are generally fair—are more likely to be wired than those who are less content.

• Those who feel they have control over their lives are more likely to be wired than those who feel they do not have much control of their lives.

• Those who read newspapers, watch TV, and use cell phones and other technologies are more likely to use the Internet than those who don't.

A special look at the disabled and the Internet

• 38% of disabled Americans go online, compared to 58% of all Americans. Of the disabled who do go online, a fifth say their disability makes using the Internet difficult.

• 28% of disabled non-users say their disability makes it difficult or impossible for them to go online.

It may be helpful to review briefly the regular survey carried out by the Federal Communications Commission (FCC) on high-speed services for Internet access. Clearly the wave of the future is broadband connectivity because it obviously encourages such services as the downloading of movies and music. The lead sentence almost says it all: "High-Speed Connections to the Internet Increased 23% During the Second Half of 2002 for a Total of 19.9 Million Lines in Service."[83] The FCC defines two levels of service that are faster than the ubiquitous 56.6 kilobits per second, namely, "*high-speed lines* are defined as those that provide services at speeds exceeding 200 kilobits per second (kbps) in at least one direction, while *advanced services lines* are those that provide services at speeds exceeding 200 kbps in both directions."[84] The statistics reveal a continuing rapid growth rate of high-speed access[85]:

• High-speed lines connecting homes and businesses to the Internet increased by 23% during the second half of 2002, from 16.2 million to 19.9 million lines, compared to a 27% increase, from 12.8 million to 16.2

million lines, during the first half of 2002. For the full year, high-speed lines increased by 55%.

- Of the 19.9 million high-speed lines in service, 17.4 million served residential and small business subscribers, a 24% increase from the 14.0 million residential and small business high-speed lines reported six months earlier. For the full year, high-speed lines for residential and small business subscribers increased by 58%.
- Of the 19.9 million high-speed lines, 13.0 million provided advanced services, i.e., services at speeds exceeding 200 kbps in both directions. Advanced services lines increased 24% during the second half of 2002, from 10.4 million to 13.0 million lines. For the full year, advanced services lines of all technology types increased by 75%.
- About 10.8 million of the 13.0 million advanced services lines served residential and small business subscribers.

One last point is that the two current options for high-speed access, high-speed asymmetric digital subscriber lines (ADSL) and coaxial cable systems (cable modem service), grew at about the same rate in 2002, over 60%, with 6.5 million ADSL lines and 11.4 million cable modem systems at the end of 2002.

Digital Libraries

One institution that is undergoing a major change, and not surprisingly so, is the library. Given that information is what libraries are really about, the movement toward digital information has fostered a parallel movement toward the digital library, that is, a library with networked access to worldwide information and what is most important and frequently overlooked, the necessary expertise to search effectively for relevant information. Libraries face the dilemma of trying to maintain collections for the majority of their clientele that will require books for the foreseeable future, while responding to the emerging needs of those who would like to connect to the Internet as well as the hundreds of specialized databases that are available on CD-ROMs, or by online subscriptions. Academic libraries have additional burdens because of the escalating costs of journals resulting from a spiral of fewer subscriptions driving increased costs. Experiments in online journals have shown that costs could be reduced and turnaround time improved, but the case is not closed yet.

One other issue that demands attention is the problem of archiving frequently ephemeral electronic data. Should newsgroups be archived and if so who should do it and how? What about the archival media? While microfiche and microfilm have a very long lifetime, they are not a very convenient medium for search or retrieval purposes. Unfortunately, magnetic tapes, magnetic disks, and videotapes have relatively short lifetimes and are also technologies that will soon be obsolete. Optical disks will physically degrade in fewer than 30 years. Shakespeare's first printed edition of sonnet 18 dates from 1609 and is still quite readable.[86]

The Institute of Museum and Library Services issued a status report for 2002 based on the results of a survey on issues related to technology and digitization. Many of the findings are not surprising: "Library technology use is pervasive, particularly the basic technologies that automate and support services to the public."[87] Furthermore, almost all libraries, public and academic, have invested in desktop computers, access to the Internet, E-mail, a computerized catalog of the library collection, and even a Web site, for academic libraries. In ranking the primary goals of digitization, museums place increased access to the collections and collection records first and preserving materials of importance or value second. Public libraries place the preservation function first but rank the goal to increase access to books, journals, documents, and other materials second, while the top two goals of academic libraries are the reverse of the public libraries.

Given that most of the discussion so far has focused on the U.S., we might turn briefly to Europe in order to determine the library situation there. At a meeting held in Portugal, in March 2003, representatives from 36 countries with over 150 million registered library patrons "agreed on priorities to support the contribution of public libraries towards developing the information society." It was agreed that support of libraries and museums would be beneficial in the four following ways[88]:

- First, such measures would promote democracy and citizenship, as libraries provide community focused support and are attuned to the special requirements of groups such as those with disabilities, teenagers, the elderly, the unemployed, and those living in rural areas. Through the provision of Internet access, libraries can also support the take up of e-government, e-health and e-learning services.
- A second key benefit is the contribution of libraries, museums and archives to lifelong learning. Institutions should develop their roles as centres for de-institutionalised and informal learning, the participants said, and continue to promote literacy using all means, including the Internet.
- As Europe's most popular public Internet access points, libraries also have a key role to play in economic and social development, through providing access and training to those in risk of e-exclusion. Participants suggested that public institutions work together with local businesses to support the growth of the knowledge economy in Europe by providing valuable information services.
- A final aim for support initiatives should be the preservation of cultural diversity, say delegates. In particular, libraries should aim to support ethnic, cultural, linguistic and religious identities through the creation of a 'community memory' of digital resources available to all.

The roles of libraries and museums in fostering ethnic, linguistic, and national knowledge and pride cannot be overestimated, and the transformation to digital storage and access should be instrumental in increasing the effectiveness of these institutions.

One of the leading proponents of the digital library is Michael Lesk of Bellcore, who has written a series of papers on many of the technical and social issues facing the development of digital libraries, the economics of digital information flow, and the problems of digitizing images. A summary of Lesk's position is given as follows[89]:

1. Digital libraries are now economically efficient, and the area is booming
2. Digital technology offers great advantages for libraries
3. The adoption of digital information will mean changes in the role of libraries, and in how we manage them.

Rather than an extensive treatment of Lesk's arguments (which are available at his Web site, http://lesk.com/mlesk), the conclusion to the work referenced above is offered as a succinct summary of a very persuasive point of view[90]:

> In summary, it is clear that digital libraries are coming, both in free and commercial versions, and in both image and ascii formats. This is an opportunity, not a threat. Digital information can be more effective for the users and cheaper for the librarians. Access will become more important than possession. But this must be used to encourage sharing, not competition. The real asset of a library is the people it has who know how to find information and how to evaluate it. It must emphasize its skills in training, not in acquisition. If we think of information as an ocean, the job of libraries is now to provide navigation. It is no longer to provide the water.

PROSPECTS FOR THE INTERNET AND THE INFORMATION HIGHWAY

> In another dimension, the effect of the Information Superhighway on communities is likely to be extraordinary—and highly beneficial. The Council believes that dispersed communities, such as those in rural areas, will be brought together; that distressed communities, such as those in the inner cities of many metropolitan areas, will be joined in helpful communication; that neighbors will be better able to help neighbors online; that family members will keep in touch via e-mail; and that many people will join "virtual communities" of like-minded individuals wherever they may be. Similarly, the Information Superhighway will invite disabled persons to reenter the workplace, to enjoy entertainment with others, and to become full-fledged members of the emerging electronic community.[91]

In Chapter 1, a brief introduction to the Information Highway (IH) was presented. As envisioned by both the U.S. and Canadian governments, the IH was to be an ambitious, all-encompassing, broadband system, linking homes, schools, libraries, workplaces, and institutions of all kinds, and providing opportunities for business, government, and the public at large. Although the Internet is a work in progress, the IH is a vision in progress, and a great deal has been written and said that is pure speculation. Currently, as mentioned earlier, this vision has disappeared from the public agenda; so only a brief overview will be presented.

Government Views

Canada

The final report of the Canadian Information Highway Advisory Council was issued in September 1995. It contained a large number of recommendations on 15 different areas of vital concern. Some eight months later, the Canadian government responded with its commitment to the development of the IH. So many issues were covered that a brief review is bound to trivialize many important ones and ignore many others, but there are a few major concerns that have come to the fore. The Council was guided by three objectives and five principles[92]:

Objectives
- creating jobs through innovation and investment in Canada
- reinforcing Canadian sovereignty and cultural identity
- ensuring universal access at reasonable cost

Principles
- an interconnected and interoperable network of networks
- collaborative public and private sector development
- competition in facilities, products and services
- privacy protection and network security
- lifelong learning as a key design element of Canada's Information Highway.

Canada's objectives and principle are similar to the those of the U.S. except for Canada's concern with its "sovereignty and cultural identity." As a close neighbor of a country with 10 times its population and powerful international entertainment media, Canada has had a long-term concern with supporting its creative artists and providing ready access to its media. The IH could be seen as yet another powerful channel funneling U.S. content into Canada and overwhelming indigenous culture. Of course, Canada's concern is mirrored around the world as the global influence of U.S. culture is pervasive and threatening to many countries. It should be noted that the U.S. is not immune to such concerns, as U.S. law limits the degree to which its telecommunications companies can be owned by foreigners.

In response to the Advisory Council's report, the Canadian government issued a report in May 1996, in which it acknowledged its continuing commitment to and responsibility for the development of the IH. It would support Canadian content in a variety of ways, make sure all Canadians benefit by supporting learning and social networks around the country, make government services and information dissemination easier and faster, and protect privacy: "The ministers of Industry and Commerce, after consultation with the provinces and other stakeholders, will bring forward proposals for a legislative framework governing the protection of personal data in the private sector."[93] This was done in 2000.

U.S.

The United States Advisory Council on the National Information Infrastructure delivered its final report at the end of January 1996. It was only one of many committees and agencies charged with the responsibility of outlining and preparing detailed studies of the many dimensions of the IH, or the National Information Infrastructure (NII), from technical, commercial, social, and legal perspectives. The following are "five fundamental goals" the Council "urges the Nation [to] adopt"[94]:

> First, let us find ways to make information technology work for us, the people of this country, by ensuring that these wondrous new resources advance American constitutional precepts, our diverse cultural values, and our sense of equity.
>
> Second, let us ensure, too, that getting America online results in stronger communities, and a stronger sense of national community.
>
> Third, let us extend to every person in every community the opportunity to participate in building the Information Superhighway. The Information Superhighway must be a tool that is available to all individuals—people of all ages, those from a wide range of economic, social, and cultural backgrounds, and those with a wide range of functional abilities and limitations—not just a select few. It must be affordable, easy to use, and accessible from even the most disadvantaged or remote neighborhood.
>
> Fourth, let us ensure that we Americans take responsibility for the building of the Superhighway—private sector, government at all levels, and individuals.
>
> And, fifth, let us maintain our world leadership in developing the services, products, and an open and competitive market that lead to deployment of the Information Superhighway. Research and development will be an essential component of its sustained evolution.

Another informed vision of the NII was the product of a quasi-government agency, the National Research Council. In attempting to characterize so elusive a target as the NII, especially when projected several years into the future, the NII 2000 Steering Committee deliberately chose a very broad and inclusive definition[95]:

The national information infrastructure (NII) is the collection of all public and private information services, both facilities- and content-based, operating as a complex, dynamic system. It exists today but is and always will be in a state of flux.

This definition suggests that the NII is not a structure but rather a concept that can be used "to focus thinking about a very important set of resources whose value to society depends on their connectivity, accessibility, and functionality for many important purposes." Some of the tenets of the Information Society as compiled in this report are the following: broader and more user-oriented modes of information to be communicated, use of wireless systems for text or video communications, an erosion of the distinctions among home, work, and school because of the pervasiveness of communication networks, and the expansion of professional services over networks, as well as increased citizen participation in the political process in as yet unpredictable ways.

RISK AND SECURITY

Knowledge of the world and those who would do us harm is what is needed. Knowledge does not come from the accumulation of random data, but rather it is found in thoughtful and informed inquiries. Great progress can be made just with sensible, straightforward use of relatively simple tools and already-collected data. Inexpensive data checks, strategically planned, should have been able to prevent the 9/11 attacks. Yet, then, the government lacked the capacities to perform them. Now, more than a year later, the government still has not acquired them.[96]

On September 17, 1991, AT&T long-distance service in New York failed, resulting in 5 million blocked calls and a paralysis of the air traffic control systems. America Online's breakdown took place on August 7, 1996. In later years, denial of service attacks occurred, demonstrating the vulnerabilities of the Internet to dedicated and skilled hackers. Calls for increased security were heard more frequently but on the whole, few concerted efforts were mounted until that fateful day, September 11, 2001. Two commercial airliners crashed into the twin towers of the World Trade Center in New York, toppling the towers and killing nearly 3000 people, and another plane crashed into the Pentagon, in Washington. A new age of worldwide terrorism had begun and it was anticipated that the Internet and connecting networks would become prime targets, given the degree to which global commerce is dependent on the Internet. (See Chapter 11 for additional discussion of this topic.)

These and many other smaller, similar events, including breakdowns of more traditional communications networks, are reminders that the information society is supported by a fragile infrastructure of computers and communication networks, or perhaps more precisely, by complex and frag-ile software, as hardware breakdowns are rarely the cause of system fail-ure. As technology increases in complexity, the possibilities of accidents also increase and the results may be staggering. Witness such serious calamities as Bhopal, Challenger, and Chernobyl. Information systems underlie most of the present and future technologies at work, home, and play. As the requisite software increases in complexity, it becomes almost impossible to test it sufficiently to guarantee against failures that could occur under a rare combination of circumstances. Furthermore, current software, subject to repeated "patches," is itself quite fragile and likely to crash. Systems may fail for a variety of reasons such as human mistakes, both in the design and operation of the system, rare acts of nature, hard-ware breakdowns, events unforeseen during the design phase, overload, or various combinations of these.

Given that humans are subject to lapses of memory, periods of inatten-tion, and occasional physical disabilities, it is incumbent upon designers to foolproof systems as much as possible and to include clean, error-recovery procedures, because accidents will occur. The problems of developing strategies for risk management and reliability are difficult but obviously of growing importance if technological disasters are not to become a com-mon occurrence.

One major early source, still relevant, on computer risks and security is the book, *Computer Related Risks*, by Peter G. Neumann, who is the mod-erator of the well-known Internet Risks Forum, a clearinghouse of tales of warnings, disasters, risks, and remedies. In discussing where to place the blame, Neumann notes that, "most system problems are ultimately and legitimately attributable to people. However, human failings are often blamed on 'the computer'—perhaps to protect the individuals. The attribu-tion of blame seems to be common in computers affecting consumers, where human shortcomings are frequently attributed to 'a computer glitch.' Computer system malfunctions are often due to underlying causes attribut-able to people; if the technology is faulty, the faults frequently lie with peo-ple who create and use it."[97]

Neumann makes specific reference to the National Information Infrastructure (NII) and some of the associated risks to be incurred when vir-tually every computer in the U.S. and subsequently the world is potentially linked. The dimensions of risk are overwhelming, multiplying the traditional concerns: "It encompasses many now familiar risks and increasingly involves human safety and health, mental well-being, peace of mind, per-sonal privacy, information confidentiality and integrity, proprietary rights, and financial stability, particularly as internetworking continues to grow."[98] Finally, taking the highway metaphor seriously suggests a number of analo-gies to computer network malfunctions[99]:

traffic jams	congestions
crashes	system wipeouts
roadkill	bystanders
drunken drivers	accidents waiting to happen
carjackers	malicious hackers
drag racers and joy riders	bogus E-mail and switched vehicle identifiers
speed limits on the Autobahn	as well as the Infobahn
onramps and gateways	controlling access, authentication, and authorization
toll bridges	usage fees
designated drivers	authorized agents
drivers' licenses	system registration and inspections

As a conclusion to this section, the following advice of the social critic Jerry Mander as condensed from his "Ten Recommended Attitudes About Technology," is well worth considering[100]:

1. Since most of what we are told about new technology comes from its proponents, be deeply skeptical of all claims.
2. Assume all technology "guilty until proven innocent."
3. Eschew the idea that technology is neutral or "value free." Every technology has *inherent and identifiable* social, political, and environmental consequences.
4. The fact that technology has a natural flash and appeal is meaningless. Negative attributes are slow to emerge.
5. Never judge a technology by the way it benefits you personally. Seek a holistic view of its impacts. The operative question is not whether it benefits you, but who benefits most? And to what end?
6. Keep in mind that an individual technology is only one piece of a large web of technologies, "megatechnology." The operative question here is how the individual technology fits the larger one.
7. Make distinctions between technologies that primarily serve the individual or the small community (e.g., solar energy) and those that operate on a scale outside of community control (e.g., nuclear energy). The latter kind is the major problem of the day.
8. When it is argued that the benefits of the technological lifeway are worthwhile despite harmful outcome, recall that Lewis Mumford referred to these alleged benefits as "bribery." Cite the figures about crime, suicide, alienation, drug abuse, as well as environmental and cultural degradation.
9. Do not accept the homily that "once the genie is out of the bottle you cannot put it back," or that rejecting a technology is impossible. Such attitudes induce passivity and confirm victimization.
10. In thinking about technology within the present climate of technological worship, emphasize the negative. This brings balance. Negativity is positive.

FINAL REMARKS

> From the time of Gutenberg, and even before, information production has been controlled and has led to social stratification based on unequal access. What is of special significance about the current situation, is the centrality of information in all spheres of material production, as well as its increasing prominence throughout the economy. Today, information increasingly serves as a primary factor in production, distribution, administration, work, and leisure. For these reasons, how information itself is produced and made available become crucial determinants affecting the organization of the social system.[101]

That we, the U.S., Canada, Western Europe, and Japan, are moving toward an Information Society seems to be accepted dogma, even if the shape of that society is not well-defined. Throughout this book the various building blocks of the emerging information society have been discussed and associated societal implications described. It may be useful, at this point, to step back and attempt to assess some of the major overall features and large-scale impacts of that envisioned society.

Aspects of Information Society Research

One way to identify the important issues is to extract them from the body of research developed over the years. Consider the following characteristics so identified[102]:

Information Materialism, or Information as an Economic Commodity. From discussions throughout the book, it is clear that services are gradually increasing their share of the economy and that throughout the economy the role of information is assuming a dominant position. But it is not just improved information processing as a means to increase productivity that is of interest here; rather, it is information as a commodity, as a product in its own right. Various scholars have discussed this phenomenon, including Fritz Machlup, Daniel Bell, Marc Porat, and Andrew Oettinger.[103] There exists a problem of definition in this area, as information seems to be all-inclusive: information "goods" such as video cassette recorders, personal computers, and television sets; information gathered for one purpose reconfigured for another, for example, motor vehicle records used to identify potential purchasers for upscale products. Furthermore, although bought, sold, borrowed, or stolen information is neither durable nor intrinsically valuable, its commercial exchange does create a need to treat it as property.

Widely Diffused Information Technology. The development of global communication networks to instantaneously transmit information around the world holds enormous possibilities and is a major theme in any analysis of the Information Society. From McLuhan's global village to Ellul's technological society, computers and communications may well have eliminated geography as a factor in human society and perhaps real difference and choice as well.[104] Computers have become pervasive and virtually unchallenged as the leading edge of technological change. It seems almost impossible to think of the Information Society without the integral role played by computers.

Many Messages and Channels. An enormous number of devices that receive, send, and manipulate information have become ubiquitous in American homes: telephones, telephone answering machines, televisions, radios, VCRs, audio cassette recorders, compact disc players, home computers, modems, printers, and more recently, Fax machines, copiers, and laser printers. In addition, large and growing amounts of paper are flooding homes in the form of mail, newspapers, magazines, and advertisement circulars. They are indicative not only of the vast amount of information available to Americans but also of the power of the media to shape and influence public opinion.

Interconnectedness. Because of the power and growth of the new information technologies, boundaries and distinctions among institutions have begun to disappear. The facilitation of information flow has created unlimited possibilities for companies to extend their activities beyond their original purpose. Thus overlapping financial services are available from an ever-increasing number of companies: banks offer credit cards and credit card companies offer banking services. Many of these possibilities have resulted from the growing number of interconnected channels for carrying information, such as cable, satellites, direct broadcasting, personal computers for electronic mail, bulletin boards, and videotex.

A Large Information Workforce. Along with the growth of information industries is an obvious growth in the associated workforce. Through a variety of approaches, it can be established that the largest percentage of the workforce is clearly involved in the manipulation of information, not in the manufacture of goods. This situation surely has some important implications for the structure of society.

The Special Status of Scientific Knowledge. Scientific knowledge describes the language that scientists employ in discussing their work and communicating ideas. Given the importance of science to the development of technology and hence societal change, science must be supported as a special and privileged domain of inquiry. Thus scientific knowledge represents in economic terms "intellectual capital," difficult to measure but obviously fundamental to growth and progress. Note that social scientists are included, as their activities support the direct relationship between product development and market acceptance.

Information as a Commodity

Of all of the above issues, we wish to focus on the commoditization of information, or perhaps in a more felicitous description, information as a commodity. As mentioned elsewhere, the rapid growth of computers, telecommunications, and software has initiated a transformation in kind rather than degree; that is, it is not just that old things can be done faster but that new possibilities are created, that new markets are opened, and that new uses for old "products" are developed. Thus, information within companies is increasingly being used for purposes that transcend internal needs to external markets. Information as a commodity is not new, but technology has accelerated the pace at which new markets are created, and furthermore, the existence of vast amounts of information in both private and public databases has provided additional motivation.

A longtime critic of the power and influence of the communication and information industries is Herbert Schiller, who has noted, "the information sphere is becoming the pivotal point in the American economy. And, as the uses of information multiply exponentially by virtue of its greatly enhanced refinement and flexibility—through computer processing, storing, retrieving, and transmitting data—*information itself becomes a primary item for sale.*"[105] [original emphasis] The growing commercialization of information has some important effects on the role of public institutions, such as libraries, universities, and the government itself. As long as the costs of gathering, storing, and disseminating information were non-recoverable, the public was expected to bear the expense, but as soon as it was possible to profit from the information, as a product, demands were heard to remove government from the marketplace and to permit business to do its job. Thus the government is under pressure to privatize its information-distributing agencies or at least limit their roles to bulk distribution, permitting private companies to provide customized services, usually electronically, over the Internet.

SUMMARY

The gathering, processing, storage, and transmission of ever-increasing quantities of information is becoming the major activity of economically advanced societies. It is possible to connect, from the home, to a wide variety of computer networks, including, of course, the Internet and the World Wide Web, that provide services ranging from home banking to stock market trading. Electronic mail and bulletin boards are becoming popular far beyond their early audience of researchers and computer buffs, for communicating over long distances.

With the exciting world of Web pages and their glitzy graphics, sounds, and video, it is sometimes overlooked that earlier experiments, many unsuccessful, laid the foundations for current systems. One such experiment, called videotex—a two-way communication network—was intended to provide a wide range of information services, including shopping, banking, home security, education, and so forth. In many countries, especially France, but not the U.S., government-managed telephone companies assumed an active role in stimulating the growth of videotex. The most successful videotex system in the world was and is France's Minitel, whose growth was linked to the financial support of the telephone company. Minitel is still widely used in spite of the growth of the Internet. There was some concern that videotex would be controlled by a few large corporations and that its potential benefits would thus be compromised. A similar concern is held by some critics today.

Communicating online has become a way of life for many millions worldwide, whether by e-mail or by a host of other more sophisticated services. Synchronous communication via chat rooms, ICQ, or instant messaging has attracted many people including children, who find these services a necessary extension of their social lives. However, there are associated dangers as some adults have found these fora to be useful environments to lure children and other vulnerable individuals into potentially dangerous offline relationships. The online life is also rife with flaming and spamming, the bombardment of unwanted e-mail.

The growth of the Internet has fostered the parallel growth of virtual communities, that is, distributed networks of individuals who associate by communicating over the Internet to exchange information; support shared political, social, religious, ecological beliefs; and even to engage in make-believe games and relationships. Some have hailed these interactions as exciting ways to explore self (by assuming new personae), gender (by assuming the opposite), and any other variation on one's real-life situation. Many different selves can be projected to others, who are simultaneously exploring their repressed other personalities. These games are supposed to be liberating and to provide alternatives to difficult times in one's real life, but they could also be seen as avoidance and escapism.

Since 1993, there has been considerable discussion and publicity about the Information (Super) Highway (IH) and the changes it will bring to society, although much of the discussion under this term has virtually disappeared since the late 1990s. Governments have invested considerable resources in committees, conferences, reports, and books to outline projected benefits of the IH. It will connect the nation's homes, schools, libraries, community centers, and workplaces. New jobs will be created, new and unpredictable technologies will emerge, and those who have traditionally been silent will be given a voice. Such are the claims, but it will be necessary to first provide the required equipment and access or the silent will remain silent.

As the nation's economic infrastructure depends increasingly on computers and computer networks, the risk of breakdowns, with their associated costs, becomes a matter of serious concern. Much intellectual effort is being invested in improving techniques for building stable and fault-resistant systems, but it must be acknowledged that with complexity goes risk. The future is certainly exciting, but as societies prepare for such natural disasters as earthquakes, tornadoes, and floods, they must also prepare for disasters associated with the breakdowns of large, complex systems, especially when compounded by the threats of terrorism.

The Information Society has been a topic of study for many years. Concerns have arisen about the power of information and especially those countries that control its flow. Information itself has become a commodity, to be bought and sold, beyond its importance within companies as a means to improve productivity. As systems become larger and society more dependent upon them, the problems of failure become more serious. Whatever the future holds, the role of technology is crucial and the study of its impact must include the associated social effects.

NOTES

1. Michael Pastore. "PC Forecast Gets a Lift," CyberAtlas, March 20, 2002. Available at http://cyberatlas.internet.com/big_picture/hardware/article/0,1323, 5921_995051,00.html
2. The formal definition of videotex, adopted by the International Telecommunication Union, International Telegraph and Telephone Consultative Committee in 1984, in *New Telecommunication Services: Videotex Development Strategies*, ICCP, Information, Computer and Communication Policy Series (Paris: OECD, 1988), p. 9.
3. Jean Devèze. "Minitel™ and Its Residential Services," in Felix van Rijn and Robin Williams, (Eds.) *Concerning Home Telematics*, (New York: North-Holland, 1987), pp. 62–63.
4. James M. Markham. "France's Minitel Seeks a Niche," *The New York Times*, November 8, 1988, p. 29.
5. Riccardo Petrella. "Experiences in Home Telematics," in van Rijn and Williams, *Concerning Home Telematics*, p. 15.
6. Dermot McGrath. "Minitel: The Old New Thing," *Wired*, April 18, 2001. Available at http://www.wired.com/news/technology/0,1282,42943,00.html
7. Catherine L. Harris. "For Videotex, the Big Time Is Still a Long Way Off," *Business Week*, January 14, 1985, pp. 128, 132–133.
8. "Domain Survey Notes," Net Wizards, July 1996. Available at http://www.nw.com/zone/WWW/notes.html

9. *Ibid.*

10. "Internet Survey Companies and Constituencies," Last updated June 17, 1996. Available at http://www.nua.ie/choice/Surveys/SurveyLinks.html

11. *Ibid.*

12. John Perry Barlow. "A Declaration of Independence for Cyberspace," February 8, 1996. Available at http://www.eff.org/~barlow/Declaration-Final.html

13. David Manasian. "Digital Dilemmas," Survey: The Internet Society, *The Economist*, January 23, 2003. Available at http://www.economist.com/surveys/showsurvey.cfm?issue=20030125&CFID=11620703&CFTOKEN=6ffe0d-9687f683-841f-4429-b0a6-ca6cdbe20354

14. "The Accidental Superhighway: A Survey of the Internet," *The Economist*, July 1, 1995. Available at http://www.economist.com/surveys/internet/intro.html

15. *Ibid.*

16. Russell Kay. "A History Lesson," *Computerworld*, November 12, 2001. Available at http://www.computerworld.com/softwaretopics/software/groupware/story/0,10801,65574,00.html

17. Robert H. Anderson, Tora K. Bikson, Sally Ann Law, and Bridger M. Mitchell. "Universal Access to E-Mail: Feasibility and Societal Implications," RAND, MR-650-MF, 1995. Available at http://www.rand.org/publications/MR/MR650/

18. *Ibid.*

19. *Ibid.*

20. "C=}>;())" *The Economist*, October 6, 1990, p. 104. Different cultures may use different symbols; for example, the Japanese use (∧_∧) for smile as compared with :-) in Europe and North America. Happy is (∧o∧) as compared with :-)) for very happy. Exciting is (*∧o∧*) and cold sweat is (∧∧;). See Andrew Pollack, "Happy in the East (∧_∧) or Smiling :-) in the West," *The New York Times*, August 12, 1996, p. C5.

21. Russell Kay. "Emoticons and Internet Shorthand," *Computerworld*, January 14, 2002. Available at http://www.computerworld.com/softwaretopics/software/story/0,10801,67313,00.html

22. J. A. Savage. "Nonprofit Firm Seeks to Create Low-Cost Networks," *Computerworld*, October 8, 1990, p. 60.

23. Felicity Barranger. "Electronic Bulletin Boards Need Editing. No They Don't," *The New York Times*, March 11, 1990, p. 4E.

24. "History of Instant Messaging," Show.kit, (No date). Available at http://www.show-kit.com/download/samples/with/internet/html/slide6.html

25. Yuval Dror. "U.S. Awards ICQ Founder Patent for Instant Messenger Software," *Haaretz*, December 17, 2002. Available at http://www.haaretzdaily.com/hasen/pages/ShArt/

26. Jeff Tyson. "How Instant Messaging Works," HowStuffWorks, 2003. Available at http://www.howstuffworks.com/instant-messaging.htm

27. *Ibid.*

28. Available at http://www.webopedia.com/TERM/b/blog.html

29. Robyn Greenspan. "Blogging by the Numbers," CyberAtlas, July 23, 2003. Available at http://cyberatlas.internet.com/big_picture/applications/print/0,,1301_2238831,00.html

30. Jack Kapica. "Notes Toward a Theory of Flaming," *The Globe and Mail* (Toronto, Canada), August 2, 1996, p. A5.

31. Norman Z. Shapiro and Robert H. Anderson. "Towards an Ethics and Etiquette for Electronic Mail," RAND, July 1985. Available at http://www.rand.org/areas/r3283.html

32. Ed Korthof. "Spamming and Usenet Culture," *Bad Subjects*, Issue #18, January 1995. Available at http://english-www.hss.cmu.edu/bs/18/Korthof.html

33. Definition for "Spam (or Spamming)" taken from The Full Glossary. Available at http://www.matisse.net/webgen/glossary/pages/Definition.87.htm

34. A. Michael Froomkin. "An Introduction to the 'Governance' of the Internet," University of Miami Law School, 1995. Available at http://www.law.miami.edu/~froomkin/seminar/ilsx.htm

35. Detective Letha DeCaires. "Chat Room Liars," Honolulu Police Department, Crime Stoppers Honolulu, September 11, 2001. Available at http://www.crimestoppers-honolulu.org/tips/chatroom.html

36. "Raising Kids Online: What Can Parents Do?" New York State Division of Criminal Justice Services, 2002. Available at http://www.criminaljustice.state.ny.us/missing/i_safety/guid_pa.htm

37. "Declaration on Freedom of Communication on the Internet (Strasbourg)," *Adopted by the Committee of Ministers at the 840th meeting of the Ministers' Deputies* (Member States of the Council of Europe), May 28, 2003. Available at http://www.coe.int/T/E/Communications%5Fans%5FResearch/Press/News/2003/20030528_declaration.asp

38. George du Pont. "The Criminalization of True Anonymity in Cyberspace," 7 Mich. Telecomm. Tech. L. Rev. (2001). Available at http://www.mttlr.org/volseven/dupont.html

39. "Anonymous Remailer FAQ," Andre Bacard, September 4, 1996. Available at http://www.well.com/user/abacard/remail.html A FAQ (Frequently Asked Questions) is a guide to some arcane Internet topic usually structured in the form of a series of questions and answers, and maintained by a knowledgeable Net regular.

40. *Ibid.*

41. "Anonymity: Remailers: Cypherpunk remailers," Arnoud "Galactus" Engelfriet, September 4, 1996. Available at http://www.stack.urc.tue.nl/~galactus/remailers/index-cpunk.html

42. *Op cit.*, "The Closing of anon.penet.fi" August 30, 1996.

43. Front page of *The Observer*, August 25, 1996. Available at http://scallywag.com/obsfront.jpg Note that this item is a photograph of the actual front page. The stories, on page 16, are available at http://scallywag.com/obsin.gif

44. *Ibid.*

45. "Johan Helsingius Closes His Internet Remailer," Press Release, August 30, 1996. Available at http://epic.org/privacy/internet/anon_closure.html

46. Xeni Jardin. "Giving Sharers Ears without Faces," Wired.com, July 1, 2003. Available at http://www.wired.com/news/culture/0,1284,59448,00.html

47. Sherry Turkle. "Who Am We?" *Wired*, 4.01, January 1996, pp. 148–152, 194, 196–199.

48. Mark Slouka. *War of the Worlds: Cyberspace and the High-Tech Assault on Reality* (New York: Basic Books, A Division of HarperCollins Publishers, 1995).

49. *Ibid.*, p. 10.

50. *Ibid.*, pp. 61–62.

51. *Ibid.*, p. 63.

52. *Ibid.*, p. 66.

53. *Ibid.*, p. 68.

54. *Ibid.*, p. 97.

55. Lindsay Van Gelder. "The Strange Case of the Electronic Lover," *Ms. Magazine*, October 1985. Reprinted in Charles Dunlop and Rob Kling (Eds.), *Computerization and Controversy: Value Conflicts and Social Choices*, (San Diego, CA: Academic Press, 1991), pp. 364–375.

56. John Suler. "Identity Management in Cyberspace," *Psychology of Cyberspace*, April 2002. Available at http://www.rider.edu/~suler/psycyber/identityman age.html

57. "Frequently Asked Questions (FAQs): Basic Information About MUDs and MUDding," Posted in the newsgroup, rec.games.mud.announce, on August 31, 1996.

58. *Ibid.*

59. "The Characters in MUDding," Sheffield University, United Kingdom, (no date). Available at http://www.shef.ac.uk/uni/academic/I-M/is/studwork/groupe/chara. html

60. John Suler. "Do Boys (and Girls) Just Wanna Have Fun?" Gender-Switching in Cyberspace, *Psychology of Cyberspace*, April 1999. Available at: http://www.rider.edu/~suler/psycyber/genderswap.html

61. Shannon McRae. "Coming Apart at the Seams: Sex, Text and the Virtual Body," 1995. Available at http://dhalgren.english.washington.edu/~shannon/ vseams.html

62. *Ibid.*

63. Herb Brody. "Session with the Cybershrink: an Interview with Sherry Turkle," *Technology Review*, November 1995. Available at http://orca.csudh.edu/ ~jjeffers/courses/hci-turkle.html

64. *Ibid.*

65. "Discover Dialogue: Social Scientist Sherry Turkle, A Psychologist in Cyberspace," *Discover*, June 2003. Available at http://www.discover.com/ june_03/breakdialogue.html

66. "Online Communities: Networks that nurture long-distance relationships and Local Ties," Pew Internet & American Life Project, October 31, 2001. Available at http://www.pewinternet.org/reports/pdfs/PIP_Communities_ Report. pdf

67. *Ibid.*

68. Janelle Brown. "Life and Death on the Well," Salon.com, April 17, 2001. Available at http://www.salon.com/tech/review/2001/04/17/well/index. html

69. Let the buyer beware.

70. "Silencing the Net: The Threat to Freedom of Expression On-line," Human Rights Watch, 8(2 G), May 1996. Available at gopher://gopher.igc.apc.org: 5000/00/int/hrw/general/27

71. "The Internet Under Surveillance," Reporters Without Borders, 2003 Report, Available at http://www.rsf.org/IMG/pdf/doc-2236.pdf

72. "Reply Comments of Benton Foundation Before the Federal Communications Commission In the Matter of FCC 96-93, CC Docket No. 96-45, Federal-State Joint Board on Universal Service," April 12, 1996. Available at http://www.benton.org/Goingon/uniserv-replycomments.html

73. Michael Lesk. "Libraries and the Web," 1995. (To appear in *Libraries and Information World Wide*, 1996.) Available at http://lesk.com/mlesk/liww/liww. html

74. Peter Lyman and Hal Varian. "How Much Information?" School of Information Management and Systems, The University of California at Berkeley, 2000. Available at http://www.sims.berkeley.edu/how-much-info/how-much-info.pdf

75. *Ibid.*

76. Mike Yamamoto. "Legacy: A Brave New World Wide Web," News.com, April 14, 2003. Available at http://news.com.com/2009-1032-995680.html

77. David Becker. "Future: Is There Life After the Browser?" News.com, April 16. Available at http://news.com.com/2009-1032-995683.html

78. "Complaint Requesting Investigation of Various Internet Search Engine Companies for Paid Placement and Paid Inclusion Programs," Federal Trade Commission, June 27, 2002. Available at http://www3.ftc.gov/os/closings/staff/commercialalertletter.htm

79. "Report No. DC 96-21, Commission Establishes Joint Board and Initiates Rulemaking for Consideration of Universal Service Issues Pursuant to Telecommunications Act of 1996," Federal Communications Commission, March 8, 1996. Available at http://www.fcc.gov/Bureaus/Common_Carrier/News_Releases/nrcc6019.txt

80. *Ibid.*

81. "E-rate: A Vision of Opportunity and Innovation," Education and Library Networks Coalition, 2003. Available at http://www.edlinc.org/pdf/ErateReport070803.pdf

82. "The Ever-Shifting Internet Population: A New Look at Internet Access and the Digital Divide," Pew Internet & American Life Project, April 16, 2003. Available at http://www.pewinternet.org/reports/pdfs/PIP_Shifting_Net_Pop_Report.pdf

83. "Federal Communications Commission Releases Data on High-Speed Services for Internet Access," Federal Communications Commission, June 10, 2003. Available at http://www.fcc.gov/Bureaus/Common_Carrier/Reports/FCC-State_Link/1AD/hspd0603.pdf

84. *Ibid.*

85. *Ibid.*

86. Jeff Rothenberg. "Ensuring the Longevity of Digital Documents," *Scientific American*, January 1995, pp. 42–47.

87. "Status of Technology and Digitization in the Nation's Museums and Libraries," Institute of Museum and Library Services, 2002 Report, May 23, 2002. Available at http://www.imls.gov/reports/techreports/2002Report.pdf

88. "Ministers Highlight Role of Public Libraries in Strengthening the Information Society," Cordis RTD-News, March 26, 2003. Available at http://dbs.cordis.lu/cgi-bin/srchidadb?Caller=NHP_EN_NEWS&ACTION=D&SESSION=&RCN= EN_RCN_ID'Col'19977.htm

89. Michael Lesk. "The Future Value of Digital Information and Digital Libraries," A lecture given 9 November 1995 at the Kanazawa Institute of Technology Roundtable on Libraries and Information Systems, Kanazawa, Japan. Available at http://lesk.com/mlesk/kanazawa/kanazawa.html

90. *Ibid.*

91. *A Nation of Opportunity: A Final Report of the United States Advisory Council on the National Information Infrastructure*, Key Roles Section, January 1996. Available at http://www.benton.org/KickStart/nation.home.html

92. *The Challenge of the Information Highway: Final Report of the Information Highway Advisory Council*, Industry Canada, Ottawa, Ontario, September 1995. Available at http://info.ic.gc.ca/info-highway/ih.html

93. *Building the Information Society: Moving Canada into the 21st Century*, Industry Canada, Ottawa, Ontario, May 1996. Available at http://info.ic.gc.ca/info-highway/ih.html

94. *A Nation of Opportunity*, A Final Report of the United States Advisory Council on the National Information Infrastructure, January 1996. Available at http://www.benton.org/KickStart/nation.home.html

95. *The Unpredictable Certainty: Information Infrastructure Through 2000*, NII Steering Committee, Computer Science and Telecommunications Board, National Research Council, (Washington, DC: National Academy Press, 1996). Also available at http://www.nap.edu/nap/online/unpredictable/

96. "Protecting America's Freedom in the Information Age," A Report of the Markle Foundation Task Force," October 10, 2002. Available at http://www.markletaskforce.org/documents/Markle_Full_Report.pdf

97. Peter G. Neumann. *Computer Related Risks*, New York: ACM Press and Reading, MA: Addison-Wesley, 1995, p. 286.

98. *Ibid.*, p. 299.

99. *Ibid.*, p. 301.

100. Jerry Mander. *In the Absence of the Sacred: The Failure of Technology & the Survival of the Indian Nations.* (San Francisco: Sierra Club Books paperback edition, 1992).

101. Herbert I. Schiller. "Paradoxes of the Information Age," an address to a conference on microelectronics, Santa Cruz, CA, May 1983, as quoted in George Gerbner, "The Challenge Before Us," in Jorg Becker, Goran Hedebro, and Leena Paldan (Eds.), *Communication and Domination: Essays to Honor Herbert I. Schiller* (Norwood, NJ: Ablex Publishing, 1986), p. 233.

102. Jorge Reina Schement and Leah A. Lievrouw (Eds.). *Competing Visions, Complex Realities: Social Aspects of the Information Society* (Norwood, NJ: Ablex Publishing, 1987), pp. 3–9.

103. Fritz Machlup, *The Production and Distribution of Knowledge in the United States* (Princeton, NJ: Princeton University Press, 1962). Daniel Bell, *The Coming of the Post-Industrial Society: A Venture in Social Forecasting* (New York: Basic Books, 1973). Marc U. Porat, *The Information Economy, Volume 1: Definition and Measurement* (Washington, DC: U.S. Department Of Commerce, 1977). Anthony Oettinger. "Information Resources: Knowledge and Power in the 21st Century," *Science*, July 4, 1980, pp. 191–209.

104. Marshall McLuhan. *Understanding Media: The Extensions of Man* (New York: McGraw-Hill, 1964). Jacques Ellul, *The Technological Society* (New York: Alfred A. Knopf, 1964).
105. Herbert I. Schiller. *Information and the Crisis Economy*, (Norwood, NJ: Ablex Publishing, 1984), p. 33.

ADDITIONAL READINGS

Introduction

"America's Online Pursuits," Pew Internet & American Life Project, December 22, 2003. Available at http://www.pewinternet.org/reports/pdfs/PIP_Online_Pursuits_Final.pdf

Birkerts, Sven. *The Gutenberg Elegies: The Fate of Reading in an Electronic Age*, (Winchester, MA: Faber and Faber 1994).

Rushikoff, Douglas. *Cyberia: Life in the Trenches of Hyperspace*, (New York: HarperCollins Publishers, 1994).

The Making of the Online World

Berners-Lee, Tim. *Weaving the Web: The Original Design and Ultimate Destiny of the World Wide Web*, (New York: HarperSanFrancisco, 1999).

Dibbell, Julian. "A Rape in Cyberspace or How an Evil Clown, a Haitian Trickster Spirit, Two Wizards, and a Cast of Dozens Turned a Database Into a Society," *The Village Voice*, December 21, 1993, pp. 36–42. Available at gopher://jefferson.village.virginia.edu/00/related/NVR/VillageVoice

Godfrey, David and Chang, Ernest (Eds.). *The Telidon Books* (Victoria, Canada: Press Porcepic, 1981).

Nie, Norman H. and Erbring, Lutz. "Internet and Society, A Preliminary Report," Stanford Institute for the Quantitative Study of Society, February 17, 2000. Available at http://www.stanford.edu/group/siqss/Press_Release/Preliminary_ Report. pdf

Sigal, Efram et al. *The Future of Videotext* (White Plains, NY: Knowledge Industry Publications, 1983).

"Trends in the Evolution of the Public Web, 1998-2002," D-Lib Magazine, April 2003. Available at http://www.dlib.org/dlib/april03/lavoie/04lavoie.html

"The Web Maestro: An Interview with Tim Berners-Lee," *Technology Review*, July 1996. Available at http://web.mit.edu/afs/athena/org/t/techreview/www/articles/july96/bernerslee.html on July 26, 1996.

Communicating Online

Bower, Bruce. "Survey Raises Issue of Isolated Web Users," Science News Online, February 26, 2000. Available at http://www.sciencenews.org/20000226/fob8.asp

Canter, Laurence A. and Siegel, Martha S. *How to Make a Fortune on the Information Superhighway*, (New York: HarperCollinsPublishers, 1994).

Carnes, Patrick, Delmonico, David L., and Griffin, Elizabeth. *In the Shadows of the Net: Breaking Free of Compulsive Online Sexual Behavior*, (Center City, MN: Hazelden Information & Educational Services, 2001).

Davis, Carrie. "Kiss Your Privacy Goodbye: Online Anonymity Post-9/11," *The Internet Law Journal*, January 21, 2003. Available at http://www.tilj.com/content/ecomarticle01210302.htm

McCullagh, Declan. "P2P's Little Secret," News.com, July 8, 2003. Available at http://news.com.com/2100-1029-1023735.html

Shirky, Clay. "Social Software and the Politics of Groups," InternetWeek, May 10, 2003. Available at http://www.internetweek.com/story/showArticle.jhtml? articleID=7600047

Virtual Communities

Benedikt, Michael. *Cyberspsce: First Steps*, (Cambridge, MA: The MIT Press, 1991).

Bruckman, Amy. "Finding One's Own in Cyberspace," *Technology Review*, January 1996. Available at http://web.mit.edu/afs/athena/org/t/techreview/www/articles/jan96/Bruckman.html

Davis, Carrie. "Kiss Your Privacy Goodbye: Online Anonymity Post 9/11," *The Internet Law Journal*, January 21, 2003. Available at http://www.tilj.co/content/ecomarticle01210302htm

Froomkin, A. Michael. "Anonymity and Its Enmities," *Journal of Online Law*, 1995. Available at http://warthog.cc.wm.edu/law/publications/jol/froomkin.html

Grassmuck, Volker. "'Don't Try to Control the Network Because It's Impossible Anyway,' Interview With Johan Helsingius on Internet Remailers," *IC Magazine*, December 1994. Available at http://www.race.u-tokyo.ac.jp/RACE/TGM/Texts/remailer.html

Grossman, Wendy M. "alt.scientology.war" *Wired*, 3.12, December 1995. Available at http://www.hotwired.com/wired/3.12/features/alt.scientology.war.html

Heim, Michael. *The Metaphysics of Virtual Reality*, (New York: Oxford University Press, 1993.)

Hertz, J. C. *Surfing on the Internet: A Nethead's Adventures On-Line*, (Boston: Little, Brown and Company, 1995).

Rheingold, Howard. *The Virtual Community: Homesteading on the Electronic Frontier*, (Reading, MA: Addison-Wesley, 1993).

Turkle, Sherry. *Life on the Screen: Identity in the Age of the Internet*, (New York: Simon & Schuster, 1995).

Access

Bennett, Matthew. "A Broadband World: The Promise of Advanced Services," The Alliance for Public Technology, The Benton Foundation, 2003. Available at http://www.benton.org/Library/broadband/broadband-world.pdf

Bush, Vannevar. "As We May Think," *The Atlantic Monthly*, July 1945. Available at http://www.isg.sfu.ca/~duchier/misc/vbush/

"Connected to the Future," A report on Children's Internet Use From the Corporation for Public Broadcasting, 2003. Available at http://www.cpb.org/ed/resources/connected/03_connect_report.pdf

"The Deep Web: Surfacing Hidden Value," BrightPlanet, White Paper, July 2000. Available at http://192.41.24.235/download/deepwebwhitepaper.pdf

Digital Libraries: Universal Access to Human Knowledge. President's Information Technology Advisory Committee, Panel on Digital Libraries, February 2001. Available at http://www.itrd.gov/pubs/pitac/pitac-dl-9feb01.pdf

"Digital Libraries," Special Issue, *Communications of the ACM, 38*(4), April 1995.

"Federal and State Universal Service Programs and Challenges to Funding," United States General Accounting Office, GAO-02-187, February 2002. Available at http://www.gao.gov/new.items/d02187.pdf

Kling, Rob, Fortuna, Joanna, and King, Adam. "Real Stakes of Virtual Publishing: Transformation of E-Biomed into PubMed Central," Center for Social Informatics, SLIS, Indiana University, No. WP-01-03, October 3, 2001. Available at http://www.slis.indiana.edu/csi/WP/wp01-03B.htm

McClure, Charles R., Ryan, Joe, and Bertot, John Carlo. "Public Library Internet Services and the Digital Divide: The Role and Impacts from Selected External Funding Sources," Information Use Management and Policy Institute, Florida State University, January 2002. Available at http://slis-two.lis.fsu.edu/~jcbertot/DDFinal03_01_02.pdf

"A Nation Online: How Americans Are Expanding Their Use of the Internet," U.S. Department of Commerce, National Telecommunications and Information Administration, February 2002. Available at http://www.ntia.doc.gov/ntiahome/dn/anationonline2.pdf

National Research Council. *A Digital Strategy for the Library of Congress.* (Washington, DC: National Academy Press, 2000).

"The New National Dream: Networking the Nation for Broadband Access," Report of the National Broadband Task Force, Industry Canada, 2001. Available at http://broadband.ic.gc.ca/Broadband-document/english/images/Broadband_e.pdf

Prospects for the Internet and the Information Highway

"America in the Age of Information: A Forum." Committee on Informational Communications, National Science and Technology Council, July 1995. Available at http://www.hpcc.gov/cic/forum/CIC_Cover.html

Bennett, Matthew D. "A Broadband World: The Promise of Advanced Services," The Alliance for Public Technology and The Benton Foundation, 2003. Available at http://www.benton.org/Library/broadband/broadband-world.pdf

"Information Superhighway: An Overview of Technology Challenges." U.S. General Accounting Office, GAO/AIMD-95-23, (Gaithersburg, MD: U.S. General Accounting Office, January 1995). Available at http://nii.nist.gov/pubs/gao.txt

"The Internet Society," Survey, *The Economist*, January 23, 2003. Available at http://www.economist.com/surveys/showsurvey.cfm?issue=20030125&CFID=128 37840&CFTOKEN=190f5b8-3a01f412-7956-4b7f-8be6-f8d3c356c2d2

Risk and Security

Anthes, Gary H. "Hackers Step Up Attacks," *Computerworld*, June 10, 1996, pp. 65–66."Global Information Security Survey 2002," Ernst & Young, 2002. Available at http://www.ey.com/global/vault.nsf/Global_Info_Security_Survey_2002.pdf

Arquilla, John and Ronfeldt, David (Eds.). *Networks and Netwars: The Future of Terror, Crime, and Militancy*, (Pasadena, CA: Rand. 2001). Available at http://www.rand.org/publications/MR MR1382/

"CERT/CC Statistics 1988-2003." CERT Co-ordination Center, April 16, 2003. Available at http://www.cert.org/stats/cert_stats.html

Denning, Peter. *Computers Under Attack: Intruders, Worms, and Viruses*, (New York: ACM Press and Reading, MA: Addison-Wesley, 1990).

"Digital Security." *The Economist*, Technology Survey, October 24, 2002.

"How Americans Used the Internet After the Terror Attack." Pew Internet & American Life Project, September 15, 2001. Available at http://www.pewinternet.org/reports/pdfs/PIP_Terror_Report.pdf

Final Remarks

Berleur, Jacques, Clement, Andrew, Sizer, Richard, and Whitehouse, Dianne. *The Information Society: Evolving Landscapes*, (New York: Springer-Verlag, 1990).

de Sola Pool, Ithiel. Technologies of Freedom (Cambridge, MA: Harvard University Press/Belknap, 1983).

Katz, Raul Luciano. *The Information Society: An International Perspective* (New York: Praeger, 1988).

Miller, Stephen E. *Civilizing Cyberspace: Policy, Power, and the Information Superhighway*, (New York: ACM Press and Reading, MA: Addison-Wesley, 1996).

Mosco, Vincent and Wasko, Janet (Eds.). *The Political Economy of Information* (Madison University of Wisconsin, 1988).

15

ETHICS AND PROFESSIONALISM

Why be moral?	*Socrates*
Do the right thing!	*Spike Lee*
You know what's right!	*My mother*

INTRODUCTION

"Ethics has to do with what my feelings tell me is right or wrong."
"Ethics has to do with my religious beliefs."
"Being ethical is doing what the law requires."
"Ethics consists of the standards of behavior our society accepts."
"I don't know what the word means."[1]

Throughout this book we have discussed a wide range of issues associated with the use of computers and especially the Internet. Many of the examples have pointed to applications which might have detrimental effects on some segment of society. Among these examples are the following:

- The expanded role of computers in the office with the result that some employees, usually women, may lose their jobs or discover that their working conditions have changed for the worse: monitoring of their work patterns, reduced social interaction, fear of harmful effects of repetitive work, or restricted upward-mobility options.
- Computer-aided instruction causes some teachers to feel threatened because they know little about the subject, have not been properly instructed themselves, and are concerned about the impact on their students.

- Enormous expenditures on high-technology medicine—CAT, PET, and MRI scanners, for example—may limit the amount of money available for preventative medicine, which has a significant impact among poorer people.

- Governments maintain large numbers of databases, with information of all kinds about their citizens, and this information may or may not be strictly controlled. Either carelessness or maliciousness may result in the disclosure of personal information damaging to individuals or groups. (The terrorist attacks of September 11 have exacerbated this situation.)

- Someone breaks into a computer system via an Internet connection and just "looks around," copies some information onto his or her own computer, destroys one or more files immediately, or inserts a program, a virus or worm, to destroy files later in both this system and in others with which it communicates.

- Your daughter is a regular user of instant messaging to keep track of her school friends. But suddenly she has become secretive about some of her online activities and you think she might be involved in a chat room conversing with strangers.

- A company purchases a new spreadsheet program and several employees make copies to take home so that they can do some of their work there. Some spouses and children discover this new program and decide it will be useful for their clubs, or other purposes, and also make copies to share with their friends.

- A credit bureau releases information to a reporter on one of the consumers in its database, which causes considerable embarrassment and possible financial loss to that consumer.

- You are prepared to buy a new CD of a favored singer, but first you go to Kazaa to download a few songs, and then you download the whole CD.

- A worker is refused a new job for which she is well-qualified because the prospective employer discovers, via a commercial database to which he subscribes, that she has been involved, in a previous job, with a group attempting to organize a union.

- A group concerned about racist Web sites urges an Internet service provider to terminate the account of a client that it believes manages one. The provider refuses, claiming that he has no responsibility for the content of Web pages on his system.

- It's Monday and the essay is due tomorrow but you don't know where to begin. A friend mentioned a Web site that sells university essays on a wide range of topics; so what harm is there in having a look?

In all of these examples, to a lesser or greater degree, individuals or organizations have had to make decisions that affect their own lives as well as the lives of others. How these decisions are made, what the essential ingredients are, and to what principles, if any, appeals are made, form part of the subject of this chapter, namely, ethics and professionalism.

In the last few years, the concern with ethical behavior has moved from academia and religious institutions into the public consciousness, propelled by a number of events, some of which have been conditioned by recent technological innovations. Probably no area has had a greater impact, nor received more publicity, than the investment industry and big business in general. The spate of insider trading and stock and bond violations has given the impression that honesty and ethical behavior are in short supply when big money is concerned. Consider the following remarks taken from those who either comment on, or who are intimately involved in, the business:

- What is this—the business news or the crime report? Turn over one stone and out crawls Boesky's tipster, investment banker Dennis Levine, dirt clinging to his $12.6 million insider-trading profits. Turn over another and there's a wriggling tangle of the same slimy creatures, from minute grubs like the Yuppie Gang to plump granddads like jailed former Deputy Defense Secretary Paul Thayer.[2]
- As the revelations of illegality and excesses in the financial community begin to be exposed, those of us who are part of this community have to face a hard truth: a cancer has been spreading in our industry. . . . The cancer is called greed.[3]
- Not since the reckless 1920s has the business world seen such searing scandals. White-collar scams abound: insider trading, money laundering, greenmail. Greed combined with technology has made stealing more tempting than ever. Result: what began as the decade of the entrepreneur is becoming the age of the pin-striped outlaw.[4]
- The Justice Department is considering almost doubling the office's securities fraud staff . . . there is enough business there to support doubling the current effort.[5]

The public also had some strong feelings about insider trading—the trading of stocks based upon information not available to stockholders or the general public—and more recently, the vast financial losses finally reported by WorldCom and Enron. When given a selection of reasons that some brokers engaged in illegal activities, even though many were legitimately making hundreds of thousands of dollars a year, those surveyed in a *Business Week*/Harris Poll, taken during August 1986, answered as follows:[6] pure greed (56%), many others on Wall Street were doing it (21%), they made too much money at too early an age (11%), they were criminal by nature (6%). Most were not surprised by the revelations; when asked how common insider trading was, 63% said very common or somewhat common, 21% said it only occurred occasionally, and 5% said it was not common at all. Finally, 80% said that the news about insider trading had not made much difference in their opinion about people who work on Wall Street. This last result indicates either a surprising degree of cynicism by the general public or a level of sophistication and realism beyond that revealed by breast-beating market analysts who seem considerably more surprised than warranted, given their supposed expertise. One of the highest profile cases of the 1980s was Michael Milken of Drexel Burnham Lambert, who practically invented junk bond trading. He was convicted, heavily fined (although he managed to hold onto about $500 million), served a jail sentence, was barred from returning to his previous activities upon release, and was on the cover of *Fortune* to celebrate his return to an active and financially advantageous lifestyle.[7] It may be difficult to mount a convincing ethical argument to aspiring business school graduates that such activities as those engaged in by Milken should be avoided.

Some 10 years later, enough stories of financial misbehavior are reported that it does not seem that much has changed, although greater amounts of money must be involved to make the story newsworthy. For example, John Jett, head government bond trader at Kidder Peabody, was fired in April 1994, after having "concocted $350 million of phony profits over a 29-month period. He claims to have been acting with the knowledge of his superiors. The scandal led Welch [General Electric's CEO] to sack the Kidder [GE-owned brokerage unit] Chairman, Michael Carpenter."[8] The first three stories in the top 10 list of business stories, as rated by the Scripps Howard News Service for 2002, are the following[9]:

1. The $107 billion collapse of WorldCom—the largest bankruptcy in U.S. history—got Congress and President Bush to OK the most sweeping corporate governance bill since the Depression in hopes of restoring investor confidence. WorldCom eventually fessed up to fraudulently inflating its books by at least $9 billion.
2. Former WorldCom executives David Myers and Scott Sullivan, Enron chief financial officer Andrew Fastow, Adelphia Communications founder John Rigas and ImClone CEO Samuel Waksal were among those made to do perp walks for the press that prosecutors traditionally reserved for the toughest murderers and mobsters.
3. The Bush Justice Department won conviction of Arthur Andersen, the Big Five accounting firm found guilty of shredding documents detailing alleged abuses by Enron, the nation's top energy trader that went bankrupt late last year. The verdict shattered Andersen, accounting's longtime gold standard.

Another area of growing concern for applied ethics is the impact of recent developments in reproductive medicine, including in vitro fertilization, cloning, surrogate motherhood, frozen embryos, the use of fetal tissue in the treatment of Parkinson's disease, control of genetic defects by gene insertion, and planned pregnancies in order to obtain compatible bone marrow for older siblings. All of these technologies, as well as those on the horizon, challenge traditional views of parenthood and raise serious ethical issues for prospective parents, physicians, and of course the judicial system. The courts have already dealt with cases in which the surrogate mother, whose egg was fertilized by the husband of the couple wanting the child, changed her mind about giving up the infant. More recently, a surrogate mother, whose uterus was, in some sense, rented to carry an externally fertilized egg to term, petitioned for joint parenthood and was denied.

What if we knew more about the kind of person a fertilized human egg would eventually develop into? Which gender? What size? How high, or low, the IQ? Which illnesses would necessarily, or with known probability, plague this person? Gender can be determined *in utero* and it is not uncommon in some cultures for females to be aborted. Consider the following possibility of genetic testing[10]:

> New genetic tests are moving rapidly from research laboratories into doctors' offices, where they are being marketed as a way to predict people's chances of getting common diseases such as colon cancer, breast cancer and Alzheimer's disease.
>
> But instead of offering clear views of the future and strategies for altering it, genetic tests have raised the specters of DNA-based discrimination and loss of health insurance, and the prospect of people learning just enough to scare them but not enough to cure them.

Clearly there are serious ethical questions to be resolved, such as what is the responsibility of the physician to tell a patient that there is a 70% chance of a certain illness developing, when this may have a devastating effect on that person's siblings or children. There is more[11]:

> The stakes are high on both sides of the issue. The fledgling genetic testing industry, which foresees soaring profits in the next few years, is pushing hard to get its tests to market, arguing that patients have the right to learn about their own genes even if the information is incomplete or inconclusive. Similarly, health insurers desperately want the right to peek at their clients' genes to help predict their medical fates—and to set their insurance rates accordingly—in part because they are afraid that people who discover they have faulty genes may try to take out large policies.

Such cases in medicine and in business, and others in government, law, and science, have heightened the concern about ethics and professional conduct and raised such questions as whether there has been a decline in ethical conduct; if so, what are the contributing factors, how can the situation be improved, and what responsibility do the professional schools bear? In the wake of the insider trading scandals, several major corporations donated large amounts of money to business schools to endow chairs in applied ethics, presumably to raise the consciousness of future business leaders. Special commissions and panels were formed by government and professional societies to hold hearings, articulate the relevant issues, and form policies to help professionals deal with difficult problems. Many of the professions have codes of ethics, or codes of professional conduct to provide guidance and to serve as standards against which charges of inappropriate or unethical behavior can be evaluated. Even such a young discipline as computer science has developed codes both for academic practitioners and information-processing professionals. The form and purpose of these codes will be examined later in this chapter, as will some of the issues associated with professionalism.

Professionals have a responsibility to their clients—or patients—to their profession, to themselves, and to society at large. In some cases these responsibilities clash, and it is often difficult to resolve the competing interests. In the public's perception, professional societies tend to protect their members rather than to censure them and bring their actions to the public's attention. On those rare occasions when professionals cannot persuade their superiors that current practices violate ethical or professional standards and feel compelled to "blow the whistle," their societies are not always eager to defend their interests. Such an image has lessened the regard in which many professional societies are held.

How are professionals to acquire knowledge of what constitutes ethical behavior or proper standards of conduct? How can they recognize that they are confronted with an ethical problem and then do the right thing? Are the ethical decisions that a professional must make fundamentally different than those facing the ordinary citizen? The questions are numerous and relatively concise but the answers are long, involved, and often ambiguous. That is, there is rarely a situation in which the right thing to do is obvious.

ETHICS

> Whatsoever things I see or hear concerning the life of men, in my attendance on the sick or even apart therefrom, which ought not be noised abroad, I will keep silence thereon, counting such things to be as sacred secrets.
>
> Oath of Hippocrates, 4th Century, B.C.E.

It is obviously not possible to include an introductory course on applied ethics with a special emphasis on computer technology-related problems in the limited space available, but some important issues can be introduced, discussed, and pointers provided to more detailed and comprehensive treatments. In its most simplistic form, ethics deals with right and wrong. Among the earliest questions considered by philosophers were: How should one know what is good? How should one act to achieve it? The task has gotten no easier over the centuries. For the doctor, lawyer, and engineer, the ethical responsibilities of the ordinary citizen are compounded by professional responsibilities. Or are they? A brief overview of approaches to ethical behavior may be helpful.

Approaches to Ethical Behavior

> There can be no question of holding forth on ethics. I have seen people behave badly with great morality and I note every day that integrity has no need of rules.[12]

Most ethical theories are normative in character; that is, they attempt to define, by a variety of methods, what people should, or ought to, do in given situations. The breadth of such theories is determined by how comprehensive and principled they are. Other approaches are descriptive; that is, they describe what actually happens in the world and are supposed to be evaluated in terms of appeal to the real world. A statement that describes a situation as true or false could be answered presumably by looking for empirical evidence. Throughout this book many examples have been given of how individuals and institutions use computers, accompanied by comments that certain instances may be problematic whereas others seem to be socially useful. In the absence of an ethical framework, all such comments may be seen as gratuitous, as emerging from an unknown author, with questionable consistency. As the philosopher of computer ethics, Deborah Johnson notes, "ethical theories provide a framework for (1) getting at the underlying rationale of moral arguments, (2) classifying and understanding various arguments, and (3) most importantly, defending a conclusion about what is right and what is wrong."[13]

For the present purposes, we will explore some general issues related to ethics and ethical theories. Consider the following attempts to answer the seemingly simple question: What then is ethics?[14]

- First, ethics refers to well based standards of right and wrong that prescribe what humans ought to do, usually in terms of rights, obligations, benefits to society, fairness, or specific virtues. Ethics, for example, refers to those standards that impose the reasonable obligations to refrain from rape, stealing, murder, assault, slander, and fraud. Ethical standards also include those that enjoin virtues of honesty, compassion, and loyalty. And, ethical standards include standards relating to rights, such as the right to life, the right to freedom from injury, and the right to privacy. Such standards are adequate standards of ethics because they are supported by consistent and well founded reasons.
- Secondly, ethics refers to the study and development of one's ethical standards. As mentioned above, feelings, laws, and social norms can deviate from what is ethical. So it is necessary to constantly examine one's standards to ensure that they are reasonable and well-founded. Ethics also means, then, the continuous effort of studying our own moral beliefs and

our moral conduct, and striving to ensure that we, and the institutions we help to shape, live up to standards that are reasonable and solidly-based.

While we have suggested a variety of issues that may require ethical analysis and decision making, it may be interesting to sample the current sensibilities of the American workforce with respect to concrete concerns. A relevant survey was conducted in March 2001 of some 1130 respondents "required to use a desktop or laptop computer, e-mail, or the World Wide Web for business purposes, whether they worked from home, on the road, in a traditional office or in some combination of these settings."[15] Some of the relevant results, for the present purposes, are as follows[16]:

Behaviors considered at least somewhat unethical by the largest majorities (over 90%) of respondents are:

- Sabotaging systems/data of former employer
- Sharing proprietary company information with outsiders
- Listening to a private cellular phone conversation
- Visiting pornographic Web sites at work
- Exchanging vulgar or offensive e-mail messages
- Accessing private computer files without permission

Over half of the respondents believed the above six actions were highly unethical. Using company e-mail for personal use, Web-surfing, Internet shopping and playing computer games at work appear to be viewed as ethical transgressions by about half or less of the respondents.

Perhaps nowhere else in this study is the generational divide etched as sharply as it is with respect to perceptions of ethical behavior. Older technology users are much more likely than younger ones to consider each behavior as highly unethical. While there is a fair degree of consensus regarding the top four offensive behaviors, the biggest generational divides (20 points or more) appear in the following areas:

- Using work hours to search for another job
- Copying the company's software for home use
- Exchanging vulgar or offensive e-mail messages
- Blaming errors on a technological glitch
- Personal Web surfing or shopping at work

[T]he following are viewed as likely to be at least somewhat effective [at limiting undesirable behavior] by over 60% of the respondents:

- Banning all games from company computers
- Guidelines on personal use of company resources
- Warning notices to employees misusing company resources
- Monitoring Internet usage, e-mail transmissions and computer files
- Corporate training on ethics

These findings clearly show that people working with high-tech equipment are well aware of a variety of possibly ethical decisions that they may have to make. Are there any guidelines or tools that can be provided to help them? First, it is necessary to be aware of current approaches to ethics and then to focus on the more promising ones or those approaches that reflect what are the most popularly held positions and try to understand how effective they might be in spite of their limitations. One group of approaches is given below.[17]

The Virtue Approach
Focuses on attitudes, dispositions, or character traits that enable us to be and to act in ways that develop our human potential.

The principle states: "What is ethical is what develops moral virtues in ourselves and our communities."

The Utilitarian Approach
Focuses on the consequences that actions or policies have on the well-being ("utility") of all persons directly or indirectly affected by the action or policy.

The principle states: "Of any two actions, the most ethical one will produce the greatest balance of benefits over harms."

The Rights Approach
Identifies certain interests or activities that our behavior must respect, especially those areas of our lives that are of such value to us that they merit protection from others. Each person has a fundamental right to be respected and treated as a free and equal rational person capable of making his or her own decisions. This implies other rights (e.g., privacy free consent, freedom of conscience, etc.) that must be protected if a person is to have the freedom to direct his or her own life.

The principle states: "An action or policy is morally right only if those persons affected by the decision are not used merely as instruments for advancing some goal, but are fully informed and treated only as they have freely and knowingly consented to be treated."

The Fairness (or Justice) Approach
Focuses on how fairly or unfairly our actions distribute benefits and burdens among the members of a group. Fairness requires consistency in the way people are treated.

The principle states: "Treat people the same unless there are morally relevant differences between them."

The Common Good Approach
Presents a vision of society as a community whose members are joined in a shared pursuit of values and goals they hold in common. The community is comprised of individuals whose own good is inextricably bound to the good of the whole.

The principle states: "What is ethical is what advances the common good."

We will explore three common ethical positions: ethical relativism, held unknowingly by many people and groups; utilitarianism, favored by those who believe it is consistent with the operation of democratic societies; and deontological theories, holding the moral high ground—exceedingly difficult to make workable in the real world.

Ethical Relativism

When philosophers wish to disparage an opposing ethical theory they occasionally describe it as ethical relativism. Simply put, this doctrine claims that there are fundamental differences between the ethical principles of individuals, in the sense that even if agreement could be achieved on all the properties of the concepts being defined, there would still be disagreement on the principles. For example, in anthropology, a version of ethical relativism called cultural relativism holds that all disagreements follow cultural lines, although some may also derive from the differing constitutions and personal history of individuals. From this position it follows that there are no universal principles of what is right or wrong, that each individual's behavior must be viewed as relative to his or her own culture. One argument against this approach is that just because people behave in accordance with their culture's normative principles does not automatically mean that they should. For example, suppose at some university called Comp U., it is common practice for computer science students to attempt to gain entry into the files of all their co-students and leave behind a message indicating their success. At the end of the year, the student with the maximum number of verifiable coups is given an award. A graduate of Comp U. attends another university and upon being discovered attempting to enter a student's files, offers the explanation that at Comp U. it is accepted, and even encouraged behavior.

Utilitarianism

This term is most often associated with the English philosopher of the late 18th and early 19th century, Jeremy Bentham, but other British philosophers such as David Hume, John Stuart Mill, and Adam Smith are also connected to this ethical theory. The short-hand version of utilitarianism is that one must always act to achieve the greatest good for the greatest number. This definition obviously requires the definition of good, and the computation of the greatest good as well the greatest number for that good—not an easy task under the best of conditions. Bentham proposed a psychological theory involving pain and pleasure, from which a definition of happiness as the excess of pleasure over pain emerged. Maximizing happiness is equivalent to achieving the greatest good, or in Bentham's own words, the general principle of utility: "approves or disapproves of every action whatsoever, according to the tendency which it appears to have to augment or diminish the happiness of the party whose interest is in question." There are problems with the definition of happiness, as well as the calculus to compute overall good, but nevertheless the political consequences of the movement inspired by utilitarianism were positive in bringing about legislative reforms in England. The theory also places public good over private good without justifying this preference, implicitly arguing that what benefits society at large is better than what benefits the individual.

We should note that utilitarianism is just one branch of the more general theory called consequentialism, which argues in favor of actions that maximize good consequences. There are many other branches of consequentialism, such as act consequentialism which chooses that act that maximizes the good, and rule consequentialism, which chooses an act according to a set of rules such that the act maximizes the good.[18] It is important to realize that morality and ethics are substantial subjects that have a long and distinguished history and that this presentation barely scratches the surface.

Deontological Theories

In utilitarianism, it is the consequence of acts, not the acts themselves that are right or wrong. Deontologists, however, take the act itself to be prime and to carry moral weight. Thus, although under a utilitarian approach the happiness of some people may have to be sacrificed to achieve a greater good, for deontologists acts of this sort, as well as others, will have to be rejected. Deontological theories derive in part from the philosophy of Immanuel Kant (1724–1804), whose ethical theory is the most important rival of utilitarianism. Other philosophers associated with this approach, one version of which is referred to as the social contract, are John Locke of England and Jean-Jacques Rousseau of France. Kant's theory is built on three principles: the examination of the facts of moral experience, the analysis of the logic of ethical judgment, and the formulation of the metaphysical principles presupposed by ethical judgments, as distinct from scientific generalizations.[19] What has come to be thought of as most lasting about Kant's theory are his moral or categorical imperatives. A moral, or genuinely categorical imperative is a rule that commands a type of action independently of any desired end, including happiness. Kant's greatest contribution is the criterion of universality, "that is, the logical possibility of requiring universal obedience to a rule of action (logical for 'strict' duties and psychological for 'meritorious' duties). It expresses more precisely and unambiguously the 'golden rule' to be found in all the great religions."[20] Deborah Johnson expresses it as, "Never treat another human being merely as a means but always as an end in himself or herself."[21]

The obvious objection to Kant is that surely no one would agree that any one rule should always be followed, without exception. Sissela Bok, in discussing Kant's arguments in support of the maxim "Do what is right though the world should perish," notes that in Kant's time no one took such a maxim literally because no action of any individual could bring the end of the world. However, now such an act is a real possibility and certainly sheds a new light on the absolutist position.[22] Given an order to fire his nuclear missiles, should a submarine commander have second thoughts if he believes that the order is ill-advised under the current circumstances. "If we accept the need for exceptions to moral principles in emergency conditions, it becomes necessary to take every precaution to avoid the dangers that Kant rightly stressed—of self-delusion, misunderstanding, lack of moral concern, shortsightedness, and ignorance on the part of government leaders and advisors."[23]

Generally acknowledged to be the most influential political theorist of the 20th century, John Rawls, who died in November 2002, had much to say about morality, ethics, and justice. His work follows in the tradition of Locke, Rousseau, and Kant. Although it is impossible to capture such a complex philosophy, a brief quotation reveals much about the goals of his work.[24]

> Each person possesses an inviolability founded on justice that even the welfare of society as a whole cannot override. For this reason justice denies that the loss of freedom for some is made right by a greater good shared by others. It does not allow that the sacrifices imposed on a few are outweighed by the larger sum of advantages enjoyed by the many. Therefore in a just society the liberties of equal citizenship are taken as settled; the rights secured by justice are not subject to political bargaining or to the calculus of social interests.

A very clear rejection of utilitarianism is presented in these few words by Rawls at the outset of his major book, *A Theory of Justice*.

PROFESSIONALISM

> Computers have a central and growing role in commerce, industry, government, medicine, education, entertainment, and society at large. Software engineers are those who contribute, by direct participation or by teaching, to the analysis, specification, design, development, certification, maintenance, and testing of software systems. Because of their roles in developing software systems, software engineers have significant opportunities to do good or cause harm, to enable others to do good or cause harm, or to influence others to do good or cause harm. To ensure, as much as possible, that their efforts will be used for good, software engineers must commit themselves to making software engineering a beneficial and respected profession. In accordance with that commitment, software engineers shall adhere to the . . . Code of Ethics and Professional Practice.[25]

The emergence of professionalism—at first through associations, or guilds, of individuals in the clergy, law, and medicine in 11th-century Europe—has bestowed special privileges and special duties upon their members. In North America, the movement toward professionalism seems to be a necessary step to legitimize practitioners of a given skill. Along with doctors, lawyers, dentists, engineers, and others, computer professionals have seen the need to establish standards for membership in their community.

The major distinguishing (and controversial) feature of professionalism is the self-regulatory function of professional societies or organizations. Such societies define a separate group, with membership determined by standards they set and expulsion solely determined by them, as well. By maintaining high standards, societies hope to assure the public that all practitioners can be relied upon to serve the public responsibly and competently. For the most part, the public is well served, and in fact places considerable confidence in most of its professionals—especially doctors, dentists, teachers, and engineers. However, there is some sense that the major functions of professional societies include the maintenance of high income levels and the protection of members accused of improper actions. Societies attempt to proclaim their responsibility by disciplining wayward members, however infrequently, and by publicizing their stringent membership requirements. However, it should be kept in mind that the professional's allegiance is frequently divided: "Now the engineer's professional obligation to protect the well-being of the community, as well as to shun participation in deceptions, conflicts with another obligation: to serve as a faithful agent of his clients."[26] Another step taken in recognition of having achieved a professional status is the design of a code of ethics or standard of conduct by the society.

The philosopher, James Moor, argues for computer ethics as a special branch of applied ethics. He proposes the following definition: "*Computer ethics* is the analysis of the nature and social impact of computer technology and the corresponding formulation and justification of policies for the ethical use of such technology."[27] The term computer technology is meant to be quite comprehensive and includes hardware, software, and communication networks. This definition clearly focuses on the study and analysis of social impact, not overtly on responsibility and ethical behavior, although in his subsequent discussion Moor does include behavior: "A central task of computer ethics is to determine what we should do in such cases, i.e., to formulate policies to guide our actions." One question that immediately comes to mind concerns the actual need for a special branch of ethics related to computers. Why not automobile ethics, or camera ethics, or telephone ethics? Each of these technologies certainly raises a variety of social concerns and particular ethical problems, but those associated with the computer seem to have a special and far-reaching quality.

Those who are involved in developing the discipline of computer ethics are really attempting to respond to the concerns, within and outside of the field, about a class of ethical problems that seem to be tightly linked to computers, large and small, as well as computer networks, such as the Internet. Also of prime importance is the process of diffusing the accepted results into the educational system to inform both teachers and students about their power and responsibility.

Professional Codes of Ethics

> As an ACM computing professional I will . . . give comprehensive and thorough evaluations of computer systems and their impacts, including analysis of possible risks.[28]

Probably the best known and oldest code governing professional behavior is the Hippocratic oath, for the medical profession, attributed to the Greek physician Hippocrates (approximately 460–370 B.C.). For the computing profession, scarcely 50 years old, a code of ethics may be somewhat premature, as relevant issues are still emerging. Nevertheless, there exist many concerns specifically related to computers—such as the responsibility for gathering, verifying, storing, protecting, and distributing information—that seem to argue for the establishment of a code of ethics. Some applications of computers are sufficiently controversial that an ethics code seems to have intrinsic merit. Motivated by engineering concerns, Stephen Unger has suggested a number of features of such a code, as follows[29]:

- A recognition of the responsibilities of individuals
- An attempt to create a general recognition and acceptance of ethical behavior
- The establishment of readily accessible guidelines
- Justification for actions taken in opposition to directives by superiors
- Useful in lawsuits that may follow certain actions
- A statement to the public at large that the profession is concerned about the actions of its members.

A major problem in enacting codes is how to restrict them to matters of professional concern, without being influenced by political, economic, or religious opinions. For example, the U.S. Army Corps of Engineers used computer models to formulate economic policy with respect to the construction of large dam projects. The Department of Defense runs computer war simulations as a fundamental part of its planning requirements. Computer Professionals for Social Responsibility (CPSR) has focused on the role of computers and automated decision-making by the military in determining a rapid response to a possible attack by strategic missiles. CPSR has acted to make their colleagues aware of how their research might be used, to serve as a pressure group to influence public opinion, and to lobby the government. One's response to working on these projects certainly depends on one's political and social beliefs. Thus, drafting a code of ethics requires extreme care, treading a line between professional responsibility and personal belief, among many issues which must be considered. More on this topic later.

Mark Frankel identifies three types of codes of ethics: aspirational, a statement of lofty principles toward which members should aspire; educational, a pedagogical approach to explanation and guidance; and regulatory, with enforceable rules to govern behavior and determine compliance.[30] He also provides a list of eight functions that codes of professional ethics may perform[31]:

1. Enabling document. So that professionals may make informed choices
2. Source of public evaluation. So that the public knows what to expect of professionals

3. Professional socialization. To reinforce solidarity and collective purpose
4. Enhance profession's reputation and public trust
5. Preserve entrenched professional biases. It may be difficult to introduce innovations
6. Deterrent to unethical behavior. Code may provide sanctions and monitoring provisions
7. Support system. Against debatable claims by clients or intrusions by government
8. Adjudication. To deal with disputes among members or between members and others.

Some Codes of Ethics for Computer Professionals

Codes of ethics and standards for professional conduct have been adopted by the following major organizations that represent computer professionals:

Association for Computing Professionals (ACM). The oldest association for computer professionals, with considerable representation among academics, has a new Code of Ethics and Professional Conduct for computer scientists that was adopted by the ACM Council on October 16, 1992.

Institute for Electrical and Electronics Engineers (IEEE). Although it is primarily an organization for engineers, the proportion of the membership involved with computers has increased dramatically in recent years. The IEEE Board of Directors endorsed a simplified Code of Ethics, which includes coverage for computer engineers, in August 1990, which took effect on January 1, 1991. The new Code is shorter, clearer, and more attuned to a worldwide membership, according to a past president of the IEEE, Emerson Pugh, who initiated the revision.

The IEEE Computer Society and the ACM adopted the Software Engineering Code of Ethics and Professional Practice in 1999.[32] Because of its length, it is not included with the other codes.

Data Processing Managers Association (DPMA). The DPMA has adopted a Code of Ethics and Standard of Conduct for the managers of computer systems and projects.

Institute for Certification of Computer Professionals (ICCP). The ICCP offers a voluntary certification program for computer professionals and has a Code of Ethics and Codes of Conduct and Good Practice for certified computer professionals.

Canadian Information Processing Society (CIPS). CIPS adopted a brief Code of Ethics in 1975 and a more comprehensive version in 1984.

Other organizations related to information processing that either have codes or are in the process of adopting or revising them include International Federation for Information Processing (IFIP), American Society for Information Science (ASIS), and Information Systems Security Association (ISSA).

The ACM code is given in its entirety in Figure 15.1 (but without the associated guidelines), the IEEE Code of Ethics in Figure 15.2, the DPMA Code of Ethics in Figure 15.3, and the ICCP Code of Ethics in Figure 15.4. Not included here is the forward to the DPMA code, the associated standards of conduct and the extensive standards of conduct enforcement procedures, or the ICCP codes of conduct and good practice. C. Dianne Martin, former president of the ACM Special Interest Group on Computers & Society, and her husband, David Martin, identify a number of common themes in these codes,[33] of which the first six appear in all four codes: personal integrity/claim of competence; responsibility to employer/client; responsibility to profession; confidentiality of information/privacy; public safety, health, and welfare; increase public knowledge about technology. The following four appear in at least two codes: personal accountability for work; conflict of interest; dignity/worth of people; participation in professional societies.

A cautionary note about all these codes is that they lack procedures to deal with emerging issues resulting from technological advances. They vary in their success in integrating ethical behavior into daily activities and this must be an important concern, as computers continue to play a growing role in our lives. Other critics question the effectiveness of ethical codes and even the reasons for adopting them. Among the most prominent is Samuel Florman, engineer and author of the best-selling book, *Blaming Technology*. His opinion is expressed forcefully as follows[34]:

> Engineers must be honorable and competent. Agreed. But engineering ethics cannot solve technical problems or resolve political conflicts. It cannot determine which tradeoffs should be made between safety or economy or between growth and environmental protection. It cannot provide consistent guidelines for individuals who are troubled by conflicting loyalties. In sum, engineering ethics cannot cover up differences of opinion that are deep and heartfelt. . . . Engineers owe honesty and competence to society. The rest of engineering ethics is a matter of taste—which is to say, political choice.

Whistleblowing

One response to a situation involving an ethical dilemma may be the need to appeal to the public at large, because all avenues available internally seem to be blocked and there is no prospect that any change will be forthcoming. It is not an action taken lightly, for a great deal is at risk—personal reputation, career, professional status. Why do some people blow the whistle? Perhaps the situation they find themselves in is so intolerable, so offensive to their ethical standards that they cannot remain silent, they cannot walk away, they must inform the world[35]:

> "Whistle-blower" is a recent label for those who . . . make revelations meant to call attention to negligence, abuses, or dangers that threaten the public interest. They sound an alarm based on their experience or inside knowledge, often from within the very organization in which they work. . . . Most know that their alarms pose a threat to anyone who benefits from the ongoing practice and that their own careers and livelihood may be at risk.

Preamble. Commitment to ethical professional conduct is expected of every member (voting members, associate members, and student members) of the Association for Computing Machinery (ACM).

This Code, consisting of 24 imperatives formulated as statements of personal responsibility, identifies the elements of such a commitment. It contains many, but not all, issues professionals are likely to face. Section 1 outlines fundamental ethical considerations, while Section 2 addresses additional, more specific considerations of professional conduct. Statements in Section 3 pertain more specifically to individuals who have a leadership role, whether in the workplace or in a volunteer capacity such as with organizations like ACM. Principles involving compliance with this Code are given in Section 4.

The Code shall be supplemented by a set of Guidelines, which provide explanation to assist members in dealing with the various issues contained in the Code. It is expected that the Guidelines will be changed more frequently than the Code.

The Code and its supplemented Guidelines are intended to serve as a basis for ethical decision making in the conduct of professional work. Secondarily, they may serve as a basis for judging the merit of a formal complaint pertaining to violation of professional ethical standards.

It should be noted that although computing is not mentioned in the imperatives of section 1.0, the Code is concerned with how these fundamental imperatives apply to one's conduct as a computing professional. These imperatives are expressed in a general form to emphasize that ethical principles which apply to computer ethics are derived from more general ethical principles.

It is understood that some words and phrases in a code of ethics are subject to varying interpretations, and that any ethical principle may conflict with other ethical principles in specific situations. Questions related to ethical conflicts can best be answered by thoughtful consideration of fundamental principles, rather than reliance on detailed regulations.

**1. GENERAL MORAL
   IMPERATIVES**

As an ACM member I will . . .

1.1 Contribute to society and human well-being.

FIGURE 15.1 ACM Code of Ethics and Professional Conduct.*

1.2 Avoid harm to others.

1.3 Be honest and trustworthy.

1.4 Be fair and take action not to discriminate.

1.5 Honor property rights including copyrights and patents.

1.6 Give proper credit for intellectual property

1.7 Respect the privacy of others.

1.8 Honor confidentiality.

2. MORE SPECIFIC PROFESSIONAL RESPONSIBILITIES

As an ACM computing professional I will . . .

2.1 Strive to achieve the highest quality, effectiveness, and dignity in both the process and products of professional work.

2.2 Acquire and maintain professional competence.

2.3 Know and respect existing laws pertaining to professional work.

2.4 Accept and provide appropriate professional review.

2.5 Give comprehensive and thorough evaluations of computer systems and their impacts, including analysis of possible risks.

2.6 Honor contracts, agreements, and assigned responsibilities.

2.7 Improve public understanding of computing and its consequences.

2.8 Access computing and communication resources only when authorized to do so.

3. ORGANIZATIONAL LEADERSHIP IMPERATIVES

As an ACM member and an organizational leader, I will . . .

3.1 Articulate social responsibilities of members of an organizational unit and encourage full acceptance of those responsibilities.

3.2 Manage personnel and resources to design and build information systems that enhance the quality of working life.

3.3 Acknowledge and support proper and authorized uses of an organization's computing and communication resources.

3.4 Ensure that users and those who will be affected by a system have their needs clearly articulated during the assessment and design of requirements; later the system must be validated to meet requirements.

3.5 Articulate and support policies that protect the dignity of users and others affected by a computing system.

3.6 Create opportunities for members of the organization to learn the principles and limitations of computer systems.

4. COMPLIANCE WITH THE CODE

As an ACM member, I will . . .

4.1 Uphold and promote the principles of this Code.

4.2 Treat violations of this code as inconsistent with membership in the ACM.

---

*Bylaw 15 of the Constitution of the Association for Computing Machinery. © Association for Computing Machinery. October 16, 1992. Reprinted by permission.

FIGURE 15.1 *Continued*

We the members of the IEEE, in recognition of the importance of our technologies in affecting the quality of life throughout the world, and in accepting a personal obligation to our profession, its members, and the communities we serve, do hereby commit ourselves to the highest ethical and professional conduct and agree:

1. To accept the responsibility in making engineering decisions consistent with the safety, health, and welfare of the public, and to disclose promptly factors that might endanger the public or the environment
2. To avoid real or perceived conflicts of interest whenever possible, and to disclose them to affected parties when they do exist
3. To be honest and realistic in stating claims or estimates based on available data
4. To reject bribery in all its forms
5. To improve the understanding of technology, its appropriate application, and potential consequences
6. To maintain and improve our technical competence and to undertake technological tasks for others only if qualified by training or experience, or after full disclosure of pertinent limitations
7. To seek, accept, and offer honest criticism of technical work, to acknowledge and correct errors, and to credit properly the contribution of others
8. To treat fairly all persons regardless of such factors as race, religion, gender, disability, age, or national origin
9. To avoid injuring others, their property, reputation, or employment by false or malicious action
10. To assist colleagues in their professional development and to support them in following this code of ethics.

*The Institute, A News Supplement to IEEE Spectrum, October 1990, p. 2.

© 1997 IEEE. Reprinted, with permission, from The Institute of Electrical and Electronics Engineers.

FIGURE 15.2 IEEE Code of Ethics*

As Sissela Bok further notes, three factors make whistleblowing a particularly unsettling act, for everyone concerned[36]:

Dissent. By whistleblowing private dissent becomes public.

Breach of Loyalty. The whistleblower acts against his or her own associates, or team. What about implicit or explicit oaths of loyalty and the sense of betrayal that their violation arouses?

Accusation. It is the charge of impropriety itself that most upsets people. Individuals or groups are singled out as having behaved badly, as having violated the public trust, as having turned their back on responsible behavior.

In spite of the terrible costs involved, whistleblowing is not a rare event. It happens in government bureaucracies, in large companies, and in other institutions. Motives may be political—to expose hidden government policy as in

I acknowledge:

That I have an obligation to management, therefore, I shall promote the understanding of information processing methods and procedures to management using every resource at my command.

That I have an obligation to my fellow members, therefore, I shall uphold the high ideals of DPMA as outlined in its International Bylaws. Further, I shall cooperate with my fellow members and shall treat them with honesty and respect at all times.

That I have an obligation to society and will participate to the best of my ability in the dissemination of knowledge pertaining to the general development and understanding of information processing. Further, I shall not use knowledge of a confidential nature to further my personal interest, nor shall I violate the privacy and confidentiality of information entrusted to me or to which I may gain access.

That I have an obligation to my employer whose trust I hold, therefore, I shall endeavor to discharge this obligation to the best of my ability, to guard my employer's interests, and to advise him or her wisely and honesty.

That I have an obligation to my country, therefore, in my personal, business, and social contacts, I shall uphold my nation and shall honor the chosen way of life of my fellow citizens.

I accept these obligations as a personal responsibility and as a member of this association. I shall actively discharge these obligations and I dedicate myself to that end.

Data Management, October 1981, p. 58. © 1981 Data Processing Management Association. All Rights Reserved.

FIGURE 15.3 DPMA Code of Ethics*

Certified computer professionals, consistent with their obligation to the public at large, should promote the understanding of data processing methods and procedures using every resource at their command.

Certified computer professionals have an obligation to their profession to uphold the high ideals and the level of personal knowledge as evidenced by the Certificate held. They should also encourage the dissemination of knowledge pertaining to the development of the computer profession.

Certified computer professionals have an obligation to serve the interests of their employers and clients loyally, diligently, and honestly.

Certified computer professionals must not engage in any conduct or commit any act which is discreditable to the reputation or integrity of the data processing profession.

Certified computer professionals must not imply that the Certificates which they hold are their sole claim to professional competence.

Your Guide to Certification as a Computer Professional, Institute for Certification of Computer Professionals, © 1973 ICCP.

FIGURE 15.4 ICCP Code of Ethics*

the case of Daniel Ellsberg and the Pentagon Papers—or because of a perceived violation of accepted professional standards. A 1993 report by the U.S. General Accounting Office (GAO) noted that, "A survey of federal workers who have sought whistleblower reprisal protection from the Office of Special Counsel (OSC) found that the vast majority were frustrated with the complaint process and did not believe that investigators gathered all of the information needed to examine their claims."[37] GAO called for an education program for federal workers to improve their awareness of "their right to protection from whistleblower reprisals." The very existence of the government's whistleblowing program is encouraging but somewhat paradoxical given that the government is setting rules for its employees to inform against it and be protected as well.

If any institution demands complete loyalty in the chain of command, it is the military, and breaches of this central and hallowed injunction are neither taken lightly nor treated lightly when discovered. Hence, the 1988 Military Whistleblower Protection Act, if seriously intended to protect those with sufficient courage to reveal serious problems must also prove to be effective in its execution. Not surprisingly, all was not smooth and the GAO was called in to review the quality of protection provided by the Act.[38] One of the interesting features of the Act is that only those whistleblowers who complain to the Department of Defense's Inspector General fall under its protection. Of particular interest to this study is that allegations existed that some whistleblowers had been subject to mental health evaluations. Very few cases were available for investigation but the GAO concluded that reprisals for whistleblowing did occur. The use of mental health examinations is interesting because in the heyday of the Soviet Union, dissenters were frequently placed in mental institutions to undergo evaluations. Queries from the West were met with responses that, no, they were not being punished for their political beliefs, but were merely undergoing standard psychiatric evaluations, which required considerable time and effort. These examples reinforce the widely held belief that, in the case of whistleblowing, doing the right thing can be dangerous.

Another GAO report released in 2000 presented results of a survey at the Department of Veterans' Affairs. In 1994, the Whistleblower Protection Act amendments had been enacted "to inform employees about their rights to protection against reprisal when reporting misconduct." The GAO had discovered among other things the following somewhat disturbing result[39]:

> Despite VA's actions, our survey results indicate that the majority of VA employees had limited, or no, knowledge about their rights to whistleblower protection. For example, about 57 percent of VA employees had not received, or did not know whether they had received, any information from VA about their right to protection from reprisal when reporting misconduct in VA. About 43 percent of VA employees reported that they were not

aware or only somewhat aware that laws exist to protect them if they "blow the whistle" on misconduct. These survey results are one measure of the effectiveness of VA's efforts to inform its employees about whistleblower protection.

On their willingness to report misconduct, 83 percent of VA employees supported from a great to very great extent the idea that VA employees should report misconduct, but a smaller number, about 50 percent, would be either generally or very willing to report it if they became aware of misconduct. Our survey results concerning the willingness of VA employees to report misconduct indicate, however, that a fear of reprisal in the existing organizational culture could deter VA employees from coming forth with allegations of misconduct. For example, only about 21 percent of VA employees reported that protection against reprisal is generally or very adequate.

Some Thoughts on Ethical Codes for Computer Professionals

The previous discussion suggests a number of features that ethical codes for professionals should contain, with special emphasis on computer-related issues. The following list is illustrative rather than exhaustive, but it does indicate a variety of concerns that an effective code must address:

Readability, Elegance, and Generality. The code should be easily understood or it will not be useful. Elegance is a bonus but generality is a necessity; otherwise, the code will be extremely lengthy and unwieldy. In this regard, the IEEE Code is a model. The ACM code, however, is considerably longer especially if the associated guidelines are included, but the explanatory sections (not included in Figure 15.1) are very helpful in understanding the intentions of the various imperatives and responsibilities.

"Living" Code. It must be the original intention of the society that the code is written to be used and therefore its use must be regularly monitored and it must be regularly updated.

Responsibility of the Society for the Ethical Behavior of Its Members. Enunciating a code is just a first step. The society must respond to questions and problems raised by its members, quickly and effectively. It must use its good offices with employers and act as an ombudsman for its members.

Legal Liability of the Society for the Actions of Its Members and for the Enforcement of Its Code. Some important issues must be settled with respect to what, if any, legal liability the society has for the actions of its members.

Responsibility of the Society to Educate, Train, and Inform Its Members of Their Rights and Responsibilities. The society must provide regular training and educational sessions to upgrade the professional qualifications of its members, to assure that they meet minimal standards of performance, and to guarantee that they are fully aware of their rights and responsibilities under the Code of Ethics.

Problems Specific to Computer Professionals Must be Addressed. There are a number of issues of special interest to computer professionals that should be addressed at the risk of violating the injunctions about elegance and generality. Among these are ethical behavior with respect to intellectual property (when software should be copied), privacy (awareness of issues associated with databases, their development, maintenance, and use, electronic mail, and electronic monitoring), computer crime (viruses, worms, and hackers), and computer risks (system security and breakdowns).

Additional Responsibilities for Professional Societies

The existence even of a carefully crafted code does not begin to exhaust the responsibilities of professional societies to their members. Simply put, what can a professional expect by way of support if he or she encounters difficulties in attempting to follow his or her reading of the code? In attempting to respond to this basic question, two professional societies were compared, ACM and IEEE, in terms of how well they advertised their responsibilities to their respective members on their Web sites. As a result of this examination, the following recommendations were proposed, involving in part a new or existing ethics committee[40]:

- Ensure that incoming members are made fully aware of the Code and are responsible for a basic understanding of its import.
- Advocate a variety of ways in which the Code could be brought to the attention of new and existing members and be responsible for implementing them.
- Advertise to the membership that it is available for consultation and advice. Guidelines should be drawn up by the society's executive with respect to the legitimate activities of the ethics committee in this regard.
- Report annually to the membership via the society's major publication about the nature of the cases it has dealt with and the major issues that have arisen, respecting confidentiality of course.
- Hold regular meetings, both nationally and internationally, to discuss issues and report to the membership at large.
- Promote speaker tours to inform students and faculty about its activities and the possibilities of curriculum development in this area.

- Serve as the repository for ethics cases and develop a recognized group of advisors and consultants, whose expertise can be used for a number of purposes.
- Make recommendations to the society's executive for revisions to the Code, that will become inevitable, given the dynamic nature of most active disciplines.
- Serve as the public voice of the society for questions of ethics and professionalism that may arise in the future.

This paper concluded with a call for professional societies to fully exercise their responsibilities: "Professional societies must provide advice, counseling, support, and advocacy for their members and surely this goes beyond the promulgation of a code of ethics and/or professional standards. They must ensure that their members are regularly informed about what is expected of them as professionals and make available to them their expertise, experience, and support where useful and appropriate."[41]

Political Actions by Professional Societies

Professional societies are supposed to represent the best interests of their members. Of course, what is best is usually determined by the executive committee of the organization and may involve appeals to the general public to explain recent actions by members or to drum up support for actions to be taken. The government may be petitioned to implement certain procedures and regulations that affect the working lives of the professionals or it may be lobbied with respect to procedures and regulations that affect society at large and about which the professional society has some expertise. This latter situation brings to the fore a pivotal question about the role of professional societies: What responsibility, if any, do they have in engaging in political activity that is not directly related to the professional lives of their members? Of course some organizations have been formed by professionals to carry out political lobbying and public education and obviously people join because they believe in these activities. The question is directed only at traditional professional societies. A few examples might help in answering it.

In March 1991, the ACM issued a statement on privacy urging its members to observe the privacy provisions of its Code of Professional Conduct, affirming its support for the Code of Fair Information Practices, and supporting "the establishment of a proactive governmental privacy protection mechanism in those countries that do not currently have such mechanisms, including the United States, that would ensure individual privacy safeguards."[42] Four years later, the presidents of five leading U.S. computer organizations, American Association for Artificial Intelligence, ACM, Computer Professionals for Social Responsibility, IEEE Computer Society, and Society for Industrial and Applied Mathematics, wrote a letter to Senator James Exxon expressing their concern about the proposed

Communications Decency Act. In part they noted, "this legislation would impose unreasonable technical and financial burdens on the increasing number of institutions, large and small, that rely on the Internet for communication. We believe that these burdens will significantly harm the technological and communications opportunities now emerging from the Internet."[43] Of course, a year later this legislation, as part of the Telecommunications Act of 1996, was enacted. Subsequently, in 1997, parts of the Act were found unconstitutional by the Supreme Court.

That the lobbying efforts initially failed is not the issue. What is important is that professional societies engaged in vigorous lobbying efforts to influence the shape of legislation that would affect all Americans. Presumably individual members of these societies had differing opinions about the merits of the Communications Decency Act as well as the actions of their societies. But many members must have felt that their professional society was acting in accordance with its code of professional conduct, or its equivalent, and were encouraged to see what many had felt to be abstract principles being put into practice. Such actions could not help but reinforce a sense of professional responsibility in the minds of the members of these societies and further encourage them to act responsibly in their own individual professional lives. It should be noted that the ACM and other societies also took actions with respect to the government's proposals on copyright (Information Infrastructure Copyright Act, H.R. 2441) and encryption, by supporting the legislation introduced by Senator Conrad Burns (Encrypted Communications Privacy Act) to counter the Clinton administration's proposals.[44]

PEDAGOGY AND ETHICS

A man's ethical behavior should be based effectually on sympathy, education, and social ties; no religious basis is necessary. Man would indeed be in a poor way if he had to be restrained by fear of punishment and hope of reward after death.

Albert Einstein (1879–1955)[45]

What is the expected outcome of a program to instruct soon-to-be computer professionals in ethics and professionalism? To answer this question, one must acknowledge that computer scientists, like other professionals, face situations that require coming to terms with conflicting goals that may seem equally worthwhile. It is impossible to make an informed decision without first understanding, as well as one practically can, the issues involved, their interrelationships, and their impacts, no matter how convoluted these may be. This section may therefore serve as an introductory *Guide to the Perplexed*,[46] by suggesting some ways in which difficult decisions can be made, given the prior requirement, that the existence of one or more problems is perceived and acknowledged. Assuming responsibility for one's actions is at the heart of the matter and clearly beyond the scope of pedagogy. Exploration, identification, discussion, analysis, and appeal to social, legal, historical, philosophical, and yes, religious principles, are all part of the process of growing and nurturing ethical antennae, but the translation to action depends ultimately on personal choice, and that is as it should be.

Recent proposals for teaching applied ethics to computer science and information systems students will be presented in the context of the kinds of issues that arise in computing environments such as the office, the school, and the Internet. A series of representative case studies will be introduced and analyzed as part of the process of developing abilities to recognize situations that do require ethical analysis and how to proceed in that endeavor. Two important concerns must be kept in mind: The discussion is not to be viewed as a handbook and it is not and cannot be exhaustive. If one is left feeling uncomfortable, it should not be surprising. Knowing when to do the right thing is difficult, and *doing* it is even more difficult.

Teaching Ethical Behavior in Computing

Project Impact CS

An attempt to create a meaningful ethical component in the computer science curriculum, Project Impact CS, was undertaken in 1994 under the leadership of C. Dianne Martin (George Washington University) and Chuck Huff (St. Olaf's College) and involved a steering committee of prominent computer scientists and applied ethicists. Since then it has produced a series of reports that include a particular strategy in presenting the social issues that arise in computer projects and implementations and the ethical and social principles and skills necessary to deal with them. The issues that motivate the development of the ethics curriculum are similar to those discussed previously. For example, consider the following questions[47]:

- Who is accountable when bugs in medical software result in patient deaths?
- Is being an imposter on a bulletin board system, creating violations of trust mitigated by the fact that some positive result is also achieved?
- When a multimillion-dollar software project is behind schedule, should technical staffers who doubt it can be rescheduled and completed as promised inform the client organization?
- Should there be limits to how managers and owners of private firms examine the movements of their employees?
- Are computer scientists morally responsible for anticipating and publicizing the problems that could result from the systems they designed?

A general framework for organizing the relationship between topics in ethical analysis and levels of social analysis can be thought of as a chart in which the columns are divided into classes, namely, Responsibility (individual and professional) and Ethical Issues (quality of life, use of power, risks and reliability, property rights, privacy, equity and access, and honesty and deception), and the rows are categorized as individuals, communities and groups, organizations, cultures, institutional sectors, nations, and global structures. Thus the entire framework could be represented as a series of charts, each one headed by a particular technology, such as medical, computer-aided manufacturing, or electronic communications, with individual relevant intersections identified where appropriate.[48] Identifying which levels of social analysis are relevant to which topics of ethical analysis for a given computer-related technology is an important exercise in understanding the complexities of social impact and ethical responsibility. Obviously, there is much more, but for the present it is useful to list the important ethical and social principles and skills that the Steering Committee highlighted[49]:

Ethical Principles
- Ethical claims can be discussed rationally.
- Ethical claims must be defended with reason.
- Ethical choices cannot be avoided.
- Some easy ethical approaches are questionable.

Ethical Skills
- Arguing from example, analogy, and counter-example.
- Identifying ethical principles and stakeholders in concrete situations.
- Identifying and evaluating alternative courses of action.
- Applying ethical codes to concrete situations.

Social Principles
- Social context influences the design and use of technology.
- Power relations are central to all social interactions.
- Technology embodies value decisions made by designers.
- Empirical data is crucial to the design process.

Social Skills
- Identifying and interpreting the social context of a particular implementation.
- Identifying assumptions and values embedded in a particular design.
- Evaluating, by use of empirical data, a particular implementation of a technology.

Learning about ethics and professional codes and standards provides a rich library of acknowledged principles that can subsequently be employed in the tasks described above. As noted, the professional lives of many computer scientists will not be empty of ethical challenges, and it is hoped that by providing a rich and integrated program of instruction they will be equipped to undertake a useful examination of these challenges and discover approaches to confront them.

Teaching Business Ethics

Business schools have been involved in the attempt to make ethics a meaningful part of the curriculum for quite a while, with mixed empirical results. Consider the problem facing instructors of ethics courses in business schools[50]:

> For long-term survival, any economic system requires a moral component. This assumption leads to the call for teaching ethics courses in our business schools. . . . However, because America's free-enterprise economic ideology assumes no vocabulary of ethics, students come to our classes without categories for ethical reasoning in the context of business. Given the importance of teaching business ethics, it is incumbent on business school professors to devise effective pedagogical methods for stimulating the moral imagination of their students who enter business ethics courses without a vocabulary permitting them to discuss business decisions and dilemmas in moral terms.

At the risk of quibbling about the assumptions underlying this enterprise, we question the first sentence of this quotation and the necessary inference that "teaching business ethics is important." Some would argue that the only moral imperative of business is to succeed, that is, be profitable, and from this, good things will follow. To be fair, the authors note later in the paper that, "Because the amoral theory of business holds sway today, business students enter our courses without a vocabulary of ethics for economic relations." One version of this "amoral theory" is that obedience to the law is all that is required of a business; another version is that since no universal ethical theory exists, individuals can decide for themselves what is ethical or that narrow selfish interests are sufficient. The authors believe that more is necessary and propose ways in which ethics and morality, admittedly used interchangeably, can be made significant and useful in the lives of business students. Their use of the term vocabulary is somewhat confusing, as they intend it to be much more inclusive than its usual interpretation as a collection of words and phrases.

The authors of the above quotation employ the method of the cautionary tale or the morality play as found in literary works from all historical periods. This method assumes that a carefully constructed exposure to important literary works can influence ethical behavior in the lives of business professionals. Examples presented in this paper are the television play and later the 1957 movie, *Twelve Angry Men*, the novel, *The Great Gatsby*, by F. Scott Fitzgerald, the play by Friedrich Durenmatt, *The Visit*, and the classical Greek play, *The Clouds*, by Aristophanes. Many more examples are presented and each literary work is discussed in terms of the lessons that it teaches with respect to ethical dilemmas and their solutions. The authors are quite realistic in terms of their aims and expectations[51]:

> Of course, exposure to this vocabulary of ethics—including the minimum conception of morality, the barriers to morality, and the three dominant moral theories of our day—does not ensure that students will think or behave ethically. A grasp of this vocabulary, however, does provide students: the opportunity to develop an ethical perspective they can apply to business life; the ability to recognize an ethical business dilemma when they are confronted with one; the capability of discerning ethical (or unethical) styles of others within and between organizations; an awareness when consciously choosing to behave ethically or unethically in a business situation; a conceptual line of defense against immoral business decisions made unwittingly; and finally, an understanding that the amoral paradigm, which assumes economic relations to be a morally neutral part of social life, provides a mental and emotional cover for immoral decision making.

This an admirable statement that all those involved in the enterprise to teach and understand ethical responsibility would be well advised to adopt. Of course, the real measure of success cannot be effectively determined, no matter how high the grades that are achieved. So the basic article of faith is that such a course makes a difference in the world, a difference that improves the lives of people and their environment.

Case Studies

Another method of teaching professional ethical behavior, after an introduction to ethical principles, is to explore a variety of supposed real-life situations, or scenarios, in order to isolate potential ethical dilemmas, then to determine various approaches to deal with them, and finally to select the most appropriate, if possible. If enough different situations are studied in a principled fashion, it is held, students will acquire skills to identify ethical problems, and tools to deal with them. There are obviously no guarantees that a case-based approach will be successful, but then it is virtually impossible to measure success. The general public, as shown above (in the *Business Week* poll on the public's view of stockbrokers), has no illusions about the ethical standards of Wall Street traders. As calls for improvements in the education of future business leaders have grown in volume, the usual response has been to establish applied ethics courses, a bonanza for philosophy professors. Will they result in a decrease in business crimes, in a reduction in sudden plant closures, in a reduction in privacy violations of employees, in a practical recognition of the worth of employees, in the termination of bribes to foreign governments, in a limitation on significant cost overruns on government contracts, in a reduction in special deals with government agencies, and so on?

In any case, the examination of a few scenarios in engineering and information processing will at the very least highlight some of the ethical problems likely to confront practicing computer professionals. The analyses of these cases will vary in depth and detail. In some cases they will be left as exercises for the reader, teacher and student alike. If possible, the ACM code should be studied and sections identified that may be relevant to the questions at hand.

Case 1

The City Council of Cyber City, USA, is debating a new program: the Cyber City Network, a service that would allow residents to access a wide variety of municipal and school services from their home computers. If the program is approved, residents will be able to scan the city's job listings, apply for building permits, ask questions of the police department, or get their children's homework using the Internet.

City Council agendas would be posted, and citizens could testify at council meetings from offsite computers. Recreation Department schedules would be available on the network, and parents could sign their children up for sports teams online. Parents could also communicate with teachers. Businesspeople who require city permits and licenses could apply for them via the Cyber City Network.

About a third of Cyber City's 45,000 residents own computers equipped with modems, which would allow them to log on to the network from their homes. The city has promised to provide 10 additional computers at elementary schools, senior centers, and libraries for those who do not have ready access at home.

You have been asked to testify at City Council about the ethical implications of the Cyber City Network.

Will you urge the members to vote yes or no?[52]

At first glance, the City Council seems to have identified and dealt with relevant issues. For example, it is adding 10 computers to those already available at public places. However, in this move toward local E-government, it is important to make sure that the new way of doing business does not totally replace more traditional ways, at least until there is strong evidence that no one is left out. But probably the crucial question is how will those uncomfortable with, or lacking knowledge of, the necessary technology be made more at ease and more knowledgeable. Typical of plans to introduce new technology into the workplace or schools is the limited amount budgeted for education. As general moral imperative 1.4 of the ACM Code states, "Be fair and take action not to discriminate." Surely someone on the City Council might have raised the issue about educating the citizenry to properly and effectively use the proposed systems. So I would urge the members to postpone their vote, or vote no, until adequate provisions are in place to deal with this issue.

Case 2

John and Sally "meet" on a bulletin board provided by a commercial network operator and then begin corresponding through e-mail. The operator has a "standard" set of acceptable use policies that prohibit sending (through e-mail) or posting (on either type of bulletin board) any "defamatory, obscene, threatening, sexually explicit, ethnically offensive, or illegal material." John receives a private e-mail note from Sally's husband saying: "I know what's going on between you two, and I'm not putting up with it. It's too late to save her. She's a gonner." John notifies the operator and forwards a copy of this note, requesting that the operator notify the local police in Sally's home town (since John has no way of knowing where Sally lives).[53]

Associated with this case are several questions, which follow, that highlight the crucial issues and raise some legal concerns:[54]

- Does the operator have any legal responsibility to notify the police? If John had not contacted the operator, would it have any liability or responsibility?
- Should the operator provide John with Sally's address so he can notify the police if he wishes?
- If the operator decides to notify the police and they arrest the husband, only to find out that a prank was played by Sally, does the husband have any claim against the operator?
- If the operator decides not to notify the police and it turns out that Sally was killed by her husband a day after John notified the operator, does the operator have any liability to Sally's heirs? How do "Good Samaritan" laws apply in this case?

In this case, professional issues are not involved, given that John and Sally are just two people who have met through a bulletin board.

Case 3

A university is connected to the Internet. Under a joint effort of its alumni relations and industrial liaison program, the university also provides library and Internet access for Company X, a small start-up business founded by university alumni, in return for stock options in Company X. To facilitate private communications, the university provides RSA-based, public-key encryption software on its host computers, encourages the software's use, and maintains databases that facilitate the lookup of the public keys of all users using the university as a node. ("RSA" refers to a type of highly secure public-key encryption scheme that is widely available in the U.S. and elsewhere. Software that implements RSA encryption/decryption algorithms may be subject to U.S. export control laws.)[55]

The questions that follow define a series of increasingly complex situations that primarily raise legal issues and responsibilities resulting from them. Clearly, the university had not anticipated what its responsibilities might be in acting as an Internet Service Provider for a private company. It also appears that security measures were not adequate, especially with respect to storing public keys and sensitive software. All in all, this case is a recipe for several possible disasters.[56]

- A foreign national in Iraq accesses the university system and downloads the encryption software. Who has violated what law? What obligation does the university have to report the incident? To configure its system to prevent a recurrence?
- Encrypted messages are sent from Company X, based in the U.S., to a client located in Brussels. The client uses decryption software obtained locally. Any violation?
- The FBI requests access to the university's records regarding who has requested the public keys of a particular client of Company X. Should the university cooperate? Must the FBI use any particular process to compel disclosure? What standard should apply to such requests? Is the standard different if the request is made to Company X?
- The FBI determines that a staff member of the university and a client of Company X, unbeknownst to these institutions, are using the electronic communications system to plan a terrorist act. The FBI demands access to the private keys that will allow them to monitor encrypted communications between the parties. They have a search warrant. Is it feasible/lawful to comply? May the system providers require registration of private keys for purposes of allowing compliance with such warrants? May the government require such registration?
- Company X uses the authentication capability of public-key encryption to determine that requests for assistance actually come from its clients. The university, which administers the database of public keys, does a sloppy job, and a prankster obtains the private keys of the officers of Company X. In consequence, a student prankster sends a request for information that appears to be from a client of Company X, but is not. Company X discloses confidential information to the prankster, who then reveals this information publicly. As a result, Company X incurs costs, based on its assumption that the message is genuine. Who is liable to whom?

Case 4

Since the terrorist attacks on the U. S. on Sep 11, 2001, many individuals have had their sense of safety and security challenged. In response to a perceived public demand for action regarding national security, the government has enacted new laws which permit increased surveillance by the federal government. Many feel that this increased governmental power will help track and apprehend those individuals who might be intent on terrorist actions and keep our society safer. On the other hand, unpopular though it is, some have chosen to speak out against this more intrusive role by the federal government. The citizens of some foreign countries have routinely accepted this high-level governmental surveillance and either don't care that it is being done or recognize that their protests could be interpreted as an act of sedition and therefore punishable. In either case, the type of system being considered for our country appears to work well in other similar parts of our new world.[57]

This case presents a challenge to ordinary citizens in general, and in particular, civil liberties advocates, computer specialists, and of course politicians. The challenge of combating terrorism in democratic societies is serious because basic rights may come under attack. It has been said in the U.S. that the Constitution is not a suicide pact. That is, preserving liberties at all costs to the detriment of national security cannot be what the founding fathers had in mind. And so the challenge is to act ethically, keeping in mind that on occasion it may be necessary to make compromises. What is important is to deal with each situation on its own terms and to be prepared to justify actions taken. Rights cannot be categorically abrogated under a general claim that the Republic is under threat. After all, rights once weakened may be difficult to restore; the U.S. presents itself as a nation of laws, not men.

Case 5

Jean, a statistical database programmer, is trying to write a large statistical program needed by her company. Programmers in this company are encouraged to write about their work and to publish their algorithms in professional journals. After months of tedious programming, Jean has found herself stuck on several parts of the program. Her manager, not recognizing the complexity of the problem, wants the job completed within the next few days. Not knowing how to solve the problems, Jean remembers that a coworker had given her source listings from his current work and from an early version of a commercial software package developed at another company. On studying these programs, she sees two areas of code which could be directly incorporated into her own program. She uses segments of code from both her coworker and the commercial software, but does not tell anyone or mention it in the documentation. She completes the project and turns it in a day ahead of time.[58]

The issues in this case focus on intellectual property, both in terms of ethical behavior as well as legal concerns. Hence, with respect to the ACM code, sections 1.5, 1.6, and 2.3 clearly apply. A fuller analysis would require a more detailed articulation of how the Code applies. But it is clear that using someone else's work without proper acknowledgment is unethical and it may be illegal depending on the legal status of the work copied.[59]

Case 6

> A computer company is writing the first stage of a more efficient accounting system that will be used by the government. This system will save taxpayers a considerable amount of money every year. A computer professional, who is asked to design the accounting system, assigns different parts of the system to her staff. One person is responsible for developing the reports; another is responsible for the internal processing; and a third for the user interface. The manager is shown the system and agrees that it can do everything in the requirements. The system is installed, but the staff finds the interface so difficult to use that their complaints are heard by upper-level management. Because of these complaints, upper-level management will not invest any more money in the development of the new accounting system and they go back to their original, more expensive system.[60]

What's the problem? Sometimes systems don't work as expected or at all, in the worst case. However, this case lacks any information about first expressing requirements, test runs, consultations with user groups or affected parties, or a cycle of test, modification, retest, consultation. Just producing a system and then seeing if it works violates basic principles of software engineering and ethical behavior. For example, consider ACM Code imperative 3.4: "Ensure that users and those who will be affected by a system have their needs clearly articulated during the assessment and design of requirements; later the systems must be validated to meet requirements."[61]

Other Guidelines to Appropriate Behavior

The codes and standards of professional societies are only binding on their members. In some environments, such as the Internet, long-time users have developed behavioral norms that users, old and new alike, are expected to follow. The term netiquette is commonly used to describe the Internet's acceptable etiquette. Violations are usually met with rapid and typically unsympathetic responses, as newcomers, or newbies, are severely chastised for their "stupid" mistakes. However, various organizations concerned with both the rights and the responsibilities of Internet users and with an eye to the future, have formulated policies to create equitable online environments. Clearly these are not binding on anyone because they are intended to apply to the diverse Internet community, but since such policies are usually formulated by groups of committed users, they do represent operating norms reflecting years of experience. They generally differ in the emphasis placed on particular activities and perceived rights.

EDUCOM's Bill of Rights and Responsibilities for Electronic Learners

"EDUCOM, founded in 1964, is a nonprofit consortium of higher education institutions which facilitates the introduction, use, access to, and management of information resources in teaching, learning, scholarship, and research."[62] Given this statement of purpose, it is not surprising that EDUCOM proposed this "Bill of Rights" to articulate in some detail what users can expect and what is to be expected of them while using the Internet for educational purposes. The Bill has four major divisions or articles: Individual Rights, Individual Responsibilities, Rights of Educational Institutions, and Institutional Responsibilities. In order to get a flavor of this document, samples of the sections of each division will follow[63]:

Article I: Individual Rights
- **Section 1.** A citizen's access to computing and information resources shall not be denied or removed without just cause.
- **Section 4.** The constitutional concept of freedom of speech applies to citizens of electronic communities.
- **Section 5.** All citizens of the electronic community of learners have ownership rights over their own intellectual works.

Article 2: Individual Responsibilities
- **Section 1.** It shall be each citizen's personal responsibility to actively pursue needed resources: to recognize when information is needed, and to be able to find, evaluate, and effectively use information.
- **Section 2.** It shall be each citizen's personal responsibility to recognize (attribute) and honor the intellectual property of others.

Article 3: Rights of Educational Institutions
- **Section 1.** The access of an educational institutions to computing and information resources shall not be denied or removed without just cause.
- **Section 3.** Each educational institution has the authority to allocate resources in accordance with its unique institutional mission.

Article 4: Institutional Responsibilities
- **Section 3.** The institution shall treat electronically stored information as confidential. The institution shall treat all personal files as confidential, examining or disclosing the contents only when authorized by the owner of the information, approved by the appropriate institutional official, or required by local, state or federal law.

- **Section 4.** Institutions in the electronic community of learners shall train and support faculty, staff, and students to effectively use information technology. Training includes skills to use the resources, to be aware of the existence of data repositories and techniques for using them, and to understand the ethical and legal uses of the resources.

This document is interesting and important in that it is intended to apply to both users and the institutions that supply them with services. The access to information is a two-way process, and the associated rights and responsibilities should reflect this reality. Of course, the Bill is purely voluntary and no one is bound by it; however, its existence establishes certain expectations about what are reasonable rights and under what conditions such rights may be exercised.

Ten Commandments of Computer Ethics

Since 10 is such a congenial number, it is not surprising that a fairly well-known code for promoting ethical behavior should be cast as 10 injunctions, or rather in keeping with a Judeo-Christian perspective, 10 commandments. The Computer Ethics Institute, located in Washington, DC, proposed the following pithy commandments in 1992[64]:

1. Thou shalt not use a computer to harm other people.
2. Thou shalt not interfere with other people's computer work.
3. Thou shalt not snoop around in other people's computer files.
4. Thou shalt not use a computer to steal.
5. Thou shalt not use a computer to bear false witness.
6. Thou shalt not copy or use proprietary software for which you have not paid (or been given authority to do so).
7. Thou shalt not use other people's computer resources without authorization or proper compensation (includes using computers or telephones for personal business, or printing nonacademic materials with university-owned printers).
8. Thou shalt not appropriate other people's intellectual output.
9. Thou shalt think about the social consequences of the program you are writing or the system you are designing.
10. Thou shalt always use a computer in ways that insure consideration and respect for your fellow humans.

This code expresses moral principles that have been extended to the computer world. Its limitation is that it has very little to say about the Internet and its host of special concerns.

Responsible Use Policies

Most institutions, including schools, colleges and universities, and libraries, have devised a set of rules that all members or patrons must be aware of and follow when using the information technology systems. They vary in length, detail, and comprehensiveness and are typically situated within a nexus of regulations, ethical principles, and laws. One example is "Policy #104: Responsible Use of Information Technology Facilities and Services,"[65] which took effect in November 2000 at the University of British Columbia in Canada. It was the result of about one and a half years of effort by a facultywide committee representing the administration, professors, and students. At the outset of the statement, in the Policy section, this notification appears: "All users must adhere to University policies and all laws that govern the use of the University's computing and communication facilities. Applicable legislation includes, but is not limited to, the Criminal Code of Canada, the B.C. Civil Rights Protection Act, the B.C. Freedom of Information and Protection of Privacy Act, and the B.C. Human Rights Code." The following issues are extracted from the complete policy statement[66]:

Privacy and Security
1. Users must preserve the privacy of data to which they have access; respect the privacy of others by not tampering with e-mail, files, or accounts they use; and respect the integrity of computing systems and data.

Intellectual Property
1. Users must respect the legal protection provided by copyright laws for computer programs and data compilations and for all other works (literary, dramatic, artistic or musical). Also, users must respect the legal protection provided by trademark law and the common law for names, marks, logos, and other representations that serve to distinguish the goods or services of one person from another.

Freedom of Expression
The University does not and will not act as a censor of information available on our campus network but will comply with applicable legislation. To the extent that the latter requires specifically identified information to be banned pursuant to a court order, the University will comply.

Discrimination and Harassment
Users must recognize that the University, as a community sharing a commitment to study and learning, upholds the principles of academic freedom, mutual respect and equality of opportunity for all.

Examples of Illegal Uses
The following are representative examples only and do not comprise a comprehensive list of illegal uses:
- Uttering threats (by computer or telephone)
- Distribution of pornographic materials to minors
- Child pornography
- Pyramid schemes
- Copyright infringement.

Examples of Unacceptable Uses

The following are representative examples only and do not comprise a comprehensive list of unacceptable uses:

• Seeking information on passwords or data belonging to another user
• Making unauthorized copies of proprietary software, or offering unauthorized copies of proprietary software to others
• Copying someone else's files, or programs, or examining such information unless authorized
• Attempting to circumvent computer security methods or operating systems (e.g., subverting or obstructing a computer or network by introducing a worm or virus).

This policy represents a conscientious effort to deal with a host of potentially conflicting principles in an environment committed to respect for privacy, intellectual property rights, and freedom of expression.

OTHER ISSUES

Silence is the language of complicity.

Anonymous

Hacker "Ethics"

Hackers were discussed in Chapter 11 with respect to their violations of computer system security and their strong belief in their inalienable right to access information anywhere and any time. Stephen Levy in his book, *Hackers*, outlined what he called the "hacker ethic," an approach to computers and information at odds, apparently, with much of the foregoing discussion on ethics. Consider the following statement of this "hacker ethic" and some of the additional features[67]:

The Hacker Ethic. Access to computers—and anything which might teach you something about the way the world works—should be unlimited and total. Always yield to the Hands-On-Imperative!

Implications:
• All information should be free.
• Mistrust authority—promote decentralization.
• Hackers should be judged by their hacking, not bogus criteria such as degrees, age, race, or position.
• You can create art and beauty on a computer.
• Computers can change your life for the better.

Adherents to this "ethic" have increasingly come into conflict with the law and most of the other people associated with computers. Abrogating to themselves the right to enter systems at will, and to freely distribute information discovered there, places them beyond the pale. As an embattled minority, possessing advanced computer skills, their self-righteousness borders on the hysterical at times. Their facile dismissal of privacy rights and property rights has obviously not won them many friends. Many hackers do not recognize software ownership and believe all software should be freely available. The "hacker ethic" seems to constitute an "anti-ethic" to most established ethical codes and hackers themselves are usually viewed as anarchists, if not outlaws. In their concern with the individual's struggle against the establishment, hackers do strike a responsive cord among many who feel isolated and occasionally oppressed by the power of large institutions.

The distinguished computer scientist Dorothy Denning has written at length about hackers and has characterized their motives and activities in ways that differ substantially from the typical media portrayals. For example, in reporting on the initial findings of a study on hackers, Denning suggests that[68]

> hackers are learners and explorers who want to help rather than cause damage, and who often have very high standards of behavior. My findings also suggest that the discourse surrounding hacking belongs at the very least to the gray areas between larger conflicts that we are experiencing at every level of society and business in an information age where many are not computer literate. These conflicts are between the idea that information cannot be owned and the idea that it can, and between law enforcement and the First and Fourth Amendments.

She claims that all the hackers she encountered "said that malicious hacking was morally wrong . . . and that they themselves are concerned about causing accidental damage." Furthermore, although they believe that information should be shared, it is not personal information that they have in mind, but rather corporate and government information. Some five years later, after more interviews, especially with law enforcement officials, Denning's views altered somewhat.[69] Hackers cause more disruptions than they are willing to acknowledge, even if one accepts their protestations of non-malicious intent. By providing detailed knowledge about how to crack systems, they encourage novices to engage in such activities, with little understanding of the impact of their actions. She is far less inclined to take their views at face value, especially that victims are responsible for being victimized, and no longer recommends working with hackers to find solutions to the "hacker problem."

Ethics of Online Research

The Internet is assuming an important role as an area of study for social scientists, but the online world presents a number of problems, including the following[70]:

Public versus private forums

Much of the information useful for Internet research is treated as public information, which can be viewed by any person at any time, without obligation of any sort. However, the often-personal nature of the messages that are posted to these groups can have potentially negative repercussions for the posters if they are singled out and published in an article or journal. The conflict between the researcher's traditional right to publish materials obtained from public sources, such as television, radio, books, and open records and spaces, and the ethical research principle of beneficence, or maximizing possible benefits and good for the subject while minimizing the amount of possible harm and risks resulting from the research, leads to confusion.

Naturalistic studies

One of the most exciting things about Internet research is also one of the most ethically troubling: the possibility of conducting completely naturalistic, non-reactive research. Participants in online discussions can be observed without their knowledge, and thus without affecting their actions. They can even be observed without the attention of the researcher, who can let his computer analyze data that it downloads automatically and review the results. Taking it a final step farther, discussions can be observed years after they take place.

Obtaining informed consent

The researcher, having decided that getting consent will be necessary, is presented with a choice. He or she may attempt to gain consent before gathering data or after gathering data and before publishing (the former is preferable but not always possible, especially in naturalistic studies). If the researcher prefers to obtain consent before studying a certain group, it follows that consent must be given by the whole group. Similarly, if the group itself is to be identified, then it would seem necessary to obtain consent from the whole group (Even if consent is obtained from the group as a whole, because of the fluid nature of groups on the Internet, many of the group who consent may not be part of the group who are to be studied, and vice versa).

Confidentiality and data security

One question that has its roots in the very nature of the Internet is the problem of confidentiality and data security. Any communication over the Internet or data stored on a computer connected to the Internet is susceptible to hacking, or to receiving inadvertent publicity because of an error by a researcher (or otherwise—in the U.S. there is a growing precedent for employers to legally read employees' e-mail). However useless research data may be to hackers (other than maverick Internet researchers) if it contains PII [Personally Identifiable Information] or sensitive information, it should be given reasonably strong protection.

Fortunately, a growing body of knowledge related to these issues is starting to appear but it will face an environment such as chat rooms in which the coin of the realm is deception. Given that participants present themselves in arbitrary ways with respect to gender, age, and occupation, how can any demographic information be determined? For that matter, what can one learn by studying the transcripts of interactions among people for whom it is impossible to conclude anything with certainty? A set of guidelines and approaches was released by the Association of Internet Researchers in November 2002. It attempts to cope with the issues raised above and much more in a pragmatic and principled way.[71]

Computer Scientists and Society

The most sophisticated and well-meaning of ethical codes will have very little influence on individual behavior if society at large is unsympathetic, non-supportive, or actually hostile. In the midst of large bureaucracies, individual responsibility can sometimes fade and disappear. History is rich with examples of individuals either standing up for their principles, at great risk, or immersing themselves in the whole and abrogating any sense of personal responsibility. Large computer systems, in their regular use, provide a bureaucratic excuse that can relieve the individual of any reason to accept blame or to provide explanations. Responsibility is diffused and individuals become mere cogs in a great machine. This response is precisely that which Adolf Eichmann's defense argued in his 1961 trial in Jerusalem. Eichmann's responsibility was to ensure that the trains carrying victims to the extermination camps during World War II ran efficiently in the context of the larger transportation system. What happened to the "passengers" was not his concern. Hannah Arendt, the esteemed social critic noted: "As for the base motives, he was perfectly sure that he was not what he called an *innerer Schweinehund*, a dirty bastard in the depths of his heart; and as for his conscience, he remembered perfectly well that he would have had a bad conscience only if he had not done what he had been ordered to do—to ship millions of men, women, and children to their deaths with great zeal and the most meticulous care."[72]

Langdon Winner, in commenting on the impact of large systems on traditional concepts of ethical behavior, writes: "What is interesting about the new ethical context offered by highly complex systems is that their very architecture constitutes vast webs of extenuating circumstances. Seemingly valid excuses can be manufactured wholesale for anyone situated in the network. Thus the very notion of moral agency begins to dissolve."[73] And this is the great fear that in large systems, of all kinds—no one person either takes or receives responsibility. Unless ethics codes can combat this tendency, they will become mere window dressing, if they are not so already. One example of personal integrity may stand as a beacon for computer professionals everywhere.

David Parnas, a distinguished software engineer with a long history of consultation to the U.S. Department of Defense, was asked in 1985 to serve on a $1000/day advisory panel on Computing in Support of Battle Management, a "Star Wars" project. Two months later he resigned publicly, although he had previously expressed support for any approach that would remove nuclear weapons as a deterrent factor. It is important to note that Parnas believes that people with a strong sense of social responsibility should work on military projects. A statement of his position on professional responsibility follows[74]:

> Some have held that a professional is a 'team player' and should never blow the whistle on his colleagues and employer. I disagree. As the Challenger incident demonstrates, such action is sometimes necessary. One's obligations as a professional precede other obligations. One must not enter into contracts that conflict with one's professional obligations.

The basic question is how did work on this project violate Parnas's sense of his professional obligations. Is there a general principle in force that will be helpful to others in similar circumstances, or is this an instance of idiosyncratic behavior? Again Parnas's own words are necessary and instructive[75]:

> I solicited comments from other scientists and found none that disagreed with my technical conclusions. Instead, they told me that the program should be continued, not because it would free us from the fear of nuclear weapons, but because the research money would advance the state of computer science! I disagree with that statement, but I also consider it irrelevant. Taking money allocated for developing a shield against nuclear missiles, while knowing that such a shield was impossible, seemed like fraud to me.

> When I observed that the SDIO [Strategic Defense Initiative Organization] was engaged in "damage control," rather than a serious consideration of my arguments, I felt that I should inform the public and its representatives of my own view. I want the public to understand that no trustworthy shield will result from the SDIO-sponsored work. I want them to understand that technology offers no magic that will eliminate the fear of nuclear weapons. I consider this part of my personal professional responsibility as a scientist and educator.

This statement conveys a strong sense of honesty, responsibility, and commitment, both personal and professional, especially given his past record of involvement in military research and development. Parnas's negative evaluation of the prospects of success of Star Wars have been challenged, but for the present purposes, it is his strong action and public statement that are important.

The final words of this section will be given by Joseph Weizenbaum, viewed by some as the conscience of computer science and by others as just a cranky nuisance. Weizenbaum makes it clear that he is not arguing against technology itself, which can be used for good or ill, but rather for responsible, informed decision making[76]:

> Today it is virtually certain that every scientific and technical result will, if at all possible, be incorporated in military systems. In these circumstances, scientific and technical workers have a responsibility to inquire about the end uses of their work. They must attempt to know to what ends it will be put. Would they serve these ends directly? Would they personally steer missiles to their targets and watch people die?
>
> Many . . . scientists say that the systems on which they work can help take astronauts to the moon and bring them back as well as guarantee that missiles aimed at a city will actually hit it if fired. How then can they be held responsible for their work's consequences? . . . But the attitude, "If I don't do it, someone else will," a thinly disguised version of this disorder, cannot serve as a basis of moral behavior, or else every crime imaginable is so justifiable.

The Social Cost of Technology

We live in age of serious contradictions. Technological development is accelerating, and without doubt the benefits to society have been massive and persuasive. To list some of them is to stand in awe of human ingenuity; electrical power, airplanes, space exploration, television, communication networks, microelectronics, genetic engineering, and computers and the Internet. Surely, the improvements in health, food supply, longevity, living standards, safety, working conditions, and so forth are real and largely attributable to discoveries in science and technology. This fact applies to the industrial and burgeoning post-industrial countries of the world. Many other countries, to a greater or lesser degree, are facing such basic issues of survival that the debate over the benefits and dangers of technology is largely irrelevant.

Most attempts to describe and analyze the impact of technology on society inevitably produce a list of putative good effects, a shorter list of obvious bad effects, and an assurance that we can ultimately control how the actual technology will be used. Perhaps the choice is ours, although in many cases, the reverse is true, but in certain areas control seems elusive at best. Nuclear power is an example, in both its peaceful and military contexts. Compared to the potential holocaust of nuclear war or serious power-plant accidents, all other issues fade into insignificance. The use of the technology of nuclear or thermonuclear weapons could result in the destruction of most of the planet. Up to fairly recently, control has rested on a delicate balance of mutual threats and assured destruction. With the dissolution of the Soviet Union, part of this threat has dissipated; unfortunately, as a byproduct there is some uncertainty that Russia, the Ukraine, and other former republics, still exert effective control over the weapons in their possession. Thus the apparent lessening in tension is not a result of a reasoned decision to "bury the bombs."

Having created such weapons of mass destruction, humanity still lives under a shadow that affects every person's life, albeit a reduced one and one not particularly a matter of concern to most people. Here is an example of a technology that seems to control us. A study of the history of the atomic bomb reveals that many of the scientists involved in its original development assumed that they would be consulted about its uses. Such was not the case. Decision making was assumed by the executive branch and the military, surely an obvious step, and the bomb became an instrument of national policy. Although some of the scientific team had opposed its initial use at Hiroshima, preferring a demonstration blast to convince Japan to surrender, most were certainly opposed to a second explosion, at Nagasaki, believing that not enough time had been allotted to permit the full implications of the first blast to sink in. But as noted, it was not up to them; they had built the weapons and their job was over. It is a fact that technological innovators rarely continue to exercise authority over their invention or discovery after it leaves the laboratory. If technology can be controlled for the benefit of society, we must therefore ask, controlled how and by whom?

Even the peaceful uses of nuclear energy have not met the initial optimistic expectations of very low-cost safe power. Plant costs have escalated, and the environmental protection movement has rallied public support to limit the growth of the nuclear industry. Anxiety about the safety of nuclear reactors for power generation has been translated, in North America, into a marked reduction of plant construction. In this regard, events at Three Mile Island in the U.S. and Chernobyl in the Ukraine have been decisive. The impact of aroused public opinion has been effective in this area and demonstrates the possibility of an aware public exercising its political power. Other technological concerns currently reaching public awareness include global warming, reproductive technologies, genetic engineering, and human cloning. In each of these cases, growing political activity may result in the enactment of controls to protect health and safety, or not, if the consequences seem remote and the costs of enforcement and affected economic activities are deemed too severe.

Meeting the Challenge

It is a formidable undertaking to evaluate the effect of technological change on social, political, and economic institutions. A study of the past is informative and necessary, but predictions of the future have not been particularly accurate, notwithstanding the emergence of a forecasting industry and such powerful tools as large computers and refined simulation techniques.

In a book on computers and culture, J. David Bolter makes the following forceful statement[77]:

> Until recently, however, our technical skills were so feeble in comparison with the natural forces of climate and chemistry that we could not seriously affect our environment for good or ill, except over the millenia. High technology promises to give us a new power over nature, both our own nature and that of our planet, so that the very future of civilization depends upon our intelligent use of high technology.

He further notes that the crucial element in high technology is the computer. Clearly, the attempt to locate the computer in the history of technology, to survey its applications, is to probe associated benefits and problems, and to assess the future impact is a worthwhile and in fact necessary exercise.

As with most technological innovations, the choice of when and how to proceed is not usually left up to the individual members of society. Governments and companies, both large and small, multinational and local, have the power and resources to make the important decisions. As ordinary citizens, we live in a world that for the most part is not of our making. Nevertheless, an informed and sufficiently aroused public can make a difference. In discussing the nature of a liberal democracy, the Canadian political scientist C.B. Macpherson analyzed the opinions of the American scholar, John Dewey, as follows[78]:

> He has few illusions about the actual democratic system, or about the democratic quality of a society dominated by motives of individual and corporate gain. The root difficulty lay not in any defects in the machinery of government but in the fact that the democratic public was "still largely inchoate and unorganized," and unable to see what forces of economic and technological organizations it was up against. There was no tinkering with the political machinery: the prior problem was "that of discovering the means by which a scattered, mobile, and manifold public may so recognize itself as to define and express its interests." The public's present incompetence to do this was traced to its failure to understand the technological and scientific forces which had made it so helpless.

SUMMARY

Many of the decisions chosen by computer professionals have serious social repercussions and affect the well-being of many individuals. The past few years have also witnessed serious ethical dilemmas in reproductive biology, including in vitro fertilization and surrogate motherhood, and ethical breakdowns among major players in the financial markets, mainly associated with insider training and financial misdeeds. All of these issues have awakened an interest in ethical behavior and have stimulated the academic field of applied ethics.

Three major approaches, with of course many subdivisions, have emerged. These are ethical relativism, utilitarianism (with the important area of consequentialism), and the class of deontological theories. They all attempt to characterize ethical behavior for individuals but additional questions are raised when the behaviors of doctors, lawyers, and other professionals are included. There is some debate about how a professional's responsibility to self, client, profession, and society at large can be reconciled. Examples are given of how computer professional societies have entered the political arena to defend positions or to oppose proposals that they feel do a disservice to their members as well as society at large.

Most professional organizations have adopted codes of ethics or standards of behavior to guide their members and to announce to the public the level of conduct that can be expected of their members. Such codes attempt to resolve the potential conflict between social and professional responsibility. Six case studies explore a variety of situations that may arise when engineers and information systems specialists encounter ethical problems. These may serve to illustrate the distance between theory and practice. Under some circumstances, it may be necessary for individuals to "go public" and become whistleblowers, however painful that may be, because institutions are unresponsive to genuine misdeeds. Less formal guidelines are also in place, such as responsible use policies, to govern the behavior of non-professionals in computing environments.

Computer science departments have long been concerned that their students enter the workplace with adaptable skills that will serve them and their employers well, both immediately and down the road. They are gradually becoming convinced that among such technical skills, there must be the ability to identify potentially problematic situations as well as the skills to deal with them appropriately.

A certain group of computer addicts, sometimes called hackers, seems to operate under a set of "principles" at considerable odds with those held by the vast majority of the information processing community. Computer scientists, in general, may be faced with difficult choices about the immediate and long-term implications about computers and networks. Especially troublesome are military applications; cautionary remarks have been addressed to computer scientists by Joseph Weizenbaum, a critic of the technological imperative, and David Parnas, a vigorous proponent of professional responsibility.

NOTES

1. "What is Ethics?" The Markkula Center for Applied Ethics, Santa Clara University, (No date). Available at http://www.scu.edu/ethics/practicing/decision/whatisethics.html
2. Myron Magnet. "The Decline & Fall of Business Ethics," *Fortune*, December 8, 1986, p. 65.
3. Felix Rohatyn. "The Blight on Wall Street," *The New York Review of Books*, March 12, 1987, p. 21.
4. Stephen Koepp. Harry Kelly, and Raji Samghabadi, "Having it All, Then Throwing it All Away," *Time*, May 25, 1987, p. 26.
5. Robert Taylor. "U.S. May Boost New York Office Staff to Pursue Mounting Securities Fraud," *The Wall Street Journal*, January 19, 1988, p. 12.
6. The *Business Week*/Harris Poll, August 1986. *World Opinions Update*, September 1986, p. 108.
7. Jeanie Russell Kasindorf. "What to make of Mike," *Fortune*, September 30, 1996, pp. 86–88, 90, 94, 96.
8. John Greenwald. "Jack in the Box," *Time*, October 3, 1994. Available at http://pathfinder.com/@cmfBwAQA1h49I53p/time/magazine/domestic/1994/941003/941003.business.html
9. "The Year in Review: WorldCom, Enron Fallout Lead the Way in Scandal-Filled 2002," Scripps Howard News Service, *Naples Daily News*, December 30, 2002. Available at http://www.naplesnews.com/02/12/business/d776419a.htm
10. Rick Weiss. "Tests' Availability Tangles Ethical and Genetic Codes," *The Washington Post*, May 26, 1996, p. A 1. Available at http://wp2.washingtonpost.com/cgi-bin/displaySearch?WPlate+3629+%28ethics%29%3Aheadline
11. *Ibid.*
12. Albert Camus. *The Myth of Sisyphus* (New York: Knopf, 1957), p. 65.
13. Deborah Johnson, *Computer Ethics* (Englewood Cliffs, NJ: Prentice-Hall, 1985), p. 6. (A 3rd edition was published in 2001.)
14. *Op. cit.*, "What is Ethics?"
15. "Technology & Ethics: Perspectives From Americans Who Rely on Information Technology in the Workplace," Society of Professional Service Professionals, March 2001. Available at http://www.financialpro.org/press/Ethics/Technology_Ethics_survey.pdf
16. *Ibid.*
17. "Approaching Ethics," The Markkula Center for Applied Ethics, Santa Clara University, (no date). Available at http://www.scu.edu/ethics/practicing/decision/approach.html
18. R. N. Johnson. "Primer on the Elements and Forms of Utilitarianism," Philosophy 213, University of Missouri, 1996. Available at http://Web.misouri.edu/~philrnj/utilnote.html

19. Raziel Abelson. "History of Ethics," In Paul Edwards (Ed.), *The Encyclopedia of Philosophy, Volume Three* (New York: Macmillan, 1967), p. 95.

20. *Ibid.*

21. *Op cit.*, Johnson, *Computer Ethics*, p. 17.

22. Sissela Bok, "Kant's Arguments in Support of the Maxim 'Do What is Right Though the World Should Perish'," in David M. Rosenthal and Fadlou Shehadi (Eds.), *Applied Ethics and Ethical Theory* (Salt Lake City: University of Utah Press, 1988), pp. 191–193.

23. *Ibid.*, p. 210.

24. Jon Rawls. *A Theory of Justice*, (Cambridge, MA: The Belknap Press of Harvard University Press, 1971), pp. 3–4.

25. "Software Engineering Code of Ethics and Professional Practice," *IEEE Computer*, October 1999, p. 85. Available at http://computer.org/Computer/code-of-ethics.pdf

26. Stephen Unger. *Controlling Technology: Ethics and the Responsible Engineer*, (New York: Holt, Rinehart and Winston, 1982).

27. James H. Moor. "What is Computer Ethics?" *Metaphilosophy*, 16(4), October 1985, p. 266.

28. Rule 2.5 of the Association for Computing machinery Code of Ethics and Professional Conduct. Available at http://www.acm.org/constitution/bylaw17.txt

29. *Op cit.*, Unger, *Controlling Technology*, pp. 32–55.

30. Mark S. Frankel. "Professional Codes: Why, How, and With What Impact?" *Journal of Business Ethics*, 8(2&3), February—March 1989, pp. 110–111.

31. *Ibid.*, pp. 111–112.

32. *Op. cit.*, "Software Engineering Code of Ethics and Professional Practice."

33. C. Dianne Martin and David H. Martin. "Comparison of Ethics Codes of Computer Professionals," presented at an Ethics Symposium organized by the Special Interest group on Computers and Society of the Association of Computing Machinery, Washington, DC, September 1990. An earlier version appeared in *Social Science Computer Review*, 9(1), 1990 and *Computers and Society*, 20(2), June 1990, pp. 18–29. Note that the ACM Code Of Ethics and Professional Conduct and the IEEE Code of Ethics used in this paper have been superceded by the ones in Figure 15.1 and Figure 15.2, respectively.

34. Samuel C. Florman. "A Skeptic Views Ethics in Engineering," *IEEE Spectrum*, August 1982, p. 57.

35. Sissela Bok. *Secrets: On the Ethics of Concealment and Revelation*, (New York: Pantheon Books). (Source: Vintage Books paperback, p. 211.)

36. *Ibid.*, pp. 214–215.

37. "Whistleblower Protection: Reasons for Whistleblower Complainants' Dissatisfaction Need to Be Explored," U.S. General Accounting Office, GGD-94-21, December 15, 1993. Available at URL:http://www.access.gpo.gov/cgibin/waisgate.cgi?WAISdocID=193859675+72+0+0&WAISaction=retrieve

38. "Whistleblower Protection: Continuing Impediments to Protection of Military Members," U.S. General Accounting Office, GAO/NSIAD-95-23, February 1995. Available at http://thorplus.lib.purdue.edu:8100/gpo/GPOAccess.cgi?gao/PDF/33476/3=0%20-33476%20/diskb/wais/data/gao/ns95023.txt; 7=%00;

39. "Whistleblower Protection: VA Did Little Until Recently to Inform Employees About Their Rights," United States General Accounting Office, April 2000. Available at http://www.gao.gov/new.items/d0070.pdf

40. Richard S. Rosenberg. "Beyond the Code of Ethics: The Responsibility of Professional Societies," *Proceedings of the Ethics and Social Impact Component, ACM Policy '98*, Shaping Policy in the Information Age, May 10, 1998, Washington, DC, pp. 18–25.

41. *Ibid.*

42. "ACM Statement on Privacy," Association for Computing Machinery, March 1991. Available at http://www.acm.org/usacm/privacy.html

43. "Computer Society Professionals Oppose Internet Censorship," ACM Press Release, March 22, 1995. Available at http://www.acm.org/usacm/EXON. HTML

44. Letter to Carlos J. Moorehead, Chairman, Subcommittee on Courts and Intellectual Property, House Judiciary Committee, ACM, February 15, 1996. Available at http://www.acm.org/usacm/hr2441_statement.html Letter to Conrad Burns, Chairman, Subcommittee on Science, Technology and Space, Senate Commerce, Science and Transportation Committee, ACM and IEEE, April 2, 1996. Available at http://www.acm.org/usacm/burns_letter.html

45. From an online collection. Copyright: Kevin Harris, 1995.

46. *Guide to the Perplexed* is a three volume work completed in 1190 by the Jewish physician and philosopher, Maimonides, as an explanation of the philosophy and theology of Judaism.

47. Chuck Huff and C. Dianne Martin. "Computing Consequences: A Framework for Teaching Ethical Computing," *Communications of the ACM*, December 1995, pp. 75–84.

48. In some sense, this approach is both a generalization and an extension to ethical issues of the representation given in Figure 1.1, Chapter 1 of this book. The author was a member a of the Impact CS Steering Committee.

49. *Op cit.*, Huff and Martin.

50. Jon M. Shepard, Michael G. Goldsby, and Virginia W. Gerde. "Teaching Business Ethics Through Literature," *The Online Journal of Ethics*, 1(3), Article 1, 1995. Available at http://condor.depaul.edu/ethics/gerde.html

51. *Ibid.*

52. Thomas Shanks, S. J. "The Case of the Cyber City Network," Markkula Center for Applied Ethics, Santa Clara University, (no date), Available at http://www. scu.edu/ethics/dialogue/candc/cases/cybercity.html

53. "Sample Scenarios Used for Teaching the Issues Surrounding Internet Privacy," The Online Ethics Center for Engineering and Science at Case Western University, Sample Scenarios from the Computer Science Telecommunications Board, (no date). Available at http://onlineethics.org/privacy/scene1.html

54. *Ibid.*

55. *Ibid.* Available at http://onlineethics.org/privacy/scene4.html

56. *Ibid.*

57. "Ethics Cases and Assignments, Case 3–Privacy versus security" Dr. Edelbach's SET Seminar Page, The College of New Jersey, February 2003. Available at http://www.tcnj.edu/~set/ethics/ethics-cases.htm

58. Professor Rob Kremer. "Nine Cases that Call for Ethical Decision Making," CPSC 451: Practical Software Engineering, The University of Calgary, 1998. Available at http://sern.ucalgary.ca/courses/cpsc/451/W99 /Ethics.html#case1
59. *Ibid.*
60. *Ibid.* Available at http://sern.ucalgary.ca/courses/cpsc/451/W99/Ethics.html#case4
61. *Ibid.*
62. EDUCOM Programs as presented in every issue of the EDUCOM *Review.*
63. "Bill of Rights and Responsibilities for Electronic Learners," EDUCOM *Review,* May/June 1993, pp. 24–27. Available at http://www.luc.edu/infotech/sae/bill-of-rights.html
64. "Ten Commandments of Computer Ethics," The Computer Ethics Institute, Washington, DC. It appeared in *Computerworld,* June 7, 1993, p. 84. An annotated version was available at http://spigot.princeton.edu/net/ethics.html
65. "Policy #104: Responsible Use of Information Technology Facilities and Services," The University of British Columbia, November 2000. Available at http://www.universitycounsel.ubc.ca/policies/policy104.html
66. *Ibid.*
67. Stephen Levy. *Hackers: Heroes of the Computer Revolution,* (New York: Doubleday.). (Source: Dell paperback, 1985, pp. 39–49.)
68. Dorothy E. Denning. "Concerning Hackers Who Break into Computer Systems," *13th National Computer Security Conference,* Washington, DC, October 1–4, 1990. Available at http://www-swiss.ai.mit.edu/6095/articles/denning_defense_hackers.txt
69. Dorothy E. Denning. "Postscript to 'Concerning Hackers Who Break Into Computer Systems'." Available at http://guru.cosc.georgetown.edu/~denning/hackers/Hackers-Postscript.tx
70. Paul Schuegraf and Richard S. Rosenberg. "Research Ethics and the Internet," ETHICOMP2001, *The Social and Ethical Impacts of Information and Communication Technologies,* Technical University of Gdansk, Poland, June 18–20, 2001, pp. 274–284.
71. Charles Ess and the AoIR Ethics Working Committee," Ethical Decision-Making and Internet Research: Recommendations from the AoIR Ethics Working Committee," November 27, 2002. Available at http://www.aoir.org/reports/ethics.pdf
72. Hannah Arendt. *Eichmann in Jerusalem: A Report on the Banality of Evil, Revised and Enlarged* (New York: The Viking Press, 1964), p. 25.
73. Langdon Winner. *Autonomous Technology: Technics-out-of-control as a Theme in Political Thought* (Cambridge, MA: The MIT Press, 1978), pp. 303–304.
74. David Lorge Parnas. "Professional Responsibility to Blow the Whistle on SDI," in M. David Ermann, Mary B. Williams, and Claudio Gutierrez (Eds.), *Computers, Ethics & Society* (New York: Oxford University Press, 1990), p. 360.
75. *Ibid.,* pp. 364–365.
76. Joseph Weizenbaum. "Facing Reality: Computer Scientists Aid War Efforts," *Technology Review,* January 1987, pp. 22–23.
77. J. David Bolter. *Turing's Man: Western Culture in the Computer Age* (Chapel Hill: The University of North Carolina Press, 1984), pp. 3–4.

78. C. B. Macpherson. *The Life and Times of Liberal Democracy* (Oxford, England: Oxford University Press, 1980), p. 73.

ADDITIONAL READINGS

Introduction

Berleur, J. and Whitehouse, D. (Eds.). *The Ethical Global Information Society: Culture and Society Revisited.* (London: Chapman & Hall, 1997).

Ermann, M. David; Williams, Mary B., and Gutierrez, Claudio. Computers (Eds.). *Ethics & Society* (New York: Oxford University Press, 1990).

Johnson, Deborah G. and Nissenbaum, Helen (Eds.). *Computers, Ethics & Social Values* (Englewood Cliffs, NJ: Prentice Hall, 1995).

Kevles, Daniel J. and Hood, Leroy (Eds.). *The Code of Codes: Scientific and Social Issues in the Human Genome Project.* (Cambridge, MA: Harvard University Press, 1992).

McCullagh, Declan. "Hold Technology Creators Liable?" News.Com, May 12, 2003. Available at http://news.com.com/2010-1071-1000673.html

Teitelman, Robert. *Gene Dreams: Wall Street, Academia, and the Rise of Biotechnology,* (New York: Basic Books, 1989).

Ethics

Bowyer, Kevin W. *Ethics and Computing: Living Responsibly in a Computerized World,* 2nd Edition, (Piscataway, NJ: IEEE Press, 2001).

Dejoie, Roy, Fowler, George, and Paradice, David (Eds.). *Ethical Issues in Information Systems,* (Boston: Boyd & Fraser, 1991).

Edwards, Paul (Ed.). *The Encyclopedia of Philosophy ,* Vol. 3 (New York: Macmillan, 1967), pp. 69–134.

Floridi, Luciano. "Computer Ethics: Mapping the Foundationalist Debate," University of Oxford, 2001. Available at http://www.wolfson.ox.ac.uk/~floridi/pdf/cemfd.pdf

Iannone, A. Pablo. (Ed.). *Contemporary Moral Controversies in Technology* (New York: Oxford University Press, 1987).

Johnson, Deborah G. *Computer Ethics,* 3rd Edition, (Upper Saddle River, NJ: Prentice Hall, 2001).

Spinello, Richard. *Cyberethics: Morality and Law in Cyberspace.* (Sudbury, MA: Jones and Bartlett Publishers, 2000).

Spinello, Richard A. and Tavani, Herman T. (Eds.). *Readings in CyberEthics.* (Sudbury, MA: Jones and Bartlett, 2001).

Professionalism

Andrews, Kenneth R. (Ed.). *Ethics in Practice: Managing the Moral Corporation,* (Boston: Harvard Business School Press, 1989).

Baird, Davis. "Testimony," Presented before the U.S. Senate Committee on Commerce, Science, and Transportation Hearing on Nanotechnology, May 1, 2003. Available at http://commerce.senate.gov/hearings/testimony.cfm?id=745& wit_id=2012

Benson, George C. S. "Codes of Ethics," *Journal of Business Ethics* 8(5), May 1989, pp. 305–319. "DMA Guidelines for Ethical Business Practice as of March 2002," Direct Marketing Association, Available at http://www.the-dma.org/library/ guidelines/ethicalguidelines.shtml

Fleddermann, Charles B. *Engineering Ethics*, (Upper Saddle River, NJ: Prentice-Hall, 1999).

Friedman, Batya (Ed.). *Human Values and the Design of Computer Technology.* (New York: Cambridge University Press, 1997).

Gotterbarn, Don, Miller, Keith, and Rogerson, Simon. "Computer Society and ACM Approve Software Engineering Code of Ethics," *Computer*, October 1999, pp. 84–88. Available at http://computer.org/computer/code-of-ethics.pdf

Hoffman, W. Michael and Moore, Jennifer Mills (Eds.). *Business Ethics: Readings and Cases in Corporate Morality, Second Edition.* (New York: McGraw-Hill, 1990).

Johnson, Deborah G. and Snapper, John W. (Eds.). *Ethical Issues in the Use of Computers* (Belmont, CA: Wadsworth, 1985).

Lewis, Philip V. "Ethical Principles for Decision Makers: A Longitudinal Survey," *Journal of Business Ethics*, 8(4), April 1989, pp. 271–278.

On Being a Scientist: Responsible Conduct in Research. Committee on Science, Engineering, and Public Policy, National Academy of Sciences, National Academy of Engineering, Institute of Medicine (Washington, DC: National Academy Press, 1995). Available at the National Academy of Sciences Web site with URL:http:// www.nas.edu.

Schlossberger, Eugene. *The Ethical Engineer*, (Philadelphia, PA: Temple University Press, 1993).

Wilder, Clinton and Soat, John. "The Ethics of Data," InformationWeek, May 14, 2001. Available at www.informationweek.com/837/dataethics.htm

Pedagogy and Ethics

"An Information Bill of Rights," The Aspen Institute, Communications and Society Program, July 1995. Available at http://www.aspeninst.org/dir./current/Infobill.html

Dahlbom, Bo and Mathiassen, Lars. *Computers in Context: The Philosophy and Practice of Systems Design*, (Cambridge, MA: NCC Blackwell, 1993).

Epstein, Richard G. *The Case of the Killer Robot*, (New York: Wiley, 1997). "Ethics and Computer Use," Special Section of the *Communications of the ACM*, 38(12), December 1995.

Loch, Karen D. and Conger, Sue. "Evaluating Ethical Decision Making and Computer Use," *Communications of the ACM*, 39(7), July 1996, pp. 74–83.

Rinaldi, Arlene H. "The Net User Guidelines and Netiquette," Academic/Institutional Support Services, Florida Atlantic University, July 1994. Available at http://www. toyama-u.ac.jp/tya/library/netiquee.html

Riser, Robert and Gotterbarn, Don. "Ethics Activities in Computer Science Courses," *ACM Computers and Society*, 26(3), September 1996, pp. 13–17.

Other Issues

"Ethical and Legal Aspects of Human Subjects Research on the Internet," A Report of a Workshop, American Association for the Advancement of Science, November 1999. Available at http:/ /aaas.org/spp/dspp/sfrl/projects/intres/report.pdf

"Ethical and Policy Issues in Research Involving Human Participants," Volume I, Report and Recommendations of the National Bioethics Advisory Commission, August 2001. Available at http://bioethics.gov/human/overvol1.pdf Volume II, Commissioned Papers and Staff Analysis. Available at http:/ /bioethics.gov/human/ overvol2.pdf

Forester, Tom and Morrison, Perry. *Computer Ethics: Cautionary Tales and Ethical Dilemmas* (Cambridge, MA: MIT Press, 1990).

Hester, D. Micah and Ford, Michael J. (Eds.) *Computers and Ethics in the Cyberage*, (Upper Saddle River, NJ: Prentice Hall, 2001).

Lackey, Douglas P. (Ed.). *Ethics and Strategic Defense: American Philosophers Debate Star Wars and the Future of Nuclear Deterrence*, (Belmont, CA: Wadsworth, 1989).

Mnyusiwalla, Anisa, Daar, Abdallah S., and Singer, Peter A. "'Mind the Gap': Science and Ethics in Nanotechnology," *Nanotechnology 14*(2003) R9-R18. Available at http://www.utoronto.ca/jcb/pdf/nanotechnology_paper.pdf

— Appendix —

MAGAZINES, JOURNALS, ASSOCIATIONS, AND WEBSITES

POPULAR MAGAZINES

Computer & Internet

- *Computerworld.* Tabloid format. For business users. Reviews of major trends, government policies, and frequent discussion of many social issues, including privacy and free speech. (http://www.computerworld.com/)
- *Datamation.* Sold primarily by subscription. For business professionals. Wide coverage of the industry. Primarily devoted to technical issues with occasional articles on social issues. Renowned for its annual list of the world's top 100 information processing companies. (http://www.datamation.com/)
- *Information Week.* (http://www.informationweek.com/)
- ZD group of magazines: *PC Week, PC Computing, MacWeek, Mac User, InternetUser, Family Computing, PC.* (http://home.zdnet.com/home/filters/main.html)

Technology

- *Discover.* A Time Warner Publication with a wide coverage of scientific and technological developments, including a section on computers. (http://www.discover.com/)
- *New Scientist.* A British publication with wide coverage of scientific and technological innovations. Somewhat oriented to British issues. (http://www.newscientists.com/)

- *Scientific American.* The most prestigious popular science magazine in the U.S. The articles are written by prominent scientists, with excellent graphics. Computers and related technologies are treated infrequently but very well. (http://www.sciam.com/)
- *Technology Review.* Published by the Massachusetts Institute of Technology. Well-written and interesting articles on a wide variety of issues. High level of social concern. Some articles cannot be read without a paid subscription. (http://technologyreview.com/)
- *Wired.* The most trendy and glitzy magazine appealing to Internet users. Interviews and articles on all the major technical and social issues related to the Internet and the Web. (http://www.wired.com/)

Business

- *Business Week.* Regular, extensive coverage of technological developments and associated business, labor, and economic issues. Frequent in-depth studies of the Internet, the Web, computer and communications issues, as well as social issues. (http://www.businessweek.com/)
- *Fortune.* Well known for the *Fortune* 500 list of leading U.S. companies. Excellent coverage of technology. Good records of spotting trends and anticipating problems. (http://www.fortune.com/fortune/)
- *Wall Street Journal.* Primarily business-oriented but with frequent in-depth articles on computers and applications. Requires a paid subscription for online access.

General

- *The Economist.* British magazine similar to *Time* and *Newsweek*, but much deeper analyses and regular special surveys of finance, telecommunications, and computers. Many articles can only be accessed with a paid subscription. (http://www.economist.com/)
- *Time, Newsweek.* Regular, limited coverage of developments in computers. (http://www.time.com/time/; http://www.msnbc.com/news/NW-front_Front.asp)
- *The New York Times.* Excellent treatment of business, technical, and social problems. Requires registration to access and articles more than a week old, in many cases, cannot be accessed without a paid subscription. (http://www.nytimes.com/)
- Times Newspapers: *The Times, The Sunday Times, The Times Higher Education Supplement* (United Kingdom). (http://www.thetimes.co.uk/)
- *The Washington Post.* Similar to the *New York Times* in the depth of its treatment on many business, government, and social issues. Requires supplying some personal information for registration. (http://www.washingtonpost.com/)

Technical Journals

- *Computer*. A publication of the Institute of Electrical and Electronics Engineers (IEEE). Covers technical issues in papers written by academics. Special issues on such topics as security and Cad/Cam. (http://www.computer.org/)
- *Communications of the ACM*. A publication of the Association of Computing Machinery (ACM). Includes state-of-the-art articles by leading figures in computer science. In-depth analysis of many social issues.
- *Ethics and Information Technology*. A new journal with a growing reputation for important and relevant articles.
- *The Information Society*. The leading journal for a wide variety of social issues related to computers and the Internet.
- *Science*. A publication of the American Association for the Advancement of Science. Most of the articles deal with advanced research topics in biology, chemistry, physics, and so forth. Periodic serious coverage of technological innovations and their social impact. (http://www.sciencemag.org/)
- *IEEE Spectrum*. Important technical journal, published by *IEEE*, that treats serious topics at a non-specialist level. Special issues on social impact of technology. (http://www.spectrum.ieee.org/)
- *Harvard Business Review*. Coverage of important issues associated with computers in business. Regular treatment of management information systems, impact on labor, and Japanese management techniques.
- *Sloan Management Review*. Similar to the *Harvard Business Review* but with the MIT perspective.
- *Privacy Journal*. Not really a journal, in spite of its title, but rather a newsletter with up-to-date information about privacy issues, legislation, and trends. (http://www.privacyjournal.net/)

Useful News Sites

- *Cnet*. Excellent coverage of technical and social issues. (http://news.com.com/)
- *eWeek* Good industry coverage. (http://www.eweek.com/)
- *Wired* The online *Wired* magazine with lots of good news and access to *Wired* archives. (http://www.wired.com/)
- *Canada.com* Access to Canadian newspapers across the country. (http://www.canada.com/)
- *SiliconValley.com* Access to interesting stories about Silicon Vally, including new technologies. (http://www.siliconvalley.com/mld/siliconvalley/)
- *Salon.com* Well-written feature pieces on technological issues but requires a paid subscription for most articles. (http://www.salon.com/)
- *Google.news* Easy access to news headlines. (http://news.google.com/)

- *BBCNews* World news from the British Broadcasting Corporation offers an alternative view to North American sources. (http://news.bbc.co.uk/2/hi.html)
- *PoeNews* Eclectic selection of news stories around the world. (http://www.poe-news.com/)
- *FindLaw* Detailed coverage of legal issues with access to judgments. (http://www.findlaw.com/)
- *ZDNet UK* Wide coverage of technology stories worldwide. (http://news.zdnet.co.uk/)
- *InfoWorld* Technology and industry focus. (http://www.infoworld.com/)
- *TechWeb* Focus on business and technology issues. (http://www.techweb.com/)
- *Slashdot* "News for Nerds, Stuff that Matters." A non-standard view of the high-tech world provided by contributors. (http://slashdot.org/)

PROFESSIONAL SOCIETIES AND ORGANIZATIONS

- *Professional Societies*
  ACM Special Interest Group on Computers and Society (SIGCAS) (http://www.acm.org/)
  IEEE Society on Social Implications of Technology (SSIT) (http://www.ieee.org/)

- *Privacy and Free Speech Organizations*
  ACLU Freedom Network (http://www.aclu.org/)
  American Communication Assoc. (http://cavern.uark.edu/comminfo/www/ACA.html)
  American Library Association (ALA) (http://www.ala.org/)
  Anonymous Surfing (The Anonymizer) (http://www.anonymizer.com/)
  CCSR (Centre for Computing and Social Responsibility) (http://www.ccsr.cse.dmu.ac.uk/)
  The Center for Democracy and Technology (CDT) (http://www.cdt.org/)
  Computer Professionals for Social Responsibility (CPSR) (http://www.cpsr.org/)
  EFF – The Electronic Frontier Foundation (http://www.eff.org/)
  Electronic Frontier Canada (EFC) (http://www.efc.ca/)
  Electronic Privacy Information Center Home Page (http://www.epic.org/)
  GILC—Global Internet Liberty Campaign (http://www.gilc.org/)
  Privacy International Home Page (http://www.privacy.org/pi/)
  Reporters Committee for Freedom of the Press (http://www.rcfp.org/)

- *Family Values*
  Christian Coalition of America (http://www.cc.org/)
  Family Research Council (http://www.frc.org/)

- *Online Access*
  Alliance for Public Technology (http://www.apt.org/)
  Benton Foundation Projects (http://www.benton.org/)

- *U. S. Government*
  Bureau of Labor Statistics (http://stats.bls.gov/)
  Government Accounting Office (GAO) (http://www.gao.gov/)
  Office of Technology Assessment Archives (http://www.wws.princeton.
  edu/~ota/)
  The White House (http://www.whitehouse.gov/)
  The House of Representatives (http://www.house.gov/)
  The Senate of the United States (http://www.senate.gov/)
  Current Bills and Past Legislation (http://thomas.loc.gov/)

- *Women*
  The National Organization for Women (NOW) (http://www.now.org/
  index.html)
  WITI Campus Women in Technology International (http://www.witi.
  com/)
  ACM's Committee on Women in Computing (http://www.acm.org/
  women/)

- *Labor*
  AFL-CIO Home Page (http://www.aflcio.org/)
  International Labour Organization (http://www.ilo.org/)
  United Automobile Workers (http://www.uaw.org/)

INDEX